ADVERTISING COPYWRITING

GRID SERIES IN ADVERTISING AND JOURNALISM

Consulting Editors
ARNOLD M. BARBAN, University of Illinois
DONALD W. JUGENHEIMER, University of Kansas

Barban, Jugenheimer & Young, *Advertising Media Sourcebook and Workbook*
Burton, *Advertising Copywriting,* Fourth Edition
Burton & Miller, *Advertising Fundamentals,* Second Edition
Francois, *Beginning News Writing: A Programed Text*
Francois, *Introduction to Mass Communications and Mass Media*
Michman & Jugenheimer, *Strategic Advertising Decisions*
Patti & Murphy, *Advertising Management: Cases and Concepts*
Pickett, *Voices of the Past: Key Documents in the History of American Journalism*
Quera, *Advertising Campaigns: Formulations and Tactics,* Second Edition
Rotzoll, Haefner & Sandage, *Advertising in Contemporary Society: Perspectives Toward Understanding*
Simon, *Public Relations: Concepts and Practice*
Simon, *Public Relations Management: Cases and Simulations,* Second Edition
Simon, *Publicity and Public Relations Worktext,* Fourth Edition
Smeyak, *Broadcast News Writing*
Zeigler & Howard, *Broadcast Advertising: A Comprehensive Working Textbook*

OTHER BOOKS IN THE GRID SERIES IN ADVERTISING AND JOURNALISM

Francois, *Mass Media Law and Regulation,* Second Edition

ADVERTISING COPYWRITING

Fourth Edition

Philip Ward Burton
J. Stewart Riley Professor
School of Journalism
Indiana University

Grid Publishing Inc., Columbus, Ohio

Contents

Getting and Keeping Attention
Types of Commercials
Watch Your Timing
Live or Taped?
Call for Action at the End
Now—To Sum up

Foreword

Several years ago I wrote a foreword for the third edition of *Advertising Copywriting*. It was a pleasure because I thought it was a good book.

Now that the fourth edition is about to make its appearance, I've been asked to write the foreword again. I see no point, however, in writing another because the foreword for the third edition applies extremely well to the fourth edition.

In looking over the manuscript for the fourth edition, I find that the book has been strengthened in many sections. Current issues such as comparative advertising, market segmentation and consumerism are spotlighted. Such important areas as television advertising and business advertising have been made stronger than ever.

In short, I think Professor Burton has made a good book even better, so this foreword seems even more appropriate for the fourth edition.

Anthony C. Chevins
President
Cunningham & Walsh, Inc.
April 14, 1977

It had always seemed strange to me that no one had written a good, definitive book on advertising copywriting. Imagine how embarrassing it was to find that there not only was one, but that it was written by my very own former advertising professor. Obviously, this occurred several centuries ago at Syracuse University.

Writing a book on advertising copywriting must be, in some ways, like writing a how-to-do-it book on sex. You can choose to be very brief and general, and therefore of little practical use to anyone except as a kind of cheerleader, or you can be thorough and detailed. Having made the latter choice, however, you had better be right in what you say. And you had better not leave out anything that counts.

In this fourth and extensively revised edition of *Advertising Copywriting*, I am happy to report that the author has left out almost nothing that I believe is important. And the details, as well as the overall focus, seem right to me.

Like any thorough text, this one provides far more answers than the novice has questions. What makes a good headline? What about body copy? Should your commercial be produced on film or tape? What's the maximum number of words in a 30-second spot? What about music?

These and all the other answers unfold, in their proper context, in a book that is notably lucid and well-organized.

Those persons who are not cut out to be copywriters (and they are legion) need read no further than the first chapter.

However, the thorough reader will find intelligent analysis of what makes good copy (and there are many different kinds); of the disciplined thinking required to write good copy; of the dynamic but delicate relationship between the writer and art director and how important this team-work is to singleminded advertising.

In telling detail, the book also shows how the copywriter works with account people, clients, researchers, and even lawyers. Does this make the copywriter's job sound difficult and complex? Well, it is. Otherwise, there would not be such a shortage of really good professionals.

In the second edition of this book the authors made many astute judgments that stood the test of time. For example, they correctly sensed a trend toward believability in advertising. Today, as this fourth edition appears, that trend has turned into a stampede, not only because advertising people are smarter, but so are consumers. And let's not forget the Government (a not-quite-disinterested-enough bystander that seems to be turning into an overactive participant).

As you would expect, this new book contains many outstanding examples of print and broadcast advertising. Most of them are current; some are classic. There are also new sections on farm advertising and different forms of business and professional advertising. The book also covers retail advertising and direct mail, and manages to do it without being superficial.

Overall, I don't know of anyone in advertising who could not learn something from reading this book. (And I know some fairly smart, and very successful, people.) Its value to the novice, therefore, should be enormous—and to a professional, whether practitioner or professor or both, should be substantial. Anyone who takes the trouble to understand what is in this book can save himself a lot of work, a lot of problems, and perhaps, at some point, even his job.

As any copywriter knows, that's a strong selling argument for any book.

Preface

Change is a constant in advertising. So it is with books on advertising. Although books that relate to advertising copywriting are subject to less drastic changes than books about advertising media, each edition of a book on advertising copywriting does, nevertheless, represent some change. As I worked on this fourth edition, it was surprising to discover how much I *wanted* to change. Thus, this preface, while retaining much of the material from the third-edition preface, reflects the substantial additions, deletions, and changes that have occurred.

Only a few persons know who did the writing of any advertisement. Yet, copywriting, more than any other advertising activity, provides an opportunity for personal expression. In the words of the body copy, in the headline, and in the art ideas conveyed to the artists, copywriters unmistakably stamp their personality, or their lack of it since the copy may be stylized, inventive, deft, pedestrian, eloquent, persuasive, enthusiastic, lackluster.

Authors of books on copywriting likewise put more of their personal stamp upon those books than authors of other books on advertising such as those on media, research, principles, and budgeting, for example. Most often authors of copywriting books are telling you what has worked for them. The style they favor is their style and the copy appeals they list are those that they have worked into their own advertisements. It is unthinkable, in fact, that authors of copywriting books could avoid putting so much of themselves into a book on the subject since they have been living in the field or, more prosaically, working in it.

As I have continued to write advertising copy, I have continued to learn more about it—what to do and what not to do. These learning experiences show up in the fourth edition. Copywriting is a craft in which you never stop learning no matter how long you practice it.

The same learning process is true of the teaching of advertising copywriting. As more students sit in your classrooms, the more you discover about what subject matter arouses student interest. You see, too, how presenting subject matter can aid the learning process. Thus, this new edition reflects new truths about teaching advertising copy, as well as writing copy. Those of us who work with students are privileged because some immensely skilled practitioners of copywriting cannot convey their skill to the beginner because they cannot think like students. Theirs is an intuitive ability, based on quick, swift judgments. It is difficult, if not impossible, for them to work on the level of uninformed, plodding learners. Yet, much of a book on advertising copywriting, must be addressed to these people. It must recognize their limitations and it must bring them along step by step.

Despite this talk of change in the book, it is a striking fact to see as one revises a book on advertising copywriting, how much about advertising copywriting stays timeless and constant. Most of the suggestions, made many years ago by such old masters as John Caples, are applicable today. Many, many suggestions appearing in the first edition of this book are likewise valid today. Since copywriters write for people and since the basic "people" appeals stay largely constant, a book written in recognition of this fact is not going to discard all the original material in succeeding editions.

Despite the retention of much of the material from the earlier editions, there are significant changes in the fourth edition. Examples are new material on positioning, market segmentation, and strategy considerations in creative planning. There is additional material, too, on psychological factors in advertising copywriting.

Comparative advertising, so much in the news today, is given much attention, along with the consumer movement and the group sensitivities of which the copywriter must be aware. Masculine pronouns have been used for succinctness and of course, are intended to refer to both men and women.

In the third edition, the television section was greatly strengthened. The fourth edition has an even stronger television section. Both of the television chapters offer much new and additional material. This attention to television appears elsewhere in the fourth edition as in the research chapter in which ways of pretesting television are discussed, and in the chapter on local advertising that tells the copywriter how to prepare material for low-budget local users of television.

Very frankly, when I began to revise the third edition, I had thought that this would be a once-over-lightly task that would consist chiefly of getting new illustrations. I can smile wryly now that the work is over. It turned out to be so much more than I had planned because in chapter after chapter I cut, altered, added, and rewrote. Many of the changes resulted from suggestions of teachers who had used the book. Some student input appears, too. Accordingly, I'm hopeful that the students will find the fourth edition more interesting and more usable, and that the teachers will find it even more teachable.

Acknowledgments

No man is an island when he writes an advertising textbook. He accepts help from those whose contributions can result in a better book.

For this fourth edition, I'd like to thank two men particularly. One is Dr. Paul Lyness, long-time friend and former president of Gallup & Robinson. Dr. Lyness made many helpful suggestions about the chapter on research. The other is Sidney Diamond, a leading authority on communications law and a member of the law firm of Kaye, Scholer, Fierman, Hays and Handler. In addition to rewriting the chapter on advertising law for the second edition, Mr. Diamond has helped in the revisions of the chapter for the third and fourth editions.

Special thanks are also given here to five persons who contributed heavily to former editions. That their contributions were first-rate is shown in the fact that much of what they wrote can be found in the fourth edition. These persons are Albert E. Ametrano, Melvin H. Goodrode, Rosemary Smith, Joseph Sollish, and Richard S. Taylor.

Print and broadcast material has been supplied by many firms and individuals. I certainly want to acknowledge their generosity. Also, other persons made suggestions and offered ideas. The following list names firms and individuals who contributed in any way to the book. By no means, however, do I want to imply that because their names appear here that they necessarily endorse all the material in the book. They were, however, good enough to contribute in one way, or another, and for this I'm grateful.

Paul Abbott, Elanco Products; Lawrence Adams, B. F. Goodrich Company; T. R. Albright, Olay Company; Peter Allerup, Pabst Brewing Company; Richard Altman, ThermaSol, Ltd.; Jane C. Arkus, Lando, Inc.; J. Avrigean, Wheeling-Pittsburgh Steel Corporation; Charles Barden, Green Giant Company; W. P. Barton, International Business Machines; Ian W. Beaton, Campbell-Ewald Company; Maria Beltrametti, Batten, Barton, Durstine & Osborn; Russell M. H. Berg, Hewlett-Packard Company; G. M. Blase, LeBlond Machine Tool, Inc.; Larry Blostein, Radio Shack; Thomas E. Bohan, Benton & Bowles, Inc.; David L. Bowman, Ralston Purina Company; Alice Boyer, Douglas Leigh Transit Advertising; A. G. Brandt, Watkins Products, Inc.; W. H. Brown, Sharon Steel Corporation; Robert L. Bunting, Pentel of America, Ltd.; J. J. Burgdoerfer, The Hertz Corporation; Tom Burgum, Armstrong Cork Company; Jay Burzon, Woman's Day; William M. Buter, Saks Fifth Avenue; John Cadenhead, Sakowitz, Houston; Conrad R. Cain, Bonwit Teller; Toni Callahan, E. F. Hutton & Company; Joseph Caminiti; Starch INRA Hooper; Jan Campbell, Land O' Lakes, Inc.; F. R. Cawl, Outdoor Advertising Association of America, Inc.; Helen V. Chaplin; Beverly Wilshire Hotel; Richard A. Cohen, May Company; Peter B. Cooney, Needham, Harper & Steers, Inc.; Robert H. Crawford, Kearney & Tracker Corporation; Max Crowder, Elanco Corporation; Robert Cudworth, T. A. Best, Inc.; Cunard Line; Lorraine D'Aleo, Benton & Bowles, Inc.; Thomas Delph, Hardware Retailing; Steve D. Dinsmore, General Foods Corporation; Joseph J. Doherty, Owens-Corning Fiberglas Corporation; Lawrence E. Doherty, Advertising Age; William Edgley, The Pillsbury Company; William T. End, L. L. Bean, Incorporated; Robert B. Ferguson, The Sperry & Hutchinson Company; Martin D. Fischer, Botsford Ketchum, Inc; Fran Foley, Marshall Field & Company; Robert C. Freeman, Hotel & Motel Management; Jane Fry, T. A. Best, Inc.; D. M. Furman, Bic Pen Corporation; Nic Goeres, Eastman Kodak Company; B. Gooden, Swift & Company; Bart C. Grabow, Public Service of Indiana; Tina Grant, Bergdorf Goodman; Benjamin S. Greenberg, The Advertising Council, Inc.; Steve Gritton, Leo Burnett U.S.A.; Norman F. Guess, Dartnell Corporation; Marvin P. Hammer, Continental Grain Company;

George W. Hayden, The Advertising Council, Inc.; Patrick J. Higgins, Craft, Kennedy & Higgins, Inc.; Gerald E. Holmes, Saginaw Steering Gear Division, General Motors Corporation; Jane A. Holmes, American Dairy Association; G. L. Hoobler, Warner & Swasey; Charles Horn, Bost Enterprises; Sherry Hudson, Walker Research; Cynthia Huffman, Leo Burnett U.S.A.; Saralee Hymen, Radio Advertising Bureau; Arthur C. Iaia, Jr., Castle Company; Dan R. Indgjerd, Norm Thompson Outfitters; Mark Johnson, Lanier Business Products; Robert H. Jurick, John Blair Mail Marketing; Richard Keith, N. W. Ayer ABH International; William Kendall, Arvin Industries; J. D. Kerr, Star-Kist Foods, Inc.; Charles J. Klopf, Successful Farming; Jack Lane, Jack Lane Studio; Stuart H. Lane, Hormel & Company; Ashton R. Lee, Leo Burnett U.S.A.; Arnold G. Lockwood, A. T. Cross Company; Robert M. Lustgarten, Colorite Plastics Company; F. Bradley Lynch, N. W. Ayer AHH International; Paul Lyness, Lyness Research; Carole Lyons, L. S. Ayres, Inc.; Andew R. Magnuson, Aeroquip Corporation; Les Margulis, Benton & Bowles; Robert Mercer, National Potato Promotion Board; Louis D. Methfessel, American Olean Tile Company; J. D. Mitchell, Indiana Bell; Merlin E. Morris, Amana Refrigeration, Inc.; Stephen Novick, Grey Advertising, Inc.; Joseph Palastak, Transit Advertising Association; George C. Perry, Mobil Chemical Company; Roy W. Peterson, Economics Laboratory, Inc.; Ralph M. Pinkerton, California Avocado Advisory Board; Ronald Polomoff, N. W. Ayer, Inc.; Natalie Posner, Hamilton House; W. E. Pritchett, Pfizer Agricultural Division; Richard J. Ratcheson,

Pabst Corporation; Peter Reader, Pepsi-Cola Company; Hugh A. Roger-Smith, Eastman Kodak; Royal Copenhagen Porcelain Corporation; Frances Saia, The Gillette Company; Elly Schoenfeld, Mercedes-Benz of North America, Inc.; Jack Schwartz, Renfield Importers, Ltd.; Brian D. Scott, Kimberly-Clark Corporation; R. T. Scott, Rumrill-Hoyt, Inc.; Brian Seavoy, Kenyon & Eckhardt Advertising; Dorothy Sirotin, Grey Advertising, Inc.; Brian Sitts, Rumrill-Hoyt, Inc.; Barry C. Smyth, Gulf Oil Company; Barney Spaulding, New York Subways Advertising Co., Inc.; Trish Spear, May Company; L. E. Sport, Delta Airlines; John H. Steinway, Steinway & Sons; Carmin Timpanelli, Stanley Tools; Vincent L. Tofany, National Safety Council; Henry Townsend, Frank J. Corbett, Inc. Communications; Robert Turflinger, Kinser Lumber Company; Douglas R. Toler, National-Standard Company; Robert Van Brundt, Underwriters' Laboratories, Inc.; Robert Vanderstok, Young & Rubicam West; W. L. Vande Water, AC-Delco Company; R. J. Vilt, True Temper Company; Clarence Wage, Mirro Aluminum Company; R. J. Wean III, Wean United; Bernie Webb, Hospitals Magazine; A. W. White, Communications Programs; R. E. Widiger, Shell Chemical Company; Donald C. Williams, Donald Williams Advertising, Inc.; J. W. Williams, Minnesota Mining & Manufacturing Company; Jane Wolchonok, Church & Dwight Co., Inc.; Robert S. Yates, Timken Company; Mary A. Yontz, Kirkhill, Inc.; Jerry Zaret, Grey Advertising, Inc.

Finally, I would like to thank Marcie Clark, Elaine Garver, and Lois Yoakam of Grid Publishing.

Copywriting

What you can expect to learn
by reading a book about it.

You'll find it's a *Yes* and *No* situation.

Yes—you can learn to distinguish good copy from bad copy. You will learn the do's and don'ts that can save you time and trouble on the job.

Yes—you can learn the terminology of the field of copywriting and of advertising.

Yes—you can learn what motivates people to buy and what appeals to use.

Yes—you can learn the technical requirements that are peculiar to the different media so that you can proceed confidently whether you're writing a 10-second television commercial, a 4-color magazine spread, or a 24-sheet outdoor poster.

Yes—you can learn the special requirements of the different forms of advertising such as retail, mail order, industrial, professional, trade, and others.

Yes—you can learn what a copywriter must know about research and law, and how a copywriter can write copy that is in keeping with the tenets of consumerism, yet can sell efficiently for the advertiser.

Yes—you can learn how a copywriter cooperates with, and learns from, artists and production people.

—but—

No—you cannot learn from a book the ability to come up with an inspirational idea that forms the basis of an outstanding campaign, or of a memorable, award-winning advertisement. Some people have a heaven-sent ability to think creatively and originally. They have this, book or no book. A copywriter can be trained but there are some who are naturals. They are born with the ability to spark original ideas just as there are artists, poets, and musicians whose talent shines through almost from birth.

No—you cannot learn from this, or any book, how to write first-draft copy speedily and under pressure. Such speed is learned on the job and is developed from constant practice.

A book on copywriting can point you in the right direction. It can give you a helping hand in a course in advertising copywriting, and it can help you significantly during those first days on the job. It can help you even after you've had working experience because all writers need to go back to the fundamentals occasionally.

There may be moments when you experience doubt and insecurity. Perhaps this book can help you get through such moments. If it does, it will have justified itself.

ADVERTISING COPYWRITING

Copy Is Salesmanship—and More

Ask a group of people the meaning of "copy" as used in advertising and you'll be given a number of definitions. One member of the group may be unkind enough to refer to the dictionary definition of the word—"imitation." He would, of course, be right to some degree since much advertising copy is imitation. It is reasonable to assume, however, that most of the group will tend to think of advertising copy in terms of its function. They will, accordingly, call it "salesmanship in print." According to the views of these people, advertising copy that does not present a product to the public for purchase and does not offer reasons why the purchaser should buy, is not salesmanship but subtle persuasion and impression building. Others maintain that the salesmanship-in-print definition is too narrow—that it reduces the advertising person to the role of merchandise peddler. They point to advertising's place in the total marketing process. Advertising properly used is, they say, a force for mass consumer education and a tool for effecting social change. It is almost insulting to copywriters, they add, to assume that their only interest in writing copy is to sell something or somebody.

These viewpoints are interesting, challenging, and possibly debatable. Yet, it hardly seems questionable that the overall objective of almost all advertising copy is to sell. Rarely is an advertisement found that does not have a sales motive somewhere behind its writing. True, as one looks at many advertisements it is difficult to find any obvious sales message. Many advertisements, for example, that appear in print media or in broadcast media are written to build a feeling of good will, to strengthen public opinion, or to break down a possible negative public opinion. Such advertisements, often called "institutional advertisements," normally do not offer products or services for sale. The copy , nevertheless, is selling copy just as surely as is product-selling copy. It is merely selling something different. If you are a salesperson and you invite a customer or a prospective customer to dinner, to play golf, or to see a ball game, you are engaged in a form of selling. Perhaps you aren't actually clinching your order—possibly you make no attempt to talk business—but you are selling your company or yourself, or both. The impression you create in the mind of your client is almost certain to have an important bearing upon the ultimate signing of the order.

So it is with advertising copy. In almost any type of advertisement you are asked to write, remember that you have something to sell to your readers. Otherwise, there would be little reason to spend thousands of dollars, or anything at all, for the space or time in which to deliver your message.

WHAT'S BEYOND SELLING?

Can we, accordingly, agree that copy is merely salesmanship in print? Is that as far as the definition goes? No—it isn't half defined—especially as far as you, the copywriter, are concerned.

Copy can be the voice of the advertiser, boasting about the product, shouting its merits in bald, unlovely terms, damning the competition, gaining attention through sheer weight of words and extravagant claims, making the most noise.

Or copy can be the voice of a friend—a trusted adviser offering help to the consumer in purchasing problems—clear, arresting, interesting, honest.

Copy can be the enthusiasm of salespeople—echoing their words, reflecting their pride in their products, opening doors for them, easing their jobs. It can be your contribution to the merchant who knows what he wants to say but doesn't know how to say it. It can be a primer for the dealer, the jobber, and the distributor—a means of preconditioning their selling. Copy can be an instrument of better living, easier living, happier living. Through copy that stimulates mass sales, the whole economy of a field of enterprise

There was a time when supporting black education could have cost your freedom. Today it just costs money.

In 1833, Prudence Crandall, a young Quaker, opened a school for black girls in Connecticut. The villagers tried to burn it, they refused to sell her food or medicine.

Still, black children from all over New England came to the school.

Then the state passed a law prohibiting the establishment of Negro Schools. Miss Crandall disobeyed and was sent to jail.

The law didn't stop blacks from learning. And it didn't stop others from helping them, despite very real danger to their lives and liberty.

Thanks to a continuing tradition of support for black education, the United Negro College Fund has been able to help thousands of black students change the course of their lives at UNCF schools.

Please continue a great American tradition. Support the United Negro College Fund.

Give to The United Negro College Fund

500 E. 62nd St.
New York 10021 A mind is a terrible thing to waste.

A Public Service of The Advertising Council

FIGURE 1-1

Public service advertising.   Worthy causes, as well as products, are sold through advertisements such as this one. Some of the outstanding creative people in the United States contribute their talent free in support of such campaigns.

Courtesy of The Advertising Council, Inc.

may be improved by price reduction and product refinement. Copy is a social and an economic force. And the way <u>you</u> create it is the true way it may be defined.

WHAT COPY MEANS TO DIFFERENT PEOPLE

It is well at the outset to establish a literal interpretation of the word "copy." To the newspaper reporter, copy is simply the text of the story. It is the only thing he is responsible for. He needn't worry about headlines, subheadings, typography, illustrations.

Copy, to him, is what he writes—the main body text of the article.

Advertising has a different idea of copy. If you are speaking formally, copy means everything that appears in an advertisement. When you are asked to prepare copy for an advertisement, you are expected to write everything required for the complete advertisement. If the man or woman to whom you turn over

the finished job asks you, "Is the copy ready?" he or she expects that you have completed headline, subheadings, body text, captions, blurbs, signatures, and even copyright notices. To you, copy means every word that is to appear in your finished advertisement, depending upon its format.

Usually, in an informal working session, copy includes nothing more than the headline, main body text, and possibly subheads, if any.

ELEMENTS OF COPY

Occasionally you will find one advertisement that contains all the different elements of copy. This is rare. Normally, your advertisements will be made up of two or three of the common copy elements. You may sometimes find it necessary to employ all of them but very seldom. There is certainly no rule of thumb by which you can predetermine exactly which elements you'll use and which you'll not need.

When preparing a campaign for a client or a prospective client, a copywriter may often need but two elements of the complete advertisement in order to convey the basic campaign idea or approach. These elements are the headline and the illustration. A number of layouts may be prepared that show the client different headlines and illustrations. If the client approves the campaign idea, as demonstrated in these layouts, the copywriter will then supply the body copy for the advertisements, plus the subheads, or captions, or other elements needed to complete the advertisements.

Main headline

Any reader of news stories, or magazine material is aware of headlines that use larger type than any of the material underneath. Often the reader sees these headlines tied up with illustrations, the combination attracting maximum reader-attention. In advertisements, you will use headlines in the same manner as the story editors do.

Normally, the headline of an advertisement will present a selling idea or will otherwise serve to intrigue the prospective purchaser into a further and more exhaustive reading of your advertisement.

Headlines can and do fall into many varied patterns. It is not necessary, for instance, for a headline to be big. Some headlines—notably in newspaper advertisements—are set in very large type and in general resemble regular newspaper headlines. Others, however, may be quite small in type size, and qualify as headlines by their leading position in the advertisement. Still another common form of headline is the blurb or balloon, in which a character is supposed to be speaking. Headlines do not even have to say anything. A company name, for instance, might be used as a headline. So might a familiar brand or signature. But practically all advertisements have headlines of one sort or another, and their primary function is to attract immediately the attention of the reader.

Overline

In some advertisements, you'll see an advertisement that is topped by a combination that looks like the following:

Here's a way to keep cool this summer.
(This is an overline. It is set in smaller type than the main headline that follows.)

Install a KUL-AIRE attic fan.
(This is the main headline.)

As you see, the overline, often called a "lead-in," is placed over the main headline and is almost always in smaller type. In the example shown here, the copywriter may have found, as he experimented, that if he put the two lines together in one main headline, he would have to reduce the type size in order to fit into the space. If the type were thus made smaller, the attention-getting value of the headline would be reduced. He elected, therefore, to make an overline of the first line. Thus he could call for big type in the relatively few words now used for the main headline.

FIGURE 1-2

Advertising agency advertisement stresses fundamentals. Any copywriter, new or experienced, can profit occasionally from the advice given here by one of the world's leading advertising agencies.

Subheads

In writing an advertisement you will often have some important facts you wish to telegraph to your reader, but which require more space than you care to use in the display of the headline, or possibly they are not quite so appealing as attention attracters. When such information is displayed in smaller type than the headline, yet larger than the body text of the advertisement, it is known as a "subhead." Subheads may be three or four lines of copy underneath the headline, or they may be display lines throughout the text, or in other places in the advertisement.

In our nation of quick readers, who so often are more picture-minded than print-minded, the subhead serves an important function. It tells the readers quickly what is coming in the copy and enables them to judge whether they want to continue. In most advertisements, nothing is lost if the subhead causes readers to skip the following copy. Usually, the headline and illustration, plus the signature of the advertiser, have already enabled the readers to judge whether it's to their self-interest to read the body copy.

Six questions to ask before you approve an advertisement.

1. Is there a big idea?

Nothing else is so important to the success of an advertisement. A genuine selling idea transcends execution. Before you approve any advertisement, ask yourself if it really has a big idea and if that idea emerges clearly, emphatically, and single-mindedly. Ask yourself: Is it an *important* idea—such as Scope's "medicine breath," the positioning of Pledge furniture polish as a dusting aid, or AMF's "We make weekends."

2. Is there a theme line?

A theme line that presents your selling idea in a memorable set of words can be worth millions of dollars of extra mileage to your advertising. Provocative lines like "When E.F. Hutton talks, people listen," "Please don't squeeze the Charmin," "We really move our tail for you" (Continental Airlines) make it easy for the customer to remember your selling message. Incidentally, when you get a great one, treasure it and use it prominently in every print ad and television commercial you run.

3. Is it relevant?

If your advertising is remembered but your product forgotten, you might as well run "compliments of a friend." Jokes that steal attention from the selling idea, inappropriate entertainment devices, celebrities who have no logical connection with your product, and other irrelevancies can be devastating. Look for relevance in every advertising execution.

4. Is it hackneyed?

Is the advertisement fresh, innovative, and original or is it merely a pale carbon copy of somebody *else's* advertising? Too much advertising is look-alike, sound-alike advertising. These advertisements are often costly failures. Don't run the risk of being mistaken for your competitor. Demand an execution that is all your own.

5. Does it demonstrate?

Nothing works harder or sells better than a demonstration of your product's superiority, especially in television. Look for every opportunity to demonstrate. If you can't demonstrate, at least show the product in use. Demonstrations—such as the simple exposition of how the Trac II razor works or the coating action of Pepto-Bismol—are convincing ways to sell.

6. Is it believable?

Does the advertising overpromise? Does the selling idea sound a false note? An advertisement can be totally truthful, yet sound unbelievable. Better to underpromise and be believable than to overpromise and lose credibility.

We know that great advertising is not made by rules nor created by guidelines. It comes from creative people. However, we also know from experience that most successful advertising has certain readily identifiable and wholly predictable qualities. We have listed six. There are others. We would like nothing better than to show you some of the advertising that illustrates these points.

Please call or write Jack Bowen, President, Benton & Bowles, Inc., 909 Third Avenue, New York, N.Y. 10022. Telephone: (212) 758-6200.

Benton&Bowles
New York, Chicago, Los Angeles, and other major cities worldwide.
It's not creative unless it sells.

A subhead, on the other hand, will normally lure readers into the following copy. In the case of very long copy, it will break up type masses and make the advertisement look easier to read. This is especially true of advertisements that do not sell products, but instead talk about the company or its point of view. These institutional advertisements, or "corporate" advertisements, usually obtain low readership. Well-written subheads can help make the advertisements look more interesting.

In some places, particularly in department store and other retail advertising operations, subheads are also known as "captions." This is not usually the case, however. Caption normally has a meaning all its own, as will be discussed shortly.

Body copy

Sometimes "body copy" is called "body text." Either way, it is the main message of your advertisement. Your selling is done in the body copy. Here is where you reason with the reader and show how persuasive you can be. Your body copy, if you structure your writing properly, is an extension of the idea conveyed initially by the headline and the illustration.

You have probably heard salespeople talk about "getting a foot in the door." Well, your headline is your foot. The body copy is the follow-through on that foot. Some advertisements actually have no body copy, from a technical standpoint. That is, they contain no major unit of type. Advertisements built around a comic-strip style, picture-and-caption advertisements, and others fall into this category. Since the entire story is told in these advertisements by other than the usual means, they will be discussed later as a highly specialized form of body copy.

Captions

Captions are the small units of type used with illustrations, coupons, and special offers. They are generally less important to the main selling points of the advertisement than body copy and are usually set in type sizes smaller than the body text. Now and then you will want to plan an entire advertisement in picture-and-caption style, presenting your sales points by illustrating them and explaining them at the same time, much the way a magazine handles news stories. Here, of course, the caption assumes far greater importance and must be considered as body text.

Blurbs

A "blurb," or "balloon," is the advertising profession's term for copy set up so that it seems to be coming from the mouth of one of the characters illustrated in the advertisement. It is most often used, as is the caption to punch across some secondary feature in the story you are telling, but sometimes it too can constitute the complete body text, as in the comic-strip style. Blurbs are often used as headlines. When

so employed, they are not changed in any way except to be displayed in larger-sized type and placed at the head of the advertisement. They are still known as blurbs or balloons.

Boxes and panels

You'll hear copywriters and artists referring regularly to "boxes" or "panels." These, as their names imply, are simply captions which obtain greater attention value by being placed in special display positions. A "box" is a caption around which a rule has been lined, singling it out from other copy. A "panel" is a solid rectangle of black or color, in the center of which is the caption, either in white or "reverse" type, or centered in white space. Boxes and panels are usually used in advertisements using such features as coupons, special offers, and contest rules. These will often be set apart from the rest of the advertisement by means of such devices. Boxes should be used sparingly.

Slogans, logotypes, and signatures

Many times you will meet a client whose company uses a slogan of years' standing and which he insists must appear in every advertisement. Too, almost all advertisers logically demand that their company name be displayed in its familiar form. This display of the company name, seal, or trademark is called a "logotype" and is a common part of most advertisements. The term is often abbreviated in advertising jargon to "logo," "sig," or "sig cut." Copyright notices, too, are often required for legal reasons and must be included in all copy prepared for such advertisers.

An important point to remember is that everything that appears in print in an advertisement must appear on the copy sheets that the copywriter prepares. These sheets serve as a guide to the artists and typographers and other production people who will be working on the advertisement after the copywriter has finished. If the copywriter leaves some element out of the copy, the whole advertisement may be held up later and a publication date missed because the advertisement may need to be reset.

One way to make sure of including the various elements is to set up the copy neatly and logically on the copy sheet by labeling the different elements on the side. Many copywriters are sloppy in their execution. An example of an ideal copy sheet is shown in Figure 1-4. If all copy sheets were handled in this manner, there would be fewer mistakes in production.

Broadcast copy must be included, too

All the attention in this chapter has been concentrated on print copy for newspaper and magazines. Most of what has been said will apply to other forms of print such as leaflets, folders, catalogs. For these forms of print, however, more elements may be included. These will be discussed in later chapters.

FIGURE 1-3

Use of balloons, as in this example, helps to emphasize points
an advertiser may wish to stress.

Also, to be discussed later will be the requirements for broadcast copy in radio and television. The same attention to form must be observed in writing radio commercials and in preparing material for television. In the latter, the writer must think in two dimensions, sight and sound. He encounters an entirely different vocabulary from that used for print. Since, in many advertising agencies, the copywriter creates broadcast commercials as well as print advertisements, he must be equally familiar with the terminology and form required in this kind of advertising.

(Illustration occupying approximately top 2/3 of advertisement consists of long, open box of pastels and, propped against the box, a picture presumably executed with the pastels)

Overline: A special introductory offer for only $2.98

Headline: 60 PROFESSIONAL OIL PASTELS

Subhead: New professional dustless type

Copy A: A huge assortment of pastels with no two colors the
            same. These professional dustless pastels can be
            mixed and blended but never make a mess. They are as
            convenient as pastels yet have the brilliance and
            color depth of oil paints. Sticks will not crumble
            or break easily and can be used on paper, board, cloth,
            stone or plaster. They are excellent for quick
            sketches as well as finished drawings and paintings.
            You may also use turpentine to blend colors and
            heighten the oil effect. Completed oil pastel
            paintings do not require fixing and can be framed like
            a water color painting. Nontoxic composition makes
            them perfect for adults or young "Picassos"! Great
            for portraits, landscapes, anything at all. A great
            gift and a great buy for only $2.98.

Subhead: Offer will not be repeated this season

Copy B: Supplies are limited and orders will be filled first
            come, first served, so we urge you to order right now
            to avoid disappointment. The price is right and offer
            will not be repeated this season.

Coupon   Mail 10-day no-risk coupon today.
copy: Greenland Studios
            5165 Greenland Building
            Miami, Florida 33054

            Please send me #9760 Oil Pastel sets checked below. I
            understand if not delighted, I may return for a prompt
            and complete refund. Enclosed is check or m.o. for
            $_____.
                       #9760 Oil Pastel sets
            _____ @$2.98 (Add 50¢ postage each)

            Name _____
            Address_____
            City_____
            State _____ Zip_____

            _____ Save $1. Enclose only $5.96 for 2 Oil Pastel sets
            and we will pay the postage. Extra set will make a
            wonderful gift.

FIGURE 1-4

Example of properly executed copy sheet.

HOW MUCH OF A WRITER IS A COPYWRITER?

The answer must be that he may be an ordinary hack writer, or he may, indeed, be a first-rate writer by any standard. Copywriting, if done well, is one of the most exacting forms of writing. It requires not only a command of the language but also an ability to coordinate persuasive, colorful writing with music, photography, artwork, printing, engraving, vocal intonations, and acting.

All this skill and coordination takes place within stern limitations of time, or space. Copywriting thus requires the writer to be precise, clear, and persuasive in relatively few words compared to most other forms of writing (always excepting poetry, of course). Furthermore, the good copywriter brings to the craft a knowledge of psychology, salesmanship, merchandising, marketing and purchasing habits.

Like any writer you try to make each piece of copy as perfect as possible but "perfect" often means that what you have written has produced sales rather than memorable prose. Many of the best advertisements will never win writing awards, but they'll make the cash registers sing. In most copy you strive for sales, not literary recognition. Instead of concentrating on literary excellence, you're thinking of the copy's suitability to the media used, the market for the product, and selling points. Often "fine" writing would be incompatible with a nuts-and-bolts type of product, or service, being sold.

Yet, there are times when your copy can be almost poetic in its execution; other times it will be prosaic and businesslike. The following examples were in advertisements in the same magazine. Each was aimed carefully at its audience. Each is executed well, but note the total difference in writing style.

Parure. It is a word which is difficult to translate. One could say "ornament" or "adornment" but one would be missing the point.

It is "Ornament" only in the sense of a jeweled tiara from Tiffany's. It is "adornment," but in the sense of an aura, creating a presence which is felt more than seen.

Parure is a fragrance of exquisite femininity. A fragrance evoking a season of lilacs and plums, the vigor of cypress, the charm of amber. It is lingering, opulent, and stunning. It is a perfume that says exactly what you want it to say.

In contrast to the foregoing is this second example from the magazine:

There are plenty of things you won't see when you look at a Kodak Moviedeck projector. But they're all there. Things like automatic threading, rapid reel-to-reel rewind, permanently attached takeup reel, elevation control and the capability to show both super 8 and 8 mm movies.

You might even miss the special pull-out viewing screen on Models 455, 465 and 475. It gives you the option of looking at your movies without setting up a big screen or turning off the room lights.

Marsteller Inc.
CHICAGO   As Recorded

RADIO COPY

Date typed:	March 25	Revision number:
Client:	LANIER BUSINESS PRODUCTS	Date recorded:
Program:	"Missing Person"	Air date: As Recorded
Length:	60	

ANNCR: Here's Stiller & Meara for Lanier Dictating Equipment.

STILLER: May I come in?

MEARA: Who are you?

STILLER: I'm your husband.

MEARA: Oh yeah, George. The guy who works late every night. I'm married to a missing person.

STILLER: I finally got caught up.

MEARA: Say hi to your son, Ronny.

STILLER: How's my little cub scout?

MEARA: He's in law school. He grew up.

STILLER: Ha ha. Still wearing that funny little hat, huh?

MEARA: Listen. If you don't start coming home earlier, I'm going to put us all up for adoption.

STILLER: I can't help it. I work as fast as I can.

MEARA: We need Lanier.

STILLER: Who's Lanier, a marriage counselor?

MEARA: Lanier is dictating equipment.

STILLER: I've never used dictating equipment.

MEARA: Dictating is 6 times faster than writing. With Lanier's Action Line, you'd be home at 5:00 instead of 10:00. And with a Pocket Secretary portable, you could bring work home!

STILLER: I think Lanier can bring us back together.

MEARA: Oh terrific! Now you'll be more to Ronny than just that strange little man in our wedding picture . . . . I'm so happy!

STILLER: I'm happy too, Donna.

MEARA: Donna? Who's Donna?

STILLER: I don't know. I made it up.

MEARA: Oh, George.

STILLER: Elaine . . . Phyllis . . . give me a hint!

ANNCR: Get more done with Lanier Business Products. In the Yellow Pages under dictating machines.

The first is ethereal and interpretive. It is concerned with mood instead of fact. The second is informative and common sense in its approach. Would you say the writing in the first advertisement was better than that in the second? Ask that question of laypeople and they'd probably answer yes. They would be impressed by the color of the words, the sensory appeal, the emotion. Advertising people however, would say "To each his own." They would mean that the second advertisement was just right for the product and the market. To attempt the approach of the first advertisement in the second advertisement could be detrimental to sales.

It is possible that the copywriter who wrote the second advertisement devoted more time and thought to the copy than did the copywriter who turned out the first. The writing you do must be tailored with precise craftsmanship to fit the job in hand.

FIGURE 1-5

Humorous radio commercial.   If the writing of copy was simply a straightforward assembling of facts, you would not see advertising such as this. Copywriting, however, often takes the kind of imagination shown in this commercial—an ability to use humor and yet not to forget to sell. As part of a campaign, this commercial succeeds in selling and in humor—a difficult accomplishment because writing acceptable humor is a very challenging task.

Judgment and versatility are other attributes that stand high in the requirements of good copywriting. As an agency copywriter especially, you will be expected not only to pace your copy correctly, but to write copy which differs in approach and feeling as radically as do the foregoing two examples.

It should be pointed out that some agencies and many retail establishments and mail-order houses consider the neophyte copywriter little more than a space-filler. In other words, you may start to work for a company whose policy will not permit you to do much creative thinking on your own for some time. During the preliminary phases of your training you may be asked simply to write the body text, captions, or other parts of advertisements for which the major planning has already been done by others. No attempt is made here to determine whether this system is better or worse than that which calls for the beginner to jump into the business of thinking out entire advertisements right from the start. Both have produced, and are still producing, successful copywriters. It is somewhat a question of temperament. Some copywriters like to have their assignments blueprinted for them—others find their satisfaction in being their own copy architects.

CREATIVE WORK IS EXCITING

To spin something out of your mind as you do in creative work is exciting. Then, to see your idea on the television screen, to hear it on radio, or to see it in a four-color magazine spread is deeply satisfying. That excitement and pleasure never disappear completely, and shouldn't. But you're concerned with something more than a personal satisfaction. Also, there is the effect of what you've created on that big market reached by the media, on the sales curves of your clients, on their salespeople, on the retail stores that sell their goods. If you think beyond those words that you've committed to paper, you'll see that there's another creative thrill to be obtained as an advertising copywriter, one that matches or even outdoes that of many writing artists whose work touches very few people.

One evidence of the right of advertising copywriting to be considered a legitimate example of writing art is in the number of writers of contemporary literature who began as advertising copywriters—especially as advertising agency copywriters. The exactness, the economy of phrasing, the requirement for subtle shadings in word meanings have given many copywriters the precise training they needed for their subsequent literary efforts.

It is not surprising then to discover how many well-known writers spent their early years behind a copywriter's desk. A few of these are such writers as Richard Powell, Cameron Hawley, Sinclair Lewis, and Sherwood Anderson. Many successful writers have, like Richard Powell and Cameron Hawley, produced best-selling novels or plays while they were still employed in advertising. This accomplishment is beyond most copywriters who find all the creative challenge they need in turning out good copy day after day. It is not recommended that persons enter the copywriting field as a preparation for producing literary works. It is true, nonetheless, that numerous literary people have found such preparation valuable.

One agency head had this to say about copywriters who write outside of their copywriting jobs: "Let 'em moonlight as poets, novelists, or freelance article writers. Just so they don't drain themselves so much creatively that they have nothing left for their copy jobs, I'm all for it. It's sort of a two-way street. Working in copy can make someone a better poet or novelist. And doing literary stuff can make copywriters better ad writers. All I ask is that they don't do these literary productions on company time."

2

Know Your Market Before You Write

You have a title—copywriter. This identifies you as a person in advertising. Also, it means that you're in marketing. Never forget that advertising is only a part of the much bigger activity of "marketing," the total process of getting goods from the producer to the user. Your job is a small, but important, part of that marketing process.

Although this book deals almost entirely with copywriting and the copywriter's duties, you should understand some of the marketing questions that must be investigated and answered before your advertising copy can be fully effective. You must know the basic sales strategy, since it establishes a definite set of boundaries into which you fit your writing and the planning of your writing.

You may never have much to do with the establishment of the basic sales strategy unless you happen to work on a new product promotion; or possibly the product is one that needs a complete promotional overhauling. In either case, you might sit in on meetings during which the sales setup of the company is established or reorganized. Usually, however, you will do most of your creative work for organizations which have been operating profitably and whose sales strategy is well established.

Part of your job will consist of studying this policy. You will need to understand why it was established. This will be accomplished through a thorough examination of what might be termed "the Three P's": the product, the prospects, and the purchases. To write effective copy, you must know your three P's well. Whatever product you're writing about, consider it in the light of the following analysis.

P IS FOR PRODUCT

Does the product fill a definite need or desire? An automatic washing machine, for example, fills a definite need. Several, in fact. It enables a person to wash the family's clothes cleaner, with less effort, in less time, and with less wear and tear on the clothes. If a person had been sending the laundry out prior to the purchase of the automatic washing machine, such a machine will also save money. Thus, an automatic home laundry can fill five basic needs!

Perfume or shaving lotion, on the other hand, does not fill a specific need. It does fill a very strong natural desire felt by many people to be attractive. People use these products to fulfill a wish—to feel better groomed.

Then there are products that fall in-between. For some, they fill a need. For others, they fill a desire. Such a product is the CB radio that caused a buying wave in the mid-70s. Only a relative few in the population really needed CB radios, but millions desired them and this latter group formed a vast market. Many other products fall into this in-between status. Examples are snowmobiles and ten-speed bicycles that are needed by few and desired by many.

Almost all successful products fill either a need or a desire. Unfortunately, however, a continuous flow of products on the market fill neither need nor desire. These are usually spawned by "mad" inventors or by others whose imagination is spent on fashioning the inventions—not in figuring out a real use for their creations. Without seeking competent advice from persons experienced in marketing, they blindly rush into production "before someone steals the idea." Their reasoning, if it may be called that, seems to run something like this: "There's no product on the market like it! Therefore, it's bound to be a best seller!" They fail to see the reason there is no similar product— because there's no real need or desire for one. Typical of this type of "predoomed" product would be a left-handed shoehorn. Such a gadget might amuse you, but you wouldn't buy it. The marketer of such a product would soon run out of prospects because it fills neither need nor desire.

Just the same, there is—and undoubtedly will continue to be—a constant flow of novelty products which manufacturers introduce with the full knowledge that—because they do not fill any lasting need or desire—the products can only hope to enjoy flash sales over a short period and then almost die out.

The objective is to whip up a desire for their product through its novelty. If it catches on, sales sky-rocket; but they usually plummet a short time later as illustrated by "soapless" soap bubbles, hula hoops, and pet rocks which piled up sales for a brief time and then were seen no more. Such products come and go. They're freaks and not to be likened to the normal, stable products which are your primary concern as an advertising person. Once it has been established that your product fills a valid need or desire, the next thing you should want to know is:

Are most users satisfied with the product? It is a fundamental of marketing that a product must live up to the buyers' expectations if it is to be a successful repeat-sale item. Living up to expectations is probably even more important in the case of low-cost, nondurable products. Bread, hair oil, soft drinks can't attain sustained success, no matter how sound your advertising may be, unless a good percentage of buyers constantly and quickly repeat their purchases when the initial purchase needs replacement. In the case of the printing press it is important to the continued success of the manufacturer that the product live up to its claims. Repeat orders for $100,000 printing presses, however, would come at very long intervals. Few printers would make such a huge investment without first finding out from companies already owning similar presses whether they were satisfactory—thus the buyer of such an item would be satisfied in advance of purchase that the product was all right. Regardless of the nature of a product, then, it must represent honest value if it is to obtain lasting success. Next, you will want to know:

Does the product possess any exclusive features of benefit to the user? The answer to this question is important. When your product does possess exclusive advantage over competition, it often will give you an advantage over the copywriters working on the competitive accounts—a knockout punch they don't have.

Crest toothpaste, with fluoride, is an example. It was a success from the start, vaulting into first place almost overnight. Polaroid's instant camera offered another exclusive benefit that made the copywriter's job easy. The remote control device introduced on Zenith television sets is still another product-exclusive to which the public responded. The lesson? Give people a meaningful exclusive benefit and they'll buy.

Other "firsts" or product exclusives were the Ford convertible hardtop, Sanka coffee (caffeine removed), and the original mentholated cigarettes. Speaking of mentholated cigarettes, although you may not recall when they were first marketed, you certainly have been aware of the results of imitation. The first mentholated cigarettes were followed by a parade of new cigarettes featuring everything from dry ice to crème de menthe.

Many products have exclusive features. Unless, however, their advantages are rather obvious to prospective buyers, these exclusives may be difficult to write about and thus far less effective as selling tools. That a product differs from competitive ones does not mean, of course, that the difference necessarily will sell more merchandise—the difference must be a definite plus value of demonstrable importance to the buyer.

Be careful that you are not lulled into a pleasant dream by the glowing description you may get of a product from its maker. Human nature being what it is, almost any advertiser may be overly enthusiastic about what he has to offer. He may endow the product with advantages that actually don't exist outside his own imagination. Only your own close study of the product, independent laboratory tests, or large-scale sampling studies can give an unbiased comparison between two or more similar products, insofar as possible consumer reaction and your copy approach are concerned.

Such laboratory tests or samplings, though they may be fairly expensive, often prove to be excellent investments. If, as a result, the product lives up to expectations, buyers will respond more readily to copy backed by impartial comparisons than to copy filled with unproved claims. For instance, in these days of energy conservation, the car that delivers greater proved mileage; the washing machine that has proved it uses less hot water; or the tire that has proved it lasts longer give the advertisers powerful material for advertisements.

Is the product or service "positioned" correctly? Positioning a product simply means that you and others concerned with product promotion examine that product to determine just what it is you are offering, and to what kind of people, and how you want these people to think of the product. Out of these three findings is born much of your creative strategy.

Few products are intended for everyone. In today's market segmentation, there are specific products for specific groups and subgroups. Advertising is directed to these. The same is true of services. A bank, for example, might position itself as the "young family" bank that aims at those who are buying homes and furnishings, taking loans, and are generally on the way up—and going into debt to get there.

In the same city, another bank is positioned as a "solid, conservative, business-oriented" institution. Its advertising and media choices (no radio stations featuring rock, country western, or bluegrass) zero in on the older, more affluent group. The stress in advertising is on the bank's understanding of the needs of business people and investors.

A new hair cream for men might position itself as a superior hair grooming preparation that offers the good grooming of hair cream without the greasiness often associated with these creams. The segment of the market at which the advertising is directed is the

15–34 male audience that buys three-fourths of the total output of hair creams. Once more, the product is positioned against the proper market segment.

A complexion soap uses cold cream as an ingredient and positions itself as a skin-care product for the segment of the population who suffer from dry skin. To further separate themselves, the company avoids calling the product a "soap." The emphasis is on skin care rather than mere cleansing.

So it goes. First, you determine what your product really is and what needs it will satisfy. After this, you position it in relation to your prospects. At that point, you can more surely find an advertising strategy that will convince the prospects that the product is suited to their needs and that it will answer their problems better than competing products. This separation from the competition is vital. Thus you might well call "positioning" a search for the product's proper identity in the marketplace.

P IS FOR PROSPECTS

When you have examined the foregoing product considerations, you will have explored only one area of the precopy approach. Now that you have thought about the product, what about the people you hope will buy your goods instead of your competitor's? You must know these people equally well.

In many instances, you will know clearly who your best prospects are. In many others, what you may consider obvious may be wrong. You might think that men would be your best prospects for men's shirts. You may find that they are not. To your surprise you may find that so many wives shop for their husbands that women buy more men's shirts than men do!

Never ride a wild conclusion when determining who are your best prospects. Get the facts—from actual sales studies. Find out:

Are your best prospects men or women? For maximum effectiveness, your copy must be aimed at your best prospects—not at just anyone. Certain copy approaches appeal especially to men, others to women. When you write to women, for example, your copy should be consistently directed to women only if it is going to be fully effective. If, as with cigarettes, both sexes are large buyers, your copy will be written to appeal to both. To sum up: Decide whether your product will appeal to men, women, or to both men and women. Having determined this, key your writing to fit the group.

Are they young, middle-aged or old? And why is this knowledge of value? Because, as people grow older—as they proceed from grade school, to high school, to college, to business, to marriage, to family, to middle age, and possibly on to grandparenthood—both their needs and desires for products change. Children, certainly, are your best potential customers for bubble gum. Children are your worst prospects for automobiles—the law and the family budget see to that. Young married couples buy the largest percentage of baby necessities, but they put up strong resistance to the cemetery-lot salesperson. People over thirty-five are fine prospects for home improvement products, but would laugh if you tried to sell them boxing gloves or popsicles. So birthdays are important—not only to the people themselves but also to the copywriters who can make money out of birthdays if they key their copy to the age.

Are your best prospects rich, poor, or average? Who, would you say, would be your best prospects if you were writing an advertisement for fur coats—women of wealth, women of average means, or working women? The answer to that question would depend on what kind of fur coats you were writing about! You'd know that Park Avenue or Gold Coast women would be your best bets for ermine evening wraps. You'd know, too, that the Park Avenue prospect would shudder at the low-priced, dyed-rabbit coat that a store clerk would go without lunches to buy. Sex, age, and income thus are important factors in the movement of many types of merchandise.

Where do most of your prospects live? If your product is burglary insurance, your best prospects would be among city dwellers, because statistics show that a huge percentage of burglaries occur in cities. Small-town people, on the other hand, would probably be more interested in your copy story on home canning equipment than would urbanites. Farm families, logically, are your audience if you're writing about agricultural equipment. Again you may say, "But all those things are obvious." You're right. Throughout this entire chapter you have been given examples that would be obvious to any thinking person. Why? Because when you and the next person and the next person write copy, you tend to forget what was once so obvious to you. You forget the simple truths—the obvious thinking that makes your copy sell. You get so wrapped up in technique and the ultra refinements of the copywriter's art that you forget these obvious truths and facts that sell merchandise. This section, accordingly, has not endeavored to be subtle. You have been told, "When writing to women, then write exclusively to women," "When writing about a home canning product, then write primarily to small town or country dwellers." If you learn these obvious stratagems early in your copy career—and remember them—you'll be a better copywriter.

To show you how the obvious can be overlooked, wouldn't you think that it would be a waste of money for an advertiser to take large space in California newspapers to warn motorists to "Get Set Now for Winter's Sub-zero Blasts!"? But one major advertiser did just that! The illustration showed Old Man Winter blowing an icy breath. It failed, however, to chill the sun-tanned spines of Californians. The copy pushed antifreeze, tire chains, high-powered heaters, and other arctic equipment—all of which the average Californian has as much use for as he has Florida oranges—unless he plans to spend the entire winter skiing in the Sierras.

Remember where your prospect lives. His location has a direct bearing on how he lives, and often affects wants or needs.

What are your prospects' tastes—in reading, in TV, in radio? If you have been able to determine the sex, age, income, and habitat of your prospects, you have covered some of the important points of their private lives. You will still want to know something about their preferences in reading and in TV and radio. What kinds of newspapers and magazines do they usually read? Do they read the *New York Times, Harper's, Fortune,* and the *Wall Street Journal,* or perhaps a tabloid newspaper, *True Story, Playboy,* and *Variety?*

When they watch television, do they lean toward high drama or low comedy, sports, news, or westerns? In radio listening are they likely to be hearing your commercials in the car driving home from work, or at home doing the ironing?

FIGURE 2-1

Advertisement aimed at high-level market.   After considering the market and the product carefully, the advertiser placed this advertisement in the *New Yorker* magazine. Notice that the copy level is appropriate for the product and the medium.

1860 Life Mask

Two years before Abraham Lincoln became President, Chicago sculptor, Leonard Wells Volk, greatly impressed by Lincoln's debate with Douglas, sought his permission to make a life mask. It was not until 1860, just prior to his nomination, that the opportunity came to do so during a Lincoln visit to Chicago.

From this original life mask Volk made a plaster cast now in my private collection. I am making available a limited edition of 1,000 solid bronze castings from this life mask. Each one is carefully hand finished under my direct personal supervision, and comes to you in a handsome hand made walnut case or with a distinctive stand.

In these days of fragile and tenuous heroes, Lincoln's greatness endures unblemished. As surely as the sculptor Volk captured his exact likeness, this bronze emanates a life of its own so strongly as to be almost mystical. This bronze, made with the admiration and respect deserved, will serve as an inspiration to all who view it.

I think it is a rare opportunity to share the spirit of this great man, whether as a personal possession, corporate or community gift.

$1200

Jack Lane

Write for details, brochure and color photo of the Bronze Lincoln Life Mask.

JACK LANE STUDIO
29 WEST HUBBARD STREET,
CHICAGO, ILLINOIS 60610 · 312-337-2326

In cross-section studies of potential consumers, the equal appeal of a product to different groups often necessitates diversified radio or television advertising. This wide appeal is particularly true of products such as cereals, which are equally enjoyed by children and adults. You'll agree that a cereal television commercial written for use on a show produced for young children is not likely to have much selling appeal for the TV viewers of one of the cereal maker's adults shows.

How much do your prospects already know about the product? Are most of your best prospects already familiar with the product, as most people are now familiar with home permanents, for instance? Or is it a new product, whose utility or other benefits must be clearly explained as Toni Home Permanent originally had to be explained? How much potential buyers know about the product, and how well they know it, will definitely affect your copy.

Starting your copy in either case will give you certain difficulties. If your product is well-known, you either say the same thing over and over again hoping to sell through repetition, or work for new ways to start your copy. If you use this latter technique, copy will "start" out of your inventiveness and your application of the P's. You'll strain to give an old story a new fascination in each advertisement.

On the other hand, your problem with a new product is that you can assume so little. You're not entirely sure of your prospects, since you cannot tell by any previous sales record, as in the case of an already marketed product, how the consumers react to your product and copy message. The reader will not know your product name, how it works, what it's made of, who makes it, and just what it will do for the buyer. You must explain and sell, and you must do your best to gauge the reader's interest in and knowledge of the type product you are advertising. If he is already acquainted with the type of product, for instance, it will make your copy job easier even if your product is being put on the market for the first time. It may mean that you will need to do less selling of the need for the product. Advertising of similar products may have given your type of product an acceptability to the general public. Thus you may start off your copy confident that you don't need to stress the need for the product so much as the qualities of your product that make it superior to other similar ones on the market.

P IS FOR PURCHASES

You now have arrived at the point where you may think you have done enough analyzing to enable you to create campaigns that will ring the cash registers of every store in the country selling your product. Perhaps you're eager to get your ideas down on paper—but wait just a minute! You may know a good deal about your product. You may know fairly well the people who should be your best prospects. There are still, however, some important points you haven't touched that affect the actual buying of the product.

Where do customers buy the product? Early in their careers copywriters must recognize that most people are *not* particularly anxious to buy the products for which they're writing copy. During World War II, when shortages existed, a single whisper from a salesperson to a friend could have sold a carload of nylon stockings. That's because there weren't enough nylons to go around. Normally, in peacetime there's more than enough of all commodities. There's plenty of your product and plenty of your competitors'. The public, under normal conditions, won't react to your selling message with a fraction of the mad greed they displayed for nylon stockings years ago.

Today it is not enough to sell people merely on the desirability of your product. You must be a sort of remote-control Pied Piper and lure them from their easy chairs right down to the store. You must make it as easy as possible for them to buy. Unless the product is one that is so well established that everyone knows where he can buy it, you'll want to tell him where it is sold—whether at drug stores, hardware stores, grocery stores, or all three! Never leave any question in his mind, since, unless you're selling diamond rings for a dollar, few people will be so anxious to purchase your product that they will be willing to go out and search for a place that handles it! Tell your readers or listeners where they can buy it! And be as specific as possible. Don't rely on such empty phrases as "sold by leading stores everywhere" or "get it at your nearest dealer's."

The first of these statements possibly has some vague value as advertising. It may enhance the prestige of the product in the minds of a small percentage of prospects. Some people may reason, if they take the trouble, that if leading stores carry it, it must be good. But this type of statement is sometimes no more than an expression of wishful thinking on the part of the advertiser, and it often backfires to his disadvantage. To illustrate, picture a man reading a shoe advertisement in a national magazine. The shoes look good to him, and he wants to buy a pair. The advertisement explains that he can get them "at better stores coast to coast." He concludes from that phrase that Macy's carries this particular brand. Certainly, Macy's is a "better store," so he goes down to Macy's. He finds that Macy's doesn't carry the brand in which he's interested, and what happens? While in Macy's he eyes a pair of shoes by a different maker and decides to buy them instead. The copywriter who wrote the shoe advertisement that appealed to this man actually ended up by making a sale for a competitive brand! Wouldn't it have been much wiser if this manufacturer (as so many do) had clearly listed the dealers in the classified section of the phone book and advised readers to "see the classified section of your phone book for name of your nearest dealer"? Or run in the advertisement a list of stores in the country that sell the shoes?

Similarly, the phrase "Get it at your nearest dealer's" is meaningless if a prospect doesn't have any idea where his nearest dealer is. He might be seventy-five miles away for all the reader may know! You have to tell him where he can buy all but the most commonplace products. If he can get your brand only at Safeway stores, tell him so. If all good stores carry it, tell him so. If he can get the name and address of his nearest dealer by calling a telephone number, tell him so. If he can order by mail, tell him so. Do everything within your power to make it easy for prospects to buy!

Are purchases primarily seasonal or for special occasions? Most products sell well all year round. Many are sold as seasonal items. You'd know that snow shovels, Christmas tree lights, and ice skates aren't bought in June; and you wouldn't be surprised that lawn mowers, flower seeds, and sun shades would sell poorly in winter. But what about electric light bulbs? Do they sell equally well throughout the year? Offhand, if you didn't stop to analyze it, you might well answer yes to that question. But, because it is dark earlier in winter—which means more use of electricity and more burned-out bulbs—sales are naturally greater during the winter months.

Similarly, you might reason that because people must know the time every day, watches wouldn't be subject to any sharp rises and falls in sales. But you'd be wrong because watches—and perfume, jewelry, and candy, to name but a few—are largely bought as gifts for Christmas, graduations, birthdays, and wedding anniversaries. Thus they are referred to as "special occasion" items.

Why is it important that you know whether the products for which you are writing copy sell more readily in one period than another? Or are bought primarily as gifts? The answer is—to help you avoid misdirecting your copy. For instance, suppose you are an agency copywriter and you are assigned to write copy on watches. The contact person, or account executive in charge of the account, is so familiar with the peculiarities of the market that he may take it for granted that you know the slant your copy should take. Without knowing that most people receive their watches as gifts, you might naturally assume that your primary object would be to persuade readers to buy a watch for personal use. In actual practice, you'd probably have much better results if you told them the watch would make a wonderful gift for a coming graduation.

If there's the slightest question in your mind as to whether a product falls into one of these specialized categories, ask, don't guess, in order that you can be sure you're aiming at the right market! Be humble and remember that although you might think candy bars sell in about the same volume every month of the year, actually they don't.

Is purchase premeditated or impulsive? Any major purchase, such as a car, fur coat, refrigerator, or stereo component system, is usually made only after lengthy consideration. Before buying, people usually debate their actual need for a new stove. They ask themselves if, instead of buying a new sofa, they might not have their old sofa repaired. In the purchase of an automobile there is usually a long deliberation as to the family's ability to pay for a car. Even after a decision has been made to buy the super-deluxe, they still take their time before actually making the purchase. Almost any major purchase is made slowly. The buyers shop around, comparing one radio-phonograph against several others, one pressure cooker against its competitors.

Even some relatively low-priced items are bought this way. Phonograph records, for example. People listen—often to half a dozen or more recordings of the same popular tune—before they buy.

Such sales are made only after the buyer has weighed the facts. Thus they are termed "premeditated purchases," to differentiate them from what are known as "impulse purchases." In this latter classification falls such merchandise as chewing gum, soft drinks, cigarettes—and any and all other goods people normally buy without going through the long, involved process of reasoning that precedes a "premeditated purchase." A typical impulse buyer is the person who inserts a coin in the Coke dispenser in a service station. He drives in for the sole purpose of getting gas, but when he sees the Coca-Cola cooler, he decides to have a cool drink. This purchase is completely impulsive.

To show the extent of impulse buying, various researchers interested in grocery buying habits have pointed out that more than 50 percent of women shoppers buy one-third of their groceries on impulse. Does your product come within this one-third group?

You should learn into which category a product falls if you hope to attain maximum effectiveness in your copy. You can be flippant and capricious—and deal in generalities—in an advertisement for a bubble bath. The technique changes when you're persuading a person to part with thousands of dollars for a Cadillac. This person wants fact, not foolishness—sincerity, not flippancy.

If you want to "win friends and influence people," be sure your copy is always tuned in the right key.

How does the price of your product compare with prices charged by competitors? If a buyer has a choice between two products he considers to be of equal merit and equal renown, and finds that one is priced appreciably lower than the other, he is almost certain to take the one that costs less.

Price, especially in times of economic distress, is an important factor in the selling of merchandise. You are handicapped if you don't know how the price of your product compares with the prices of competitive goods. If your price is appreciably higher, then you will want to explain, as convincingly as you can, why it's higher. If it's lower, you'll want to tell your readers or listeners that they not only can get good service from your product, but also that they save money by buying it rather than some other make!

SEGMENTATION AND THE COPYWRITER

Closely allied with positioning, discussed earlier, is segmentation that is involved with all three of the P's. This term refers to breaking the total market into

units of various types. Segmentation has many definitions, and appears in many forms as you will discover in reading the numerous articles and books on the subject.

Sometimes the segmentation breakdown is geographic. Regional magazines recognize this form of segmentation. Then there is Zip-Code marketing that can be geographic and demographic in enabling the marketer to zero in on certain areas and certain demographic groupings. For the copywriter the demographic segmentations are more important. It is important to know that people of similar interests tend to cluster and that they tend to exhibit common buying habits and attitudes. Such people will likewise have similar goal-related characteristics.

Another segmentation is by rate of usage of a product. The market, accordingly, may be broken down into heavy users of a product, light users, and potentially heavy or light users among those not presently users.

Usage might have ethnic overtones. For example, one study of rice consumption showed that in New York City the Puerto Rican 12 percent of the population consumed 55 percent of the rice.[1] Blacks consumed another 33 percent of the total.

In Miami, Florida, Cubans, who make up 22 percent of the population, consumed 66 percent of the rice. In Los Angeles, the high consumption of rice was among Mexican-Americans and blacks while in San Francisco the product was consumed largely by Orientals and blacks.

Mayonnaise, the study revealed, has a consumption index of 24 in Des Moines, 204 in Atlanta. Likewise, regular coffee with a national average of 15.1 percent is consumed at a 3.7 percent level in Portland, Oregon but reaches a 34.6 percent level in Charlotte, North Carolina.

These variations, of intense interest to the marketing and sales departments of the manufacturer, will ultimately be of concern to the copywriter who shapes an approach to what market research has revealed—especially if markets are developed on a section-by-section basis.

Still another segmentation breakdown is psychographic, referring to the life styles or personality characteristics of buyers within the segment. According to psychographics, the market might be described in such terms as: religion-obsessed, radical chic, buttoned-down-conservative, macho, white-Anglo-Saxon-Protestant, executive, militant, activist, women's lib, ski bum, hippie, back-to-nature, and in a myriad of other ways. Some of these are easily defined and thus easy to write to; others have blurred profiles that make it more difficult for the copywriter to write to them effectively.

Although segmentation is more directly pertinent to the marketing strategist than the copywriter, it is, nonetheless, one more factor in your search for understanding of those complex, fascinating prospects

[1]Harry Wayne McMahan, "Baptists Researching $1,000,000 'Peace of Mind' TV Campaign," *Advertising Age*, December 20, 1976, p. 20.

to which you address your copy messages. The more you understand of such matters as positioning and segmentation, the more confident you can be in your writing. Some aspects of segmentation and positioning you already know through observation and experience; others you learn as you go along.

FIND OUT FOR YOURSELF—THEN ACT

If a copywriter collected personally all the data needed for an analysis similar to the one presented, he would be taking too much time from his writing job. No copywriter would be expected to gather it all. Much of it may have been already well established by previous experience with the given product. Most of the rest will come from research studies. You can take an active part by doing what has for many years been popularized as "The Hat Trick." That is, you should put on your hat and go out and do some first-hand research on your own hook. Make a representative number of the interviews yourself. Ask questions—not among your own friends, but of the ordinary people on the street. Talk to dealers and wholesalers. Talk to people who use your product and like it. Find out why they like it! Talk to people who have tried your product but now use something else. Find out why they didn't like your product! Do "The Hat Trick"—often and thoroughly.

Your study of the basic strategy is now completed. And you have gone out and done enough personal research to give you a good feel of the problem.

You now have what seem to be all the pertinent facts.

You have determined what seem to be your best selling points. You've identified what seem to be your best prospects. And you've come to a decision on how best to reach these prospects.

You are ready now to start building a good, sound advertising program that will sell more of your goods to more and more people.

STRATEGY CONSIDERATIONS

Strategy is defined as "employing plans toward a goal." A plan for advertising, if it involves a campaign, is invariably written. Sometimes it is called a "copy platform," and may take weeks, or months, to work out. It can be very long but usually is short, a mere outline, in fact. Brevity is desirable. If the plan is very long, it is more difficult to use on a day-to-day basis. Also, it can be subject to more misinterpretation.

One point is certain. If a client and the advertising agency have a plan, or copy platform, through weeks or months of hard work, the agency copywriter deviates from the plan at his peril. Although creative plans, copy platforms, or enunciations of copy strategy differ, all have certain common points. Following are three examples called:

Creative Planning Guide
Creative Strategy
Written Advertising Plan

Any one of these will be useful in helping you determine the direction of your creative efforts, no matter what it is called.

Creative Planning Guide

1. Overall, what do we want to accomplish: Increased sales? Bigger share of market? Favorable opinion toward company, or product? A change of public attitude toward company, or product?
2. To whom are we addressing our message?
3. What do we have to offer that is unique? If we have nothing unique, what is our strongest selling point? Supporting points?
4. What media will carry our advertising?
5. How do we position our product (or service)?
6. What is the best creative strategy—hard sell? Soft persuasion? Strong identification approach?

Creative Strategy

1. Objective—what the advertising should do.
2. Target audience—who is your consumer?
3. Key consumer benefit—why the consumer should buy your product.
4. Support—a reason to believe in that benefit.
5. Tone and manner—a statement of the product "personality."[2]

Written Advertising Plan

1. Statement of advertising objectives.
2. Written advertising strategy.
3. List of reasons for buying.
4. Product positioning statement.
5. Creative blueprint.[3]

THE CAMPAIGN THEME

Once the basic sales strategy for any product or service is established, the next step is to develop a campaign theme. This is the vehicle in which you deliver your selling points to the public. It's the central idea—the imaginative spark plug—that will give your advertisements continuity, recall value, and thus, extra selling power.

Your theme is the life line of your campaign, and its development will largely be your responsibility as the copywriter. So take your time: make sure you develop a good theme. The success of the entire campaign may well hinge on the effectiveness of your theme.

Copywriters working on the national level almost always are looking for big ideas, or themes, that can be repeated in many advertisements as part of the long-run campaign. Even on the local level, the copywriters for such organizations as banks and dairies will work mightily to come up with a strong

[2]Kenneth Roman and June Maas, *How To Advertise* (New York: St. Martin's Press, 1976), p.3.
[3]Steuart Henderson Britt, ed., *Marketing Manager's Handbook* (Chicago: The Dartnell Corporation, 1973), p. 935.

campaign theme that will be used many times with effectiveness. The writer who consistently presents campaign themes or ideas is the one who shoots ahead in advertising, not the one who thinks only in terms of "one-shotters." In the following material you will be given some suggestions for utilizing certain basics from which powerful advertising themes spring.

You have already determined from your basic strategy planning why people might buy yours and similar products, what they want and expect for their money. Your first interest is to develop a theme that will, over a long period, influence a large number of people to want and buy your product instead of that of a competitor. To accomplish this you want to appeal to their own selfish interests.

INTERESTS, DRIVES, AND APPEALS

Psychology is often named as one of the most important subjects a copywriter can study. Certainly when he begins to consider consumers' selfish interests, their drives, and the basic appeals that can motivate them, he is drawing upon psychology. He may ask himself, for instance, "Aren't the basic human appeals used by a copywriter simply the means by which we satisfy consumer drives?" He can, of course, neither pose that question nor answer it unless he understands "drives" to mean urgent, basic, or instinctual needs. Or sometimes such drives may be defined as culturally acquired concerns, interests, or longings.

He knows that human beings do what they do because of certain stimuli. An advertising copywriter is not likely, however, to talk of stimuli or drives. He talks instead of basic human appeals or simply "advertising appeals." Each of us is motivated consciously or subconsciously by these psychological stimuli each day. Every copywriter hopes that his copy can trigger the proper stimuli that lead to buying action, and they draw upon his understanding of human appeals to accomplish this.

Copywriters are not limited in their appeals to the truly basic, or primary, appeals of hunger, thirst, and the sex drive. (But some psychologists insist that all human appeals stem from fear, love, or hunger.) He uses these and many others. How many appeals he utilizes depends on what school he went to or what list he cares to use as a guide. When trying to determine a definitive list of basic human appeals, it is too limiting to utilize only the truly basic, or primary, appeals. On the other hand, some authorities offer lists of twenty-four such appeals or more. A copywriter will find such long lists unworkable.

It may be understood, therefore, that no one list of basic human appeals has been agreed upon by everyone. You are offered the following list, ample enough to be useful, but brief enough for convenience. Each appeal is powerful enough to supply the stimuli previously referred to and each may be found in advertisements, some more than others, of course.

In studying these products and relating their sales stories to the basic appeals, you will again be aware that almost all of them employ multiple appeals. In many cases one appeal can be made unmistakably dominant. Many advertisements, however, seem to put equal stress on two or more appeals. A Goodyear tire advertisement might, through illustration and headline treatment, put over a smashing stress on fear. The copy will carry out this theme but will do so through a strong appeal to family love. The father will be urged to protect his wife and children against the hazards of a blowout. A copy section at the bottom of the advertisement emphasizes a strong third point—economy.

In many products you will find it possible to develop a theme that will intermingle appeals so that it is difficult to say just which is dominant. In one advertisement, for example, the headline reads, "How to be safe—and save 31¢ on our flashlight batteries." Which is stronger—the appeal to fear or to acquisitiveness?

Although it is difficult and sometimes impossible to develop a theme which falls unmistakably into one appeal classification, it is best to try to come as close to this goal as possible. A "shotgun" theme which embraces several appeals may often fail to carry out your basic sales strategy by weakening the punch of your copy message.

All advertising, of course, is not built on such attention-catching themes as those given as examples. All advertising, however—even one-time insertions—should be built on a central theme that appeals to the prospect through one or more basic human interests. The important thing to remember is to choose the appeal or appeals that will have the greatest interest for the greatest number of your prospects.

BASIC HUMAN APPEALS

As you go over the following basic appeals, evaluate each one as it applies to yourself. Not until you do this can you fully appreciate the wide extent of their power in influencing people to buy the goods you have to sell. You will discover something more in going over these appeals—that they often overlap. Thus an advertisement will contain several basic appeals. Possibly all of them are equally strong, or it may be that one appeal clearly dominates.

ACQUISITIVENESS. Desire for money, power prestige, efficiency, material possessions.
COMFORT. Desire for physical comfort, rest, leisure, peace of mind.
CONVENIENCE. Desire to eliminate work, to do tasks more easily.
CURIOSITY. Desire for any kind of new experience.
EGOTISM. Desire to be attractive, popular, praised.
FAMILY AFFECTION, TOGETHERNESS, AND HAPPY HOME LIFE. Desire to do things as a family unit, to please members of the family, to help children in their growing years.

FEAR.   Of pain, death, poverty, criticism; loss of possessions, beauty, popularity, and loved ones.

HEALTH.   Desire for good health, longevity, youthful vigor.

HERO WORSHIP.   Desire to be like people we admire.

KINDNESS, GENEROSITY, AND UNSELFISHNESS.   Desire to help others, our country, our church.

LOVE AND SEX.   Desire for romantic love, normal sex life.

MENTAL STIMULATION.   Desire to improve mind, to broaden mental horizons.

PLEASURE.   Desires fulfilled through fun, travel, entertainment, enjoyment in general.

SENSORY APPEALS.   Desire for any stimulus received through any of the five senses.

To show how the foregoing may be used in developing advertising campaign themes, in Figure 2-2 is a list of familiar products whose advertising consistently reflects one or more of these basic appeals. You will recognize immediately the association between the appeal and the product sales story, even though through the years, different words and different slogans and copy approaches have been used to express the idea.

U.S.P., suffering points, and point of difference

Some years ago Rosser Reeves, a prominent advertising agency executive, stirred the advertising world with his book *Reality In Advertising*. In this short book he made a number of powerful points that caused endless discussion in advertising circles. One of the most important phrases to come from that book was "Unique Selling Proposition," or U.S.P. To paraphrase from the definition in the book, the U.S.P. is a proposition each advertisement makes that is powerful, unique and not offered by the competition. Sometimes the uniqueness lies in the product or in a claim that is made for the product. An example of the latter was Colgate's "Cleans your breath while it cleans your teeth."

What you must do in those minutes or hours before writing your copy is to look for the U.S.P. Sometimes it jumps right out at you. Consider the attributes of the four following products:

Product No. 1:   A power lawn mower that cuts tall grass evenly even when the grass is soaking wet.

Product No. 2:   Canned cream that tastes exactly like real cream.

Product No. 3:   An alarm clock that plays Brahms Lullaby.

Product No. 4:   A magnesium tray that polishes silver without rubbing.

Can you always find a distinct U.S.P. in a product or service? No. If you're ingenious enough, however, you may be able to devise a unique claim such as that mentioned for Colgate. But suppose you can't seem to dig out any usable U.S.P.? Here is where you might rely on the suffering points approach.

A "suffering point" is the need of the consumer that possession of the product will satisfy. Remember that people do not buy products; they buy uses of the product that will take care of some problem they have. A product may take care of a consumer's suffering points without having U.S.P.

For example, after Teflon-coated frying pans became common, these products still answered a suffering point—the tendency of food to stick to frying pans. To take another product, a suffering point voiced by millions of nonprofessional painters was the dripping of the paint and its regrettable habit of running down the paintbrush when the brush was held above shoulder level. DuPont's Lucite answered this problem.

Look for the suffering points in every product you advertise and bring them up humanly and believably. Suffer with the reader. Sympathize. Let him or her know that you appreciate the problem and then tell how your product solves that problem.

And then we come to the "point-of-difference." While this would seem to be another way of saying U.S.P., it isn't necessarily. It may not be the U.S.P. that makes your product different from your competition's but merely a quality or product feature that makes it sharper, longer lasting, cheaper to run. It could be a brighter picture tube in the television set or a more sensitive tuning device.

Since advertising is so intensely competitive, every copywriter before he begins to write will ask the account executive, the advertising manager, or someone else who should know: What do we have that's different? Is there a point of difference?

He has a sinking feeling if the answer is no. If he is given such a difference he immediately, if it's important enough, considers it for use in the headline, the opening copy, and the illustration.

If the difference is not very important, it simply becomes one of the selling points of the advertisement. If it's important enough to be considered a U.S.P. of the product, the copywriter will usually build the whole advertisement around it because, of course, the best point of difference is a U.S.P.

The most powerful type of advertisement has a strong U.S.P. slammed home to the reader by having it stressed in headline, illustration and opening copy. Yet, too often, we see advertisements that stress the most powerful point in headline and illustration but neglect it in the opening copy, or push it in headline and opening copy but let the illustration go off in another direction. All advertisements should have three-way power—headline, illustration, and opening copy working together.

FIGURE 2-2

Basic human appeals and advertising campaigns.

Appeal	Headline of advertisement	Product or service	Advertiser
Acquisitiveness	Go a little crazy. Get a lot of music. Any 10 records or tapes. $1.00 plus shipping and handling.	Records and tapes	Columbia House
	Get the best . . . best sellers . . . best authors . . . best buys.	Books	The Literary Guild
	Dream on . . . Dream on . . . Someday you'll own one.	Watch	Lambert Brothers
	Win $10,000 for the perfect time of your life— from the coffee that's perfect every time.	Coffee	Max-Pax®
	How to get extra income from your stocks.	Finance	Merrill Lynch
Comfort	Come home to Barcalounger.®	Furniture	Barcalounger® Recliners
	L'Eggs® Knee Highs. Put you up to your knees in comfort. Our extra wide comfort band does it.	Stockings	L'Eggs® Knee Highs
	Goose Down sox keep feet warm.	Sox	Eddie Bauer®
	The new glamour sweatshirt. The ultimate cover-up to snuggle into after a shower, a swim, now and forever.	Clothing	Glamour
	The most comfortable shoes you've ever worn or your money back!	Shoes	Norm Thompson
Convenience	How to get on and off a jet without a lot of checking, waiting, rushing or crushing.	Luggage	The Carry-Ons by Hartman
	To make the shopping almost as easy as the giving.	Credit card	Master Charge®
	Fast food can be good food. Ronco spaghetti in a skillet.	Food	Ronco®
	It's easy to have smooth, creamy frosting.	Food	Betty Crocker®
	Stairs? . . . Who cares!	Elevator	Inclin-ator®
Curiosity	Exploring strange waters and seldom seen landfalls is a daily experience aboard the M/S Lindblad Explorer.	Travel	Lindblad Travel, Inc.
	You could borrow a classic film, get help finding a job, stay in shape, trace your family tree, get fast answers, or get books by mail. At the library? At the library. Come see what's new besides books.	Library	American Library Association
	Send for the who? what? when? where? why? and how? of the year in sports.	Almanac	The Official Associated Press Almanac
	The exhibit you've been waiting for since 1325 B.C. Treasure of Tutankhamun.	Art museum	Exxon
Egotism	Want to look as young as you can?	Cosmetics	Oil of Olay®
	For people who are still individuals—the Irish country hat.	Hat	Norm Thompson
	How to stand out in a roomful of minks.	Fur	Swakara
	What owning an original print says about you.	Prints	Original Print Collectors Group, Ltd.
	For the person who enjoys being different.	Pen	Lamy
Family affection, togetherness, and happy home life	Treat your family tonight. 5 great ideas from Betty Crocker.	Food	Betty Crocker®
	Brunswick—where family fun begins.	Games	Brunswick Company
	Kodak sound movies. To the family, from the family, for the family.	Movie camera	Eastman Kodak
	If they could just stay little till their Carter's wear out.	Sleepers	Carter's
	Kids and Moms never grow out of Cream of Rice.	Cereal	Cream of Rice

Appeal	Headline of advertisement	Product or service	Advertiser
Fear	Having hospital insurance is fine—but what about when you're laid up at home?	Insurance	Commercial Travelers
	Stop thieves! Hide-a-Gate prevents forced entry.	Home protection	Himco National Inc.
	The natural gas shortage could mean your job.	Natural gas	American Gas Association
	Safe or sorry? Don't let fire rob you of your valuable records and home documents.	Home protection	Sentry®
	Going gray scares me. But peroxide scares me even more.	Hair color lotion	Clairol
Health	The time has come for a new way to treat your child's colds. It's here.	Medicine	Contac Jr.
	For cold and flu relief nothing's changed.	Medicine	Bayer® Aspirin
	Constipation: relief without fear.	Medicine	Ex-lax
	A sleeping tablet that's even safer than aspirin.	Sleeping tablet	Compoz
	Arthritis sufferers: are you cheating yourselves?	Medicine	Anacin
Hero worship	Tennesse Williams—signs it with a Sheaffer.	Pen	Sheaffer®
	How does your mouth feel after brushing with Colgate, "Dr. J"?	Toothpaste	Colgate®
	The hands, Eric Sloane. The watch, Rolex.	Watch	Rolex
	Chris Evert for new Astringent Shampoo.	Shampoo	Helene Curtis
	Are you anxious when Edwin Newman is eager?	Dictionary	American Heritage
Kindness generosity and unselfishness	Read this and cry.	Charity	Christian Children's Fund, Inc.
	You can help save Julyi Latemoon for $16 a month. Or you can turn the page.	Charity	Friends of SOS Children's Villages, Inc.
	Help your children. Help their school get the playground equipment it needs.	Cereal	Post's®
	Help save this vanishing American.	Conservation	World Wildlife Fund
	The Metropolitan Opera's next performance could be its swan song. Unless you give a quarter.	Charity	U.S. Pioneer Electronics Corp.
Love and sex	The passionate perfume from Spain.	Perfume	Pertegaz
	The glow of love.	Liqueur	Sambuca Romana
	The most romantic gift of fragrance a man can give a woman.	Perfume	L'Air du Temps
	Put her in the right mood.	Perfume	Mood Fragrances
	Clean is sexy.	Cosmetic	Cover Girl
Mental stimulation	Who says you can't speak another language in 60 days?	Lessons	Linguaphone
	We've just made learning a new language more fun for less money.	Lessons	Berlitz®
	Catch up on the books you have promised yourself to read.	Books	Book-of-the-month Club®
	How to wake up the financial genius inside you.	Investment	Mark O. Haroldsen
	When was the last time you read something you couldn't wait to tell your friends?	Newspaper	National Observer
Pleasure	Palm Springs will make you feel a lot better about winter.	Vacation	Palm Springs Conventions and Visitors Bureau
	Instead of sloshing through the slush in your galoshes this Christmas, dig your feet into Florida's soft, warm sand.	Vacation	Florida Division of Tourism
	Let her carry you to the Cities of the Dawn.	Travel	Carras
	It'll drive you happy.	Automobile	General Motors
	Turn ordinary evenings into a cultural event.	Pearls	Mikimoto

Appeal	Headline of advertisement	Product or service	Advertiser
Sensory Appeals	Clairol® Herbal Essence shampoo. It's a fresh kind of clean that you can see and feel and smell.	Shampoo	Clairol®
	The fresh, clean scent of baby powder—now in the extra-rich hand lotion.	Hand lotion	Desitin Pfizer
	Can you pass the soft-to-touch skin test?	Skin lotion	Vaseline Intensive Care Lotion
	We're sure you can't taste the difference Morton Lite Salt® makes in your recipes.	Salt	Morton Lite Salt®
	This year, let Christmas ring to the sound of music gifts from Reader's Digest.	Records	Reader's Digest

3

Creative Equals—Artists and Copywriters

Joe Fredericks, a competent copywriter, is vaguely dissatisfied with the copy he has just turned out for a cereal manufacturer. He has written the headline, the opening copy paragraph and a short description of the illustration. Frowning, he examines the copy sheet for a few minutes. Finally, he's convinced he needs help.

Strolling down the hall from his office he pushes through the door of Bob Grenshaw, the agency art director. Tossing the copy on Grenshaw's desk, Fredericks says: "I'm stuck, Bob. I've got some good words here but I just can't think of an art treatment that fits the situation. I'd like to see what you can come up with."

For the next few minutes the two work together. Ideas are tossed back and forth. During the session Grenshaw worked up several very rough layouts in which he kept rearranging type and suggested illustration elements. Suddenly, Fredericks exclaims: "That's it! Just exactly what I was looking for. Bob, can you polish this one up a bit so I can take it over to the client's this afternoon? He's going to love it. Boy, I don't care if you art guys are odd types, you sure come in mighty handy at times."

This creative session with Joe and Bob demonstrates the point that you can work up the most effective advertising campaign ever conceived, copywise, and see it fail as a selling tool simply because of inferior layout and art handling. On the other hand, many advertising campaigns presenting no new or fresh copy treatment prove outstanding in selling power because of brilliant art work.

There is no sure way to determine whether the effectiveness of any piece of advertising is based on copy or art. One can very rarely stand by itself. Advertising graveyards are full of the gravestones of copywriters and artists who never learned the fundamental fact of teamwork.

It is teamwork—between you and your art associates—that will result in sound, selling advertisements, properly executed for maximum impact upon readers. There is no room for the "I-can-do-it-alone" technique. If you learn quickly how to get along with your art people, you will have taken a major step toward your creative goal.

HOW MUCH COPY INVOLVEMENT FOR ARTISTS?

Some excellent artists have strayed from their creative field and have assumed positions of importance in executive capacities other than art direction. A few have become heads of advertising agencies, large and small. Others are in charge of the advertising activities of department stores and other retail operations. Art people will usually deny special interest in any part of the advertising business but their own. The varied and complex business matters which you, as a copywriter, must know to do your part of the creative job properly, have less bearing upon the work of your art director from his standpoint, though many of them have definite bearing upon the general layout and character of the advertisement itself. Proper emphasis, for example, of certain sales points or policy matters, are most often not a part of the art director's responsibility but yours. If the art director does interest himself in these matters—fine, but they are "musts" for you.

COPYWRITERS AND ARTISTS BLEND THEIR SKILLS

Probably the most common error that copywriters make in attempting to cooperate with artists is to assume too much responsibility in "art direction." The average copywriter will usually resent his art colleague's telling him how to write copy, or criticizing the manner in which he has already written it.

Yet that same writer, who has written the headline, has suggested an illustrative device, and has made a very amateurish sketch of what he thinks the layout should look like, will sometimes sit at his director's elbow and will try to tell him exactly how to proceed. He may offer advice on styles of artwork, typography, lettering, and decoration. He will insist on photography when the artist believes drawings or paintings to be more satisfactory. He will reject layouts over which the artist has spent hours because he personally prefers something "just a little different." The result of all this is that he will have an association with a key coworker that is a contest to see who has the last say.

FIGURE 3-1

Industrial advertisement with unusual illustration.   It takes a certain amount of daring to depart from the conventional illustration in industrial advertising, but now and then it can pay off in getting attention for an advertisement. Usually much discussion between the art and copy departments precedes such a departure.

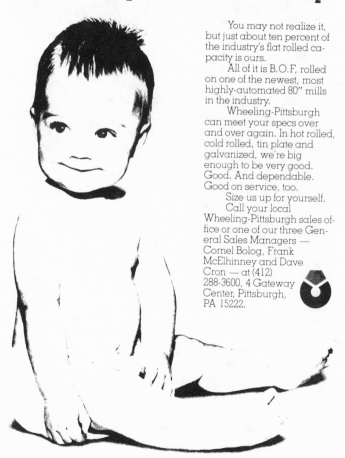

One of every ten tons is our baby.

You may not realize it, but just about ten percent of the industry's flat rolled capacity is ours.

All of it is B.O.F. rolled on one of the newest, most highly-automated 80" mills in the industry.

Wheeling-Pittsburgh can meet your specs over and over again. In hot rolled, cold rolled, tin plate and galvanized, we're big enough to be very good. Good. And dependable. Good on service, too.

Size us up for yourself. Call your local Wheeling-Pittsburgh sales office or one of our three General Sales Managers — Cornel Bolog, Frank McElhinney and Dave Cron — at (412) 288-3600, 4 Gateway Center, Pittsburgh, PA 15222.

Just big enough to be very good.
Wheeling-Pittsburgh Steel

S-7610

Remember that you are not an art director. There is no doubt that you can and should offer valuable suggestions about your layouts. From you, the art director must obtain all the essential information about what elements are most important to the ultimate selling job. From you, he can gain the background of the problem—background which he must understand to get the proper "feeling" into the work. Not only can he use this sort of assistance from you, but he can't do justice to his own job without it. If he is capable, however, he will almost always turn out a better layout and supervise a better job if he is permitted to use his own imagination without heckling from you.

The goal is to produce advertising of which you both can be proud—you of the thinking behind the advertisement, the power and clarity of the selling ideas, and he of the physical execution of these ideas.

Art directors will welcome suggestions from you upon which they may improvise. Artists see, in you, art of another sort. Most of them will admit that they're glad they aren't faced with the responsibility of conceiving the original copy ideas. Artists are, after all, specialists in translating those ideas to layouts and illustrations and they are much better at it than any copywriter or group of copywriters.

Regardless of the type of copy work you do, if your art associates realize that you consider the creation of advertising a job of close and friendly teamwork—if you can establish a method of joint operation with them—you will discover a richness in the routine of your daily work that many copywriters never find. Such richness will help produce good advertisements. The success of your career as a copywriter depends in a large measure upon your knowledge of human psychology. Don't let that knowledge apply only to the people who read your advertisements. It will pay off fully in your dealings with your art directors.

HOW MUCH TO KNOW OF ART

Beginners in copywriting generally feel that a thorough working knowledge of art and layout is a good thing for them to have. Some young men and women, aspiring to be advertising writers, even study art in art schools to better grasp the problems they think will be confronting them. It may be better for copywriters to know nothing at all of art than to know just enough to make them think they know a lot. Alexander Pope's "A little learning is a dangerous thing" applies very well here.

This is certainly true from the standpoint of economy of effort. Wherever you work—agency, department store, retail shop, direct-mail or mail-order house—you will have available the services of men and women trained in making layouts and supervising artwork. They take your ideas and make attractive and compelling layouts from them. If you, the copywriter, have a wide knowledge of art and layout, you will tend to spend time which should be spent in copywriting, making rough layouts that will neither be used nor appreciated by the artists. After all, no two artists will ever see a layout job exactly the same way.

Far better to set your ideas down on paper, <u>write</u> your suggestions for illustrations, supply the <u>other</u> necessary elements, such as headlines and subheads, and then forget them until you have something to look at done by a specialist. Then, if you have suggestions to make—if you would prefer to see some slightly different style of handling and you really feel that your criticisms are justified for the good of the advertisement—then is the time to take them up. You'll get along better that way with the person it's most important to get along with. You'll have more time for your own job, copywriting. Also, copywriters' roughs often make lazy artists. They are tempted merely to "dress up" copywriters' ideas instead of applying their specialized knowledge of layout to designing the advertisement as it should be designed.

Assuming that you have reasonably sensible taste, all you need to know about art is what you will normally learn working with and around artists.

Most of your important relationships with the art department, wherever you work, will be concerned with print advertising.

Many advertising agencies, however, maintain specially trained and talented art directors whose duties are entirely confined to television visualization. In no phase of creative advertising is a person expected to be so versatile and flexible as in the creating of television "storyboards." Although concentration in this chapter is on the need for copywriter-artist cooperation in turning out good print advertising, the importance of TV creation must be mentioned here but full discussion will be given in the television chapters.

Certain important fundamentals of art which can influence the success of your advertising will be covered very briefly here. Other than learning these few basic facts and terms, however, you'd better be a copywriter first and an artist last.

LAYOUTS

An idea for a proposed print advertisement may be presented for approval by a client by a drawing called a "layout."

A layout, as its name implies, is the physical grouping of all the elements in an advertisement, as originally conceived by the artist. There are several types of layouts: thumbnail sketches, roughs, finished, and comprehensives.

Thumbnail sketches

The type of layout often used in advertising operations that has the least drawing detail is called the "thumbnail sketch." (See Figure 3-2.) This is a very rough layout, done in one-half or one-fourth size by the artist, and is normally used when you are considering several different ideas for a new campaign. From thumbnail sketches, it is possible for you and your art director to determine quickly whether an

FIGURE 3-2

Thumbnail sketch.   Artists can do a number of such small trial layouts in a few minutes. Such layouts enable them to visualize the more elaborate layouts to follow.

idea has possibilities. You may find, however, that the various units won't fit and that it would be a waste of time to go into further layout attempts.

Rough layouts

When you have decided upon a headline, subheads, captions, and illustrative suggestion for an advertisement, you will present the artist with this material, pointing out which selling points are to get the main emphasis, and in what sequence the other elements of the advertisement should logically follow. From this information, the artist will then arrange the advertisement in an orderly, balanced manner, roughing in your headline and making a very rough sketch of your illustrative suggestion (or a different one, if he thinks it would work better). This is called a "rough layout" or "visual," and from it you can determine whether the final job will maintain the place you desire, will focus proper attention on the right parts of your message, and, in general, whether your idea is going to jell.

During your early years as a copywriter, you may be working under a copy chief or supervisor, with whom you will be required to clear your ideas before passing them on to members of the art department.

When the artist has made the rough layout, you will then discuss it with your superiors, and the three of you will decide whether it is okay to proceed or whether more roughs are needed. Possibly, especially if you are working in an advertising agency, the rough layout or layouts will also be shown to others who are working on the account—contact people, account executives, and on some occasions even representatives of the client's advertising department.

FIGURE 3-3

Rough layout.   After being guided by the thumbnail sketch shown in Figure 3-2, the artist makes a rough layout. This can be used around the agency to show the copywriter, the account executive, and others. If the clients are the kind who can visualize the finished advertisement, they might be shown the rough layout. Usually, however, they see a more finished layout.

Finished and comprehensive layouts

Once the rough layout is approved by all those who are concerned with its formative stages, the artist is ready to do a "finished layout" or "comprehensive layout." Finished layouts are more complete than "roughs." Lettering is done rather carefully and pictures may be sketched. The client can obtain an accurate idea from the finished layout just what the printed advertisement will look like.

FIGURE 3-4

Semicomprehensive layout.   From this layout anyone engaged in approving the advertisement can obtain a solid idea of what the finished advertisement will look like, in typography, size and placement of elements, and the illustration.

The "comprehensive" is a layout which carries the elements of the advertisement into a more refined stage. It serves two purposes. One is to present the elements to the people who have the final say in okaying them for publication. Two is to solicit new business or to present an entirely new departure for an old campaign.

When advertisements are presented formally, all major elements in the advertisement appear as nearly as possible the way they will actually look in the printed advertisement. Since most of your clients will not possess the trained imagination of you and your art director, they may be unable to visualize the published advertisement from a rough layout. In finished and comprehensive layouts, therefore, the standard procedure is to letter in carefully the headlines, subheads, and caption headings, and to include a fairly accurate sketch of the illustration. The comprehensive must be accurate enough to be followed easily by two more persons who turn out advertisements: the commercial artist who creates the finished artwork or photograph; those who handle the printing and engraving and who must know exactly how to position the elements mechanically.

FIGURE 3-5

Finished advertisement.　　　Here is the advertisement as it appeared in print that evolved from that thumbnail sketch in Figure 3-2.

This machine communicates over 150 words per minute across oceans at less than 1½ cents per word.

And also listens, reacts, sympathizes, charms, persuades, pleads, cajoles, apologizes, needles, soothes, explores, informs, explains and does whatever else it takes to solve the problem or close the sale.

Call overseas. Your voice makes the difference.

Ⓐ Bell System

Comprehensive layouts are done with precision because of their use in presenting a new campaign idea or soliciting new business. Finished layouts, in contrast, are usually just "slick" enough to give a graphic idea of how the final job should look. When you ask an artist to make a comprehensive layout, the artist will very often ask you, "How comprehensive?" Then, according to the nature of the job, the production time element, and other considerations, you will describe just how far he is expected to go. A five- or six-word headline for a comprehensive layout can be lettered in by a good lettering person in a few minutes, but where you wish to show an exact type style or other precision lettering, the job may require several hours.

In some places, the rule is that you should spend your time writing body copy and captions while the layout is being made, so that your entire advertisement will be ready for study at the same time. You can then take up any final copy polishing while the finished or comprehensive layout is with the art department.

This "rule" depends, however, on the situation. As mentioned in a preceding chapter you may, when presenting campaign ideas, merely write headlines and suggest ideas for the main illustrations. The body copy can be done later.

If, however, you know what you want to write and you have done the needed background thinking and investigation, you may prefer to write all the copy in the advertisement before you give it to the artist, along with your illustration ideas. By so doing, you will help him since he will know how much space is to be occupied by the copy and can do his layout accordingly.

Sometimes, when the layout technique for a campaign has already been decided upon, you will write the same amount of copy for every advertisement since the illustration size will be the same in every instance and the space for the copy will not vary from advertisement to advertisement. Thus, you might set your typewriter to write fifteen lines of sixty-five characters. While writing copy to such exact specifications can be irksome to some copywriters, the practice results in copy that will fit precisely into space allotted.

ARTWORK, PRINTING, AND ENGRAVING

After the layout and copy for your advertisement have been okayed by all those whose approval is necessary, it is ready for production.

Production of any advertisement requires the following procedure:

1. The art director calls in whatever type of commercial freelance artist is needed to make the final art. Usually this requires a specialist in some phase of art, depending upon whether the illustration is to be a careful line drawing in ink, a painting, a cartoon, a photograph, or a wash drawing. (See glossary at end of chapter.) Your art director could possibly do this artwork himself, but it is normally the job of a specialist, and in any event the art director probably wouldn't have the time to do this in addition to other duties. In many agency operations it is the custom for the art directors to farm out the actual artwork in this manner. Although some retail advertising departments use the farming out method also, some have staff artists who do the final artwork. Except in rare cases, it is the function of the art director to supervise the creation of the final art. The director may ask your opinion on certain points, and you certainly are privileged to offer any suggestions you may have, but the responsibility for the job rests with the art department.

2. The art director in most cases is also responsible for the direction of typesetting. He will make, or have made, what is called a "type mechanical"—a tissue-paper tracing of the area into which type is to be set. This is attached to the

piece of copy to be sent to the printer, and shows the printer exactly how wide and how deep to set the type, specifies the type face and size to be used, and gives the printer all other specific instructions on the job.

3. Once the artwork is completed and okayed and copy is set and okayed, the job passes on to the engraver, who makes the plates from which the advertisement is printed. This, again, in most operations is watched carefully by the art director. In many large advertising agencies and retail operations there are subdepartments which specialize in mechanical production and which are responsible for all printing and engraving. Even where there are such experts on hand, however, the supervision of the production of the advertisement remains in the hands of the art director.

FIGURE 3-6

Rough layout for full color advertisement.   This is the beginning point for what you will see in Figure 3-7 and Figure 3-8.

WHAT ABOUT MECHANICAL PRODUCTION?

As in the case of art, you, as a copywriter, do not need to be an authority on production. It would take years of working closely with printers and engravers to give yourself even the most modest background in

FIGURE 3-7

Comprehensive layout that followed rough layout shown in Figure 3-6.

the lore of that field. You can and should, however, have a "working knowledge" of the operations of these trades. You should learn exactly what happens to your advertisements after they gain the okay of your superiors and/or clients.

You should know the fundamentals of printing and engraving, the use and production of electrotypes, zincs, mats, and the mechanics of typesetting. You should be familiar with various styles of typefaces. It will help you to find out the many things that can be done to obtain special effects in the printing of your advertisements. You won't be called upon often to use this information, but it will help you to know just what you can expect in the way of reproduction of your ideas, and to know what is and is not possible from a production standpoint. Also, some copy jobs call for more production knowledge than others.

Don't use too many typefaces

If you take a job as a beginning copywriter in a retail store, you can save yourself embarrassment if you move slowly in the matter of using a variety of typefaces. If your advertisements are set by the newspaper, you will do well to find out how many typefaces and families are available to you through the newspaper. Most newspapers don't offer much variety, so if you ask for faces such as Bernhard Cursive, Weiss Roman, or Trafton Script you may be told to limit your type recommendations to faces handled by the newspaper. Actually, a good many retail department stores buy fonts of special faces and keep them at the newspapers ready for use.

A beginning retail copywriter is often inclined to think that advertisements will gain interest if he employs many typefaces and families. If you fall into this trap, climb out fast. You will do much better to avoid showing how many typefaces and families you have learned. Many retail people feel that it's undesirable to have more than two typefaces in one advertisement, and they recommend that the variations occur within one type family. This is the sort of advance information you should get about production in order to do a more intelligent job.

FIGURE 3-8

Finished four-color advertisement that had its beginning with the rough layout shown in Figure 3-6.

Know typography

In a good many places, of course, your copywriting duties won't require you to specify type. If so, consider yourself lucky, especially as you read the following laments voiced by two young copywriters who found out sorrowfully that they did have to know something about type when they started their copywriting careers. After working a couple of months in their new positions, they had some interesting observations to make on the need for knowledge of type. The

FIGURE 3-9

Effect created by typography.   An atmosphere of exclusiveness is created through the use of distinctive typography associated with the famous names shown in this advertisement.

first excerpt is from a young female copywriter in the advertising department of a very large department store. She wrote back to her school:

> Because the copywriter here does have a "finger in the pie" as far as layout and typefaces are concerned, a sound knowledge of typography is invaluable. I recall that in school I talked my way out of the typography requirement . . . I rue the day now. To show how type knowledge is always with us, we use a different advertising approach for our basement departments than for the upstairs sections. Typefaces are different along with artwork.

And from the other copywriter:

> One course I could not get into and which I'm sure every advertising student could use is typography. It would certainly be a big help to me if I knew more about the subject.

Copyfitting. An aspect of typography which some copywriters learn automatically and which troubles others is copyfitting. As printers are fond of saying, "Space isn't elastic." If you write 350 words for a copy block big enough for 50 words, you are going to look just a little foolish. As a beginning copywriter, you are likely to run into copyfitting trouble much more than the experienced person who has developed a "feel" for how much type will go into a given space.

FIGURE 3-10

Effective use of space.   By taking one-third of the space on each side of the page, the advertiser achieves full-page dominance at less than full-page cost. Each advertisement helps the other. A decision to employ such a strategy can be a team decision of the artist and copywriter.

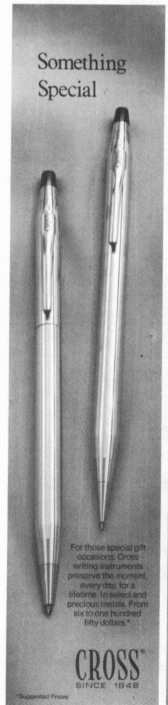

The rules of copyfitting are simple. Sit down sometime and you can learn in a few minutes the character-count method of copyfitting. It will pay off when you stare at your layout and wonder whether the space allotted for copy will take 50, 100, or 150 words. There are methods other than the character-count system for use in copyfitting. Learn some method so that you'll be able to save yourself the painful job of rewriting copy just because you had no idea of how much copy you could write for the space allowed.

The following simple method enables you to fit type if you know the size of the space to be filled:

1. Find an advertisement that has:
   a. Type of the size you think is suitable for the advertisement you are preparing.
   b. The kind of spacing between lines you want.
2. Now count the characters (including spaces and punctuation marks) per inch on the line of type you have selected as suitable. Then multiply by the number of inches in the line that you are going to use in your advertisement. (Thus if there are sixteen characters to the inch, you can set your typewriter at fifty-six if your line is to be 3½ inches.)
3. Next, measure how many lines of this type will fit into a vertical inch. In step 1-b, you selected an example that was suitably spaced (leaded) between lines. When you measure, you find that the lines so spaced fit eight lines to the vertical inch. (Thus if the space to be filled is 4 vertical inches, you will be typing thirty-two lines of copy, each line having fifty-six characters.)

Another simple method is to utilize a "type specimen" book that shows type in different faces and different sizes. Using this book, you can follow the procedure described in the foregoing section.

20 BASIC GUIDELINES FOR TYPOGRAPHY

The following guidelines were condensed from approximately 1,100 words, Staff Memo at Benton & Bowles:

There are exceptions to every one of the following guidelines, but, on the other hand, there is a good solid reason behind each. In general, the rules of typography follow custom. We find that what we are most accustomed to read is what we read most comfortably and easily.

1. A line should be 1½ to 2 alphabets long. The longer the line, the harder it is for the eye to follow.
2. Body text should not be set in smaller than 10-point. Some folks wear glasses.
3. Use one typeface throughout, for display lines and text. This is an esthetic consideration. An ad looks more homogeneous, less busy, less distracting, when so set.
4. A long copy block must be broken up! This is one rule you will hardly ever want to break.

FIGURE 3-11

All-type advertisements.   Sometimes when doing serious, newsworthy advertisements on important issues, artwork and illustrations can be omitted in favor of an advertisement that has an editorial look. Such an approach gives impact to the advertisement. It is especially desirable in advertisements of this type to use headlines that are big physically and challenging in content. The headlines shown here satisfy on both counts.

Second in a series of reports on Marble Hill nuclear project:

The most dangerous thing about nuclear power is not having any.

Nuclear power plants today produce 10% of all the electricity Americans use. Commercial plants—63 now are licensed to operate—have logged over 300 reactor years of service. And not a single person has been injured as a result of their operation—a safety record unmatched by any other industry.

Yet much is being said against nuclear power these days—at home and abroad. It's not strange that the people who know most about nuclear power are its strongest supporters.

Since you will have a nuclear neighbor in the 1980s when Public Service Indiana expects to have its Marble Hill nuclear station in operation), you have a right to know just what kind of a neighbor it will be. And we're here to tell you.

We intend for Marble Hill to be the safest industrial facility in the state. Only other nuclear power stations will come close to its safety performance. How can we be so sure?

Never in the history of American technology has an industry developed into maturity with as safe a record as nuclear power. Safety systems upon safety system, backup upon backup, is designed into every nuclear plant in order to meet the strictest kinds of regulations ever imposed on any industry.

Safety redundancy is inherent in all nuclear facilities in recognition of the fact that human error is possible. That is, a nuclear plant like Marble Hill is designed to operate safely in spite of human error. You've heard some of the fears voiced by critics. Let's examine a few of them as they relate to Marble Hill.

FEAR: A nuclear plant might explode.

FACT: All but the most uninformed critics concede that there is no way a nuclear plant can explode. At Marble Hill, heat to make steam to spin turbine-generators will be produced by a carefully controlled loosening, or splitting, of atom particles in the reactor. Nuclear fuel for this purpose is very weak in fissionable material compared with bomb grade material. (Reactor fuel contains about 4% enriched uranium. Bomb material is almost pure enriched uranium.)

FEAR: Nuclear plants give off harmful radiation.

FACT: Natural background radiation from the sun, the earth, the soil, together with medical x-rays exposes the average person to 200 millirems per year. Nuclear power plants will add a small fraction of 1 millirem to the average person's annual exposure. Someone living in Jefferson County (even if they camped on the property line at Marble Hill) will be exposed to more than 5 millirem a year and probably far less ... about the same as you'd get from cosmic radiation on a plane trip across the country.

FEAR: Harmful radioactive waste will be stored at Marble Hill.

FACT: No radioactive waste will be permanently stored at the site. When refueling of the reactor is scheduled about once a year, one third of the total fuel loading is replaced with fresh fuel. The used fuel bundles will be held in a closed-circuit water tank until ready to be transported to a reprocessing plant. High-level waste removed from fuel reprocessing will go to federal government storage facilities for long-term storage and eventual beneficial use.

FEAR: Radioactive discharges from Marble Hill will contaminate the Ohio River.

FACT: All discharges from the plant will be well within the limits set by state and federal authorities for total protection of man and the environment. These limits have been proven adequate to prevent any harmful effects.

FEAR: No method for storing wastes that will remain radioactive for thousands of years has been developed.

FACT: Governmental delay in taking final steps to construct permanent waste storage facilities has caused some to believe no solution is at hand. The technology needed to solidify these wastes and seal them in canisters buried in salt formations that have remained stable for millions of years is at hand. Only political decisions are needed. The problem isn't pressing since the amount of waste to be stored is so small. High-level radioactive waste from one year's operation of Marble Hill will fit into a cube 2½-feet square.

FEAR: Nuclear plants aren't safe or you could buy insurance coverage for your home.

FACT: Most homeowner's policies do have a "nuclear exclusion" clause simply to channel such damages into the nuclear insurance pools set up to do this job for the property owner. Premiums for private insurance coverage as well as premiums for government coverage under the Price-Anderson Act are paid by each nuclear utility. Total coverage for any single nuclear accident is $560 million. And because of the unmatched safety record of nuclear plants, the insurance pools have already made significant refunds to utilities.

FEAR: Nuclear material can be stolen and used for blackmail or sabotage.

FACT: Nuclear material used at Marble Hill will be of little value to thieves. Fissionable materials needed for an explosive device are found only in very dilute form. Terrorists have no practical way to handle and convert low-grade reactor fuel into a weapon.

We've covered several of the major fears raised by nuclear critics—but not all. If you would like our response to other specific issues, please let us know. Write: Public Service Indiana, 1000 East Main Street, Plainfield, IN 46168.

Next: Is nuclear power really cheaper!

⚡ PUBLIC SERVICE INDIANA

5. Avoid setting the body copy in reverse whenever possible. Reverse type will cut down readership.
6. If the paragraph leads are not indented, more leading is required between paragraphs.
7. Don't print text over tint blocks. It's harder to read that way.
8. Don't print the text over illustration or design element. It is a signal to the reader that the copy really isn't very important.
9. Use lowercase instead of caps in display lines. Lowercase is more legible.
10. Body copy should always have an even left-hand margin for easier reading.
11. When there are several copy elements, align them wherever possible. This is to avoid a cluttered, busy look to an ad.
12. Use numerals instead of bullets where possible.
    a. All bullets do is to signal that you have a list.
    b. Numbers do the same job better, add interest, make your list seem more important.
13. Never run a picture without a caption. (Well, hardly ever.)
14. Try to run a cutline under every main illustration.
15. Don't be afraid of "widows!"
16. Use normal punctuation. Commas, semicolons, periods and dashes serve a useful purpose in guiding the reader through your copy. Leaders (those nasty little dots . . .) usually are merely a crutch for proper punctuation. In addition, they make copy look messy and uninviting.
17. Don't overdo the bangs. Exclamation points are often the refuge of the writer who can't think up exciting thoughts.
18. Keep your sentences short. They make copy look less formidable. They lend a feeling of urgency and conviction.
19. Use italics sparingly. Italics are good for occasional emphasis. A lot of italics in a piece of copy make it paler, look weaker, instead of adding impact.
20. Sans serif type is better in display than in text. That's because this cleaner, more modern-looking face is easy to read in big size, not so easy in running text.

COLOR OR BLACK AND WHITE?

Unquestionably, advertisements printed in full color normally get better attention than those which appear in black and white. If a rule must be given, the conclusion is inescapable. There are, however, certain basic principles which can help you decide whether to plan any advertisement or series of advertisements in full color, one or more colors, or black and white.

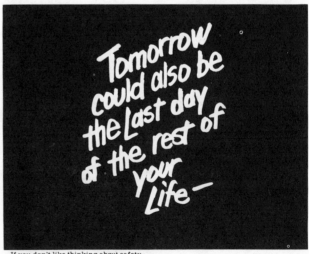

If you don't like thinking about safety, think where you might be without it.

National Safety Council

A reminder from the National Safety Council. A non-profit, non-governmental public service organization. Our only goal is a safer America.

FIGURE 3-12

Illustration-less advertisement.   Occasionally, the creative team might agree to omit the illustration. In this instance, this public service advertisement's somber warning is given added impact through the use of an all-type format on a black background.

Your common sense may tell you that while the generality is often true that "the more color the better," it is more true with some types of products than others. The addition of one or more colors to insurance advertising, for example, will probably gain a few more readers, but can scarcely enhance the sales power of the advertisements enough to warrant the extra expense involved. Food products and automobiles, on the other hand, customarily direct their advertising punches directly toward the sensory nerves and are not only more likely to be noted if color is used, but are much more salable. They're selling "beauty," and there's beauty in color.

Generally speaking, you can let your product dictate whether color is to be considered in planning its advertising. That is, you can do so if your advertising budget permits a choice. To use color for attention-value and impact only is mighty expensive. On the other hand, it would be foolish economy <u>not</u> to use color if the sales of your product depend upon it. The Armstrong floor covering campaign, to illustrate, has been expensive with its lavish use of color. Yet the use of color is absolutely necessary with this product, which would look dull and lifeless in black and white. Color adds real sales power here.

WHEN TO USE ARTWORK OR PHOTOGRAPHS

Photography is most often going to be used in advertising illustration because of its realism. This is true whether you are concerned with consumer or business advertising. Thus under normal circumstances, you will call for, or expect, photography for your advertising illustrations.

Still, artwork <u>is</u> used and may be suitable if:

- Exaggeration is desirable, as in the case of some high-fashion advertising in which the models have a fashionably elongated look never found in real life.
- A schematic, or cross-section, is wanted, as may be the case in an industrial advertisement aimed at engineers.
- A seasonal illustration is needed in the off-season such as a snow scene in the summer or a farm spring-plowing scene in the harvest season.
- It is difficult, or impossible, to find the right people as models for photography. These might be current people, or historical figures.
- Speed is important. It may take a long time to get the proper photographic shot, but a good artist can sketch what is needed quickly, and on order.
- Cartoon treatment is desired. This treatment might be especially suitable for comic page advertising, or for advertising to children.
- Way-out mood, or atmosphere, is needed. Horror, exclusiveness, or satire may often be conveyed more starkly or subtly through artwork.

FIGURE 3-13

Good use of small space layout.   The technique used here is good for magazines or newspapers. Catch attention with the main illustration. Then demonstrate a product's multiple uses with small panels containing line drawings or sharp photographs. The additional pictures and captions cut out the need for long, explanatory copy.

IF YOU MUST DO ROUGH LAYOUTS

Here are some suggestions if you are a copywriter who works in small organizations—agencies, companies, or retail stores—which expect you to do rough layout work.

1. Make sure you supply a dominant element, something for the reader's eyes to focus upon and to attract his attention. This element will usually be the illustration, but sometimes it can be a big headline. Above all, avoid making layouts that have no impact because you've cluttered them with a number of different elements of equal size.
2. Make your headlines and illustrations competitive in size and character with other advertising. This suggestion is especially important when your advertisement is to be on a big newspaper page with advertisements that are equal in size, or even bigger.
3. In most advertisements, make the logotype big enough, or distinctive enough, to stand out. Now and then the mood of the advertisement or the nature of the product is such that the logo can be relatively small. Usually, however, it must be commanding enough to insure that readers know the advertiser, or the product, being advertised.
4. Keep copy elements out of illustration area—items such as headlines, subheads, price figures. When such elements intrude into the illustration area, they distract from the illustration and they give a cluttered feeling to the advertisement.

5. Don't play tricks with copy and headlines by putting them in circles, wavy lines, upside down, or in odd shapes. Such tricks will cost you extra typesetting charges. Furthermore, whatever attention value you achieve will be offset by loss of readership and by the annoyance felt by many readers who don't like it when the advertiser makes the message hard to read.

SOME COMMON ART AND PRODUCTION TERMS

Following is a brief list of terms used almost daily in connection with the art and mechanical phases of advertising production. It is by no means complete, and the definitions offered are far from comprehensive, since this is not a book on art and production. If, however, you become familiar with these few terms and their meanings you will be equipped with a reasonably good vocabulary with which to start your career as a copywriter, whether it be on a newspaper, in a retail store, advertising department, agency, or elsewhere.

AGATE. Once merely the name of a size of type, it is now the unit for measuring the depth of advertising space. There are 14 agate lines to the inch.

AIR BRUSHING. Blowing a liquid pigment onto photographs or wash drawings. Results in smooth, tinted surfaces.

BEN DAY PROCESS. A medium for use in photo-mechanical engraving for adding tints, shading, or stippling to line engravings. The important result is that it gives line plates a halftone tonal appearance. Its use eliminates hand shading of a drawing, thus avoiding irregularities. The ordinary method of indicating on the drawing the portions to be shaded is to attach a transparent flap upon it and mark the areas of each Ben Day with appropriate colors.

BLEED. Printed matter runs right to edge of page. This creates an illusion of size and gives a natural appearance. It may add to cost—about 10 to 15 percent in some magazines. It is usually not available in regular press runs of newspapers.

BODY TYPE. Refers to type sizes generally used for the composition of body matter. The sizes are 6 to 14 point.

BOX. An element that has four rules that has art or type inside. Should not be used too often because it gives advertisement a mechanical appearance. Good occasionally, however, to focus attention on that part of the advertisement.

BROADSIDE. This is a large printed sheet used as a circular and folded into a size that can be used for mailing. It differs from a folder in that its printed matter runs across the sheet, regardless of the fold.

CAMERA-READY COPY. A pasteup that's ready to be photographed by the platemaker. It is the last step before actual production.

CAMP ART. This is art that is self-consciously so bad that it has become acceptable, especially in youthful circles. It has a strong element of humor.

CARBRO. A carbro is a photographic print in full color, as distinguished from a black-and-white print that has been retouched in color. Carbros are ideal for use as artwork on subjects that are likely to require retouching or idealization. They are not as satisfactory for "snapshot" or "candid" color illustrations because of the length of exposure time needed.

COLD TYPE COMPOSITION. Copy composed for photo-mechanical reproduction by means other than the use of metal type; usually by the typewriter.

COMBINATION PLATE. The combining of a halftone and line plate in one engraving.

CONTRAST. A difference in tonal values in an illustration which gives strong highlights and shadows.

CRIB FILE. Also called "swipe" file. This is a collection of illustrative material filed by advertising artists. The files are usually crammed with many advertisements that may be under different headings such as: Babies. Animals. Machinery. If the artist is stuck, he can refer to the file for ideas. He can use what he finds as a point of departure, or he may lift the idea bodily.

CROP. To cut off or trim an illustration to make it fit into a space.

CUT. Any plate used for printing.

DISPLAY TYPE. Larger type, usually starting with 14-point, that is used for heads and subheads and other material that is to stand out.

ELECTROTYPE. A duplicate of an original engraving or type form. These are used when the same advertisement is to appear in various publications and save the expense of making separate engravings for each. "Electros," as they are called, are useful for long runs, for color work, and for fine engravings. They are electrolytically reproduced from the original type and/or engraving. Since they are expensive to make and costly to ship because of their weight, they are not used as often as mats and plastic plates.

ENGRAVING. A metal plate of copper or zinc upon which is etched the lines from which an advertisement is reproduced.

FACE. The printing surface of a piece of type is called its face. The same word is used to describe a style of type.

FONT. A complete assortment or font of any one size and style of type. It contains all the characters—capitals, small capitals, lowercase letters, numerals, punctuation marks, etc.

HIGHLIGHT. Light areas in an illustration. Term is used very frequently in photographic work and is understood to be the opposite of shadow.

INSERT. A page, either type matter or illustration, printed separately from the regular sections and tipped in later between the pages. In newspapers these are often called color preprints and are associated with Hi-Fi and Spectacolor process.

ISLAND POSITION. An advertisement is in this position when it is entirely surrounded by editorial matter. Such positions are found most often in magazines.

LEADING. The spacing between lines of type that is achieved by the placing of metal strips between the lines. It varies by a point system such as 2-point leading, 3-point leading. If there is no leading, the type is described as "set solid."

LINE DRAWING. Drawings made with pen and black ink are commonly called line drawings. In this class are included drawings made in line, stipple, or brush strong enough in color to be reproduced in the line etching process. In line drawing there is no continuous blending of color from light to dark as in photographs or wash drawings. It consists of solid blacks and pure whites.

LOWERCASE. The small letters in a font of type as distinguished from the capital letters.

MASKING. The use of material to protect or block out certain areas on a proof or plate.

MAT. Abbreviation for matrix. A duplicate of an original engraving, made on heavy paper matting. Used principally in newspaper work. The mat is really a mold. Hot lead is poured over it, thus forming a stereotype. Keep in mind that the printing is done from the stereotype, not from the mat. The stereotype can be used only for a limited number of impressions because of lack of durability. A "mat service" provides retail stores with copy and illustrations for ads, or parts of ads, which the store may run in local newspapers over its own name.

MECHANICAL.   When a client approves copy, a "mechanical" is made which explains to the typographers the typefaces required and the position of copy in the advertisement. The mechanical is really a tracing of the layout in outline form. The art director dictates the style of type which in his judgment will be consistent with the design of the page. The copy is measured by actual count of characters that can fit into the space allotted on the mechanical. The typographer follows this mechanical exactly.

MONTAGE.   Refers to the putting together into a single unit of several photographs or drawings. The term is also used in television when several scenes are shown together, or follow each other in rapid succession.

MORTISE.   A mortise is a place in an engraving where part of the plate has been cut out to insert type or other illustrative material. Mortising is the cutting away of the part of the block, usually in a space that has been left for the insertion of type matter.

MOUNTED PLATE.   An engraving plate which is mounted "type high" (0.9186 of an inch). The mount may be metal or wood.

OPAQUE.   A water-soluable paint applied to negatives to block out areas by making them nontransparent.

OVERLAY.   In producing layouts, sometimes alternate suggestions and ideas for arrangements of headlines, copy, or illustration may be desired. A transparent overlay is made and attached to the original, showing these alternates. Very often overlays are made on drawings or paintings to show the engravers the position of lettering, type, or supplementary art to be superimposed when engravings are being made.

PASTE-UP.   When various pieces of art, lettering, design, and typography are ready for final assembly, a paste-up of these units is necessary for positioning. This paste-up is necessary for two reasons:

  a. to give the art director a chance to make any necessary adjustments because of changes, corrections, or additions to art or copy after original layout was made;

  b. to get the client's approval. If artwork is made up of a number of separate pieces, it shows the advertisement as a unit before plate-making begins.

PHOTOSTAT.   A photostat is a photograph-like copy of any two-dimensional object or print by a special photographic machine. (Very bad distortion will result when three-dimensional objects are used.) Where permanency is not essential, this method of reproduction saves expense and time. The first step is a paper negative which is really a positive, but with values reversed (white on black). The second step is a paper print which has the appearance of a normal photographic print.

PICA.   In printing, a pica equals 12 typographical points or 1/6 inch. On a typewriter the key size is either pica or the small elite size.

PROGRESSIVE PROOFS.   Made from separate plates used in color-process work to show the printing sequence and the result after each additional color has been applied. They are furnished to the printer by the engraver.

REPRODUCTION PROOFS.   Often called "repro proofs," these are proofs of great sharpness. They can be used for reproduction.

RETOUCH.   Change a negative or photograph through art techniques. May eliminate or tone down some sections.

REVERSE PLATE.   A line plate in which the whites come out black and vice versa. Thus the letters will normally be white against a black background. Such technique is especially useful in small advertisements that must flag attention. Don't use this for long copy since it is hard to read.

RUN-IN.   To set type without paragraph breaks or to insert new copy without making a new paragraph.

SCALING.   Working out measurements for art that is being reduced, or enlarged, to fit a space.

SCRATCHBOARD DRAWING.   Drawing made by scratching a knife across a previously inked surface.

SCRIPT.   Script lettering will sometimes bring distinctiveness to headlines or other text as well as provide a style of lettering to harmonize with a special design or special space. It is a continuous form of letters into words. Typographers are able to set type designed especially to imitate a hand-lettered script character.

SELF-MAILER.   A direct-mail piece that can be mailed without an envelope.

SET SOLID.   Type composed with no lead between the lines.

SPECTACOLOR.   This is an advertisement printed by rotogravure in another plant for later use in a newspaper. Unlike a preprint advertisement, a SpectaColor advertisement has clearly defined margins.

STOCK ART.   This is art that usually falls in many categories, listed alphabetically, that the artist may draw upon for particular situations. Many companies supply books of stock shots that may be found in the offices of artists. If the artist wants a certain shot, he orders it by number and gets back a glossy photograph for a modest price. The danger is that some other agency may be ordering the same shot at the same time for use in the same publication.

STRIP-IN.   Patch placed in an engraving containing correction for original plates. The metal is cut away and new metal, engraved with the correction, is inserted and locked in.

TOOLING.   Hand-cutting of white areas in engraving for retouching purposes.

WASH DRAWING.   A drawing in sepia, India ink, or transparent colors. The color or shading is "washed" on as with a brush. Suitable for halftone. Most wash drawings are made in "black and white"—that is, they are made on white drawing board usually in tones of color running from black to very light grays or pure white in the highlights. In making an opaque wash drawing an opaque pigment is used. The composition is first worked up in masses or all over and then the artist adds lights and shade as may be necessary to emphasize the right detail. This ability to place emphasis where needed makes wash drawings better than photographs for many types of products—especially where great detail is needed.

WIDOW.   A very short line carried over to the top of a newspaper column or magazine page. Sometimes a copywriter will be asked to rewrite a piece of copy in order that the widow can be avoided and a full-length line used instead.

The foregoing list gives you only a few of the terms you will encounter when you are discussing advertising that is to be printed. Advertising television production requires a separate and extensive set of production terms that you will have to learn if you are working with that medium. This knowledge will be picked up easily if you are working daily with television.

Attracting Attention with Headlines, Part A

Picture Mr. Jones who has settled down to read a magazine. His interest is in the articles and short stories (if any), not the advertisements. Somehow he must be attracted to the advertising. His attention must be diverted, however briefly, from his absorption with the editorial material.

And there is Mrs. Jones. Typically, she has more interest in advertising than her husband. She might actually seek out the advertising and read it before reading the editorial material. If this is the situation, then the advertiser hopes that he can get her to pause over his advertising before that of his competitors or, at least, in addition to.

In either situation, the advertiser relies on headlines to flag the reader and to create enough interest to force that pausing over the advertisement. The headline doesn't convince the reader; that comes later. It says in effect: "Here's something interesting," "Here's news," "Here's a useful item," "Here's something profitable for you," or "Here's an easy way to do something."

When you've written your headline, you've taken your first step toward the sale. It's a vital step because if you fail to attract Mr. or Mrs. Jones to your advertisement or your message, you're out of the action completely. You must get that initial attention and that initial sparking of interest.

HEADLINES AND ILLUSTRATIONS WORK TOGETHER

Arguments between copywriters and artists about which does the better job of gaining the reader's attention—the headline of the advertisement or the illustration—fail to settle the issue. Sometimes the illustration is the principal attention-getter. Sometimes the headline wins.

Actually, you have only three ways of shouting "Stop & Read" to your prospects:

- Headline alone.
- Illustration alone.
- A combination of both.

You will find that—often enough to be called standard technique—this last method will prove to be most logical. Headlines fall into certain categories or types. You will see how, in each type, the words and illustration are usually so closely allied that often neither the copywriter nor the artist could tell you which was the original thought.

Your relationship to your art associates is one, as already discussed, that can and will have an important bearing upon the success you attain. Functioning as a team you can contribute immeasurably to the quality of the work the other turns out.

A LOT OF THINKING GOES INTO HEADLINES

Most copywriters will tell you that once they've worked up a good headline, the rest of the copy seems to fall in line. The creating of a clever, or sales-producing headline is usually sheer, hard work and you'll never know before you start a headline-writing session how long it will take you to write the one that satisfies you. Occasionally, the very first headline that rattles off your typewriter may be what you use. Then again, you may work for hours or days without results. Most of the time you'll write many heads to get the one you'll finally use. You'll drop words, add words, change words and shuffle words until finally the headline falls in place. Yet, you often end with the feeling that somewhere within you an even better headline is crying for release.

It always happens so fast.
    And, this time, you're right. It did happen to "the other guy."
    You know: The guy who wouldn't hurt a fly, turn down a friendly drink—or take a cab home instead of driving. A nice guy who'd now and then smoke in bed, maybe swim out a little too far, sometimes hurry a little down the stairs.
    We know you knew him. And that you'll miss him.
    We just don't want you to join him.
    "Oops" is a pitiful epitaph.

National Safety Council

If you don't like thinking about safety, think where you'd be without it.

A reminder from the National Safety Council. A non-profit, non-governmental public service organization. Our only goal is a safer America.

FIGURE 4-1

Advertisement without a headline.   There is so much drama in the illustration that a headline in this public service advertisement might actually weaken the message. Although generally it is better to include headlines in advertisements, here is an exception.

MOST HEADLINES USE BASIC APPEALS

For much of your creative time you will be writing headlines that must start to sell at once, at the same time that they are attracting attention. You will often use as attention-getting means, the "sales appeals" of your product. You must stop your audience by offering something they want, thus inviting their interest in further exposition of those appeals.
    For example:

Your whole week's wash done in 30 minutes
. . . While you shop!

There is little chance that such a headline resulted from creative genius! It tells the entire story—yet is pretty sure to flag the eye of most homemakers as it does so.
    On the other hand, consider this second one:

What it's like to be in love.

Also a good stopper for most women and men, it could be equally effective as a headline for almost any number of products—perfume, candy, clothes, deodorants, or a travel agency. It is an imaginative and fanciful headline, designed to lure the reader to the copy, where it is discovered that falling in love is highly akin to owning a certain brand of silver.
    Most copywriters prefer writing unusual headlines. They seldom get this chance. Day in and day out, your job will be much more prosaic than that. It will be a matter of stating the facts, stating the facts, stating the facts.
    Headline writing varies a great deal with types of markets and types of media. The same techniques that are successful in one may not work well in others. Certain specialized principles apply to each of these fields—fashion, direct mail, catalog, trade and industrial, and retail newspaper advertising. For the moment, consider only the agency copywriter who has a client with a product of national distribution, normal appeal, and reasonable price, and whose problem is to write headlines that will sell the product to the general public through magazine or national newspaper advertising.
    Almost every author who has written a book on copywriting has compiled a list of the various types of headlines. As in the listing of the basic human appeals, some name four or five types, while others discover as many as fifteen or twenty. Although it is tempting to omit headline classification, it is of some value for copy beginners to organize their thinking about headlines in an orderly manner.

This list is presented to help you understand headlines, their creation and function. It will sometimes serve as a source from which you may pull the right approach to a given advertising problem.

DIRECT OR INDIRECT SELLING?

In reviewing types of headlines that will be presented in the succeeding pages, keep in mind the differences between direct and indirect selling. All advertising headlines definitely fall into one of those two selling categories, regardless of which type of approach or appeal is used.

A "direct-selling" headline uses one or more of the primary sales features of your product as both attention-getters and sales-influencers. An "indirect-selling" headline merely stops the reader to get him to read past the heading.

The two examples given previously illustrate the point:

Your whole week's wash done in 30 minutes
. . . While you shop!

is direct selling. The main attraction or sales potential of automatic washing machines is used to gain the reader's interest. While

What it's like to be in love.

doesn't sell anything except an intriguing thought.

You may ask, "When do you use a direct-selling approach, and when an indirect one?" That depends almost entirely upon what you have to sell. If you can discover features in your product strong enough to arouse interest and stimulate sales response, then, by all means, headline them. If you can attract your reader by telling him of the specific advantages your product has over others, you have a good chance to make an actual sale. He is enough interested in what you have to offer to read further. If, however, he must be caught by a nonselling device, you still aren't sure you won't lose him when you present your sales story.

As you review the types of headlines, note how many of them may be used directly or indirectly. Only in the "news" and in the "slogan, label, logotype" headlines will you find that either one or the other is a must. Those two, by their very nature, call for direct selling.

TYPES OF HEADLINES

Advertising headlines may be classified into the following categories (although many headlines can be in two or three categories at the same time).

News	Gimmick
Direct benefit	Curiosity
Emotional	Hornblowing
Directive	Slogan, label and logotype

Most of these titles are self-explanatory. "News" headlines, for example, are headlines in which the featured offer is handled in the same manner as though it were a newspaper item of timely interest to the reader. "Curiosity" obviously refers to headlines which pique the reader's interest without telling all.

Often a headline will embody two or more of these so-called types. For instance, it is possible to write a headline that combines both "emotional" and "curiosity" characteristics. It is unwise to depend too much upon any breakdown of headlines into types. If you learn to improvise upon a basic approach, rather than try to remember a long list of possible types, you will create your own types. You then will not be depending upon a list that exists only in some other copywriter's mind.

You will observe two more points as you look over this classification of headlines: a) that there are some headlines that do not classify under any heading presented here; and b) that many headlines have no real meaning, and hence no classification, without being considered with the illustration. Each is wholly dependent on the other for meaning, or classification.

FIGURE 4-2

Curiosity headline.   When this striking headline hits the reader's eye, an irresistible urge is stirred to read the copy to find out the meaning of the headline. An outstanding illustration and good copy complete this attention-getting advertisement.

Courtesy—The Potato Board

NEWS

The most common method of direct selling in headline treatment is the news approach. This technique calls for the same devices used by the person in the "slot" or on the copy desk of a newspaper in preparing headlines for the stories the reporters turn in. That is, to select the outstanding features you have to present quickly, clearly, and attractively. In writing news headlines, more than any others, a high value is placed on sentence structure because you usually have more than one thing to say yet you must use a minimum of words. Brevity is a powerful virtue in all advertising headlines, but you can't afford to be so brief that you omit important sales features or fail to state your case with clarity.

Consider the following headline:

Dust and soot roll off new
snow-white curtains and chairs.

This headline followed an illustration showing a salesperson demonstrating a chair covered with an easy-to-clean material. It should attract and hold the attention of homemakers and most men. Although the headline is simple, the writer has not sacrificed the copywriter's prerogative of being imaginative. How much more vivid to say dust and soot "roll off" than to use any of the more ordinary phrases such as "easier to clean," "saves time, work," and so forth.

Note one further point about this headline. There is no exclamation point at the end, even though a rather astonishing statement has been made. When you are writing a somewhat sensational headline, don't assume that it needs the added emphasis of the exclamation point. In many cases, the character of the headline itself, as in this example, is such that the exclamation point is out of place. If your headline is strong to begin with, there is little need of the additional emphasis of an exclamation.

Use a news head only for genuine news

When you plan on using a news approach, determine quickly whether or not you really have a news story. Headlines announcing new features, sensational developments, unheard of low prices, or any of the other selling points must be backed up. You cannot afford to write a headline that will attract the attention of your readers because of its news value and then fail to gain conviction as you develop your later copy. If you announce "a new amazingly low price," be sure that your price is amazingly low—not just lower than the highest-priced product in the same field, but low clear across the board.

Here, for example, are two headlines; each tells a news story, each offers a statistic or two, yet each presents a different degree of that all important "believability."

Doctors prove 2 out of 3 women
can have lovelier skin in just 14 days.

Without question, a headline designed to attract the attention of a majority of women, young and old. It tells them something they wish to know, something that they'd like to believe, and that doesn't appear to be too impossible. Furthermore, it is a headline which can be backed up by factual evidence, presented in a straightforward manner.

Now consider this statement:

50% Faster!
200% Smoother!

That's a headline about a razor—a product with which most men feel pretty familiar. Now it is within reason to suppose that male readers of that headline will believe the "extra speed" promise. The nature of the razor seems to make that possible, even though the average man would have trouble believing he could actually cut his shaving time in half. It's doubtful, too, if the second part of that headline ever attracted anything more than a hearty laugh. 200% smoother! In the first place, it's a quality that can hardly be measured. Secondly, the average man is a cynic when the percentage figures climb too high. "Shaves smoother" is a statement to be accepted. "Shaves 200% smoother" asks for disbelief. Be careful in your presentation of news. It must be believed if it's going to sell.

In writing news headlines it is well to consider key words such as "amazing," "new," "sensational," "at last," "what you've been waiting for," and others.

There is nothing wrong with using these words and phrases if they are true. Many copywriters, however, avoid them because they feel they have been overused—clichés that have lost their selling value in modern advertising. If these words are judiciously headlined, in cases where the products they sell actually do bear out their claims, they can and will regain stature as respected elements of good headlines. Certainly in cases where a product (or its characteristics) is in reality "amazing" or "sensational" news to the reader, it is reasonable selling technique to say so.

A product, for example, of possible volume sales among the hundreds of thousands of men who use electric razors appears to have real news value because of characteristics that are both believable and very much desired. The copywriter announces this with the word "amazing" in a key position in the headline.

The copywriter backs up "amazing" not only by stating the facts which make it so, but also by presenting the testimony of several men who agree. The whole feeling of the headline is one of important news that is supported with dignity and credibility.

On the other hand, here is another news headline:

New . . . A history-making advance in the annals
of electric clockmaking!

Sounds as if the least you could expect would be a clock that ran by radar or played Brahms. But, on reading further, the "history-making" advance turned out to be a simple improvement in design.

As you read through magazines and newspapers, give a rating to the news headlines you see. Judge them from the standpoint of how quickly, clearly, and forcefully they slam home selling facts. Grade them on how well you think they perform their primary function—attract attention while starting to sell. And, finally notice whether they are believable.

The following headlines utilize certain standard words that flag the reader quickly and unsubtly. After all, why be subtle when you have an interesting point to make?

Mercedes-Benz presents a singular new achievement.

Aquasport introduces its new all-fiberglass self-bailing family runabout.

Exxon heads to sea—to open a new frontier of energy.

Amazing improvement in oven cleaning.

Now—you can enjoy butter flavor without worrying about cholesterol.

DIRECT BENEFIT

A direct benefit headline, of course, can be combined with straight news headlines, with directive headlines, or the hornblowing type. It is a simple statement of the most important benefit offered by the product to the reader. For example:

At last—a copying machine that uses regular bond paper, and prints unlimited copies in a wide range of sizes.

When you have a strong benefit such as this, why be cute? Why try to arouse curiosity? A straightforward statement of fact is your most powerful selling weapon.

In today's ingredient-conscious world, the following direct benefit head carries a strong message for the reader. Set in big type; it commands heavy readership.

Wesson Oil Is 100% Pure Vegetable Oil.
   No chemicals.
   No preservatives.
   No coloring agents.

Two more observations can be made about this headline. One is the use of the product name. There are some advertising authorities who declare that every headline should carry the name of the product or advertiser. While this statement is extreme, it is true that flagging readers with product or company name in headlines will result in higher identification for either, and better "Advertiser Associated" figures in Starch readership figures described in the chapter on advertising research.

The second observation is that the use of the subheads strengthened an already powerful and seemingly complete headline.

Beginning copywriters, thinking that they must always be clever, shun direct benefit headlines as unimaginative and dull. They forget that a strong benefit is never uninteresting to the reader who reads advertisements for benefits, not for cleverness and entertainment which are strictly by-products.

People in the car-buying mood will find it fascinating if you tell them directly in the headline that the car you're selling has front-wheel drive that will provide better winter driving handling. Nothing dull about this to anyone who drives in the snow-belt areas.

Suppose you have no special advantage over a competing product. Should you, as so many copywriters do, avoid the direct benefit headline in favor of pure cleverness? Not so. You can still use the direct benefit headline, but you will combine it with a twist, an interesting phrase, or a different way of expressing the benefit. In that way you can satisfy your urge to be clever while simultaneously giving the reader a strong reason to buy. An advertisement for heat-and-serve salisbury steak demonstrates this two-way type of headline:

"Heat and serve" isn't the best part
(eating is).

Another example of a copywriter's finding an interesting way to headline a direct benefit is offered by an advertisement for a rich looking but relatively inexpensive carpeting. The writer might have written a headline that said:

Here's carpeting that looks
expensive but costs little.

Although this headline would attract readers and sales, the copywriter preferred a headline that would express the benefit with more flair and imagination. The headline actually used was:

Bigelow's sculptured elegance for the woman
who likes to feel extravagant—but isn't.

Notice once again the use of the company (and product) name in the headline.

A third example of a direct benefit headline that uses the name of the product and incorporates an interesting—and in this case, humorous—twist is the following:

TASTER'S CHOICE® makes
fresh coffee in seconds.
Our competition is still boiling.

Examples of direct benefit headlines:

Improved Easy-Off cleans faster, easier,
better than any leading brand.

. . .without all those fumes.

A good, hot family dish with meat.
Now about 24¢ a serving.

Better insurance coverage on your home
without increasing the premium.

EMOTIONAL

A common approach to headline writing is to appeal directly to the emotions of the reader. It could probably be argued that all selling, in headlines, in copy, and in artwork, does this in varying degrees.

Unlike the news headline, which usually is used only in making a direct sales presentation, the emotional headline can be either direct or indirect. These two headlines illustrate this point.

He'll be helpless in your hands
with this new miracle lotion.

One little whisper shattered my pride!

In one, though it makes capital of strong emotional appeal both visually and in the headline, a claim is advanced. In the other, the headline has no direct-selling virtues. It does have sales value, in that it sets up a situation which, in itself, is representative of the campaign strategy. But, as a headline, it sells only curiosity and attention value. Both headlines capitalize on the reader's interest in anything that can be linked to personal problems. Certainly love and pride are two strong emotions with which to lure the reader into further examination of the advertisements.

It will be obvious to you that certain products, or types of products, lend themselves particularly well to emotional approaches and you will find that the emotional approach is used in their advertising. Your job is one of interpretation. Almost all products used in the intimate daily lives of both men and women are well adapted to this type of approach. In the campaigns behind tooth paste, soap, perfume, tobacco, hair tonic, shaving cream, deodorants, and similar items you will find emotional appeals headlined.

If you are selling an automobile, a cigarette, or a typewriter, a straight emotional headline will be used less frequently. The difference in selling appeal should be clear:

No good night kiss for Charley!

might present a very good reason why Charley should buy himself a mouth wash—but it would be pretty hard to use it as a sound sales argument for smoking a brand of cigarettes.

Many headlines featuring emotional appeals represent statements from either real or imaginary people. It is easier for the reader to identify himself with a person of some resemblance to himself, who is saying something familiar, than with the impersonal words of an advertiser. Furthermore, your reader is much more ready to apply the sales psychology to himself if someone else is "guilty," than if you come right out and tell him he has terrible teeth or bad breath.

One of the most important points to remember in writing headlines with an emotional slant is that they must be realistic. Don't put words in the mouths of characters in your headline that your reader would

FIGURE 4-3

Emotional headline.   Sometimes, as in this instance, the emotional values in a headline are due to the headline-illustration combination, not to the headline alone. Furthermore, this headline could also be classified as a "directive" type. See how this same advertisement was used as an outdoor poster in Chapter 16.

The Advertising Council, Inc.

not say himself. The more human and down-to-earth you can make your headlines, the more attention you will get, and the more believability. If you were the reader, what would *you* think of the following headlines?

EXCELLO is the best car anyone ever owned, regardless of price.

And for you, pup, good old-time BARKIES.
They're packed with nutrition.

It's this Double-Action tonic for my active family.

It should not be assumed that all good headlines of an emotional approach must be testimonial types or purport to be the words of actual people. There are many ways to reach the reader's emotions—and most of them are good, provided they are based on sound psychology.

You have much more latitude in writing emotional headlines than is possible with the news approach. For example, no woman would actually believe that any lotion on her hands would render her sweetheart "helpless." Still this headline attracts attention. It is not intended by the copywriter to be taken literally by readers, and they realize that. But they associate the exaggeration with the fact that hand lotion makes hands soft, and soft hands are appealing.

Certain types of emotional headline writing must be done with special care. Insurance, at least life insurance, represents one of the most common fields of advertising in which the emotional approach is used. Yet, because the subject is anything but frivolous, and because the investment involved is more than the price of a bar of soap, great care must be taken to stick to the facts.

Examples of emotional headlines:

As the years roll on
memories become more important
. . . sometimes they're *all* we have left
The warmth of a fireplace,
The soft patina of a fine old table . . .
These are the things that bring beauty
and a sense of history to the homes of readers of
Early American Life

How long has it been since you promised her the moon?

Why horror movies
are more horrible on the
Quntrix II color picture tube.

For a rare and wonderful
feeling—try saving a life.

The remaining types of advertising headlines will be considered in the next chapter.

5

Attracting Attention with Headlines, Part B

As discussed in Chapter 4, advertising headlines may be classified into many categories. Some do not classify under any heading, and many headlines have no real meaning and no classification. Let's, however, now look at those which may be considered as directive; gimmick; curiosity; hornblowing; and slogan, label, and logotype. Again, you will find that many of these titles are self-explanatory.

DIRECTIVE

Now and then you will have occasion to use the command, or directive, approach in writing headlines. This type of headline is more often found in retail advertising, where you wish to get immediate action from your readers. Normally, when you are preparing advertising for national magazines, you will not expect to have your readers leap from their chairs and dash to the nearest drug store or grocery store to act on your sales message. You will not, therefore, have much reason usually for addressing them in such terms as

Go now!
Don't wait!
Call in your order!
Act while they last!

and all the hundreds of other command phrases found in retail copy.

Occasionally directive headlines are effective for magazine advertising campaigns. Directive headlines formed the basis of a long and successful series of advertisements and radio commercials for a soft drink company:

Keep up to date!
Look smart!
Be sociable!

This is not a command to immediate action, it is true, but it is a definite directive and one that has a particularly effective tie-in with its product.

Another directive headline, again part of a series designed to increase unit sales, was this one, for a headache relief:

Buy 2 instead of 1, and save.

Directive headlines are effective if you can give reasonable support to your command. There certainly is no faster way to tell people to do something than simply to tell them.

Directive headlines don't necessarily, however, require prompt buying action.

Plan your home for family comfort.

is a command that cannot immediately be complied with by most of us. Neither can

NEXT TIME TAKE THE BUS
and leave the driving to us.

In fact, you will rarely write a directive headline that will be expected to bring immediate action. This, as mentioned earlier, is more true of national advertising because such advertising is farther removed from the customer-store situation than is retail advertising.

However, there is no formula by which you can determine when and where to use directive headlines. Because they are strong and direct, because they require a minimum of words, and because they often make up in forcefulness what may be lacking in an illustration, such headlines are common in advertising. The directive headline is a general type of headline, and is presented as such. When you will use the type, just as with all the others, is something that you cannot be taught.

Examples of directive headlines:

Cover it up! Light it up! Quiet it down!
With a new Armstrong suspended ceiling.

<u>Stop taking harsh laxatives.</u>

Now.   Look younger,
            longer!

Come to the tropical island
with only one hotel.

GIMMICK

During the previous discussions of headlines, you have gathered the importance of taking a sane, sound, common-sense attitude toward your creative work particularly when you are writing news and direct benefit headlines.

Give her a ring tonight.

You don't have to be a big spender to give your out-of-town love a ring tonight.
    In fact, if your love is as far away as New York City, a 10-minute long distance call direct-dialed without operator assistance after 5 p.m. costs only $2.31. And if you call after 11 p.m., or anytime on the weekend until 5 p.m. Sunday, that same 10-minute call costs only $1.42.
So if you miss your out-of-town love, say so . . . by long distance.

 Indiana Bell

FIGURE 5-1

Pleasant directive headline with a clever twist.   A combination of an interesting layout approach and a headline that ties in cleverly lifts this newspaper advertisement out of the ordinary. It has strong human interest without showing any more of a person than the hand holding the illustration element.

But there are times when you will be able to pull out all the stops on your imagination and be the kind of copywriter the movies depict. Now and then you will reach that rare state of delight when you can use a gimmick. What's that?

Well, it's hard to say. A gimmick is a common word in an adman's daily life. It's used to describe practically everything that defies easy definition. Perhaps it's a trick television idea. Perhaps it's a type style. Possibly it's an art device or a gadget or a spoken phrase. And, it may be a headline. You may not like the word "gimmick," but it does describe a headline which is an attention-getter and uses for its appeal something that has no <u>apparent</u> relationship to the product involved, even though you eventually discover that there is a connection.

You will usually use the gimmick-type headline when you find yourself with a product that has few important competitive advantages to shout as news and that lacks sales appeal of the emotional type. You can expect to interest many readers who, intrigued by your headline and illustration, expose themselves to your copy story while they linger over your gimmick.

The most important thing to remember about the gimmick type is that it is successful only in certain circumstances. Gimmicks should not be used if you can be sure of getting attention through a straightforward approach.

Examples of gimmick headlines:

A marshmallow a day
keeps your freckles on straight.
(Illustration shows freckle-faced boy holding a cup of cocoa topped with marshmallows.)

Cooking secrets from the C.I.A.
(Illustration of two chefs. C.I.A., it turns out, is the name of a cooking school.)

How to have identical twins with Rit® Dye.
(Illustration of twin beds.)

Look at it this way:
Your daughter paid $85.00
for a dress that
used to be a petticoat.
And you're still
drinking ordinary scotch?
(Illustration of Pinch bottle. The headline, in this instance, is all the copy presented. The advertisement is part of a campaign using headlines of this type.)

The Asschaffenburgs'
home has seventy-five
bedrooms and a great kitchen
(No illustration in this small advertisement but a logotype for The Pontchatrain Hotel in New Orleans.)

CURIOSITY

The curiosity headline is closely akin to the gimmick, but it must be considered in a class by itself.

Every gimmick, whether it be a headline or an illustration, is designed to excite the curiosity of the reader but gimmick headlines arouse curiosity about nothing in particular. Curiosity headlines, on the other hand, definitely arouse curiosity about the product or service they are advertising. For example:

> He whirls a white hot
> "rope" of stainless steel.

is a headline (and imagine the dramatic illustration with it!) that was written to make readers curious enough about "a 'rope' of stainless steel" that they would go on and read the rest of the advertisement. Another good curiosity arouser:

> C'mon now! What other coffee
> ever gave you all this?

Nothing particularly tricky about that headline, yet it is a curiosity headline. People are not inclined to think of coffee as embodying many varied appeals or advantages. Normally, readers could be expected to read further because they were curious about what was meant.

> What . . . No cord?

is a good curiosity headline for an electric iron, yet it sticks with the selling points of the product. So is this one, which offers a selling point for a canned meat:

> 8 Years without a moment's privacy.

Both curiosity and gimmick headlines are methods of indirect selling, one a little less indirect than the other. Both should be used when the same general conditions prevail as far as the product's characteristics and appeals are concerned. If you have any means of direct selling at your command—any logical, believable approach to the reader's interest through a straightforward presentation—*use it*. If you have not, if you are selling an idea, an institution, or a product which fails to offer any attention-getting appeals, then it is good copywriting to examine the other means of approach.

Examples of curiosity headlines:

> When was the last time you were told
> to wash your face!
> *(Illustration of a hand holding a bar of soap. The advertiser is an institute for skin care.)*

> What your home could
> have in common with the Met,
> the Tate, and the Louvre.
> *(Illustration in this small advertisement shows a print of a famous painting. The advertiser is a company that sells prints of paintings.)*

> Down with love!
> *(Illustration of a young couple under quilt filled with European goose down.)*

> "Dear General Foods,
> People are what they eat.
> So why should I eat
> propylene glycol monostearate?"
> *(Small illustration in this page advertisement shows different foods and their chemical names. Advertisement explains why additives are needed.)*

HORNBLOWING

When you can be specific, be specific. If your product has really outstanding selling points, take advantage of them in your headlines. Use them as attention-attracters. If you can find no such headline appeals in the product itself, you may find it advisable to lure the reader with other devices—the gimmick or the curiosity headline.

Sometimes, however, you must decide what to do if neither of these approaches seems to be right. This situation can arise from a number of reasons. The product may compare favorably with all competitive products, in every respect, and still lack any unique qualities. It may actually have some advantages which, for one reason or another, are not important enough to warrant building an entire advertisement around. It may be that a gimmick or a curiosity-arouser, per se, would seem to detract from the dignity of the product or its manufacturer.

In modern advertising, therefore, you will see many headlines which simply speak in general terms about the merits of the products they are advertising. These are called "hornblowing" headlines. The term is not used in a derogatory sense. It is true that many such headlines lack power and sales appeal and might be better handled some other way. But many, also, are examples of strong selling. Consider for example the following headline:

> It isn't easy to improve a Cadillac.
> But we did.

Pride of craftsmanship has been a characteristic of Cadillac advertising over the years and to millions of car buyers the Cadillac has come to symbolize a high standard in the automotive world. This headline, therefore, while saying nothing specific about the new automobile, reinforces the quality image built up over the years. Coming from a lesser manufacturer, the headline would seem empty and pretentious. Moral: be sure your stature is high enough before you use a hornblowing headline.

Sometimes your product has a definite advantage. You may decide in such a case to use a hornblowing headline as a simple statement of fact. You are the best in some respect so you reason that it is pointless to be modest. An example of a headline that points up its specific advantage is the following:

> Mazola: The only leading brand
> that's pure corn oil.

In contrast, many advertisers use a hornblowing headline to give an opinion that they are the best. If said often enough, the people in the market might eventually believe what the headline is telling them. Studies made by the Gallup & Robinson research organization, however, suggest that what they term the "brag and boast" headlines do poorly in readership and in achieving conviction.

A hornblowing headline based upon opinion follows:

Avon introduces
Candid
the most beautiful coloring
ever created
for a woman's face . . .

Automobile advertising and cigarette advertising are two fields in which the hornblowing headline is almost standard procedure. Thumb through a magazine and note the similarity between advertisements for these two products.

Such headlines as the following have become expected in cigarette advertising to the point where the consumer is numbed by the conflicting statements and, unfortunately, either loses interest in the advertising or disbelieves it.

Of all menthols:
Carlton
is
lowest.
(The reference is to Carlton's being lowest in tar.)

Why is Tareyton better?
Others remove.
Tareyton improves.

Each period of new automobile introductions finds print advertisements and television commercials full of the same tired-out boasts for the new cars:

Most comfortable.
Most miles per gallon.
Most beautiful.

Such overuse of the hornblowing headlines tears down believability in advertising and emphasizes the point that such headlines should be used sparingly. In fact, the boastful headline should be the last headline considered.

When a beer is advertised as being

Preferred for Mellow Moments

or a candy bar because it is

The Center of Attraction

or a razor because it is

America's No. 1 Shaver

it is fairly safe to assume that the "idea" department is slowing down. While many hornblowing headlines are part of a carefully worked-out plan and represent sound thinking and sales strategy, others are only too obviously the result of a failure to discover a better way to do the job.

Remember the function of the horn on your automobile. There are plenty of times when it is the most important part of the car. Used properly and at the correct time, it serves you well. But blowing the horn just for the purpose of making noise can accomplish only one thing—it will wear down your battery.

Examples of hornblowing headlines:

The unbelievable
Dodge Aspen.

The Leica® CL
The incomparable compact.

Best "diet" a
skin can have.
(Product is a medicated soap.)

Arpège
Very simply, the most beautiful
gift in the world.

SLOGAN, LABEL, AND LOGOTYPE

Often a campaign for the promotion and advertising of a product will have as a basic purpose the getting of as much recognition as possible for either a slogan or the product or the company name.

Normally, you might consider that advertisements that feature signatures and slogans as the major display units still carry headlines using one of the various approaches already discussed, since subheadings usually carry on and get into the selling story. Such advertisements are frequently found. But if you remember the primary function of the headline—to attract the reader's attention—you will see that these subheads, given less display space, could not be termed headlines in the true sense of the word.

When copywriters use the slogan-label-logotype approach, they do so with one of two ideas in mind. First, they feel that the name of the product or company is, in itself, their most important attention-attracter, or they are willing to sacrifice a potentially more intensive reading to pound home a name or an idea.

Many successful advertising campaigns have stressed "name" emphasis. An outstanding example of how consistent name advertising can pay off as well, if not better, than a succession of clever selling ideas is typified by the Florsheim Shoe Company. For many years, Florsheim has advertised in the nation's magazines, with one main objective, one basic selling idea—an illustration of a good-looking pair of shoes and the name Florsheim. That their theory has been successful is evident from a look at the Florsheim sales record and growth.

Slogan headlines are good devices to obtain sales and to get attention provided the slogan is a "selling" slogan.

The slogan-logotype headline is best adapted to products whose advertisements depend more upon constant reminder than upon the weight of competitive advantages. That's why you'll find them featured often in advertising for beverages, candy bars, cigarettes, and other items which sell in volume across the counter and for low cost and rarely have any demonstrable superiority over their competitors.

Obviously, you needn't worry about the actual technique of writing this type of headline, because it is already written for you. But it does represent a percentage of the headlines that appear regularly, and should be recognized as one of the important approaches.

Examples of slogan, label, logotype headlines:

You've come a long way, baby
Virginia Slims.

les must® de Cartier

HALSTON
for Fieldcrest

A great newspaper is more
than a paper towel.

ABILITY TO WRITE HEADLINES DIFFERS

As you mature in copywriting, you find that certain types of headlines are easier for you to write than others. You may never be a good creator of gimmick headlines because you just don't think that way. Don't be discouraged. Many competent copywriters don't think that way either, but they may have strong talent for writing other types of headlines—powerful news presentations, for instance, or they may have an unerring feeling for emotional headlines that will reach out to the reader.

Although many headlines are of the straight news or direct benefit type that do not call for the gimmick type of thinking, you will go farther in this business if you can add the little twist, or the touch of cleverness, to such headlines to make them stand out on the page. Otherwise, the world of copy would start to become a bit dull with every copywriter churning out straight headlines that had nothing to distinguish them from all the other straight headlines. (An example is a headline for a clock that reads: Give her a clock like this and she'll have the time of her life.)

Despite the fact that creativity in headline writing is a quality admired and rewarded in advertising, such creativity isn't always allied with "cleverness." Straight thinking, clear writing, and a deep knowledge of what moves consumers—these are all important, too.

OFTEN HEARD QUESTIONS ABOUT HEADLINES

Beginning copywriters in school and in business consistently run into the same snags in writing headlines. They ask the same questions. With regularity they make the same mistakes. The following section is a discussion of some of these questions and mistakes.

Get a group of young copywriters, or potential copywriters, together. They'll usually get around to questions on the headline, because headlines are more spectacular than most body copy. Furthermore, every advertising writer has been fed figures relating to the astounding percentage of readers who read nothing but headlines. Here are some of the questions that beginners so often ask about headlines, and the answers to them. Remember as you read the answers that no rules are given as inflexible—it is a matter of fitting the answer to the situation, and in the "gimmick" headline, anything goes. You may consider the answers as observations rather than rules.

Don't let my beauty mislead you

Arvinyl's "skins" are tough, too. Our vinyl-metal laminates resist scratching, scuffing and abrading. They provide good protection against corrosion and give years of service under normal — and not-so-normal — use. During fabrication, these tough skins securely bonded to the base metal, stand up under a wide range of fabricating steps. Want more information on Arvinyl's beautiful-but-tough skins?
Call or write Arvinyl
Division of Arvin Industries, Inc.
Columbus, Indiana 47201 • 812-372-7271

West of the Rockies, call Fullerton, Calif., 714-871-9143

FIGURE 5-2

A change-of-pace headline and illustration combination.   A disarming headline and a gaze-riveting illustration make this advertisement stand out from its business magazine competitors. The advertisement won a first-place creative award. Notice the strong, straightforward copy that follows the whimsical treatment at the top.

Is the question headline wrong?

No. The question headline is very useful. It can get directly to the point that is in the reader's mind. In such cases it serves as a lively opening into the discussion that answers the question. For instance, an

Arrow Shirt advertisement that attracted much attention was headed by the question, "Which one wears it?" A woman was pictured looking unhappily at three different men in three separate panels who were wearing sloppy collars obviously not Arrows. Each caption explained how an Arrow collar could have improved the man's appearance. Finally, in panel four, a man is pictured wearing the trim Arrow collar. The caption for this panel triumphantly breathes, "A-h-h-h! This one wears it—the Arrow white shirt that has everything! Etc., etc."

The question headline was admirably adapted to this advertisement. It is doubtful whether any other type of headline could have been as suitable for the light touch handled so well in Arrow advertisements. Yet, many capable copywriters tell other copywriters never to use questions for headlines. These writers distrust the question headline because so many copywriters misuse it.

Too often the question is phrased so that the reader can answer it with an impertinent no! and, thus losing interest, he goes on to the next advertisement. A question of this type might ask directly, "Would you like soft, lustrous hair?" Many readers, being human, would give the negative answer flippantly and that would end the advertiser's chance to entice them into reading further.

On the other hand, here's a question head that gives the reader no chance to make a retort:

How does your mouth feel after
brushing with Colgate, "Dr. J"?

Another question headline, this one a direct question, asks

Want perfect coffee?

In almost the same breath, the advertiser follows with:

Try A.D.C.—one coffee all four
recommend.

The quick follow-up is desirable for such direct questions. Examples:

Bad Break?
Super Glue® 3
makes it good in just 10 seconds

Why smoke Now?
(Immediately the advertiser provides a reason in the form of recent tests.)

Dry lips?
Medicated Blistik

An interesting way to use the question is shown in the following:

Who says Dynamo® works better
than Tide?
I do
(Answer comes from a woman pictured in the advertisement.)

Perhaps the suitability of the question headline hinges upon the ability of the question to draw the reader into the body copy for the answer. If the reader can answer the question without further reference to the advertisement, you'd better look your question over. Be especially careful with direct questions. This warning is doubly emphasized in radio and television commercials.

All of us have, at one time or another, sassed announcers when they asked directly, "Wouldn't you like to double your income?" Despite the fact that all of us do want to double our income, it is hard to resist saying no when the question is asked. Keep that in mind when you write your question headline. Also, the question headline is often overused by beginning copywriters. Make sure that the question headline is the best device for putting over your copy message, and be sure to shape your question to get the answer you want.

Should headlines be short?

There is no firm answer that can be given to this question but it occurs frequently because it has been an axiom of advertising that headlines should be short and that they should not tell too much of the story. There are still many who believe that the headline should say just enough to entice the reader into the following copy, and no more.

If you feel comfortable with the short-headline philosophy, what about the following headlines? Are they wrong?

Will you live
as well as you do now
when you are on
Social Security?

The Lincoln can help you save taxes
on $15,000 a year and retire rich!

Timesavers!
Hints on how to avoid "touch-up"
ironing jobs. How to keep socks and such
from disappearing in the wash. And more.

Azure waters tranquilize it.
Snow covered slopes
harmonize it.
You can sun,
ski and revive in it.
Spain.

Our $26.50 gift box has mini
Quiche, hens with wild rice,
Chicken Kiev, Cannelloni and crepes.
You'd pay more than double
in a fine restaurant.

Mattel Preschool. A merry collection of grins,
giggles, squeals, chuckles, whoops and tee-hees.

New No nonsense®
Comfort Stride™ panty hose.
So your legs can feel
as good as they look.

TURN CENTRAL PARK INTO THE TUILERIES, THE SUBWAY INTO THE METRO. YOU'RE GOING TO BE LIVING WITH CACHAREL THIS SUMMER. CHECK OUT THE ENVIRONMENT IN DESIGNER SPORTSWEAR.

FIGURE 5-3

Bold, attention-getting headline.   There is boldness in the size, language, and length of this headline for a page advertisement of Bonwit Teller, the well-known retail establishment. Sometimes such a headline is called a "grabber" because it cannot be ignored.

With the
Toastmaster System III
you can cook a chicken
in ten hours
or one.

What Hidden Valley Ranch™
did, to make a fresher, livelier
Italian salad dressing, would
shock an Italian.

Just remember this, if you begin to worry about the rule "Headlines must be brief" that your prospects are assaulted by so much advertising that only those headlines with big, informative, catchy headlines and illustrations may have enough attention-getting quality to make readers pause and partly sell them. Today's headlines do more preselling of the reader than was true in the past days when headlines had completed their mission if they had attracted the reader's attention.

Despite all the defense in this section of the long headline, it is desirable normally to write short, interesting headlines that say much in a few words. Certainly if you wish to use large type in the headline, you are forced to keep it brief unless you have a big-space advertisement.

There is a certain drama in the punchy one or two-word headline—a memorable quality that is lacking in the very long headline. Volkswagen advertisements over the years have specialized in such headlines, achieving an impact that has caused them to be discussed, admired, and imitated.

Do headlines always have to use verbs?

Hardly anything must always be done in copywriting. That is true of the use of verbs in headlines. Almost every authority in copywriting will tell you that it is usually better to use a verb in a headline. Some writers will tell you that every headline should have a verb, or an implied one. Although this book agrees that in the main it is better to use a verb in a headline than not to use one, there have been many fine heads that are verbless. The famous war-time headline, "The Kid in Upper Four," which came out in World War II, had no verb but it is one of the best-remembered heads of all time.

Although the following head may not go ringing down through the years, Breck shampoo has used it effectively. Note that it is verbless:

Now . . . both dandruff control
and beautiful hair

Such headlines admittedly lack the vigor of headlines using verbs. There is less life and direct action. There is less chance that the headline will make you move. Just the same, depending upon the campaign, the illustration and the body text, there are advertisements for which the verbless headline seems suited.

Even though a defense has been made for the verbless headline—use a verb as often as you can. The headline "News about Lucite" is pretty drab, for instance, compared to "Lucite makes news," or "Here's news about Lucite," or "Lucite is news." A headline with a verb seems to go somewhere; a headline without a verb often sits passively in the advertisement. Occasionally, because of its appropriateness with the illustration, a headline such as "The Kid in Upper Four" does its job satisfactorily. Usually, however, a headline that is all right without a verb would be better with one.

Do directive headlines sometimes cause resentment?

Yes. Americans dislike orders or commands. Printed advertisements and radio and television commercials are constantly telling us:

Don't scrub your hands with harsh soaps.

Take liver pills for upset stomach.

Don't take chances with your tires.

Orders get under anyone's skin after a while. On the other hand, the average reader is inclined to move only after prodding. What does the copywriter do when he considers that the reader may resent an order but won't make a buying move unless he is given some sort of push? The answer is that the copywriter must pitch the headline in the right "tone."

All through life you have probably found that one person asks you to do something and you do it willingly, whereas another person may ask you to do exactly the same thing and you resent his doing so. Perhaps it was the latter's tone of voice—the *way* of asking—that caused your resentment. It is your way of phrasing that causes success or failure in your directive headlines.

Usually you'll do better to suggest than to command. The words "stop" or "don't" often sound unpleasant to the reader. From childhood to the grave someone is using those words. If you start your headline with them, the reader may react instinctively against your product.

Also, be careful not to offend him by assuming in your directive headline that he is doing something foolish. Headlines of this type would be "Don't waste your money," or "Don't be careless with your child's health."

What about using quotation headlines?

The quotation headline is often a pleasant variant of the straight headline. When you remember that dialogue enlivens almost any book, you can see how quotation headlines can be useful in advertisements.

A headline using a quotation has human interest. It often enables the advertiser to make a product claim more believable; a quotation headline has an element of storytelling about it. Most of us like a story, so when we read the headline—

"We had visions of
producing a sort of
off-Broadway television . . ."

—we want to find out the background. Did whoever made the statement succeed in the entertainment goal sought?

"Testimonial" copy is, of course, the most logical vehicle for the quotation headline. Too many of the persons pictured in advertisements seem unreal. The quotation headline can humanize them.

In view of the foregoing, what possible objection can be made to a quotation headline? When it is used by experienced copywriters, there will usually be no objections, since they will probably use it with discretion. The beginning copywriters, on the contrary, will be inclined to overuse such headlines. Not being able to write effective straight headlines easily, they constantly make the people in advertisements do the talking. Since the quotation headline is especially desirable as a change from the conventional headline, the copywriter robs it of its freshness by using it too often. It has been observed in college classes in copywriting that, left to their own devices, the young copywriters would rarely write anything but question or quotation headlines. Such headlines are easy to write and that's that.

Examples of quotation headlines:

"I switched from clay litter
to Litter Green®. . .
when some friends asked
if I kept my cat's litter box
under the sofa."

"It's thicker and zestier than Ragu."
(Illustration shows man eating spaghetti that is covered with a rival product to Ragu.)

"Mother Nature gave me plain hair.
I gave it pizazz."

"Gracious! We thought you said
to come at lunchtime!"
(Illustration shows two grandmother types showing up unexpectedly at the front door of a house.)

"My Orville Redenbacher's®
Gourmet Popping Corn
will blow your top!"
(Illustration shows Mr. Redenbacher with two bowls of popcorn. One bowl of his product; the other of a rival.)

Look at the foregoing. No. 1 and No. 5 followed up the headline by having the person pictured provide all the body copy as well as the headline. The other three advertisements used the characters shown merely to deliver the headline.

Although you will see both techniques used, in general it is better to let the quotation headline suffice. That is, do not have the person delivering the headline also deliver the whole copy message. It is difficult to keep such advertisements believable. A single, short statement about a product is about all you can expect from a testimonial-giver. When such a person also provides copy for an entire advertisement, he or she tends to sound like a copywriter.

"Hanging" headlines—should they be used?

First, to make clear what is meant by a hanging headline. It is the type of headline that is not complete unless the reader reads the first words in the body text. An example would be:

Headline: What is . . .
Body Text: . . . the most sensational advance
                  in television today? Why it's the
                  new automatic tuner, of course,
                  etc., etc.

When you examine the foregoing example, you see that the headline doesn't make sense unless the reader immediately reads the first words in the body copy. Neither does the body text beginning mean too much if the reader hasn't read the headline.

Now the inconvenient part of all this is that readers fail to follow neat paths in their reading. Some will start with the headline and skip to the logotype. Others will start with the first line of body text, look at the illustration, and then glance at the bottom of the advertisement. It is difficult to predict just how the reader will read your advertisement.

If you have used a hanging headline, therefore, you may lose much force in your advertisement. Headline readers may look at the meaningless fragments you have written and not bother to find the first line of body text to complete the headline's meaning. They may be irritated if they start the body text and find that they must backtrack to the headline to find out what you're talking about.

Even if you lay out your advertisement scientifically, using every possible device to lure the reader from the headline to the first line of body text, you will often fail to do so. This situation is made even worse in layouts that separate the head and body text widely by illustrations and other elements.

Generally, therefore, it is sounder practice to avoid hanging headlines. Unless your headline and body copy are completely independent of each other for meaning, and unless each will make sense by itself, you will be treating the readers more kindly if you avoid hanging headlines.

All this advice about hanging headlines is aimed directly at the beginning copywriter because the experienced writer simply isn't going to use the technique. If you examine hundreds of advertisements, you may not find one example of a hanging headline. Yet, initial advertisements turned in by beginners will almost always include one or two hanging headlines.

YOU'VE WRITTEN A HEADLINE— NOW HEAR THIS . . . (Ten tips)

1. Ask yourself: Is this the most powerful headline I can write? Or, is it the most interesting?
2. See that the headline is important looking. This is a matter of type size and/or type style. Check with your art colleagues on this point. Make your wishes known, or you may end up with an anemic-looking headline.
3. Be sure your clever headline is truly clever and not baffling. Cleverness defeats itself if you, or a tight little group of insiders, are the only ones who understand your headline. Prefer clarity to cleverness unless, of course, you can devise a clever head that's also clear.
4. Try to write a headline in such a way that the readers know at a glance what your big point is, what benefit you're offering, or simply what you're advertising. In short, hook them quickly.

5. Be sure your headline appeals to the reader's self interest more than your own. Too many headlines are company or product-oriented—not reader-oriented.
6. Decide whether you should include the name of the product or the name of the advertiser in the headline. There's no rule that says you must do either, but often you'll get better product or advertiser identification if you do. Do not, however, force the name into a headline that may be clever or forceful in its own right (and might be more effective without the inclusion of the product or advertiser name).
7. Consider giving your headline an editorial look instead of an advertising look. This "look" may result from the kind of the type that is used, as well as the content of the headline.
8. If you have a particular segment of your market in mind, aim the headline directly at this segment. It may be young mothers, the Geritol set, or the macho group. If you know your target, let them know from your headline that you're talking directly to them.
9. Question the overuse of capital letters in headlines such as:

   YOU'LL GET BETTER MILEAGE

   or

   You'll Get Better Mileage.

   Readers favor printed messages that give them what they're used to seeing. Accordingly, why not write the foregoing heading like this:

   You'll get better mileage.

   If you do, you're following the advice of the readability experts who frown on capitals, italics, and other artificial forms.
10. If in doubt, use a strong news headline with an appealing benefit. This is an all-powerful combination. Look for the news value in your product and find its most appeal benefit. Join them in a strong headline that can still, if you're clever, provide a twist that sets it apart from other headlines. But remember. News and benefits. They're always good and always in style.

6

You Put It All Together in Body Copy, Part A

Look upon the headline as the piquant sauce whose enticing aroma arouses your salivary glands. Now you're interested in the meat and potatoes that follow. Body copy is the main course of the copywriting meal. Headlines, illustrations, subheads, captions, slogans, and logotypes are important elements in the meal. Your sales-clinching argument, however, must be done in the body copy. It is here that you present your facts, or your reasons-why-to-buy material.

In some advertisements, it is true, the chief objective is merely to identify. Where this is the case, headlines, illustrations, and logotypes carry the advertising burden. Advertising for perfumes, soft drinks, sugar, and salt usually fall in this category. Body copy plays a minor role, as a rule, in promoting these products.

Should selling be required, however, body copy assumes a major role. While an illustration of a new car model can certainly interest prospective buyers, they usually need more than an attractive picture to get them into the dealer's showroom. They need to know what is under the hood, what improvements have been made, what kind of mileage to expect, whether power steering is offered, and on and on. Your body copy does the same sort of persuasive work for a host of other products. In a television commercial, "body copy" is normally a powerful combination of video and audio although sometimes all of the selling can be done by video, or by video with a minor contribution by audio.

WRITING FOR NEWSPAPERS AND MAGAZINES

You will not find separate chapters in this book on the writing of newspaper and magazine advertisements because the material on appeals, headlines, and body copy applies fundamentally to both. Newspaper and magazine readers respond to the same basic appeals. As for writing approach, many advertisers use similar advertisements in newspapers and magazines and certainly utilize the same campaign approach in each.

If, however, you make certain assumptions about the magazine reader, you may in the light of those assumptions write copy somewhat differently for magazines and newspapers. Assumptions: That magazine readers tend to be somewhat better educated and of a higher income level. That they read magazines in a more leisurely fashion over a longer period, and that during this period they will pick up and put down the magazine a number of times. This is in contrast with newspaper readers who read quickly and tend to finish their reading at one sitting.

What implications are there for you in these assumptions? One, of course, is that the language level in newspaper copy may sometimes be a trifle lower than for magazines, especially selective magazines aimed at an obviously upper-level audience. Headlines can be more direct and localized, and the following body copy should likewise be direct and localized. The body copy may tend to be brisker and more telegraphic than magazine copy. Because newspaper readers go through the publication so speedily, it is well, if the copy is at all long, to break it up with subheads in order to hold their attention.

Once more, however, usual copywriters do not need to make a sharp distinction between the way they write for newspapers or magazines. The rules for writing headlines and body copy apply by and large to both. This is especially true of mass circulation magazines and newspapers. Differences will become pronounced only when the advertisements are to be placed in publications appealing to high-level audiences.

52

**Look at it this way:
Your wife's spending $250 a month
on meditation lessons to forget
$12,000 worth of college education.
And you're still
drinking ordinary scotch?**

BODY COPY DIRECTION IS DICTATED BY HEADLINES AND ILLUSTRATIONS

Copy direction and the type of copy will be set by the direction of the headline and illustration. Once you have decided upon a good headline and illustrative device, the selection of the body copy style will not require much planning. For example, if you use a direct selling, factual headline, your body text will usually be most effective if it, too, is factual. Make it back up your headline claims immediately.

Likewise, if you employ a gimmick or a curiosity element in your headline and/or illustration, your body copy should explain the connection before you can get into your selling arguments.

Setting the direction of your body copy requires common sense. Logic will show you that effective body copy must, in the main, follow the pattern established by the headline and illustration.

HOW IT BREAKS DOWN

Once again a list is given to you, this time of body copy types. It's a short list because body copy can be categorized rather well in six types. Each has its own advantages and difficulties. It's up to you to decide which will do best in helping you reach your sales objectives and copy platform objectives.

Straight-line copy, in which the body text begins immediately to develop the headline and/or illustration idea in direct selling of the product, using its sales points in the order of their importance.

Narrative copy, the establishment of a story or specific situation which, by its nature will logically lead into a discussion of a product's selling points.

"Institutional" advertising, in which the copy sells an idea, point of view, service, or company instead of presenting the selling features.

Dialogue and monologue copy, in which the characters illustrated in your advertisement do the selling in their own words (testimonials, quasi-testimonials, comic strip and continuity panel).

Picture and caption copy, in which your story is told by a series of illustrations and captions rather than by use of a copy block alone.

Gimmick copy, unclassified effects in which the selling power depends upon humor, poetry, foreign words, great exaggeration, gags, and other devices.

FIGURE 6-1

Humorous (gimmick) advertisement.   With its engaging, utterly different approach, it is difficult to classify this advertisement into a standard list of advertisement types. The copy, all in headline form, commands attention as does the striking illustration. The product is not the kind that needs long, serious copy. Thus the headline and illustration can carry the entire creative burden.

Perhaps it would be well here to repeat that this chapter talks about the primary copy of advertisements rather than about their general format. For example, the format of an advertisement on skin care might call for an illustration of a pimply young person bemoaning, via a blurb, some romantic failures. If the entire advertisement were to be classified in one of the preceding six categories, this would come under "dialogue and monologue," since the character in the advertisement is doing some of the selling in his own words. The body copy, however, in which the young person's plight is amplified and then solved by the use of the product, would probably be "narrative."

In many advertisements you will be able to discover more than one type of copy. Pictures and captions, for instance, very often are used as an amplification of the selling ideas, although the main block of copy is straight-line and factual. The same is true of all other classifications.

Although occasionally you may find some advertisement that defies classification, almost always the six preceding listings can be used for classification purposes. To check this out, 222 advertisements in a copy of *Family Circle* (published at the time this new edition was being prepared) were examined carefully. Each advertisement was classified.

Thirteen of the advertisements contained no body copy. Generally, these contained only headlines, illustrations, and logotype. In the remaining 209 advertisements, the classifications were as follows:

Straight line	146
Narrative	16
Institutional	8
Dialogue/monologue	11
Picture/caption	7
Gimmick	12
Combination	9
	209

Notice the great dominance of the straight-line copy style. It would be surprising not to find such dominance. Every examination of an entire issue of a publication reveals the same utilization of straight-line copy.

BETTER NOT SPECIALIZE

You are going to discover—if you are like most copywriters—that you write one or more types of copy better than you do others. The question then arises: Should you attempt to make yourself a specialist? Should you try to limit your writing to those types of copy you do best? The answer is no!

No matter what kind of copywriting you get into—agency, retail, mail-order, direct-mail—you will find that your daily routine may call for all types of copy. The products you will be asked to sell will not lend themselves to one specific style of copy, or headline-illustration-copy treatment. If you try to specialize, you may have more fun writing what you do write, but you'll soon be writing strictly for fun and no longer for cash. There are few places for a "one-shot" copywriter in the nation's big advertising operations today. To be more sure of your future, you should be versatile. Naturally the advertisements decorating your sample book will demonstrate the type of copy you write best. Your seniors in the business will certainly recognize your skill in handling certain types of work and will make that recognition evident in the assignments they give you. Just the same, become proficient in writing keyed to all the various categories.

FIGURE 6-2

Institutional advertisement with a public service message.   In this personally written institutional advertisement is a powerful message that defines the problems posed when industries attempt to meet environmental standards. The strong headline and the hard-hitting message make this a fine example for the writer of institutional advertisements.

"We spent $1,178,000 to clean up the air in Vandergrift, Pennsylvania. If things keep going the way they are, there won't be anyone around our plant to breathe it!

COPY AND RHETORIC

Many beginners ask how much background of English grammar is needed by a copywriter. The answer is—a lot or a little.

No one will deny that a thorough knowledge of the fundamentals of grammar and sentence structure is helpful to a copywriter. Yet you will find that many times a piece of copy will sound better and more sincere if it does not quite meet the standards of perfect prose. Remember that most of the people reading your advertisements, who will eventually buy the products you are selling, do not sport Phi Beta Kappa keys. Give them simple talk, not fancy language. But one caution is needed here—usually you will not violate good grammatical usage. Your readers will soon see through your attempt to write "on their level."

The word "usually" was employed in the preceding sentence because some successful advertising has resulted from the copywriter deliberately violating grammatical rules. A celebrated instance of this is the much deplored but hugely successful "Winston tastes good like a cigarette should" that made the bells ring at the cash register while simultaneously infuriating the grammarians.

Another example is the advertisement that told the readers in the headline that, "It ain't hard to speak good English."

Despite these successful violations, most copywriters observe the rules of writing and grammar without being pedantic. Most good copywriting has a conversational tone. While such easy, informal writing might offend the purists and the authors of social science text books, it is admirably suited to advertising that communicates with a mass audience composed of people who vary greatly in educational background.

Your writing style in advertising should be interesting, yet simple. It is straightforward, yet subtle. You should abhor dull writing above all else.

One writer had these words about achieving interest through observance of a number of writing niceties. His hard-boiled, commonsense suggestions should be read very carefully.

What do I mean by writing style?

Just this. The simple sentence starts with a subject. Then the simple sentence has a verb. Then the simple sentence has an object. The simple sentence ends with a period. The simple sentence gets boring as hell after you've read three or four of them. And you just did!

Let's try again. By hanging a phrase out in front of the subject, you can add an extra thought, and more interest to a sentence. And by starting sentences with a "non-th" word, ("th" words are the, then there, etc.) you make your copy flow more smoothly . . . read more easily. Of course, ending a sentence with a question mark helps, too, doesn't it? Exclamation points are even better!

If you're the copy-writer, become the copy-reader. Read what you write with a red pencil in your hand. Be brutal. Cut out meaningless words and useless phrases. Combine some sentences and eliminate others. Give the reader a long flowing sentence that combines several thoughts and presents facts which are of average importance. Then use a shorter sentence to quicken the pace for the reader.

And then . . . hit him in the eye! Shock him. It's amazing how short sentences can catch people. They stir the imagination. They create desire. And produce positive action.

Of course, there's more to good writing than varying the length of your sentence. Vary the length of your paragraphs, too.

Like this.

Simple, isn't it?[1]

Free flowing, easy-to-read copy will be more effective than will writing that is self-consciously stiff and precise—whether you're selling cologne or corn plasters—or even a book on English grammar.

At one time a brilliant young Frenchman completing his education in the United States enrolled in a copywriting course at one of our major universities. His academic record was high, his personality and imagination exceptional, and his use of the English language impeccable. Yet the university professor whose copywriting course he took was baffled by his work. Every copy assignment the student turned in was a precise and correct piece of prose. He made no grammatical errors and his choice of words was irreproachable. The ideas behind his copy were good. Yet the copy itself simply lacked the vigor, the enthusiasm, the "aliveness" that is evident in the top-notch advertising messages found in our magazines and newspapers today.

"It stopped me," the young man's professor commented. "It was my first experience in criticizing something for being too perfectly written!"

Obviously, what was lacking was a familiarity with American talk, American thinking, American psychology. The copy was excellent from a grammatical standpoint, but it lacked the humanness, the ease, and the familiar, informal, and idiomatic language written and spoken by the average American.

STRAIGHT-LINE COPY

Straight-line or factual copy is naturally the most-used type because, in a majority of cases, magazine or newspaper space is bought for just one purpose— to tell people about something for sale. That space costs money—a lot of money! From the standpoint of getting satisfaction for your advertising dollar, straight-line copy is like a white shirt— correct for any affair—whereas testimonial copy, picture-and-caption copy, gimmicks, and the other forms of copy are not always suitable for every purpose. This does not mean that straight-line copy is ideal for all advertisements—simply that it can be used for any approach, whereas the other types have more specialized functions.

Glancing back at the results of the check on a single issue of a magazine, you will note that better than two-thirds of all the advertisements in this issue fell into the straight-line classification.

Straight-line or factual copy is copy that proceeds in a straight and orderly manner from beginning to end. It does not waste words, but starts immediately to sell the product on its own merits, and directly following the headline.

One to grow with.

"We'll buy a cheaper piano. Then if she stays with it we can always buy a Steinway."

It sounds logical. And yet. . .

If you take her ambition seriously enough to buy the Steinway,* will she take it more seriously herself?

If you buy the cheaper piano will she hear and feel what a piano is truly capable of? Will she develop the musical values necessary to move ahead?

Is the cheaper piano really more affordable? Your Steinway dealer or an astute banker can surprise you on that score.

Buy the Steinway and you have selected the finest instrument of its kind . . . the one found in conservatories and practice rooms everywhere . . . a piano she can start with, grow with, and stay with even after her debut . . . and, a piano that will suffer less depreciation than the cheaper piano, should she lose interest and you decide to sell.

The least expensive piano isn't always the least expensive piano.

For information about Steinways write to one: John H. Steinway, Steinway Hall, 109 W. 57th St., New York 10019.

Steinway & Sons

FIGURE 6-3

Straight-line copy with an emotional twist.   The picture of the cute little girl sitting on a telephone book is combined with persuasive straight-line copy to make a powerful advertisement for affluent parents who read the *New Yorker* magazine.

When to use straight-line copy

The style or type of copy you write for advertisements must follow the pattern and pace established by your headline and illustration which are, in turn, paced by the theme idea of your campaign. If you are selling a product that has certain competitive advantages over other similar products, or lends itself to interesting uses, or does something unusual (glows in the dark, for instance!), the chances are that your theme idea will capitalize upon those facts in its plan. Your headline will flag the reader's attention with the most appealing and interesting facts.

[1]*Copy Service Newsletter*, International Newspaper Promotion Association, February, 1973, p. 7.

FIGURE 6-4

Unusual straight-line advertisement.   Selling an expensive, prestige product such as a Steinway is made much easier when one can list well-known users of the product. The list shown here is persuasive testimony for the product. Notice the difference between this straight-line advertisement and that used in another Steinway advertisement shown in Figure 6-3. Despite the difference, this advertisement is also suited to the *New Yorker* readers.

Year after year the great majority of piano soloists who perform with major orchestras appear in concert at the Steinway. The 1976-77 concert season is no exception.

STEINWAY & SONS

The body copy of your advertisement must maintain the momentum already established.

All copy—all body copy—regardless of product, medium, or market, must be written to keep alive the interest that the headline and illustration have created. Nowhere is this of more immediate importance than in the straight-line type of copy. Straight-line copy will almost always follow a headline and possibly a subhead which has used a product feature to gain the reader's attention. It must not fail to maintain that interest, and yet it cannot logically confine itself to one feature, if the product has more than one. This type of copy must be a rapid-fire form of selling—starting with one idea, or one sales point and quickly putting others across. The most important fact to remember in writing straight-line copy is

this: <u>Most often, if you have something to say to your readers that you have reason to believe will interest them, it pays to say it at once.</u>

Occasionally, however, it is not necessary to do this. The following copy from a magazine advertisement must be considered straight-line, since its primary function is the sale of a product and its overall job is to tell what the product will do.

It's Johnson & Johnson quality that has earned for BAND-AID Adhesive Bandages the confidence of millions.

More families use BAND-AID Adhesive Bandages— more doctors recommend them than any other brand.

Every bandage comes to you sterile, sealed in an individual envelope. Keeps out dirt; helps prevent infection, avoid irritation.

Keep one box at home—one at work.

You will notice that the lead paragraph is not a powerful direct-selling statement, but a general claim of quality and brand distinction. Actually, from the standpoint of salesworthiness, the second paragraph of this advertisement is far stronger than the first. This product happens to be a recognized leader. Its brand name is almost a generic term. "Generic" in this case means a brand or trade name which, through constant advertising and usage, becomes identified by the public as being the name of a type of product, rather than one specific product. Thus people think of "Band-Aid" as any small adhesive bandage, rather than the particular one made by Johnson and Johnson. Undoubtedly, the thinking behind this advertisement dictated a policy of protecting that name against the advances of competitors. The selling of the product for its many uses was probably a secondary consideration.

Ordinarily, straight-line copy is, as its name implies, a series of statements of fact which will impel the public to desire and buy a particular product for the selling reasons given.

Your thinking must be organized

Straight-line copy, like all other types, demands good, sound preliminary organization before an advertisement is written. "Organization" means a careful review of all the selling points you may wish to get across to the reader and a close study of the importance of each.

You have probably already gone through much of this operation in the original planning of your advertisement. You have selected the most outstanding feature your product has to offer and have worked out a clear, forceful headline built around that feature. Your opening copy should now be aimed at the feature also. <u>Immediate follow-through on the headline</u> is nearly always vital to top-notch straight-line copy. Whether your copy actually fulfills its function and maintains interest and selling power largely depends upon how you carry on from there.

Practicing copy men and women have various methods of organizing their thinking before writing, depending upon their temperament and manner of working. Some simply close the office door and think. They keep the different angles of their sales story in mind until they develop a clear picture of how it should unfold. Others write a preliminary piece of copy with little attention to sequence, point of order, or emphasis and then, when they decide what they want, they rewrite in order to obtain sufficient continuity and strength in the sections lacking those qualities.

Neither of these methods is ideal for producing the best in copy. One places too much burden on the copywriter's memory, the other often causes a stilted style of writing. Nothing seems to work so well as a simple checklist of selling points. To see how you may compile such a list, look at an actual advertisement and see what steps the copywriter might have taken in writing it.

Notice that the advertisement will usually follow a list of the points of importance. As a result, it has a continuity and a simplicity that make it easy to read and understand. It gives primary emphasis to the sales ideas the copywriter wished to feature, yet one point leads to another in logical progression.

Making a list of what you want to tell the reader before you write a word of copy seems like a great deal of extra work, but it will result in clarity and continuity. After you have worked out your campaign and written a number of advertisements within its pattern, the list-making will, of course, be less important since experience with a given product and a given sales approach will so familiarize you with what you have to say that reminders won't always be needed. In most cases, once you have established your list, you need never change it unless:

- Product is improved.
- Audience aim is changed. You might have started out with a homeowner campaign and then decided to advertise to carpenters through business papers.
- You decide upon an entirely different approach.

For your first attempts at straight-line copy close reference to your checklist is an excellent means of keeping your copy on a straight line. It is a system used successfully and continuously by some of the nation's most experienced men and women copywriters.

BE BELIEVABLE

One of the most common errors made by copy people is that of overselling. When you create an advertisement, you have two objectives. One, to wrest the attention of your readers from whatever else they may be thinking about, and two, to persuade them into some sort of action or belief. Your job is highly competitive, since you are bidding not only for a sale of your product against the editorial material of the

magazine or newspaper, but also against the ingenuity and skill of other trained and imaginative copywriters.

In this competitive situation, it is easy for copywriters to be foolishly enthusiastic in making claims which simply cannot stand up. They are often encouraged in such extravagances by clients, who may take a somewhat inflated view of their own product's attributes.

Overselling is certainly not confined to straight-line copy. In almost every one of the major copy categories you can find examples of flagrant violations of good taste and sound selling principles. Copy that is intended to represent the endorsement of someone, real or imaginary, is a particular offender. Since, however, claims for a product seem somewhat less bombastic if they appear to be made by a user of the product rather than by its manufacturer, the testimonial is less likely to be weak in the matter of sincerity and believability than the straight-line

FIGURE 6-5

Newspaper advertisement using celebrity presenter.   A celebrity attracts attention to an advertisement, especially as in the case of this cooperative advertisement, when he is promoting the product in television as well as print media.

copy story. Overselling, however, is something to be avoided in every piece of copy you write, regardless of its style.

If you are writing advertisements for a soft drink, for example, be certain that what you say about that soft drink is recognizable to people when they try it. Straight-line copy simply cannot promise more than the product offers. It must do more than produce a consumer. It must produce a satisfied consumer, or it fails to accomplish the job for which it was intended. If you say of your soft drink—

Once you taste the completely new and different flavor of Gulpo, all other drinks will seem flat and insipid.

—you are guilty of the worst kind of overselling. Your own experience, common sense, and practical analysis of what's in that beverage will tell you that the public will not get that kind of reaction from a bottle of Gulpo, or any other drink. If they have been led to suppose that Gulpo has some magical qualities of life and sparkle that other beverages don't have, the disappointment will be sharp when they find that Gulpo is just another soft drink. You will make your first sale, but you will have left the people with a feeling of having been deceived—thus your repeat sales will suffer. You have sacrificed the good attributes your product has to offer for an extravagant claim that can't be backed up. A more modest claim might have led the way to repeat business.

To illustrate the kind of unbelievable, exaggerated statements that cause the general public to say too often "That's just 'advertising' talk," here are a few lines culled from national and local advertising. This list could have been expanded by hundreds of examples, but the point is made clearly after you read but a few examples:

The only way to get anywhere is with a new (name of car).

Victory employees are the most courteous anywhere.

The purchase of a mobile home at Oakridge is the smartest investment a couple can make.

(Name of car) makes any trip more fun.

Every meal's a feast when you serve 7-Up.

Biggest little treat in all the land.

This beer is the most enjoyable companion for any time and any occasion.

Chewing Doublemint Gum doubles the pleasure of everything you do.

Nothing tastes as good as a cold Ballantine Beer.

Quality takes a back seat these days unless you shop at Acme.

Not one of the foregoing statements stands close inspection. Not one is illegal but not one is credible to any thinking person. When advertisement after advertisement uses such flagrantly unbelievable, unprovable assertions, it is no wonder that so many of the public look upon advertising practitioners as a bunch of glib "con" men. Occasionally, you would do well to look over this list of statements to remind yourself to keep your copy believable.

Many copywriters suffer from what is called the "Alka-Seltzer complex." That is, they are sometimes inclined to project "immediacy" into their copy that the product cannot substantiate. Alka-Seltzer or any of the effervescent salts can be sold on the basis of the immediacy with which they act to help relieve unpleasant ailments such as headaches of certain types, gas on the stomach, indigestion, and others. To use the same sort of appeal for bacon, cigarettes, beer, or ball point pens would seem to make little sense, yet a glance through any magazine will bring to light plenty of examples in which copywriters have tried to do so.

At the first captivating taste you'll recognize this beer as tops in master brewing.

Even the aroma of this marvelous bacon convinces you instantly of its quality.

Just a few words written with this precision instrument will prove to you that it's the peak of pen craftsmanship.

Are any of those statements true, do you think? You may fancy yourself as an expert on beer, but could you recognize any beer as "tops in master brewing" with one taste? Of course not, so why lead your consumers to think they're going to get a beer so outstandingly different that they'll be able to do so?

Anyone who happened to be in the market for a new pen might be impressed with "precision instrument" and "peak of pen craftsmanship," but do you believe that these abstract boasts could be proved by a few scrawled words on a piece of paper? Hasn't the pen's leakproof quality, or its shape, or its appearance, or its capacity anything to do with such claims?

Don't be a "baloney artist," as copywriters many times are called. Far too many copywriters have already sacrificed believability and sincerity for the one unit sale that exaggerated selling can and will bring—men and women who have turned their typewriters into tripewriters! When you write straight-line copy, make sure that it is straight in honesty, and in presentation of product points. Your job is to build a sales curve of steady customers and the only way to do that is to advertise your product for its merits alone.

Straight-line copy is not difficult to write if you keep straight-line "selling" in mind. "Sell," with the words you choose, in exactly the same, direct, uncomplicated, and sincere manner you would use if you were selling in person. Naturally, you should use care and consideration in the selection of the right phraseology—observe the rules you learned long ago that make writing smooth flowing and smooth sounding—but remember, in all good straight-line copy the overall aim is simplicity.

Included in this chapter are examples of straight-line copy. You will benefit by analyzing carefully how these writers wrote how they emphasized their selling points, how they maintained clarity and order, and how they stayed within the bounds of good judgment in making their claims.

PICTURE-AND-CAPTION COPY

In an earlier chapter "caption" was defined as being a small unit of type employed descriptively in connection with illustrations and other parts of an advertisement. When such captions are the principal means of telling a copy story, the advertisement is said to be a picture-and-caption advertisement. Reference is made here only to advertisements in which the captions are the sole selling copy.

No rule will tell you precisely when to plan advertisements of a picture-and-caption style. That can depend on the type of product you are advertising, the type of sales features the product has to offer, and the physical space for your story, as well as other factors.

One point to remember is that picture-and-caption advertisements lend themselves much better to sizable space than to small space. Magazine quarter-pages usually don't allow enough room to produce top-quality illustrations in series, together with headline, subhead, caption, and logotype. Even in half-pages, the problem may be difficult unless your captions are so brief as to be almost classified as subheads. You will find that if you try to put more than one or two illustrations in the space of one-half page or less (still speaking of magazines), you will tend to be cramped for room to give adequate display to your copy, or to say all the things you wish to say. In addition, unless you plan to illustrate something very simple, the illustrations will suffer by being reduced too much.

As a generalization, caption copy goes best in advertisements where you have a page or more to tell your story. Like all generalizations, this statement can be challenged by advertisers who go ahead and defy the principle by using less than page units for picture-and-caption advertisements. Despite this, you would probably do better to plan most of your picture-and-caption advertisements in page sizes—it will be less strain on the ingenuity of your layout people.

The type of product you are advertising may influence your use of caption copy. If you are working out a campaign for an automobile, for example, you'll agree that the reader is likely to be more interested in the looks of the car and more attracted to your advertisement if the predominant portion of it is given over to a large illustration showing the beauty of the car, than if you show a series of illustrations and captions concerning its brakes, mileage, upholstery, and driveshaft. Shoes provide another good example of products that do not lend themselves particularly well to picture-and-caption advertising. The points of interest to the reader in shoe advertising are primarily style, price, and name. Since illustrations of these features would be dull, the use of picture-and-caption copy is eliminated.

FIGURE 6-6

Picture-caption advertisement.   A quick, effective message is conveyed with short copy and inviting illustrations. Using picture-captions is especially sensible when the advertiser is featuring a number of products—in this case, seven.

SPAM GIVES YOU SEVEN MEATS FOR THE PRICE OF ONE.

This special blend of pork shoulder with ham is more than just a popular sandwich meat.

Before you plan to break down the selling points of your product into pictures and captions, be very sure a) that those selling points will be of personal interest pictorially, to most of your readers; and b) that the captions you write for the illustrations back up the promise of the illustrations.

Some time ago the manufacturers of a new-type automotive lubricant inaugurated a series of picture-and-caption advertisements in which the features of this lubricant were highlighted. Illustrations, dramatic and interesting, pictured what happened inside your car when the product went to work. Captions backed up the illustrations with hard-selling copy.

The public response to this campaign was sluggish and disappointing. Finally aid was asked from one of the nation's top advertising men. He had no quarrel with the pictures and thought the copy was well written and strong. "But," he said, "people just aren't interested in the mechanics of what goes on inside their cars."

The reason for this, of course, is that the average person doesn't know enough about motors to understand anything even vaguely technical. The advertising expert wrote a headline which stated "Cuts Your Repair Costs in Half!" used a big block of straight-line copy telling how, and the lubricant immediately became a sensational seller. If you are going to use pictures and captions, be positive that the pictures reflect the self-interest of the readers or your finest copy in the captions will not sell.

Research people will tell you that, generally speaking, advertisements of a picture-and-caption style will get more thorough reading of the copy than will advertisements that contain a big block of body text. This may be true, because people are interested in pictures and will read short captions. It is only true, nevertheless, if the advertisements you are comparing are both good advertisements. A good headline and all-type advertisement, for instance, will usually get better reading than a picture and caption advertisement with a poor headline and dull, unimaginative pictures.

Caption writing is easier

You will find it easier, usually, to write captions for picture-and-caption advertisements than to write straight-line copy. The reason is clear. In straight-line copy, you must develop your story in a strong, orderly progression of ideas, one leading smoothly to the other, but you have no such problem with caption copy. Here, once you have selected the specific sales points to be illustrated, your job is to sell each point by itself. You do not have the "transitional" type of writing which carries you easily from one point to another as a straight-line copy.

One of the great weaknesses of beginning writers is that their copy lacks flow and transition. They fail to make their ideas and sentences connect.

If the pictures in picture-and-caption copy have been arranged in a logical sequence, the transition is assured. The writer merely writes the captions independently as dictated by the pictures.

An example would be a versatile garden and lawn tool that performs many tasks. Supposing in analyzing its functions you discover that it does the following:

Trims hedges	Shapes bushes
Edges walks	Mulches leaves
Prunes trees	Destroys crabgrass
Cuts grass	Cuts branches
Mows weeds	

Now, you devise a headline that stresses the versatility of the unit and points out that it can do nine lawn and garden tasks. You then call for illustrations that will demonstrate each of these nine functions. You arrange the illustrations in a sensible order and write each caption without any reference to the preceding and following caption.

Your advertisement is tied together by the headline that tells of the overall function of the unit—to perform many lawn and garden tasks. From then on, if you have arranged the pictures logically, your advertisement will be a smooth, flowing production.

Major and minor captions

In planning picture-and-caption advertisements, evaluate first the nature of the claims you want to make in selling your product. If you discover a single particularly outstanding feature that distinguishes your product from the competition and you are sure that this feature will be important to prospects, discard the picture-and-caption idea in favor of a smashing presentation of that certain feature. You can always illustrate other features in minor roles, with captions, but a good strong block of straight-line body copy can do the best job of selling one specific feature.

Picture-and-caption technique is best adapted to products with multiple sales features, no one of which is outstandingly potent.

It is possible, of course, to use picture-and-caption copy and still gain major emphasis on one point in a series of product advantages. The emphasis is gained by displaying the major illustration in larger size than the other illustrations and by running the lead caption in larger size type. Such treatment may be considered as almost a combination of straight-line copy if it does not confine itself to selling the one feature involved in the picture, and if it presents a complete story. It must be considered a caption, regardless of the length of copy and what size type it appears in, if it does not stand by itself as a complete and all-inclusive sales story.

Avoid covering too many ideas in captions. If you are using a picture-and-caption technique, be sure that your caption completely covers the illustration to which it is keyed and does not wander off into selling other features that have no bearing upon what is illustrated.

Every extra idea that you insert in your individual captions should have a direct relationship to the main point you're trying to get across in that specific caption. Also, each idea maintains the connection with the main selling ideas written in the headline. Use this technique to prevent your advertisements from being disconnected and incoherent. If you have hooked the prospects into reading each caption solely on the basis of what they see in the picture, don't lose them by failing to give them a direct and powerful sell on what they are interested in in the first place (through the overall theme set by the headline).

Lead-in lines and headings

If you had enough space to work with, every caption would have a headline that highlighted what it was going to say. Rarely can you afford, however, to give that much space to minor headlines. Copywriters, therefore, use three means of gaining immediate attention to key words and phrases. One of these techniques should be used in the writing of every caption.

- You may display a word or two as lead-in, running it in heavier, slightly larger type.
- You may simply have the first few words of your caption set in boldface type, or color, if color is used.
- You may number captions to help greatly in increasing readership.

All these devices help the advertisement from two standpoints. They serve to gain just that much more sell, in case the reader looks at the illustration but fails to go on to the copy; and they help dress up the page, mechanically speaking.

When you write your captions, keep this lead-in idea in mind. Put down your most interesting words first, thus giving them the added strength of the extra weight or color.

7

You Put It All Together in Body Copy, Part B

When an advertisement features a person who is talking about a product—usually praising it and telling how it worked—you may have a smashing success, or you may arouse cynical disbelief.

In the successful advertisement, you will undoubtedly have a strong, believable statement delivered by a person whose credibility is unquestioned.

In the advertisement greeted by disbelief, you may have: a) a statement that doesn't ring true because it makes a salesperson out of the person delivering it; or b) a statement delivered in artificial or unnatural language (where a homemaker talks like a Ph.D. in chemistry about a personal product such as a cleansing cream, a household detergent, or a cold remedy.)

LET OTHERS SELL FOR YOU— IN DIALOGUE AND MONOLOGUE COPY

Testimonials, when judiciously handled, have proved their ability to produce outstanding results. The trick is to write testimonial headlines so that the message retains its selling power and at the same time is natural sounding when placed in the mouths of human beings. The same problem is of constant concern to copywriters when they carry the testimonial type of advertising into the body copy.

If you use personalized selling in your headline, whether the statement of a real person or that of an unidentified person, it does not mean that your copy must also continue with personalized selling. Very often you will want to use a testimonial headline from some well-known person as a means of attracting attention, and then develop your own sales message in straight-line copy, captions, or other copy approaches. One of the most famous of all success stories in testimonial advertising often featured headlined praise from popular movie stars, but confined its selling messages to straight-line copy. When this method is followed, your body copy should be handled no differently than if your headline were a straight selling message.

Often, however, you will wish to use more dialogue or monologue copy than is possible to put into a headline. You may do this by letting your featured character do the complete selling job, clear through the advertisement, or by including additional endorsing remarks in captions.

You will be called upon to write three different types of copy for personalized advertisements: a) true testimonials, in which you prepare statements for real people to "say;" b) quasi-testimonials, in which you illustrate, by photography or artwork, supposedly real persons but do not identify them by name; and c) comic-strip and continuity-panel advertisements, copy for blurbs or balloons where obviously fictitious people are speaking.

TRUE TESTIMONIALS

The longer the statement, the more danger of incredulity—this assertion is almost axiomatic in testimonial writing. You start off fast in testimonials because in the first exposure to the advertisement your audience is influenced by the name and picture of the celebrity. In fact, the stopping value of a celebrity testimonial is in the person's name, not necessarily what he or she says.

After the first statement is cleared, however, and the reader settles down to what purports to be sincere talk about the product by the testimonial-giver, plain talk is necessary. Movie stars, lion tamers, baseball heroes, or ballerinas shouldn't be presented as experts on nutrition, engineering, or economics. At least you cannot expect the public to believe they are or to care very much.

FIGURE 7-1

Straight-line copy.   Very directly and conversationally, the copy in this advertisement gives useful background information about the product and surmounts the interesting message with an attractive illustration.

It is possible that thousands of American readers will buy a certain brand of soap because a famous movie star says he or she uses the soap and likes it. In the copy that goes with such a statement the prospect can be reminded that movie stars, to help preserve their beauty, require fine soap, and the fact that movie stars use a certain brand of soap is good evidence that it is of fine quality. The readers can be also urged—in straight-line copy—to use that soap on the reasonable assumption that it will help them, also, to be more beautiful. Ingredients of the soap and other factors that make it a quality product may be discussed also.

The moment, however, that you attempt to put such selling into the mouth of an alluring Hollywood star you are injecting a phony note into something that otherwise might be easily believable and salable. There is a huge difference between the following

two statements, when you are asked to believe that a screen personality said them spontaneously:

I think Blank soap is just <u>wonderful</u>! It seems to leave my skin extra soft and smooth. I never use any other brand but Blank soap.

That is believable, but who could seriously believe that a person would normally speak in the words of this testimonial:

Blank soap is the perfect soap. The cottonseed oil in it keeps my skin soft and smooth. None of us in Hollywood would think of using any other soap.

Now notice the difference in those testimonials. In one, the person speaking does not make any claims other than having a very strong liking for a brand of soap and giving her own personal reactions to using it. That is enough to gain power from the name of the celebrity as far as influencing the public is concerned. In the second statement, however, the testimonial attempts to take in a lot more territory.

The endorser is claiming more than she could possibly be expected to know. She says, "It's the perfect soap." She asserts that the "cottonseed oil in it" is what keeps her skin smooth and soft, yet so far as the public is concerned, she would have no understanding of the action or effect of any of the ingredients, even assuming she knew what they were. After all she's a name star, not a dermatologist. Furthermore, she makes a completely unbelievable claim concerning the soap-using habits of her Hollywood colleagues. There is a big difference between saying that you prefer a certain product and crediting everyone else with the same sentiments.

If you are writing a testimonial for use in cereal advertising, it is logical to have your endorser say that the product has "finer flavor" or is "crisper" or "stays fresh longer," or even to make a general claim about its being "good for you."

It is not logical to have the endorser refer to the actual nutritive qualities of the cereal, such as claiming that its wholesomeness comes from "niacin and Vitamin B_1," or that children will thrive on it because it has a high protein content.

Testimonials for candy can indicate a natural preference for its "delicious goodness," its "nutty, crispy, crunchy, chocolaty, chewy, delicate, or otherwise luscious flavor," but they are on thin ice if they present normal citizens talking about "dextrose" or "rich in food energy."

A testimonial for a whiskey advertiser demonstrates the folly of putting "expert" words in the mouth of the endorser:

"I tried it and it's true."

"(*Product name*) true bourbon taste comes from the finest grains, long, lazy years of aging in charred oak barrels and the priceless know-how of (*name of distiller*). It's a true value."

It is very easy to let yourself drift into such errors in writing testimonial copy, because you know more about the products you are advertising than does the general public. If you are responsible for writing advertisements for men's clothing, for example, you know how those clothes are made, what percentage of wool they contain, how they are styled and tailored, and other features that only someone close to the operation could know.

If one of your friends asked you, "What's so good about these clothes?" you would undoubtedly answer with a run-down of the features that most impress you. If the same question were asked of a man who had been wearing one of the suits, he would probably reply in the simple but enthusiastic way in which American men talk: "It fits well," "I get lots of compliments," "I like the style and the price." You can usually avoid this problem of causing your endorsers to talk too expansively and/or technically in testimonial copy by taking two precautions:

1. Associate the copy you are writing with some real person whom you know well and ask yourself what he or she would say about the product if giving an endorsement. Remember that the person with whom you identify the product does not know much about it beyond having a high regard for its qualities in general. If you can easily imagine your friend saying what you'd like to have the advertisement say, then the chances are you have created a good, believable testimonial statement.

   If you can have this friend actually make a statement to you, or read aloud what you have written, you'll be aided even more.

2. Test your copy on somebody not in the advertising business, preferably a person who already uses the product you are advertising. Let this person read the statement and tell you whether he or she would make such a remark. Only in one or both of these two tests can you be sure you are not, because of your knowledge of your product, putting words into the mouths of real people—words that sound strained, insincere, or too expert.

Testimonials must be honest

Testimonials should be used to gain the name of some prominent person only if that person actually uses the product regularly and he or she subscribes wholeheartedly to the feeling about it you wish to get across.

The Federal Trade Commission, the various advertising organizations, and other groups interested in better advertising frown upon the practice of writing testimonial statements without regard for the identity of the endorser, and then paying someone a large sum of money for the use of the name and for signing the statement. You may look foolish and dishonest if one of these operations backfires, as they often have, and it is learned that your prize endorser actually uses some rival-brand product. Know your endorsers. Talk to them, if possible—get their own honest appraisal of your product before you write anything. You'll come up with better selling copy and you'll save yourself embarrassment.

You will be responsible, usually, for the writing of the testimonial statements your endorsers sign. Usually they won't care much, and you will be expected to do the writing for them. Just remember, make all testimonial statements sound like normal people talking. On rare occasions, endorsers insist upon making their own claims, and refusing to sign anything else.

QUASI-TESTIMONIALS

In planning an advertising campaign you and your associates may decide that the story may most effectively be told in the first person—testimonial style. Yet for one of many reasons you may not wish to use the statements of actual personalities. The increased costs of paying for testimonials may be one reason. Availability of well-known people who might be interested in endorsing the particular product may be another. The most common reason for discarding the true-testimonial approach is simply that the product does not lend itself particularly well to the endorsement of a celebrity. In this case, you may decide to use the "quasi-testimonial." In the quasi-testimonial you have a copy approach, and also the sort of product (or service) which might be sold by an unidentified person as well as an identified person.

You might have what appears to be an endorsement of a certain type of insurance and an insurance company by an average-appearing man of late middle age. The headline and practically all the body copy are of testimonial character, with the selling story handled in the first person singular. Yet nowhere is this man identified. He is used solely as a type with whom every man of fifty-five can conceivably associate himself. It would be worthless to use the endorsement of a well-known person here, since most readers would not believe that any celebrity could or would "retire" on $400 a month.

Secondly, most people who have retired would be reluctant to publish the facts concerning their income from an annuity or elsewhere. To gain, therefore, the added human interest of the personalized copy, those responsible for this advertisement decided to go ahead and write it just as if this were to be a signed testimonial but to use a photograph of a professional model rather than that of a real endorser.

An interesting slant to this advertisement is that the headline is written with a "you" approach to capture the personal interest of every reader, while the body text is entirely within the testimonial pattern. If the copywriter had used a headline, "How I retired at 55," he would have sacrificed readership from those men who might automatically say to themselves, "Well, maybe he could do it, but I'll never be able to retire." The you approach flags interest; the testimonial technique provides believability.

This type of copy is one of the most frequently used and most successful tools of copywriters. Just remember, though, that you must keep such copy material simple, believable!

"I put a fabric softener in my dryer 5 weeks ago, and it's still doing a terrific job."

"It's terrific Free n' Soft.®

"You stick it on a fin in the dryer just once, and leave it there, for 40 to 50 really soft, static-free loads.

"You don't have to remember to add a softener to the wash or rinse cycle. And you don't have to stoop down to spray your dryer before every load either.

"Know what else? Free n' Soft costs about half as much to use as most other big name softeners.

"Wasn't I right? Isn't Free n' Soft terrific?"

Free n' Soft. The only fabric softener that works in your dryer automatically, and economically, for 40 to 50 loads.

Quasi-testimonials give you more freedom

You will have more latitude in writing statements for imaginary people to "say" than for real ones. In the first place, you eliminate all worry lest the endorsers not really believe what they say and actually are not boosters of your product. Secondly, and this is especially true when the illustration of the "endorser" is shown in a painting or a drawing rather than in a photograph, the public has become familiar enough with the quasi-testimonial treatment to understand its motives.

People will not be so critical of the statements of imaginary characters in advertising as they are of those supposed to be said by real ones. However, don't let this comment lead you astray. The difference is very, very slight, and you will be wise to treat the copy in quasi-testimonial advertisements exactly as you would if you were writing for a quotation by a real individual. Keep it natural! Keep it simple! Don't try to sell!

Personalized copy can sometimes get so far afield that the foregoing rules don't apply. If you are preparing advertisements for a dog food, you may want to show a talking dog, and let him do your selling for you. You may use an illustration of a baby for a soap or talcum advertisement, putting grownups' words in baby's mouth. If you look through magazines and newspapers long enough, you can find examples of almost every conceivable kind of object brought to life for advertising purposes—railroad trains, cats, clocks, fish and fowl, vacuum cleaners, and hundreds of others.

These advertisements represent an imaginative use of personalized copy, in which the copywriter is working more for the humorous and attention-getting value of the unusual.

Morris the Cat and Charlie the Tuna have become famous spokesmen for their brands. Because of the humorous way they do their selling, full attention will be given the sales message in contrast to the half attention that is, unfortunately, given to so many commercials. Despite the fun-and-games approach used in commercials delivered by nonhumans, copywriters must remember that they cannot have a cat or a tuna making statements that aren't literally true even though they may be delivered in an unrealistic atmosphere such as Charlie's statements coming from the bottom of the sea. In short, as a consumer you don't have to believe that the message is coming from the ocean depths, but you have every right to believe that whatever Charlie says is as true as what the president of the company might say.

FIGURE 7-2

Quasi-testimonial.   Instead of using an identified person as the endorser, advertisers often prefer to use an unidentified person in the illustration who looks typical of a wide range of users. The statement given by such a person is likewise representative of what users might say about the product.

To sum up this particular point: When writing for human beings, make their statements and language realistic. When writing for cats, dogs, fish and so on, don't worry about realism but do make certain that product claims are wholly true.

COMIC-STRIP AND CONTINUITY-PANELS COPY

The practice of making advertisements resemble comic strips or editorial cartoons is widespread and successful. Researchers have provided considerable evidence that such formats for advertisements often gain greater attention from readers, especially in newspapers, than those designed in a more conventional format.

The success of one format or another in getting closer reading depends upon what is being advertised, where, how, and how often. The number of times you write comic and continuity copy will undoubtedly be few, but there may be occasions when you will have to know the technique.

There is not much variation between the comic-strip and the continuity-panel advertisement. Both are normally planned to tell a story that stresses the selling features of a product. Both usually involve a character or group of characters whose actions present a problem to be solved. The problem is then solved through purchase of the product being advertised. Both types feature copy displayed in blurbs or balloons, and in many cases this copy accomplishes the entire job of telling the story, reaching the happy ending, and selling the product. Often, however, either a straight-line copy block or selling caption under each panel is used in addition to the balloons.

Newspaper comic-strip advertisements should be designed to resemble, as closely as conditions permit, an editorial comic strip. They should be of the same size and horizontal shape, if possible, and carry a heading and title just as regular comic strips do.

Continuity-panel advertisements may use a horizontal or vertical arrangement of panels, which tell a type of story similar to that of the comic strips, but often carry a headline, a large illustration, and a logotype. In many advertisements you will see a series of comic-strip and continuity-panel advertisements of various kinds. Note that there is no set pattern for their construction. Some use the last panel for a display of the product and a straight-line copy story, while others depend on the payoff of the blurb continuity to carry all the sell.

All these points about this style of advertising are mentioned because in both comic-strip and continuity advertisements your job requires a greater amount of creative ingenuity than is needed in many other forms of advertisement writing. Since success of panel advertisements depends upon a logical, believable story, you must plan the illustrations and the action before you write your copy. In creating most other advertisements you can often count on plenty of help from your art associates to get a good illustrative device, and your main task will be the

At Meow Mix, we've received numerous letters about our product from satisfied customers.

Most of them from people with cats.

Some of them from cats with people.

At least, they're signed by cats (some even have paw prints).

Cats writing letters?

If that seems unheard of maybe it's because, in Meow Mix, they finally have a cat food worth writing home about. Or writing away about.

One cat, who claims to be a gourmet, says she eats nothing but Meow Mix.

Another cat (Klondike, by name) says that when his favorite supermarket ran out of Meow Mix, he went on a hunger strike.

Other cats spoke glowingly of the taste of Meow Mix, the convenience, the price and the fact that they could get their three favorite flavors (tuna, liver and chicken) in one package.

They all agree that Meow Mix tastes so good they ask for it by name. Practically every time they open their mouths.

There was more, too. Which we won't go into now. Somehow, it seems that what cats couldn't put into words about Meow Mix, they put into letters.

Oh, people said some nice things about us, too.

But, after all, that's easy for them to say.

TASTES SO GOOD CATS ASK FOR IT BY NAME®

CATS DON'T JUST SAY THEY ASK FOR MEOW MIX, THEY PUT IT IN WRITING.

writing of headlines, subheads, and body copy. In the strip or continuity-panel advertisement, you'll have to go way beyond that. Your job here can almost be likened to that of a movie scenario writer rather than a copywriter, although it is actually a twofold proposition, since in addition to artistic creation you are, of course, trying to sell something.

The Bureau of Advertising of the American Newspaper Publishers Association has given advice to copywriters interested in improving their copy for comic-strip advertisements. Following is a discussion and enlargement of some of their suggestions:

■ Follow editorial style. If you are writing a comic-strip advertisement, make it look as much as possible like a real comic strip. Do not include panels that look like little advertisements. Do not vary the size of the panels. Remember that you are trying to hook readership on the basis of public familiarity with and liking for comic strips. You will not obtain this bonus readership if your advertisement doesn't look like a comic strip.

■ Keep your first panel interesting—humorous or action-packed. By doing so you gain impetus in leading your reader along into the next panel and through to the conclusion. Sometimes you will see examples of comic-strip advertisements that beg for further reading and that do not offer enough excitement about what is coming to lure maximum readership.

■ Change focus. Comic-strip artists and writers have discovered that it attracts attention to mix up long and short shots of characters in the strip. The same technique is true of comic-strip advertisements.

■ Keep blurb copy short. If you can't set up your situation, develop it, and sell the product in short, natural-sounding blurbs, don't try to use the comic-strip style. You will repel the reader if you jam your blurbs with long, involved copy in order to establish your story. Your characters are supposed to be speaking, and the things they say must be things anyone would say in similar circumstances. If they aren't, you will lose selling power even though all the other directions have been carefully followed.

Most of the foregoing comment on comic-strip copy is also applicable to continuity-panel copy, except, of course, for the requirements of staying within the physical confines of the actual comic-strip format. Continuity panels are used when it is felt that the comic-strip technique is desirable, but for one reason or another—usually space limitations—the true size and shape of the comic strip cannot be followed. Continuity panels, for instance, will be used in magazines, rather than the familiar comic strip,

FIGURE 7-3

Quasi-testimonial.   An entertaining variation of the conventional testimonial is to have it delivered by a nonhuman, in this case, a cat. Dogs, horses, fish, and all manner of creatures have delivered advertising messages in this manner.

FIGURE 7-4

Continuity-panel advertisement.   Although sometimes photographs are used for such advertisements, more often artwork is used as in this example.

since readers of magazines are not accustomed to seeing comics in them; and, too, magazines do not sell space the size and shape required for comic strips. The continuity panel is also often used in newspapers when larger space than the standard comic strip is considered necessary.

Both these types of advertising depend, for their maximum effectiveness, upon their ability to lure readership rather than to compel it. The closer they can be designed and written to resemble the editorial features after which they are patterned, the better chance they have of succeeding.

FIGURE 7-5

Narrative advertisement.   Often the copywriter can put over a message more effectively by giving it a story quality, as in this instance.

"It's pretty spooky rowing around inside a supertanker in a rubber boat."

"That's me in the back of the rubber boat," says Chief Mate George McShea. "We're not rowing on oil, but on a saltwater lake in the belly of a supertanker. And it's one aspect of life on a supertanker I can't get used to.

"Sure, a supertanker is three football fields long, and twelve stories high. But after a while those are just numbers.

A lake in a cave

"This tank inspection is something else. After the tanks are cleaned and the residual oil retrieved and stored, they're flooded with seawater, and inspection crews go inside, checking structural integrity.

"It's like a lake in a cave, but it's inside a ship at sea. It's a big job, and sometimes it gets pretty spooky. But it has to be done, to protect the ship, the oil and the ocean. Gulf tankers have a fine record; we do all we can to keep it that way.

Most efficient

"Supertankers are the most efficient way to move so much oil such distances. It's a real challenge working on them. But it's important work, and I think we do it well."

Gulf

Gulf people: meeting the challenge.

Supertankers—some almost as long as the Empire State Building is tall—are the most efficient way to ship so much oil such great distances.

Gulf Oil Corporation

NARRATIVE COPY

Narrative copy, in one respect, is closely allied to most dialogue and monologue copy—in its requirement for setting up a situation or story prior to getting into the selling copy. As you have discovered, most of the personalized copy approaches conform to this pattern. The story and often the selling as well are handled in dialogue between the characters in the advertisement, or in a monologue by one character.

When it is necessary to establish a situation or tell a story, you often will not wish to personalize the copy. You will then be writing narrative copy. The most common type of narrative copy establishes a background for the presentation of specific sales appeals for a product.

Your job becomes much broader when you are following a format that requires narrative copy. Your writing problem is no longer one that can be solved with a clear, straightforward, well-organized summary of your product's sales features. You must also create a "preface," a prologue to your selling story, and one which is not only calculated to select the proper reading audience, but which fits into the overall sales plans of the product you're selling.

Take, for example, an advertisement for a $300 wristwatch. Copywriters may reason that $300 watches are not very often sold by simply pointing out how pretty they are or how well they run. They also know that few men who would be reading their advertisements in a popular weekly magazine would actually be live prospects for such an expensive watch, regardless of what superlatives they could think of. Neither do they consider as prospects the women who want to give a watch to their husbands or sweethearts. Straight-line copy, accordingly, is out. So is testimonial copy, because while Mr. America possibly will wear jeans because a theatrical figure does, he will not be likely to spend $300 for a watch because anybody does.

No, the problem here is to write an advertisement which will hand-pick those men and women from the millions who read it who could afford a $300 watch and to offer them a subtle enough sales message to make them wish to do so. The entire selling power of this copy lies in its ability to cause a small group of people to act. By adroit writing alone, this copywriter appeals to the good taste of the successful executive, the ego of the semisuccessful executive, the wishful thinking of the newly rich, and the desire of many people to make an impression upon others.

Narrative copy in product selling does not, however, require such unusual products as $300 watches. You will find that narrative structure, while it may be used effectively for almost any kind of product, is best adapted to products that can be sold on a highly emotional basis. Insurance, deodorants, toothpaste, jewelry, cosmetics, clothing, antiseptics, and similar articles or services may be described in their most appealing light when you can dramatize the results they produce.

Narrative copy—long or short?

If you are writing an advertisement in straight-line style, be as brief as possible while still giving adequate emphasis to all the sales points you wish to make. If you have only one thing to say and you can say in three words, then three words is all the copy you should write. If you are preparing a piece of narrative copy, on the contrary, you can't very well confine it to a few words or sentences, although your coy may be every bit as or even more powerful from a sales angle than a terse, telegraphed message.

Don't waste time worrying about whether copy should be long or short. When you have convinced yourself and your associates that the approach is right, tailor the copy to do the job, regardless of the number of words you use.

Narrative copy is fun to write

Product selling, narrative style, is usually more fun for copywriters than any other type of copywriting because it allows a freedom from rules and regulations that sometimes will inhibit copywriters in doing straight selling copy. Few people will argue, for instance, that insurance cannot best be sold to a person who is "in the mood" to buy insurance. You can scarcely get a person in the mood to take on another policy by reciting a cold, hard series of facts and figures unless they are sensationally interesting. You may, however, start someone thinking about insurance needs by painting a word-picture of some of the unpleasant events that could happen if that person did not have enough insurance. By using a) an illustration of sufficient strength and human interest that he can easily associate it with himself or his own family, and b) a poignant story that also could well be his own, you can precondition someone to listen to your offer much more receptively than you could if you started in by saying, "Look, I have an insurance policy here that, etc., etc."

It's fun to let your imagination wander into such writing, away from the fetters of product features, laboratory reports, scientific tests, advertisers' do's and don'ts, and other qualifying factors which regulate much of a copywriter's daily work. Narrative copy gives you a chance to write a "story."

Emotion isn't always used

Don't get the idea that all product-selling narrative copy is, or should be, filled with pathos or fear or one of the other great emotional appeals. The only factor that makes narrative copy "narrative" is its requirement for telling a story before selling the product. It doesn't need to establish fear or uncertainty in the minds of its readers. Yet it does maintain a very definite air of self-association for most people. It sets up a situation of normal, everyday nature—notably, self-criticism.

Product selling in narrative copy is best adapted to products of a certain type. This, you will probably agree, makes sense, because most such narrative copy is based upon emotionalism. Even the narrative copy for the $300 watch was emotional.

Have fun, but don't forget to sell

Narrative copy, then, is fun for copywriters to write. It is a challenge to creative imagination. It is a fine way to establish a good selling situation—sometimes.

Watch out for this—be very sure that the story you tell in your narrative has a quick and easy transition to your selling message, and be sure your selling message sells hard. Don't waste space to tell a story that does not give a powerful springboard into the sales arguments that you wish your reader to hear. Once you make that transition, leave the characters of your playlet to themselves. Do as the veteran copywriter does. Turn your guns on the reader. Get

back on the straight line to show how your product is needed to overcome the problems you have presented.

INSTITUTIONAL COPY

Even more common than narrative copy is the type of copy you have probably heard called "institutional." In many cases, institutional copy is narrative in style, because under normal conditions you are not trying to sell a specific product or service.

At one time, defining institutional advertising as "all advertising that attempts to sell the company instead of its product or service," seemed to satisfy advertising people. In recent years, however, the definition has seemed too narrow. Thus we now have "idea" advertising, "corporate" advertising, "public relations" advertising and "management" advertising. While each of these designations has merit, the term "institutional advertising" is still the most commonly used term by those describing advertising that does not sell goods or services of a corporation.

One criticism of the term, of course, is that a considerable amount of advertising that is called institutional advertising is conducted in behalf of hotels, hospitals, and other organizations that fall under the heading "institutions." In this chapter we are not referring to this type of advertising.

Why institutional copy is used

Before copywriters begin to write an institutional advertisement, they must have a clear idea of what it is trying to accomplish. In the usual product advertisement their objective is relatively clear and simple; they are trying to sell the product. Objectives in institutional advertising are not so clear-cut and often are quite subtle. Ordinarily, however, those objectives will fall into one of the three following:

1. To create confidence in the company that will help sell its products. This confidence may be required because:
    a. The company makes so many products that the institutional campaign serves as a sort of umbrella. Thus if confidence is engendered, it is not so vital that the public remember individual selling points for each of the products. Instead, if the institutional campaign has done its job, public reaction will be: "I don't know much about this product, but if it's made by the ABC Company, it must be good." Such thinking is especially valuable when quick buying decisions must be made by supermarket or drug store shoppers.
    b. The company makes the kind of product that will never be bought if the consumer doesn't have strong faith in the reliability, integrity and skill of the maker. Pharmaceuticals, such as remedies and medicines, require consumer belief. Squibbs, Lederle, and Eli Lilly are advertisers whose great growth has largely developed because of the public trust they have enjoyed through the years.

Delta is an air line run by professionals.
Like Captain John Richards. John, who has been
with Delta for 17 years, has flown just about
every airliner from the DC-3 up. He spent 9 years in
Delta's Training Department, where he helped train
about a third of Delta's 3,200 pilots. Now he's back to his
first love, flying full-time as a 727 captain.

John's job is getting people where they're going. Taking
a family to a vacation resort. Whisking a busy executive to an
important meeting. Bringing a college student home for a visit.
When it comes to people, John Richards couldn't care more.
And that goes for all 28,000 Delta professionals.

Delta is ready when you are.®

*This is Delta's Wide-Ride® L-1011 TriStar,
a $21 million superjet. Cabins are almost 19 feet
wide. All seats are two-on-the aisle.*

FIGURE 7-6

Institutional advertisement that puts emphasis on a person. The very personal approach used in this advertisement gives a warm and human appeal often lacking in institutional advertisements that do not focus on people. Also, such an approach is more interesting because people like to read about people, especially people engaged in interesting work.

2. To explain the company management's stand about such pressing matters as a labor dispute, a bad product, or a drastic price rise. Such advertisements have a public relations flavor and very often are tied in with news releases published at the same time. Sometimes they are signed by top officials of the company although written by the copywriter. Exceeding care must be exercised in the writing of such "policy" advertisements which are scrutinized closely not only by the company's advertising department but also by top management, by the company's public relations agency, and by the corporation lawyers.

3. To express the company's philosophy about government, politics, or other aspects of society. Enlightened management executives in a corporation feel keenly the need to speak out on the pressing issues of the day—ecology, the drug problem, education, slaughter on the highways. Advertisements are often used to give voice to these feelings. Once again, critics will be looking over your work to be certain that it expresses accurately what management intends to convey.

What has probably driven more companies to institutional advertising has been the increasing difficulty of impressing advertising messages for individual products on the minds of prospective buyers. The profusion of brands, coupled with the similar profusion of advertising messages, has made it increasingly difficult for advertisers to register their selling points. Research of print and broadcast advertising has revealed a dismaying lack of product-point registration and, equally as alarming, poor identification of the advertisers paying for the advertising.

Interesting institutional advertising, not designed to sell but to do one thing only—to create a favorable feeling for the advertisers and hence any product they promote—has been viewed as a possible way out of the "too-many-products, too-many-advertising-messages" impasse. Copywriters writing institutional advertising, accordingly, face a stern challenge in their writing task.

Your study must be studied

Give extra long and careful study to the subject about which you are to write. If you are going to sell your firm to the public on the basis of its ability to help develop a jet engine, be very sure that what you write about that jet engine makes sense, not only to

people you think don't know, but to jet experts. If you are going to go after readership with the story of an antibiotic, get your information from unimpeachable sources. There is no room for extravagant claims in institutional advertising. If you lose believability, you lose everything. Be sure of what you're writing before you start to write, and check it after you've finished with the same unimpeachable sources.

In this type of copy, again, the nature of the firm or product you are advertising has a lot to do with the selection of the style of the format, and, therefore, the body copy style. Institutional copy is used mainly by four kinds of advertisers:

1. By organizations such as drug firms that serve the public's vital needs. It lends itself very well to building good will and prestige.

2. By companies whose products require precise engineering or research, the oil companies or the automotive industry. Thus an advertisement based on "creative imagination" sells Chrysler Corporation's ability and ingenuity rather than the separate merits of the individual Chrysler-built cars. These, of course, are advertised in other campaigns planned individually for each car.

3. By advertisers (discussed earlier) who either because they make a great many products themselves, or because they are discouraged by the difficulty of fighting for recognition against the myriad of advertising products, decide to strive for company-name registration as a form of advertising umbrella.

4. By "association" advertising or advertising paid for by a group of independent operators in the same industry. Thus the fruit growers of California advertise Sunkist rather than their own names. The Washington State Apple Association advertises the merits of the big red beauties grown in Washington. And the National Association of Life Insurance Underwriters uses copy which sells "life insurance," not that of any particular insurance company. This category of institutional copy many times promotes sales of a certain type of product. A beer advertisement run by the U.S. Brewer's Foundation, even though it cannot describe the good features of any brand of beer in competitive beer selling, can sell beer in straight-line copy, and sell it competitively against other beverages.

Write to reader

Beware of the outstanding peril of institutional copy. That peril is the tendency to write in terms of products and sales and not in terms of prospects and purchases. Writers, especially beginners, get so wrapped up in the traditions of the company, in its astounding (to them) manufacturing processes, in the details of its operations, that they completely forget the reader. The copy becomes chest-pounding in its boasting, and the "you" approach is entirely replaced by the "we."

How close can you come to eternity?

Perhaps when you look into the heart of a diamond, you can begin to understand.

Although this photograph captures one beautiful moment of this diamond, no photograph can capture, in split second time, the true nature of this elusive, spontaneous beauty. Because every color is there. Everywhere. Never seeming to be in the same place twice. Jumping from a slash of red, to a glint of green, a glimmer of orange and yellow, then into a flash of blue. Over and over again. With an intensity and a "fire" that never dies.

An infinity of prisms and mirrors with no beginning and no end. Created over a million years ago, to be alive a million years from now. Like this 2.45 carat diamond. Very large, and very rare. Valued at approximately $18,000.* With no equal, because no two diamonds are ever created the same. It reaches out as only a diamond can, seeming to hold back the sands of time.

A diamond is forever.

*This price refers to this specific stone. Other stones of the same size will vary in value, sometimes much higher or lower, according to the individual characteristics of each stone. De Beers Consolidated Mines, Ltd.

This is a 2.45 carat round solitaire. (Enlarged for detail.)

FIGURE 7-7

Institutional advertisement with emphasis on the product. Another in a series of a long-time, famous campaign noted for the almost lyrical quality of the copy and handsome illustrations. A strong headline engages the reader's attention immediately.

Such copy often results from the urging of a self-satisfied executive of the advertiser's company who finds it difficult to believe that the success story can fail to be as fascinating to the readers of the advertisements as it is to him. Remember then—keep in mind your readers interest and never let your reader become subordinated by the urge to stress "us" and "our" and "we."

A poem, deriding institutional advertising, appeared in the magazine *Advertising & Selling* some years ago. This irreverent verse, after pointing out that the advertiser may be interested in the factory and the company history but that no one else is, ended with the following almost bitter admonition:

So tell me quick and tell me true
   (Or else, my love, to hell with you!)
Less—How this product came to be!
   More—What the damn thing does for me!

Memorize these words and they may keep you from going the way of a good many copywriters when they tap out institutional copy on their typewriters.

Be interesting—it's vital

Picture some typical readers of an institutional advertisement. They turn the page, and there is your creation. It has no product that will make their lives easier or more pleasant or more profitable. There are no prices to arouse their interest or product selling features to compare with other products.

In short, your advertisement is likely to be viewed as a big fat nothing that offers not one reason for their taking the time to read it. If it follows the lead of too many institutional advertisements it is likely to be dull, self-centered, stuffy, overly-long, and full of "we" and "our" and the board-of-directors language.

You have a vital obligation to be interesting because you won't be read if you're not. Institutional advertising characteristically is at the bottom in readership figures.

To get readership, pull out all the stops. Entertain, shock, amuse, fascinate, be unusual and even bizarre. Grab attention with your headline and reinforce it with a different, exciting illustration.

Except for unusual situations, forget dignified prose. Be human. Write relaxed, conversational copy. Concentrate on the "people" approach. Reduce the awesome corporation to a person—possibly a person who works for it, or a person it serves. The telephone company has done this for years. AT&T is a monstrous corporation in size but the advertising for this company has consistently over the years focussed on people and usually each advertisement spotlights one person. The corporation is thus reduced to dimensions to which the readers or viewers can relate, and which they can understand.

From the writing standpoint, to repeat because it's so important, your most vital single job is to be interesting. Then, and only then, will you force readership of your institutional advertisement—an advertisement most readers would rather "not read" than "read."

GIMMICK COPY

If the discussion on gimmick headlines is not fresh in your mind, it might be well to review it briefly, since the term "gimmick" is used also for body copy for which it is difficult to find a better term. Any copy not falling into one or another of the foregoing categories may be termed gimmick copy. You are familiar with advertisements written as limericks or jingles or formal poems. Those are gimmicks. So are advertisements in which the copy is set to music or written in pig Latin or set upside down and sideways.

They are rare because, despite the type of headline treatment you use or the unusual or bizarre illustration you and your art associates may plan, the body copy is usually a place for sober selling. And you can't get much selling out of an advertisement written backwards.

Gimmick copy is seldom used except in cases where you have no need for telling a straight, hard-selling story and you wish to gain added attention and continued interest in an already interesting situation. You aren't shown any fundamentals of writing gimmick copy in the section because there aren't any. It's a case of the person with the first idea having the best one—or the worst. At any rate, you won't have many occasions to worry about it.

ADDITIONAL THOUGHTS ABOUT BODY COPY

This discussion of body copy would be incomplete without a reemphasis on the importance of simplicity, sincerity, and honesty in all the copy you write. If you have the natural ability to write clearly and well, if you have the desire to write and the needed information concerning your product, you need not spend much time on categories of copy or copy types. As pointed out previously, the style of your body copy will almost always be determined by the style of your advertisement. How you write it depends upon you—and plenty of practice.

Make pictures in words, as well as illustrations, to which the reader can relate. Too much copy is impersonal because there is no use of the "suffering points" mentioned earlier. Body copy should involve readers by picturing situations they have encountered. Consider the breakable thermos, for example. Anyone who has used one has heard that dread tinkle when the thermos falls off a table, rolls off a bench, falls out of the car, drops from a picnic table, or is knocked over on a table. In your copy, bring in those happenings if you happen to be selling an unbreakable thermos. Don't just talk about the steel construction. Show what that steel construction means in terms of solving everyday problems.

Let's say that you're selling a cordless, battery-powered lawn mower. Now, what pictures are evoked? There's the tangle of the cord on the conventional electric lawnmower that catches on every bush and wraps itself in a snake-like fashion around the feet of the user. Another picture comes to mind if you're selling against the gasoline-powered mower—the glares of the neighbors disturbed by the racket made by the mower. A contrast could be, of course, the serenity of a Sunday morning that remains unshattered because the homeowner is using an electric lawnmower.

Think in everyday pictures as you spin out your body copy because through such pictures you create empathy, involvement, and sales.

Ten excuses for not sailing The Queen to Europe.

"I don't have the money."
Then go round trip at a one-way price. Fly to Europe from anywhere in the continental U.S.A. and sail home first class on the Queen Elizabeth 2, all for no more than the one-way sea fare. Same savings the other way! Great savings in tourist class as well.* Specially priced tours also available.

"It takes too long."
Flying one way saves time. And the 5 days you do spend on the Queen Elizabeth 2 are a complete vacation you'll never forget. Continental cuisine. Impeccable British service. And an international passenger list.

"I don't have anyone to go with."
You'll make friends on the ship. Our passengers are a marvelous, easy-to-know bunch of people.

"I don't have a tux."
You don't need one. Unless, of course, you like to dress up. Some people do. Either way, The Queen will make you feel most comfortable.

"I'm afraid of being cramped."
Room for room, the Queen Elizabeth 2 has the largest staterooms, wardrobes, dressing rooms and bathrooms of any ship afloat.

"It will be too fattening a trip."
We admit to having fine food. But you can always jog it off (The Queen is longer than 3 football fields), dance it off, swim it off, or sweat it off in our gym and sauna.

"I'll be bored stiff."
Nonsense! The Queen is a Festival of Life. Celebrities and celebrated authorities have been invited on all 30 crossings. They're there to entertain, speak, dance, demon-

No excuse stands up to this – The Greatest Ship in the World."

strate, to see that you're never bored. As if you could be with 13 stories of pools, bars and nightclubs.

"I worry about seasickness."
Rough weather can get to the heartiest of sailors. But rest easy. The Queen is the largest liner afloat. She was built to smooth out rough seas, should you happen to encounter them.

"I just want to get where I'm going."
Fine. You can fly over on British Airways and sail The Queen home. You'll still get our same money-saving rates. And a chance to unwind before you meet the world again.

"What will I do with the kids?"
Nannies mind your children during the day. And if they're from 2 to 12 they can stay in your room for half price.
If you've got any other excuses your travel agent would like to hear them. Or you can call Cunard at

(212) 983-2510. For brochures, simply mail coupon below.

*A few conditions: Any first-class ticket qualifies for the full air-fare credit and any tourist-class ticket qualifies for half the air-fare credit. The routing between your hometown in the continental U.S.A. or Canada and London must be at the lowest available one-way air fare. The total duration of your air/sea trip cannot exceed 40 days.

Write to: CUNARD, 155 Allen Blvd. Farmingdale, New York 11737
☐ Please send details on Cunard's Air/Sea Savings Plan.
☐ Or send details about your bargain-priced European tours.

Name_____
Address_____
City_____
State_____ Zip_____
Phone (Area Code)_____
My Travel Agent is_____

CUNARD
Great Ships of British Registry since 1840

FIGURE 7-8

Curiosity headline and straight-line copy.   Strong interest created by the provocative headline is rewarded by the information provided in a lively way by the question-answer format of the body copy.

Humor. Yes and no. Some very good advertising people find themselves in opposing corners about the use of humor in advertising. Those who like it point to the attention-getting power of humor and the fact that if humor is well done, it provides the basis for a long campaign.

On the contrary, the sales message can get lost in humorous copy. It's easy to become so involved in the humorous story line that the product is subordinated to the humor and poor sales may result and/or poor identification. Furthermore, humor can kill you in the marketplace if it is poorly done. If it is, it has a short life and an ability to irritate enormously to the detriment of good will toward the company and its product. A poorly done humorous campaign is less likely to enrage the print audience than the radio and television audience. The wear-out factor is especially quick in the latter.

The biggest problem in the use of humor, apart from trying to judge how long to use it before you've worn out your welcome, is to judge how many people will like and respond to your particular type of humor. What makes one person laugh may disgust another person. The moral here is that a humorous approach should be tried out on many persons before the campaign is launched. Two objectives should be sought: a) to determine how well the sales message, or product identification, come through; b) to determine how well the mass audience is likely to respond to the humor.

Humor is great if it works. It can be a disaster if it doesn't. So use it with caution.

Service advertising. Your involvement. "Service" refers to advertisements that promote causes such as those turned out by the Advertising Council in behalf of education, participation in politics, conservation, and innumerable other topics related to public benefit. Such advertising, in this period of public protest and consumer advocacy, has been seen more and more even though advertisements of this type touch the average copywriter very little.

If you do have a chance to fashion such advertisements, consider yourself lucky. You have an opportunity to use advertising as a useful social tool and to write body copy that gives you a chance for more intelligent writing than you find in much of the product copy you do.

There is no formula writing here. Usually, you will be writing from the heart although, if your advertisement is concerned with economic issues it must be very rational indeed. Your copy will center around the reader's sense of fair play and justice and good will toward those less fortunate. You may wish to arouse the reader's awareness of the need to protect—those less fortunate, the environment, the political and economic traditions that have made us strong.

Such advertising, like institutional advertising, answers no selfish interests of the reader. It can be passed over very easily unless, as in institutional advertising, you: a) use strong, attention-getting headlines; b) use ample, but not overly long body

copy; c) are, above all, interesting in headline, body copy, and illustration.

Lastly, avoid reproving the readers too much. Don't be accusatory. Refrain from making the readers feel ashamed of themselves. It's easy to cause resentment in such campaigns. Assume that the readers have done well in their contributions to causes. Your advertisement should lift them to new levels in their contribution to whatever worthy cause you're promoting.

What about those advertisements that have "Advertisement-Advertisement-Advertisement" inserted by the publisher to warn readers? Despite the warnings, such advertisements obtain good readership because they have the editorial look. The secret is to be consistent. Be editorial throughout—in headline, body copy, and illustration. Avoid the hybrid—part editorial and part advertising. Usually, the one departure from the wholly editorial approach is the use of the logo. Even this can be sacrificed on rare occasions.

Sometimes you eliminate the illustration. If the "advertorial" advertisement is small, for example, there is little point in jamming an illustration into the space, especially if by so doing you destroy the editorial look.

In other cases, you may cut the illustration because you're announcing an important new product breakthrough, or a new service to be offered. The use of the usual illustration will detract from the news-article feeling.

Your writing should have the news flavor throughout. In making your important announcement, write like a newsperson instead of like an advertising copywriter.

One last suggestion—if the magazine will permit such a technique. Some of these Advertisement-Advertisement-Advertisement type of advertisements can adopt the makeup of the magazine in the type style, kind of headlines, and writing style in the body copy. In short, the reader can hardly detect the difference between your advertisement and the magazine's editorial material. This makes it imperative that your advertising material is so interesting and important that readers won't feel tricked when they realize that they're reading an advertisement, not one of the publication's features.

Ending this chapter are two topics everyone in advertising is thinking about these days— comparative advertising and consumerism. Sometimes the copywriter is deeply concerned with each. Sometimes, they will not enter the copywriter's daily routine. Still, no body copy chapter would be complete if it did not consider the possible involvement of the copywriter with these two subjects.

COMPARATIVE ADVERTISING

When you buy a product in a retail store, you're accustomed to having the salesperson show you competing brands. If you buy a toaster, for example, you check such points as the pop-up feature, controls for light-medium-dark, the appearance of the unit, and so on. Or, if you're interested in a General Electric refrigerator, for example, the salesperson will tell you what features this brand offers that make it superior to the Amana, the Coldspot, Westinghouse, and other brands. You take such comparisons for granted when you buy any item in a store. Indeed, you would not feel very intelligent if you did not insist on these comparisons.

Despite the acceptance of product comparisons in the shopping situation, the use of comparative advertising has become one of the most talked-about and controversial issues in the field of marketing. On one side, it is considered a beneficial development by many in the consumerism movement and the FTC looks indulgently upon it.[1]

---

[1](So long as there is no clear-cut deception or unfairness and advertisers can substantiate their claims, the FTC is not likely to take action because of the Commission's feeling that product comparisons serve a useful consumer function. For a brief discussion of comparative advertising from the legal point of view, see Chapter 22.)

Within the field, however, advertising people revile it or praise it. As for consumers, some don't know what to think although many feel that it isn't cricket to name competitors in an advertisement. Furthermore, as comparative advertising is used increasingly, consumers seem to find it more difficult to make judgments when they are assailed by so many contradictory claims.

Looking at comparative advertising from the researcher's point of view, the president of Gallup & Robinson pointed out in a television workshop of a 1976 meeting of the Association of National Advertisers that a study of ninety-seven brand contrasts showed that such advertising produced a 22 per cent premium in recall among viewers and that the technique performed significantly better among men than women. Warning that comparative advertising does not guarantee success, the researcher recommended that comparative advertising should emphasize product benefits and attributes rather than just price alone.

Despite this testimony for comparative advertising as used on television, the Ogilvy & Mather advertising agency measured the effectiveness of the advertising of six packaged goods brands, each represented by a noncomparative and a comparative commercial. The conclusions were reported widely in the trade press. Also, they were given in a booklet of the American Association of Advertising Agencies. This booklet contained speeches made on comparative advertising during the 1976 annual meeting. Here were the conclusions made from the Ogilvy & Mather research:

- Comparative television advertising does not offer any advantage to the packaged goods advertiser.
- It does not increase brand identification.
- It makes consumers more aware of competitors.
- It results in lower belief in claims.
- It results in increased miscommunication and confusion.
- It is not more persuasive.

Others echo the Ogilvy & Mather findings and say that you simply can't make valid product comparisons in 30-second commercials. At least, they say, use print advertising if you must use comparative advertising. In print, it is asserted, the consumer has time to weigh the facts, the claims, and counter-claims.

Thus it goes. As a copywriter, you may or may not be asked to write comparative advertising. Also, you may believe, as many do, that comparative advertising reduces advertising's credibility, or you may believe with many consumerists that its use is giving buyers solid information that enables them to make buying decisions based on something other than entertainment, jingles, and fact-less advertisements.

Whether you feel pro or con, comparative advertising is riding high just now. Thus if you write such copy, you should see that it is done sensibly and honestly. To aid you in that objective you would do well to follow the guidelines of the American Association of Advertising Agencies issued in 1974 (after being revised twice before). Should you follow these guidelines, there is a reasonable chance your copy should gain the approval of consumerists, the lawyers, and even most present critics of comparative advertising. The following guidelines have been widely printed in the advertising press:

Guidelines For Comparative Advertising

1. The intent and connotation of the ad should be to inform and never to discredit or unfairly attack competitors, competing products or services.
2. When a competitive product is named, it should be one that exists in the marketplace as significant competition.
3. The competition should be fairly and properly identified but never in a manner or tone of voice that degrades the competitive product or service.
4. The advertising should compare related or similar properties or ingredients of the product, dimension to dimension, feature to feature.
5. The identification should be for honest comparison purposes and not simply to upgrade by association.
6. If a competitive test is conducted it should be done by an objective testing source, preferably an independent one, so that there will be no doubt as to the veracity of the test.
7. In all cases the test should be supportive of all claims made in the advertising that are based on the test.
8. The advertising should never use partial results or stress insignificant differences to cause the consumer to draw an improper conclusion.
9. The property being compared should be significant in terms of value or usefulness of the product to the consumer.
10. Comparatives delivered through the use of testimonials should not imply that the testimonial is more than one individual's thought unless that individual represents a sample of the majority viewpoint.

Lastly, in a letter to clients in 1975, NBC placed particular emphasis on the need for care in price comparisons, an issue that worries many in marketing.[2] The letter made three points that serve as additional guidelines for you to follow:

1. Comparisons of retail pricing may raise special problems that would tend to mislead rather than enlighten viewers. For certain classifications of products, retail prices may be extremely volatile, may be fixed by the retailer rather than the product advertiser, and may not only differ from outlet to outlet, but from week to week within the same outlet.

    Where these circumstances might apply, NBC will accept commercials containing price comparisons only on a clear showing that the comparative claims accurately, fairly, and substantially reflect the actual price differentials at retail outlets throughout the broadcast area, and that these price differentials are not likely to change during the period the commercial is broadcast.

2. When a commercial claim involves market relationships, other than price, which are subject to fluctuation (such as, but not limited to, sales position or exclusivity), the substantiation for the claim will be considered valid only as long as the market conditions on which the claim is based continue to prevail.

3. Whenever necessary, NBC may require substantiation to be updated from time to time.

COPYWRITERS AND THE CONSUMER MOVEMENT

To avoid criticism from the advocates of consumerism and the numerous federal and state consumer bureaus, you should write copy that is not only legal (see discussion in Chapter 21), but also is socially responsible—copy that recognizes the responsibilities of business in today's changing and contentious world.

What are the consumer attitudes toward business and hence toward advertising that affect how you write your copy? Some of these attitudes are expressed in the anti-business gripes that follow:

The Major Anti-Business Gripes

1. Business provides materialistic quality in American life, but does not necessarily advance the quality of life.
2. Business appears too impersonal and selfish, and "humanity" is sacrificed to efficiency in the pursuit of profits.
3. Business too often fails to meet the basic needs of poor markets, as in the ghetto areas, or charges exorbitant prices to these essentially captive markets.
4. The market mechanism is restricted in some cases where the danger to consumers is open to speculation (e.g. marijuana, pornography), but is allowed to function without restraint for many products which do affect the safety of others (e.g., guns and overly powerful cars).
5. The value added by marketing is difficult to justify, both in terms of high markups on many goods, and in exorbitant prices.
6. Marketing misallocates resources by encouraging the consumption of "non-necessities."
7. Marketing breeds contentment with mediocrity (it offers nothing "higher"), and does not serve markets (e.g., ballet, symphony, chamber music, etc.) if they are not directly profitable.
8. Marketing, through restyling and poor quality in production, encourages and engages in planned obsolescence.
9. Many products in an individual product category are not very different, if at all. An excess of products in one product category represents a misallocation of resources and also breeds consumer bewilderment.
10. Consumer recourse for defective products is sadly lacking.

---

[2]In the same year, as reported in *TV Guide*, October 2, 1976, p. 46, CBS, in a review of 490 comparative commercials rejected 238 as being "too pushy," or as needing further judgment. Evaluating the acceptability of comparative advertising has become, it is obvious, a major problem for the media.

11. Advertising creates false needs and manipulates the consumer.
12. Advertising and other promotion efforts, including packaging and labeling, are often deceptive, false, and misleading. Many products are not as distinctive or as differentiated as the promotion implies. Many advertising claims are voided by obsolescence (advertisements induce dissatisfaction with past purchases).
13. Producers foul public resources for private profit. Lumber companies destroy beautiful forests. Firms pollute once beautiful rivers. Neon signs and outdoor advertisements blight once pleasant thoroughfares.[3]

FIGURE 7-10

"Issue" advertisement.   Industry is speaking out more and more these days on issues that concern the country. Many advertisements, such as this, explain industry's position and viewpoints, and its place in our business and social system. Only in a minor way do they call attention to the sponsoring company and its products.

Who profits most from profits?

About seventy five years ago a good many men were going into the business of making automobiles—not to benefit humanity but to make money for themselves.
      "Terrible", the reformers said.
      Most of these men lost every cent they had, a few made some money. A very few made millions, became extremely rich, built up huge corporations out of profits.
      "Terrible", the reformers said.
      Those huge corporations and the companies they help support, provide more than 14 million jobs in America today, jobs for workers who are among the highest paid in the world.
      Those 14,000,000 jobs would never exist if it had not been possible to make *and keep* profits in the past.
      Profits like that cannot be made today and, even if made, could not be kept. The reformers have had their way.
      But the millions of jobs we'll need tomorrow are not being born. That's a terrible price for "reform" that your children will have to pay.

Unique Warner & Swasey Automatic Computer Controlled Grinding Machine performs complete multiple-diameter grinding automatically from load to unload without operator intervention. (Coolant splash guards removed to show machine detail.)

 WARNER & SWASEY

Productivity equipment and systems in machine tools, textile and construction machinery
© 1977 THE WARNER & SWASEY COMPANY   *Executive Offices:* 11000 Cedar Avenue, Cleveland, Ohio 44106

This ad appears in Iron Age, January 3, 1977

Obviously, if you're a socially attuned copywriter you'll be conscious of these consumer sensitivities when you write about certain products or services. You will do well to keep in mind the following comments by Donald Jugenheimer:

Consumerism

Although the consumer movement may already have peaked, it certainly is far from being on the wane. Consumers now know what they can and should expect from marketers. Consumers know that advertising can help them become better buyers by using the information contained in the advertisements to help them buy more efficiently and more economically. Some advertising spokesmen have suggested resisting this consumer trend; they want advertising to stand up for its "rights." What these people seem to be missing is the point that advertising is as much a servant of the consumer—the buyer—as it is of the seller.

Why should the seller of a product or service be the only one to benefit from the huge amounts of time, energy, and money which go into advertising? If a product or service really meets a want or need on the part of consumers, why can't the advertising for those items point out these benefits? One key to successful advertising is to find a suitable benefit and to present it as an appropriate appeal to the consumer. Why, then, go only half way and talk only about the benefits of the products and services? If they are to provide consumer benefits, why shouldn't the advertising which supports them also provide consumer benefits?

In the future, advertising must realize that there are two ends to the communications channel, and that the other end, the consumer's end, has much more economic power than the advertiser's end. Consumerism can help advertising to do a better job of serving both the advertiser and the consumer, but the advertising industry is going to have to recognize this opportunity first.[4]

Group sensitivities must be heeded

Allied with consumerism is the heightened sensitivity of so many groups in America these days. Copywriters who are careless with words will sooner or later offend one of these groups. Women, especially, have developed a new militancy and are quick to resent words or situations that seem to demean them or their status. Examples: Using "chairman" instead of "chairperson," or "salesman" instead of "salesperson," or implying that the chief concern of all women is running a home while failing to recognize the importance of women in industry, politics, and other facets of American life. Depicting women as being wholly dependent upon men is another sore point. (For a full discussion of objectionable sexist advertising, see *Advertising Age*, April 21, 1975, p. 76.)

---

[3]Y. Hugh Furuhashi and E. Jerome McCarthy, *Social Issues of Marketing In The American Economy* (Columbus, Ohio: Grid Inc., 1971), p. 9.

[4]Ronald D. Michman and Donald W. Jugenheimer, Strategic *Advertising Decisions: Selected Readings* (Columbus, Ohio: Grid, Inc., 1976), p. 413.

This period of militancy and social activism is a perilous time for advertisers who must in their advertising be very much aware of minority groups, environmentalists, and all the others who are asserting their rights and who seem constantly to find new words, phrases, and situations that cause offense. In utmost innocence copywriters may use such words or phrases in their copy and learn to regret it. You must, therefore, as a copywriter in this pugnacious world have a keen knowledge of the social currents and cross-currents. Your lack of knowledge and vigilance can cost your clients goodwill and sales.

Consumerism—it can be good or bad for your copy

Despite the cries of persecution from some advertising writers, as a copywriter you should be grateful for the critical, skeptical looks given copy these days. Writing copy in today's climate is more than writing copy that is pure legally. In addition, you must be credible. You avoid the careless statement,[5] the almost dishonest claim, or the claim not backed by proof, even though the claim is technically correct.

Watchful for the consumerist's baleful glance, you try to eliminate simplistic portrayals of your product as the answer to all domestic problems. You're conscious of the need for copy that is not offensive—that

---

[5]In this category was the claim of milk producers using a slogan "everybody needs milk." The slogan was changed when doctors protested, saying that some people are allergic to milk. Legal objections were not raised to the slogan, but it was changed nonetheless because of the concern of the medical profession.

is in good taste as well as defensible legally. You try to write copy that is useful because it helps the consumer arrive at a rational buying decision.

With all this good stemming from consumerism, how can the movement be bad for copy? The answer is simple enough. Rather than take a chance with strong claims and aggressive advertising, the copywriter may play it safe with innocuous copy, or often downright silly copy. Humor is substituted for information and possibly challengeable claims. Copy becomes bland and boring, or if not boring, it relies on cleverness for cleverness sake.

Sometimes it is easier to go institutional in advertisements rather than to dig up hard facts about the product. Accordingly, with an eye out for the consumerists, we find as a substitute for "selling" advertisements, a myriad of campaigns that boast of the advertiser's contributions to the solving of world problems—anything from environmental concerns, to economic panaceas, to population control. These are "safe" campaigns although, unfortunately, even they must be executed with exceeding care or the consumerists may attack them for oversimplifying complex issues.

Summing up. The demands of consumerism are not outrageous. You are asked merely to write about your products in a way that you would approve if you were a consumer instead of a copywriter. With this in mind you should approach each copy assignment with two viewpoints, the copywriter's and the consumer's. You will omit the latter at your peril.

Slogans, Names, Publicity, and Other Items

It's late Friday afternoon. You're tired. It's been a rough week. Lots of tight deadlines, copy conferences, and a demanding mixture of copy to turn out for television, magazines, newspapers, radio, and dealer brochures. What with a series of demands for TV 10-second commercials with "sell and sock" and print headlines with the same qualities, you're drained creatively.

But wait. There's more.

A memo marked RUSH has just landed on your desk. It reads:

> Jones Bros., our client, is not satisfied with any of the names suggested for their new product. By Monday, therefore, we'd like to give them some new, interesting names to choose from.
>
> Please contribute a list of names by Monday at 9 A.M. Furnish all the names you can think of, keeping in mind the unique attributes of this new product. Try for a fresh approach.

You become aware once more that there's much more to your copy job than merely writing commercials, body copy, and headlines. There are many odd byways into which your title "copywriter" will lead you. Some of these will take little of your time, others may swallow many of your working hours. Most copywriters learn very quickly that these "odd jobs" of copywriting can sometimes be the most important in a day's work. A copywriter turning out a client publicity story, for example, may discover that sometimes a client may be more impressed by a five-inch publicity story in the newspaper than by his full-page advertisement running in the same issue. He may learn to his chagrin that the same client will overlook the truly excellent creative work in an advertisement if something about the company's signature displeases him. Thus, these "little jobs" that a copywriter does are very frequently "big" when viewed through the eyes of a critical client. Let's look over some of these miscellaneous activities that you, as a copywriter, may do but which may not be mentioned as part of your regular duties in a formal job description.

- Providing the dialogue for executives taking part in a closed-circuit sales meeting.
- Writing the copy for window or interior displays for stores.
- Preparing a feature magazine article about a client's business. This will appear in a national magazine and will be signed by a top executive of the client company.
- Writing the copy for a company's bulletin board.
- Preparing speeches for various client executives, or for the members of the advertising staff.
- Organizing and writing a taped interview in which the client will take part, or possibly someone in the advertising agency such as the agency president.
- Helping out the account executive by writing a presentation to be given at a client meeting. This will describe creative, media, and marketing plans for the forthcoming six months or a year.
- Writing copy for salesperson-portfolios. Contained in these may be sales talks, examples of advertising and display aids, and a boost for the advertising support.
- Putting together comments, talks, or remarks to be made by agency or client personnel at regional or national sales or dealer meetings.
- Inspiring dealers or salespeople with pep letters, urgent bulletins, or telegrams.
- Writing the sales portion of package copy (the legal material will be furnished by lawyers).
- Preparing booklets, or even short books, that concern the client's products, history, or personnel.
- Turning out promotional pieces for the advertising agency that can be left with prospective clients.
- Writing a house organ for the client, or preparing articles for it, or acting as its editor.

The foregoing are the more unusual tasks you may be asked to perform, but in the following material will be described the more conventional duties of a copywriter.

SLOGANS ARE IMPORTANT, BUT . . .

Talk to the typical nonadvertising person. You'll find that this person thinks that slogan-writing is the most important part of the copywriter's daily work. Television shows and Hollywood do nothing to dismiss this belief.

Today's advertising copywriters spend little time creating slogans. Rarely do they sit down deliberately to write a slogan and, if they did, their chances would be slight for evolving a truly good slogan.

Some of advertising's most famous slogans have been the result of spur-of-the-moment inspiration, but they are exceptions. Packard automobile's "Ask the man who owns one" was one of the exceptions. Mr. Packard, himself, was credited with the slogan so long identified with the automobile that for many years was a famous name among American automobiles. Back in the early days of the automobile, so the story goes, Mr. Packard was seated at his desk working. His secretary came in to report that a prospective customer had inquired about the merits of the Packard car. When she asked Mr. Packard how she should answer the customer, he replied, "Tell him to ask the man who owns one!" Thus was born one of the best known, most enduring of all advertising slogans. It was a clever slogan, but could not have endured on that basis alone. Packard's slogan also had "sales power." Sales punch is a "must" for slogans today. Mere cleverness is no longer enough.

Today most of the new slogans coming into advertising are the product of evolution rather than inspiration. Some started out as full-blown campaign themes. After filling the requirements of the time, a new theme was headlined, the former one being retained as a slogan. An example:

Promise her anything but give her Arpège.

Other slogans have first appeared deep in the middle of a paragraph of copy. This was true of Morton Salt's "When it Rains, it Pours." Its copywriter said: "If you want to find a good slogan, write some good copy, and the slogan will pop out at you." Recognized as an especially deft turn of words, a phrase may be picked up and repeated in subsequent advertisements. If it still seems to wear well, it may be used again and again. Finally, it may be displayed apart from the copy block. Eventually it may evolve as a campaign theme that will become a household term. But regardless of how slogans come into being, you should look at slogan writing as just another part of your job. In prejudging a phrase you think might be an effective slogan, ask yourself these questions:

Does it make a specific claim or promise a believable benefit? A good example of such a slogan is "Tegrin Moisturizes and Medicates." When you have such a specific promise for persons who suffer from skin ailments, your slogan repeated over and over again becomes a powerful sales tool. The direct promise can be more effective than mere cleverness.

Another benefit slogan that promises much to a busy cook is "Chef Boy-Ar-Dee Spaghetti Dinner. Everything You Need Is In The Package." Clever? No. Effective? Yes.

Then there's the slogan for a wet-dry heavy-duty power vacuum:

It's a buy!
Cleans up wet.
Cleans up dry.

In these few words is the basic benefit of the unit expressed in an easy-to-remember rhyme.

Does it contain a command to action, a direct appeal to buy? This type of slogan has merit because it has vitality. Likewise, it involves the reader directly in the action. Placed at the bottom of the advertisement, it ends the advertisement with an urge to action, always a desirable technique. Examples:

The American Express Card.
Don't leave home without it.

Come to where the flavor is.
Come to Marlboro Country.

Give your dog
the "people food" dog food.

Does it create a favorable identification or image for your product, service, or company? Newspapers have provided some outstanding slogans that answer this third question. Some of these:

New York Times	All the News That's Fit to Print.
Philadelphia Bulletin	In Philadelphia . . . Nearly Everybody Reads the *Bulletin.*
Atlanta Journal	Covers Dixie Like the Dew.

Certain writing attributes of slogans appear in the examples that have been offered here. For instance, most of them have a strong sense of the vernacular, of a conversational style that is breezy, informal, and offhand. A slogan talks "people" language. It is rarely literary in tone and it almost never uses a word that will make anyone reach for a dictionary.

It is rare, too, to find a long slogan. To be memorable a slogan must almost always be brief. A world of copy strength can be packed into a few words as "It's toasted" and "It floats" will testify.

A further aid to memorability is the use of rhyme and alliteration. "Be sure with Pure" is more likely to be remembered than "Be certain with Pure" although the meaning is the same for both. If you used alliteration by writing "Pick Planters Peanuts," you'd achieve more memorability than if you wrote "Choose Planters Peanuts."

If your proposed slogan doesn't meet these requirements, see if you can't come up with a phrase that does—if a slogan seems definitely indicated by the particular set of circumstances, such as a local appliance dealer whose print and broadcast advertising proclaims:

We sell the best
And service the rest.

In any event, don't confuse cleverness with selling power; it's a most unreliable guide. Bear in mind, too, that many of advertising's most noteworthy successes have been achieved without the continuous employment of slogans. Slogans are by no means a prerequisite for sales. Remember, also, that a good slogan is not always successful nor is a slogan always good. The long usage of a slogan, or the way it is presented, can sometimes establish it in the public consciousness. A successful slogan, accordingly, is not necessarily a good slogan when measured by stern creative standards.

COPY FOR PACKAGES

Because copy on product packages is infrequently changed, this, again, is an assignment you will be given only on rare occasions. Since package copy, however, is retained for such long periods without revision, it is doubly important that occasional jobs of this type represent your best efforts.

Following is a checklist of some of the more important elements of package copy. Some are "musts" for all packages, while others are included only under certain conditions.

- Brand name. This, obviously, is a "must." It's the headline of your copy.
- Nature of product. Let buyer know what the product is—whether coffee, cheese, or a mattress.
- Specific nature of product. If product is tea, give exact type—whether green tea, black tea, Ceylon tea, or India tea. If coffee, tell what kind of grind—drip or regular. If aspirin, indicate how many grains are contained in each tablet.
- Uses of product. If use of the product isn't obvious, give its use clearly. For example, although you might presume that everyone would know that Betty Crocker is used for cake mix, the manufacturer doesn't take this for granted. In letters almost as big and bold as the product name itself you'll find the words "cake mix."

  If the product has multiple uses, give these other uses. The Cascade package, as an example, points out that Cascade can be used for washing dishes, aluminum, and silver. A package containing a food product ordinarily consumed as a result of further preparation will often carry recipes. Your purpose in listing multiple uses or recipes is, of course, to induce the consumer to "run through" a package of the product quickly, thus hastening the repeat purchase.
- Sales claims. If the product has some definite sales point, highlight it. To illustrate, Comet "bleaches out stains." It's Crest toothpaste "with Fluoristan." Beautiflor wax "cleans as it waxes."

- Directions. If special directions must be given for use of product, state them clearly and simply, avoiding all scientific or technical terms, or any words that might not be immediately understood by a person of limited education.
- "Family" products. If the manufacturer makes other allied products, call buyer's attention to them. For example, every box of Kellogg's corn flakes mentions that Kellogg also makes other cereals.
- Premium offers. If premiums or contests are being offered by the manufacturer of the product—and he is planning to continue this policy long enough to justify its mention on the package—it's sound strategy to do so, provided the package offers you enough space.
- Ingredients. Food and drug products are required by law to state their composition on the package. Copy of this nature, however, is usually prepared by a lawyer so is of but passing interest to you.
- Nutrition information per serving. This information is another legal requirement that doesn't require any creative work from you. It is sufficient that you know that such information must appear on food packages and cans because of regulations established by the U. S. Food and Drug Administration.

Probably the best advice anyone can give you regarding package copy is to "make your package a good advertisement." That's what it is or should be. Don't clutter it with words at the sacrifice of good design, but don't keep your product's good points a secret either. When a person picks up a can of peas to inspect it, sell with the copy you've written.

TRADEMARKS AND BRAND NAMES

In addition to writing the types of copy already described, you may even, in isolated instances, be asked to think of a name for a new product for which you will later write the copy.

Product names are commonly known in business as "brand names" or "trademarks." The terms can be synonymous.

Brand names, as we shall refer to them, are not necessarily registered as trademarks. They may become so, however, once they have been used on goods shipped in interstate or foreign commerce, and provided they violate no governmental restrictions applying to trademarks. (Pictorial representations may also be registered as trademarks. These will be discussed later in this chapter.)

Because a new product obviously must be highly developed prior to its introduction into retail channels, its naming is an assignment met more often by those copywriters who work in agencies or for a manufacturer than by writers in the retail field. It is only an occasional assignment at most, but one whose importance cannot be overemphasized. On the brand name rests much responsibility for distinguishing one product or family of products from any and all others; of making a given product (or line) stand out above the mass of competitive goods or services—in the soap field, for instance, any new name competes with Ivory, Dial, Lux, and the numerous other soaps now being manufactured.

Usually, you will not be charged with the full responsibility of creating a new brand name. You will be asked to get up a list of as many suitable names as you can think of. Other people in your organization will be asked to do the same thing. The advertiser's employees as well as those of the agency—from top brass to office clerks—may contribute ideas. Sometimes, as an incentive, a bonus rewards the person who offers the name finally selected. The selection of a brand name is so important that getting a good one is worth almost any effort.

Brand names are picked carefully

Selection of a brand name is a serious matter on which a final decision should be reached only after long consideration. Names that come as brilliant "flashes" should be used only after analytical comparison with many suggested alternatives. Experience has shown that even products and services of exceptional merit have little chance of survival, much less marked success, if they are burdened with unappealing, inappropriate, or hard-to-pronounce brand names. Remember that changing a brand name once a product has been put on the market and advertised is a costly and involved procedure. It necessitates writing off as a loss the advertising expenditures made prior to such a change. Satisfied users, accustomed to calling for the product under the abandoned name, must be made aware of the change. Thus if you start with a name you must usually continue with it.

The firm establishment of a distinctive brand name protects the consumer and producer alike. In the "cracker barrel" days great grandmother had to ask for products in terms applicable to all merchandise of similar nature—the good as well as the bad. (Many types of meats, fruits, cheeses, and vegetables must still be called for by their generic names.)

When great grandmother needed oatmeal, she could ask for "oat-meal" only by that name and hope that it would be satisfactory, not full of chaff, vermin, or other foreign matter. Today grandmother can ask for Quaker Oats and know that the quality is high— that every subsequent purchase will meet the same high standard.

Brand names simplify the making of repeat purchases of satisfactory brands and help us to avoid the repurchase of those brands we have found to be unsatisfactory. They insure against the unscrupulous substitution of merchandise of questionable quality on which the retailer's profit margin might be higher. They insure the advertiser from loss of sales that would result from any such widespread substitution for the product. A distinctive brand name further aids manufacturers by helping to clinch for them the sales created by their own advertising. Many of these sales might be lost to a competitor if the manufacturer's product did not possess an easily recalled name the public remembers without effort.

HINTS FOR BRAND NAME SELECTING

There are many guideposts to follow in the selection of a good brand name. There are, nevertheless, numerous brand names now known in every corner of the world that violate many of the suggestions you will be given here. As these come to your mind, remember that they have, for the large part, been constantly advertised over a long period of years. It has taken millions of repetitions and millions of dollars to win for them the eminence they enjoy today.

Make it distinctive

Since a brand name's first function is to identify one product from others, it should be, above all things, distinctive. It should be different, preferably different from all other products, but certainly entirely different from the brand name of any product which might be considered even remotely competitive. To be distinctive does not necessarily mean that a brand name must be clever or tricky. The name Goodyear is simple and ungarnished. Yet, because it is an uncommon surname, it is distinctive. Many other family names, on the other hand, lack such distinction.

Be careful, when submitting suggestions for brand names, to avoid names similar to those of established products. In the early days of brand names some brand names almost identical to established ones were intentionally chosen. The purpose, of course, was to attempt to capitalize on the established product's reputation; to try to capture a portion of a competitor's sales by confusing the public. Actually, such sharp practice has almost invariably harmed rather than helped the imitator. The similarity in names, in fact, usually confused the public so much that upon reading the newcomer's advertising, people assumed these advertisements were boosting the established product rather than the new one. Purchases were thus made automatically for the well-known brand, defeating the imitator's purpose and causing the advertising to lose a large degree of its effectiveness.

Not only is it dishonest and poor business to trade on an established leader's name, but also costly lawsuits for infringement are almost certain to be instituted. Every possible precaution should be taken to learn whether a proposed brand name has been previously registered by someone else as a trademark. Such preliminary checks may be made by contacting any one of the various trademark services found in most large cities.

Another possibility is the Trademark Bureau of the U.S. Printing and Lithograph Company, Cincinnati, Ohio. This company, for a slight fee, will check its files to see if your proposed trademark has been used before. The file is the largest independently owned collection in the country. It must be noted that, while such organizations make fairly comprehensive searches, their findings are not an absolute guarantee that the name is not already in use. This can be officially determined only after the U.S. Patent Office has passed on the application for trademark. The

Cincinnati files, however, include U.S. Patent Office trademarks almost as soon as they are recorded by that agency.

Make it easy to remember

First, as we have pointed out, a brand name should be distinctive.

Additionally, it should be easy to remember. If it is not, it will take longer and be more expensive to win widespread public recognition for it. Models of brand names extremely easy to remember are Duz, Seven-Up, and Spry among many others.

The ease with which a person can remember a brand name is of great importance. To illustrate, let us say that a person goes into a drug store for a hair tonic. The night before, he had read about a certain brand and was impressed by the benefits it promised him, but now that he is in the store, he can't quite recall the product's name. "It's right on the tip of his tongue," but he can't remember it. As a result, Vitalis or Wildroot gets the sale, a sale a competitor's advertising actually created.

It's unfortunate, but true, that if people have to think to recall the name of your product, they will buy a competitive brand bearing a name that comes to mind automatically, without requiring any thought.

Make it pronounceable

Still another very important consideration regarding brand names is that they should be easy to pronounce by consumers and by announcers in the broadcast media. As the makers of Baume Bengué Analgesique (now simply Ben-Gay) learned, the general public is reluctant, to say the least, to ask for a product whose name it finds difficult to pronounce. There is a very sound psychological reason for this. All of us, without exception, fear ridicule. Consequently, we resist putting ourselves in a position where we might appear ridiculous in another's eyes, even though that person may be a completely impersonal clerk whom we may never again see.

A customer might well hesitate to ask a druggist for Hexylresorcinol. Its name only a scientist might be expected to pronounced with any facility. Recognizing this, the makers of this product wisely gave it an additional name—S. T. 37—which a child could easily remember.

If you had never heard the name Sal Hepatica pronounced, there's a possibility that you might have trouble pronouncing it. Constant advertising, however, has familiarized a huge section of the population with its correct pronunciation. Still, Sal Hepatica may well be losing sales it could make if its name were easier for all people to pronounce.

Even the name Hormel has been subject to widespread mispronunciation. The Hormel family accents the first syllable, but such a large number of people chose to pronounce the name Hor-mell accenting the second syllable, that the announcers on radio programs the company has sponsored have had to take cognizance of both pronunciations in order to make sure that everyone listening was aware that Hormel was the sponsor.

The peculiar exception to this rule regarding ease of pronunciation seems to be among names of perfumes, cosmetics, and a few other luxury items. Many manufacturers of such products seem to feel that the use of foreign, scientific, or other difficult words—words not ordinarily in the average person's vocabulary—does not handicap sales. They feel, rather, that such names are assets. It would be interesting to check sales figures to see whether the successes of luxury items with simple names disprove this theory or not.

Directions are often given for the pronunciation of a product's name. If you feel the need for such directions in connection with any brand name you are planning, you can be reasonably certain that you can find a name that is better if you will dig a little deeper.

Keep brand names simple. Selling, at best, is difficult—don't add further to your problems by shackling the sales power of your advertising with names the public will forget, or shun as too difficult to pronounce.

See that it has pleasant associations

The fourth "must" in the selection of a good brand name is associations. Unpleasant associations should be avoided. The initials DT might, to illustrate, seem an acceptable name for a coffee made by a man named Daniel Thompson. Here is something short, distinctive, easy to remember, and easy to pronounce. In seeing the name of the product in print, or in hearing it mentioned on the air, however, many would instantly think of drunkenness, not coffee. Others might possibly think of DDT, the insecticide. In either instance, unappetizing mental pictures would be created, instead of the pleasant thoughts which should be associated with the product.

"Balloon" would be a very poor name for a girdle (even though it might be made of balloon silk) because it calls up thoughts of large, ballooning hips rather than the more alluring picture of svelte, slim hips that the woman is thinking of when she buys a new girdle.

Avoid dating your brand name

Unless you are trying purposely to establish a product as of old-fashioned vintage—obviously the case in the selection of Old Spice as a name for a line of toiletries—brand names that too closely ally a product with a certain era are best avoided. For instance, although "23 Skiddoo" might have been a "stopper" as a name for a mosquito repellent in grandmother's day, the term is now almost meaningless because it is out of vogue. Two generations ago a perfume called "It" might well have sold like the proverbial hotcakes. Today, since "it" is no longer used as a synonym for sex appeal, the name has lost its significance. If a cat food named "Hepcat" had been introduced in the 1940s, it might have enjoyed success for some time, but as jitterbugging went the way of the bunny-hug and the Charleston, the term would have lost its meaning. The danger of becoming passé is always present in any name adopted to take advantage of a current craze. When the craze is over, your name then becomes unintelligible, or old-hat.

Brand names—new and old

One of the most frequent objectives in the creation of brand names today is to make the name suggestive of some property or benefit of the product—an example is Flit. You can surmise, also, from the name Filter Queen that this vacuum cleaner filters the air. It is a benefit in which you can easily see merit, and your name blares forth the virtue. Mum or Ban are two other examples of desirable names. Such names are of special advantage during that period when a new product is fighting to win wide recognition. This is particularly true if the product is one that is entirely new, or one that has definite properties or benefits exclusively its own.

Once the product has become firmly established, however, the full significance of its name is often lost. Illustrative of this is the fact that when you refer to the brand name Frigidaire, you aren't actively conscious of the fact that you are, in essence, saying "air that is frigid." At least you aren't if you are like most people. The same principle is true with other such well-known brand names as Beautyrest, Kissproof, and Eveready.

Numbers and initials. Many famous brand names are built on numbers or initials, or both. For example, 3-in-1, S.T. 37, PM, ABC, and ZBT. These are easy to pronounce, and, because of their brevity, allow for a proportionately larger logotype, both in advertisements and on the package itself, than do brand names that are longer. But they, again, are often difficult to obtain as one's own exclusive property.

Geographical or patriotic names. Columbia, Liberty, American, Hartford, Waltham, and Palm Beach are foremost examples of brand names in this group. Such names have been popular in the past, but, because they lack true distinctiveness in most instances and are not subject to exclusive proprietorship, they are not considered among the best type for new products.

Coined names. Another rich source of brand names is tapped through coining words. Coined brand names may be divided into three types:

1. Those devised by uniting various components of the comany name to form a single word. Exemplifying this are Nabisco (National Biscuit Co.), Alcoa (Aluminum Corporation of America), Duco (Du Pont Co.) Such contractions or abbreviations, if easy to spell, pronounce, and remember, often make excellent brand names that have the added advantage of calling to mind the full name of the producer. Armco (American Rolling Mill Co.) and Texaco (The Texas Co.) are contractions that proved so successful the companies eventually changed their corporate titles and now are known legally by what once were just their brand names.

2. Those such as Tenderleaf, Treet, Perma-Lift, Holeproof, Palmolive, and Rem. These are created in several ways:
   a. They may be shortened versions of common words, as is Rem (for "remedy").
   b. They may be phonetic spellings, such as Kool and Duz.
   c. They may be created by combining two or more words, or parts thereof, employing either orthodox spelling or simplified variations. For example, Spam (from "spiced ham"), Pepsodent, Car-Nu, and Noxema. Among these are many of those brand names which spotlight some benefit or property of the product. Nofade and Pye-Quick promise definite benefits, while Bromo-Seltzer and Pepto-Bismol are semi-scientific descriptions of properties of the products.

3. Those brand names that are out-and-out inventions, such as Keds, Kodak, Dic-a-Doo, and Drax.

Coined names are today among the most popular brand names. Good ones have numerous advantages. They are distinctive. They have high recognition value, are easy to pronounce, easy to remember, and timeless in their durability. Full legal protection may usually be obtained for them, making them the exclusive property of a single company or individual.

You must beware of certain easily committed faults when coining such brand names. You must, for instance, avoid cleverness for the sake of cleverness alone. Never become so enthusiastic over an ingenious turn of a word that you lose sight of your goal: a name that will help your advertising influence the greatest number of sales to the greatest number of people, a name the public will understand, remember, and respond to.

If you use simplified spelling, make sure that your simplification doesn't confuse. Remember that people are used to seeing the word "Quick" spelled in the standard manner. "Kwik" is unfamiliar, and may not be "kwikly" understood. Keep brand names always simple, pleasant, easy to remember, and timeless in their appropriateness.

Some names such as Cellophane, Linoleum, Aspirin, Kerosene, and Shredded Wheat have become so firmly associated with a product that they have become generic—that is, part of the language. When this happens, the user often loses the exclusive right to the name. Call it the penalty for having a really excellent name. The only protection is constant watchfulness by the advertiser.

One of the most determined corporations in the protecting of its trademark is the Coca-Cola Company. This organization reminds others constantly that when they refer to Coca-Cola in its abbreviated form that they will keep the meaning "clear" if the

"Coke" is spelled with a capital C. This, the company explains in its advertising, will help protect a "valuable trademark." It is obvious that the Coca-Cola Company recognizes the peril confronting its trademarked abbreviation if editors and others are not reminded that the word Coke is the trademarked property of the Coca-Cola Company and not merely a convenient, and generic term for a general class of soft drink.

Even though the true meaning of suggestive names may after a time no longer consciously register in the minds of customers, their value in the initial stages of a product's development can be considerable. So long as the benefit or promise contained in the brand name is both important and believable, it is difficult to see how it can be other than an asset in promoting sales.

Classes of brand names

Following is a cataloguing of a number of famous brand names by classification. With each classification is incorporated a brief analysis of the type of brand name represented. This analysis will indicate why some types of names are usually considered more desirable than others.

General designation of quality. Excel, Royal, Ideal, Perfection, Acme, Hi-Grade, Apex, Superior, A-1, and so forth are included among those brand names which may be said to give a general designation of the quality of the product. These are not the best of names. They are not distinctive. Actually among the many brands emblazoned with the name Acme, to name but a few, we find Acme pencils, Acme paint, Acme oil burners, carbon paper, card cases, fire extinguishers, snap fasteners, shower curtains, scissors, wire, stepladders, thermostats, tables, chair seats, and gasoline. And that list could be enlarged with ease. Another point against such general descriptions is that constant usage has caused the average person to become oblivious to their literal definitions. Thirdly, the claims to superiority implied by such names are so lofty as to lack credibility. In addition, being common words of the public domain, it is almost impossible to protect such names adequately.

Family names. More numerous perhaps than those in any other one classification are products named after the founder or owner of the company marketing them. Among those most advertised currently are Parker, Heinz, Borden, Westinghouse, Bendix, Pabst, and Remington.

There are three reasons why it is often well to avoid family names: a) Often they lack distinctiveness. b) They may be difficult to spell or pronounce, such as is Ghirardelli, the name of a large West Coast Chocolate producer. c) They are hard to protect. Any person of the same name can enter business in direct competition with you and use the name you both possess. Sometimes if another person's so doing will obviously cause damage to your business, the courts will rule against this practice. In the past, however, a number of unscrupulous firms have deliberately hired people having the same names as leading competitors. Giving these people the title (in name only) of head of the firm, they were thus able to use their competitor's name as their own brand name and still argue that they were technically within the law.

Fictional, historical, or heroic names. Robert Burns, Chesterfield, Victor, Admiral, King, De Soto, Pontiac, Maxwell House, Aunt Jemima, and Bo Peep all fall into this category. There is nothing wrong with such names so long as they fulfill the requirements of distinctiveness (which Admiral and King certainly lack), ease of recall, ease of pronunciation, and pleasant associations. They are, however, difficult to protect. Care must be taken when you choose such a name to make your selection from those characters, events, or places whose durability has been firmly established. If you select the name of some person, place, or event of recent prominence you may find that such fame will have passed in the years to come.

Animals, minerals, vegetables. Among the first examples of brand names in this classification that come to mind are Camel, Caterpillar, Blue Boar, Walnut, White Owl, and Swansdown. Again, some such names lack distinction and in some cases are difficult to spell, pronounce, or protect. One virtue, however, is that they usually are of more pictorial interest—much more so, for instance, than are brand names based on the name of the company founder.

Familiar objects. Names based on common objects generally are not so distinctive as some others. In that respect they are like brand names in group number one—Hi-Grade, Acme, Ideal. For example, in addition to Arrow shirts, we have Arrow mucilage, Arrow shovels, Arrow desks, Arrow golf balls, and Arrow needles, to mention but a handful. Such names as Diamond, Anchor, Star, and so forth are similarly duplicated on products of almost every conceivable variety. These names usually do, however, have the advantage, like the animal-mineral-vegetable group, of being translated easily into a pictorial form that increases the recognition value of the name. Nevertheless, they are best avoided.

TRADE CHARACTERS AND PICTORIAL TRADEMARKS

"One picture," you have read or heard a thousand monotonous times, "is worth 1,000 words." Whether this ratio is entirely fair to the expressiveness of the English language is open to debate. Pictorial trade characteristics or symbols do, however, have an extremely high degree of recognition value in advertising.

Such trade personalities or symbols as Aunt Jemima, the Pontiac Indian head, and the Fisher Body coach are often employed to give extra and continuous recognition value to a company's advertising. When such characters or symbols are also affixed to

WIN A CLASSIC EXPERIENCE!

ENTER THE PENTEL ROLLING WRITER SWEEPSTAKES.
WIN PRIZES WORTH WRITING HOME ABOUT
FROM THE PERFECT PEN TO WRITE HOME WITH.

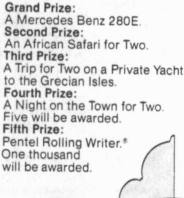

The experience of a lifetime can be yours just by reading the rules and sending in your entry.

A unique writing experience can be yours when you try the Pentel Rolling Writer. It's a feeling of smoothness you've never had with a pen before because it doesn't just write, it rrrolls!

The Rolling Writer Sweepstakes and the Pentel Rolling Writer. Get into both right away.

Grand Prize:
A Mercedes Benz 280E.
Second Prize:
An African Safari for Two.
Third Prize:
A Trip for Two on a Private Yacht to the Grecian Isles.
Fourth Prize:
A Night on the Town for Two. Five will be awarded.
Fifth Prize:
Pentel Rolling Writer.®
One thousand will be awarded.

Pentel of America, Ltd.

PENTEL SWEEPSTAKES RULES

1. To enter, fill out an official entry blank. Or, on a plain 3" x 5" piece of paper, hand print your name, full address and zip code. Also, state whether you could or could not find the Rolling Writer at your favorite store and include the store name and address. 2. Enter as often as you wish, but each entry must be mailed separately to: *Pentel Sweepstakes* P.O. Box 10580, Santa Ana, Calif. 92711. All entries must be postmarked by April 25, 1977 and received by April 30, 1977. 3. Winners will be determined in random drawings by Promotion Center West, an independent judging organization whose decisions are final. The odds of winning are dependent upon the number of entries received. 4. No cash alternate or other substitution for prizes is offered. All applicable federal, state and local taxes and licenses or passports of any kind related to the prizes are the sole responsibility of and are to be paid by the winners. 5. **NO PURCHASE NECESSARY. 6.** Sweepstakes open to residents of the USA except employees and families of Pentel, its subsidiaries and affiliated companies, its advertising agency and Promotion Center West. Void in Missouri and wherever prohibited or restricted by law. All federal, state and local laws and regulations apply. 7. Major prizes will be delivered to the winners with no warranty representation or guarantee by Pentel either expressed or implied in fact or law, relating to such prize. 8. Entrants agree that if they are a winner they will participate in awards presentation ceremonies and/or in post-sweepstakes publicity without charge or compensation. 9. Random drawings will be conducted no later than June 1, 1977. Winners will be notified by June 15 and must respond by July 15. Failure to do so for any reason will result in a forfeiture and the prize will be awarded to an alternate winner from a random drawing. 10. All prizes will be awarded. Only one prize will be awarded to any one person or household. 11. For a list of winners send a stamped, self-addressed envelope to Pentel Winners List, P.O. Box 11866, Santa Ana, Calif. 92711.

Pentel®
Pentel of America, Ltd.

NAME:_____

ADDRESS:_____

CITY:_____

STATE:_____ ZIP:_____

I could____could not____find
the Rolling Writer® at my favorite store.

STORE NAME:_____

ADDRESS:_____

Mail to. PENTEL SWEEPSTAKES
P.O. BOX 10580 SANTA ANA, CA 92711

FIGURE 8-1

Sweepstakes advertisement.   Unlike many sweepstakes advertisements, this one not only pushes the sweepstakes vigorously but also sells the product.

the product or package (as are all of those just mentioned), they build a close-knit bond between the advertising and the product itself. Application to the product or package, where practicable, helps to create instantaneous recognition in the minds of consumers the moment their eyes alight on the product on the shelf of a store, on the hood of an automobile, or on a gasoline pump in a service station. Many products are actually called for by description of the pictorial trademark on the package rather than by name. That is, a customer might ask for "the cocoa with the lady on it" instead of saying "Baker's Cocoa."

The actual designing of suitable trade characters or symbols is plainly a job that requires the talents of an artist. But more often than not, these illustrative devices are based on ideas sparked by copywriters. Here are a few do's and don'ts for you to remember should you ever be confronted with an assignment of this nature.

Review those requisites of brand names which are also applicable to things pictorial. That is, an illustrated trademark should be

a) simple, yet distinctive;
b) easy to remember;
c) subject to legal protection.

You should avoid unpleasant associations and current fashions (which might appear ludicrous ten years hence).

If such a trademark can depict a property or benefit of the product without detracting from the mark itself, such inclusion might be advisable. Prominent among pictorial trademarks that do this is the familiar "Iron Fireman"—a robot shoveling coal. If the subject is something the passage of time might make obsolete, it should be avoided. An example is the use of the radiator design of an automobile. Because these designs are changed periodically, any trademark showing one would necessarily also have to be changed from time to time, appreciably reducing its recognition value.

Whether for newspapers, magazines, or a 24-sheet poster, the placing of an illustrated trademark is a point to be decided by you and your art associates, usually on a basis to be determined by individual circumstances. It is almost impossible to establish fixed rules for such procedures. Basically, you must remember, it is to be seen. Don't put a trademark on a counter display in such a position that it might be blocked by other merchandise.

WRITING ADVERTISEMENTS FOR SWEEPSTAKES (AND CONTESTS)

Sweepstakes in which sometimes almost fabulous prizes are awarded in exchange for a box top can be tremendously effective sales stimulators. Many advertisers run such sweepstakes year after year. (Although the more commonly used sweepstakes are stressed here, the points given apply equally to contests.)

If you should ever be assigned to write a sweepstakes advertisement, there are several points you will want to know. For instance, there are two schools of thought on the subject of such advertising. One believes that a fair part of the advertisement should be devoted to the regular copy story on the product itself. The second is convinced the entire advertisement should be used to sell the sweepstakes—the sweepstakes being the "product," in such an instance.

The first school reasons thus: a) Every reader isn't going to enter the sweepstakes. You should make an effort to sell such readers the product on its own merits. b) Straight product copy is necessary to sell that "undecided" segment of the audience. These people who question their chances of winning must be persuaded that they have nothing to lose by entering—that they will get their full money's worth

for what they spend in buying the product even though they don't happen to win a prize.

The second school reasons that more entries (and thus more purchases) are obtained when the entire space is given over to selling the sweepstakes. The inclusion of straight product copy, they feel, divides the reader's interest because it presents two separate thoughts to be considered—equivalent to advertising two different products in the same advertisement!

FIGURE 8-2

Contest advertisement.   In this interesting contest advertisement, we have the appeal of a well-known name, an imaginative first prize, and many additional prizes.

Regardless of which of the two foregoing patterns your sweepstakes advertisements take, here are some copy points worth remembering:

- Most readers think in terms of winning the first prize—so play up your major prize—stress it. Use a big headline to do so.
- Generally speaking, a long list of secondary prizes has been found more effective than a small group, even though the total cash value in each case is the same. If you have an impressive list of such prizes, don't merely say "50 prizes." Instead, give that fact extra appeal by saying "50 chances to win!"

FIGURE 8-3

Sweepstakes advertisement.   A lively format, use of the word "win" in the headline, and featuring of the secondary prizes make this a strong advertisement of its type.

- Spotlight total retail cash value of all prizes if this is an impressive sum.
- "Win" is a magic word, so headline it.
- In a subhead drive home how easy it is to win.
- In your copy get over in a hurry how easy it is to enter the sweepstakes.
- Give examples of jingles, sentences, and puzzle solutions that might be typical of prizewinning entries if you are writing contest copy.
- List rules simply and clearly, leaving unanswered no question that might come to a reader's mind. Always include the specific date on which the sweepstakes entries close.
- Be sure to tell readers they may enter as often as they wish if this is the case.
- Urge readers to enter "NOW."
- Warn that offers are void where prohibited by law.
- Make clear that all prizes will be awarded.

PROMOTING WITH PREMIUMS

In considering premium offers, remember that such things as free booklets on the product or samples of the product do not constitute premiums. A premium is normally some item more or less unrelated to your product. It is offered to the buyers of your product either in exchange for evidence of a purchase of the product, or such evidence plus a nominal sum of money.

As with sweepstakes, sometimes an entire advertisement is devoted to the selling of the premium. More often, however, such advertisements also include strong product copy.

Tips for copy on premium offers:

- Highlight the cash retail value of the premium (if this is sufficiently high).
- If premium is offered as part of a "combination offer"—as a $3 floor mop might be sold in combination with a 89¢ can of floor wax for a total, say, of $2.89—pop the fact that it is a "regular $3.89 value for only $2.89.
- Sell the premium—dramatize it, make it appealing.
- If no money is required, subhead the fact—"Send no money!"
- Always include statement of time limit for which offer is good.
- Urge readers to take advantage of offer without delay.

In designing the premium advertisement avoid the trap so many copywriters fall into. Somehow, in order to achieve excitement for the offer, the writer of the premium advertisement often devises a cluttered, frantic sort of advertisement. The layout is messy and the headlines are black, screaming horrors. Keep the layout clean and make the illustration of the offer stand out. Use of color is often useful in getting attention for the advertisement and for making the premium itself more alluring.

If you are looking for a heavy return of boxtops, about two-thirds of the advertisement should concentrate on the selling of the premium. For fullest effectiveness this copy should be situated at the top of the advertisement.

In the competitive years ahead premium advertising, already responsible for stimulating billions in premium business, will maintain its present importance. If you are concerned with the movement of low-cost goods to the national market, you will almost inevitably be drawn into premium-promotion activity.

SIGNATURES AND LOGOTYPES

When you are writing copy you will ever be conscious of the signatures and logotypes used in your advertisements, yet you'll have little creative work to do in connection with them. Both are involved with company policy, both are closely connected with layout design, and both remain with little change once established. Yet, each is so important that this chapter would not be complete if a signature-logotype discussion were not included.

The signature

A signature is just what the word implies. It tells you who makes the product that is advertised. Often the maker's address is also included.

The signature, including the address, may be set off by itself to give it prominence, or it may be inserted at the close of a block of copy. There are no inflexible rules on how it is included or where it is placed. The treatment of the signature may be dictated by managerial policy, layout design, space limitations, or any of a number of other factors.

Signatures are used for one or more of three primary reasons: a) To build greater acceptance for a product or service, which is not already universally established, by acquainting the public with the fact that it is offered by a company of known reputation for quality and fair dealing. b) To provide the address that must always be included when a sample, descriptive booklet, or any other offer is made. c) To enable people to write for any further information they may desire concerning the product or service. Such communications are naturally more to be expected in regard to major purchases such as lawn mowers and washing machines than when the product is an inexpensive, day-to-day purchase such as canned peas, chewing gum, or adhesive tape. The latter represent such minor investments that few people would trouble to write about them. If additional retail outlets are desired, both signature and address should be included to make it easier for interested dealers to write for complete information about product, profit opportunities, and so forth.

The signature is purposely left out in many instances. It may be assumed in such cases:

a) That the product and where it may be purchased are so generally known that there is little likelihood of any reader needing to write to the maker for further information regarding it.

b) That dealers will know where to inquire if they wish to add the product to their stock.

To illustrate: If an advertisement for Absorbine Jr. carried the signature "W. F. Young, Inc., Springfield, Mass.," the inclusion or omission of the company name and address would probably have absolutely no effect on the selling power of the advertisement. Almost everyone knows what Absorbine Jr. is, knows that it is widely popular (so must be satisfactory), and knows where to buy it. The name Absorbine Jr. itself is so well-established that the mentioning of its manufacturer's name could not enhance its reputation to any marked degree.

Every dealer, similarly, knows the facts about Absorbine Jr. and the wholesale trade channels through which it may be obtained.

On the other hand, inclusion of such a line as "Another Fine Lever Brothers Product" on a new item in a well-known company's line would immediately endow it with a certain prestige it might otherwise take years for the new product to win on its own.

FIGURE 8-4

Advertisement offering a premium.

The logotype

When an advertisement does not carry the company's name, its "signature" is usually the product's name. (With such family names as Campbell and Heinz, the product name is actually part of the company name. That is, the brand name, Heinz, is derived from the full firm name, H. J. Heinz Co.)

The style of type or lettering in which the name of a given company's product is displayed sometimes varies from one advertisement to another. Most often though it is given a distinctive design, and almost without exception it is used in this particular style in every advertisement and in all other promotional material, including the actual product label.

When the product's name is thus treated, it is referred to formally as a "logotype" and informally as a "logo." Excellent specimens of such logotypes are those for Sunkist, Palmolive, Larvex, Coca-Cola, Van Heusen, and Valvoline, to cite but a few.

Under most circumstances, it is preferable to use one consistent design in the logotypes. This makes for far greater recall value than when the style of type or lettering is frequently changed. Readers accustomed to seeing the product name in one distinctive "dress" will recognize it more readily when they see it in similar form in subsequent advertisements or on the packages containing the product.

Creation of a logotype, being primarily a matter of design, is not the direct responsibility of the copywriter. As creative "general," nevertheless, you will often make suggestions and offer criticism of logotypes. A little knowledge of logotypes will enable you to tell whether the finished logotype is sufficiently simple, easy to read, and distinctive.

As with company signatures in which the name and address of the manufacturer are given, there are no specific rules that must be strictly adhered to in the placement of the logotype. You will recall, for instance, that in the chapter on headlines, it was pointed out that the logo is often used in the headline itself especially in department store advertisements. Customarily, however, it is placed toward the bottom of the advertisement. This is usually for reasons of balance and design, not because it is necessarily more effective saleswise.

Since the logotype is of a distinctive style, and ordinarily unlike the type in which the body text is set, it is rarely included within the actual copy block. Although you will not design the logotype or the signature, as the copywriter you may want to insist that they be displayed in type that is big enough to be seen easily by readers.

Readership studies consistently show that many readers of print advertisements are unable to recall the name of the advertiser or the product. Quite often this is due to a silly delicacy on the part of advertisers about displaying their names in a type size that they think is vulgar. Possibly the delicacy traces back to the art department that is more concerned with artistic integrity than such mundane considerations as registering company or product names.

Naturally, judgment must be used. An advertisement for Tiffany's, for example, will use restraint in the kind and size of type used for the logotype. For most advertisers and products, however, it is better to be conspicuous than to be delicate and unseen.

In the chapter on research you will find much attention paid to Starch readership studies. One of the measurements used in these studies is the Advertiser-Associated figure, referring to the percentage of readers recalling the name of the advertiser or the product in the advertisements they read. Low Advertiser-Associated figures can frequently be traced back to logotypes or signatures that were set in type too small to be noticeable.

As the copywriter you have a stake in this matter. You have the right to question the inconspicuous logotype or signature. Make your voice heard or that low readership figure will be blamed on your copy and not on that diminutive logotype or signature.

WRITING PUBLICITY STORIES

Publicity is of increasing importance as an adjunct of advertising. You may well, from time to time, be called upon to write publicity stories to be released to newspapers, magazines, and trade papers. Because publicity releases will not be published unless they meet accepted editorial standards, you must write them as straight news stories, avoiding the jargon of the advertising business and any attempt at high-pressure selling. Publicity stories are run free by publications, but only if they are newsworthy and if the editor happens to have some space to spare at the time. Don't, above all, attempt to make publicity stories thinly disguised advertisements.

What kind of situations produce publicity stories of real news value? Here are some:

- An executive of a company makes a speech of some importance.
- A company builds a new plant or wins a safety award.
- An executive is promoted.
- An old-time employee of many years' standing retires.
- An employee wins a big national contest.
- A company makes an important change in a product that is well-known nationally, regionally, or locally.
- A company announces the introduction of a product totally different from anything on the market.
- An employee wins a big suggestion-box award.

All these are legitimate news stories. Don't lose sight of that word "legitimate" because any publicity story without real news value is doomed to end in the editorial waste basket. Do you really know what "news" is? Editors may disagree with you in defining the word. They may, in the way of editors, refuse to run an item you think is the story of the century.

What is important to you, or to your client, may be wholly unimportant to editors because they feel your "news" will not interest enough of their readers. A newspaper editor will refuse a story that a trade magazine editor will accept and vice versa. Each story, then, must contain news of consequence to the readers of the publication in which we'd like our story to run.

Knowing just what constitutes news is the whole crux of successful placement of publicity material. One test, of course, is to ask yourself this question: Would I (or anyone) have any interest in this story if I didn't already have a personal stake in it?

The writing of publicity copy, sometimes disparagingly called "puff" copy, requires a sound knowledge of news procedure. After you have determined that your story has real news value, you must prepare it in accepted news style. It should be ready to insert in the news columns as you have written it. If it is a general release going to a great many newspapers, you may send out one version of the story, since in most cases there will be no duplicate readership. The papers may or may not rewrite your copy; it makes little difference here. Say, however, that you are sending a story of interest to the grocery trade and that you send the same version of the story to three magazines. All these magazines may have high duplication of readership. If the readers read the same story in the same words in all the magazines, they will be bored and disgusted. Furthermore, the editors will be resentful when they discover that you were too lazy to write the story differently for each of the publications.

To be able to write the same story in three different versions and make each version interesting will test your ability in news writing. If you have done some reporting, you won't have much trouble. If you haven't, a publicity release may cause you some anxious moments. Principal things to keep in mind:

- Follow the usual news style in all but out-and-out feature stories of putting essential facts high in the story. One way to accomplish this is to use the well-known 5-W's approach; that is, tell who—what—when—where—why early in your story.
- Remember that because of makeup requirements a story may be cut to fit a space—the space won't be stretched to fit the story. Write your copy so that it can be cut at the end of any paragraph and still make sense—all the more reason for getting important material high in the story.
- Make paragraphs, sentences, and words short, and write so that it will be easy for the copy desk to dig out a headline for the story—in other words, say something significant and say it quickly.
- Don't worry too much about style rules, but if in doubt, use a "down" style for newspaper stories since most newspapers are inclined toward that

style. A "down" style uses a minimum of capitals—an "up" style newspaper capitalizes heavily. (The *Associated Press Stylebook* offers a handy guide for style rules to follow.)

- If possible, get a picture to send along with the story and write a snappy caption for the picture (8 x 10 glossy prints are best).
- Avoid too many references to your company or client. If you can put over your idea without any direct mention of your product name or company, all the better. If not, tread very easily. Many editors will throw a story out as soon as company or product is mentioned.
- If your story has an interest for a special section of the newspaper, send it to the editor of that section, such as financial editor, or automotive editor.
- Be accurate—if your facts aren't correct your first story will be your last. Don't kill your chance for future publicity.

Here's an extra note about the 5-W's approach previously mentioned. If you're wondering what elements might properly go under each of the W's for a publicity release, here are a few ideas for you. These are, of course, but a few of the many points you might consider.

- WHO—are the people involved in the story?
  Names
  Titles
  Departments
  Interesting history or accomplishments
  Newcomers or old timers
  Quotes from important people involved
- WHAT—has happened?
  Is this the first time?
  Is it a major event in the field?
  Is there anything different about it?
  Does what happened fill a long-felt need?
- WHEN—did it happen?
  Has it already happened?
  Is it taking place over a period of time?
  (How long a period?)
  Is it going to happen?
  Exact date (and time, if necessary)?
- WHERE—did it happen?
  At the plant?

Is it local, or did it happen at a number of places simultaneously?
- WHY—is it happening?
  What is the story behind the event?

Writing feature publicity stories

The foregoing material has stressed the writing of straight news-publicity material. You may, however, be asked occasionally to write a feature story. Normally, this will be a longer piece suitable for publication in a newspaper or magazine. If the latter, very often you will write it for the signature of an executive in your client's company, all the way up to the presidential level.

When doing a feature style, you forget the 5-W approach for the lead. In fact, whether for a newspaper or a magazine, the feature story resembles magazine articles in writing style and general structure.

Especially important and distinctive is the feature lead. This may stress human interest, an oddity, an historical event—anything that is interesting enough to capture quick attention.

Throughout the feature story you maintain this magazine style but manage to incorporate enough hard news value that the editor will approve what you have done. Quite often, if the piece you are writing is a magazine feature, it may be quite acceptable to refer to your company, personnel, and products frequently because your feature is being sent to a publication that serves the client's field. Thus if your client is a bank, the article could discuss in *Banking* magazine the inner workings of your client's bank. There is no need, unlike the straight news release, to hold back the references to the client.

It is especially desirable when placing feature stories to accompany the material with good photos and lively captions. In fact, the magazine will often request photographs or illustrative material.

As a copywriter in a small or medium-sized agency, or in a company advertising department, you may be expected to do both news and feature publicity stories. If, however, you work for an agency or company big enough to have a separate public relations department, such work will normally be assigned to that department.

9

Writing Selling Copy on the Local Level

At 9 A.M. Wednesday, Ginny Smith is writing copy to appear in an advertisement for the biggest retail establishment in the city, the Excelsior Department Store. The product is a new line of drapes.

About the same time Jack Lapham, a copywriter in Wales, Inc., a big furniture store down the block, is putting the final touches on a page advertisement that will offer at sale prices a variety of living room and bedroom suites.

Just over the city line in Roxwell Heights, a city suburb, Brad Lincoln, of the Lincoln Hardware Company, is planning a 400 agate line advertisement to run in the suburban edition of the city newspaper. Lincoln and the newspaper sales people are working up the advertisement together because the hardware store manager lacks enough confidence in his writing ability to do the creative work by himself.

All three of these people have a couple of satisfactions denied the writer of national advertising. One, to see an advertisement prepared on Wednesday in print on Thursday. Two, to learn on Thursday how successful their Wednesday creative efforts have been. No other phase of advertising permits the writers to deal so directly with their merchandise, and their customers, and to learn firsthand how effective their approach and methods have been. In this chapter on retail copywriting the emphasis is on department store advertising because it provides the most diversified picture of such copywriting. Most of the principles can be applied to other forms of retail selling, too.

Retail copywriters usually turn out more copy at a faster pace than do the usual agency copywriters working on national advertisements. Furthermore, the power of their copy is checked immediately by sales results, whereas the copy written by national copywriters is seldom measured by the sales results obtained by one advertisement.

When retail copywriters spin out selling copy for a $369.95 washing machine, or a ten-speed bicycle at $89.95, they know just how many units were sold by the advertisement. If many, they have quick gratification. If few, they're depressed despite the fact that some other factors may be responsible for the poor sales figures. Thus retail copywriting is exhilarating, demanding, satisfying, and exhausting. Above all, it's exciting because it's where the action is, at the consumer buying level.

In the material immediately following, you'll find suggestions for the actual writing of retail advertising. Before the writing begins, however, there are many people involved in the advertising, buying, and selling process with whom copywriters must work, or who influence their work. The fairly complicated superstructure into which the copywriter fits is taken up in the conclusion of the chapter.

SOME PREWRITING QUESTIONS TO ASK YOURSELF

Who is my customer for this merchandise? Obviously, if it's a very high-priced pair of shoes, you appeal first to the person who can afford to pay that price. That consideration is going to govern your entire approach. Your advertisement is dignified. Your appeal must be to pride and a desire to wear the best of everything.

If the shoe is a moderately priced item, you know it will have general appeal to all people. If it's a sale item, you know again that it will have general appeal, but now you concentrate on the price feature. You will be determining meanwhile whether it's the type of shoe worn by young college students or dignified bankers. Perhaps your market is the rugged outdoor type, or possibly the shoe is the sort of slick stuff fashion-conscious people like to wear. These and other factors will be learned from sifting through the material gathered from your buyer and through your own observation.

What benefits does this merchandise offer? This is part of, yet different from, the actual description of the merchandise qualities. The shoe is described as soft and pliable—these are qualities—but you must translate these words into copy that is meaningful to the people who will wear the shoes. Saying "soft and pliable" doesn't mean so much to Mr. Smith as saying that the shoes will allow his feet to bend properly, thus easing foot fatigue. Saying that the leather is durable is not the same as reminding the prospective customer that the shoes will take all sorts of rough treatment and bad weather, and that they will last a long time. Saying that the shoes are handsome is not so strong as saying that they're the latest thing out of *Esquire*, or that they'll really make his wardrobe stylishly complete.

The idea of benefits is tied up with the idea of knowing who your customers are and what they expect to get out of the merchandise you want them to buy. Translate the buyer's cold facts into personal benefits that your reader wants—foot comfort, value for money, prestige, and admiration.

How shall I attract the reader's attention? This is most vital, particularly in a newspaper where your advertisement—whether it's eight columns full or two columns by 50 agate lines—is competing vigorously for the attention of the man or woman who paid money to read the news stories in the paper. Remember, a good many of your readers did not pay their money to read advertisements, although a considerable number did. Since many people are interested in news, not advertisements, your advertisement itself must be news if you want to interest such readers.

You must get those factual benefits up where they can be seen. You stop readers with benefits and you can stop them with advertising headlines—just as news headlines catch the readers' eyes and cause them to pause for a news story. Your advertising headline is the copywriter's method for stopping readers and getting them to read your advertisement. Layout and illustration will stop them, too—but merely stopping the readers is not enough. Well-chosen words in the body copy, captions, or subheads must instantly tell them the story of your merchandise and get them to recognize that this merchandise is what they've been looking for; that this merchandise fills a need they have; that this merchandise is what they're going to buy.

Your headline, in this instance, has stopped the readers and has caused them to read in the body text why they should buy these particular shoes—but that's not enough. Your shoes are for sale at one place and one place alone as far as you're concerned. You must convince the customers not only that they should buy these shoes but also that they should buy them at your store.

How shall I identify the store? Some stores merely put the sig or store name logotype at the top of the advertisement and let it go at that. You will usually make your advertisement more effective if you mention the store also in a subhead or lead-in line, and then refer to the store as often as you can in your body copy. In all retail advertising this matter of identification is vital because in this day of "famous brands," competitors on every street in town may be carrying the same brands. Without proper identification of your store as the place to buy, you're often merely running an advertisement to help your competitor sell his merchandise.

Your main points then are:

1. Determining who your prospective customer is.
2. Presenting the appeals of your merchandise in the form of direct benefits.
3. Presenting those appeals to attract and hold the reader's attention.
4. Identifying the store so that it will be linked immediately with the benefits to be obtained.

Headlines must attract and identify, must feature main appeals, present facts vividly to stop the reader and get him to understand why this advertisement is of personal interest to him. Body copy must repeat the main appeals, once again identifying the store as much as possible. Facts should be presented to support claims made earlier, to make your story truthful and believable. The urge to buy the product advertised must be the ultimate end of your copy—to stimulate the reader into coming to your store to buy your goods.

HOW RETAIL COPY DIFFERS FROM NATIONAL COPY

Writing techniques and formulas of the type just given you are only two of the things for you to think about if you do retail copy. Although no one will deny that all copy—national, retail, radio, direct mail, newspaper, and magazine—has certain basic similarities, it is also true that retail copy has some characteristics that set it apart. A retail copywriter, especially one who has been familiar with the national field, should be aware of these characteristics along with the beginner who has had no experience. You will find the characteristics in varying degrees in copy for small, medium, or large stores.

Imagine that you have had some experience with other types of copywriting but that you have decided to try retail copywriting. At the moment you are seated across the desk from the advertising manager of the department store for which you are going to work. Knowing your background in other types of copy, the manager is discussing retail advertising. You realize that he is very diplomatically indicating to you that although you were competent in other forms of copywriting, it doesn't follow that you can automatically write retail copy. He is giving you the same briefing he would give anyone entering retail copywriting.

It isn't your writing the advertising manager is concerned about; he's aware that you're a good technician. Rather, he's anxious for you to understand the basic concepts of the retail approach—some of the important differences between the writing you have been doing and the kind you'll do in the retail business.

A methodical person, the advertising manager ticks off points for you. He says, "We're glad to have you with us. Also, I'm glad that we have a few minutes now to talk about this retail business. I'm well aware of your background. I know you can write so we'll forget that. What I do want to make sure of is that you get something of the retail picture before you type a word of copy. Some of the things I'm going to tell you may be obvious, but they bear repeating because their very obviousness often causes them to be overlooked, even by us who have grown up in retail.

"First of all, and I'm not sure that I wouldn't list this as the one and only point I'll make—a retail store is part of the community—a big part. You fellows and gals who write the copy share the community with your readers. You swelter in the same heat and get nipped by the same frost. You enjoy the same football team, and the current crime wave is a mutual worry. The financial ups and downs of your city and county are of acute concern to all of you. The retail business is, except in the case of some very large stores, a 100 percent local affair. This fact you will feel in all the copy you write. Let's see how this affects your thinking."

The advertising manager then makes the following points. He tells you that in retail advertising three facts must be recognized:

Urge to "buy now" is stronger. There is immediacy in most retail copy. Stores depend upon turnover of stock. The best kind of stock is the kind that is "here today and gone tomorrow." Retail copy, for the most part, should be slightly breathless and urgent. You should push generally for the quick sale. In retail advertising you expect a quick response to your copy and you must get it. Thus your copy should ever be prodding the customer, sometimes subtly, and sometimes with all the subtlety of a meat-ax. Get the readers to come to the store; get them to telephone; get them to bring their money down for a quick purchase. Phrases like "Come in today," "Buy while they last." "See them today," or "Get yours now while quantities last" are important in retail advertising. Sometimes you push people more delicately, but almost always there is some sort of urge to action—immediate action. This urge is much more pointed than in national advertising, which usually doesn't expect or need such immediacy of purchase on the part of the reader.

Readers are more price-conscious. People who read retail advertising want to know the price of merchandise. They have become accustomed in national advertising to price-less copy, but in much of retail copy, price is all important. Consciousness of cost creeps into all your copy. It weaves a web around the customers until they ask themselves, "Can I afford not to spend my money?" When you think of price in retail copy, you don't think of price figures. Instead, you look upon your entire advertisement as building justification for the moment when the customers dig into their pockets and say, "I'll take that."

There are very few stores that aren't price-conscious down to the last word in the last line of copy. Big stores, little stores, exclusive stores, and bargain stores—all of them use price as the wedge for sales. You should get in the habit when you finish a piece of retail copy of looking it over and asking yourself whether your words would make you buy if you were the ordinary reader to whom dollars are mighty important. You have few chances in retail copy to forget that all the words you write simply act as background music for that all-important tag line which reads, "Only $00.00 while they last."

Developing of store personality is a must. Taken as a whole, you probably don't look much different from the people around you. You have the usual number of limbs, eyes, and ears. Compare yourself with the next-door neighbor. Based upon appearance, there isn't much to choose between you, yet you may have many more friends. Credit your personality.

Likewise, you can credit successful retail stores with personality. Development of the personality of your store is a never-ceasing copywriting job. Ability to write "personality" copy is something you acquire on the job. You don't learn it the first day. It comes after you have studied your store's advertising; after you have got the feel of the place; after you have talked to other store employees; after you have been around a while.

Those saucy Gimbel's advertisements, those dignified productions of Lord & Taylor's, those slam-bang sales-producers of Goldblatt's—they reflect personality. Personality in your advertising is what makes people come in to see your merchandise instead of going to your competitor's store to see the same merchandise. Remember that most stores can match goods with their competitors these days. If all you have to offer is merchandise, you may fall back of your competitors who have found a personality and let it shine through their advertisements. The basis of store personality is found in many things—friendliness, bargain prices, service, dependability, long establishment in the community, size of operation, or perhaps a combination of some, or all, of these.

Personality marks you as different from your competitor. Downtown streets are lined with famous stores, each striving to be different from its neighbor. Saks is different from Bonwit Teller. Bergdoff Goodman differs from I. Magnin, and Neiman-Marcus is different from Bloomingdale's, and no one would mistake a Lord & Taylor advertisement with one from Ohrbach's. Each store works hard to be different, especially from its closest rival. A celebrated rivalry

First impressions

Impressions of our newly redone First Floor...
An airy, welcoming feeling, amid tones of
apricot and ivory. Beams and panels of warm
natural pecan. Elegant brass moldings. The floor
itself, pearly Italian marble.

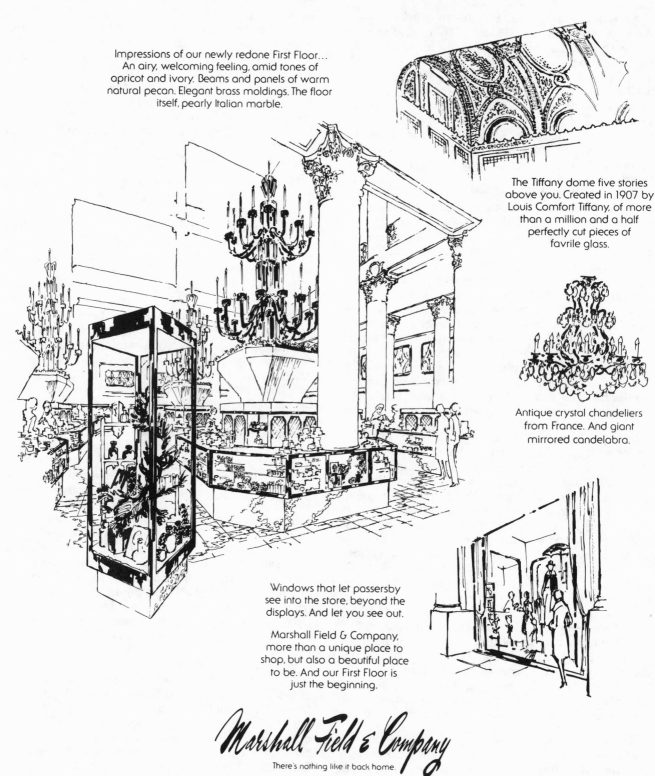

The Tiffany dome five stories
above you. Created in 1907 by
Louis Comfort Tiffany, of more
than a million and a half
perfectly cut pieces of
favrile glass.

Antique crystal chandeliers
from France. And giant
mirrored candelabra.

Windows that let passersby
see into the store, beyond the
displays. And let you see out.

Marshall Field & Company,
more than a unique place to
shop, but also a beautiful place
to be. And our First Floor is
just the beginning.

Marshall Field & Company

There's nothing like it back home.

FIGURE 9-1

Institutional advertisement for famous store.   This advertisement, appearing in the *New Yorker* magazine, conveys through illustration and copy the unique essence of the store. Advertisements such as this help to establish Marshall Field & Company as a retail personality.

exists between Macy's and Gimbel's in New York. Although both stores use effective selling copy, many little differences exist which enable the reader to recognize a Gimbel's advertisement from one out of the Macy copy department.

Personality comes also from the creative technique—from the borders you use, the twist on words, the art treatment, the typography, the repetition of certain copy points or phrases such as the celebrated "Nobody, but nobody but Gimbel's" and the well-known "It's Smart To Be Thrifty" of Macy's.

Companies engaged in national advertising develop personality in their campaign themes but they are not usually forced into doing so, as are retail stores. The normal retail store has certain natural rivals who sell the same kind of goods at the same prices to the same type of customers. Rivalry between these stores is very personal. It is a matter of frantic interest to the stores that the stores themselves and their advertising reflect an individual personality which make the customer differentiate one store from the other.

When you work in a retail store, you may find that your toughest assignment is to capture your store's special personality in your copy. It's tough, because the personality is made up of so many little things. Be sensitive to those little things and be observant, and one day you'll find that you have pinned down the elusive spirit that spells your store to the customers. If you don't capture this spirit, you'd better move on.

THE LANGUAGE OF RETAIL ADVERTISING

Your language in a retail advertisement walks a tightrope. Normally, retail copy goes out after the sale. Yet this hard-smacking sales copy must be clothed in friendly, good-neighbor talk because of the personal relationship of the store to its customers.

Note: What is said here does not apply directly to an important segment of retail advertising—high-fashion promotion. Such copy operates in a rarefied atmosphere that removes it from many of the rules affecting the ordinary retail copy. Certainly it's true that a hat for $7.98 won't get the same copy treatment as will a mink coat. It is also true that many high-fashion writers could often profit from getting back to the less ethereal writing which moves mass merchandise out of retail stores. Regardless of the merits or failings of high-fashion copy, it is a part of its little, tightly circumscribed, glittering world. This discussion of retail language does not, in the main, refer to such copy. It does refer to the copy for less prosaic merchandise such as hardware, shoes, home furnishings, and haberdashery.

The specific words are the ones that sell. If you're selling moderately priced items like hats, "Prices cut in half" punches harder than "Huge savings." Perhaps the line "Save $5 to $10" may sell the best of the three because it gets even more specific.

A salesperson is specific in talking to a customer—you can be, too. Naturally there is some difference between printed sales messages and those spoken by the person behind the counter. The clerk can be more specific, more pointed, and more down-to-earth because the clerk is not held down by space limitations of a newspaper page. Just the same, a better sale will usually be made if you talk in your copy in the specific language of the salesperson, and not in the words of a copywriter reaching for the "well-turned" phrase and the empty adjective.

JUDGING HOW MUCH TO WRITE

You'll be faced in retail copy, as in other types of copy, with the problem of how much copy to write. As in other copy, your solution is obvious—write enough copy to do the sales job. For instance, suppose you are writing an advertisement that is describing several items. You have decided to use a main copy block and several subsidiary copy blocks which will serve as captions for the multiple items being advertised. You'll defeat your advertisement if you try to jam too much copy into the main copy block, trying to describe in detail all the sales points for all the items in the advertisement.

In short, here is a case where you would be writing too much copy. You would do a better sales job if you made one overall sales point covering all the items in an interesting way, thus luring the reader into the specific selling copy in the captions. In such a case, the main copy block might be more effective if it had six lines of copy than if it had twenty.

Judging the right amount of copy is the mark of the skilled, experienced copywriter. As the young copywriter soon finds out, it is often easier to write a page advertisement than a one-column, three-inch advertisement. Most people have more trouble "compressing" than "expressing." You may find it mighty hard at times to keep from writing too much copy. Suppose, for example, you have a really sensational promotion—really "hot" merchandise. The natural tendency is to write your head off. You and your buyers get excited. You load yourself with so many interesting facts that you could write a campaign for the product. Sadly, however, you realize that all these facts, and all this enthusiasm are going to be earthbound by the fact that you have just one advertisement in which to do your sales job.

In such a case, don't lose your momentum. Go ahead—write your head off—then start the sifting process. Get rid of the fluff. Get rid of the long-winded explanations that attempt to make clear this remarkable value. Tell the story straight, like a newspaper reporter. Remember your customers and their lack of interest in your writing ability. Remember your customers and their desires and wants and needs, all of which you're attempting to stimulate.

Knowing when to stop in the writing of copy is especially difficult in the writing of institutional copy. Such copy, in which you explain store policy, pricing, service, and other facets of store operation, can easily become too long. You can get so wrapped up in the store that you forget the customer. Institutional copy can be fascinating copy, but if you write too much it can easily be the dullest copy for readers because you may take many words to talk about something in which they are not basically interested.

SPACE-FILLER OR COPYWRITER?

A good copywriter rarely can sit in an office and write about merchandise two floors below—without personal contact with the merchandise. That's why you should school yourself to follow the entire process from start to finish—from the buying of the merchandise, if possible, to the investigation of the effectiveness of the advertisement you wrote. If you can possibly find the time, you should get to the selling department after your advertisement has run. Find out the reaction. If a crowd of shoppers flocks in at the opening bell and rushes to the department using your advertisement, you have a good idea that your copy was effective.

Later, again granting that you have time, check with the buyer and the salespeople to find out what they've sold. At the end of the day, ask again and keep a record of the dollar volume, and the advertised items sold off your advertisement. Some stores will actually require that you attach a form listing these results to a tear sheet of the advertisement. You then turn this in to the advertising manager.

Whether or not your boss requires it, make it your business to keep in touch with your advertisements all the way through. If an advertisement doesn't click, find out why. If you ask the buyers, they'll more than likely say it was a poor advertisement. A buyer might tell you, for instance, that the item is one that is usually bought by the husband and wife together. He might show you rather pointedly that your advertisement is slanted too much on one side—that you failed to recognize that both parties share in buying responsibility.

Perhaps you'll say the merchandise wasn't salable. Puzzle out the trouble. You might even rewrite the copy. Some copywriters have actually rewritten advertisements, asked that they be run again with the new slant, and hit the jackpot on the second running.

HELP FROM THE OUTSIDE

Copywriters in a retail organization do not have to depend on their brains alone for ideas. In small

stores, especially, where the copywriter may be a person with a thousand jobs, outside material may be a lifesaver. In big stores or small stores, however, be careful that you don't use so much material from your merchandise sources—often called "resources"—that you forget how to turn out advertising on your own.

Agencies, manufacturers' advertising departments, newspapers, magazines—everybody wants your store to work cooperatively in promoting their products. Magazines will give you tie-in promotional material complete with copy and illustrations for use in your newspaper advertisement. Agencies and company advertising departments will send you brochures full of information, mats, glossy prints, radio spots, copy ideas—and they're all yours to use or discard.

How much you will use and how much you will discard depend upon several factors. The most important factor is the soundness of the ideas offered to you. Sometimes these outside sources forget that you are operating in retail advertising. They seemingly forget that on the retail level, when you talk with your chin right up against your customer's, you must be direct and careful in your use of ideas—often even more careful than in national advertising. For instance, a national campaign on girdles and furs may be built around the distinctiveness of a certain brand—the exclusiveness of its makers. Played up in color, in fine art treatment, such a story may be interesting and effective, and may do much to keep the firm's name connected with prestige and dignity.

On the retail level, your customer is primarily interested in how that fur will go with her fall outfit and what that girdle will do for a bulging figure. Out go the fancy words and tricky, cute expressions, and vague references. Your language is direct. Chances are that in all the material provided you'll find something to hang your "direct" advertisement on— something about the variety of sizes, prices, shapes, and so on and that will be your springboard.

DIRECT MAIL—A RETAIL SALES-BUILDER

You'll find that most retail organizations think almost exclusively in terms of newspaper advertising. Buyers will talk about a "spread" in their favorite evening paper. Most of the store's budget will be spent in newspapers, because the store can see what it's doing and can depend on reaching a healthy circulation guaranteed by the newspaper. Because it's a proved medium, you'll find that most of your time will be spent writing newspaper advertisements. Such copy will use much of the technique employed in copy for magazines and direct mail. Some differences do exist, however, in the tendency toward greater simplicity, shorter sentences, and use of news style in copy and headlines.

In larger stores you'll find much direct-mail advertising, too. Some stores have had great success with direct mail. Many have built big orders with simple post cards or bill inserts sent out to inform charge customers that a certain item will be offered. With no other advertising of certain items, some stores have found selling departments jammed with customers who responded to mailing pieces. Stores have also enjoyed great success in response to mailers which invited the customers to phone or mail in coupon orders.

You should understand the basic differences between direct-mail copy and newspaper copy. Though the selling purpose may be the same, your direct-mail piece may necessarily lack the forcefulness of illustration that your newspaper advertisement could command. Size, alone, can make a big difference. A full newspaper page, for instance, has the wallop of a pile driver—a wallop that direct mail can hardly match. Since newspapers have this "impact" advantage, your words in direct mail, whether in letters, post cards, or insert, must be even more carefully chosen. Remember, although the newspaper itself had some attraction for the customer (in its news value), your insert comes entirely uninvited into the home—the letterhead or store name itself may be enough to cause it to be thrown away without being read.

Be just as specific as you can. Avoid being cute. Make your letter friendly, newsy, interesting. Get out what you have to say as quickly as you can, catching the reader's eye and imagination with a fact that is of personal interest to him. Avoid printing letters upside down, or employing other such tricks. Devices of that sort only irritate and confuse.

Much direct-mail material can be obtained from the manufacturer of the goods you advertise—a fact of great value to the small store, especially. Almost all companies produce mailing inserts for the use of their retail outlets. Some are given to the store free—others can be bought on a cooperative basis. Be sure the store name is imprinted on any mailing piece you buy from a national source, and avoid mailing pieces that lack a local, personal flavor. After all, your purpose is not so much to sell the national brand, but to sell the national brand in your store.

Follow the same principle with the mats that companies send you. Read them carefully. Make sure that your specific merchandise is described in such a way that your store will be identified as the seller. In fact, it's usually a good idea to use the artwork on a mat—if you like it, or if it's more expedient and economical—and have the newspaper reset the copy matter to conform with the type style and approach of your store. This helps continue the "family" relationship among all your advertisements. It should be followed similarly through direct-mail advertising as much as possible.

Direct-mail copywriting for retail stores may require you to write many things in addition to letters. You may do copy for post cards, illustrated invitations to fashion shows, announcements, and college booklets. You'll find an interesting variety usually.

RETAIL RADIO WRITING

Writing for retail radio is so similar to writing for national radio that there is no attempt to detail how to write radio copy for a retail store. The suggestions found in the radio chapter will apply to retail radio writing.

One caution might be observed, however. You might remember that, as in the case of local newspaper advertising, you will do well to capture the local flavor in your radio commercials. You can be a shade friendlier and more intimate. The very fact that you are mentioning a local store in your copy immediately establishes a rapport difficult for the national advertiser to match.

The following commercial with its mention of the local department store illustrates this built-in advantage of the hometown advertiser. This commercial with its frequent push on price was successful in the small town, in which the store is located, in selling 244 pairs of the corduroy pants that were mentioned in the copy.

FIGURE 9-2

Humorous radio commercial aimed at boys.   With all the humor in this commercial, there is much sell, too. The tone of the copy matches the light-hearted feeling of the Christmas season.

```
YOUNG BOY'S LEVI RADIO    :60

NOW YOU MAY NOT KNOW ME PERSONALLY.  BUT YOU'VE PROBABLY HEARD OF
ME.  MY NAME IS BLITZEN.  I'M ONE OF SANTA CLAUS' REINDEER.  AND
I'VE GOT A PROBLEM WITH SANTA.  I MEAN IT'S NOT A REAL DOWNER OR
ANYTHING LIKE THAT.  SANTA'S PROBABLY THE NICEST GUY A REINDEER
COULD WORK FOR.  IN FACT HE'S ABOUT THE ONLY GUY A REINDEER CAN
WORK FOR.  BUT HERE'S MY PROBLEM.  SANTA CLAUS DRESSES LIKE A
SLOB.  I MEAN RED BAGGIES ARE DEFINITELY OUT.  JUST BECAUSE HE'S
SEVERAL HUNDRED YEARS OLD HE DOESN'T HAVE TO LOOK IT.  AND HE
KNOWS THERE'S BETTER STUFF AROUND.  I MEAN HE SPENT WEEKS IN THE
BOYS' DEPARTMENT AT MAY COMPANY PICKING OUT LEVI'S STUDENT CUTS.
I KNOW A LOT OF LEVI'S STUDENT CUTS ARE FOR THE SLIMMER GUYS BUT
THE MAY COMPANY'S BOYS' DEPARTMENT ALSO HAS HUSKY SIZES.  THEY
HAVE LEVI'S SLACKS AND JEANS IN REGULAR AND PREWASHED DENIM,
BRUSHED DENIM, CORDUROY...MAY COMPANY EVEN HAS VESTS AND JACKETS,
I MEAN AFTER SEEING THE LEVI'S IN THE BOYS' DEPARTMENT AT MAY
COMPANY YOU THINK SANTA WOULD WANT HIS OWN.  NOW WOULDN'T THAT
BE TRIPPY.  THERE'S US REINDEER IN THE SKY, YOU KNOW, WITH THE
SLED AND ALL AND THERE'S SANTA.  DECKED OUT IN LEVI'S BELLS,
COORDINATED VEST, EVEN A JEAN JACKET.  I MEAN AFTER HE'S SEEN THE
LEVI'S IN THE BOYS' DEPARTMENT AT MAY COMPANY...AND HOW ABOUT A
BELT WITH SEQUINS, A LEATHER HAT, BOOTS WITH STARS ON THEM.....
```

Mother, does your son play hard? Then shop BIGELOW'S for tough-as-nails corduroy pants, regularly $4.49, now just $3! Yes, for boys who play hard, there's just no substitute for thick-set, long-wearing durable corduroy pants. What's more, he's sure to get extra wear out of these pants—because they have a double knee for extra wear and tear! Choose from navy blue, brown and green, in sizes 6 to 12. And remember, these are a $4.49 value for just $3 at BIGELOW'S. You'll also like the cuffs on these pants, the zipper openings, and the elastic top with the belt, all for the amazing price of just $3. So, for value that means money saved, for quality that means hard wear, get your son durable, thick-set corduroy pants, regularly $4.49, now at the value-packed price of just $3, in the Boys' departments on the Third Floor of BIGELOW'S.

Here is another example of retail store selling through the radio medium. Notice how the writer localized the approach in the beginning of the commercial and then proceeded with the sales talk. Once again the store name adds a localizing touch.

Every hour of every day fire destroys a home. The recent Elm Street fire shows that it can happen here. And your home could be next. That's why it's so important to have a Protexall fire extinguisher in your home—ready to stop a little fire before it grows to be a home-destroying big fire. You'll find the Protexall featured today in the 4th floor hardware department of Johnson's Department Store. It's made by American La France, world's largest manufacturer of fire fighting equipment. This handsome extinguisher comes in four decorator colors that will fit beautifully into your home design. And the Protexall is as efficient as it is handsome. In seconds, Protexall will put out any type of fire—grease, electrical, or wood. Fire can strike any time so come <u>soon</u> to get your Protexall. It'll give you extra peace of mind to know that Protexall is guarding your home and your family. See it today in the hardware department of Johnson's Department Store.

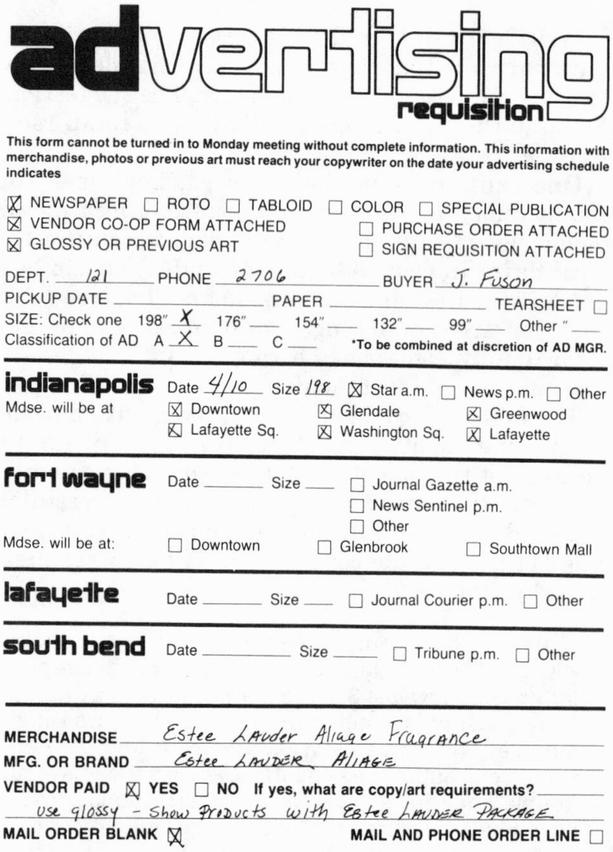

This form cannot be turned in to Monday meeting without complete information. This information with merchandise, photos or previous art must reach your copywriter on the date your advertising schedule indicates

☒ NEWSPAPER ☐ ROTO ☐ TABLOID ☐ COLOR ☐ SPECIAL PUBLICATION
☒ VENDOR CO-OP FORM ATTACHED   ☐ PURCHASE ORDER ATTACHED
☒ GLOSSY OR PREVIOUS ART   ☐ SIGN REQUISITION ATTACHED

DEPT. _121_ PHONE _2706_ BUYER _J. Fuson_
PICKUP DATE _____ PAPER _____ TEARSHEET ☐
SIZE: Check one 198" _X_ 176"___ 154"___ 132"___ 99"___ Other "___
Classification of AD A _X_ B ___ C ___   *To be combined at discretion of AD MGR.

indianapolis Date _4/10_ Size _198_ ☒ Star a.m. ☐ News p.m. ☐ Other
Mdse. will be at: ☒ Downtown   ☒ Glendale   ☒ Greenwood
                   ☒ Lafayette Sq. ☒ Washington Sq.   ☒ Lafayette

fort wayne Date _____ Size ____ ☐ Journal Gazette a.m.
                                        ☐ News Sentinel p.m.
                                        ☐ Other
Mdse. will be at: ☐ Downtown ☐ Glenbrook ☐ Southtown Mall

lafayette Date _____ Size ____ ☐ Journal Courier p.m. ☐ Other

south bend Date _____ Size ____ ☐ Tribune p.m. ☐ Other

MERCHANDISE _Estee Lauder Aliage Fragrance_
MFG. OR BRAND _Estee Lauder Aliage_
VENDOR PAID ☒ YES ☐ NO If yes, what are copy/art requirements? _____
use glossy - show Products with Estee Lauder Package
MAIL ORDER BLANK ☒   MAIL AND PHONE ORDER LINE ☐

FIGURE 9-3

Buyer's requisition (also called "buyer's copy"). If such forms are filled out fully and properly, they can be of great help to the retail store copywriter. The good advertising manager will insist that buyers do their part by giving full information on such requisitions.

Sometimes a department store that uses radio vigorously will run many spots, long and short and throughout the day. An example of a short spot is the following:

Your daughter will appear at her perkiest in the over-blouse and skirt look . . . . One dress your size 7 to 14 girl will like is the red printed dress with the red printed overblouse. The price: $10.98 . . . Dress your daughter in the style she knows is new. . . . From Woodward & Lothrop, Washington. Open today til 6 . . . and Woodward & Lothrop, Chevy Chase, Seven Corners and Alexandria, open til 9:30.

A typical spot of this store includes a description of the item, its price, the department in which it is sold, and the store hours.

High-pressure radio is used less in retail copy than in national copy. The "irritation-type" commercial—the kind that slams the message home over and over again—is not keyed so well to the homespun friendliness of retail radio. Your national accounts don't have to live with their customers. Let them use the sledgehammer—you use a more relaxed approach generally. You'll wear better that way. The push to buying may be in your message, but clothe it in warmth and good-neighborliness for the most part.

Since many retail stores handle radio programs through agencies or through the stations' commercial departments, you may not have a chance to write commercials for a retail radio show. If you do get into retail radio writing, there is a good chance that the only kind of commercials you will write will be spot commercials—anywhere from 30 to 60 seconds. A good set of spots can sell a lot of merchandise. You can build an institutional story with spot announcements, but you'll probably write them to put over the quick sale, the unusual bargain, the get-them-while-they-last approach. In these spots you often won't be "relaxed," as suggested previously. You'll find a real challenge, however, in turning out these dramatic, selling spot announcements.

RETAIL TELEVISION WRITING

Although television is being used by many retail advertisers, it still is too expensive and too specialized for many other retailers. The retailers using television tend to employ simpler, less costly techniques than the national advertiser. Not for them the expensive animation and elaborate live-action film settings used by the big-budget national advertisers.

The retail advertiser is more likely to use live studio shots, or possibly syndicated open-end commercials. More elaborate productions may be possible, however, through cooperative arrangement.

Retail copywriters then are very often required to create television within the framework of a limited production budget. This means the retail writer will

FIGURE 9-4

Reverse side of buyer's requisition shown in Figure 9-3.

advertising requisition

This form cannot be turned in to Monday meeting without complete information. This information with merchandise, photos or previous art must reach your copywriter on the date your advertising schedule indicates

☒ NEWSPAPER ☐ ROTO ☐ TABLOID ☐ COLOR ☐ SPECIAL PUBLICATION
☒ VENDOR CO-OP FORM ATTACHED ☐ PURCHASE ORDER ATTACHED
☒ GLOSSY OR PREVIOUS ART ☐ SIGN REQUISITION ATTACHED

DEPT. _121_ PHONE _2706_ BUYER _J. Fuson_
PICKUP DATE _____ PAPER _____ TEARSHEET ☐
SIZE: Check one 198" _X_ 176" ___ 154" ___ 132" ___ 99" ___ Other " ___
Classification of AD A _X_ B ___ C ___ *To be combined at discretion of AD MGR.

indianapolis Date _4/10_ Size _198_ ☒ Star a.m. ☐ News p.m. ☐ Other
Mdse. will be at ☒ Downtown ☒ Glendale ☒ Greenwood
☒ Lafayette Sq. ☒ Washington Sq. ☒ Lafayette

fort wayne Date ____ Size ____ ☐ Journal Gazette a.m.
☐ News Sentinel p.m.
☐ Other
Mdse. will be at: ☐ Downtown ☐ Glenbrook ☐ Southtown Mall

lafayette Date ____ Size ____ ☐ Journal Courier p.m. ☐ Other

south bend Date ____ Size ____ ☐ Tribune p.m. ☐ Other

MERCHANDISE _Estee Lauder Aliage Fragrance_
MFG. OR BRAND _Estee Lauder Aliage_
VENDOR PAID ☒ YES ☐ NO If yes, what are copy/art requirements? _____
use glossy - show products with Estee Lauder Package
MAIL ORDER BLANK ☒   MAIL AND PHONE ORDER LINE ☐

most often depend upon local station talent and production facilities. There will be much use of slides, stock shots if film is used, and simply staged studio shots.

Videotape, however, has opened up many new opportunities for the retailer using television commercials. If the local station happens to have videotape facilities, the retailer may, because of lower costs, make more use of television advertising. The writer will find that although the creative possibilities are expanded, videotape used on the local level is essentially live-action studio production except that rehearsals can eliminate the mistakes that have so harassed studio production before videotape was perfected. Too, the writer now finds that optical effects employed with videotape can make the commercials more interesting.

Although television has been used successfully by many kinds of local businesses such as banks and automobile dealers, it has always found it difficult to make real headway in retail businesses such as department stores. Where such enterprises have used the medium profitably, they have found certain creative procedures are effective while holding down

cost—the latter being the stumbling-block for so many retail advertisers. Thus it is suggested that:

- A commercial should star the product, use the camera skillfully and avoid the use of high-priced on-camera talent.
- Use a good voice—male or female—for voice-over presentation even though the general rule is that on-camera voice is more effective.
- Develop a distinctive logo.
- If several commercials are to be used, produce them all at one session to cut production costs.
- Use music in public domain.
- Shoot in 16mm instead of 35mm.
- Hold down editing or use no editing in videotaped commercials.
- Use actual advertisements for artwork, as is often done on local shows in which commercials are presented live by station announcers.

Because the writing of television commercials has so many ramifications, there will be no attempt in this chapter to tell the retail writer just how such writing should be done. If you are writing on the local level, it is suggested that you read the chapter on television writing for suggestions. Although this chapter is largely centered on writing for national television advertising, the principles you will find can be applied to retail television.

THE COPYWRITER'S PLACE IN THE RETAIL STORE

Despite the importance of your work, as a copywriter in a big department store you may sometimes feel crushed by the weight of that superstructure over you, and by all the people who can have some influence over your work.

A department store is a subtle, vital organism composed of many parts. You find immediately that you must learn those parts and how to fit your skills and efforts into this complicated structure of which you've become one of the smaller parts. Always, however, you have the ultimate comfort.

Your words are going to be visible on those newspaper pages, or in the direct-mail pieces. If they're clever, bouncy, persuasive, elegant selling words, they'll be noticed. And if you turn them out day after day, you can be assured that no matter how massive the retail structure you're going to get recognition and an escape from anonymity.

Who's in charge
of your work?

You have three bosses in retail advertising—your advertising boss, the buyer who buys the merchandise, and the salesperson who stands behind the counter selling the goods you're writing about. If the salesperson works on a bonus or percentage basis, his very living may depend upon the skill with which you do your job—that makes you mighty important, too.

In some forms of national copy the copywriter doesn't need to acquire a personal working relationship with all members of his organization. Retail copy can't be written without close relationship of the copywriter and the store personnel inside and outside the advertising department. Since no retail department store writers can do the job well unless they understand their relationship to the departments and people with whom they must work, you will find in the following material a description of some of the activity going on about you in a typical department store. You will find more details of the work of those people who are so important to you—such as the advertising manager, the buyer, and the comparison shopper.

Examine the organization of a large department store to get an idea of the extent of your copywriting duties. Keep in mind, too, that despite differences stemming from the type and size of the store, the advertising budget, and the size of the advertising department, the situation is basically the same in all retail establishments.

Much of the following description of the duties of department store personnel is derived from big stores, but the positions listed carry similar duties in all stores. Other department stores might not use exactly the same organizational set-up but will, in a great many cases, have the same basic pattern.

Advertising manager. The advertising manager's job is to oversee the entire advertising operation and to plan future campaigns on a top-management level. He is in direct contact with the store manager, in most cases, and translates management's wishes into actual printed or spoken advertising. Many times he is a "yes-man" to management. Other times he may come up with fine ideas which he "sells" to the management.

The advertising manager usually makes up the entire month's advertising schedule in advance—or he might even plan two or three months ahead. All advertising goes through his hands for final approval, whether it's a newspaper advertisement, a television or radio commercial, or a mailing insert. He controls all personnel in the advertising department, including you.

Section chiefs. Large department stores often employ section chiefs or divisional advertising managers to head the various copy sections such as homewares, men's furnishings, downstairs store, fashions, and others. These people are responsible for actual planning within their divisions. They work with buyers and their merchandise managers, check advertisements as they are written by copywriters, consult with the art department on layout suggestions and art treatment. In effect, they are the advertising managers for a group of "clients" within a division of the store.

Merchandise managers. Each major division within the store has a merchandise manager who may control as many as thirty buyers. He is responsible for their buying plans and their spending and sales figures. In an advertising sense, his job is to allocate money from his monthly budget to the various selling departments in his division. He also turns in a tentative monthly schedule to the advertising manager—which is used to make up the entire store's schedule for the coming period.

A merchandise manager passes on individual advertisements for his department, and sees that buyers provide full information to the copywriters preparing the advertising.

Buyers. These men and women go into the market to buy the goods you write about. Some of them gladly cooperate with the writers who must turn out selling copy about their goods. They provide "buyer's copy" to tell the writer about merchandise. They give the copywriter every chance to see, feel, try, and test the goods. The buyers are, in a sense, the copywriter's clients. You will respect their wishes as long as they result in good advertising.

Regrettably, a good many buyers give copywriters the poorest kind of cooperation. They must be begged for information. Not seeming to care about the copywriter's side, they give information only about the obvious things such as colors, sizes, and prices. Your job will require you to dig for more than these bare facts. Desperately you'll hound the buyers for more help than the scanty facts they give you in their buyer's copy. Though some buyers will be a real help to you, rely on your own effort and ingenuity to get facts for writing your copy. Buyers have their own problems to worry about and copywriting is not among them. If they give you complete information—fine. If they don't, you get it yourself.

Comparison shoppers. Almost all large stores maintain a comparision shopping department to check the truthfulness of statements made in the store's advertisements, to determine whether quantities of merchandise on hand warrant advertising, to act as liaison between the buyer and the advertising department, and to shop in other stores in the community for comparable values and comparative store activity. "Comparison" usually has the final word on all advertising, especially on descriptions that may go counter to policies of the store and trade principles as laid down by the Better Business Bureau.

In addition to being in contact with the buyers, section managers, and the others mentioned, during the advertising day, you will also work closely with the art director, who is responsible for layouts, finished art, and photographs; the production manager, who marks the type, handles the proofs, enters corrections, and sends all material to the newspapers; the clerk, who controls the flow of merchandise that is sent up for sketching or photography.

As you can see, a great many people contribute to the preparation of every advertisement, from the warehouseperson who hauled furniture for a camera shot to the clerk who checked copy for accuracy. The combined activity is slanted toward one end—to create advertisements that produce—advertisements that sell!

WRITING COPY FOR THE SMALLER STORE

Of course, the foregoing operation differs in some respects from that of other big stores. The general procedure, however, is similar enough to that of a great many of them that the description will give you a fairly good picture of your duties in the typical big store.

The procedure in thousands of small and medium-sized stores, however, is much different. In a small store you may be a copywriter, advertising manager, production chief, and display manager rolled up into one very busy person. Often, in such a job, you will not write much original copy. A good portion of your writing will consist of revising, shortening, or lengthening the "canned" copy that accompanies the mat material from the mat services or from the manufacturer of the goods you are advertising.

Many small stores depend upon mat services and proof books to provide them with layout and copy ideas. Very often, also, small stores let their newspapers do copy-layout work for them. If you land in a store like that you won't find much challenge to your copywriting ability. In other stores, however, you may write much copy, since you will wish to key your advertisements to the local situation. You may use mat material, but just as an occasional help.

One thing you can almost be certain of—in a small store you will usually find that there is not enough copywriting to fill all your working hours. This means you will fill out the rest of the time doing practically anything that comes along.

Take the case of an advertising-school graduate, for instance, who was hired as a "copywriter" in a small retail store. True enough she did write copy. She also did all the layouts, planned the monthly advertising schedules, gave the space orders to the newspapers, and worked with the store manager in determining the advertising budget.

In addition, the "copywriter" helped out on the floor occasionally, filling in as a sales clerk. Regularly, too, she helped put up window displays. She even made talks on fashion trends to local women's groups.

Although all small or medium-sized stores might not expect so much from their young copywriters, you will probably find, if you enter such work, that writing copy will be just one of your duties.

STEPS IN EXECUTING A RETAIL ASSIGNMENT

Now to get down to the actual procedure of writing an advertisement. Suppose the buyer of men's shoes has an advertisement on his schedule and that he's supposed to have his "buyer's copy" up to you by a certain date (you usually will work anywhere from six to fourteen days ahead of publication date). Ultimately, after the buyer has sent his material through his own merchandise manager and then through the

advertising manager, you and the other staff members will discuss this advertisement along with others when you confer about advertisements about to be put into work.

Some stores may have such discussion for each advertisement. Others may simply determine general treatment for a group or series of advertisements and leave it up to the copywriter to develop copy for individual advertisements according to this overall plan. General copy meetings in such stores may be called only for special promotions.

During your meeting, suggestions for treatment may come from any of the copywriters, from the advertising manager, from the art director, from the production manager—from any advertising person at the copy meeting. Perhaps it may be decided that the advertisement is to be hard selling, that it will emphasize the variety of styles. You and the art director will discuss the tie-in of illustration and copy. You'll agree that the illustration should feature many shoe styles. You are to write captions for the numerous shoes pictured. After much discussion, you leave the meeting with a rough idea of the copy and art approach. You're ready to go to work.

Talk to the art department

One of your most important jobs at this point is telling the art department what sort of layout treatment the advertisement requires. You discuss the merchandise being advertised, suggest the type and the number of sketches, tell what your headlines and subheads will be—even prepare a rough layout or thumbnail sketch of the advertisement. This last item will be even more vital in a smaller store where the copywriter may be called on to turn in a complete "visual" of the advertisement.

The instructions to the art department are not the final word, of course, since the layout must be approved by the advertising manager before any finished art can be started. Probably the best way to tell the art department exactly what you have in mind is to write the entire advertisement—write every word that you want to have in the advertisement so that the layout person knows how much of a copy block you need, how many and how long the display lines must be, how many items you will have in a listing of merchandise, how many figures must be illustrated, and so on. Your providing the actual copy assures you that the layout you get from the art department will be much closer to your wishes than if you had merely turned in some vague directions about "large copy block required," or "big display head," or "generous copy space." If you were the artist, what would "generous" mean to you? Just as you need complete information from your buyer in order to describe the merchandise, the layout people need complete information in order to turn out the right layout for that merchandise.

Remember, however, that many stores do their artwork first and then the copywriter goes to work. In such stores you would write copy that would fit the character of the artwork, and that would fit into the space that wasn't taken up by illustration. As a copywriter, it is much more satisfactory to work in the situation where you, rather than the illustrator, will be controlling the makeup of the advertisement. Unfortunately, there are probably more stores in which the art treatment comes first. You might as well realize this right now and be prepared to adjust yourself to playing second-fiddle to the art department if you happen to land in a store that gives the art people principal authority in the construction of advertisement.

All right—the layout's made and approved, and the art is to be prepared. This time the shoes were photographed in the photographer's studio after the buyer had delivered them to the studio. In the case of big items, such as furniture, the photograph will usually be taken after hours in the department involved. If you can, it's desirable for you to be around when your merchandise is being photographed or sketched. You might be able to make useful suggestions.

Start writing

While all this art activity is going on, you're supposed to be writing the copy. In large departments you'll be given a copy of the layout as it was actually approved, and the headlines will be represented properly along with copy space and listings. Perhaps you may have some simple adjustments to make. You may need to cut your copy slightly, or change your headline somewhat. The important thing is that this layout is no stranger to you. Most of your planned thinking has been done.

Sometimes, of course, your original ideas may be thrown out completely and you will have to start from scratch when you receive the final layout. Now assume that this is the case with the advertisement in question. You had what you thought was a fine idea but someone along the line—the advertising manager, or sectional manager, or perhaps both—caused your "fine idea" to be dropped into the wastebasket. Now you see the fresh layout in front of you. You're really starting all over again because a new slant has been thrown at you.

Recheck facts

Pick up the buyer's copy—the sheets containing all the information that the shoe buyer had to offer. First ask yourself: What am I selling? No, the answer isn't shoes alone, because everybody sells shoes. What's the idea behind this advertisement? What's the story behind all the illegible writing on the buyer's sheet? Dig down into the buyer's copy. Digest what was given to you. Call him up or go see him. Ask to see the shoes. Ask to see any manufacturer's data on the product, or any promotional material. Why does he want to advertise these shoes? How does he happen to have this merchandise? Is it a new brand, a special price, a new idea? Get all the facts before you sit down to write!

Get back to writing

When you're loaded with information, you go back to your typewriter and start to write. First, write the story out for yourself from start to finish. Put it all down on paper so you can go back and refer to it for the facts you'll need. It might be a good idea to make a check list to use in preparing any advertisement, whether it's newspaper, radio, or direct mail.

Understand that the preceding procedure represents the ideal. Sometimes you may be so harried with little tasks that you can't find time to go through this suggested process. If you can, you'll write better copy. When you first write retail copy, you should try especially hard to follow this checklist. Later, when you've become adept, you'll do the right thing automatically—it won't make any difference then if you get so busy that you don't consciously think in terms of the following checklist points. You'll do the right things by habit. If you're a beginner in retail copy (or any other type), however, you can't help profiting if you check yourself carefully before you start to write.

801 SOUTH BROADWAY, LOS ANGELES, CALIFORNIA 90014   488-4141

Dear Sportswear Customer:

Because you've shopped in our sportswear shops, we would like to invite you to a special preview sale of Evan Picone Sportswear at 33 1/3% savings on Friday, December 24th. It's a special courtesy day for our Better Sportswear customers. This sale will begin for the general public on Monday, December 27th.

Evan Picone always has a new way to go simply everywhere. Tailored classics that are timeless and in the best of style. Each piece is an investment in a wardrobe of impeccable taste and endless possibilities. It's the way you want to look today. Our collection of compatible separates includes: pants, skirts, blazers, vests, shirts and sweaters in novelty plaids, wool flannels, checks, harris tweeds, velveteens for you to add and multiply.

        Pants, were $41 to $55, now $26.99 to $36.99
        Skirts, were $37 to $51, now $24.99 to $33.99
        Blazers, were $79 to $93, now $52.99 to $61.99
        Vests, were $43 to $47, now $28.99 to $30.99
        Shirts, were $27 to $43, now $17.99 to $28.99
        Sweaters, were $27 to $33, now $17.99 to $21.99

Remember, your special courtesy day is December 24th...yours for one day only...in the Forecast shop at all May Co stores. Visit us early to be sure you get the best selection of Evan Picone sportswear at 33 1/3% savings.

Sincerely,

Judy Gmur

Judy Gmur
Evan Picone Buyer

P.S. Friday, December 24th all May Co stores are open
      from 9:00 to 6:00, except Downtown L.A. 9:30 to 6:00.

FIGURE 9-5

Department store sales letter.   A retail store's best opportunities lie in former customers. This letter makes such customers feel "special."

BUT WHAT ABOUT OTHER FORMS OF LOCAL ADVERTISING?

Retail advertising and department store advertising are inclusive terms that take in big department stores, small department stores, millinery shops, shoe stores, variety stores, furniture stores, photographic shops and the myriad of business enterprises that operate in the downtown areas, shopping centers and neighborhoods of the cities, towns, and villages of the United States.

In these same locations we have huge sums being invested in advertising by enterprises that cannot be called "retail." These include banks, real estate firms, dairy companies, hotels, car dealers, and many others.

The principles of good copywriting for the department stores (about which you have just read) can be applied by these advertisers and, in the case of banks, are often applied exceedingly well. This excellence is largely due to the fact that most bank advertising is prepared by advertising agency copywriters. This is likely to be true, also, of large dairies, hotels and car dealers, and some other local enterprises that invest substantially in advertising. Unfortunately, however, there is much local advertising that is not done well.

MUCH LOCAL ADVERTISING COPY IS POOR TO MEDIOCRE

An examination of advertisements in newspapers (with the exception of first-class establishments in big cities) reveals a depressing picture. Too often the copy is prepared by persons in the establishments who have had no training in advertising, or by newspaper space salespeople who do the copy because they are expected to write copy as part of their overall selling duties. It is obvious from their copy that many space salespeople should concentrate on their selling and leave the writing to better qualified persons.

The result of the inexpert approach is advertising on the local level that has these common faults:

1. Telegraphic copy that has no flow or character.
2. Label headlines that don't lure readers into reading the body copy.
3. Impersonal writing that doesn't reach out and involve the reader.
4. Little, or no, use of suffering points to give solid reasons for buying.
5. Product-oriented copy instead of people-oriented copy.
6. Too much mere listing of product, or sales points.
7. No localization of the copy that takes advantage of the shared experiences of the advertiser and the customers.
8. Overall dullness of the copy—a lack of sparkle, imagination and use of colorful, persuasive words.

10

It's Another World—Fashion

Poets and writers of high-fashion advertising have much in common. Both can twist the language into marvelous, often zany, shapes. Their use of imagery and mood set them apart from ordinary mortals whose writing is earthbound. A poet is viewed indulgently when he departs from conventional paths. "Poetic license" excuses much. A similar tolerance is extended to the fashion copywriter.

Most men, and even many women, do not understand much of the language of fashion advertising. Comprehension of the oftentimes stilted, haughty phrases is, however, not required. What a woman cannot understand, she can feel, often more important than literal understanding.

If you have worked up a comfortable set of rules to guide you in copywriting, you'd better drop them in the bottom drawer of the file before you begin writing fashion copy. Good creative techniques for fashion promotion will very frequently be radically different from acceptable techniques for selling ordinary goods and services. You are entering a new creative world when you begin a fashion-copy career.

SMARTNESS AND SUBSTANCE SELL FASHION

Anyone who enters fashion advertising thinking, however, that it consists of nothing more than creating mood and a series of airy, somewhat silly phrases will soon be disabused of this notion. True, fashion advertising writing uses a flip, mode (or mod) language but the moment of truth arrives when facts must be given and the fashion writer then employs tough, resultful, reason-why copy. She knows that the reader of her advertisement can't make a buying decision if she is served nothing but fluff.

A good example of a fashion advertisement is the following that utilizes a certain amount of the lan-

guage expected in fashion advertising but which has a hard core of rational, here-are-some-good-reasons-to-buy.

SPORTSWEARMANSHIP. YOU EITHER HAVE IT OR YOU DON'T

Sportswearmanship. It's a slightly irreverent flair for the informal. And Lucky Tops® has it. In the print jumpsuit below, $32. Accented by the solid tunic. $16 in 10 colors, and the more classically casual striped tie-belt top and slacks on the right. The top, $14, the slacks, $14. Both in 10 colors. The slacks, size 5/6-19/20. All other styles P-S-M-L-XL. All made with generous attention to detail in 100% celanese Fortrel® polyester. All machine washable . . .

Another example of this same sort of approach in which the fanciful is mixed with the practical is the following. Note that the beginning captures attention through the dream-date reference to the Rolls Royce but notice, too, how quickly the writer gets down to the practical details needed for a buying decision.

"My latest Leslie Fay."®

When he told me he'd pick me up in his car, I never dreamed it would be a Rolls.

What do you wear in a Rolls? Leslie Fay knows. This dress and jacket outfit was perfect.

It has a navy and white arnel triacetate and nylon knit tank top with a white arnel triacetate skirt pleated all around.

The red linen-like jacket, of 100% polyester, is softened with a drawstring belt.

Also available with red and white tank top, white shirt and navy jacket. Sizes 8-18. About $54.

It's my latest Leslie Fay.® And I love it.

109

*I out-dazzle
the sunset,
dim the stars.
One billow of
my cloudburst...
and the pulse
quickens.*

Anthony Muto's
cumulation for Marita:
A graceful gathering of
Qiana® nylon, in pink
champagne for sizes
8 to 14, '100.
Fifth Avenue Shop.

Saks
Fifth
Avenue

What is fashion copywriting, and how can you learn to write it successfully? Like all other types of copy, it has its tricks. You must learn those tricks. Also, before you can learn to write fashion copy, you must first learn what fashion is. At the outset, then, you will pursue the illusive fashion.

Perhaps you'd better start by thinking of fashion a) as exemplified in high-fashion periodicals and in advertisements for exclusive stores, b) as exemplified in volume selling in department and moderate-price stores. When you have thought about these two divisions of fashion, you will be ready to absorb a few do's and don'ts of fashion writing.

You probably have surmised already that fashion is a capricious commodity. What is and what is not fashion almost defies analysis. Every few years some scholar comes out of research activities to write a new and learned treatise proving that fashions stem from wars and the general economy of a country. In the broad, overall view he's probably right. However, in view of fashion's inherent ephemeral quality and because the motives and causes underlying changes in fashion are as subject to change as the fashions themselves, it is of no great importance to pin it down, dissect it and catalog its component parts.

Consider what happened to fashion after World Wars I and II. When women began bobbing their hair after the first war, it was supposedly to assert equality with men by looking more boyish. It was even argued that since women had shared the hardships of war as Red Cross workers, nurses, and so forth, they intended to share the rewards. Ostensibly, the generalization to be drawn from this example is that women express their emancipation after a war through more masculine fashions, but this analysis does not work out. Many thousands of women also served in the World War II. Again, when the war was over, they swarmed to have their hair cut shorter. This time the motive was changed. They clipped it off not to look more boyish but to achieve a fluffy, feminine look. The war had made fashion static, imposed regulations, prescribed tailored suits, demanded practical, mannish clothes. The outburst of the new, the curved, the longer skirted silhouette, as well as of the short coiffures, was an expression not for equality, but against the deadly regimentation of war.

The approach in fashion is so personal that many feel that it takes a female copywriter to sell another woman. A man can understand how important it is to a woman to wear a skirt three inches longer (or three inches shorter) than last season, but he's at a distinct disadvantage in having to guess how she feels in it. A woman knows. She sells the feel of fashion, of low waists or high waists, flared skirts or straight skirts, or whatever, almost before she sells the specific merchandise.

Fashion moves in cycles. If you're an aspirant for a top job in fashion copy, you'll need to read as much as possible about the clothes of all periods. While you're at it you'll profit also from exposure to the humanities, history, literature, and the economics of the world. Writing fashion advertising is less inspiration than it is a comprehensive knowledge of what made the world turn in Cleopatra's time and what keeps it spinning today.

Fashion is emotion. You must live with it. It is your job to begin where the photograph or illustration leaves off. Your work is good when you give the reader the feel of fashion, when you make a coming dinner party inviting by letting a woman know how it will feel to appear in an original by Yves Saint Laurent.

IT'S THE FASHION TO CHANGE

Keeping up with fashion is your joy and despair. One moment it's the peasant look, at prices far beyond the "peasant's" ability to pay. Gone is the tunic over pants and the graceful drape of chiffon. Suddenly, the sumptuous look takes over in place of the simple chiffon or jersey dress. "Importance" has become the word.

Because the dress must look important, the swing may be to velour fabrics. For originals, the price is important, too, at $950; less, of course, in copies. So understated elegance is out, and the change can occur at a dizzying pace. For example, one high fashion store, less than two weeks after a Paris showing by a renowned designer, presented the new style in New York. Eight dresses at $500 were sold the first day and the store continued to sell the new fashion at the same brisk pace.

Unless your antenna are quivering ceaselessly, significant changes may catch you unaware. When they occur, you need to call upon new words and to evoke new moods. Meanwhile, amidst all the newly coined elegance, you may still be selling denims with a fashion flair and at prices unmistakably in the fashion range.

So much for fashion in general. Now to point up the distinctions between high-fashion advertising and volume-fashion copy.

HIGH-STYLE FASHION WRITING

High-style fashion writing can be fairly formal, as on the pages of *Vogue* or *Harper's Bazaar*. Formal, as it is in the advertisements of Marshall Field's, informal, as in *Mademoiselle*. Or formal or informal, as in the top fashion advertisements of Lord and Taylor. Whichever it is, this copy is authoritative; it sets the fashion.

From these editorial pages and advertisements spring the words and phrases that articulate the fashion. Through the years, the words associated with fashion have been as essential to the fashions themselves as the very fabrics from which they are cut. For instance—the Gibson Girl shirt, the hobble skirt, the swing skirt, the D'Orsay pump.

High-fashion copy is designed primarily to sell the idea of the coat of the moment, rather than a specific coat in stock. The importance of this objective must not be underestimated. Writing for this type of advertisement is an exacting job.

Newspapers and magazines from time to time carry striking examples of superb advertisements. Quite a number, by their originality and daring, have started whole new circles of advertising thought. In New York, for example, Lord and Taylor runs newspaper advertisements written by copywriters who have distinguished themselves by being able to put down on paper just a few really thought-through words. These writers are masters of the art of saying a lot by writing little. It isn't easy. Years of apprenticeship and hard work are necessary before a writer can hope to achieve this skill.

Nothing has been said here about the fashion artists as important members of the creative team. In many eyes they are more important than you in inducing sales. Fruitless and unending arguments can be held on this point since words and illustration must ultimately work together. Each can enhance the other. Make no mistake, however. Recognize that illustration, as important as it is in other forms of advertising, is still more important in fashion advertising in conveying mood and authenticity. Fashion artists are usually superior artists. Such artists will provide you with a strong creative challenge—to do as well with words as they do with art. The test is whether the art embellishes the copy, or vice versa—or does each match the other perfectly?

A study of high-fashion advertisements will reveal these characteristics:

- They are directed toward people who set the pace.
- Their appeal is prestige.
- They speak with authority (usually written in third person).
- They strive toward mood and illusion.
- Their concern with details, if any, is secondary.
- They contrive to make the readers feel they are influencing fashion, rather than being influenced by it.
- The copy is usually brief—and always enhanced by dramatic artwork and distinctive type faces.
- The words themselves are fresh as an April leaf, highly dramatic and descriptive.

FIGURE 10-2

High fashion advertisement.   Unusual copy and a graceful illustration impart a distinctive feeling for the offering and the store.

Notwithstanding the fact that good high-fashion advertising has these characteristics, there is a regrettable amount of high fashion advertising appearing in magazines and newspapers that does not measure up. One criticism is the sameness in the sleek illustrations and the copy's artificial sheen—the bright, insincere patter that has confused shallowness for sophistication.

There is the tendency, too, for fashion advertisers to fall in love with prettiness. Advertisements are judged as pretty or not pretty—whether or not they have ideas or selling arguments. The advertisements—copy and art—show and talk about merchandise but make no real attempt to sell it.

FASHION COPY FOR VOLUME SALES

Whereas high-fashion advertising is designed to set the pace, volume-fashion advertising is directed to selling the people who must keep the pace. The student looking forward to a career in advertising will very likely start here. This does not mean that volume-fashion advertising is easy, nor does it imply that the techniques involved are less exacting. It does mean that there are more opportunities in this phase of advertising because this is the category into which most advertising falls. The stores and agencies engaged in promotional work to move stocks of merchandise are in the thousands. In contrast, the smart shops and periodicals whose concern is high fashion are relatively few.

You must realize that a flair for writing is not enough for writing fashion advertising that sells. You must understand selling techniques, adaptations of style, human nature, and above all, you must have an intimate knowledge of the people who buy and wear the clothes you are writing about—the people who do the volume-buying upon which all stores depend.

In one sense, your knowledge of peoples' buying habits, their whims, and their enthusiasms is more important than your writing skill. If you don't have the former, you're just another writer spinning out glib, bright patter that fails to convince and thus fails to sell. Although there are vast differences in the markets and in the writing techniques used, a fashion writer and an industrial writer have a lot in common. Each must have an intense personal interest in his specialized field and must be able to turn out copy precisely geared to that field.

As mentioned earlier, you must, above all, be breathlessly intrigued with fashion change and fashion detail. In the illustrative part of your advertisement it must be important to you how a glove stops at the wrist, and where the flower is pinned on the dress. It is easy to be wrong in these details. Likewise, it is exceedingly difficult to recover the confidence of the reader who looks over your advertisement and finds that you, seemingly, have less interest in these details than she does.

FIGURE 10-3

Fashion advertisement.   In addition to an intriguing copy style, this advertisement provides a strong inducement in the offering of an exclusive.

EYES ON EYELET
Spotting a trend,
that's the Sixth Sense!
The trend? The bare
little sundress.
White cotton eyelet.
Feminine.
Romantic. Beguiling.
Ours alone from France.
Sizes P,S,M,L, 70.00
The Sixth Sense,
Sixth Floor

On the Plaza in New York and White Plains
BERGDORF GOODMAN
Mail to 754 Fifth Avenue, New York 10019 (212) PL3-7300
Please add 1.55 beyond our delivery area.

The writer engaged in volume-fashion advertising must correlate three factors: selling techniques, human nature, forceful style.

Effective volume-selling, like other forms of selling, is based on six rather commonly accepted objectives: to attract attention, to hold interest, to create desire, to overcome obstacles, to stir to action, and to give satisfaction and pleasant reaction for money spent.

Although the precepts of effective selling can be learned in Psychology 201 or in basic courses on salesmanship, human nature cannot be so conveniently catalogued. Textbooks can give you general knowledge about the woman consumer. All people want recognition, want response, work for security, and yearn for new experience. But—the woman you are trying to reach considers herself less as a member of a particular group and more as an individual who is different and has different problems You must know and understand this woman in particular. Recognize her problems. If your copy is to sell, you must show her how to dress attractively, but you must be aware, too, that she is concerned with making her budget stretch, and that she is determined to keep healthy.

Your job is to sell her fashions. Dozens of considerations and economies are pulling against you. Hundreds of commodities are competing with your dress for her attention, and to make your selling job tougher a dozen stores are competing with you to sell her that same $45 dress.

If your advertisement is successful, you will attract her, persuade her, and bring her into your store to buy the dress you describe. You will have found a way to say it better. You will have convinced her. You will have made your dress her most compelling consideration.

A successful advertisement, you see, is good writing plus a point of view that enables your copy to begin where the reader is.

ELEMENTS OF VOLUME-FASHION COPY

Significantly, the appeals in volume-fashion advertising are quite different from the specialized appeals in high-fashion advertising. The message is toward the woman who must keep the pace. A volume advertisement:

- Helps a woman to feel she is buying and wearing the new, the smart, that she is *keeping* pace.
- Assures her that she is well dressed. (Note: not because she is imitating, but because she has the good judgment to recognize "smart fashion.")
- Does not chide her for waiting to be assured that the fashion she is buying is the established fashion; it helps her feel she showed good sense.
- Emphasizes what is new about the dress you are advertising, and shows her why it will be becoming to her.
- Indicates that her standard of dressing is parallel to "best dressed" through the merchandising or designing abilities of your store—her store. (Note: it's always a good idea to sell the store or the label in addition to the merchandise. In the long run, if the merchandise is good, it will add to sales by making that manufacturer's line, or that store, a habit with the woman you have sold);
- Connotes fashion in terms of her activities.
- Answers her implied questions on wearing qualities, washability, and so forth.
- Tells more of the details—width of seams, fabric, colors, sizes. A woman may be looking for a dress or coat in pink wool. She reads carefully. Nothing is said about color—nor about the fabric. Remember, by supplying information about the color and fabric of the merchandise you do not necessarily detract from the atmosphere of "style."
- Gives more stress to price. While you should certainly be aware that price gains more prominence as it drops lower and lower, watch out for basing

fashion copy wholly on an economy appeal. "Now—a woolen suit for $39.98" probably will not appeal. Women prefer not to identify themselves with $39.98 even if that's all they have to spend.

Although interesting style is pretty much a personal matter, there are, nevertheless, some precepts and rules that cannot be ignored. Since copywriting is a craft—like building a bench or cobbling a shoe— you should think in very clear terms of problem solution. Every block of copy, whether it pertains to mink or walking shoes, has a message to convey. You decide what is to be said and why—and you must say it exactly the way it should be said.

You must do justice to the fashion in terms suitable to your reader audience, its age, its tastes, its way of life. The medium and the audience set the slant for the copy. An advertisement scheduled for *Seventeen*, must be written to dovetail with its reader's way of speaking or thinking. This is not the way of speaking or thinking of a woman who reads *Vogue* or *Harper's Bazaar*. The fashion writer knows to whom the eyes peering at the page belong.

You must have facility with words, a sharp ear, attuned to the turn of a phrase, and the perception to recognize gestures, and attitudes of readers. If you're good, you visualize the reader before you attempt to reach her with your copy.

Call attention to designers

Designers are the glamor types of fashion. Fashion advertising, therefore, profits from capitalizing on designers' names. The following copy section from a fashion advertisement of Cotton, Incorporated, demonstrates the technique of utilizing the power of a designer's name.

> At a time like this, you'll thank Larry Levine for making it with cotton.
>
> Sweet-talk time:Time to keep cool under a barrage of compliments. Larry Levine makes the compliments happen. Then helps you keep your cool. He tailored this safari pantsuit in 100% cotton corduroy by Crompton.
>
> Cotton corduroy breathes. Just as you do. So stay comfortable. Larry Levine knows that 80% of American consumers (like you) think of comfort first when they buy clothing. Gather all the compliments you can. Cotton keeps you cool. Larry Levine Safari Pantsuit, approximately $64. Poppy red, navy, or champagne. Sizes 5 to 13. At Marshall Field, Neiman Marcus, I. Magnin, Filene's.

FASHION WRITING'S YEAS AND NAYS

Here are some do's and don'ts on interesting writing style. You will do well to remember them.

- Do . . . make your caption sound smooth and unstilted.

- Do . . . whenever possible, use an active verb for description instead of a descriptive adjective. Verbs make a caption stronger, give it movement. NOT: The black skirt has circular bands around it. BUT: Black ribbon bands encircle the skirt.

- Do . . . keep your sentences simple, whether long or short. Be careful that your modifiers fall as close as possible to what they modify.

- Do . . . avoid the phrase that's crushingly last year's. Catch phrases of the day can be effective, but bear in mind whether you are writing for a daily newspaper or a periodical. The smart phrase that's on everyone's lips now is likely to become completely passé in the long interim between writing and publication of a periodical.

- Do . . . be light and gay and humorous if you can. Don't try to be if you can't.

- Do . . . digest thoroughly all information on merchandise (study the photograph or layout intensively if you can't see the merchandise yourself) before you put your pencil on paper. You can't write interestingly if you don't write knowingly.

- Don't . . . use a tired simile. It's even more soporific than the tired adjective. Don't say "crisp as lettuce, sleek as a seal, striped like Joseph's coat." Say "bright, like a fire-engine; fresh as a four-year-old's cheeks; gala as the evening that starts with an orchid."

- Don't . . . rely on a clutter of lush adjectives. When you do use adjectives, make them as specific and fresh as possible. Embellishments "pretty, marvelous, charming, wonderful, divine" don't really accomplish anything. "Slouch looks, tunnel waistline, popcorn-cardigan, ruffly necklines"— these all give you a definite picture and a definite association. These adjectives have feeling.

- Don't . . . imitate someone else's style. Read other people's advertisements for the ideas they contain—but when you have an advertisement to write on the same dress, write in your own way. Be fresh. Remember that fashion is the "Fresh Roses" end of merchandising—and your copy should match it.

By this point in the chapter you have come to realize that the fashion copywriter must be as subtle as a glance behind a veil, and as direct as a salesclerk in Macy's basement; as factual as a catalog sheet, and as imaginative as a mystery writer. Fashion writers must have a strong love for fashion, and for glittering, human, persuasive words—and most of all for ideas around which they wrap the words with precision and that mysterious quality called "flair." Possessed of all these qualities they may survive, and even thrive, in the demanding, volatile field that is fashion copywriting.

BUT DON'T FORGET THE MEN

At one time men smiled indulgently at women's concern with fashion, cosmetics, and other feminine enthusiasms. The woman's world was far from the

BEGIN THE CEREMONY. DUSK GLIDES IN, SPREADING
WINGS OF SHADOW. DISCOVER YOUR INNER SERENITY.
MEET BILL TICE AND SEE HIS ORIENTAL PERSUASION IN LOUNGEWEAR.

DRAWINGS BY JIM HOWARD

Light flickers on a tapestry of unfolding blossoms.
The quiet time has arrived. Balance is achieved and grace has meaning.
In the soft flow of fabric, the delicacy of design, the interrelationship
of color and line. Bill Tice's new collection for Swirl has arrived.
Side-tied caftan, in yellow and blue, one size fits all, 45.00.
Zippered kimono with contrasting turn-back sleeves, in blue and white,
for 8 to 16 sizes, 45.00. Wrap with lined ceremonial sleeves,
in cream with blue, for 8 to 12 sizes, 70.00. All in pure cotton.
Loungewear, Fifth Floor.

Come meet Bill Tice Monday and Tuesday, informal modeling from 12 to 4.
And do see the collection previewing in our 56th Street windows.

BONWIT TELLER

New York Manhasset Scarsdale Short Hills Philadelphia Wynnewood Jenkintown Chicago Oak Brook Boston Troy Palm Beach Beverly Hills

Add 1.35 outside delivery area and sales tax where applicable. Call (212) EL 5-2600 any hour.

world of clean-shaven males who wore dark suits, sober ties, and short, neatly clipped hair.

In the last decade, however, men have burst into the fashion scene. Ruffled shirts, colorful suits, and platform shoes have taken over a sizable portion of the men's world. In the new unisex era, we have become accustomed to seeing males with shoulder length hair. We shrug as they daub themselves with colognes and perfumes, and apply makeup. Clothing and personal grooming ideas are dictated by *Playboy, Esquire,* and the many men's magazines that have caused much of the departure from male conservatism in dress and personal habits.

How can the fashion writer create advertising for this newly emerged male butterfly? First, she must understand she is addressing three markets.

One is the still conservative, young-man-on-the-move market. Her target is the young executive whose clothes have a quiet distinction suitable for the appearance of the investment broker in the board room, for the account executive who must present a campaign at a client meeting, for the young lawyer in a prestigious Boston law firm. This man's well-groomed hair may be slightly longer than in the past, but he is much the same in dress as he always has been.

Copy for this market is subdued and deferential. It recognizes the importance of the impression that the reader's attire must make on his associates. The stress is not so much on what is new as what is appropriate. This man doesn't want to be innovative in dress so much as quietly, and possibly—expensively—correct.

FIGURE 10-4

High fashion advertisement.   Every element of the true high fashion advertisement is present here. A bold, imaginative headline. An invitation to meet a celebrated designer and to see his creations. Copy with flair that uses words complementing the striking illustrations. Enough detail to satisfy the practical side of the high fashion shopper. Artwork instead of photography fits the mood of this advertisement.

Two is the swinging market. This is the machismo male who glories in his virility and attractiveness to females. Copy directed at him, whether for musk oil scents or colorful, flared slacks, has sexual overtones. Sometimes, the copy can poke fun at the image ala the Joe Namath approach for many products. Fun, or not, our male target is moved by self-gratification and a desire to impress the women he meets. He has a self-image that is largely created by the clothes he wears, the hair styling he adopts, and the cologne he splashes on himself. The *Playboy* reader, typical of this market, is highly conscious of styles, is innovative, eager to try the new, and blanches if described as conservative.

In writing to this market of males, you pull out all the stops. Your words are colorful to match the styles and you cater to the fantasies and self-image of these men who have broken the shackles that inhibited men's styles for so many years.

Three is the casual market. Here we have men who dress to please themselves, not others. Clothes selection is easy-going with the accent on comfort—open collars, sport shirts, denims, slacks with sport coats, slacks with sweaters or denim jackets, loafers.

Copy matches the mood of this man. You recognize his easy-going lifestyle, his interest in sports, and his desire to be individual in his dress. He likes to put combinations together to suit himself. You "suggest" to this person. You don't tell him that he must dress according to a fixed or prescribed mode.

Men's fashions have become subject to some of the volatility that has always characterized women's fashions. An illustration of this was shown by what happened when President-elect Carter announced that he would be wearing jeans at the White House. The story was headlined in all print media and given full treatment in broadcast media. Denim manufacturers, already worked to capacity, anticipated an avalanche of additional sales once the White House became the locale of scores of photographers snapping pictures of a denim-clad President of the United States. Denim, already a phenomenon for its acceptance by both sexes and its use for all occasions, was thus given a further boost up the ladder of total acceptability.

11

Writing Mail-Order Copy for Results, Part A

At this very moment, the owner of a small mail-order business deep in Vermont may be preparing an advertisement for maple syrup. This will be a small advertisement to run in the back pages of such magazines as *Better Homes and Gardens,* or *Ladies' Home Journal.* Another mail-order entrepreneur in Virginia is describing in enticing terms the delights of the succulent Virginia hams he would like readers to send for. He, too, uses small space advertisements to invite orders.

Thousands of hopeful people, running small businesses, seek sales through mail order for a staggering variety of goods. Sadly, many do not succeed. Perhaps their products are not right for the market or the times. Most often their advertising has no magic pulling power because the writers simply don't know how to do an entire selling job through advertising.

To balance these failures there are many successes. Currently, mail-order buying is reaching new peaks. There are many reasons for this. Costs for transportation and for fuel continue to rise, making trips to stores more expensive. More and more women are working and have less time to shop. Lastly, buying by mail order has achieved a general acceptance and this acceptance becomes even greater as the variety of purchases through mail order widens. In addition to a complete range of conventional goods, the mail-order business now includes many luxury items and even food, including meats, poultry, and gourmet items that are mailed packed in dry ice.

If you write mail-order copy for any of these items, you must do the complete sales job through words and illustrations alone. This means that those words capture interest, spur want or desire, overcome objections, and persuade the prospect to sign the order. In mail-order selling you have no alternative. There is no sales force to carry the burden. You are the sales force. If you don't create sales, you're a failure and your business fails, or if you're working for someone, that person goes out of business.

This direct responsibility for results is not necessarily the curse it may seem to be since mail-order selling produces such a prompt reaction—or lack of it—that you have an almost instant measure both of the effectiveness of your idea and of the success of your message. If they've proved "pretty good," you may be able to inject into your next message just the right touch needed to make it produce excellent results. If your first message obviously has proved "not so hot", you know at least that you'd better try another version of your idea or even a new idea. You may then, through analysis of the results of the first message, be able to spot the exact flaw.

Of course, you won't ignore the possibility that a poor reaction to a piece of mail-order selling and the accuracy of any analysis you may make of that reaction may depend somewhat on two other factors not basically a part of the advertising-sales effort—"product" and "prospects." If the product is poor or if the prospects are not reasonably well defined (and therefore not reached), reaction is fairly certain to be discouraging.

The single most important factor in mail-order success is the product. You must have a product people want. A poor product will hurt you more than poor copy in attaining results. Superb copy, on the other hand, can't sell a poor product.

MAIL ORDER ALSO SELLS SERVICES

Because of the nature of the selling method—mail order—the product offered is usually some item of merchandise. A service may, however, be sold by the mail-order method. Examples: a personal income-tax computing service, a manuscript

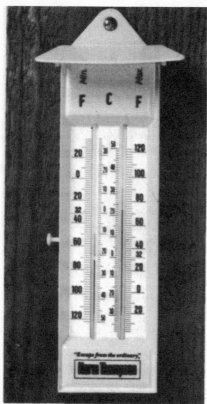

Gives you the day's high and low temperatures at a glance in both Fahrenheit & Centigrade.

Norm Thompson's new mini-max thermometer!

For use in greenhouse, lab, wine cellar…anywhere temperatures must be monitored and maintained.

We've never seen anything quite like this unique new contraption. It is actually two thermometers in one. You get a reading of the day's high and low temperatures and of course, the current temperature. The rising mercury pushes the indicator on the right to show the highest temperature, while the marker on the left records the day's low. Each indicator remains at the respective extreme of the day until the thermometer is reset with the pushbutton on the side of the case.

Great for both home and business.

Our new thermometer is useful anywhere temperature is a factor…in your greenhouse, home, lab…or for keeping your wine cellar at the correct temperature. For outdoor use, it features a removable, rotating weather shield to protect it from sunlight, snow or rain.

Easy to read … Centigrade and Fahrenheit.

The black and white graduations and blue minimum-maximum markers are simple to read and give you a reading in both Centigrade and Fahrenheit, which will come in handy when the U.S. converts to the metric system.

Built for accuracy and long life.

This new thermometer has no springs or magnets to get lost or wear out. There are no screws or bolts to work loose or rust. It's precision-made to give accurate readings and last a long time.

Order your thermometer today. Examine it carefully. See how it works. If you're not completely satisfied we'll refund your money in full. (See P. 2) .

No. 9330 . . . . $15.00

FIGURE 11-1

Mail-order advertisement.   Notice the stress on uniqueness and the emphasis on the all-around utility of the product. Also, an extra sales push is given in the reference to the thermometer's suitability when the metric system is adopted.

Parma Advertising for Norm Thompson Outfitters

---

criticism-correction service for amateur writers, and —yes—a mail-order copywriting service (on a fee basis) for small businesses which have no advertising agency or creative personnel of their own. Normally, such a small percentage of mail-order selling is of services—and so much of tangible goods—that throughout this discussion the terms "product," "item," "merchandise," and the like will be used to designate anything sold by mail order.

YOU WRITE TO SUIT THE MEDIUM

As in all advertising, in addition to knowing everything possible about product and prospects, you need the answer to one other major question before beginning to write your mail-order sales message, "How— through what medium—am I going to tell my prospects about my product?" The medium used affects not only the physical requirements of your message—its length, its layout, its illustration, its space for and location of headline, and so forth—but also the handling of your message. This handling may include the approach your copy takes, the use of attention-getting words and copy devices, the relative emphasis of appeals, and the inclusion (or exclusion) of other copy elements. You can see that you must ask, "What medium am I writing for?"

MAIL-ORDER KING—THE CATALOG

The "king" of mail-order media—at least the classic one, the "bible" of mail-order selling—is the mail-order catalog. Catalogs vary greatly, one from the other. Most famous are those merchandising tomes typified by the semiannual "big book" editions of Montgomery Ward & Company, Sears, Roebuck & Company, and J. C. Penney, their lesser "flyers" and other seasonal or special sales books. There are also the slimmer major volumes of the smaller general merchandise firms that sell by mail, together with their supplementary catalogs.

Next come the issues of still lesser houses which may limit themselves primarily to definite but still relatively broad fields. The increasingly famed fall and spring catalogs of L. L. Bean, of Freeport, Maine, exemplify this type. Another is Norm Thompson, Portland, Oregon. For luxury items, there is the Horchow Collection.

Finally come the specialty catalogs limited to one line or type of merchandise, such as seeds. Burpee's and Vaughan's are examples.

MAGAZINES AND NEWSPAPERS ARE IMPORTANT, TOO

Another important medium of mail-order selling is that of publications—magazines and newspapers—in which the advertiser buys space just as for any other advertisement. The difference, however, is that the mail-order advertiser hopes to receive immediate orders as a direct result of each advertisement, unlike many publication advertisers who build up desire for products over a period of time.

In the magazine field, typical publications in which appropriate items are successfully offered for sale by mail include many that on first thought might not be considered good mail-order media at all—high- and medium-class consumer specialty magazines in the home furnishings and fashion fields. *House and Garden, Better Homes and Gardens, Vogue,* and *Glamour* customarily devote special shopping sections to mail-order advertisements. The advertising columns of general magazines occasionally carry successful mail-order offerings, usually in small space advertisements because of the high rates of wide circulation publications.

Somewhat more commonly associated perhaps, with the mail-order selling of specialty types of merchandise, are those magazines appealing to certain classifiable economic, occupational, avocational, and/or social segments of the population. Typical examples of these might be:

- The pulp groups of movies, romance, adventure, and detective magazines appealing mostly to the people of modest education and income.
- The farming and livestock publications such as *Farm Journal.*
- Comics, and the children's and youth magazines.
- Sports and body-building publications and out-of-doors periodicals.
- Hobby publications such as home mechanics, amateur photography, arts, and antiques.
- The lower income and/or small town and rural magazines such as *Grit.*
- Publications appealing to specific racial groups such as *Ebony.*
- Magazines whose paid advertising columns are composed largely of mail-order offers—and whose readers over the years have come to regard them as "marketing places."

Newspapers, although handicapped by a relatively short life, offer many opportunities for successful mail-order advertising, especially in comic sections and Sunday magazine pages. The former have been important in reaching the youth market with box-top premium offers. An example of a strong mail-order Sunday magazine is the one that appears in the *New York Times*. A huge variety of mail-order offers appears in the pages of this publication.

MAIL-ORDER SELLING THROUGH DIRECT MAIL

A third general category in the field of mail-order media is that of mailing pieces, which usually make from one to several offers (a larger number, of course, would become a small catalog). Here is where the two branches of "remote control" advertising meet—in fact, are synonymous. This is direct mail mail-order selling. By joining the two "mails" you might merely call it "direct mail-order." Such pieces may take many forms, some of the more common ones being leaflets, circulars, return post cards (today usually with postage payment guaranteed by the vendor), letters, broadsides, booklets, brochures, envelope stuffers, and the like, or combinations of any two or more of these forms.

These may be sent in reply to a paid (or unpaid) response to some other advertising. Often they go out as individual mailings. At other times they are grouped with similar pieces making other offers and are sent out to mailing lists either maintained by the merchandiser himself, or rented or bought from a mailing-list service or another advertiser. Often, too, they are used as enclosures, perhaps with a department store's monthly statements to its charge account customers, or possibly enclosed with other purchases being sent from the store or from a mail-order house such as Alden's, Sears, Spiegel's, or Ward's.

USING THE AIR WAVES FOR MAIL ORDER

Some successes have been recorded in radio and television mail-order selling. For example, a small farm magazine through radio built up its paid circulation—in just a few months' time—by several hundred thousand subscribers. Each subscription was mailed in with a $1 bill. The subscribers lived in thirteen of the poorest states in the country. Radio coverage was only partial in several of the states and was supplied by a single radio station!

Individual stations are the mainstay of radio broadcast mail-order selling. Except for occasional premium or similar offers by national advertisers on network programs, most mail-order selling is done over local stations serving relatively limited areas, or, at the widest, perhaps over small sectional networks.

Television would seem to be the perfect medium for the mail-order advertiser with its ability to show the product better than in publication advertising and to show it in action. Then add its ability to demonstrate in the prospects' home, and you would seem to have an irresistible mail-order advertising force.

Unfortunately, there are problems. With the 30-second commercial the standard unit, there simply isn't time to do a full selling job needed for mail order and to spell out how the prospect should send for the item. Ordering instructions alone can swallow up most of the time.

Escalating television costs have also made the medium unappealing to mail-order advertisers who know very well that a great portion of the viewers exposed to the usual mail-order offer are not going to be interested. Thus television advertising becomes even more expensive because of the great waste circulation, unlike print advertising that can be directed selectively to a specific audience.

FIGURE 11-2

Mail-order radio commercial.   Desire for the product is built up through a series of questions. Also, the copy tells what the listener will get if the listener sends for the offer. A strong urge for action closes the commercial.

```
YOU KNOW THAT HIGH-FIBER DIETS ARE VITAL TO YOUR HEALTH.  BUT DO
YOU KNOW WHY?  DO YOU KNOW WHICH CEREAL PRODUCTS--BY BRAND NAME--
CONTAIN THE MOST FIBER?  AND--SINCE YOU CAN'T EAT ALL DAY LONG--
WOULDN'T YOU LIKE TO KNOW WHICH HIGH-CALORIE FOODS ARE ALSO RICH
IN FIBER?  AS WELL AS WHICH HIGH-CALORIE FOODS YOU CAN EAT--
WITHOUT ADDING WEIGHT?  SIMPLY BECAUSE OF THEIR HIGH FIBER?
THESE FACTS--AND MANY MORE--ARE IN A NEW, FORTY-TWO PAGE REPORT
CALLED FABULOUS FIBER, YOURS FREE FOR TRYING "PREVENTION"--THE
WORLD'S LARGEST HEALTH MAGAZINE.  FIND OUT WHY ALMOST TWO MILLION
HEALTH-CONSCIOUS SUBSCRIBERS DEPEND UPON "PREVENTION."  FIND OUT
NOW WHEN YOU GET A SPECIAL PRICE:  12 MONTHLY ISSUES FOR ONLY
FIVE-EIGHTY-FIVE, PLUS FABULOUS FIBER AND THIS GUARANTEE:  IF NOT
SATISFIED WITH THE FIRST ISSUE, JUST WRITE "CANCEL" ON THE
INVOICE YOU RECEIVE, AND RETURN IT.  YOU'LL OWE NOTHING.  YOU
ALSO KEEP THE FREE REPORT.  SEND NO MONEY NOW.  JUST PHONE
581-4200 IN NEW YORK.  THAT'S 581-4200.  OR WRITE "PREVENTION,"
CARE OF WOR, NEW YORK 10018.  TODAY!
```

AS MEDIA DIFFER— WRITING AND PROSPECTS DIFFER

If a pair of decorative wall plaques were to be advertised in magazines such as *House and Garden* and *Grit*, your copy would differ not only because your prospects were of a different economic and social status, but also because your advertising, to be effective in the medium in which it appears, must conform to the makeup of that type of medium. An advertisement planned, designed, and written for *Grit* will frequently look out of place if used in *Home and Garden*, and vice versa. With few exceptions, an advertisement that is out of its element will not produce successful results.

Assume, similarly, that the same product was being sold by radio or television mail order to different groups of prospects in the same general area. Not only would your programs differ but possibly your time of broadcast and the stations you use. Your copy, likewise, would probably be geared to each group despite the fact that the basic appeal to each group might be almost the same.

Assume for the moment that you are writing commercials for a large phonograph-record retailer, located in a medium-sized midwestern city. He handles a complete line of the records and volumes of all the major recording companies. He does a large mail-order business, but sells at regular retail prices (including postage, however).

It has been decided to push three types of records—classical music, jazz, and country western. This means three distinct markets must be reached, perhaps at three different times of the day or week. Depending upon the coverage and listening patterns of your local radio stations, you may use more than one of them to reach your markets.

Yet your programs will be similar in that all of them feature recordings (naturally!). So, too, will your commercials be similar, and yet they will vary widely. Your basic appeal to all three markets is almost certain to hinge on one idea—the convenience of getting any recordings you want without the bother of going to a store. Yet, just as you will vary your programs—although all will be music—to appeal to lovers of symphony, to youthful addicts of popular tunes, and to bluegrass devotees, so must you vary the appeal in your commercials to suit the varying situations of your audiences:

- To the rural audience: "Shop from your fireside—no need for a special trip to town; and avoid disappointment—our stocks are always complete."
- To the teen-agers: "Just drop us a note (or fill in an order blank—if they've been distributed) between classes or in the evening—don't miss that important class meeting, play rehearsal, or basketball game just to come downtown (or into town) to buy a record."
- To the serious-music appreciator: "A new concert's just as near as your desk (or your phone—if charge accounts are permitted or C.O.D. deliveries encouraged)—avoid a long bus ride, traffic jam, and parking worries downtown."

To everyone, of course, goes the general story of "same-day" service, of quality products at standard prices including packing and mailing costs, of satisfaction or your money back—and perhaps a long-life needle as a premium with each order of so many dollars. Most likely you will write even such "standard" parts of the commercials in a different style and in different words for each audience. If you do, then you've adapted your copy to your media; and, other factors being favorable, you should have a set of successful mail-order commercials.

MAIL-ORDER WRITING

Assume, now, that your product is one that can be sold to your prospects, and that the medium selected is an effective one for reaching the prospects at low cost. The next question is how to induce those prospects to make purchases. What are you going to do that will make the potential customer order? The results depend on how effectively you present the merchandise.

Like running a store by mail

Since you are the salesperson, compare your job with the selling process of the owner of a small specialty shop. The shop owner first of all creates an inviting window display to attract the casual shopper or passerby into the store. Assume that he does go in. The shop owner gives him a close-up view of the merchandise—opens it up or takes it apart, giving a sales talk point by point. He answers the customer's questions and meets his objections. Finally, as the customer is about convinced to buy, he presents his final sales point—the clincher—an irresistible reason for not postponing the purchase. Then, ideally, the customer says, "I'll take it," and lays his cash on the counter.

That's the ideal sale. It's exactly what you hope to do with your mail-order offering. Your show window that stops your prospect is your display (in type and illustration), or the opening words of your commercial. Your copy (and detailed views, if any) comprise your close-up of the product, and your sales talk. Next, because you're not face-to-face with the prospect, you have to anticipate what his questions and objections are most likely to be, and work the answers into your sales talk (keeping them in a positive vein, of course) as you write. Then you weave in your clincher— why it's important or necessary to order now—frequently a matter of limited supply, a special price for a short time, or perhaps a premium for promptness. So far you've pretty well paralleled the retail sales procedure.

At this point your retail customer would say, "Wrap it up" and dig into his wallet. You'd take his money and hand him the change and his parcel. It's not that simple in mail-order selling since the customer—the prospect—still has one more step to take on his own. He has to make out his order (perhaps getting out paper, envelope, and a stamp), probably write a check (or quite possibly going to a bank or post office to buy a money order), and then mail the order to your firm. Not only do you have to make these extra steps simple and easy as possible, but you must also make your whole offer seem so attractive that the customer doesn't mind the extra work.

The extra attraction you must weave into your mail-order copy is difficult to define but might be explained by saying that you write in a somewhat "higher key" so that your copy reads or is heard at a higher pitch. Perhaps some of this is the result of your urge to immediate action. This feeling, nevertheless, is often an integral part of the entire advertisement. Perhaps a careful look at each element of the mail-order sale will show what's required to give the entire advertisement its high pitch. Begin with the headline.

Your display windows—headlines

Although you have already read a discussion of headlines, the mail-order headline presents enough

4 pages from your daily newspaper can cook a steak to perfection in less than 6 min.

About 15 years ago, on our first trip to Africa, we saw natives in the northern frontier district of Kenya broiling meat on strange looking pots with holes in the bottom. Using rolled up balls of grass for fuel, they were really cooking up a storm.

Needless to say, we were intrigued. We did a little looking, and found that a British engineer stationed in Johannesburg had also observed this unusual device and perfected it by using a rolled steel barrel and newspaper. We know it's hard to believe, but this thing really does work. We like to call it the Zulu's answer to microwave ovens . . . only a lot cheaper version. In fact, if you consider the money you'll save on charcoal and lighter fluid in just one season, Norm Thompson's Shikari Grill will literally pay for itself.

Fast and efficient . . . the Shikari Grill cooks just about anything.

We guarantee it . . . a succulent steak, medium broiled to tasty perfection over live flames in just 6 minutes. There's no charcoal or lighter fluid to mess with, no waiting for coals to glow. Just crumple newspaper into a ball, light a match, and instantly you're cooking.

Steaks, hamburgers, hot dogs, chops, spareribs, fish and chicken . . . you can even boil water. Meat cooks in its own juices over scientifically air-controlled flames. (The Shikari Grill works on the principle of controlled combustion. Natural fat dripping over charred paper keeps the fire going.) You get better tasting food and it's actually more healthful because you use fat for fuel instead of eating it.

Compact and completely portable.

Norm Thompson's Shikari Grill comes in a compact heavy cardboard box that serves as a carrying case. It measures only 12"x12"x8" so it's really easy to take along . . . anywhere! It's great for just about anything from a summer picnic at the beach to a winter barbecue at a ski resort.

Safe and easy to use in your fireplace.

This is one outdoor grill you'll want to use year 'round. Use it in your fireplace for delicious outdoor flavor any time. And

since combustion is complete, there's little or no mess to clean up afterwards. That goes for utensils too! There's no need for forks or spatulas because the entire grid turns over rather than turning each piece of meat. The unique "stay-cool" handles simply don't get hot, so you won't even need hot pads.

Transform ordinary food into delicacies.

There's probably nothing more ordinary than the good ol' hot dog. But even the hot dog can be turned into a delicacy on the Shikari Grill. Just wrap each tube steak in a strip of bacon and secure it with a toothpick. Put it on the grill, light a match, and in about 3 minutes you'll be eating the best hot dog that you've ever had.

Completely guaranteed.

Order your Shikari Grill today and test it any way you like. If you're not completely satisfied in every respect, simply pack it up and send it back to us. We'll refund your money . . . no questions asked. You get everything you need . . . 3 section barrel, nickel plated grid, and instructions.

No. 9005 . . . . $15.00

You can use the Shikari Grill in your fireplace for delicious outdoor flavor anytime.

Compact carry case measures only 12"x12"x8".

Shikari Grill

57

FIGURE 11-3

Mail-order advertisement.   Several points are noteworthy here. First is the headline that combines benefit with curiosity. Second, there is the interesting narrative opening that provides a background for the unusual product. Third, there is the enthusiastic copy that rushes along knocking down all possible doubts and questions. Fourth, the selling subheads keep the prospect reading to the end.

Parma Advertising for Norm Thompson Outfitters

individual problems to make it worth some extra attention. Whatever appears in display-size type in your advertisement can be considered headline material. It's the "show window"—the attention-getter—of your "shop." It may be more than merely the first display line; it may consist of several such lines placed in various parts of the advertisement. Most frequently, it includes a large display price—sometimes the most prominent display element of all.

Why you should buy your shearling lamb-skin coat <u>by mail</u> from Norm Thompson.

We've spent more than 16 years testing and comparing shearling coats from all over the world. Our goal has always been to offer our customers the finest coats available for the best possible price. We don't like to be called experts, but we think our experience makes us a pretty good judge of quality and value when it comes to shearling lambskin coats. On the following pages you'll find what we consider to be the "cream of the crop." Compare them to any other coats of their kind on the market. We're confident you'll find they're the best to be found anywhere, at any price.

■ **Style:** We make sure the styles we offer are classics. Fine shearling coats like these have been known to last 25 years and longer ... so it just doesn't make sense to risk a gimmicky design that may become dated after just one or two years.

■ **Handcraftsmanship:** Luxurious shearling coats require scores of hand operations to be made properly. Machines simply can't perform the intricate stitching and finishing that it takes to insure perfection. Norm Thompson shearling coats are handcrafted by a firm with more than 300 years of experience. From start to finish they expend six weeks and over 600 individual steps to produce each coat.

■ **Practicality:** Here's where our 16 years of experience really become important. We maintain strict controls on the production of each coat. They're fashioned from the lightest, most supple lambskins available. There's no restriction or binding ... just natural comfort you can wear from the first crisp days of autumn to the last chilly evenings of spring. And Norm Thompson shearlings **will not waterspot** ... we guarantee it. A special tanning process eliminates this problem. And unlike most suede fashions, soils can be simply brushed away. Your shearling can be drycleaned, although it'll rarely need it.

■ **Sizes:** We make sure our coats are cut to fit true American sizes, and we stock a full range for both men and women. Men's even sizes: 36-50 reg., 38-50 longs. Women's even sizes: 6-20. We've learned how to give our customers a proper fit by mail so you can expect to receive a coat that looks and feels great.

Backed by our uncompromising guarantee of satisfaction.

Order your shearling coat today. When it arrives, really test it. Experience the unordinary comfort and downright good looks of natural shearling. If for any reason you aren't completely satisfied with it, simply return the coat to us insured, postage prepaid and we'll refund your money.

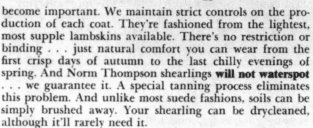

To assure perfection, master craftsmen hand-cut each coat.   Carefully matched skins are marked to fit American standard sizes.   For complete flexibility, edges are trimmed to eliminate bulky seams.   Each coat is hand-finished and carefully inspected by experts.

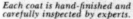

Luxuries you don't have to treat like luxuries.

A lot of people have a tendency to think of a genuine shearling coat as a luxurious garment that requires constant care and grooming. They're half right. It is a luxurious garment, but a Norm Thompson shearling coat is made to be worn and enjoyed.

We're not suggesting that you invent ways of abusing your coat, but you don't have to treat it like a fragile piece of crystal either.

Cut for action ... made better for many years of wear.

One of the most important things we look for when choosing a shearling coat to offer our customers is practicality. And you can bet that we test each style to make sure

it meets our standards. The coats featured in this catalog are specially designed for people who want to do more than stand in the corner and look good ... they're built for action.

Don't let it just hang in the closet ... wear it!

Go ahead. Take a walk in the rain. Tackle your husband or wife this winter and roll them around in the snow. Really use your shearling coat ... that's what it's for. When you're finished playing in it, give it a good brushing and wear it to the most elegant restaurant in town. We guarantee it'll attract many admiring glances. It's a very practical luxury.

FIGURE 11-4

Mail-order advertisement.   Here is mail-order selling at its finest and most persuasive. This page introduces a number of pages that show and describe shearling coats. Because these coats cost from $200 to $385, they must be sold. Notice the intensely personal character of the copy as in the section that says "Go ahead. Take a walk in the rain. Tackle your husband or wife . . ." Although the copy is long, detailed, and specific, it is so lively and intimate that readership is almost insured.

Parma Advertising for Norm Thompson Outfitters

Considered alone, this physical handling (layout) of the headline material imparts a large measure of its high pitch—its aura of urgency. Mail-order headlines are frequently written in a more exciting style than for usual consumer advertising. They may be exhortative, like:

Don't Give in to Gray Hair

Save on Farm Income Taxes Before April 15th

Look Taller Instantly

Make Beaded SEQUIN Lapel Pins—Easy at Home

Now! Be Stunning in a Rainstorm

Remove Any Stump

Treasure Your Baby's Tooth

Each one is a command to action as well as an appeal to some need or desires.

Others, by brevity alone—a sort of terse index quality—impart a feeling of urgency:

Nylon Parachutes (*not for aviation use*)

Delphinium

New Miracle Wall Cleaner

Feet Hurt?

Gardenia Plants

LAW

Orchard Fresh Holly (*for Christmas*)

Wristwatch—Military Style

Some of these index headings include a selling word or two; others none, except possibly by inference. Display lines in other advertisements rely for their excitement primarily on exclamatory sentences or phrases:

At Last You Can Throw Away Your Worn-out Mop for a New All-Purpose DeFold Cleaner

Two Bushels of Ripe Tomatoes from One Vine

3 Crochet Beauties Easy to Make

Lifetime Knife Cuts Anything

The Oriental Symbol of Power

At Home, Your Own Manufacturing Business

For Lusty He-Men

Stops Moth Damage for 5 Years or Pays the Damage

The attention-getter—price

Price is frequently a compelling element of attention-getting display type. Most of the headlines quoted so far have not relied on price display to compel attention. Most of those cited, however, could have done that, too. Probably more mail-order selling is dependent upon price appeal for compelling interest than on any other one factor. A few examples in each of the headline categories cited above will show you how price is an important if not dominant display factor in much mail-order selling. Price may be a part of the exhortative display:

Print Your Own Post Cards—Complete Outfit Only $9.50

Embroider Add-a-Squares to Make a Priceless Linen Tablecloth—Inexpensive Starting Kit Only $2.00 Postpaid.

Dutch Bulbs—Plant this Fall!—Dollar Specials (*Followed by nine offerings each with $2 prominently displayed*)

Men! Appear Slim'n'Trim in Only 5 Seconds with this Amazing Abdominal Supporter Belt! Only $6.98.

The index heading is often combined with, or even dominated by, price:

12 Hardy Phlox $2 Postpaid

Hemstitcher—Button Holer—Both for $2.00

New "Shooter's Bible" $2.50 Postpaid

65 Gorgeous Tulips Only $2 Postpaid

Carpenters and Builders Guides—4 Vols. $6.—($1 per mo.)
(*the "$1" alone appears in type almost as high as the heading*)

Price often complements the exclamatory display treatment and sometimes provides its climax:

New Easy Way Makes Button Holes, Hemstitches, with Your Own Sewing Machine—Special Offer, Reg. $2 Value, Both for Only $1.
(*The two attachments offered are listed in small type under "Special Offer."*)

Compare this entire display treatment with the index-plus-price display for a similar offer:

At Last! Shirts that Kiddies Can Truly Call Their Own—Personalized Polos—$2.65 Postpaid.

A Lot of Greenhouse for $264.

For the first time—the design of fabulous earrings costing up to $3300 copied to look like the expensive originals to cost you $1, $2, & $3 pr. Can you tell the difference?
(*The prices in huge, black type*)

Irresistible Offer! Flowering-Size Darwin Tulips, 100 Bulbs $3.69.

Yes, price is certainly an important display element in attracting attention to a mail-order offering.

"Implying" price is effective

Attractive values or prices are sometimes merely implied in the wording of the display copy—a more subtle method but effective if adroitly handled. Two or three illustrations can make this technique clear:

Buy Direct from Factory—Seamless Plastic Garment Bags

Now . . . a Home that "Grows With Your Income"— Total Cost of Materials . . . Less than $8,000" (*Selling house plans for $2 to $5*)

Easy to Make Beautiful Rugs from Old Clothing (*A patented hooking-type needle.*)

New Direct Mail Plan Saves You Big Money (*For auto seat covers, with their low prices in relatively small display type.*)

Note the economy appeal implicit in " . . . for your money," "buy direct from factory," " . . . rugs from old clothing," and others.

Naturally, no law or custom dictates that every piece of mail-order display must fall into the exhortative, index, or exclamatory classifications. Not only may plenty of examples of advertisements that stray from these categories be seen any time, but often, too, any or all of them may be combined effectively. An abdominal belt advertisement display might, for instance, read something like this:

Men! It's Amazing! Send only $6.98 at Once for this Abdominal Belt that Makes You Appear Slim 'n' Trim in Only 5 Seconds! Don't Delay—Act Today!

Corny, sure. Probably effective, too, with certain prospects.

Pulling orders through catalogs and direct mail

Mail-order display lines quoted thus far have been extracted primarily from publication advertisements, but most of them would be "at home" in many direct-mail-order pieces or in mail-order catalogs. In many of these pieces and catalogs, it is assumed that at least a certain portion of the reader's attention already has been obtained. Certainly in the case of a direct-mail-order piece, hundreds of other items, plus a lot of interesting editorial matter, are not screaming for his attention. As for the catalog, once he's opened the cover, you know the reader has at least some interest in your collection of offerings or he wouldn't have got that far. In such cases, unless price, or perhaps something essentially emotional, is your basic appeal, you will probably use material for your major display that either tells some pertinent fact about your product or else identifies it categorically, and perhaps includes at least a mention of one or two of its features.

A direct-mail-order mailing to a list of business-people, for example, includes a small six-page folder with the following display (and illustrations) on the first three pages as the piece is unfolded:

Page 1	How Will Washington's Next Move Affect *You*? (*Uncle Sam's hand reaches for knight, presumably on a chess board.*)
Page 2	It Will Pay You to Know! *Today*, More Than Ever Before, You Need Reliable Facts and Forecasts from the Nation's Capital. (*The Capitol, set on a chess board.*)
Page 3	Plan *Your* Moves Wisely . . . Safely with Kiplinger Washington Letters. (*Following this is an opening half-page of body copy.*)

The salutation on the letter accompanying the folder reads, "This May Be What You Have Been Waiting For . . . ," followed by an "invitation" to accept a special three-month trial subscription offer. Also included in the mailing are a current copy of the forecast, an order card ("We accept your invitation . . . etc."), and a return envelope, postage to be paid by addressee.

A similar mailing—this time a publisher's offering sent out by local bookstores to their own mailing lists—includes a nearly business letter-size six-page folder (folded once more for mailing)—almost a broadside. Profusely illustrated by extracts from the book being sold, this mailing piece also makes use of dominating type displays which frequently ignore the folds to streak across two or more pages. Heads and subheads comprising the major display elements read like this:

| Page 1 | The Largest, Most Complete Book of Maps Ever Published in America . . . Self-Revising Feature . . . Actual size 13½ by 20. (*Large illustration of man using the book, its title, Hammond's New World Atlas prominently displayed.*) |
| Pages 2 3,4 | Opens to a Size Much Larger Than Your Daily Newspaper! . . . This Atlas Measures Fully 27 Inches Across . . . and 20 Inches Deep! Size Closed, 13½ Inches by 20 Inches. (*Most of this three-page spread is devoted to illustration of a typical spread from the atlas.*) |

In all, this folder-broadside contains only six blocks of body copy and only three of these are large. It relies almost entirely upon display headings, subheads, and illustration to get its message across—swiftly, interestingly, completely. This piece is accompanied only by a return (postage guaranteed) postcard, on its order side, in prominent display: "Mail This Card to Secure Your Copy of Hammond's New World Atlas."

If you have seen any mailings of some of the smaller mail-order houses, you will know that the display copy they use can be just as exhortative and exclamatory as the most extreme of mail-order offerings advertised in publications. That this treatment is effective for those prospects to whom such product offerings are most often sent is proved by the fact that the style of presentation has not changed in the years which have seen mail-order catalog advertising, for example, assume a great deal more dignity.

Catalog copy is quieter these days

Mail-order catalog display—especially by the larger houses—is no longer generally typified by the exhortative, exclamatory headlines (except perhaps in special sales editions) so often formerly associated with them. Where catalog display copy now exceeds purely index headings, more often than not it uses the phraseology more typical of many newspaper retail advertisements by national advertisers. Some examples picked at random from a Sears, Roebuck catalog will illustrate:

Fit for a little king! Luxury quality Honeysuckle Crib . . . with full, rounded panels, toe-touch drop sides, maple or birch finish.

Twice As Warm . . . double-woven wool fleece over-coats.

Sears proves that fine bags can be low priced.

You'll feel lovelier, wearing Luxurious Lace-Trimmed Slips.

Dress Forms . . . Handy Stand-ins to streamline your sewing, make fitting easier.

Protect your gun from dirt, moisture, scratches.

Use Sears Laboratory Approved Packaging Materials for freezing foods . . . for freshness, flavor, vitamins.

It's "sew" saving to do your upholstering.

Craftsman Flexible Shafts . . . Many tools in one!

Top Carriers save space . . . More comfort inside your car.

You can now convert 10 back-breaking jobs into fast, easy, profitable farm work. (*portable power saw*)

For poultry profits, it's breeding that counts!

Blast Horns command attention.

Wash your windshield while you drive!

Readers of catalogs have built-in interest

When you write display lines for a mail-order catalog page or item, you still want to attract the interest of your prospects. Yet, they are more truly prospects than are the casual readers of a magazine, because they already are, or want to be, customers of your firm—as is evidenced by their having your catalog. When looking at the catalog, they are usually in a buying mood—at least for a certain type of product. When they turn to that item, then what you've said in your display headings about the product focuses their attention more sharply on it or its features. But if your display fails to interest them, they may turn to your competitor's catalog—or decide to go to a store to shop. Although lacking competition for attention, you still have competition for the order. What you say in your headlines (or in major subheads if the main heading is essentially the index type), and in your other display lines, may well affect the prospect's interest and so in turn influence his decision to purchase from you.

Most mail-order copy uses the direct approach

Almost all mail-order display copy is direct and to the point. Whether you say,

Develop a torso the girls will admire!

Quick-drying, one-coat flat oil paint—
one coat looks like two!

you tell something immediately about the product or the results of its use or application. You do essentially the same thing if you are just a little less direct and write, instead,

The girls never even used to look twice at me on the beach

You wouldn't think one coat of paint
could make such a difference in a room!

You'd scarcely, however, write a headline for a mail-order muscle-building course that says, "I'd Rather Stay Home With a Book," or for one-coat wall paint, "I Never Enjoyed Entertaining the Smiths Until Tonight." No, you certainly wouldn't use these as major display lines for mail-order selling. They aren't mail-order selling. They may represent a technique suitable for a campaign in which you hope to build up an impression over a period of time, but a mail-order sale, nine times out of ten, is an immediate sale—often even an impulse sale.

The first caption you write, as you rough out, experimentally, your first draft of copy, may be just as indirect as the last two examples. If so, you'll find yourself hastening almost automatically to add a second display line which tells something much more meaty about your product or the direct advantages of its use. Next you discover that you can either eliminate the first line entirely, or at least incorporate its basic idea merely as a minor lead-in element of the second line. It will then be likely that you've written a display line that's a real stopper—you've set up a "show window" that brings the prospect right into your "store."

SHOW WINDOWS FOR RADIO MAIL ORDER

A program can be a form of window but many commercials have no program connected to them. You'll have to create a window. Sound effects and music can be used very effectively at times. Usually, however, you create your show window with arresting, attention-getting words, and phrases.

Perhaps you will use a direct address:

Snowmobilers—keep warm on the trail this winter . . .

Tennis players—Jimmy Connor's advice is . . .

Football fans—like the real story behind those headlines? . . .

FIGURE 11-5

Small space mail-order advertisement.   Orders came in from better than one out of five persons who sent for the free catalog offer. This advertisement was by far the best of eight test advertisements. The magical word "free" undoubtedly helped placed, as it was, in the headline.

For a less direct approach, there are many phrases that can be used:

Here's good news . . .

At last, there's an answer to . . .

Everyone's a winner when he . . .

If you want a new experience, try . . .

Getting in a rut? Here's how to get out.

There's a sure-fire way to . . .

The first words in a radio message are important because the average radio listener is giving half-attention, or no attention, to the commercials. You need to pull him out of his indifference. Jar him to wakefulness with a statement that makes it clear that it might be profitable to listen to what the announcer is saying.

How to hold attention of radio listeners

As in print, you want the show window of your commercial to do more than merely to arouse attention. You want it to inspire interest as well—listener-interest sufficient to hold that attention throughout your message. So you write into your next sentence or sentences immediately following your stopper phrase or device some idea or thought that will be of interest to the largest group of prospects among your listeners. This opening thought is the

"display" of your commercial. See how these sample opening lines, all of them from successful mail-order commercials, are written to hold the attention of the greatest number of potential prospects for the offers which follow:

Friends, the record you just heard, and any others you hear on the _____ (an evening-long program with several co-sponsors), can be bought from _____'s Records-by-Mail. It's the new, easy way for you to buy the records you want . . ."

Ladies . . . Here's how you can easily win a complete five-piece bedroom set, a portable electric Singer Sewing Machine, and 101 additional valuable prizes . . . (Quilt-patch bundle offer, a contest entry blank accompanying each bundle ordered.)

Folks, due to a very special purchase, the makers of the nationally advertised _____ combination cigarette case and lighter . . . for a limited time only . . . will send you a remarkable three-dollar-ninety-five cent value . . . at the rock bottom bargain price of only one-dollar-ninety-eight!

Folks—wouldn't you be thrilled to win a new Ford station wagon or equivalent in cash, just by taking part in a simple, interesting game? . . . (contest sponsored by rural magazine, each contest entry to be accompanied by $1 for magazine subscription.)

Say, folks, what musical instrument do you think is the easiest and quickest to learn to play? (harmonica offer)

An extra display line may be inserted occasionally in the middle of your commercial—an additional interest pepper-upper—just in case attention to your message lags a bit after the first excitement has subsided. This is akin to a prominent subhead or second display line. About a third of the way through the commercial for the cigarette case/lighter combination, for example, we find, "But that's just the first half of this sensational offer! Second, you will receive the world's smallest ball-point pen, complete with key chain!" Here the advertiser has reserved part of his offering for use as a midway "headline."

You'll write headlines and subheads into your mail-order selling for almost identically the same purpose that you'd decorate the show window of your specialty shop—and set up supplementary displays inside—to attract and hold your prospect's attention and interest until he hears your complete message and decides to make the purchase.

These are not passive headlines and subheads. They're active, vigorous messages that inform, excite, move to action, and literally pull the reader along. The subhead comes into its own in mail-order and direct mail. Unlike so much of nonmail-order magazine and newspaper advertising that uses no subheads, the mail-order advertisement—no matter what the printed medium—uses subheads generously. Long copy will never put your prospect to sleep if it's broken up with lively subheads. This is a lesson that must be learned by those who have written other types of copy lacking the powerful, throbbing push of mail-order copy.

12

Writing Mail-Order Copy for Results Part B

HOW TO WRITE CATALOG COPY

Just as in advertising in other media, your appeal in catalog copy is based on the product's ability to satisfy the desires of your prospects. One difference, however, is that you use "tell-all" copy. This means that first you imagine all the ways your item can answer the wants or desires of your prospects. Then, you include as many of these ways as possible in your message. Your hope is that you will thus interest the majority of your potential customers.

Few advertisements in general media, such as newspapers or magazines, offer an opportunity for tell-all copy, but then such advertisements are not expected to do the entire selling task. Tell-all copy requires space and a willingness on the part of readers to read a long copy message. Catalog readers have that willingness. Furthermore, they will read a message in print much smaller than that used in the usual general media advertisement.

Some of the most persuasive mail-order copy in the United States is found in the Norm Thompson catalogs that come out of Portland, Oregon. Notice in the copy for a wool blend jacket (Figure 12-1) how all possible details are given without causing the writing to bog down. This is tell-all copy at its finest. Note, too, the use of subheads to break up the type mass.

Use the language of the prospect

Another type of mail-order catalog offering may be quite different. As was said before, not only must you know what to say to your prospects, but how to say it.

Note the illustration and listing from L. L. Bean's catalog. "But," you ask, "where are the major selling points highlighted to attract and interest the reader? There are only small pictures and an index heading!" You must remember that this is a specialty catalog

for hunters and out-of-door men and women. Here's one case, admittedly a rather exceptional one, where because of the limited appeal of the class of merchandise, the field of prospects is limited, too. Almost everyone reading this catalog reads nearly every listing on practically every page. Because this catalog enjoys this unique advantage, its manner of obtaining attention and maintaining interest in itself and in its offerings is not so apparent as in other publications.

We've taken a traditional jacket style ...combined it with our special wool blend fabric, and come up with a garment that's extremely good looking, exceptionally comfortable and surprisingly durable. We call it the Knockabout because you can wear it for just about any casual activity, give it day-in, day-out punishment and always expect to look your very best while wearing it.

The style of our new Knockabout jacket has been around for a number of years. Some historians claim that it is one of the original golf jacket designs. Others say it was developed for bicycling in the late 1800's. In any case, it is clearly a style that lends itself to active leisure pursuits.

It features a waist-length cut and a convenient zippered front. Raglan sleeves add to the roominess of the Knockabout giving you plenty of action room. Elastic inserts at the waist provide a trim fit. At the wrists you'll find a double-button arrangement that can be adjusted to keep the cold out. A storm collar provides added protection. And finally, there are

two roomy slash pockets that have been carefully placed to serve as comfortable arm rests.

As you can see, there are no frills on the Knockabout...just functional features and clean, classic styling.
Made of a lightweight wool blend.

The Knockabout is fashioned from a mixture of 85% wool with 15% nylon. This gives you the comfort and protection of natural wool with the added strength and long-wear of nylon. And, this blend breathes to keep you comfortable in a wide range of temperatures. We honestly feel this is one of the most practical fabrics you can wear because it offers the benefits of wool plus the improvements of a modern synthetic.
Your satisfaction is guaranteed!

Like every item we sell, the Knockabout is backed by our "You be the Judge™" guarantee. (See P. 2).

Color: Grey herringbone. Men's sizes: S, M, L, XL, XXL to fit 36-50.
No. 6550 . . . . **$38.50**
XXL (48-50) **$41.50**

FIGURE 12-1

Advertisement with tell-all copy.

Another unique advantage which obviates the necessity for any specifically stated claims of quality or value is the reputation of the firm and the integrity behind the name L. L. Bean, which has become synonymous over a period of years with a good buy at a fair price. These are things not easy to acquire, and lucky is the mail-order copywriter in such a situation.

FIGURE 12-2

Mail-order advertisement with a common theme. All six items relate to survival in woods. Notice the use of index heads and the simple copy that gives all needed facts to the reader—a typical page from one of America's favorite mail-order catalogs for outdoors enthusiasts.

Silva Safari Compass

Silva 16 sighting system for high-accuracy bearings. Liquid filled housing stops needle oscillation in four seconds. Rotates for setting point to point course from map or sighting. Graduation 0° to 360°. Scales on base plate in mm and inches. Size closed: 2" x 3". Weight 2 oz. Instructions included.

6386C Silva Safari Compass, $12.25 postpaid.

Ranger-type 15 Compass. Used by foresters, geologists, surveyers, scientific explorers and others demanding extreme accuracy, convenient plotting features and reliability. 2¼" diam. compass housing, large protractor plate, highly magnetized needle, luminous points (for night sighting) and sighting mirror. Built-in mechanism to adjust for magnetic declination. Scales on base plate in mm and inches. Size closed: 2½" x 4". Weight 3 oz.

6381C Silva Ranger Compass, $23.50 postpaid.

Safari

Ranger

Rescue Blanket

An emergency blanket of metallized PVC—windproof and waterproof. Unfolds to 56" x 84". Reflects more than 90 percent of the covered person's body heat. Tough enough to make a blanket litter. Orange color on one side for high visibility and silver on the other for maximum reflectivity of search and flashlights. Shirt pocket size. Weight 2 oz.

6362C Rescue Blanket, $3.00 postpaid.

"Boony Box" Survival Kit

Provides the basic needs for wilderness survival for one or two nights - a time period sufficient for most survival situations. Because it is compact and light in weight (5 oz.), it is conveniently carried (and not left in camp). In addition, several of its features, such as the compass, fire starter and sharpening stone can be used every day making the "Boony Box" doubly useful.

Sturdy 1" x 2½" x 4" ABS plastic container with top of molded rubber has a reliable, easy-to-read liquid filled "turnable" compass mounted on the side. Includes flint, tinder and striker, sharpening stone, map reading scales, moleskin and gauze bandages, signal whistle, signal mirror and a 3' x 4' aluminized blanket. Extra space for personal medicines, aspirin, salt tablets, or water purifiers, etc. Instructions included. Color: Yellow with Orange Top.

6365C "Boony Box", $11.95 postpaid.

Sportsman's Signal Kit

A compact, lightweight (5 oz.) kit containing a variety of signaling devices. To attract help when lost in any terrain, in any weather conditions. Contains a "Ten Mile" signal mirror with an optical grid for sighting, a fire starter kit, a red smoke flare (For daytime use) and two high altitude red magnesium flares visible up to 20 miles. Safe and reliable to use. Complete with instructions and orange belt pack. Size 3" x 5" x 2".

6363C Sportsman's Signal Kit, $9.75 postpaid.

Bean's Belt Pouches

Strong, three-ply waterproof fabric or soft glove tanned cowhide. Nylon zipper, leather pull tabs and metal belt loops. Designed to carry fly and lure boxes, personal accessories and small tools. Fits comfortably on belt. Size 8" long x 5½" deep x 2" wide.

5245C Waterproof Belt Pouch. Two colors: Tan. Green. (Both with leather trim.) Weight 4 oz. **$4.25 postpaid.**

5246C Leather Belt Pouch. Color, Brown. Weight 5 oz. **$7.75 postpaid.**

Also available in Fluorescent Orange for high visibility and hunting safety. Strong, water resistant vinyl coated fabric. Weight 3 oz.

5244C Orange Belt Pouch, $3.75 postpaid.

New Beef Jerky

Hand cut from pure beef flank steaks. Marinated in select spices, then smoked and dried with applewood for more tenderness and flavor. Thicker, more flavorful and individually wrapped in cellophane.

No refrigeration required. Each strip weighs ¼ oz. Several can be carried in pocket when hiking, for a handy snack or emergency use.

Box of 20 sticks, gross weight 7.5 oz.

8183C New Beef Jerky, Box of 20 sticks, $5.50 postpaid.

82 **L. L. Bean, Inc. Freeport, Me.**

Of course, it should also be noted that this firm does not seem to be overly anxious to expand its list of prospects greatly. Therein, perhaps, lies part of the reason for the seeming lack of more aggressive selling usually considered normal for any merchandising house.

Despite its seemingly naive, artless style, the copy sells hard. There is a simple directness that is persuasive and disarming.

Notice, too, the clear-cut, simple explanations that tell all. There is conviction in these words—much more than most "hard-hitting" copy could achieve in pages of superlatives. This is intelligent, mail-order copy. Much of it has been written by people who have tried in the fields and woods most of the products. For these specialized products, offered through this unique medium, to this definite group of prospects this copy is difficult to match.

ADVERTISEMENTS IN PUBLICATION

Mail-order selling in other media has the same job to do and does it usually through the same copy formula of appealing to as many of the potential prospects as can be reached in one advertisement without scattering the message so widely that it hits no one. Unless the publication itself is limited in circulation pretty much to one class of people, your display will have to do the job of attracting the attention and arousing the interest of the particular field of prospects to whom you are writing.

The hemstitcher-button holer index headline cited earlier in this chapter, just by the prominence of these words in display type, almost automatically attracts people who sew, and perhaps some who wish they could, away from what probably are less specifically or more obscurely worded headlines. Then follows immediately this fact-packed selling copy:

> HEMSTITCHER—Hemstitch on any sewing machine with this handy attachment. Does two-piece, criss-cross, inlaid, circular and hemstitching for pleats; also tucking, smocking and picoting. Makes rugs, comforters, slippers, etc. out of any material. Easy directions included.
>
> BUTTON HOLER—Makes button holes on your sewing machine instead of by hand. Also darns stockings, sews buttons, zippers; and can be used for quilting. Sews in any direction—front, back or sideways.
>
> SEND NO MONEY—Merely send your name, address and pay postman $4.00 plus postage on arrival. Or, send $4.00 with order, and we mail postage paid. You risk nothing. Satisfaction guaranteed or your money back. *(Company name, department, and address.)*

Once more—and this time in a 2-inch by 1-inch column advertisement including two illustrations and a display price—is found all the pertinent detail necessary to satisfy any sewer who has $4 to invest in a "satisfaction guaranteed or your money back" purchase. It does, within its physical limits, the complete selling job. No wonder many mail-order advertisements have no white space! In fact, the sales job can be done in even less space, as is proved by this 1-inch by 1-inch-column "Delphinium" advertisement, another of the index headline group (this time without illustration, which is hardly needed to sell non-special variety flowers to experienced gardeners):

> DELPHINIUM—Giant flowering magnificent double-type 2-year plants that have bloomed. Gorgeous colorings range from deepest blues, lavenders with pink tints to the wonderful bi-colorings that rival orchids. You will have 3- to 5-foot flowering spikes with flowers 2 to 3 inches across. 6 for $1.50; 12 for $2.50. Cash orders prepaid or sent C.O.D. plus charges. Return at once for refund if not satisfied. GIVEN with $2.50 orders "Million Dollar" Mystery Bloom Peony, $1 value. *(Company name, department, address)* Clip this.

A beginning copywriter sometimes feels insulted when he's asked to do a 1-inch advertisement. He usually gets over his feeling of injury when he finds out the difficulty of making a good small advertisement. It's an art to say a lot in a small space. The best way to get the "wind" out of your copywriting is to do small advertisements.

SELLING COPY CONTAINS DETAILS

Department stores, too, know the necessity for giving all the information needed for the prospect to make a satisfactory purchase by mail (or phone). Here are two examples from a group of bill enclosures.

Outstanding Value . . .

Wonderful Wool Sweaters for men $25 each
Two-ply French zephyr worsted . . . that's tops in wool! These handsome sweaters are firmly knit, and sized generously. Knit tapes at neck and shoulders reinforce the seams they allow to stretch. Lightweight, warm, in colors for fall: tan, maize, blue, gray or green. Small (38), medium (42) and large (46).

And—

Blue, pink or white wool for your little lamb!
baby blankets
$9.95 each
Keep baby warm in his transfers from bath to bed with this soft blanket. It's made in a lovely weave that is exclusive with our baby-pampering department! It has a deep fringe that actually will not tangle, thanks to an entirely new finish. Big enough for a crib . . . 40 by 48 inches.

Notice how many more factual details are included in these pieces of selling copy than would normally appear in a department store's newspaper advertisement for the same merchandise. Yet the facts are not just listed. Their importance is emphasized and their meaning expanded by an occasional, well-chosen word or phrase that doesn't merely tell the reader something—it sells him on the merits of the item. The sweater is not "all wool," it's "worsted"—"Two-ply French zephyr worsted" at that.

Yet the copy doesn't leave it to your knowledge or imagination to make even this categorical description of the material suffice. It doesn't dare, because the store knows that among its many customers are some who aren't acquainted with this type of wool—or who may not get the full implication of its quality by merely reading even this impressive description. It says in so many words that two-ply French zephyr worsted is "tops in wool!"

What's more, it recognizes that two common faults of sweaters often, paradoxically, are unwanted snugness and a tendency to stretch out of shape, especially around the neck and across the shoulders. Thus, beside the size listings at the end of the copy, it tells you that these sweaters are "sized generously," yet "firmly knit" and "knit tapes at neck and shoulders reinforce the seams they allow to stretch." Now these are some good, positive, product selling points specifically included to answer possible questions and objections by the store's prospects.

So, too, with the baby blanket. The copywriter knows that some of the more experienced shoppers among the prospects may shy away (and justifiably!) from a fringed baby blanket—the necessarily frequent launderings may do things to fringe that make it unattractive, but this blanket has fringe—deep fringe—as the illustrations show. Does the copy ignore that possible objection? It does not. It turns the objection into an advantage, ". . . deep fringe that actually will not tangle, thanks to an entirely new finish." The fringe becomes another selling point.

FIGURE 12-3

Mail-order advertisement appearing in a magazine.   All the elements are here for a successful mail-order advertisement—powerful headline, selling subheads, long tell-all copy, a free trial offer, an urge to act, and a coupon that sells.

TELL-ALL COPY FOR RADIO?

Of course, your radio mail-order commercials, too, must give much important detail about the products, yet probably not one out of ten prospects in a retail shop, where they can see the item, would have to have each of the product's features pointed out individually before deciding to make the purchase. Suppose, for example, that you were writing the mail-order commercial to follow the interest-arousing lead-in quoted earlier for the harmonica offer. How best can you (in one minute!) tell your prospects the features most likely to induce them to purchase? What would they want to know about the product? Now, forget you're a copywriter for a minute; instead, you're all the listeners tuned into the station carrying the harmonica offer. You're attracted and interested by the announcer's opening lines:

Say, folks, what musical instrument do you think is the easiest and quickest to learn to play? Well, I guess you'll agree when I tell you that, generally speaking, the harmonica is acknowledged as the easiest musical instrument there is for a beginner to learn to play quickly. In a wonderful offer to (station name) listeners you can get a beautiful harmonica . . .

Ah, there it is! You (the listener) can get a harmonica! "But," you say, "I can't play the harmonica." And that's exactly the point where you (the copywriter) begin to set down the selling points in 1-2-3 order that you're going to use in turning all those prospects into purchasers. Once more you set down the points that you, as a listener want to know about this harmonica:

1. Is it easy to learn to play it?
2. If so, how do I learn? How long will it take?
3. What will I play on it?
4. How much does it cost?
5. If it's an inexpensive harmonica, it'll probably fall to pieces in no time, won't it?
6. What is it made of?
7. Aren't harmonicas unsanitary? (*Mothers—hundreds of them—will ask this one.*)
8. What does it sound like—is it squeaky, tinny, whiney?
9. Can I play high and low notes on it? What's its range?
10. How much did you say it costs?
11. Suppose I can't learn, or don't like it? How about getting my money back?
12. How long did you say it will take me to learn to play it?
13. How do I get it?
14. How long will I have to wait for it to come?
15. Where do I send for it?
16. How much money, once more, did you say I had to send?
17. Come again—where do I send for it?

Answer all those questions in one minute—if you can. Yes it can be done. And it has been—almost, anyway. Here's the fast-paced commercial as written and used on the air:

Say, folks, what musical instrument do you think is the easiest and the quickest to learn to play? Well, I guess you'll agree when I tell you that, generally speaking, the harmonica is acknowledged as the easiest musical instrument there is for a beginner to learn to play quickly. In a wonderful offer to (station name) listeners, you can get a beautiful harmonica . . . a book of EASY instructions that guarantees to teach you to play the harmonica . . . 200 songs with the words and music . . . and the entire cost for everything is only $4.49! Now let me repeat that slowly. You get a harmonica . . . a book of instructions . . . and the

words and music for over 200 songs, all for only $4.49! This mouth organ is unbreakable . . . it's washable . . . it's lightweight, and it has one of the mellowest tones you've ever heard. What's more, it's 100 percent guaranteed. It's also guaranteed that the EASY instructions will have you playing it within five short days. . . . or you get your money back. Now here's all you have to do . . . Send no money . . . simply send your name and address to Harmonicas, care of (station and address). In a few days, you'll receive your harmonica, your simple-as-A-B-C instructions and the 200 songs, and you pay your postman $4.49, plus C.O.D. postage. So act today. Just write to Harmonicas, that's H-A-R-M-O-N-I-C-A-S, Harmonicas, care of (station and address).

The writer of this commercial has answered all but two of those questions, 6 and 9: "What is it made of?" and "What's it's range?" Perhaps you've noticed one other point the seller of the harmonica might have made not only to increase attention to, and interest in, the commercial, but also to add one more selling appeal as well. This item has the unique (for radio) property of being a natural to demonstrate, if only to have someone (even the announcer) run up and down the scale on it. Here would be audible proof of its mellow tone and its range. For only a little more cash outlay for talent, someone might have been hired to play a bar or two or melody or a few chords to demonstrate the playing ease claimed for the instrument.

FIGURE 12-4

Tell-all radio commercial.   Although it seems as if this commercial is giving the listener too much to remember, it is actually achieving one objective—to make the offer sound exciting enough to persuade the listener to call the toll-free telephone number. In keeping with good radio technique, the telephone number is given twice.

Did you know that the Museum of Natural History publishes a magazine and that they're making a special subscription offer right now? If you subscribe to this superb publication, you'll receive as a free gift--a fascinating 377-page book covering 40 of the finest and most famous articles from Natural History magazine. Read what it feels like to be bitten by a poisonous snake--why killer whales have been misjudged--how the floods that destroyed priceless art in Florence could have been predicted and prevented. By subscribing now, you also become a member of the museum with unlimited free admission and use of the exclusive member's lounge. In addition, you'll receive two surprise bonus gifts, plus discounts on all items in the museum gift shop. All this for subscribing to Natural History now. Just call this toll-free number: 800-228-1776. Natural History will bill you only ten dollars for your 10-issue yearly subscription plus the bonus gifts and membership in the museum. That number again: 800-228-1776. For Natural History magazine.

A caution about tell-all radio

Although the harmonica commercial was a success, radio is not the ideal tell-all medium. Instead, radio is used most effectively to put across one point emphatically, not a number of points. Listeners simply cannot absorb a number of points made over the air even though they might be (which they usually aren't) giving the commercial full attention.

Despite the fact that it seemed that the harmonica commercial was jammed with selling points, there was one big point made, and it was repeated—that the listener would get the harmonica, a book of instructions and 200 songs for $4.49. All the other words simply created excitement for the offer.

Sometimes you may make an offer on radio that consists of many points no one of which you expect to register strongly with your listeners. Your purpose is simply to make prospects aware that your product or service has an amazing number of fine attributes for the money you're asking. Although such a technique will work, it is still best to write radio commercials that register one idea overwhelmingly. If this means you don't use tell-all in your radio commercials, so be it.

SHOW-ALL—TELEVISION'S MAIL-ORDER TECHNIQUE

Television, of course, can go beyond radio in its ability to show merchandise as well as talk about it—and even more important many times—to demonstrate it. Your selling principles for copywriting are not changed by television, merely enhanced. Possibilities of television go beyond even illustrations in print, for the product can be shown in actual use, including all views of it and demonstrations of its performance. Different models, patterns, or styles available may be shown—and color selections, too, when color telecasting and receiving are commercially in use. In fact, the scope of mail-order selling by air seems unlimited when the possibilities of showing products being modeled or otherwise in use, a full range of styles or patterns—and colors, too—are considered.

Mail-order selling will merely be adapted to suit the medium and the selling advantages it offers, but mail-order selling principles will not—cannot—be eliminated, nor will their fundamental sales psychology be altered. Television's biggest asset as a salesmaker lies in its illustrative advantages, its ability to enhance verbal description—not replace it. Look at a few of the descriptive sales points extracted from the radio mail-order commercial, mentioned earlier, which offers a combination cigarette case and lighter plus the midget ballpoint pen premium:

You'll be thrilled with the new (_____) cigarette case made of richly finished, lightweight, marble-effect plastic in Hollywood pastel colors. It fits a shirt pocket or purse. IN ADDITION, there is a sure-fire, all-metal cigarette lighter built right into the top of this case. But that's just the first half of this sensational offer! Second: you will receive the world's smallest ballpoint pen, complete with key chain! This glittering, all-metal marvel is the mighty midget of the ballpoint pens! Small enough to fit a vest pocket or coin purse, it's guaranteed to do a big job of writing. If you order immediately, your cigarette case will be monogrammed with your own initial, in ornamental lettering that glows in the dark . . .

A pretty fair verbal picture, but translate these sentences into television language—actually not much of a change—and you'll see how some words are replaced or converted to take every advantage of the opportunity of visual illustration provided by the new medium:

Wouldn't you be thrilled to own (*announcer produces product in his hand from behind his back*) this beautiful new _____ cigarette case? Look at the rich finish (*turns case in close-up before camera*) or its marble-effect plastic—its Hollywood pastel colors. Notice its light weight (*flips case lightly in palm of hand*)—how it fits your pocket or purse (*slips case in and out of upper vest pocket*). AND LOOK—A sure-fire all-metal cigarette lighter (*flicks flame in close-up, on and off*) built right into the top! But that's just the first half of this sensational offer! (*Brings other hand, closed, from behind back.*) Second, you will receive this (*opens fist in close-up*) ball-point pen—the world's smallest—complete with key chain! (*Lets chain dangle and swing momentarily*) This glittering, all-metal marvel is the mighty midget (*writes large "Mighty Midget" with pen on pad of paper as he says words*) of ball-point pens! Small enough to fit your vest pocket (*tucks pen into lower vest pocket and removes again*) or purse, it's guaranteed to do a big job (*holds up pad again*) of writing. If you order immediately, your cigarette case will be monogrammed with your own initial, in ornamental lettering (*holds up initialed case as studio lights dim momentarily*) that glows in the dark! (*Initial glows, then lights come on again.*)

Actually, you've changed none of the selling points—and just enough of the words to capitalize on the actual demonstration of your product. In fact, your word count is practically the same. As in your use of any mail-order medium, you've merely used every opportunity at your command to present all your major selling points as graphically and completely as is possible within that medium. You've adapted your copy, too, to suit the medium and to reach as many of the prospects covered by the medium as you can. Your word rate is high since the commercial is fast paced and enthusiastic.

Now, to get your prospects to order

Your display has attracted the prospect's attention. He was interested enough to enter your shop, and now you've sold him on making a purchase. Here is where mail-order selling must go an extra step beyond any other kind of selling. Why? Because there's an extra step in the making of a mail-order purchase. As the mail-order salesperson you have an extra job to do, too. That job is not merely to ask for the order, but to make the purchase so easy that the prospect is willing to go to the added inconveniences inherent in ordering by mail. He will be glad to write out his order, to remit the purchase price, and to mail the two together.

Help us give you a proper fit!

Chest or bust: Run a tape well up under arms, across shoulder blades, and over the fullest part of the chest. Hold the tape firm but not tight. Be sure it's straight across your back. Stand naturally. Give measurement in inches.

Sleeves: Measure in inches from middle of back of neck, across the shoulder and around point of elbow to wrist.

Waist: Measure in inches the waistband of same style slacks or skirt that fit properly. Or measure your waist in inches over a shirt or blouse. Measure at the position you normally wear your trousers or skirts.

Hips: Run a tape around the fullest part of hips which is usually 7"-9" below the waist. Give measurement in inches.

Neck: On a shirt of the same style that fits well lay the collar flat. Measure in inches from the center button to far end of button hole. Or run a tape around your neck at the level you'd usually wear your shirt collar. Please send measurement in inches.

Shirts: Send us your neck size, sleeve length, height, and chest or bust size.

Pants: Send waist (women also send hip) measurement. All Norm Thompson pants are styled with a medium rise and shipped unhemmed for easy adjustment to your exact length.

Belts: Send us waist measurement.

Jackets or coats: Send us your chest or bust measurement, sleeve length, and your height.

Hats: Measure in inches around the largest part of your head or where you plan to wear the hat.

Shoes or boots: Send us your regular shoe size and width (AAA to EEE, not narrow, medium, or wide). Please do not send a tracing of your foot.

Norm Thompson Gift Certificates.

Norm Thompson gift certificates are welcome on birthdays, anniversaries and special holidays. They make wonderful wedding gifts, especially for those young couples who get "two of everything for the house" when what they really need is clothing. A gift certificate is ideal for those who are just plain hard to shop for...when you don't know the size or color...and for those with decided tastes who would prefer to shop for themselves.

You can make Norm Thompson gift certificates for any amount from $10 right on up. If you want the gift certificate delivered on a special date, just let us know and we'll see that it gets there on time.

With each gift certificate we send a free Norm Thompson "Escape from the ordinary®" catalog.

Please include the name, address, and zip code of the recipient if you want us to send your gift directly to them.

Norm Thompson

1805 N.W. Thurman St.
Portland, Oregon 97209 Dept. 60-04

☐ Mr.
☐ Mrs._____
☐ Miss   1st and 2nd initials   Last name

Address_____

City_____ State_____ Zip_____

Apt., suite, or room #_____ Telephone # and area code_____

☐ My personal check or money order is enclosed. (U.S. funds only)

Charge to my ☐ BankAmericard ☐ Master Charge

_____
Card number   4 digit interbank No. for Master Charge

X_____
Signature   Good thru date

☐ Send to: (if other than myself)

Name_____

Address_____

City_____

State_____ Zip_____

☐ I have moved since my last order. My former address was

Address_____

City_____

State_____ Zip_____

Your BankAmericard or Master Charge are welcome.

We want you to have a perfect fit, and it'll really help if you can supply us with the following information:

Men: Height____" Waist____" Neck____" Sleeve____" Chest____"

Women: Height____" Waist____" Hips____" Sleeve____" Bust____"

Qty.	Cat. No.	Name of item	Size	Width	Color	Price

☐ Ship via surface*
☐ Ship via air*

*Shipping, handling, and insured delivery charges:

Total order	Add for surface shipment	Add for air shipment
less than $26	$ .75	$1.50
$26 to $51	$1.00	$2.00
$51 to $75	$1.25	$2.50
over $75	$1.50	$3.00

Total _____

Thank you for your order

Prices effective until superseded by subsequent publication.

We want to give you the fastest and best possible service, so unless you specify shipment by parcel post your order will be shipped via United Parcel Service.

FIGURE 12-5

Ordering instructions for a mail-order catalog.   No chances are taken. Information must be complete.

Parma Advertising for Norm Thompson Outfitters

ORDERING DIRECTIONS ARE IMPORTANT

How do you make ordering simple, easy or even inviting? There is no single way applicable to all mail-order selling, so first look at the three principal methods of encouraging or inviting the order:

- An order blank (perhaps with an addressed postage-guaranteed envelope);
- A return post card (always self-addressed and usually, today, with postage guaranteed) and coupons;
- Advertisements without coupons; contain mere statements of ordering requirements and mailing address.

Obviously, the first two are definitely <u>ordering aids</u>. They remove some of the burden imposed upon the purchaser by the fact that he can't just hand you his money and carry off his purchase. Number 3 relieves the purchaser of none of the effort required to place an order. Which method should you use for any particular mail-order offering? The major consideration is your medium. Mail-order catalogs, for example, usually include an order blank, perhaps several, to encourage frequent ordering. Direct mail-order offerings frequently have a return post card enclosed. The coupon most often is part of a mail-order advertisement in a publication. Ordering information alone is usually used either in mail-order advertisements too small to accommodate coupons or in radio commercials. Now to discuss each of these methods.

ORDER BLANKS

Order blanks usually are the most elaborate of the methods to invite orders. Because they most commonly accompany catalogs, more than one type of item may be—and usually is—ordered on one blank; this means that often different kinds of information may be required for each item—color, pattern, finish, initials (for monograms), width, length, size, model, price each, per pair, or per set, or what-have-you.

Because general merchandise mail-order houses have so many regular customers ordering several times a season or year, these houses must have a means of keeping up-to-date information on customers' addresses, past and current.

Because they sell on several different sets of terms—cash, time-payment accounts, and open accounts are the three most common—the payment method must be recorded on the order blank. Spaces are provided for such details.

A choice of shipment methods must be provided on the blank. Then such obvious requirements must be provided for as catalog numbers, quantity ordered, name and shipping weight of each item, plus totals on the weights, prices, postage, taxes and the like.

RETURN POST CARDS AND COUPONS

Coupons and post cards are similar to each other, although the customary difference in their sizes may at first mask the resemblance. A study of their mutual requirements will show their similarity.

Very frequently both return post cards and coupons include some inducement for prompt reply—often in addition to any such urge previously incorporated into the accompanying mailing piece of advertisement. One of those you'll find most common is some variation of the magic word "Free":

Free Examination Postcard

Free 10-Day Trial Coupon!

Free Sample

Free Catalog

Don't Wait—Send Coupon Today for Approval Offer

Good for Both Free

As a rule these are in some sort of display type—quite often in a "reverse" panel—but sometimes they may be set in relatively small type, especially in small coupons. Other typical incentives for ordering include such inducements as variations of the common one, "Mail This Coupon Today!" and others a little more original, like:

Clip This Coupon—Mail Today

Order with This Handy Coupon

We Accept Your Invitation

Mail This Card to Secure Your Copy

Complete Crochet Library—Only 10¢ a Book

Get the Facts by Mail

Mail Opportunity Coupon for Quick Action

Phone—Wire—Use Coupon

This Certificate Saves You $3

All these, of course, besides urging prompt action, call attention to the coupon (or card). To accomplish a similar purpose, an arrow or some similar eye-directing device is sometimes incorporated into the advertising layout, although nowadays many layout artists tend to scorn such "corny" treatment, preferring to accomplish the same result more subtly by designing the entire piece to lead the eye "naturally" through the steps of the selling process, ending logically with the final step—the action-inducing coupon.

Another feature that most mail-order return post cards and advertisement coupons share is the inclusion of some sort of statement to make them more personal, as if the purchaser had written them himself. The one you are most familiar with undoubtedly is "Please send me . . . ," or any of its close relatives, followed by a brief restatement of the offer made in the mailing piece or advertisement, again usually phrased in the first person, supposedly the sender's words.

Prospects must know how to pay

Common also to both return post card and coupon order forms is not merely a restatement of the price but a provision for stating the method of payment chosen. Even where no choice is offered, this is included as a precaution against any misunderstanding by the purchaser. The following illustrations of typical wordings (most of them self-explanatory as to the terms offered) will show you how such statements may be handled:

☐ Charge My Account; ☐ Find Check or M.O. Enclosed; Please include 3% sales tax on orders in (*state*).

☐ C.O.D.; ☐ Money Order or Check; ☐ Charge My Account.
(Please do not send currency or stamps)

☐ Cash   ☐ C.O.D.   ☐ Charge

Check for _____ enclosed. No C.O.D.'s
Check ☐ I am enclosing $ _____ . Ship Postpaid.
One   ☐ Ship C.O.D. I'll pay postman $ _____ plus postage.

Please send me the books checked, at 25¢ each. I enclose _____ .

Mail (*title of book set*) on 7 days' free trial.
If O.K. I will remit $1 in 7 days and $1 monthly until $6 is paid. Otherwise I will return them. No obligation unless I am satisfied.

Within ten days I will either return the book and owe nothing, or send you $1.50 and the $2.00 a month for three months until the special price of $7.50, plus postage is paid.

☐ Check here if you send the full price of $7.50 with this card. We will pay the postage. Same return privilege and refund if you're not satisfied.

☐ Remittance Enclosed; ☐ Please Bill Me;
☐ One Year (26 Issues) $3.50–$3.90 single copy value.
☐ Two Years (52 Issues) $6.00–$7.80 single copy value.

Enclosed is 25¢ (in coin) and the top of a package or sack of your _____ . Please send me one of _____ .

Please enroll me as a _____ Book Club subscriber and send me at once " _____ " as a gift. Also send me as my first selection for $2.00 the book I have checked below:
(*Four choices listed, each with a check box*)
With these books will come my first issue of the brochure " _____ ," telling about the forthcoming _____ selection which will be offered for $2. (plus shipping charge) to members only, regardless of the price of publisher's edition. I am to have the privilege of notifying you in advance if I do not wish to purchase any _____ selection. The purchase of _____ selections is entirely voluntary on my part. I do not have to accept a book every month—only

four during the year—to fulfill my membership requirement. I am to receive a bonus book for every four _____ selections I purchase . . . Price in Canada, $2.20.

Many cards and coupons offer return privileges "without obligation," or perhaps a "free trial" offer, restated in the body of the card or coupon, to make sure the purchaser understands that his signature does not obligate him finally and irrevocably to buy.

Addresses must be right

All mail-order return post cards and coupons include the name and address of the seller. The cards, of course, always have them printed on the address side of the card, and sometimes repeated on the order side for the prestige they may lend the offer. The coupons include them primarily to insure that the purchaser has an accurate address for use on the envelope in which he sends the coupon.

One other use is to test the response to the publication in which an advertisement appears, or the returns on each of several mailing lists the seller may be renting. This may be done by "keying" the address. Frequently this key is a fictitious "department" designation. For instance, suppose you are running the same advertisement in *Farm Journal, Successful Farming,* and *Capper's Weekly* magazines, and want to test their relative effectiveness as order-getters. Like the rest of the advertisement, you make the coupon the same in all three publications except for the department in the addresses, which you would most likely designate as, "Dept. FJ," "Dept. SF," and "Dept. CW," respectively.

One more requirement is common to both return post cards and coupons in any mail-order offering using them. That is the customer's name and address. Illegibility is such a problem that you'll probably use the common request, "Please print." You may also say "Please use pencil" if the paper stock of the card or publication might make ink blot and run. The form and space you provide for the purchaser's address may vary with the classes or groups of people who are expected to respond.

If they are city folks, for example, you'll most likely ask for street and number (and perhaps apartment number), city, state, and zip. Perhaps you'll have to designate both, if your offer of your mailing lists for your publications may reach more than one group. In addition, you may want other information about the purchaser:

- Is "he" Mr., Mrs., Miss, Ms.?
  (three to be crossed out)
- What is his date of birth?
- Does he own a car? What make? What model? What year?
- Is he a home-owner or does he rent?
- Does he carry insurance? On himself? On his house? On his car? Other?

Perhaps you need credit references—a bank, names of two business houses where he has established credit, or names of two business people who know him. In any case, your card or coupon will have to provide space for any of these additional pieces of information which you require.

One word of caution: give your purchaser enough space to fill in the information most important to you—usually his name and address. You'll find it wiser and more profitable, to forego some information in order to give him room in which to write his name and address. If his name and address is: "Humphrey Stanislavski, Oklahoma City, Okla.," you'll get no reply if you have provided barely enough space for a customer to write: "Ned Hay, Erie, Pa." Give plenty of room for the city name.

Finally, your "miniature order blank" may have to provide spaces for information essential to proper filling of the order, if any choice is involved, or if alternate selections are offered.

ADVERTISEMENTS WITHOUT COUPONS

What about the mail-order advertisement that doesn't have room enough for a coupon, and what about mail-order commercials?

You might as well make up your mind that you aren't usually going to get so many replies from couponless advertisements as you will receive if you include coupons. But, you may say, "I don't have room for a coupon, and I don't have enough money to increase the size of my advertisement sufficiently to include a coupon, but I still have to run an advertisement for my mail-order offering. What do I do then?"

One, you can include adequate ordering information as a part of your advertisement's copy, exerting every effort to make it sound attractive enough—to sell it well enough—so that it brings in a profitable number of orders. Second, you can, besides giving complete ordering information, state the ordering requirements simply. Third, be certain that the requirements are reduced to the basic necessities—that only truly essential elements are included.

Getting paid—how to go about it

All right, so you're going to cut out all unnecessary ordering requirements from your couponless mail-order advertisements. The biggest trouble-causer is the customer's name and address. Since you certainly can't eliminate those, you move on to the next most troublesome element—the remittance, or, to speak frankly, money. Cut out the requirement. Heresy! How, you ask, can I stay in business without money?

If you read carefully the quotations from post cards and coupons a few paragraphs back, you'll recall that even with these ordering devices some mail-order merchandisers have avoided the need for a remittance with the order. Of course, this is relatively simple for a department store selling either to its charge account customers or making C.O.D. sales locally where its truck drivers can collect for the merchandise at the time of delivery. But the requirement for cash, money order, or check with the order is being omitted by more and more nonlocal mail-order advertisers who have neither charge customers nor any delivery system of their own. The C.O.D., "pay-postman-on-delivery" type of offer is becoming more and more popular since it eliminates one of the three traditional steps in ordering by mail (writing the order, enclosing the remittance, and mailing the two together).

C.O.D. orders are not so frequently invited—in fact, are sometimes definitely prohibited—by mail-order advertisers using many of the so-called class magazines. Perhaps this is due partially to the fact that readers of such publications are in the middle-to-high income groups. Probably they are primarily urbanites, and therefore more likely to have personal checking accounts. At least they aren't too much inconvenienced by buying a money order.

Some other ways to get paid

Besides C.O.D. terms, mail-order merchandisers sometimes use other means of making the payment either physically simpler than a full cash enclosure, or at least temporarily easier on the customer's pocketbook or checkbook. One means of doing this is to offer a "free trial" period, "order on approval," "bill me later," or other similar terms.

Another plan somtimes used—especially with book clubs, sets, or individual books—is a time-payment scheme by which the purchaser remits a payment each time he receives a book-club selection or another book of the set he has ordered. He may also receive the book, or entire set, upon receipt by the seller of a down payment with the order, the balance to be paid in stated installments.

Be clear and simple

Another way to maintain simplicity in couponless mail-order advertisements is to limit—preferably to eliminate—any alternate items or choices. Usually an advertisement listing more than one offer—or two at the most—will be large enough to include a coupon as well. Some physical means should be given the purchaser to indicate the exact item he wants when a selection is offered. It's the single offering, however, made in a choice of styles or colors or finishes or sizes that cause mail-order grief, effort, and money.

The cure: making clear to the customer the physical means of indicating his choice. Nevertheless, the copywriter—you—will probably encounter some adamant advertiser who won't or can't, afford the luxury of the extra space required for a coupon. In such cases, you must be especially careful to word your ordering requirements copy so that the majority of customers will be fairly certain to include all the information necessary to receive the selection they want. "State choice," "Please indicate model wanted," "Be sure to include all measurements," and similar cautions must be stated—predominantly and preferably in bold face—and stated clearly.

A page margin as a coupon?

One device is sometimes given to make ordering from advertisements more convenient—suggest that the purchaser clip the advertisement from the publication and write on the adjacent margin his name and address—and any other necessary ordering information. But first be sure that your advertisement is of such size or shape that it will be next to one of the page margins in the publication(s) in which it will run.

Getting C.O.D. orders by radio and television

As for radio mail-order commercials, relatively little need be added to what has been said about couponless advertisements in print. The same principles apply—only more so. A radio commercial is heard once—it cannot be "reread"—and in that one hearing the offer and all its details, especially the details on ordering, must be grasped completely by the listener. Because comprehension by ear is less thorough than by eye, almost never do you offer a choice of any sort. The few exceptions consist almost entirely of colors or sizes where these cannot be avoided. In the matter of payment for the order, more and more radio merchandisers have come to use C.O.D. terms exclusively.

Advertisers-by-air have gone to great lengths to simplify their ordering requirements. They try to clarify other ordering information, too, particularly the address to which the order is to be sent. You'll find the address must usually be given at least twice during even a one-minute commercial, besides the almost inevitable spelling out of the name as well.

As a further means of simplifying the address, you may imitate many experienced radio advertisers who use the station call letters as an address: "Just write to Harmonicas, that's H-A-R-M-O-N-I-C-A-S, Harmonicas, care of WQXZ."

13

Being Personal and Successful in Direct Mail

In your typewriter is a copy sheet on which you've written several ideas for a television commercial that will be seen on the network by millions of people. On your desk is a version of the same campaign that will appear in big circulation magazines. Despite your progress, you're dissatisfied. You've found it hard to invest your copy with any personal quality. How do you get personal with millions of people?

One way is to forget you're writing to a faceless mass of viewers or readers. Instead, you visualize one person in that mass. You write to him or her. Possibly this will work. Perhaps it won't. Lucky you, if you're writing direct-mail copy because there's no need to pretend. You <u>are</u> writing to one person. Herein lies the great advantage of the medium.

This personal quality is one reason why direct mail has become almost a universal medium. Of thousands of businesses, only relatively few advertise on the air, in national magazines, or in any medium but their local newspapers. Almost every firm, however, uses direct mail advertising even though it uses other media as well.

THE JOB OF DIRECT-MAIL ADVERTISING

Direct-mail advertising gets your message in print personally and individually to a selected group of prospects or customers with whom you want to do business or whose good will you want to establish or maintain. This is a truly "direct" medium, usually conveyed entirely by "mail," as opposed to mail-order, which may use radio, television, and publication advertising in soliciting mail business.

Some direct-mail pieces are also distributed in other ways. A folder, for example, devised primarily as a mailing piece to accompany a department store's monthly charge account statements, may also be used as a pick-up piece in a suitable spot in the store—probably in the department whose merchandise or service it publicizes. This kind of promotion is sometimes called direct advertising and is considered the same as direct-mail advertising. In this discussion it will be assumed, however, that you are writing to relatively sharply defined groups—in other words, you are creating direct-mail advertising.

WHY USE IT?

At one time the Direct Mail Advertising Association issued a list of forty-nine ways direct-mail advertising could be used as a part of modern merchandising methods. Although many variations in these applications can be—and have been—made, a listing of some of the most common basic uses will give you an idea of the scope of this medium and how greatly you would have to vary your writing to meet the requirements of some of these uses:

- To sell goods or services by mail. (Although this use does not necessarily anticipate return orders by mail, its purpose is primarily the same as "direct-mail-order," covered in the last chapter.
- To reach all customers regularly with merchandise offers, thereby keeping accounts active.
- To support salespeople, pave the way for them, thus backing their selling efforts and economizing on their time (and on the prospects' time and patience) when actually making sales calls.
- To bring in orders between salespeople's calls or from territories not covered by salespeople (or, in consumer selling, areas not serviced through retail outlets), or to open up new territories.
- To broadcast mailings to and request inquiries from a large group of prospects. Names thus obtained are passed on to dealers, jobbers, or salespeople for solicitation, or are further contacted by

additional direct mail. Getting names this way saves the expense of indiscriminate distribution of catalogs since requests are from definite prospects.

- To provide news and information about the firm or its products. This might include "education" of stockholders on company products, services, and policies—either from a public relations point of view, or as encouragement of their patronage, or perhaps of their word-of-mouth advertising.

- To tie-up with trade or consumer publication advertising, or to sell dealers on trade paper or consumer advertising programs. Such selling stimulates their cooperative efforts.

- To stimulate dealer sales by consumer mailings—perhaps by suggesting a visit to the prospect's "nearest dealer." Jobber sales may also be spurred by mailing to dealers.

- To induce a dealer's own customers or prospects to visit his store—or a manufacturer's customers his showroom—to see some special goods described or illustrated.

- To overcome competition threatening established customer or adverse market tendencies. The quick publicizing of a revised price list might fall into this class.

- To pretest on a limited scale contemplated offers or presentations against each other, using different lists or splitting a single list.

- To stimulate sales or to increase acceptance of the firm's merchandise or services through enclosures in all outgoing envelopes (with dividend checks or financial statements to stockholders, for example).

- To request information from prospects to determine their needs. The information will be used as a basis for further mailings or salesperson's solicitation. The items will be specifically suited to prospects' requirements.

In this incomplete list, you have a range of jobs to be done that call for many different types of copy treatment. Yet they offer you one advantage—that of knowing on any individual job the needs and wants of the prospects to whom you are writing. Because of the selective nature of direct mail, you write more surely to the prospect's interest than in general media such as newspapers, radio, and TV.

HOW PERSONAL INTEREST CAN BE ACHIEVED

One prestige retail clothing chain, for example, mails advance announcements of its seasonal traveling merchandise displays to charge customers and former cash customers. Because this is a very well-defined group of prospects already aware of the company's reputation, styles, and values, the headline of one announcement reads merely

(Company name)   Clothes for Spring and Summer

almost a pure index type headline, with institutional

and prestige overtones. Contrast this with another—this one from a nonmail order catalog cover of a chain of retail auto supply stores, based primarily on price appeal (but including some reassurance of quality):

SAVE 25% to 50% from List Price on
GUARANTEED REPLACEMENT AUTO PARTS

Here is a headline aimed unmistakably at a large—almost universal—but yet quite definite class of prospects, automobile owners, to induce them to visit their local store of the chain where the products listed may be purchased.

Ayres

Dear Sir:

I am writing a select group of men personally about a special night we are having in our Downtown Indianapolis store on Monday, December 13 from 9:00 to 11:00 p.m. We know you have a limited amount of time to shop so we have reserved this special evening for you.

We have gathered together a unique selection of distinctive gifts and fashions for the woman in your life. Most of our buyers and other knowledgeable members of Ayres staff will be on hand to assist you.

We hope the cheese, wine, and complimentary gift wrapping will make the evening not only one of convenient shopping but also relaxing.

Please present the enclosed card at our Men's Store entrance for admission and bring a guest if you wish. For your convenience park free at Merchant's Garage, 31 South Meridian. Your parking ticket should be validated at the Men's Store entrance.

We look forward to seeing you on the night of the 13th.

Cordially,

P. Gerald Mills
P. Gerald Mills
President

FIGURE 13-1

Department store letter addressed to present customers.   An important task of retail stores is to hold on to present customers and to keep them sold. This example is typical of letters that let customers know how highly regarded they are by the store.

Quite another purpose is apparent, in a two-fold, envelope-size enclosure on slick, heavy paper sent to its stockholders with their dividend checks by a large manufacturer of soaps and synthetic detergents. The mailing was sent prior to the break in national media of an introductory advertising campaign for a new shampoo. The company already manufactured a successful liquid shampoo, sold in a bottle and a transparent "creme" shampoo in a tube had been introduced in a nationwide campaign within the year just past.

Now that a third shampoo ("beauty cream" shampoo in a jar) was being launched, the manufacturer felt it necessary to explain this seeming duplication of products to its stockholders. The explanation told the readers that research had shown that a definite market for each shampoo existed. The outer fold of this direct-mail enclosure carried the headline (with illustrations of three products):

Just what customers ordered
. . . Three Fine Shampoos

Attention and interest value of the first four words is high because they imply something of vital interest to the particular group addressed—a group whose returns on its stock in this company depend entirely upon how well the company management continues to anticipate the wants of the buying public. To this select group, the entire headline is provocative of further reading to find out why and how "three fine shampoos" fulfill these wants. And the entire folder attempts to do just the one job—to "sell" the stockholders (owners) of the company on justification of the manufacture and promotion of three apparently competitive products.

A similar direct-mail piece, mailed separately to stockholders of a large corporation with several diversified manufacturing divisions, tells of the current production and market status of the products produced by three of these divisions for use in the home. Display copy reads:

Outer fold

First inner fold	(Corp. name) PRESENTS PRODUCTS FOR THE HOME
	DIVERSIFICATION IN
Inside spread, each subhead followed by explanatory copy	MANUFACTURING
	(plus explanatory copy)
	. . . FROM TELEVISION TO HEATING!
	Radio and Television Receivers
	Kitchen Ranges
	Refrigerators
	Frozen Food Cabinets
	Kitchen Cabinets and Sinks
	Residential Heating Units

The final copy paragraph on the first inner fold does not invite requests for further information on the products covered. The tone of the entire piece is more product-sales-minded than the one on the shampoos. Its purpose is dual—to report company progress, and to sell its line of products to its shareholders by bringing directly to their attention the items it makes.

Making mailings personal

The examples of display copy used in the direct-mail advertising cited thus far have not been personalized beyond the fact that the mailing envelopes were addressed by name. This is generally true of any pieces other than those sent in letter format—and

many of these do not use prospects' names even in the letters. Others have the name (and sometimes the address) filled in to match (as well as possible) a pseudo-typewritten "circular" letter. Especially in this type of letter there is usually no display copy— that is, not in display-size type—although sometimes a second color, to stimulate use of a two-tone typewriter ribbon, will be used for important elements of the copy. Yet there are ways of simultaneously personalizing a letter and giving it a tremendous attention- and interest-stimulating impact.

Arousing attention and maintaining interest must be carefully planned to fit the copy treatment. It must avoid attracting so much interest to itself that the major impression remaining with the prospect is that of the physical novelty of the piece.

Attention-getters—the gadgets

Another attention-getter and interest-arouser is the "gadget." Chosen and used with imagination it can often help dramatize your message—to get your point across quickly and effectively. Frequently, a gadget is a small copy of a larger, familiar item, but it can be any life-size item—a candy mint wafer, a vitamin pill, a burnt match (never send inflammables through the mails), a golf tee, a pair of dice, a bobby pin, a button, a nail, a nut and bolt, or a bottle cork. Samples or pieces of the actual item or product being advertised may also be used as direct-mail gadgets (not, in this case, as samples or swatches to facilitate direct-mail orders). Such gadgets may be a piece of wool yarn used in the nap of a rug, perhaps a swatch of the carpeting itself, a sample of printing paper, a page from a new dictionary, or a patented combination washer and lock-nut.

Gadgets generally are attached in some manner to the leaflet, letter, or circular to avoid their dropping out when the envelope is opened. Seldom are they merely loose enclosures. Yet, if the gadget itself contains any part of the message and if it does fall to the floor when the envelope is opened, the recipient's curiosity might be piqued and his interest increased by the part of the message he reads on the gadget as he picks it up. Usually, however, you'll find the gadget fastened on the outside of a folder or near the top of a letter—tied into the copy by a provocative headline or by the lead-off paragraph in a letter.

Sometimes these headline tie-ins are forced to the point of absurdity—pure corn. This oldie actually used—a miniature axe with the headline "Do you mind if we axe you a few simple questions?"—is not recommended as a shining example of the catchy tie-in, yet some have been written even more insulting to the prospect's intelligence and sense of humor. But, like a famous series of direct mail-letters—one of which, with two small dice attached, opened, "The luckiest buy I ever made in my life"—most tie-ins attempt to build a natural (no pun intended) bridge from the gadget to the message. Here are a few of the other headlines in the same series used successfully on a cooperative basis with its dealers. The dealer's name was used twice in the letterhead and as the signature:

Gadget	Lead Copy or Headline
False mustache	Handlebar mustaches, like this one, went out of style years ago. And so did the Zoot Suit—the peg pants, wide shouldered loose fit clothing for men.
Small spoon	You don't have to be born with a silver (*spoon*) in your mouth to be able to afford the comfort and luxury of one of our Bench Made Suits.
Full-size pocket comb	We have combed the country for the best coat value we could find.
Blue poker chip	Here's a suit that's a "blue chip" when it comes to luxury and tailoring. Yet you don't have to pay a "blue chip" price for its custom quality!

Sometimes a gadget can be so very clever that it defeats its own purpose—the prospects remember the campaign so well that they forget the advertiser's identity—or confuse it with a competitor's. Sometimes, too, a gadget idea may backfire unexpectedly (or predictably perhaps, depending upon political views). To wit: an advertiser pasted a new FDR dime (when they first were coined) on a letterhead, suggesting it be used as a partial payment on a return order for the product offered. A number of prospects were indignant at this supposed advocacy of Roosevelt and the New Deal.

Here are some cautions in the use of gadgets:

- Don't expect a gadget to sell a product that can't be sold on its own merits. A gadget is merely an attention-getter.
- Be sure the gadget fits your message and doesn't resort to bad gags or dubious humor.
- Avoid the "too clever" gadget that pushes your name and product out of the prospect's mind.
- Look for possible ways your gadget may antagonize your prospects, either by its physical connotations or by insulting their intelligence.
- Avoid anything dangerous—self-inflammables like matches, sharp objects, such as glass, inadequately protected knives, razor blades.
- Don't rely entirely on your own personal like or dislike for a particular gadget—or for gadgets in general.

YOUR BODY COPY MUST GIVE A COMPLETE MESSAGE

Unlike mail-order selling, direct-mail advertising does not attempt to do the entire selling job, right down to and including asking for the order, except, of course in the case of direct-mail-order selling. Rather, any one piece of direct-mail advertising generally is intended to accomplish only one step in completion of the sale. Referring back to the list of common uses of direct mail, you will find that, while it

usually suggests some sort of action—perhaps only passively as in showing willingness to listen to a salesman when he calls—it may actually be used merely to implant a certain idea in the mind of the recipient which calls for no action (for the present, at least) by him. Because direct-mail advertising usually is intended to further the sale, and because it is not intended to complete the sale by itself, the copy you write must be keyed to the purpose for which the mailing is intended— but must not go beyond it.

SALESPEOPLE ARE HELPED BY DIRECT MAIL

Suppose that you had the problem once faced by the Simonds Abrasive Company, a Philadelphia abrasives manufacturer. The company's primary market was 33,000 concerns in the metal working industries—foundries, steel mills, and mass-production metalworking plants such as the Detroit auto industry. Its secondary market covered a wide range of shops, plants, and trades which use grinding wheels for either production or maintenance.

This manufacturer's most economical method of distribution was through 2,000 industrial-supply distributors' salespeople. Distributor's salespeople in the past had turned in a large volume on a few items in the line, sold to a comparatively small number of large consumers. Simonds wanted to get the supply house salesmen to sell more grinding wheels. Only $500 additional sales annually by each of the 2,000 supply house salespeople would mean a million dollars a year additional business for Simonds. How to provide the spark needed to jolt these men into producing even this relatively small increase?

A direct-mail campaign was the solution decided upon. Simonds promotional campaign to industrial consumers was three-fold: business paper, direct-mail advertising, and technical publicity in articles written by Simonds engineers for publication in trade papers. What better way to show supply house salespeople the way to increased sales than to merchandise the company's advertising and publicity—to show these people how the company's promotional activities were planned to help them in their jobs, to increase demand for the line, and to provide additional profit possibilities for them?

This was done in a series of five portfolios, sent not only to the supply houses, but personally and individually to each of the 2,000 salesmen (mailed directly to their home addresses) as well. Each mailing was planned to sell the salespeople on only one of the five ways in which the company's promotional efforts helped them sell, but each contained a statement of policy (the same in all five) that repeated the theme of the entire campaign, which might be quoted as "More sales because Simonds helps you sell":

Simonds Abrasive Co. believes in the Mill Supply Distributor . . . in the service he provides industry . . . in the manner in which he operates.

Our Distributors' salesmen are our salesmen as well. If they are to do a job for us, it is our obligation to provide the selling information and sales tools that will make their success possible. That is the reason for sending you the enclosed information.

In Grinding Wheels you have one of the most popular and attractive lines handled by Mill Supply Houses. Widespread use, frequent reordering, and good profit margin—these features combine to make Simonds Abrasive a live-wire line for you.

Remember—Simonds means top quality! In Grinding Wheels that means we take second place to no one. Our product is right—our service is right and—with your help—we mean to get the business.

Each successive portfolio contained in a pouch several examples of the type of promotion that was the subject of that mailing. The titles of the mailings—which were directly to the point in their knowing appeal to salespeople and, therefore, assured the attention and interest of that audience—were, in the order sent:

Mailing to Your Prospects Helps You Sell
Advertising Helps You Sell
Trade Press Stories Help You Sell
Technical Information Helps You Sell
Factory Stock List Helps You Sell (*A stock list, brought up to date monthly, gives salespeople a knowledge of specifications and exact quantities in stock, thus providing accurate ordering and delivery information.*)

Use strong copy in each mailing

See how the copy used in the letter (on a special campaign letterhead) accompanying one of these mailings, "Technical Information Helps You Sell," furthers one step in the sale of the company's entire promotional campaign to supply house salespeople:

The test of a good industrial supply salesman is the number of prospects he can develop into good customers—and the number of good customers he can build into regular repeat customers.

A major part of our sales effort is directed toward providing you with grinding wheel prospects in the form of sales leads and inquiries resulting from publication advertising, trade-press articles and direct mail. An even more important result of our advertising effort is the increasing Consumer Acceptance of Simonds Abrasive Co. being built up in the trade—which helps you add to your regular repeat customer list.

Supplementing such a broad program is the need to supply you with actual selling data—to give you the facts about Simonds Abrasive Wheels. The enclosed "Technical Data Sheets" do just that! Note the one on "General Purpose Grinding Wheels"—the most common and widespread type of wheel used—plain straight wheels—coarse, medium and fine—the most simple product we have to sell. Use this bulletin in your daily selling and add grinding wheels to your list of regularly sold items.

Remember sales persistence, combined with product knowledge, is the weapon to break down sales resistance.

Of course, you've noted that this letter reviews briefly the contents of the three previous mailings on direct-mail and publication advertising and trade-press articles. But note, too, how this review leads up to and ties in with the subject of the current mailing, the technical information bulletins, wrapping all these sales helps into one package that carries out the main theme of the entire campaign, "More sales because Simonds helps you sell." Actually then, this mailing has really advanced only one step in the sale of this theme to its audience. It has not diluted its emphasis by incorporating more than one new idea in the message.

Avoid giving whole story in all mailings

There is another reason, however, for not telling all in many direct-mail pieces, even though they may not be one of a series or campaign, but merely a single mailing. Imagine that you are writing a "one-shot" direct-mail piece for the women's better coat department of a retail store. You are announcing to your store's charge customers, in advance of your general newspaper advertisement, the arrival of a special group of luxuriously fur-trimmed cloth coats, and you are urging the customers' advance inspection of these models for a complete selection.

Your purpose is to get women into the department. Do you tell them, then, all about the coat? Do you list all the colors available? Every kind of fur in the group? Do you illustrate every style? You do not! If you say that dove gray, white wine, forest green, plum nectar, and cinnamon brown, as well as black, are available, some of your prospects won't bother to come in because they may think they want a pearl gray, champagne, emerald green, royal purple, or chocolate brown coat. If you say that the fur trims are mink, beaver, and silver fox, some of your potential customers will stay away because they've had in mind squirrel, persian lamb, or blue fox. If you list certain specific styles, you're sure to cause some women to shun your copy because they have other styles in mind. Thus you say something like, "All the season's highest-fashion colors and most-wanted furs, in a range of next year's full or fitted styles flattering to every figure."

You must give certain facts

Of course, there are some things you will want to tell your prospects. Sizes, for example. There's no point in making the size 12 or size 44 customer angry at you for wasting her time to come downtown when your size range begins with 14 and ends at 40. In most cases, you'll list the range of prices, too, for much the same reason. If your buyer is a smart merchandiser, he will have attempted to include at least one model in the group that can be priced at a comparatively low figure, perhaps because of a lesser amount of fur used (although probably not a cheaper fur) on a coat which, because of its styling or material, seems otherwise to "belong" with the more expensive models.

Thus, instead of having to admit to a limited price range, say of $175 to $249.50, you may be able to claim that "these exclusive creations begin at the tiny price of $125, while you'll hardly believe we could sell the most luxurious models for their modest price of only $249.50."

Save something for the next step

In all direct-mail advertising that contemplates an eventual sale, remember this strategy—tell enough to interest the prospect—and to keep him interested until you have the opportunity to complete the sale—but don't tell "your all" or you may never have the chance to make that sale. This strategy applies as well to a series of related, progressive-step mailings as it does to a single one—don't weaken your next mailing by telling its story before the strategic time. It applies even when your anticipated sale, following a direct-mail campaign, will be requested by mail as well—a direct-mail order.

When you don't follow this strategy—when you rob your following mailings of their impact by anticipating their parts of the sales story early in the campaign—your prospects either become confused by the size and scope of the early bombardment, or become tired and bored with the succession of old stuff which comes in subsequent mailings. In either case you have almost certainly lost the sale.

Mailings should be self-sufficient

One caution you should remember, however, in applying this strategy: In any direct-mail campaign—despite the fact that one major impression is all you can expect to get across in any one mailing—each mailing should be complete in itself. It should not be dependent either upon earlier pieces or pieces yet to come. Even though you cannot, of course, tell all of a multipart story in a single mailing, you must stress adequately the feature chosen for emphasis in that mailing. Know exactly what purpose you want each piece to accomplish, then write your copy to achieve that purpose—and nothing more.

WAYS TO MAKE REMOTE-CONTROL SELLING EFFECTIVE

Only a brief summary of these ways will be attempted—you can easily understand them and appreciate their importance without detailed examples. If you like, however, you can readily imagine applications of them as you read.

Keep old customers sold. One of the most important of these pointers is to remember that the backbone of any permanent success in selling is the retention of the good will and the business of old customers. Much of the responsibility for keeping old customers as satisfied current customers is not the province of the advertising copywriter, but rather that of direct salespeople, sales and credit correspondents, and others. At the same time, nevertheless, the firm's advertising also has a share of the job to do in being so planned and written that the needs and wants of the old customers are not sacrificed in the attempt to win new customers as well.

Advertising also frequently plays a big part in the maintenance of friendly relations between seller and customer. During periods of raw material shortages, transportation delays, and other difficulties—even labor troubles—advertising of every sort, including both mail order and direct mail, can and does help out in the big job of explaining the situation to customers and retaining their business.

Many firms, both retail and industrial, have adopted the sending of purely good-will direct-mail letters to their entire list of customers periodically. These are sent annually at the New Year or at other appropriate intervals and times—thanking each customer for his business, hoping for uninterrupted "friendship," possibly pledging increased service and improved products, and perhaps requesting ideas for still better fulfillment of the customer's needs. And sometimes just such a simple mailing will make a customer realize that here indeed is a firm interested in him and worthy of his continued business.

Use the YOU point of view. Look at any magazine or newspaper, listen to an evening of radio commercials—with the eye and ear of the consumer, the prospect. Which advertisements or commercials have the most appeal? Ten-to-one they're those that say "you".

In mail-order selling using the you viewpoint is vital because it is your only contact with the prospects, your only chance to present your product so that he will want to make a purchase. In direct-mail advertising, it may not be your contact, but at least it is usually your introductory one—the one that must start your prospect thinking favorably about your product.

How best to inspire that favorable thought? By shouting I—me—mine—we—us—our . . . the biggest—the best—the oldest—the newest? Or simply by saying or implying "you" and "your"?

It is not important to tell your prospect that your firm is, for example, the oldest or the largest in your field. Your firm's age or size might give your prospect confidence in either the integrity of your house, or the dependability of your other selling claims. But even such a claim can be phrased in "you" language as in, "Your assurance of a quality product is Blank Company's fifty-three years of building Dinguses for over 81 percent of the Whatsis Industry." That's written from the reader's—not the seller's—point of view . . . a requisite of good selling copy.

Be truthful and believable. You may think it superfluous to stress "truth in advertising" any more in the creation of remote-control selling than in that of other types of advertising. You need only to think of the success of the great merchandising houses—mail order in particular, such as Sears and Ward's—as ample proof of the fact that truthfulness pays, and pays well. A close relative of truth is believability. Some mail order offers seem actually to ignore both these qualities, depending for both their attention value and selling impact upon startling, even fantastic, claims. These may trap the gullible once, perhaps twice, but no business lasts long when its sales depend upon such a weak foundation.

Not infrequently you may be able to make an advertising claim in all truth, but lacking in believability. If so, don't make it, for your prospects will believe you are not telling the truth anyway. Don't make it, that is, unless, as soon as you do, you back it up with proof, believable proof, that can remove any taint of even suspected untruth. This is particularly true of a new product and its advertising, which the buying public always examines with critical suspicion if not outright distrust. Particularly in selling by mail, then, must you create an aura of truthfulness and believability, for oftentimes to your potential customers your product is a new one, because they've never had the chance to see it before.

Some firms even follow the practice—and successfully too—of underselling their products on the proved theory that the customer who finds his purchase superior to its claims will be an eager repeat customer, the ideal situation for any merchandiser who plans to stay in business. At any rate, avoid exaggeration.

Statements needn't be weak or unenthusiastic—you can state a simple fact in a way that comes out strong. Stick to the truth, avoid exaggeration, and make your claims believable.

SUGGESTIONS FOR EFFECTIVE COPY

1. Keep your writing style simple and direct. Split up involved sentences. Use words your audience would use if talking about your products, or at least words it will understand. These are usually short words—although where technical language adds to copy effectiveness, don't hesitate to use it.
2. Make your subheads work. Make them attention-getters. Use a lot of them to break up your copy into easily digested ideas. Make them helpful to the reader in grasping quickly the thought you want him to get.
3. Use your two strongest statements at the start and finish of your selling talk—the first to arouse attention and interest, the latter to spur whatever action it is that you will ask the prospect to take.
4. Repeat the name of your product frequently—ignoring the niceties of English composition (if that's really how you feel about it) to achieve the repetition which brings with it retention and recognition of that name.

5. Phrase the information in your copy so that it is helpful to the prospects. If it contains more than academic information (which they'll soon forget) but information that is of some real or potential value to remember it—and your product—better and longer.
6. Help the feeling infiltrate your copy that your product is the result of exceptionally fine engineering and manufacturing care, from a house of unquestionable integrity. Keep this feeling casual, not heavily stressed, but don't be casual about seeing that it's there.
7. Just as with any copy you write, find out from those who know (before you start to write) everything you can discover about the product that makes it unique or outstanding in its field. Then, as you plan and write your copy, feature that "different" quality strongly so that your prospects cannot fail to get it.
8. If you have more than one quality or grade of a particular product, you will probably want to "sell up"—to try to interest your prospect in the better item for his own greater satisfaction and your greater profit. This situation may occur in any type of remote control selling, but most likely in mail-order.

    The larger mail-order houses have developed a most effective means of trading up their prospects by use of a "good-better-or-best" technique on all lines where a choice of quality is offered. For some time, they actually tagged many of their illustrations or item headlines with "Good, better-or-best," whichever was appropriate, but when this handling became confusing because of the addition of a fourth or even fifth price line, a refinement of the technique evolved. Now, for the most part, "good-better-or best" is implied. Illustrations may tell part of the difference between similar terms pictorially.

    Headlines help too in pointing out differences, and display copy will feature, say, three selling points for a "good" item, five for a "better" one, and perhaps seven for the "best." Body copy (plus price!) completes the comparison. The copy for a "better" product, for example, perhaps even says in so many words that this item includes every feature of item number so-and-so at the left (the "good" item)—plus thus-and-so in addition. Selling up to the next bracket, the mail-order houses have found, can be well worthwhile.
9. If any other advertising is being used for your product, tie up your efforts to it. Perhaps you are selling a nationally advertised product by mail order in a territory where retail distribution is not feasible or has not been established. Or perhaps your direct-mail campaign is supplementing another campaign in trade journals. In either case, you'll want to take every advantage of the free ride this other advertisement gives you and your efforts.

    Pick up and feature the slogan it uses, its outstanding illustrative treatment, its unique trademark or trade name. If your direct-mail literature is designed to answer requests for "further information" produced by other media, tie your theme and copy in with the advertisement or campaign that inspired the requests. In effect, this again is repetition—so important in establishing your name and position in your chosen market.

10. If you have good testimonials, use them in sales letters. They'll increase the pull. Testimonials are effective, in fact, in any medium that attempts to bring in business through mail-order. Use testimonials, however, only when they are relevant to your prospects and, if you can localize them, do so. Computer letters, for instance, when used in various promotions, drop in names and addresses of people in the same area as the prospect.This procedure is effective.

THINK OF THE PHYSICAL ASPECTS

Since direct mail takes such a myriad of forms, there is no possibility to discuss the physical aspects of all of them. Instead, we will consider two of the most common types, the letter and the folder.

Physical appearance is of great importance to mailings because the appearance causes the first reaction on the part of the prospect. He may be discouraged in that initial glance to the point where he refuses to go on. Here are some suggestions for attracting him in that first glance.

Letters

There are general rules applying to sales letters. There are many variations possible but what you read here, if applied, can help you avoid some of the great faults of direct mail letters—physically speaking and quite apart from writing technique. For purpose of this discussion, we will assume that we are talking about one-page letters and that we are using block form in which the type is flush left with no indentations for paragraphs.

Short opening paragraph. Don't smother your reader with the first paragraph. Limit it to a maximum of four lines and it can be shorter.

No paragraph longer than eight lines. When a paragraph is longer than eight lines, the sales points tend to become buried. Furthermore, the sight of long paragraphs has a depressing effect on readers—the kind of feeling they had when they were faced with long, laborious paragraphs in school textbooks. A textbook writer can get away with this because the student has to read a textbook; a prospect does not have to read a sales letter.

Paragraph length varied. A letter with all paragraphs the same length looks dull and monotonous. This observation applies whether the paragraphs are all long or all short. It is easy to vary

JOHN BLAIR MAIL MARKETING
717 Fifth Avenue, New York, N.Y. 10022 / (212) 832-6677
a division of JOHN BLAIR & COMPANY

Alden Press
American Printers & Lithographers
John Blair Marketing
John Blair Mail Marketing
Meehan-Tooker

Mr. Robert H. Jurick
1357 Boxwood Drive
Hewlett Harbor, N. Y. 11557

Dear Mr. Jurick,

Do you ever mail 50,000 pieces?...100,000?...200,000?

If you do, you should talk with us.

Why?

Well at first you might wonder what our interest could possibly be. After all we have the reputation and production capabilities for handling mailings in the millions for many of our clients. What extra benefits could we offer to a mailer of 50,000 or 100,000 pieces?

Want it in single words...know-how...efficiency... reliability...economy. Now add the word "superior" in front of all of those...because we have to provide superior performance or we wouldn't get the million-mailers' business.

"That's just a claim" you might well say. But consider these facts --

- Our people sit as experts in postal conferences, know rates and regulations and how to take maximum advantage of them.

- Our mechanics must be and are experts at adapting sophisticated folding, inserting, labelling and stamping equipment to meet diverse job requirements most efficiently.

- Our production expeditors are trained and accustomed to adhering to rigid mailing schedules demanded by major mailing clients.

- And when a mailing job is scheduled, it doesn't get bumped -- because we always have the capability of extending regular double shift hours to round-the-clock operation to provide the necessary temporary extra capacity.

So, if your basic interests are to have your 50,000... 100,000...200,000...or larger mailings performed --

- without foul-ups

- on time

- with maximum economy in production and postage

you should talk with us. And do it if you possibly can in the planning stages where our expertise can make a most significant contribution.

What have you got to lose

    Call me or any of my associates,

     anytime, at 832-6677,
     cordially,

     Lee Epstein

P.S.   As the enclosed card indicates we perform many other direct marketing functions in addition to mailings.

FIGURE 13-2

Direct-mail sales letter.   Physically this letter is easy to read. There is no depressing type mass. Paragraphs vary in length and there is a generally open look. As for content, the opening hits hard immediately. This is followed by strong proof of claims in turn followed by a strong call for action that takes up the last fourth of the letter.

paragraph length. Do it. Occasionally, you might want to use a paragraph of a single line, or just several words. This will make your letter more interesting.

OAKTON NATIONAL BANK
(The bank that makes you feel at home)
Oakton, Arkansas 79100
375-0210

Mr. L. R. Nolte
18 Sycamore Lane
Oakton

Dear Mr. Nolte:

Welcome to Oakton!

As a new resident of this city, you're probably busily engaged in learning your way around. Perhaps we can help in the banking side of this experience.

As the only full-service bank in the area, we can offer you:

    . A free checking account.
    . Five different types of savings accounts, all paying
       high interest rates.
    . Direct deposit service for your salary checks--from
       your employer to your savings account, checking
       account, or both. We provide the same service for
       Social Security checks.

But these services are just the start.

Among the other attractive offerings for our depositors are free bank money orders, free travelers checks, and a free safe deposit box (if your savings account is at a certain level). As you can see, your savings over a year can be considerable if you make good use of these free services.

Making it profitable to do business with Oakton National Bank has been a guiding philosophy during this bank's 125-year history. That's true whether you call on our loan department, the trust department, or our investment counseling services.

Coming into a new community always requires considerable adjustment by the newcomer. Please let us help you in any way we can. Drop in when you can and introduce yourself. You'll be given a warm welcome.

Cordially,

F. T. Thirlton
President

FTT/s

FIGURE 13-3

Direct-mail sales letter.   Notice how the writer has made the letter physically inviting by using:
• A short opening paragraph.
• Indented material to break up the type mass.
• Paragraphs of different length.
• No paragraph that runs more than eight lines.
• A short closing paragraph.

Type masses broken up. Why daunt the reader with a whole page of solid, unbroken type? One way to open up the letter invitingly is to use the occasional one-line paragraph already mentioned. Another effective method is to set off important material by indenting it and giving it space above and below. As an example, suppose you want to give a name and address in the letter. The preceding line might read:

When you're in Parkersburg be sure to visit:

    John G. Smelzer
    Smelzer Pottery Company
    18 W. Elizabeth Street

The centering of the name and address creates a pleasing open effect in the letter and focuses the reader's attention on the information.

The same technique can be used when you have several points to make. Supposing you are selling a typewriter. You say:

1. Operates electrically or manually.
2. Has a feather touch.
3. Can be carried easily—very portable.
4. Switching ribbons is simple.
5. Includes all features of standard office typewriter.

Once more, you have opened up your letter and you have centered the reader's attention on important material.

Short closing paragraph. You've said what you had to say, so end quickly. Three or four lines should be sufficient to end any letter.

Folders

One of the most frequently used mailing pieces is the four- or six-page folder that fits as an insert into a No. 10 envelope. It is used also as a counter piece in establishments from hardware stores, drug stores, and plumbing shops, to banks. Considering the folder page by page, here are some suggestions for physical attractiveness.

Page 1. Use a strong headline physically to catch the reader's attention. An attractive illustration is desirable accompanied by a short copy block. Save the long copy for the inside pages. In many cases, it is desirable to use some technique to create enough curiosity to impel the reader to turn to the inside pages. Your headline might do this as:

See the 10 ways this superb tool can save you time and money.

Or at the bottom of the page, an arrow can point to the inside pages and an accompanying copy line says:

Look inside for profitable details.

In short, literally force readers to turn from page 1 to pages 2 and 3.

Here are some more examples of copy lines used on the cover pages of folders that almost force the reader to turn the page because they build up curiosity about the benefits to be obtained if the reader looks inside the folder:

If you don't know beans about boilers but you think your heating system needs a new one . . .

Now . . . the incredible watch— so incredibly water tight it actually comes to you packed in water! And that's only one of the extra features of this amazing watch.

How to get the most out of your painting effort.

How to give the most for
your money this year.

How to enjoy a marvelous vacation
and save money too . . .

Because we care, here is an
important message to you, one
of our many valuable shareholders.
Please take your time and
read it carefully . . .

Page 2 and 3. Treat these pages as one. By so doing, you can use a strong headline that spreads across the two pages and you can use a big, dominant illustration that takes up part of each page. This combination of strong head and illustration will draw the reader's gaze and create a vitality missing if each page is treated separately.

In order to create excitement for these pages, use selling subheads liberally over the copy blocks. If small illustrations are used, along with the dominant illustration, give each a caption. Carry the reader through the pages by directing his reading and by infusing the section with vigor.

Page 4 (back page). Sometimes advertisers leave this space blank. This is a grievous mistake since the back page of folders receives good readership. Treat the back page pretty much as you do the front page with an omission, of course, of any urging to turn the page. Sometimes the back page is a good place to put a guarantee, a special offer, a listing of important points. Make it just as attractive as the front page since often readers look first at the first page, flip the folder over to the back page and then, if sufficiently interested, turn to the inside pages. Make the back page worth looking at.

FOLLOW SALES LEADS VIGOROUSLY

One of the great tragedies of American industry is the lack of followup. A prospect writes to a company about a product or sends in a coupon. No answer is received. Or the answer arrives so long after the inquiry that the prospect is no longer interested, or has bought a competing product.

Not only do many companies fail to follow up consumer inquiries adequately but also they fail to follow such sales leads with their dealers as they should. If a sales lead has been derived from advertising, it should be given to the dealer immediately. He should be made aware of the advertising backing that produced the lead because dealers need constant reminding of the power of advertising supplied by their manufacturing sources.

Often, too, the followup letter provides the manufacturer-supplier with a chance to resell his product and to provide the dealer with selling words and phrases that he can use on prospects who come into his store. This reselling is often needed because the dealers, carrying many, many lines can't possibly be knowledgeable in depth of all those lines.

This sales letter to the dealer is very much like an advertisement he will see in his trade magazine because it emphasizes the 3-P's of product-promotion-profit. Its chief object is to get the dealer and the prospect together so that a sale can be made. Its secondary object is to resell the advertising backing and the product.

Figure 13-4 illustrates a letter that follows a sales lead, sells the dealer, and strongly urges action that may result in a personal sales talk. Without such followup the company has wasted money in conducting an expensive advertising campaign.

FIGURE 13-4

Letter to follow sales lead.

```
September 20, 19XX


Mr. Frank R. Bilton
Bilton Hardware Company
2235 Elmwood Place
Dover, Ohio 44622

Dear Mr. Bilton:

Here's a sales prospect for you.

            Mrs. John L. Glanke
            334 Elmwood Place
            Dover

Mrs. Glanke, in answering an ad of ours in Woman's Day, has asked
for a leaflet about Quality kitchen knives.  She has been sent
the leaflet and given your name as her nearest dealer.

There may be a good number of such sales leads because of the
hard-hitting campaign we're running in such outstanding magazines
as Better Homes & Gardens, Ladies' Home Journal, Good Housekeeping
and the New Yorker.  The Quality knife story is being told to
millions of readers of these magazines, thousands of whom live in
your area.  And to cover area residents even more intensively,
we're offering you a complete co-op plan including powerful
advertising in newspapers, TV, and radio.

To justify such an advertising barrage, you need to have an
outstanding product.  According to dealers from coast to coast,
Quality knives more than live up the advertising claims.

From what these dealers tell us, their customers seem deeply
impressed by such features as the 50-year guarantee, the forged
steel construction, and the super-sharpness that makes it
possible for them to slice vegetables razor thin.  Our advertising
has put special stress on the 50-year guarantee because no other
knife in history has offered such assurance to the purchaser.

Right now, with Mrs. Glanke obviously interested in this product,
we'd suggest that you phone or write her immediately.  Get her
into your store to see the display we've provided you--it could
mean a quick sale for you.

            Cordially,

            Homer T. McQuarrie

            Homer T. McQuarrie
            Sales Department
```

PUT ENVELOPES TO WORK

Many a letter would be tossed unopened and unread into the waste basket were it not for an irresistible message on the envelope, a fact that alert direct mailers have recognized. The message, or invitation, on the envelope has become standard procedure these days. Thus, prospects are invited to "Look inside for the greatest bargain you've ever seen."

To make the message on the envelope even more exciting and curiosity provoking, many of today's envelopes have windows—round, square, rectangular—that let you take a peek at the treasures within. An example of such usage is the big envelope used by

Cheeselovers, International that has a round window. An arrow points to the cellophane window. The envelope message reads:

Mail this token to get
$6.00 worth of Delicious Imported Cheese
FREE!

Plus, your opportunity to enjoy
some of the world's great cheeses
for as low as
3¢ to 7¢ above wholesale.

Last chance—this free gift offer
will not be repeated this season.

Even in the case of present customers, the message on the envelope can be useful in keeping them sold as in the case of a Master Charge mailing to present customers that carries an envelope message reading:

Relax
You've got a Master Charge

In the competitive world of direct mail, you must operate on the principle that if there's a place to put a message, you write one and make it sell in the case of the envelope just as you sell anywhere else.

Two more envelope messages demonstrate these principles at work:

All-New!
Betty Crocker's
Step-by-Step Recipe Cards
Free Recipe Card Enclosed
Open up now—to see our free introductory
gift for you.
A $7.50 value.

Will this unusual offer be of interest to you?
There's only one way to find out . . .

This Membership Card entitles you to receive
Collectors Gemstones (*Card can be seen through window in envelope*)

FREE EMERALD
or other extraordinary
gemstones reserved for:
(*name of mailee*)

LAST CHANCE
THIS ENVELOPE CONTAINS
YOUR LAST INVITATION TO JOIN
International Gem Finders Society . . . THIS SEASON
Membership Rosters are Almost Oversubscribed
Now!

In both of the foregoing messages on the envelopes there is a strong urge to act and a clear indication of what you will lose if you don't act. Thus, you see the same direct mail and mail order principles at work on the envelope as well as in the material inside the envelope.

A SUMMING UP

As a summing up for this chapter, here is a copy-writing formula for direct mail recommended by Edward N. Mayer, Jr., for many years a leader in the direct-mail field. This advice, applies equally well to direct-mail or to mail-order. It can, in fact, be applied to much advertising that is not classed as direct-mail or mail-order. Like so many advertising people Mayer has stressed the use of copy that offers a benefit to the reader:

1. Promise a benefit in the headline or first paragraph—your most important benefit to the reader.
2. Immediately enlarge upon your most important benefit.
3. Tell the reader specifically what he is going to get.
4. Back up your statements with proofs and endorsements.
5. Tell the reader what he might lose if he doesn't act.
6. Rephrase your prominent benefits in your closing offer.
7. Incite action now. [1]

Notice how well these seven suggestions fit into the classic A-I-D-A formula of attention, interest, desire, and action.

[1] Robert Stone, "Mr. Direct Mail's Seven Rules for Success," *Advertising Age,* February 17, 1969, p.226.

14

Selling for Business, Agriculture, and the Professions, Part A

In professional football the backfield gets the most attention from the fans. Linemen are relatively anonymous. Yet, there are more linemen than backs and, as those knowledgeable of the game will tell you, the linemen are the unsung heroes.

So it is in advertising. Consumer advertising gets the attention of the public, attracting praise or censure. Millions in that same public are unaware of business advertising that, like the big professional linemen, slogs along doing hard, important work.

Certainly, consumer advertising that sells furniture, jewelry, gasoline, loan companies, milk, perfume, airline trips, and a myriad of other personal products and services is a vital concern of many copywriters. Business advertising, however, is the chief and often only concern of great numbers of copywriters, especially copywriters in advertising agencies and in the advertising departments of large manufacturing firms. Furthermore, many copy people write both consumer and business advertising.

Business advertising is often called "business paper" advertising. This is too narrow a term because business advertising includes trade, industrial, and professional advertising. Don't look for such advertising in general magazines, newspapers, outdoor posters, radio, or television. Almost exclusively it appears in business publications, a term to be preferred to "business papers."

Almost every field of United States enterprise has one or more publications serving it, a magazine or newspaper that is published periodically and contains news and information of special interest to those in the industry represented.

Thus *Bakery Production and Marketing* is an expertly managed and edited magazine, circulated to those concerned with the baking industry. Bakers, large and small, millers, wholesale and retail grocers, and others are familiar with its interesting articles, stories, news items, and advertising as they are with those of other business publications servicing the bakery industry. *Iron Age* is a famous business paper of the industrial type for the steel industry; *Progressive Grocer* is one of the many business papers of the trade type which serves the grocery field. *Men's Wear* goes to the clothing industry and *American Funeral Director* is read by most of the country's morticians.

WHAT'S THE APPROACH IN BUSINESS COPY?

Now, naturally, all these publications do not stay in business by their subscription income alone, any more than do other magazines and newspapers. They contain a great deal of advertising, often featuring products that you see advertised elsewhere in consumer copy. But the copy story behind that advertising may be different—in appeal, in technique, and in intended results.

Trade advertising. The advertisements in business publications of the trade type are designed to gain the selling and merchandising support of the dealers who offer your product for resale.

When you write this kind of copy, remember to follow the 3-P's formula—product, promotion, profit. Emphasis on one, two, or all three of these elements is characteristic of all trade advertising.

Industrial advertising. Advertisements appearing in business papers of the industrial type enable one industry to advertise to another industry, usually about items that can be used for helping production. Thus the makers of a punch press can help in their production. In contrast to trade advertising, industrial advertising is not concerned with the factor of resale.

Professional advertising. The third classification, professional advertising, which appears in such publications as *Journal of the American Medical Association, Dental Digest,* and *American Journal of Orthodontics and Oral Surgery*, is aimed at professional people who can do two things for you. They can use your product. They can recommend the use of your product.

DON'T UNDERRATE BUSINESS ADVERTISING

To avoid confusion, consider the term "business advertising" as referring only to that kind of advertising that appears in business publications—trade, industrial, or professional. Direct mail, house organs, films, specialized presentations—all aimed at the trade—will be eliminated in this discussion. For the time being, so will "collateral"—all the display or point-of-sale materials, training manuals, merchandising presentations, and portfolios—which copywriters are called upon to produce and which usually come under the heading of "trade."

Business advertising is essentially a supplementary selling force that strengthens and meshes with the merchandising and selling program of the advertiser.

Here are some facts to remember about business advertising.

- Business publication space rates are low compared with consumer media. Thus many copywriters don't consider business advertising very important. Some agencies don't consider it worthwhile to hire competent writers skilled in business copy because space commissions aren't high enough. Yet there are notable exceptions to this. One large agency, for example, has a vice-president in charge of their business publication operation.

- Some advertisers and agencies feel that "consumer advertisements alone can do the job"— that specially designed advertising to trade or industry is not necessary. Such thinking can lead to unsound and wasteful advertising, especially in trade advertising. Any retailer who knows the business can switch customers from one product to another. He can favor one product by displaying it at eye-level on the shelves and putting others down low where people have to stoop to get them. Consumer advertising can and should be supported with a good, heavy program for the trade in most cases.

Often trade and consumer advertising are similar

Sometimes trade advertising and consumer advertising aren't much different. In *Progressive Grocer*, for example, you will find many advertisements offering products used by the dealers themselves, such as paper bags, twine, and business machines. This, of

course, is consumer advertising even though it appears in trade publications. Its primary interest to them, however, is in its offering a product or service as a source of profit, because these people are in business to make money—to earn a livelihood.

Although the beautiful new color of a transparent comb, for example, may be advertised in the *Ladies' Home Journal* in terms of its vividness, glowing good looks, and newness. Advertising of the same comb in the trade papers that reach drug and department stores would also tell of the new color idea, but would interpret it in terms of why more people will want and buy the comb; how well it is advertised to create a demand; how store tests showed sales went up quickly when it was displayed—and increased all other comb sales, as well. And the advertisement might end, "If you haven't seen them . . . if your salesperson hasn't been around and told you the mighty pretty profit story we've got to tell, let us know—but quick. Better write or wire right now.

No fancy writing there. Just a straight appeal for action. But don't misunderstand. Trade advertisements can be dramatic and interesting—and you can employ all the basic essentials of effective copywriting already mentioned in previous chapters. First of all, know what you're writing about and what you want an advertisement or series of advertisements to accomplish.

Trade advertising, as previously said, is generally confined to products or services handled by wholesalers or retailers for resale. Some exceptions might be the advertising of flour and baker's supplies in bakery trade publications read by wholesale and retail bakers. Another exception is the advertising of certain equipment such as meat cases, frozen food cases, and paper bags, in grocery and meat trade papers. These products, while not purchased for resale, can very properly be advertised in trade papers as a type of consumer advertising.

Products advertised to the trade are often nationally advertised through magazines, newspapers, radio, and TV. When this is true, you may often be called upon to tell the trade the story of these consumer advertising programs, so dealers will know and appreciate the promotional help the manufacturer is giving through the national consumer campaign.

GENERAL ADVICE ON TRADE ADVERTISING

"Clever" slogans or gimmicks alone in small space will rarely pay off as trade advertising technique. Such thoughts as "Beans by Glick Always Click," run time after time in trade advertisements with the assumption that "we're doing a job with the trade," and do not offer retailers any reason at all for featuring Glick's beans. Tell the trade how it can make money with Glick's beans—how repeat sales steadily grow—how to display the product more successfully. Tell the retailers that store tests have revealed above-normal turnover and shelf velocity. Isn't that what a good sharp salesperson would ordinarily tell dealers? He certainly wouldn't come in time after time just chanting "Beans by Glick always Click."

Use as much space as possible. Only then can you give a certain amount of prestige and importance to the product. You need that space for fair readership and for a complete sales talk.

Many advertisers and agencies will often turn out poorly produced business advertisements on the grounds that "the budget won't stand better stuff." This is faulty thinking when you have something important enough to say—or when the time is critical (such as during the announcement of a new product, a price slash, and so forth). Get in there and pitch for more color, better art, or more space in your business advertising.

Which is more important—the estimated cost of the advertisements or campaign, or the job to be done? If it's the job, then be sure it can succeed—and that may require much better art and production than were first figured on.

How long should trade copy be? Like consumer copy it should be long enough to get over the message and no longer. That could be 40 words or 400. Every advertisement must be judged individually. Trade advertisements will usually require more copy than consumer advertisements since you will be much more concerned with explanatory material. Also, your profit-minded readers are more willing to read long technical material if they see value in what you say.

WRITING TRADE ADVERTISEMENTS

In the chapter on headline writing you read this:

Your whole week's wash done in
30 minutes . . . While you shop!

Obviously, that's a headline for an automatic washer. Assume that it is the headline of an advertisement in a campaign ready to break in national consumer publications. Support for this consumer advertising will be provided through a special campaign to reach the trade. Electric appliance stores, department stores, and a few special outlets will be the trade in this case.

The people who run these stores handle automatic washers for resale. To them the only value of the claim "Your whole week's wash done in 30 minutes . . . While you shop" lies in the fact that this is a powerful weapon to use in their sales talks. It helps them sell more "X" washers.

Consider the foregoing heading. The thought expressed in it will probably be the basis for other consumer advertisements and will be used to merchandise that advertising to the trade. The people who handle the "X" washer—and prospective new dealers—will thus be informed that a comprehensive and effective national advertising campaign is starting; that it will reach people and prospects in every locality; and that, naturally, it will stimulate interest

in the washer and bring people into your store for more information or a demonstration.

First of all, a selection of the most effective trade papers would be made. You might or might not have anything to do with the choosing of these, but in any event you would want to be familiar with them in order to adjust your copy style to the magazine and its readers.

National advertising support

Orthodox treatment might start out this way. First advertisement is a double spread, uses some color, and the type of news headline mentioned in the chapter on headlines.

Most powerful consumer advertising ever! . . . To help you ring up record sales on "X" washers

Subhead: New, sure-fire, full-page color
                  advertisements run in 5 leading
                  magazines—
                  aimed to reach more than 65% of
                  prospects in your own neighborhood!

Second   All through the year,
subhead   these advertisements will appear in
                  McCall's Ladies' Home Journal,
                  Better Homes and Gardens.

Illustrations might show a few typical advertisements, as large as possible, small covers of the magazines mentioned—and possibly a small chart illustrating how 65% (figure used only for example) of prospects are reached by this advertising, for the average dealer.

Copy would explain why the consumer advertisements should be effective, why women are interested in saving time, being able to shop, do housework, etc., while clothes are being washed, etc. All copy would be written from the dealer's side—how all this advertising is aimed to work for him; now it brings people into the store; how it actually pays off at your cash register. Such an advertisement might logically ask for action at the end, something like this:

Continuous advertising support in your own neighborhood is only one reason why the "X" franchise is such a money-maker for dealers. A franchise might be available for you. A special Profit Table that shows sales and profit potentials for your own locality is yours on request. Get yours—and other facts and figures you should have. Better do it now . . . before your competitor's request arrives first.

Here's some comment on this advertisement. The headlines are quite long. The headlines and the subheads, however, certainly tell the story, and that's always good practice according to highly experienced trade-advertising experts, who say that two kinds of readers see trade advertisements: a) Quick readers who seldom read more than the heads and subheads. b) Thorough readers (a small group) who will read anything and everything having to do with their business. If, in view of the foregoing, you can get your

FIGURE 14-1

Trade advertisement with emphasis on advertising and promotional backing.   A powerful reminder of the advertising behind a product line can stir dealers' excitement and encourage them to stock up to be ready for the expected consumer response.

fairly complete story into your headings, chances are you'll get high readership from both classes of readers. Of course, this reasoning, like so many other facets of advertising, is open to long and thorough discussion. It's the kind of reasoning, just the same, that should be explored by the intelligent copywriter.

The headlines contain some "you" element and mention the name of the product. The whole tone of the advertisement is on the "you"—directed straight to the dealer—and that is an essential in trade advertising, because the writer simply must explain everything the advertiser does, in terms of benefits, profits, help, and so forth, which the dealer-reader can expect from the product or service being advertised.

Stress local effect of advertising

Assuming that the national advertising is the most important message the "X" company has for dealers, the next trade advertisement in the series could well treat the "local" effect of all the advertising the "X" company does—including the new campaign. The heading for such an advertisement might be:

New "X" washer advertising "talks to"
nearly 7 out of every 10 people
Right in your neighborhood.

The whole advertisement might use "believe it or not" technique, and with several illustrations and little copy for each show how the advertising works for every dealer in his own area. This "local advertising" versus "national advertising" question is always a moot one. Lately, there has been great recognition of the need to interpret national advertising in terms of local advertising—since the local readership of national advertising is the only interest any dealer has in it. Boasting that yours is the biggest national advertising campaign ever to hit the magazines just leaves the dealers cold unless you can show them the effect this campaign will have on their own customers. The eternal question in any alert dealer's mind is, "What does this advertising do for me?"

The next several advertisements in the trade series could well dramatize store tests and store experiences of progressive dealers with the "X" washers. Advertisements would explain how the consumer advertising brought in prospects to find out how a whole week's wash could be done in 30 minutes, and how with a few little display ideas of the dealer sales of the "X" washer rose to a new high level. The purpose here, of course, is to persuade dealers reading about these experiences to think that they can do as well.

TIMING TRADE ADVERTISEMENTS

Time of the year, specific problems that arise at times, and new company policies—all these and more affect trade advertising. What these special conditions are often dictates what the advertisements will say. A few of them will be shown with special situations; the headlines of advertisements show how the situation might be met.

Suppose, for instance, users had experienced considerable difficulty with the Swirler—a patented clothes agitator of the "X" machine. Dealers were getting too many complaints; machines were returned; sales dropped ominously. One effective solution would be elimination of the Swirler and introduction of a new agitator of proved troublefree operation. Wouldn't it be big and important news for the trade to know:

Revolutionary new clothes agitator of
"X" washer eliminates service headaches!

Copy would explain how a "torture treatment," equal to five years' normal use, was set up in an independent laboratory, and that five machines out of every one hundred going through the factory were put through this test. No mention would be focused on the "troublefree new agitator" that would certainly overcome most of the previous difficulty. The same theme would be used by salespeople making their calls.

Suppose the washing action of the "X" washer is "oscillatory." Other washers use the "reciprocating" action. There is great controversy over the merits of each. If it could be proved in unbiased tests that oscillatory was far superior, tests could be set up in noted laboratories, and results of these tests would make the basis of a series of advertisements. Here's one such headline:

Oscillatory action of "X" washer
Outperforms reciprocating 3 to 1
in actual tests

You'd have to be prepared for controversy and you'd need to be very sure of your facts, but if the advertiser were strong enough, he could settle the argument positively. He might possibly devise an action that combined the advantages of both—if they were equal in varying respects—and, so to speak, work both ends. Heading:

Advantages of both oscillatory and reciprocating actions
Combined in radical new oscil-rep action of "X" washer

To the trade that's big news. And as mentioned before, you've got to know the trade, what's going on, what interests dealers—and write "to" them—so they'll know you know.

CREATING THE PROMOTIONAL PACKAGE

Here is the second way, usually much the preferred and more effective, to support the consumer advertising of "X" washers. You will start again with the series that includes the advertisement, headed:

Your whole week's wash done in
30 minutes . . . while you shop!

Now, you will create a package or a packaged promotion which will include considerable promotional material, point-of-display pieces, gimmicks, results of store tests, direct-mail and newspaper mats for dealer's use. Also, you'll include a portfolio for the salespeople who call on dealers. The portfolio explains the whole deal. Added to the foregoing, you will also promote the promotion to the trade through regular trade publications.

Mirro's White Bakeware Sale
January-February-March

BLIZZARD OF ACTION
To cash in on the swing to home baking.

This Mirro Message on Sunday, January 30 will create extra store traffic to help you turn winter into a hot selling season.

PARADE – 113 Markets

FAMILY WEEKLY – 325 Markets

plus selected Sunday Supplements in these BIG MAJOR METRO MARKETS...

New York	Memphis
Los Angeles	Miami
Long Island	Milwaukee
San Francisco	Minneapolis
Atlanta	New Orleans
Cincinnati	Oklahoma City
Cleveland	Omaha
Columbus	Phoenix
Denver	Pittsburgh
Des Moines	Providence
Indianapolis	Rochester
Kansas City	Toledo
Louisville	

Now you can cash in on the hot trend toward home baking by offering favorite aluminum bakeware items with White Teflon II interiors at 20% savings! A full color sales message in all these magazines and Sunday supplements packs the punch and prestige of national advertising *plus* the immediacy and impact of a local promotion! To help you turn winter into a hot selling season.

See the full line of even-heating aluminum bakeware items at the Housewares Show, Booths 3906 and 4008.

Winter White Sale
20% SAVINGS
on famous Mirro aluminum bakeware with White Teflon II interiors.

This Mirro message of great winter savings (in page-dominating size and full color) will reach over 104,000,000 readers!

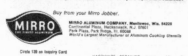

Buy from your Mirro Jobber.

MIRRO ALUMINUM COMPANY, Manitowoc, Wis. 54220

Circle 139 on Inquiry Card

FIGURE 14-2

Trade advertisement that strikes a balance between product and advertising support.   Copy has vigor and enthusiasm appropriate for this type of advertisement.

Assume the Swirler is an ingenious and exclusive agitator of the "X" machine and is the main reason why clothes wash so quickly and so clean. Also, the Swirler is one important part of the automatic operation which permits people to leave the machine while it merrily goes on with its washing. You'll then dramatize the Swirler in every way, bring it into all your promotion and advertising, and introduce a catchy theme that will be the core of your promotion. It is your U.S.P.

You may decide to use the "stop and go" light idea, which is quite suitable for this example. The slogan or keynote will be

Stop Washing
Go Swirling

In the consumer advertising, headlines would continue on the time-saving and leisure theme, as exemplified by the headline "Your whole week's wash done in 30 minutes." Copy would explain how this was possible, heavily promoting the Swirler. Somewhere in the main illustration or in an illustration of the washer or Swirler, you might show a gaily waving banner with traffic-signal-light effects and the theme words, "Stop Washing . . . Go Swirling." Already you can see how this device can be carried through all promotion and advertising—magazines, outdoor, newspapers, direct mail, display material, trade—even radio, where sound tricks would take the place of the signal lights.

Here's the promotional material you could logically include in your package and which you will promote in your trade advertising (to be explained later on).

- A series of newspaper mats and radio and TV commercials for the dealer's use, built on the "stop and go" idea.
- A series of three to six direct-mail pieces for dealers to send to selected prospects, built on same idea.
- Several large display pieces using the red "stop" and green "go" light, idea, plus possibly one life-sized cut-out figure of a traffic policeman with a red and green light above him—(they flash on and off alternately) for use in store window or inside store, next to "X" washer or washers on display.
- A series of "how to display the "X" washer suggestions. This would consist of several illustrations of putting washer on elevated floor platform, placing certain display material around it, casting colored light from a baby spotlight on it in store or window, and other similar ideas.

Then, using the same red and green light technique, all this material or pictures of it will be arranged in logical order in a salesperson's portfolio, titled

Stop Wondering . . .
Go Swirling

Next the trade advertising. With all this material ready to help the dealers and with the attention-getting red and green light treatment, we now have:

- A packaged promotion—complete and available for the dealers, to help them capitalize more effectively on the power of the consumer advertising.
- A gimmick—in the red and green lights and the slogan, which will provide immediately identity in all collateral and trade advertising.

First, the trade advertising could well announce the big consumer campaign already mentioned—bringing in the slogan and the red and green light idea in a subordinate way. In every trade advertisement—sometimes large, sometimes small—this plug would always be made: "Stop Wondering . . . Go Swirling." Use of this phrase would provide a note of recognition when the salesperson called with the same device and wording on the front of his portfolio.

Second advertisement in the trade series might be a big play on the central theme of "Stop Washing . . . Go Swirling" and explain how this catchy little selling phrase will work and work on the minds of people, wearing down sales resistance and exciting curiosity. Copy would still devote some words to the big advertising support.

Following advertisements could well run in this order:

1. Big splash on all the material available to help dealers sell more "X" machines.
2. Reproductions of telegrams from dealers telling how well the new advertising is working for them.
3. Straight appeal to dealers to "see what's in the big black book the "X" salesperson has ready to show you." This refers to the portfolio, and copy would hint of the "money-magic" that the book brings to readers.
4. Series of advertisements built on store tests, showing how successful dealers used all the material available on "X" machines and how well sales are going. In other words, success stories.

Store tests are important

You've probably noticed that the store tests are mentioned many times. Unbiased store tests are convincing to dealers. First, no dealer can overlook such data when they have to do with his bread and butter. Secondly, not many advertisers are willing to go to the expense and trouble of making the tests (and results may not be suitable for publication). When such test results do appear, they constitute material that is far from common.

All the advertisements mentioned as suitable for this series—whether based on store tests or not—would, of course, always end with a strong urge to the dealer to "wire or write, or telephone us of the 'X' salesperson who has been trying to see you—and get the full facts"—or something along that line.

It should be mentioned that when the entire campaign was approved and when the first samples of all the advertisements and material were finally available, everything was timed in order that the whole plan could be presented to the sales organization at convention, so the salespeople could sally forth into their respective territories filled with the fire and fervor of their cause. It's just as important that the sales force be sold on your advertising and promotion as the dealers or "the trade."

FIGURE 14-3

Trade advertisement with emphasis on display.   The importance of attractive and efficient display units in moving goods in retail stores is demonstrated in this advertisement.

WHY DIRECT INSTITUTIONAL ADVERTISEMENTS TO THE TRADE?

Most trade advertising tries to sell a product or service in a very direct way. Some advertisers, however, cannot always do this. Consider Hotpoint. They market many products sold through the appliance trade. If every Hotpoint product division decided to use an aggressive advertising campaign in trade magazines, a competitive free-for-all would ensue. In the case of such multiproduct advertisers it is sensible to use an institutional theme. Here, for example, the name "Hotpoint" is promoted and each product is introduced as a member of the Hotpoint family of quality appliances and the selling-theme idea may be expressed as the "quality of Hotpoint."

Merchandising the national advertising and selling the dealer on promotional assistance and institutional advertising are not, of course, the only means of using trade-paper space. Hundreds of different ideas, plans, deals, promotions, and "packages" are offered to the retailers through trade campaigns. The subject matter of your trade advertising will be dependent upon what is the most important message to get across to the trade who will resell your product.

Thus if you are marketing a brand new product, through a company with no national prestige or name, perhaps the most important single thing for you to accomplish in trade advertising is to build confidence among the dealers in your company and in its financial background. If you are introducing a new automobile, you may wish to inspire such confidence and backing by running trade advertising on your personnel, their experience in manufacturing, designing, and selling cars.

Trade advertising, as you have examined it here, is good for one major result: to gain the selling support of retail merchants. In order to do this, your trade campaigns must offer something to the dealers that will make them want to feature and sell your product.

Underlying everything, of course, is their desire to make a profit. The copy in Figure 14-4 from a trade publication stresses this point.

Discover a world of year around products for year around profits. . .

With WRAP-ON®products you now have a twelve month selling season for increased sales and more profits. Every product we sell is backed by our FREE REPLACEMENT POLICY. If any product fails to operate, it will be replaced free of charge.

FIGURE 14-4

Trade advertisement.

Still other advertisements will put the stress on the handsome display units offered to dealers. These units provide an attractive means of displaying the manufacturer's line, a very important consideration to dealers who have limited space and a pride in the appearance of their stores. Accordingly, you will find many trade advertisements that put total stress on the display opportunities they have to offer and, allied to that, the packaging is sometimes featured.

PRODUCT OR PROMOTION— WHICH COMES FIRST?

Copywriters are so product-oriented that they almost automatically think in terms of product first, and yet this can be a mistake in some trade advertisements.

Let's assume that you are selling a product without any special distinction and that there is no new product feature to exploit in the advertising. Still, the product is a steady seller in retail outlets and must be advertised to maintain its competitive position. Assume, too, that the product has an outstanding promotion behind it—big circulation consumer magazines, television, radio, newspapers.

Clearly, the promotional backing should be headlined and the bulk of the copy should concern the support the dealer can expect. The product can simply be mentioned at the top of the advertisement, but the promotion is what you dwell on.

Another situation: A new product with appealing sales features and a strong promotional support behind it. In this case, the headline and possibly an opening subhead can stress the product and the excellent advertising support. The first impression the dealer gets is that the company is offering a hot new product and is backing it with equally hot advertising. You can then follow the headline by talking first about the product, or you can start with the promotion. Either is suitable.

Another situation: General Electric is introducing a new toaster-oven, a proved seller. When the advertiser has a name so powerful as General Electric, any product it introduces is big news in itself. In this case, stress the product and then bring in the advertising support strongly.

As you can see, there are various ways to handle this question of product or promotion. The point is that promotion can be as important to stress as the product and sometimes should be stressed first and harder than the product.

Advertising backing should be sold specifically, enthusiastically and with conviction. Dealers too often aren't aware of the extent of the support; they should be told. Furthermore, because many dealers resent the amount their suppliers spend on national advertising, trade advertising should make it clear to them just how much such advertising can help them. Dealers must be sold over and over again on the value of promotion and even company salespeople need such reminding because they, too, frequently fail to realize the power of a good advertising campaign.

FIGURE 14-5

Trade advertisement. The Three Ps are demonstrated in this advertisement—Profit, Promotion, and Product with special emphasis on the first two.

X-ray, Cartography, Micrography, Laser Applications, Fiber Optics Techniques, Laboratory Measurements and Optical Display Techniques, Earth Resources, Data Processing, Image Processing, Coherent Optics, Pattern Recognition.

INDUSTRIAL ADVERTISING

Joe Ziks, an agency copywriter, was a star in the writing of copy for consumer products. For soaps, cereal, clothing, and headache remedies he created winning campaigns. His trade advertisements that tied in with the consumer products he wrote about were notable. Yet Joe was a flop in the writing of industrial advertising. He lacked the feel for technical copy. He wasn't at home in writing to engineers, technicians, factory managers, chemists, and the others who make up the industrial market.

Think about your qualifications. Then look at this excerpt from the industrial section of *Standard Rate & Data Service*. Do you feel qualified to write to the readers of this publication? Do you have the background or the inclination?

. . . Range of subject matter includes

Underwater research, Holography, Space Optics, Range Instrumentation, Image Enhancement, Optical Data Reduction, Environmental Quality, Computer Applications, Bio-Medical Research, Photographic Data Recording, Transportation Studies,

Industrial advertising is difficult to write

Good writers can usually learn quickly what they must know in order to write about most consumer products. There is no way, however, that they can learn quickly what they need to know about such products as industrial pumps or giant turbines. They can't bluff. They can't dazzle hydraulic engineers or electrical engineers with cute selling phrases. Before they write they must study the products, see them operate, talk to the plant people and the salespeople and the advertising manager. They study the specification sheets and the engineering catalogs. When finally they know thoroughly the equipment, its uses, its applications, then they might be prepared to write and only in the language of their hard-boiled market. No glib consumer approach will work here.

Forget most consumer-copy techniques. If you have technical inclinations or have had some technical or engineering training and you're a reasonably good writer, you may have a future as a writer of industrial advertising. If you switch from consumer to

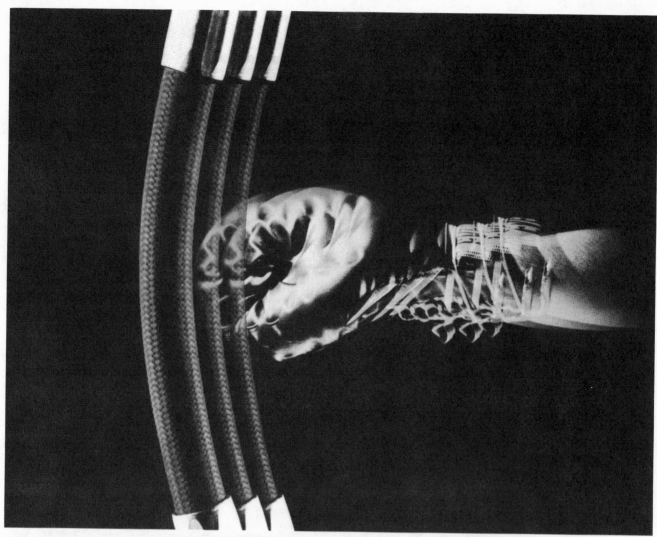

Pound a hose line 1,000,000 times at +300°F.

Revolutionary new AQP™ elastomer makes it possible

We did it to Aeroquip FC300 AQP Hydraulic Hose in hydraulic impulse pressure tests to determine how long they would last under these extreme operating conditions. They outlasted conventional hose of similar construction by as much as 5 to 1.

We also froze them, baked them, scraped them and tested them with over 850 exotic fluids including oil and phosphate ester based hydraulic fluids. The results were always the same. They outlasted their conventional counterparts in all tests.

The secret of the Aeroquip AQP Hoses is the Aeroquip-developed AQP elastomer. It was developed specifically for use in hose by a company whose specialty is hose. For more information write for Bulletin 5220. Aeroquip Corporation, Industrial Division, Jackson, Michigan 49203, *a subsidiary of Libbey-Owens-Ford Company.*

In impulse tests, Aeroquip FC300 AQP Hydraulic Control Hoses withstand 1,000,000 impulse cycles at +300°F. in all sizes, far exceeding SAE100R5 requirements.

Aeroquip turns problems into products

Aeroquip Ad No. ACI-2719 R

FIGURE 14-6

Industrial advertisement.   All the elements are used here that are needed for a strong industrial advertisement—an outstanding illustration, an interesting headline, and specific copy that provides useful information based on tests.

industrial copy, you'll notice some differences immediately:

- Your approach is generally much less informal. The "you" approach, so loved by the consumer-product writer is usually out of place in industrial advertising. You don't cozy up to a vice-president of manufacturing, a plant manager, or a safety engineer. They don't use the products you sell; they consider their purchase for use in their plant operations. Then, if they like what they read, they may ask someone else to "look into it" or to "specify" it. Because there is no personal use involved, you have little or no chance for the "you" approach, or for informal, personal language.

- Hard sell is out. You don't push industrial readers. You don't high pressure them. You don't urge action as you do with consumers or trade-advertisement readers. The industrial purchase is likely to be large. A committee may be appointed to decide whether your product should be used plant-wide. Perhaps the purchase will be in hundreds of thousands of units. Possibly six months to a year will pass before the purchasing agent is told to put through the order. In that time there may have been competitive bidding, demonstrations, tests, and presentations. Against this background you would look absurd were you to use consumer-copy exhortations of "order now," "act quickly," "don't delay," or other action phrases, the favorites of writers of consumer and trade advertising. Industrial buyers simply aren't impulsive types to be swayed by such urgency.

- As a rule you avoid the light touch.   Now and then you may invest industrial advertising with humor, or a lighthearted, consumer-type approach—but rarely. Your readers aren't poring over industrial advertisements to be amused or entertained. Your product might reduce accidents, increase production, cut down pollution, or improve morale. These are not lighthearted goals. They are approached in a serious manner and you call upon the vocabulary of the readers to tell them what your product will do for their plant or the products turned out. That vocabulary will be down-to-earth, specialized, and often difficult. It definitely is not carefree nor (usually) even cheerful. This kind of writing comes hard to consumer-product copywriters who, to this point, have prided themselves on the "easy, conversational touch."

Industrial advertising suggestions

Copy to purchasing agents, engineers, and other realists gives the facts, not the frills.

Many of the general principles given for the writing of business publication copy apply to industrial copy. You will find in the following material some additional suggestions for writing industrial-publication copy which might help you approach this market intelligently.

Purchasing agents often aren't so much concerned with long-range cost as long-range savings. Your competitor's metal tubing may cost forty cents a foot but may last only half as long as yours. Your tubing at sixty cents a foot would, consequently, be a good buy. Remember that purchasing agents are buying greater productivity for the firm—that means they are interested in saving manpower and materials. Thus, long-lasting materials and equipment are almost always their first interest.

FIGURE 14-7

Industrial advertisement featuring testimonial.   In this advertisement, the copy starts out with a testimonial, switches to straight-line copy, and then picks up the testimonial again—a good way to hold interest throughout. Often in such an advertisement, the headline will also be in quotes to get instant attention.

replaces 3 machines

"This Tape-Turn IV has replaced three turret lathes in our plant," says Marc Kinnemann (left), Chief Engineer for the Bee-Line Company, builders of auto and truck alignment equipment.

"It turns such a good finish that we've eliminated a rolling operation we used to need on these pistons for our 100-ton rams."

Bee-Line's machine is equipped with both front and rear turret, plus automatic bar feed.

"We have 350 parts we can program for it," says Rick Meeker (right), Programmer, "and I can easily program three parts in a day."

Meeker uses the LeBlond NC/LTTP system of computerized programming for lot sizes of 25 to 2,500 parts. He also uses the system to cost new parts before they're committed to metal.

It's a machine worthy of your attention. LeBlond Inc., Madison at Edwards Roads, Cincinnati 45208.

Turn it into a profit on a

LEBLOND
MACHINE TOOL

FIGURE 14-8

Testimonial advertisement for industrial product.   This is an effective use of the testimonial approach in which two persons provide statements about the product. Their statements about one machine substituting for three machines provide a powerful incentive for the prospect to look into the matter. Also, use of the actual people provides a personal touch that is occasionally welcome in an industrial advertisement.

In your illustration show the product in use. Much industrial advertising deals with equipment that looks dull when out of use but interesting when in action. If you can control illustrations for your advertisements, see that your product is not static and make your copy fit the movement of the illustration.

Don't write dull, technical details that should be in a catalog. Although industrial copy should be thorough, the reader of such copy is like anyone else in not liking dull, lifeless catalog-type copy. If your material is better suited to a specifications sheet or parts catalog, save it for those uses.

Write copy with an individual reader in mind. Have in mind a certain person—engineer, architect, company head. Point your copy message directly at that person's interests. Use his language.

Give complete information. Talk about your servicing facilities, the construction of the item being sold, the lasting qualities, the type of work for which it is best suited. Tell why your product gives better performance. Why is the material in your product superior? Remember this also: Your advertisement may be clipped and filed. It may be dragged out later to be placed next to a competitive advertisement. The copy that does the most complete job may get the sale. Industrial advertising, unlike much consumer advertising, is often referred to long after the advertising has run. Make your copy worth going back to. The typical industrial-paper reader doesn't shy away from long text—so long as it has something to say.

Use a strong news slant. Purchasing agents and others who read industrial advertising are constantly asking, "What's new?" Industrial readers are on the prowl for information that will help them or their firm do a better job. Latest developments are their meat—feed them a heavy diet. Your new product, or new use for your product, should be told about in fresh, live news style.

Case histories catch interest. The usual industrial buyer moves cautiously. Industrial advertising is largely directed to those who buy in big quantities. Successful use by another business of your product makes absorbing reading for the person going over your advertisement. Perhaps, in addition to selling him, you are helping him sell management on buying your product. Your case history of successful use of your product may often be the only sales argument that carries weight.

Get into your story quickly. Although interested readers of industrial advertising are willing to read long copy, they are not willing to waste time guessing what the copywriter has in mind. Many of your readers go through mountains of reading matter each day. Although your copy should be complete, it shouldn't be leisurely. Let the reader know immediately through headline, illustration, and first copy block what you're talking about.

Imagine all the design variables in spring wire selection...

Is it strong enough?

Will it operate in high temperatures?

Is it ductile so it can be formed easily?

Should it be small enough to hold radio crystals?

Or large enough to cushion a motorcycle frame?

Is it used in a torsional application?

Does it require high fatigue life?

Is it a carbon wire in a corrosive atmosphere?

Or a stainless wire in chloride?

And economical so it keeps costs down?

There are many design variables in spring wire selection. And we have many different types of spring wire: music, carbon, stainless, superalloy and oil-tempered. Let us help you find the right spring wire for your application. Call 616/683-8100.

NS **NATIONAL-STANDARD COMPANY**
N-S Wire Division
Niles, Michigan 49120

FIGURE 14-9

Industrial advertisement with unusual copy format.   Putting the copy in the form of questions is an effective way to get attention and, at the same time, to put over product qualities without making outright statements. The objective, in this campaign using similar advertisements, was to generate inquiries for new applications from design engineers in a broad group of industries.

Recognize a problem—then show how your product can help solve it. The readers of industrial advertising are beset with problems. Their abrasives don't hold up; V-belts break; their accident rate is too high—perhaps production is falling. If your advertisement suggests a way out of their troubles, they'll read it like a novel.

Two aspects are noteworthy in this last headline. One is the length. So much is told in the headline that anyone with the slightest interest in the product will become interested enough to read the body copy to get

The photograph you see at the left represents a dramatic breakthrough in metals machining. Here, a 3M coated abrasive belt replaces a milling machine and a vertical spindle grinder for surface dimensioning cast iron. By the method shown in the diagram, it can produce a flat, finished surface, within acceptable tolerances, at a rate up to twice as fast as conventional methods.

Abrasive machining. It dimensions castings in half the time of ordinary methods.

If you're skeptical about such a timesaving claim, consider this: one automotive foundry, now using abrasive machining on cast iron pieces, removes .080 to .115" of metal in 20 seconds with 3M Brand Resin Bond Cloth Belts. Job time per unit is 50% of the former machining time.

Could abrasive machining cut time and save money in your plant? Ask a 3M Master of Methods for a detailed, impressive case history. Or ask our pioneering Coated Abrasives Methods Center to apply its abrasives know-how to your grinding or finishing problems. For more information contact your Industrial Distributor Sales Representative or 3M Company, Industrial Abrasives Division, 3M Center, St. Paul, Minn. 55101.

3M has the method.

Leonard R. Abbott,
Account Executive,
Philadelphia, Pennsylvania

Wear eye protection
when using.

FIGURE 14-10

Industrial advertisement that offers proof.   Not only does this advertisement have a powerful benefit headline, but also it has equally strong body copy that backs up the headline claim. Advertisements such as this are respected by technically minded readers of industrial magazines.

Reprinted courtesy of the Industrial Abrasives Division, 3M Company.

FIGURE 14-11

Industrial advertisement with case history approach.

Masterpieces of IMAGINEERING

Pablo Picasso applied imagineering to develop new techniques in creating this sculptured masterpiece of metalworking art. The excellence in quality and economy demonstrated below by Kearney & Trecker is a matter of record.

Imagineering means in-depth production analysis...that's why this workpiece and this MILWAUKEE-MATIC 200 were made for each other

Kearney & Trecker's "imagineers" took up Rexnord's manufacturing assignment to reduce cycle times on a two-piece gear box unit to be used on the Rex 770 concrete truck mixer. The process involved machining two separate sections made from aluminum and nodular iron.

The precise solution was a MILWAUKEE-MATIC 200 machining center that completely mills and bores each section before joining. This in contrast to the more costly alternative of machining an assembled gear box requiring a larger machining center and a higher capital investment. KT recommendations were made only after thorough pre-sale analysis of the machining problem. And, in this case, the entire program was written by the customer's own technician after only one week's orientation.

Investigate MILWAUKEE-MATIC 200 as a solution to your parts making needs. For particulars, write

The Imagineering Company
Kearney & Trecker Corporation

11000 THEODORE TRECKER WAY, MILWAUKEE, WI 53214

the full story. Two is the use of a price figure. In industrial advertising price mention is rare, but where it is possible to bring in price, it will increase readership for an advertisement.

Copy for specialized field—agricultural, professional, and executive-management—will be discussed in Chapter 15. This chapter will also consider "collateral," the term used to include all the special pieces of advertising used in product selling.

Use important-looking, reader-interest headlines. Industrial advertising deals with heavy industry and with big purchases. It is addressed to hard-driving decision makers engaged in important work. Make your headlines reflect the character of the industrial people and their jobs—in typography (no delicate script types) and in what you write. Hit hard and specifically in attention-commanding headlines. A good example is the following long headline that offers a benefit sure to appeal to step-saving, cost-cutting industrial magazine readers.

**There must be
an easier,
cheaper way.**

1. Blank out sheet metal.
2. Punch hinge holes.
3. Bend edges once.
4. Bend edges again.
5. Insert stiffener.
6. Bend edges again.
7. Weld corners.
8. Spot weld stiffener.
9. Attach hardware.
10. Grind, file, buff, degrease.

There is.

**GE Engineering
Structural Foam.**

1. Mold it in one piece.

Other examples of industrial headlines that talk forcefully and specifically to publication readers follow. Unfortunately, there are many headlines found in industrial magazines that do not take the admirably direct approach of the headlines shown here.

At last
... a fast-acting double slide industrial door that's also a Class A 3-Hour rated fire door.

control, pull, erect, hoist, stack, lift, load, move—one wire rope line does it all
Broderick & Bascom.

Log ratio modules used to be expensive, clumsy, and hard to apply. Not any more.

Analog Devices introduces the world's first and only log ratio module that operates on either current or voltage. $42 in 100's.

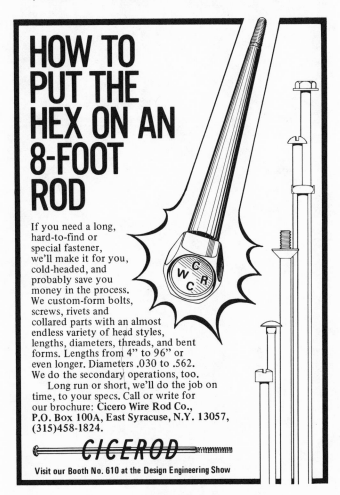

FIGURE 14-12

Small space industrial advertisement.   An unusual headline and judicious use of white space get attention for this fact-filled advertisement. The use of the word "hex" in the headline is a play on words and refers to the hexagonal head on the rod.

15

Selling for Business, Agriculture, and the Professions, Part B

Great amounts of copy are written outside of the consumer, industrial, and trade advertising areas. It is impossible to give equal discussion to all the more specialized forms of copy, but in the following sections you will find a brief discussion of the creative considerations of three of these forms.

AGRICULTURAL ADVERTISING

To write copy to people in agriculture, you should understand them. They feel isolated, put upon by government, nature, and the inexorable laws of supply and demand that affect the prices they can obtain for what they grow. You must realize that there are wide gulfs between big business farmers whose acreage is vast and equipment investment enormous and the small farmer who ekes out a bare living from his few acres. You should know that the problems vary by type of farm, too, since the dairymen have little in common with the cotton grower.

Despite the differences mentioned here, there are some general principles you can observe in writing to agriculturalists.

Watch your language. Today's farmers in a great many instances are no longer the ordinary farmers found in past rural America. Often they have gone to agricultural school. Even if they haven't, they have learned about antibiotics, animal husbandry and the fine points of difference in hybrid seed corn. You can use language, therefore, that is much above that used some years ago. Be careful, however, that you don't write like a city person trying to talk to a farmer. Use farm language and don't slip. If you do, your copy will be discredited. Remember, too, that although the farmer can be addressed in more sophisticated language than was once true, there are many, many farmers who are not college educated. Avoid literary flavor and too much urbanity.

Give them proof. Agricultural people have traditionally been skeptical. Alone much of the time and given to introspective thinking, they are cynical about salespeople and their claims. That is true of their attitude about advertising, too.

Advertiser: Shell Chemical Company
Product: Bladex® 15G Herbicide
Length: 30 seconds

VIDEO	AUDIO
1. OPEN ON CORN GROWER WALKING THROUGH GRAVEL AREA BETWEEN BARNS.	GROWER (to camera): If you're like most corn growers using a granular herbicide...
2. DISS TO NEW ANGLE AS GROWER CONTINUES.	...you're probably looking for a granular that does a good job on grasses.
3. DISS TO GROWER IN FIELD OF CORN 6" HIGH.	Well--Bladex does.
4. CUT TO CUT-AWAY OF CROSS-SECTION OF ROWS. MCU.	Look here in the middles.
5. ZOOM IN CLOSE TO GRASSES 4" HIGH.	GROWER (VO): Foxtail--fall panicum.
6. DOLLY TO CORN ROW AND SURROUNDING CLEAN AREA.	But the rows are clean.
7. CUT TO CAMERA MOVING THROUGH BROADLEAVES.	We've got broadleaves, too-- velvetleaf--cocklebur-- smartweed...
8. DISS TO GROWER WALKING OUT OF FIELD. LOW ANGLE LOOKING UP. SHOW CLEAN ROWS.	...Bladex gets 'em all.
9. DISS TO OVERHEAD OF FIELD, AGAIN SHOWING ROWS.	You got trouble with grasses-- or broadleaves--like these, you ought to be using Bladex granules. They work.
10. PECTEN AND POP ON SUPER: BLADEX® GRANULES FOR CORN. THEN ADD SUPER: ALWAYS FOLLOW LABEL DIRECTIONS.	

FIGURE 15-1

Script for 30-second television commercial aimed at farmers.

FIGURE 15-2

Television commercial aimed at the farmer.   In simple, believable words and scenes this 30-second commercial concentrates on one point and makes that point firmly. It is part of a coordinated advertising effort that includes television, radio, and print.

TREFLAN/SOYBEANS/SOUTH

② OCV: How long you been using it now?
MAN: About twelve years.

① OFF CAMERA VOICE: I see you're using Treflan herbicide again this year.
MAN: Yep.

④ OCV: Seedling johnsongrass? Crabgrass? Why you haven't had any problems with them in...oh...I don't know how long.

③ OCV: Why do you like Treflan so much, anyway?
MAN: Keeps my johnsongrass down. My crabgrass, too.

⑥ ANNCR: Treflan for dependable control of foxtail, pigweed, lambsquarters and 24 other annual grasses and weeds.

⑤ MAN: About twelve years.

Testimonials and case histories, accordingly, are useful in agricultural copy if: a) They relate to the reader's particular interest—hogs, corn, soybeans, dairy herd management, etc. b) They pertain to the reader's geographic area. The Iowa corngrower, for example, finds little in common with the California corngrower.

Instill a management feel (in some instances). This suggestion is made if your product or service is designed for the truly big agricultural establishment where the top people are business managers as much as agricultural people. They are buying big-ticket items in combines, tractors, silos and other equipment not to mention fertilizer, seed and less spectacular but still expensive items. Talk to them like management executives.

Suffer with them. With some justification farmers feel that the forces of nature, government, and economics are against them. Let them know that you're on their side and that you know their problems. This can be done subtly, of course.

PROFESSIONAL ADVERTISING

Although "professional" might include many activities such as those carried on by lawyers, architects, and teachers, discussion here relates chiefly to physicians. Many of the observations made can be applied to dentists, too. Intelligent copywriters can learn the language and problems of the agricultural man if they are observant and industrious, but it is much more difficult to achieve similar success in the medical area. Yet, there are nonmedical copywriters who write medical copy or dental copy. Here are some considerations for such copywriters.

Use the specialized language. Consider this section of copy from an advertisement in a medical magazine:

> Verequad provides this help with dual bronchodilating action to relieve smooth muscle spasm of the bronchial tree which usually interferes with the evacuation of bronchi; and expectorant action to thin and loosen tenacious mucus, aiding in its expulsion from the respiratory tract.

If you are writing to doctors or other professional people, use their language as in the example, not a simplified version of it. Their education has taught them a different vocabulary; it is your obligation to learn it and to employ it.

Avoid overly personal language. As in industrial advertising, the "you" approach should be avoided. When doctors read advertising in medical journals, they expect to be addressed in a professional manner. Don't write like an advertising copywriter. Medical people, whose writings and talks have been twisted out of shape by promoters of products, are distrustful of advertising people. Thus, they dislike "ad-dy" advertising but will accept advertising written in the style of one doctor addressing another.

FIGURE 15-3

Farm radio commercial.   As in other elements in the campaign for this product, copy is direct and simple, qualities appreciated by the target audience. Notice the very personal copy style.

Creswell Munsell Schubert & Zirbel Inc.

RADIO COPY

Client: Blanco Products Company
Product: Treflan/Soybeans/North
Comml #:   EL-76-239-97
Station: RB 25239
Program: "Johnsongrass"
Date:
Time: :30

(SOUND EFFECTS: Tractor in field coming toward us, as we listen tractor comes to a stop. The engine is shut off, footsteps of a man begin, and then fade with beginning of dialogue.)

ANNCR: You know, a year or two ago, my beans didn't have a chance when it came to that johnsongrass. But now I'm usin' Treflan. And does it do the job on that johnsongrass! I've been on this two-year special program that my Treflan dealer told me about...he said it'd take care of my johnsongrass and improve my bean yield while I was doing it. So, I tried it, and you know, he was right. Cleaned up that seedling johnsongrass the first time out...and got right to work on that rooted stuff. That johnsongrass may be tough, but Treflan...it's tougher.

FIGURE 15-4

Farm magazine advertisement.   Strong print advertisements such as this, combined with television and radio, make certain that the farmer cannot overlook the product.

Use scientific evidence. Anyone dealing in matters of life and death eschews the casual approach. They want proof, presented by recognized authorities and backed by careful investigation. Little wonder then that you must draw constantly upon evidence to back any claims you make—and woe to you if the "evidence" is not supported by proved facts.

Recognize their desire to keep up in their profession. One of the professional person's trials— doctor, dentist, lawyer, architect, teacher—is that new developments occur so rapidly that it is almost impossible to keep up. Thus the doctor is constantly attending medical meetings, reading scientific journals, exchanging viewpoints with other doctors, and in many ways trying to keep abreast of the latest advances. Your copy should recognize this need to be informed. If you have new features, stress them. If yours is a real breakthrough, make the reader a better professional person, stress it.

Recognize the reader as a user or recommender. Doctors and dentists, especially, among the professional people, may be viewed in two ways a) As persons who will use the advertised product in conducting their profession. A dentist's drill, or a surgical instrument, fall in this category. b) As persons

FROM   ADVERTISING □ MARKETING

42 east genesee street, skaneateles, new york 13152 □ phone (315) 685-5778

commercial no. 6003-1   client BEACON MILLING
length Minute radio (50 sec plus tag) product/service Hay Pre-Serv

Each year it's a race between you and the weather when haying time comes. Here's where Beacon Hay Pre-Serv can help you because it lets you hay earlier and faster. When you apply Beacon Hay Pre-Serv to baled, chopped, or stacked hay you'll prevent mold and spoilage, and hold down heating. Think of the advantage of harvesting hay earlier, with moisture up to twenty-five percent. And you can cut and store hay up to twenty-five percent, without spoilage. So you end up with a larger hay crop and less chance of weather damage. Furthermore, you'll have hay that's a lot higher in digestible nutrients -- university tests show this conclusively. Get all the facts about Beacon Hay Pre-Serv at your Beacon store and while you're there, ask about Beacon's liquid applicator and their moisture tester. Mighty handy units to have.

10 second local tag

FIGURE 15-5

Farm radio commercial.   Informative, yet conversational, copy talks farmer language and makes one point strongly while backing that point with specific material. Notice the almost inevitable reference to proof in the form of university tests—a convincing approach in the farm field.

who will recommend the product's use to patients. A drying lotion for acne, elastic stockings for varicose vein sufferers, or a mild soap for bathing babies fall into this category. Ivory Soap, as an example, has been advertised for many years in medical journals since a doctor's endorsement is so powerful with the new mother anxious to give her baby the best care.

Radio Script

Time: 60 Sec.
Script No: 10-32-1
Subject: 8630 Tractor

Attention all _____ area farmers. Here's your chance
to see real field productivity up close. _____, your
                                            (dealership)
John Deere dealer in _____ has a new John Deere Eighty-
                        (location)
Six-Thirty Four-Wheel-Drive Tractor on display now. It puts out two-hundred-
seventy-five engine horsepower and two-hundred-twenty-five P-T-O horsepower.
Those are pretty impressive numbers, but even more impressive is the way
those horses are put to work. For example, power is transmitted through
an exclusive Perma-Clutch, the virtually lifetime hydraulic clutch. Then
Quad-Range transmission takes over, gearing horsepower to any of sixteen
speeds. And remember, Quad-Range has a built-in Hi-Lo. Last but not least,
power is delivered through inboard planetary final drives. This means torque
loads are spread over three points to extend component life. The John Deere
Eighty-Six-Thirty ... it represents big power ... adaptable power ...
dependable power ... John Deere power. See the new Eighty-Six-Thirty Four-
Wheel-Drive Tractor on display now at _____ in _____.
                                        (dealership)   (location)

FIGURE 15-6

Farm radio commercials for the dealer's use.   Because most farm equipment dealers would not prepare radio commercials themselves, the manufacturer-supplier prepares suitable commercials. The dealer merely fills in the blank spots.

EXECUTIVE-MANAGEMENT ADVERTISING

We're concerned here especially with the high-level readers of business publications such as *Fortune, Wall Street Journal, U.S. News, Business Week* and the business section of the *New York Times.* These men or women feel some sense of kinship with the readers of any magazine addressing itself to management, for example, with the readers of institutional magazines in the hotel or hospital fields, or with the readers of industrial magazines aimed at management in heavy industry.

Products and services appearing in executive-management publications reflect the broad responsibilities of the readers embracing such widely varying items as computer-calculators, financial services, security-guard protection, high-speed building elevators, business insurance, corporate jets, and export banking.

150-HP
JOHN DEERE 4630

A wheatland workhorse
with moves like a show pony

150 horsepower—that's the kind of muscle you need to farm around here. But you don't need that horsepower in a clumsy, hard-to-handle tractor. That's why the 4630 is such an ideal tractor for our kind of farming. It's an ideal blend of speed, power, and easy handling. Once you've put a 4630 through its paces, you'll wonder why anybody would want a lumbering, overweight tractor. Stop in for more reasons why the 4630 is a "sure bet."

JOHN DEERE TRACTORS—
A SOUND, LONG-TERM INVESTMENT

DEALER IMPRINT

(2 col. x 6 inches) 168 Agate Lines

FIGURE 15-7

Dealer advertisement for local farm advertising.   An advertisement such as this is prepared by the manufacturer for use by dealers in their areas. The name of the dealer appears where it says Dealer Imprint. Lively headlines help to draw farmer attention to the advertisements.

Luxury personal products appear, too, such as high priced automobiles and liquor.

Aim high in the language and subjects you use. High-level, urbane language is much more evident in executive-management magazines than in any other business magazines. The men or women in the executive suite are likely to be sophisticated, well-educated, and cosmopolitan. Today they are likely to be global in their thinking. They may be in Japan one week and in Yugoslavia for a trade fair the following week.

FIGURE 15-8

Farm magazine advertisement that reports results from using the advertised product.   Farmers are interested in checking their year-to-year results and those obtained by other farmers.

While they are concerned with ecology and the impact of the industry on the environment, they are also concerned with such less broad-gauge management matters as profit-and-loss statements, plant safety, and what the stockholders are thinking. Thus, they are always receptive to advertising that tells them crisply, and sometimes entertainingly, about products and services that will result in a better-run business.

Aim your language level at people who appreciate the nuances of good writing. The discussion to this point has centered around the very top management, but you might, in the case of many products and services, be aiming at ambitious middle-management people who have heavy responsibilities but not the final word in very top-level decision making.

If you are consciously aiming at the middle-management executives, your copy may tend to include more facts and figures that the readers may use to arrive at a decision. Advertisements intended for the very top management may, in contrast, be broader and less detailed. The purpose may be to interest the occupants of the executive suites enough to cause them to send a memo down a couple of floors asking a lesser executive "to look into this."

TRADE COLLATERAL

Closely associated with trade advertising is the writing and production of what is called "collateral." Under this term are included all the special pieces of advertising used in product selling, either by the advertiser's own sales force or by the retail merchant. Such things as special mailing pieces addressed to the trade, portfolios containing promotional aids for the sales force, store display material, and other miscellaneous advertising are called collateral. Their creation represents an important and voluminous part of almost every copywriter's duties.

Much material is normally supplied to the product manufacturer's salespeople to aid them in soliciting business from the trade. If you are an agency copywriter, you will be called upon to prepare a considerable amount of this material on behalf of your clients. If you are writing copy for an advertiser in the advertising department, preparation of such items will occupy an even greater part of your time. It is important for you to consider some of the varied helps that salespeople use in their daily calls on the trade.

The way the American farmer sees it, the best buyer is the one who pays the most.

So he doesn't much care whether his crops end up on his next door neighbor's dinner table, or on a table in another country.

His attitude is understandable. After all, his livelihood depends on getting a reasonable return on his investment. And the more people (or nations) bidding for his output, the better price he's likely to get.

At Continental Grain, our job is finding the best markets for U.S. farm production wherever they exist (and in some cases creating markets where they *don't* exist).

To do this, it is helpful to operate in an open market where all buyers have an equal opportunity to compete for available supplies. And that means an absolute minimum of export restrictions.

The fact is, America's farmers produce enough crops to take care of domestic needs, with plenty left over for export.

Unnecessary export restrictions can only act as a roadblock between the American farmer and his #1 market.

Continental Grain Company, 277 Park Avenue, New York, NY 10017.

Continental Grain

His best market can be across the road or across the globe.

FIGURE 15-9

Institutional advertisement aimed at the farmer.   As part of a campaign, this advertisement with its powerful headline explains its position on export restrictions and its cooperation with the farmer in finding the best markets for farm production. It maintains a personal character through its illustration of a farmer at work.

SALES PORTFOLIOS

Perhaps the most usable collateral piece regularly supplied to a sales force is the "salesperson's portfolio," or "sales manual."

These portfolios do a three-fold job:

1. They show the dealers what advertising is being put behind the product, both nationally and locally, what display material is available to dealers for their stores, and how the combination works in preselling the product for the dealers.

FIGURE 15-10

Farm advertisement.   Anyone studying this advertisement realizes quickly that the modern-day farmer is a far cry from the "simple son of the soil" stereotype. As the long copy demonstrates, today's farmer must understand the use of antibiotics, chemicals, and scientific methods. Despite the length of the copy, the material is broken up well by hard-hitting subheads.

2. They arouse enthusiasm for the product and its potentialities in the dealer's mind, and the same emotions among the salespeople for their own advertising and merchandising promotion.
3. They offer the salesperson a complete, graphic checklist to follow in giving the dealer a sales talk.

There are two very important points to remember in writing a sales portfolio:

One is to write simply. A lot of the value that the sales force will derive from your portfolio will come while they are in routine conversations with their retailer customers. If you can write interesting, punchy, and informal copy in the portfolios you prepare, the salespeople will often find themselves picking up these expressions and using them in their daily calls. Use the kind of talk that salespeople would be likely to use.

To give yourself a working background in this trade talk you ought to spend some time on the road with a salesperson, go on calls, and listen to what is said to the dealers. If you are working in the advertising department of a manufacturing house, you will find that such trips are considered standard procedure. If you are a copywriter with an advertising agency, you may find them a little more difficult to arrange, since the agency will want to keep you busy writing. Advertising executives, though, will recognize the value of such extracurricular experience for copywriters, so you can get out if you try hard enough.

FIGURE 15-11

Farm advertisement.   Help with the many problems of farm management is always welcomed by farmers. It has become a habit to call upon experts for advice whether they are with manufacturers, agricultural schools, or with the county, state, and federal government.

The second important point to remember in writing sales portfolios is brevity. Keep your ideas simple enough to be covered in a few words. Put yourself in the position of a dealer being asked to take time to look over the portfolio, or the salesperson whose job is to show it to the dealer. Neither has time to read a lot of copy about anything. Salespeople will tell you that they can and do persuade dealers to "take a second" to glance at their company's advertising program, or the display material illustrated in a portfolio. But they can rarely pin that dealer down for a long time.

What to put in a portfolio

Any advertiser, agency, or even copywriter will have a personal technique for how best to organize a sales portfolio. There are many different techniques.

FIGURE 15-12

Professional advertisement.   Here the advertiser is aiming at the management level—at persons who need full information before making important decisions.

You can, however, learn a basic pattern that will apply to almost any type of product or market. This pattern can be almost standard except for these special points you may be asked to highlight or emphasize:

- A cover, with an illustration of interest, that tells what the portfolio is all about. If you are giving salespeople a manual covering their firm's spring and summer advertising, say so. Headlines of general interest to dealers and salespeople may be used if desired, but they are not necessary to the effectiveness of good sales portfolios. Usually, however, a breezy headline such as "Even MORE Sales Power for YOU This Spring!" is a common device to get interest in the ensuing material.

- A section devoted to the advertiser's advertising-to-come. In this part of your portfolio you will show either reprints of the advertisement, which may be slipped into a "pocket" or flap in the pages, printed right on the pages themselves, or "tipped in"—glued along one edge and inserted in the manual. Normally you will discover that the pocket method is best for advertisers who have a heavy and complete schedule of advertisements, since it enables the salesperson to carry more advertisements conveniently. It is also much less expensive than printing or tipping.

  In addition to showing the advertisements in your portfolio, you will want to give a complete schedule of where and when those advertisements will appear and how many readers they will reach. You will also want to point out to the dealers, if the campaign you show is national, that much of the national circulation is right in their town, even in their own neighborhood, so that the advertisements actually function partly as local advertising. If the operation is of a type that supplies complementary advertising to dealers for their own local use, in mat form, you will include a page or two of your portfolio to show the dealer reprints of these mats and tell him how to get them. The same is true of all phases of the advertising program—show the whole business, posters, car cards, TV and radio programs, spot announcements, and any other national or local advertising effort that is being put behind the product.

- A section devoted to merchandising. In this part of your manual you will illustrate all the various store and window display material that is made available to the dealer and tell him how to order it. You will point out how this material is designed to "tie in" with the national advertising theme, to provide recognition and recall value, and to give the final impetus to the buyer at the point of purchase.

- A wind-up page or pages where you call for the dealers support, emphasizing that it means more sales for the dealers to feature your product and is evidence of their sound business judgment.

Keep this format for sales portfolios in mind. It is not an infallible pattern that can always be used exactly as described, but is fundamentally the approach that all well-organized sales portfolios should have.

FIGURE 15-13

Executive-management advertisement.   Management people need facts and reason-why copy. They get both in this advertisement clearly aimed at the decision makers.

OTHER SALES-FORCE HELPS

In addition to portfolios, you will be called upon to write items designed to aid salespeople in making their rounds. Circulars, merchandising folders, sales letters, and post cards are among the type of material referred to. All these items will usually contain highlights of one or more of the basic elements of your sales portfolio—advertising or merchandising. Just remember that their sole function is to arouse interest among the dealers to give display prominence to the product you are advertising, to push it because they are convinced that your advertising is helping them do business.

You will also probably write items to help the salespeople directly, such as sound slide films, skits, and other dramatic presentations to be used in sales meetings and sales rallies, showing these people how

When your report isn't all good news, film is good business.

Present with film.

A presentation movie or slide show can help you put your best foot forward. It won't make excuses for a bad situation, but it _can_ make your arguments and explanations clear, concise, and logical.

Film can be warm, colorful, inviting, and entertaining. Even when the market isn't.

And when you consider the impact you get for your dollars, you'll realize that film is as efficient as it is effective.

For more information, contact an AV specialist. Or get in touch with us. We'd like to help.

FIGURE 15-14

Humorous advertisement aimed at management executives. In this award-winning advertisement, we have the proper recipe for the use of humor. Let the humor be carried by the illustration and headline, and then get down to business in the copy. As an attention-getter, well-done humor is effective even in business magazines that are not noted for the number of humorous advertisements carried.

to sell. By association with the staff of the sales department, by cultivating their friendship and understanding, you can build information on sales problems that will help you throughout your career.

Friendship with the sales department is important to copywriters in agencies or advertising departments or even in retail stores. If the salespeople don't function correctly, no matter how good your advertising may be, it doesn't look good. On the other hand, if you don't function correctly, you may make the sales department look bad. The whole business is, or at least should be, a matter of the utmost cooperation.

MATERIAL FOR THE DEALERS

Many copywriters make a mistake in giving too little attention to the creation of store display material. Because much of such creation is an art problem—simply adapting advertisements or parts of advertisements, and simplifying them to different proportions—you can easily take the attitude that it does not require much thought on your part. Many sales are lost daily because copywriters did not understand the nature of the display piece they were building and made an error that caused their work to be wasted.

Example. Suppose you are copywriter on a chocolate pudding account. You do a good job of writing and directing an advertising campaign based upon the simple idea of large heads of happy, cute children just about to take a bite of Yummy chocolate pudding. A headline may tell the special good things it has to offer. Following is more short copy and, at the bottom, a picture of the package and a logotype displaying the brand name. The campaign is fine. Everyone likes it. In the magazines or newspapers, it's sure to get lots of attention.

Now the pudding manufacturer wants you to make up a counter display card for grocery stores.

You whip up a counter card, perhaps 12″ × 14″, which is almost an exact duplicate of your advertisement. That makes good sense, you say to yourself. Cute kid eating the product. That's sure-fire for mothers shopping.

Well, the big hope for counter cards is that they are used together with a counter display of the product—card in the middle, packages around it. But

FIGURE 15-15

Advertisement aimed at management people in the institutional field.   Repeat business is vital to those in the motel-hotel field. This testimonial-type advertisement appearing in *Hotel & Motel Management* stresses the point in headline and copy.

big hopes are rarely attained. Where, oh where, is the product identification on your counter card when this happens? Yes, that's right—clear down at the bottom of the card, completely obscured by other merchandise. It's still a cute picture—still has that important appeal to mothers—but nobody has any idea what you are advertising.

That sort of mistake stems from a too hasty examination of what kind of collateral material you are asked to prepare, and an inadequate study of how it is to be used. During your career you may dream up window streamers, counter cards, display easels, wall hangers, over-the-wire banners and pennants, price cards, case display pieces, and other examples of store material. When you are assigned to prepare something of this nature, throw yourself into it.

16

Getting Noticed in Outdoor and Transit Advertising

As unlikely as it may seem, a poet and a writer of good outdoor advertising share some common abilities. Each is able to convey a powerful message in the fewest possible words. Each, likewise, will utilize emotion with telling effect upon the reader.

You may never discover these truths because the average copywriter has few, if any, requests to write outdoor copy. If that chance comes your way, welcome it because there is little in advertising that offers such a creative challenge. This is true of both outdoor and transit copy if the writer, not content with mediocre copy, tries for a creative twist that will make the copy effective, memorable, and different.

In recent times, outdoor and transit advertising have had problems, the former with environmentalists and many limiting laws; the latter because of the reduced use of inside cards on many transit systems. Yet, each survives because each offers a way to reach out-of-home prospects as they travel to buying centers. Each, while seldom a principal medium, serves as a powerful backup to major campaigns in print and broadcast. Then on the local level, outdoor advertising may be the only medium usable by the motel, hotel, or eating place that wishes to sell itself to persons traveling through the area.

POSTERS AND BULLETINS—YOUR CONCERN

As a copywriter you will probably be concerned with only two major forms of outdoor advertising:

- 24-sheet posters
- Painted bulletins and painted walls

The 24-sheet poster, the most widely used type of outdoor advertising, is what people are usually referring to when they speak of billboards. Technically,

that portion of 24-sheet poster allotted for the use of the advertiser is 8 feet 8 inches high by 19 feet 6 inches wide. Twenty-four-sheets are so called because, when first introduced, they were composed from 24 sheets of paper, each printed separately.

Although painted bulletins are gradually being standardized, painted walls have no standard sizes. Both types are bought and produced as individual units. Like posters they may or may not be illuminated, depending on whether the intensity of the night-time traffic passing them justifies the extra cost of lighting.

"Outdoor advertising," as the term is ordinarily used in the advertising business, is intended to apply only—solely and exclusively—to those companies engaged in standard outdoor advertising. That is, the companies represented by the standard well-maintained poster boards, the neat, regularly painted bulletins and "well-groomed" units—not the torn and tattered circus, theatrical, and election posters that continue to proclaim their wares months after their advertising usefulness has passed—or the rusty metal signs and crude homemade signs still seen decorating fences, buildings, and roadside pastures.

ADVANTAGES OF OUTDOOR ADVERTISING

People, generally, like to read outdoor advertising since it relieves the tedium of the long journey, or the daily commuting trip. This, of course, does not mean that people see and read every sign they pass nor does it mean that the same results would be obtained everywhere. It does, however, indicate that outdoor offers you a huge potential audience for your message—if you make it appealing enough to arouse the public's interest.

FIGURE 16-1

Play on words in an outdoor poster.   In addition to the appeal of the copy, the poster breaks away from the straight, conventional rectangle of most outdoor posters.

Outdoor advertising offers continuity. Your message will remain on the same location for a full thirty-day period and may be backing up a copy idea your magazine advertisements have established. Since most people travel and retravel the same route every day on their way to and from their work or shopping, you are able to hammer home your message to the same group of people day after day after day.

FIGURE 16-2

Play on words and appetite appeal make a strong outdoor poster.

An outdoor showing of your poster will usually be displayed simultaneously on a number of boards along major traffic arteries. As people travel down such roads, they will often see (and read) the same poster several times before reaching their destinations. This constant repetition has a cumulative effect much like that which makes a song a hit. When a tune is introduced, it usually elicits little response; but as you hear it played again and again, you find yourself unconsciously humming or whistling it as you go through the day. The repetition, not the song alone, has made a deep impression—so it is with the constant view of the same outdoor posters.

Outdoor advertising permits you to use color at relatively low cost. Because newspapers and magazines will not accept color advertisements except in large-size space, many publication advertisers who would like to use color cannot afford to do so. An outdoor advertiser, on the other hand, can easily afford to use color, even though the total advertising may consist of but a single painted wall sign.

FIGURE 16-3

Cleverness in outdoor poster.   Humor in a clever working-together of words and illustration is more effective in putting over the message than preaching. This message, seen day after day by the driver, will be accepted better than reproof. Outdoor advertising is especially good for this kind of approach.

Outdoor showings of any magnitude greatly impress dealers stocking the advertised product. Day after day they are constantly reminded of the advertising the manufacturer is putting behind the product in order to help dealers sell more of it.

Outdoor advertising is often the only medium that can successfully reach an advertiser's best prospects. The hotel posters a person sees when approaching almost every city in an automobile are a good example. They are the only economical means the hotel has at its disposal for reaching the great bulk of the motorists who plan to spend the night in the city.

FIGURE 16-4

Outdoor advertising with a play on words.   Pungent, attention-getting phrasing gets quick attention for this poster. An illustration is not needed in this instance.

Because posters are the most widely used form of standard outdoor advertising and the only type regularly requiring new designs every month, you will deal with them far more than with the others. To win an audience, in competition with all the many other things that may attract a person's attention as he walks down the street or whizzes by in his car, is no easy task. To create a poster that will do this successfully, you have to start with a good idea. It doesn't necessarily have to be a clever idea; but it shouldn't be dull. And it must be simplicity itself—usually so simple as to be obvious.

KEEP OUTDOOR POSTERS SIMPLE

Simplicity is very evident whenever effective posters are studied to determine why they are effective. You will find simplicity mentioned often as an important attribute of effective posters. There are, however, some situations in which it is possible to be more subtle in your copy situation—for instance, in a sign on a crowded city street. Such a sign could be read by walkers or slow-moving drivers. Where reading must be done more quickly, however, it is best to use a simple message.

Unfortunately, there is no set formula to follow that will enable you to hit on prize-winning poster ideas regularly. Such ideas are elusive to even the best of creative people.

A pair of quotations might be helpful here as the first guides for your poster-winning efforts. Both are

from the pen of the famous nineteenth-century editor and theologian Tryon Edwards:

Have something to say; say it, and stop when you're done.

Never be so brief as to be obscure.

Having achieved your selling idea, it is extremely important in glance-read poster copy to concentrate attention on your one idea. Don't try to make two, three, or four copy points. Be satisfied to slam one point at the readers. If it's tires, it may be safety; gasoline, mileage; bread, taste; soft drinks, refreshment; automobiles, beauty.

Each of the foregoing products has other appeals, but don't use them in combination. Stick to one idea.

MOST GOOD POSTERS USE SHORT COPY

Remember, your message must be telegraphic—so concise, yet so clear, that even people with below-average intelligence will get it the instant their eyes hit the board. You have five seconds to register if the panel is visible at 250 feet and the motorist is going thirty-five miles an hour.

One study of poster advertising examined 500 posters to see how many words of copy were to be found in each. Here is the way the analysis broke down:

Number of Posters	Percent
Without words	3.5
With one word	3.1
With two words	9.8
With three words	16.5
With four words	21.2
With five words	16.1
With six words	11.3

FIGURE 16-5

Topical humor in an outdoor poster.   The product name is registered strongly, but the chief objective of the poster is to achieve a wry humor that will create empathy with the viewers. See how much can be done with a clever combination of two words of copy and an illustration.

FIGURE 16-6

A twist on words in outdoor advertising.   The copywriter might have written "More chicken for your dollar," but by using his imagination, he wrote a phrase that will evoke a chuckle and more attention for the poster.

Like everything else in copy, however, the length of poster copy is not to be established through fixed rules. Although it is obvious that keeping your poster copy short is good sense normally, it is possible to find instances of use of longer messages.

Readability and comprehension should guide you in determining length of poster copy—not inflexible rules that limit your imagination and originality.

POSTER ELEMENTS

What are the copy and layout elements of a poster? The number varies according to the complexity of the poster, but here is a list that will serve you normally. Posters will generally be made up from some or all of these:

- Product name
- Principal illustration
- Short copy to back up illustration
- Package
- Headline (often a clever and/or selling phrase)

Other elements might have been included, but these five are found most often. To keep the list simple, such elements as trademarks, company name, and price were not included.

In many cases the package may well be the principal illustration. A headline may be a slogan or it can constitute the "short copy to back up the illustration." In brief, the elements are juggled around as demanded by the institution, the campaign, or the product itself.

The elements are clear-cut. It is your use of them that results in effective or ineffective posters. Since simplicity is so important to quick reading, attain simplicity by avoiding the mixing of too many elements in one poster. Because there are five elements listed in the foregoing does not mean you must use them all. Remember—strive for simplicity by limiting the number of ideas and elements.

HOW OUTDOOR ADVERTISING IS BORN

When you receive a request for "one" outdoor poster design, do not be misled by the use of the singular. In order to create a Grade-A poster, you may have to hatch a dozen or more ideas—and have several rough, thumbnail layouts of each sketched out on tissue by an art associate.

After these numerous rough tissue layouts are assembled, you and the other persons working on the account will give them a going over—discussing and appraising each in detail, and eliminating many. The ideas or designs that survive this first session will be revised and polished, and again be subjected to the close scrutiny of all concerned.

Posters are usually either a) direct adaptations of advertisements, using the same headlines and illustrations used in magazines or newspapers; b) semidirect adaptations, in which the theme idea is followed, but which use specially created headlines and/or illustrations or c) presentations that are completely different from the advertiser's publication or radio copy. In the last type, no attempt is made to tie-in with the campaign theme. New ideas are used, but usually a certain family resemblance is maintained.

Outdoor is an ideal medium for publicizing tradenames, trade characters, package identifications, slogans, or any idea that may be quickly stated with perfect clarity. Because it permits the use of color at relatively low cost, it affords an excellent means for putting over appetite appeal. A bowl of corn flakes and strawberries looks like wood shavings and licorice drops when reproduced in black and white. But give it color and it will look so tempting as to be almost irresistible.

FIGURE 16-7

Humorous play on words in outdoor poster.

Premium on creativity

In no other form of written advertising is it more important to be different in imagination and creativity, than in outdoor advertising. That is, of course,

FIGURE 16-8

Outdoor poster with play on words.   In addition, this poster has strong appetite appeal and package identification.

because of the nature of posters, the limited amount of space for words and illustration, the need for short, terse copy, and the requirement of product identification.

The chief function of poster advertising is to serve as a buying reminder to people who are, or will soon be in a position to buy. You are often going after what is called the "impulse sale" when you write poster copy. Since you haven't the time or space to persuade people to buy your product, you have to assume that they have already been sold by some other form of advertising; your job is to remind them of your brand in a bright, memorable and attention-compelling way.

Products such as beer, soft drinks, gasoline, cigarettes and candy are naturals for poster advertising. Your prospects are in an automobile. They are going to stop within minutes. Chances are good that they will purchase one or more of these items, or similar ones, when they do.

It must be equally obvious to you why hotels advertise so extensively on outdoor posters, and restaurants, taverns and other public services. They want to remind the immediate prospect of what they have to offer.

It is often said that the outdoor poster which advertises a grocery store product is a giant point-of-sale display. Food retailers know that a poster placed on a main traffic location near their store will serve as a quick reminder to shoppers who may very well be on their way to buy from them. These locations, near shopping centers and village business sections, are considered ideal by advertisers whose products sell through food stores.

You'll see much automobile advertising on outdoor boards. While an automobile is neither an impulse purchase nor an immediate-action type of product, remember that a large percentage of the people who see a car displayed on an outdoor poster are driving cars a year or more old. They cannot help being influenced by a sales message showing a beautiful new car. These impressions will multiply to help make the eventual sale.

Sell and entertain

Provided you adhere to the number one rule of simplicity, both in illustration and message, you can use cuteness, or cleverness, and the more of either the better. If you're bright enough to make your poster tell an entertaining story while it punches home a copy message and product identification, you have probably succeeded in creating a good poster. Remember, however, that you have to get the whole story told in five seconds, or less.

One of the most famous outdoor posters of all time was the one a number of years ago that read:

The only convertible that outsells Ford!

The illustration was a baby buggy.

The copywriter who did this poster had a perfect combination of influences. It's simple—just five words besides the name of the product. It gives a selling point of importance—more people buy Ford convertibles than any other, and it says so in a very clever, warmly human, memorable way.

Another great Ford poster violated every rule in the copywriter's book. That was the one which

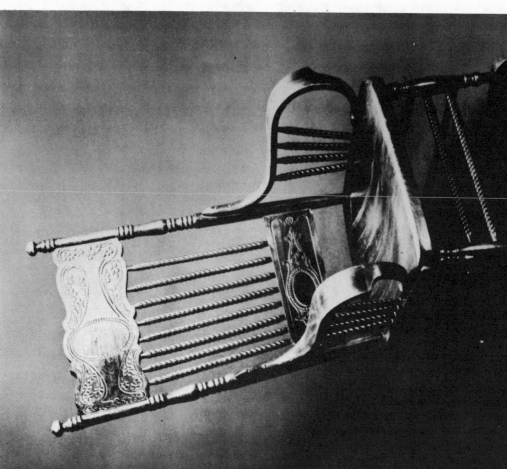

**Look at
your attitude
toward aging.**

Get off your rocker for grey liberation.

For more information write: National Council on the Aging, Inc. Box 28503, Washington, D.C. 20005

FIGURE 16-9

Clever play on words in outdoor advertising.   The symbolism of the rocking chair, combined with the twist in the bottom line of copy, evoke quick attention and a smile.

Courtesy—The Advertising Council, Inc.

showed the little boy looking longingly into a Ford dealer's window at a new model, and the only brand identification shown was the Ford name on the dealer's window, which was backward.

The Morton Salt Company has had many prize-winning posters such as one that used a short, simple, but hard-selling line that was used for an extended period:

If it's worth its salt,
it's worth Morton's

It was illustrated by luscious vegetables, melons, fruits and other food items commonly improved by the addition of salt.

Standard Oil of Indiana once won a poster competition with a poster which had just one word on it . . . TOPS! It was illustrated only with the cap worn by the Standard filling station operator. Ritz Crackers, a national sales leader, used extensive poster advertising that featured puns. One example featured an il-lustration of a happy man comfortably settling back into an easy chair with a package of Ritz and the line

I'll settle for Ritz!

You don't have to be brilliant, but often it helps a great deal to make your poster sing out from a highway lined with less imaginative efforts.

Whether you elect to be cute or whether your product and problem call for straight selling, above all keep your outdoor advertising simple, short and interesting.

You'll see a number of posters in this chapter's illustrations. Study them. See how in every case the copywriter and art director worked together for a total effect of a fast, memorable impression.

Summary

To sum up, you might keep the following in mind when you write and design posters:

1. Be satisfied generally to put over one idea in a poster.
2. Use as few elements as possible and make those elements count.
3. Be brief, but don't be brief for brevity's sake. If your copy needs to be more than ordinarily long in order to do the job more effectively, then make it longer.
4. Don't be subtle in most posters. Make your poster simple—easy to understand in glance-reading.
5. If you're promoting a packaged product, you can increase package recognition by featuring the package on your posters.
6. Use positive suggestion—although you won't use this technique in all posters, many posters will be stronger if you suggest something the reader can act upon.

FIGURE 16-10

Important reminder through outdoor advertising.   Effective even though it uses no illustration.

Courtesy—The Advertising Council, Inc.

U.S. Department of Transportation & The Advertising Council

7. Above all, try for a twist—a clever, attention-getting (often humorous) phrase that ties in with an equally clever, attention-getting illustration idea. Actually, the phrase and the illustration are one. Your object is to make the viewer react quickly—smile, frown, get angry, feel pity, make a resolution. Force the viewer to single out your message from all the competing influences around the poster.

not sound. Your transit card is traveling right along with your audience, whereas the poster must be read quickly as the automobile whizzes by. The transit card and the reader are relatively stationary. The people you are interested in reaching don't rush by your transit card at a gallop. They sit or stand near it for a long time, twenty-seven minutes per one-way trip on the average, according to studies. Readers can thus linger over your copy, if you have caught their

FIGURE 16-11

Outdoor advertising with emotional appeal.   Whether the emotion relies on humor or pathos, it arouses a quick response from the outdoor viewer—thus emotional advertising is especially suitable for outdoor posters.

Courtesy—The Advertising Council, Inc.

INSIDE TRANSIT CARDS

Although they are not literally located outdoors, transit cards are often discussed as a branch of outdoor advertising. Most advertising people feel now, however, that transit cards are not "miniature posters".

Some copywriters still look on them as such. If they would but compare transit cards and posters, they would see that except for their shape there is little similarity. Thinking of transit cards as "baby billboards" has caused many copywriters to write poor transit cards. They are not posters and should not be treated as such.

It is often mistakenly thought that it is necessary for an inside transit card, like a poster, to get its message over in the flickering of an eyelid. The thought is

eye and if you have interested them sufficiently to make them want to do so. You don't, accordingly, have to limit your copy to five or six words. Or fifty or sixty for that matter. One important restraining element on the number of words is the requirement that the message be readable three seats ahead or back of the card.

Transit cards can be so designed as to be real "traveling salespeople"—selling advertisements that can, by themselves, put over a sale instead of being mere reminders.

As you write a transit card, recall that you are not expecting to reach everyone in the car at one time. Passengers aren't going to stretch, and crane, and twist to read your copy. The only people you will usually reach at any single moment are those passengers standing or sitting close to where the card is posted. This is why it is not essential to keep copy brief, nor type kingsize. If a person can read your poster from six or eight feet away, readability is all right. A good way to test readability quickly is to place the poster on the ground at your feet. If you can read it easily, the card will probably be readable for riders in vehicles carrying transit cards.

Another point to remember about transit cards is that often they curve. Also that the bottom of the card, rather than the top, is closer to the reader's eyes; therefore, it is usually easier to read. That's why you

FIGURE 16-12

Inside transit card with a creative twist.   Humor causes a ready response among transit riders who welcome a diversion from the monotony of their daily ride.

find many transit card headlines at the bottom. Because of curvature, the upper inch or so of the card often is practically flat against the roof of the car or bus. If you put any of your copy story in this top area, make it a subordinate line, not your real selling message.

Regarding transit cards, remember—you may make them "miniature posters," if you will thus more effectively get over your message, but do not consider such practice as standard. In these days the poster often takes one technique and the transit card another.

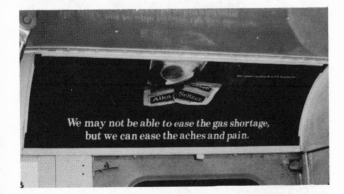

FIGURE 16-13

Inside transit card with humorous twist.   Smiles and attention are the rewards for creative people who devise transit messages such as this one.

FIGURE 16-14

Inside transit card that resembles outdoor poster.   In this instance, the wry humor of the message made the card effective even though it used minimum copy and no illustration.

OUTSIDE CARDS

In recent years there has been a falling off of the use of inside transit cards and a veritable stampede to the outside cards displayed on the ends and sides of buses. Advertisers using the outside cards obtain readership from pedestrians, motorists, and even from homes as people see the bus going by their windows.

In a sense, the outside cards are a form of traveling outdoor advertising that carries the advertiser's message into all parts of the town. For the copywriter, the outside cards constitute a strong creative challenge since the length of the sales message must be severely limited. Truly, in the case of outside transit cards, the copywriter must consider them closer to outdoor advertising than to the transit advertising represented by inside transit cards.

FIGURE 16-15

Outside transit card that uses positive suggestion.   One unusual aspect of this card is that it uses a longer message than most outdoor transit cards. The chief point of the card, however, is made in the easily read headline.

FIGURE 16-16

Outside transit card with play on words.   Many advertisers use only outside transit cards such as this one to catch the attention of pedestrians and motorists.

To write the copy for such cards, the copywriter should, therefore, follow exactly the same suggestions that were made for writing outdoor advertising. Brevity. A single compelling idea. Few elements. Simplicity.

Another form of outside card is the station poster that greets subway and train riders before they step inside the cars. These are treated like outdoor posters except that they are vertical instead of horizontal. Somewhat more copy may be written for these posters than for 24-sheet posters because reading time is longer both by people standing on platforms and by people reading the posters when the transit vehicle is discharging and picking up passengers.

IDEAS FOR WRITING TRANSIT CARD COPY

Although it has been pointed out that inside transit cards are not small posters, you should consider that there are some techniques that might transfer from one to the other.

1. As in posters, transit cards will usually be more effective if one sales point is made. An attempt to make more than one point will usually dilute your message.
2. Although your reading time is greater for your copy in transit cards, like posters, they should not have too many elements if they are to be efficient and readable.

3. A transit card can use more copy than a poster, but don't go wild. Brevity is still desirable for most cards. The use of a little white space will be helpful sometimes in giving your card a favorable contrast to the crowded cards next to yours.
4. Simplicity is another quality shared by posters and transit cards. Because of your being able to use more copy, you may indulge in more subtlety in transit cards, but don't overplay it. The

FIGURE 16-17

Subway station poster.   In big cities, station posters outside and inside are powerful selling agents. This one uses athletic talk effectively.

average rider is usually better sold by a simple message.

5. The featuring of the package is, of course, desirable in transit cards as well as posters—especially so since your card may be the last advertising contact with someone who is about to start a shopping tour.

6. Positive suggestion is a part of transit card copy, too. As in poster copy, it is not used in every advertisement, but in the right advertisements it becomes a forceful, selling technique.

Thus, in summarizing the essential differences in handling the two—posters and cards—you find that:

- Unorthodox layout tricks are often used in transit-card designing—the placing of headline at the bottom of the advertisement, for instance, the allowance for the curved surface, and other factors.
- More latitude is possible in writing transit card copy since average reading time of transit cards is about twenty-seven minutes, contrasted with the five to ten seconds' reading time of posters. The end result is longer copy and an opportunity for more subtle copy.

Both outdoor posters, and inside and outside transit cards offer you more chances to be clever in one-liners than any other advertising medium. If you have the kind of mind that is original and capable of putting a fresh twist into your writing and illustration ideas, you'll derive intense satisfaction from the creating of outdoor or transit advertising. Here are two areas of advertising where cleverness and originality pay off handsomely.

17

Making It Big in Radio

To understand how to write radio, think of yourself and others as radio listeners. You have probably listened to radio in kitchens, bathrooms, bedrooms, basements, automobiles, boats, restaurants, on the beach, in banks, service stations, airline terminals, and doctor's offices.

And while you have listened to radio you may have been: milking a cow, ironing, knitting, cooking, studying, working under a car, writing a letter, eating, driving a tractor, operating a payloader or a truck, cleaning house, painting the siding, doing woodworking, playing bridge, dusting, fishing, sitting in a ski lodge, or passing time in a hospital bed.

Radio has become the medium that reaches people while they are doing something (other than purposefully listening to radio). Radio, as the industry reminds advertisers, reaches the audience anywhere and everywhere, no matter what that audience is doing.

Awareness that the radio audience is not immobile and attentive has caused radio writers to change their writing formats. Where once the typical radio listeners tuned in to program after program and listened carefully to all of them, they are now restless, dial-changing listeners to whom radio is a background to other activities. Their attention must be captured and every device must be used to hold that attention.

Because of the flighty, inattentive listeners, radio commercials have become increasingly entertaining. Humor, much of the mad variety, holds audiences just as well as the surrounding program material. Music is used skillfully to capture attention or to create moods. Yet, despite the increase of various attention-getting and mood-creating techniques, radio commercials have become simpler. Good radio writers know that in this era of half-listening radio audiences it is vital to give the listener just one principal idea to carry away. They know, too, that details should be kept to a minimum.

WORDS ARE YOUR ILLUSTRATIONS

Although many commercials do not call for descriptive writing, the ones that do will make you realize that the greatest handicap you face in selling by the spoken word is the inability to illustrate your product. This difficulty overshadows the restrictions of writing against time and the dependence upon the imaginations of your listeners. The lack of illustrative possibilities makes commercial writing a confining form of sales writing. You must be like the storytellers of ancient times who, through ballads and skillfully told tales, made their listeners see the wonders of other lands and other peoples. Many times you'll envy the fashion copywriter who can call for a gorgeous illustration, tag a short line of copy to the art, and be off to the next assignment. If you wrote a radio commercial for the same garment, you would describe the style, the cut, and you'd use all your cunning to make the woman listener imagine how she would look in the dress, or hat, or coat.

The need for visualization in radio influences greatly your commercial writing, since you must choose selling points that can be described readily and convincingly to listeners. No longer can you depend upon artwork or photographs to help you capture and hold the attention and interest of your prospects. If, for instance, you are describing on the air the sales features of a ham, you are missing your most potent sales howitzer—the strongest, most compelling attraction of any ham advertising—a colorful photograph of a big, ready-to-eat, luscious, ham. Your job is to make those listening to your commercial see that ham through your words alone, smell it, taste it, want it.

If you are asked to prepare radio commercials for an automobile, you can't refer to the sleek, new compact parked alongside your copy in the magazine pages. You don't have that help. You must, solely by the deft use of description, put your audience in the driver's seat of that car—make them feel its lively response—its ease of handling—make them see its handsome lines.

Description is vital in many radio commercials. Perhaps you aren't an agency writer concerned with cars and hams and nationally advertised brands. Maybe your job is to turn out radio announcements by the hundreds for use on local stations to bring people into your department store—bring them in to buy shoes, and clothes, and radios, and washing machines, and toys. To the homemaker listening to the radio as she tidies up the apartment, you aren't going to offer pleasant generalities about the service offered by your store or its courteous salespeople and well-lighted aisles. If you want that woman to put on her hat and coat and come downtown to your store to buy, you've got to make her want the articles you describe. You have to make the articles appealing. And you have to do it completely with words. You can't draw a picture and then write, "Look, ma'am, isn't this a lovely coat?" You draw your picture with words.

Even good sound effects and music, as effective as they can be in enhancing a commercial, cannot substitute for even ordinary artwork. The real picture beats the word picture for putting over product detail quickly and surely. Still, the good radio writer tries to come close to art in his use of descriptive words. It's a challenge and it isn't easy because writing good description is difficult whether it's done in the writing of books, articles, or radio commercials.

Sure, you can raise calves on whole milk. But why not give 'em Be-Co-Nurse, the high energy milk replacer? You'll save big on feeding costs if you do and maybe give 'em a lot more nutrition, too. The big thing is that you want those calves of yours to get off to a fast start so you can cut down expensive growing costs. See your Beacon dealer to get the whole story on Be-Co-Nurse. It's a winner.

5 second tag

FIGURE 17-1

Conversational radio commercial.   The breezy, personal style of this commercial makes easy listening. Contractions, sentence fragments, and conversational bridges are all used here, plus a strong, action ending.

Following is a radio commercial for a paint company. Paint is a colorful product. It must be seen. Television and colorful magazine advertisements are powerful media for selling any product so visual as paint. Yet notice how the radio writer can, through descriptive words help the reader "see" the different colors of paint.

It's fall. It's beautiful. It's colorful. It's also time to paint your home before winter comes. At Every-Hue Paint Company we'll give you colors to fit the fall season and your moods. Reds like the scarlet maple leaves. Blues like soft October skies. Brilliant yellows like goldenrod waving in windswept fields. If your mood is gloomy in anticipation of the winter ahead, we have blacks as deep as cold, starless fall nights. But, why be gloomy? Every-Hue has whites to lift your spirits—chaste whites as pure and unspoiled as the snows to come. Paint to suit your mood, your home and the season—paint with Every-Hue paints.

Obviously all radio commercials don't require great descriptive powers. Neither do all of them demand writing perfection. The appearance of some products does not need description. Why describe an aspirin tablet? Or a cigarette? Or a tube of tooth paste?

Many radio commercials belong to the "see-how-many-times-you-can-get-the-public-to-listen-to-it" school, where the main object is to pound away with your product's name and perhaps one sale idea or buying reminder. Others, such as those for cosmetics and food products, require explanations and selling on what they can do for you. A third huge category, especially in department store radio advertising and other local operations, stresses price.

TRY COMMERCIALS ALOUD

The one most important rule to learn about writing for radio, whether for commercials or continuity, is that every single word you set down on paper for use over the air must be read aloud by you before you give it your personal approval.

You may not—probably won't—have a private office in which to work. Most beginning copywriters don't. It makes no difference. Even if you have to adjourn to the coatroom for privacy, find yourself an unoccupied corner and play announcer. You see, every writer always relies on seeing in print the words that are written. What looks readable may not sound the least bit so.

Embarrassing fluffs by announcers rarely will occur if commercials have been given an advance "out-loud" test. As this book was about to go to press, two commercials were heard which illustrated the need for eliminating tongue twisters before the announcer is trapped. In both instances, the announcer faltered, started again, faltered and finally gave up, passing over the incident with a quip. The writer had succeeded in making the announcer laugh, but advertisers have a very unsympathetic view of the kind of humor that may cost them product sales.

One of the phrases causing the most trouble was ". . . prepared for welcoming me in as a." Try out this phrase on an unsuspecting friend to see what trouble it can cause when it is read out loud rapidly without rehearsal. The other phrase was "fresh, flavorful, fragrant coffee." Alliteration, as you will read later, is a real troublemaker. It was, in this instance, and yet a quick reading aloud in advance of broadcast could have resulted in a correction.

To go a step beyond reading your own commercials, you should listen to the announcer as he delivers them. Here's someone reading the commercials who has had nothing to do with producing them. He is not acquainted with the thinking behind them. His reading of your commercials may reveal additional pitfalls not discovered in your own reading. Notice the mistakes and remember to avoid those mistakes in your next set of commercials.

By keeping a few rules in mind as you approach writing for radio, you can give yourself a headstart on those who walk gaily into commercial writing with the attitude that it's no different from any other kind of writing.

Whether or not you observe the various admonitions listed, keep in mind one point. Once more this advice will be emphasized, since it's all-important—Read 'em aloud!

LENGTH OF WORDS AND SENTENCES

Short words are usually the best radio words. Regardless of their pronunciation or ease of understanding, words that contain more than three or four syllables should be used only when absolutely necessary. Thus "a great car" is better than "an exceptional car"—"lovely" preferable to "beautiful"—"good" to "outstanding," and so forth. Similarly, short sentences are usually easier for the announcer than long ones. Sometimes, however, awkward sentence structure can make even short sentences poor radio. Short sentences, therefore, aren't always the final answer. A skillfully written sentence that is moderately long but well phrased can often make better listening than a poorly written short sentence.

When you make an effort to break up your radio copy into short, easy-to-read-aloud sentences, you will discover another fact about commercial writing—that certain conventional writing practices do not apply. Well-written prose has few sentences starting with the words "And" or "But." Yet these two words are standard openers in radio sentences because they preserve the flowing, conversational quality of the announcer's delivery. Likewise, they stop him enough to keep him from crowding his words and from going too fast or too breathlessly.

The frequent use of contractions is another characteristic of radio writing. In printed prose, contractions may make writing appear overly informal and undignified. In radio copy they often enhance the sincere and conversational qualities of the commercial. If you read, "Do not miss this chance to . . ." or

FIGURE 17-2

Humorous radio commercial.   Commercials such as those shown in Figures 17-2, 17-3, and 17-4 are part of a long-time campaign for the advertiser. Notice that in addition to highly imaginative humor, the commercials incorporate specific sales points. Thus the commercials get attention and good-will from the humor, and still manage to build up sales power.

Marsteller Inc.
CHICAGO   As Recorded

RADIO COPY

Date typed:	March 2,	Revision number:	
Client:	LANIER BUSINESS PRODUCTS	Date recorded:	
Program:	"Home Run Queen"	Air date:	
Length:	:60		

ANNCR: Here's Stiller & Meara for Lanier Dictating Equipment.

STILLER: Miss Kluzewski, we might just have a position for you on our team.

MEARA: In the typing pool?

STILLER: Not exactly. We're looking for a good pinch hitter.

MEARA: Oh, a vacation replacement.

STILLER: No. On our company softball team.

MEARA: Great! But I thought you needed a secretary.

STILLER: A secretary that can hit. What's your average?

MEARA: Seventy words a minute.

STILLER: Your batting average.

MEARA: Oh, .450 on my last job. But there's one small problem. I can't take dictation.

STILLER: Dictation? We use Lanier dictating equipment. Pocket-sized portable standard cassette units. We even have a Lanier phone-in system that lets you use any telephone anywhere. Lanier helps us get more work done so there's more time to play ball.

MEARA: No shorthand! Oh, terrific. When can I start?

STILLER: Practice is at 4:30 sharp. Before you leave, would you mind trying on this catcher's mask?

MEARA: Oh, sure.

STILLER: I think I'm falling in love.

MEARA: You're a sick man.

STILLER: Softball is my life.

ANNCR: You can get more done with Lanier Business Products. Look for Lanier in the Yellow Pages under dictating machines.

"You have not tasted candy until . . .," you wouldn't criticize the writer for faulty technique. The writing seems natural.

When these phrases are said aloud, however, they sound like prose. They are not phrases that you, or the announcer, or the listener would use. You would say, "Don't miss this chance . . ." and "You haven't tasted candy . . ."

Give conscious attention to contractions. They are a definite part of American speaking idiom, and that means that they are particularly good for radio use. As one caution, however, you should remember that occasionally you will want to emphasize a point, and the use of a contraction might weaken your sentence. Suppose, for instance, you are writing copy for a nonskid tire. A claim of "You cannot skid." Where a negative element needs emphasis, then you might prefer to avoid the contraction. But in most cases the contraction is desirable.

Likewise, you will find that sentence fragments will sometimes serve better than full sentences in radio. Listen to a conversation some time between two or more persons. Count how many times sentences are not completed. Yet the conversationalists understand each other perfectly. Utilize this conversational tendency in commercials, but use it carefully or you may end up writing gibberish.

PUNCTUATION

Closely associated with sentence length in radio is the use of punctuation. Punctuation, if anything, is more important in radio writing than in writing for print because bad punctuation can mislead the announcer and cause him to make a disastrous mistake over the air. To the radio writer all punctuation marks are important, but especially important are the underline, the double dash, and the hyphen.

Underline. The underline should be used sparingly and with purpose. Usually the announcer will know through experience what words to punch, but here and there you may have a word you wish to stress because of company policy or some other reason. In such cases, underline the word but—and this is important—just the *one* word. Almost never is it advisable to underline two words or a whole phrase. It is almost impossible for the announcer to put true stress on more than one word. Resolutely avoid scattering underlined words throughout a commercial because, by so doing, you overemphasize your message and you make the announcer's job more difficult.

Double-dash. A useful punctuation device is the double-dash (--) which gives a conversational flow to your writing. It gives a dramatic pause that is less abrupt than the full stop created by a period. Used correctly, the double-dash gives a graceful ease to radio writing and aids the announcer in his delivery. An example from a commercial for a savings bank reads: "But a *savings* balance--that's something else again." Notice not only how the double-dash contributes a natural pause in the delivery, but also that the underline gives vigor to the whole sentence. Note, too that all that is needed here is one word underlined. It would have been a mistake to underline "savings balance," since this emphasis would be awkward for the announcer.

Many writers use the three-dot (. . .) punctuation device in radio and print copy. Once a writer has contracted the three-dot habit, he finds it difficult to write complete sentences. Avoid this habit. If you wish to make a pause for effect, use the double-dash but do not overdo that either.

Hyphen. When you wish to join two words in order that they may modify a third word, you can use a hyphen (-). Sometimes your announcer must be guided by the hyphenated words or he will make a mistake in his reading. In the bank commercial previously referred to, the writer used a hyphen in this manner: "Open a dividend-paying savings account . . ." If the hyphen had not been used here, the announcer might have read the passage as "Open a dividend." In using hyphens, however, avoid the precious, cute, and artificial combining of words that have given advertising writing a bad name in many writing quarters. Phrases such as "bunny-soft," "cozy-warm," and "baby-cute," illustrate the point.

USE EASY-TO-SAY AND EASY-TO-UNDERSTAND WORDS

Avoid words that are hard to pronounce, even if they are easily understood words. "Indisputable" is a word that everyone would understand, but it could be a stumbling block for a radio announcer. "Applicable," "ingenious," "particularly," "demonstrable," "naive," and "detectable" would be correctly defined by most high school students, yet any of them could cause an announcer to hesitate a split second, thus disturbing the natural flow of his words.

Sometimes very innocent-looking words that are simple to pronounce by themselves can become nightmares for the announcer when they are combined with certain other innocent-looking words. A good example is a sentence actually used on the air and which very effectively tied the announcer in knots—"A government order of twenty-two stainless steel twin-screw cruisers." Too, if you put "in," "an," or "un" next to a word beginning with any of these three sounds you will give almost any announcer a moment of pronunciation juggling—example: "in an unenviable position." Say it fast and notice the mumble that results. It would be pointless for you to attempt to memorize all such sound and word combinations which might cause you trouble. Experience will teach you some of the troublemakers and reading aloud should take care of the rest.

Beware of adverbs. The suffix "ly" is a tough one for radio people to pronounce with consistent precision. If you can twist your sentence to gain the same thought without the "ly," you will usually have a better commercial. It is not as good radio to say:

The shoes that men are increasingly favoring.

as it is to say:

The shoes that more men are favoring every day.

And you might wish to say of a cereal product:

Nutritionally, too, it's the buy for you.

Much better in radio, to say:

For nutrition, too, it's the buy for you.

You don't sacrifice the swing of both, or the rhyme of one—both attributes of good radio commercials—yet

Marsteller Inc.
CHICAGO   As Recorded

RADIO COPY

```
Date typed:       August 2
Client:           Lanier Business Products
Program:          Closet Secretary
Length:           :60
Revision number:  AS RECORDED
```

ANNCR: Here's Stiller and Meara for Lanier dictating equipment.

STILLER: Miss Sharpman, Sheila, step into the closet.

MEARA: Not again, boss. I have my pride.

STILLER: It's part of your job.

MEARA: Don't shove. I'm tired of being a closet secretary.

STILLER: It's kind of cozy in here, if you don't mind the coats
          and hangers.

MEARA: It's too dark to take shorthand. Why can't I take
          dictation in the office?

STILLER: Because I want you to take my dictation, not Herman
          Oarlock's. Every time I need you, he's dictating the
          agenda for his coffee break.

MEARA: You think it's easy being a secretary for two people?
          I'm torn. Everywhere I go it's Sheila Sharpman, Sheila
          Sharpman!

STILLER: Hurry! Your flashlight's getting dim! We need new
          batteries.

MEARA: We need Lanier!

STILLER: Lanier! Can she see in the dark?

MEARA: Lanier is dictating equipment. With Lanier's Action
          Line you and Mr. Oarlock could both dictate whenever
          you want. Even when I'm busy. The Action Line is an
          intercom and a message center, too. We'd all get more
          done.

STILLER: I'll call Lanier. Are you happy now?

MEARA: I'm happy, but I don't know about Oarlock.

STILLER: Why?

MEARA: He's been waiting for me, under his desk since ten
          o'clock.

STILLER: Weird guy.

ANNCR: Get more done with Lanier Business Products. In the
          Yellow Pages under dictating machines.

FIGURE 17-3

Humorous radio commercial.

you have constructed a sentence that will be easy for the announcers to read without much chance of stumbling.

One fault you must guard against is permitting words to creep into your commercials which are similar, in sound, to other words with different meanings. One of these, for instance, is the word "chief." If you are writing a commercial about air travel, you might wish to say, "It has many advantages over all other forms of travel, the chief one being . . ."

Now you know that word is "chief." You might have used "main," or "outstanding," or some other synonym, but "chief " looks all right to you, and it sounds fine as you read it. Now consider your listener. First of all, he's not hanging on your announcer's every phrase. Secondly, he hears the word "chief "

only one time as it slips past, and he doesn't know, as you do, what comes next. It would be very easy for him to think the announcer said "cheap." You'll admit that the difference between the two words is great enough to warrant care in their use whether you're selling air travel or aspirin.

"Breath" and "breadth"; "smell," "swell," and "spell"; "prize" and "price" are other examples of words which might be misinterpreted or given a wrong meaning by the listener. It's just as easy to use a simple synonym and take no chances.

Alliteration alienates announcers

The print writer's use of alliteration in radio can cause trouble. Visually the phrase, "Prize-winners in perfectly proportioned peach halves," can't be criticized very harshly. If you saw it in an advertisement, even if you are one of those who reads everything with your lips, you might view it as a nicely turned phrase. Say, however, that you have been assigned to write some radio commercials for X peaches and you hit upon that sentence—which looks fine as it leaves the typewriter. Perhaps it looks fine also to those with whom you must clear your copy. It gets an okay and is released to the radio station. Just how do you think it is going to look to the radio announcer who is scanning the copy ten minutes before broadcast time? The way to find out how he'll like it is to stand up and read it just as you want him to read it. Do that to the peach halves atrocity right now. Read it aloud. How does it sound? Doesn't it sound a little bit like a person about to lose an upper plate?

A little bit of alliteration is certainly acceptable in radio writing. In fact, wisely used, it often helps to spark up copy. But alliteration is like dynamite—a little too much is going to blow your commercial apart. Use alliteration if you wish, but be very careful not to overdo it. Your own sense of hearing will be your safety valve. If it doesn't sound good to you when you read it aloud, change it.

Don't bark or hiss

Another thing you may discover, as you stand up and announce your first try-'em-out-loud commercials, is that you have given your copy too many hissing sounds. Radio announcers hate the "double-ess" ending and dislike it even in the middle of words because it is hard to say clearly and with force. The word "sensational"—almost a routine part of many copywriters' daily vocabularies—causes announcers to wince. Your commercials would probably sound better if you could manage to write them without ever using the letter "s" or the "z" or the soft "c."

Example. While reading the last two sentences, you are not likely to have experienced a difficulty or unpleasant reaction from the words used. Yet several times in those two sentences, you can find the soft "c" or the "s" sounds. They would not have been pleasant sounding on the air. Were this page to be read for radio, some rewriting would have to be done. Remember, too, that the particularly harsh sounds in the English language do not broadcast well. The sounds "ark" and "ack," "eesh" and "ash," "app" and "amm" should seldom be used. As you enunciate your copy, listen to your voice and try to sift out the sounds that grate on your ear. Assume that the sounds that grate on your ear as you hear them in the solitude of an office or room will sound much worse with even the minimum distortion produced by modern transmission.

WRITE TRANSITIONALLY

A radio commercial should be a unified presentation whether it's 30 seconds or 60 seconds. Each sentence should connect with and flow from the preceding sentence. Your points should be bridged by connecting words and phrases. Instead, inexperienced radio writers tend to run together a series of unrelated points. The result is a jerky, clumsy commercial that even a very good announcer will find difficult. "Difficult," here, means that they cannot achieve the smoothness of presentation that a well-written commercial makes possible.

What you should incorporate are conversational bridges that create a natural flow. Sometimes the bridge may be a single word that indicates continuity, a carrying over of a thought from one sentence to another. "And," and "but," are such words. "Furthermore," and "also," are two more. "So," is another.

Sometimes you'll use a phrase to achieve transition. Examples:

But that's only the start.

Listen to this.

In addition,

Remember, ask for

Here's something else you'll like.

If you've been needing help, think of this.

Following is a commercial that demonstrates how you can achieve unity through transitional writing:

If you live in the Midland area, you can make sure you have a great Christmas next year and get a fine gift for doing it. Here's how. Just come in before Saturday to Midland Trust to open a Christmas Club for next year, a Club that pays interest, by the way. That's right. Unlike many Christmas Clubs, this one pays regular interest. And here's another plus. When you open your Club you get a handsome, decorative hurricane lamp that'll brighten whatever spot you put it in. Just think, a valuable gift simply for opening a money-making Christmas Club. Even without the gift it makes good sense to open a Christmas Club. Bet you'll think so next year at this time when you have plenty of cash to spend in the holiday season. Better make a note

right now to open a Midland Trust Christmas Club and to get your hurricane lamp—a yuletide duo from Midland's leading bank.

Notice all the bridging words and phrases:

Here's how

Just come in

That's right

And here's another plus

Just think

Bet you'll think so

Better make a note right now

Notice two more important aspects of this commercial. One is the strong action ending. Two is the repetition of the offer at the end of the commercial. Repetition of the main selling point is one of the attributes of good radio commercial writing.

SLANG? YES, BUT . . .

When you are urged to "be conversational" in radio commercials, you are being given good counsel, but counsel that might possibly lead you astray, since the conversation of a large percentage of Americans would be unsuitable for radio usage. You will have to use your judgment in deciding what is conversational and what slips into the area of poor taste.

The inclusion of a certain amount of slang, informal phraseology, and current jargon will often lend a naturalness and spontaneity that greatly increase the believability and selling power of commercials. Whether to use such devices in your writing and how much to use them will depend pretty much on what you are trying to sell, and more than that, to whom you are selling.

On a sports program, which you could assume would interest a youngish male audience, the most logical types of products to be sold would be such items as men's clothing, beer, shaving soap, or cigarettes. If you were assigned to write commercials for such a show, it would probably be perfectly good technique to use occasional phrases such as, "a doggone good buy," "styles that are really terrific," "takes off whiskers with the speed of a jet," and similar masculine-like wordage. Such writing will be helpful in making your audience feel that the commercial is part of the show, written for them alone, and hence will be more likely to take effect. Needless to say, that kind of talk would not sound very appropriate to a person listening to a soap opera at home.

Similarly, a children's program should be liberally sprinkled with words currently being used by children. If you are asked to write the commercials for such a show, you would be very wise to do some on-the-spot investigating, and pick up the phrases and slang of the moment. Be quite sure, when you do, that you are not writing expressions that mean something

Marsteller Inc.
CHICAGO   As Recorded

___

RADIO COPY

Client: Lanier
Program: Male Secretary -- #11545
Facilities:
Date: October 1
Time: :60

ANNCR: Stiller and Meara for Lanier Dictating Equipment.

MEARA: I have your secretarial application right here, Mr.
          Piltdown.

STILLER: Call me Craig.

MEARA: Well, sit down, Craig.

STILLER: I am sitting.

MEARA: Oh, (laughter), of course you are...my you're huge!

STILLER: I played fullback for the Pennsylvania Anthrocites.

MEARA: How did you get into secretarial work?

STILLER: Well, I was a receptionist. Then one of the girls got
          pregnant so they just moved me up.

MEARA: Uh huh.

STILLER: It's not easy being a secretary. I was the only one
          around that could handle those old-fashioned belted
          dictating machines. Boy are they hard to load. You
          see, that's my specialty.

MEARA: You won't be needing that Craig. We use Lanier
          Cassettes. You've heard of Lanier cassettes?

STILLER: He played with the Texas Cowboys.

MEARA: (Laughter) No. Lanier makes cassette dictating
          equipment. Cassettes are easier to load and they
          sound better.

STILLER: No belts. Then you don't need me.

MEARA: Oh yes. I need you. I need you, Craig.

STILLER: Hey lady...

MEARA: Hmmmmmm.

STILLER: You blew in my ear.

MEARA: It's lonely at the top.

STILLER: I'm not that kind of a guy.

MEARA: You'll learn (laughter).

ANNCR: Put standard cassette speed and efficiency in your
          dictation. Give Lanier a hearing. We're in the
          Yellow Pages under dictating machines.

FIGURE 17-4

Humorous radio commercial.

___

only in one locality—one neighborhood—or, if your show is national or your spot announcements are for wide distribution, one section of the country.

Steer clear of slang words that might alienate large groups of your audience, even though at first thoug ь they might seem all right. A good example of ѕ ԇʰ a word is "darn." Now you may have used th ⸱ ҽ₅⸳ es-sion since you were two years old, heard your mother, sister and even your minister say it often. Yet to many people the word "darn" is simply another way of saying "damn," and even though he may say it

himself, you might offend one of your sensitive listeners by putting it in your commercial. There is no need to take chances with words or expressions that have the slightest chance of producing a negative effect even on a few people. Those few might otherwise all be easily sold on your product.

"Scram," "blow," "nuts," "oh, yeah," "so what," "screwy," "lousy," "stink," "jerk," "baloney," and other such words should not be included in your radio writing vocabulary. They do not represent the clean, healthy slang that makes acceptable, picturesque American talk for radio.

Before using the lighter words and phrases in your commercials, try them out on some of your more pedantic friends. If you get a lot of voluntary suggestions to do away with a word or an expression, it's probably wise to do so.

GETTING AND KEEPING ATTENTION

Mrs. Jones is stirring cream sauce while she eyes the roast in the oven and the cauliflower boiling in a pan on the stove. Little Freddy is noisily playing games with his friend, Billy, in an adjacent room.

Now, the magic moment. Your commercial sounds from the kitchen set. What will win? Your commercial, or Mrs. Jones' cooking and other distractions?

What is done in the opening seconds of the commercial determines the answer. What have you done to force listenership? Are you using music, sound effects, or an unusual opening statement by the announcer? Surely you have done something to jar Mrs. Jones into attention? If you haven't, check off another commercial that lost the attention-battle.

In addition, of course, you pull out all the stops to hold attention after you've captured it. Perhaps you've used that reliable device, the humorous man-on-the-street interview, or another old reliable, a conversation between unlikely types such as the award-winning commercial that featured a pair of voracious talking termites.

Some down-to-earth suggestions for keeping attention are given here by a veteran radio writer.

16 Ways to Capture and Hold Attention for Radio Commercials

1. Product-in-action sound effects. Coffee comes to life in the percolator, as Maxwell House proved in its radio commercials. There are sounds relevant to just about every product, waiting to be employed as creative tools. Beyond the sound itself, how it's used can also make a big difference.

2. Mix 'em up. Experiment with various combinations of jingle, dialogue, straight announcement, sound effects, music, etc., all in one commercial. Presented with this kind of variety, the listener is likely to be attentive, wondering what's coming next. The commercial can be a miniature show.

3. Symbolic character. Have a distinctive voice represent your product. If it's indigenous to a foreign country, such as spaghetti and macaroni, the voice can hold

listener attention by speaking with an accent typical of that country.

4. Tie in with stations' features. Integrate your commercials with the weather reports, time checks, musical styles, or even the call letters. Any way you can sound less like an interruption to regular programming helps.

5. Call on comedy stars.   For truly entertaining spots, you can use the guys whose job it is to be funny. But don't let it fall flat; get real comedy material, either from the performer, if he writes, or from his writers.

6. Variations on a theme.   Once you hit on the magic jingle, don't be content to present it at one tempo, over and over. See that it gets every treatment from cool jazz to old-fashioned waltz.

7. Tie in with current events.   It's going on in the world that has everyone interested? Is there a world's heavyweight championship fight in the works? Sign one of the fighters for your commercials, if the product lends itself to endorsement, by a name from the world of sports.

8. Ad libs.   For the height of realism, why not let your spokesmen call it the way they see it? Foreign actors are most articulate and convincing given the freedom to speak of their country's advantages for radio airing.

9. Speed ups—slow downs.   Often you can capture attention by tampering with the speed of sounds in radio commercials. Caution: take care that important words don't get garbled in the process.

10. Real-life interviews.   Questioning the man (or woman) in the street about your product can turn up the kind of praise which, captured on tape, can serve to activate the listening audience. Inclusion of actual street noises in the sound tract helps to heighten the realism.

11. Orchestrate sound effects.   For greater appeal to the listeners' imagination, let music simulate the sounds you're after in a commercial. You can establish the real sound, and follow with the musical treatment. The tempo of the product sound can be effectively translated to music.

12. Use real kids.   Where dialogue from youngsters is indicated, you may reach the heights of realism—and charm—by giving the part to actual children rather than character actors. With editing, the little scene stealers have been known to come up with topnotch copy through ad lib.

13. Publicity-hungry stars.   No need to spend a fortune to enlist big names in your radio commercial cause. Check into which show business luminaries are a little short on work, and anxious to get back into the limelight. Chances are you can work out a satisfactory arrangement.

14. Authoritative voice.   Radio listeners are accustomed to accepting the word of the commentators who bring them the news. That same voice—and the authority that goes with it—may be available for delivery of your sales message. Local and regional personalities may be of use.

15. Use a popular or standard tune.   If you can get the rights to a familiar tune, you've taken a giant step toward bridging the gap between entertainment and the commercial.

16. Character switch.   Play a trick or two on the listeners now and then to perk up their attention. Try introducing one type of character, say a gentle housewife, and have her enter screaming at her husband; or have a prize fighter talk like Casper Milquetoast.

TYPES OF COMMERCIALS

If you are to produce commercials for a radio program—either network or local—there are a number of different techniques upon which you may draw. Some of these are:

Straight commercial

The straight commercial is a straight-selling message devoted to the merits of your product, service, or institutional story. It might be compared with a piece of straight-line body copy and is delivered by a commercial announcer, with no outside means of attracting or holding attention.

Marsteller Inc.
CHICAGO   As Recorded

RADIO COPY

Client: LANIER
Program: "Tattoo" -- 75-3
Facilities: Stiller & Meara
Date: January 29
Time: :60

ANNCR: Here's Stiller & Meara for Lanier Dictating Equipment.

MEARA: Gee, Boss, that's an interesting tattoo. Did you get it on your trip?

STILLER: That's no tattoo. That's my expense report. You know I write on my arm when I can't find a pad.

MEARA: Oh, well, it's very attractive--when you flex.

STILLER: Here, type these notes.

MEARA: What notes? This is a dirty tablecloth. Wait--I do see writing, next to the gravy stain.

STILLER: When I get an idea, anything goes. And it's not gravy, it's chili.

MEARA: There's a missing paragraph here.

STILLER: Let's see...oh, I think it's written on an envelope in the upper right-hand pocket of my suit. Call the Hop Sing Laundry.

MEARA: Boss, working for you is like playing Chinese checkers. You need a Pocket Secretary.

STILLER: Would she mind working out of an overcoat?

MEARA: No, Boss. Lanier's new pocket dictating machine--the Pocket Secretary. It uses tiny, 60-minute cassettes, weighs only 12-1/2 ounces.

STILLER: You're probably right. But here, type one more memo from my trip.

MEARA: It says, "Use only for motion sickness..."

STILLER: Other side, other side.

MEARA: Oh...

ANNCR: Get more done with Lanier's Pocket Secretary. We're in the Yellow Pages under Dictating Machines.

FIGURE 17-5

Humorous commercial.   Humor in commercials addressed to business people is fairly rare. In this case, however, the commercials are expertly done by two skilled entertainers whose voices are distinctive. The campaign, of which this commercial is representative, has drawn much attention and is so well done that the commercials have a good reception even from people who are not in the market for the product advertised.

Many advertisers now look critically at this type of commercial since they feel that inattentive, uninterested listeners will not wait out the announcer for the full period of the commercial. Still, on thousands of radio stations, the selling messages are delivered straight and they are still selling goods and services even though artistically they are not so satisfying to creative people as other commercial types.

FIGURE 17-6

30-second straight commercial.   As in good product-selling commercials, this commercial of the public-service type uses a strong, dramatic opening to capture attention.

The Advertising Council, Inc.

```
30-SECOND RADIO SPOT #1 - "Botanic Garden"

   In Palos Verdes California, 2000 species of plant life
grow ten feet above 3-million-tons of rusted cars, trash, and
garbage.  This is South Coast Botanic Garden:  a dump transformed
into a paradise.  It proves volunteer projects can return the
land to natural beauty.

   For the name of the community team nearest you, write:
KEEP AMERICA BEAUTIFUL, 99 Park Avenue, New York, New York 10016.

   People start pollution.  People can stop it.

   A public service message of this station and The Advertising
Council.


                            # # #
```

Dialogue commercial

In a dialogue commercial the selling message is put across by means of dialogue between the announcer and others not in the cast of the show. The announcer may converse with users of the product, with experts on one or more phases of the product's manufacture, with dealers, or simply with unidentified parties. Through these conversations the various sales features of whatever is being sold are described. Most commonly used are testimonials.

The principal problem in this type of commercial is to make the dialogue believable and natural. Too often one or the other of the voices becomes a stooge for the other.

Suggested ways to make two-voice commercials believable, or at least acceptable:

If a commercial is being delivered by two supposedly real-life people such as two housewives, two husbands, a husband and a wife, or two children, it is almost impossible to deliver a number of product points without making salespeople out of the characters. Generally, such commercials make a stooge out of one of the characters. This one, possibly a housewife, will say to the other: "But Kleen-O must cost a lot." The other then replies: "Not at all, Jane. Due to a new manufacturing process, Kleen-O has been able to reduce its price to the low, low price of 78¢. And that's not <u>all</u> they've done either. Listen to this . . ."

The easiest way out of the artificiality of such two-voice commercials is to let the characters set the stage by posing a mutual problem. After an exchange of two or three lines, the announcer comes in to do the selling. This is natural because announcers are supposed to be salespeople.

But suppose you want to use the real-life characters for the whole commercial? Can you do so successfully? "Successful" here means that you maintain naturalness and believability at the same time that you are putting across enough product selling points to sell the product to the listening audience.

Here are ways to accomplish this:

- One character reads copy from the package to the other character. By reading the copy, the character avoids being a "salesperson."
- One character reads copy from a product advertisement to the other character.
- Character talks to a store salesperson. The character asks questions and the salesperson replies by giving a sales talk for the product.
- Character talks to a knowledgeable repairman or serviceman, such as a plumber, electrician, etc. The latter points out why the unit works so well, lasts so long, is so easy to repair, or needs to be repaired so infrequently.
- Character reads directions on the item itself, especially when those directions indicate the ease of operation.
- Character phones someone qualified to talk about the product—a factory employee, a dealer, a serviceman. (In television, the split-screen technique can be used for the two characters.)

Radio Script

Time: 60 Sec.
Script No: 60-11-1
Subject: 7700 Combine
             (Corn & Beans)

```
   Down corn.  Wet fields.  Weedy soybeans.  For tough harvesting, go with
a John Deere Seventy-Seven-Hundred Combine.  See _____ in
                                               (dealership)
_____.
  (location)
   The Seventy-Seven-Hundred is the most productive John Deere Combine.
It has a fifty-five-inch cylinder.  You can choose a one-hundred-forty-five-
horsepower turbocharged diesel engine or a one-hundred-twenty-eight-horsepower
diesel.  Power Rear-Wheel Drive is available for added traction in soft
and wet fields.
   Answer your toughest harvests with a John Deere Seventy-Seven-Hundred
Combine.  See _____ in _____.  And ask
             (dealership)              (location)
about crop-saving specialized headers.  Choose from corn heads.  Soybean-
saving row-crop heads.  Or platforms with bean-saving flexible cutterbar.
Go with a John Deere.
```

FIGURE 17-7

Straight commercial for dealer use.   Farmers, the target of these commercials, respond to straight, no-nonsense talk. This commercial was prepared by the manufacturer-supplier for local use by dealers handling the manufacturer's equipment.

- Two salespeople are talking about the product, mentioning points that are salesworthy.
- Sales manager conducts session with novice salesperson. He gives a demonstration of the perfect sales talk. This could well be humorously exaggerated.
- Copywriter gets reactions from his wife about sales points he's putting in his advertisement. She makes pertinent suggestions that give the woman's viewpoint that he has overlooked.
- Earnest student type is telling teacher what he's found out about product assigned as a class study.
- Same technique as in preceding example except that professor is telling class and answering questions. Again, there is possibility for exaggerated humor here.
- Two computers talk to each other. Each discusses product facts in mechanical sounding voices associated with computers or mechanical person.
- Someone presses button of computer, or of a mechanical person, and gets flood of information to each question asked.
- If product is intended for a dog, such as a dog food, two dogs talk to each other about it. Or, it could be two cats, two birds, or some other creatures.

The point to remember is that you can avoid unbelievable two-voice commercials if you try. Do so because the artificial slice-of-life commercials destroy the credibility of advertising; there is no need for this to happen.

Radio Script

Time: 60 Sec.
Script No: 60-10-1
Subject: 6602 Hillside
            Combine

Let's talk about hillside combines. If you want sure-footed stability and big productivity, then _____ in _____
                                        (dealership)   (location)
has the right combine for you. It's the John Deere Sixty-Six-On-Two Hillside Combine.

Think about stability. This John Deere Hillside has the wide wheel tread and long wheel base to give outstanding stability. On slopes as steep as forty-five percent, automatic leveling responds smoothly to keep the separator level.

Productivity is outstanding. The big turbocharged diesel engine delivers one-hundred-thirty-five horsepower. Maneuvering is easy with hydrostatic ground drive. You can choose an eighteen or twenty-foot cutting platform. A quiet and roomy John Deere cab and air conditioning comforts your harvest day. Your seat selection includes a five-way adjustable Personal-Posture seat.

Trade up to the stability and productivity you need. Choose a John Deere Sixty-Six-On-Two Hillside Combine. See _____ in
                                                      (dealership)
_____ soon.
  (location)

FIGURE 17-8

Straight commercial for dealer use.

Dramatized commercial

The dramatized commercial is an often-used type of commercial that may be compared with the narrative-copy approach. A situation is dramatized in a brief playlet, in which the product is introduced as the solution of a problem. Thus, a boy in the first fifteen seconds or so is horrified to learn that he has bad breath. Then he hears about a new kind of tooth paste, and in the twinkling of an ear you discover he wins love and romance. Then, in normal routine, the regular announcer closes with a straight product sell and a plea to buy. Dramatized commercials usually require the hiring of a professional cast, and may range all the way from a few simple, uninvolved lines of script to full-scale production, with music, sound effects, and lengthy rehearsals.

Like the dialogue commercial the dramatized commercial often becomes artificial and unbelievable. Frequently the action is humorously exaggerated to the point where the advertiser spoofs his product and audience. It can be a very effective technique if enough episodes are presented to avoid boring the radio audience. The same story presented day after day, however, can soon cause great tune-outs.

Cast commercial

Many successful programs follow the plan of using only the announcer and the cast to effect selling force. On comedy programs, in particular, one finds the cast often taking part in the commercial, especially when the product is one which can stand a somewhat lighter touch.

If the star is used in a commercial—and that star is popular—much selling power is generated. Usually, however, it is best to add the star for attention value but to let the announcer do most of the selling.

Integrated commercial

The integrated commercial has been carefully tailored to a given program. In many cases the commercial is so skillfully woven into the show that the audience is unaware that it is a commercial until the actual selling is being done. Usually, however, the integration is more in the nature of keying the character of the commercial to the character of the program.

Integrated commercials were much more common in the days of the big network shows that used one or more established stars. The technique is comparatively rare in radio these days although it is seen with some frequency in television.

Integrated plug

You have often heard radio shows in which a product claim, or "plug" as it is commonly known, has been worked into the regular script of the program. Called an integrated plug, it is one of the most effective of all radio commercial techniques when not overdone. Like the integrated commercial, however, the integrated plug is seldom used in modern radio.

Musical commercial

Sometimes this can be a singing commercial in which all or part of the sales message is delivered by song. Whether singing or instrumental music is used in whole, or in part, the musical commercial has become an increasingly common form of radio technique. This growth has occurred despite cries from the public against singing commercials.

"Jingles," as they are so often called, are hated when they are bad but among the best-liked commercials are musical commercials that have been done well. Two cautions for creators of musical commercials:

- Be sure the music is good. Especially try to use music that can be committed to memory—outstanding commercial music, such as the long-lasting Marlboro song.
- In singing commercials, make certain that the words can be understood. Otherwise, you provide the audience with a pleasant musical experience but no incentive to buy. Make the lyric memorable as well as the music; if you do, you will have a strong selling vehicle for your product or service.

SSC and B Inc. *Advertising*
575 LEXINGTON AVENUE, NEW YORK, N.Y. 10022
212-688-1600

BROADCAST	
SSC&B JOB NO.	
CLIENT	S&H
PRODUCT	Green Stamps
BROADCAST MEDIUM	Radio
LENGTH OF COMM.	
DATE TYPED	

VOCAL: You don't have to be a cowboy
          You don't have to know how to rope and ride
          All you gotta know is where everybody goes
          When they want to do their shoppin' western style
          We do the servin'
          You do the savin'
          At Western Super Markets come on in
          (That's shopping Western Style)
          You get more for your money
          (and we give S&H Green Stamps)
          At Western Super Markets
          Come on in
          (That's saving Western Style)

ANNCR: At Western Super Markets, we give you our word: you're
          going to get more for your food dollar. You won't find
          friendlier service, you won't find better quality at
          better prices, you won't find better value anywhere in
          town. Come on in. Save on our food, and save our S&H
          Green Stamps, too. That's shopping Western Style!

VOCAL: Shop at Western Supermarkets.
          Come on in.

FIGURE 17-9

Combination musical and straight commercial.   Because it is felt that straight commercials tend to become tiresome, a standard technique is to use a musical introduction, deliver a straight commercial, and then to close with music. This procedure is used here.

FIGURE 17-10

Straight commercial.   There is still a place in radio for the simply expressed message despite cries from those who sometimes seem to prefer cleverness to sales power.

SSC and B Inc. *Advertising*
575 LEXINGTON AVENUE, NEW YORK, N.Y. 10022
212-688-1600

BROADCAST	
SSC&B JOB NO.	
CLIENT	S&H
PRODUCT	Green Stamps
BROADCAST MEDIUM	Radio
LENGTH OF COMM.	
DATE TYPED	

WOMAN: I try. I may not be very good in math. But I try. Every
          time I go to the supermarket I try to figure out the best
          buys--the best values for the best price. There's just
          one catch. Did you know there are over 6,000 items in
          your average supermarket? And maybe half of them cost
          less than the other half--but you have to figure out which
          half. What's really the best value?

          You know, you could make a career out of just trying to
          save money at the supermarket. That's where I was
          heading, until one day I got smart. Now I shop at a
          supermarket that gives good value and S&H Green Stamps.
          That way I know I save something everytime I buy anything.
          Oh, I still try to get the best buys for my money--but I
          don't feel so pressured any more. I know even if I
          goof--I still get S&H Green Stamps. It's a great feeling.

LOCAL
ANNCR: Saving money is hard--but saving S&H Green Stamps is
          easy. It happens automatically--everytime you shop at an
          S&H place. Shop Store Name--it's an S&H place!

WATCH YOUR TIMING

If you are writing announcements of one-minute length and you plan them to be straight announcements delivered by an announcer, be sure that each one can be completed within one minute. An average announcer takes about one minute to read 160–170 words. But don't rely on that! Some commercials are easy to read; some hard. The hard ones take longer to read. Often you will want your message to be given slowly with exaggerated emphasis. Other times it will be desirable to have the announcer read it fast. Do not rely upon a rule of thumb. Read your announcements to yourself; time yourself to be sure.

Most straight commercials can be delivered understandably and sincerely at a rate of 160–170 words per minute. Some announcers, however, may be comfortable with a slower or faster rate than this. If you know what announcer will deliver the commercial, pace it to his style. As a rule, commercials to be delivered by female announcers should use a lower word count, preferably around 150.

The character of the offer being made might affect your word count. For instance, an announcement for a sweepstakes is usually charged with excitement. To maintain the excitement the announcer will speed up his delivery, and thus you may elect to put considerably more than 170 words in such a commercial. You do so knowing that the listeners' playback of the commercial message will suffer in terms of individual points registered. Still, if you have made the listeners aware of the sweepstakes and its glittering prizes, you will have accomplished your objective. You have made them want to enter. They can get full details later from entry blanks in stores or from magazine or newspaper advertisements.

Somewhat the same principle is at work in the frenetic two-voice commercials often heard for local firms such as tire shops. The two-person announcer team announces the message at a tremendous clip without any hope that many points will be recalled but with a very real expectation that listeners will realize that the company is offering something very special in the way of price, a variety of choice, or a dazzling new product.

Two-voice commercials may, on the other hand, be used for supposed real-life conversations between two friends, a husband and wife, a sales clerk and customer, and any number of combinations. In such simulated situations, slow down the word count. Make the conversation natural. Real-life people don't bark out words with machine-gun speed so write fewer than the 160–170 words employed in straight commercials and far fewer than for the two-voice commercials delivered by a team of two station announcers.

As Recorded

INTERVIEW WITH LINDA JOHNSON

VOICE: Linda Johnson told us how she shops for food these days.

VOICE: Do you mostly go to one store?

LINDA: Generally, I have been shopping at one store, period. This store.

VOICE: Why?

LINDA: Because it's convenient. I know that I can depend on their produce and dairy products, plus the Green Stamps.

VOICE: They give S&H Green Stamps?

LINDA: Right.

VOICE: Do you think that your prices are different because they give stamps?

LINDA: No, I honestly don't. I have compared prices in other stores and I find that the prices equal each other out... honestly.

VOICE: How many books of Green Stamps do you get a year?

LINDA: 25, maybe 30.

VOICE: What are some of the things that you've gotten?

LINDA: Recently, I've gotten an AM-FM digital clock radio from this. Oh, a toaster oven.

VOICE: Do you think S&H Green Stamps make sense?

LINDA: If the prices are balanced and I'm getting better service, better quality, plus getting the Green Stamps, why not take advantage of the store that gives the stamps? To me, I almost feel like I'm getting a gift from the store.

VOICE: Shop at Wise Markets. We give S&H Green Stamps.

END OF INTERVIEW WITH LINDA JOHNSON

FIGURE 17-11

Dialogue-testimonial commercial.   Both in radio and television advertisers are finding it useful to conduct genuine interviews with real people, especially shoppers, as is the case here.

If you want to be sure of your timing, count your words AND use a stopwatch. Most writers are content merely to use a stopwatch, but a person reading his own commercial sometimes tends to speed up his reading pace to make the commercial fit the time. The practice of counting the words will help keep him honest. On the other hand, just counting words and not using a stopwatch may cause trouble since a commercial with a fairly low word count may read long because of the use of many multisyllable words. The stopwatch helps correct for this.

When you become adept in writing for broadcast, you may let the number of lines of copy help you determine whether you're writing within your time limitations—but this is only a rough guide. You'll always be right if you double-check yourself with the stopwatch and the counting of words. For example, you might be fooled by a commercial that uses several numbers and consequently is short on lines. Each numeral, however, counts as one word. If you give a telephone number and repeat it, you may be devoting as many as twenty-five words just for this part of the commercial.

In announcements of less than one minute, you may be given a maximum number of words to use. Such directives are not given to you as a rule of thumb or as a guide or as a suggestion. They are supposed to be followed. Copywriters everywhere are careless about this request from the stations and networks. By ignoring it they cause much worry and trouble for radio production personnel.

From an advertising standpoint, it is far better to limit your message to the words that can be read with sincerity and selling strength than to take liberties with the time and length of your announcement. If you force the announcer to race through your selling message, you lose effectiveness and power.

Timing is especially important when you are taping commercials, because once an announcement is taped, it cannot be speeded up or cut. If you send a tape to a radio station that contains a "fifty-word" announcement, but which is actually longer than that, the station producers cannot do as they would in a "live" commercial and speed up the announcer's reading. Their only out is to chop off your story before it is finished, and you can easily see the wisdom of avoiding that.

LIVE OR TAPED?

Announcements are broadcast in two ways. An example will serve to illustrate these methods.

Assume you are the manufacturer of a product for general consumption, but being relatively new in the business you do not yet enjoy complete national distribution of your product. You must proceed in your marketing strategy by opening up different markets individually until each market has good distribution. You select a new city into which you wish to introduce your product and you allocate money to advertise it there. You decide that newspaper advertisements

SSC&B Inc. Advertising
575 LEXINGTON AVENUE, NEW YORK, N.Y. 10022
212·688·1600

	BROADCAST
SSC&B JOB NO.	
CLIENT	S&H
PRODUCT	Green Stamps
BROADCAST MEDIUM	Radio
LENGTH OF COMM.	
DATE TYPED	

. . . .

(WITHOUT DONUT)
"TRUCK STOP 1977" SHR 6343

MUSIC UP AND UNDER

MAN: Well I heard a breaker callin'
        There's Green Stamps up ahead
        So I kept it on the double nickel
        "Break one nine," I said.

        I said, "How about you good buddy"?
        Are the smokey's close behind?
        He said nope the stamps I'm pickin up
        Are the lick'em, stick'em on kind.

        He said we got some nice gifts
        From S&H that's great
        Things for the home and family
        That all of us sure like.

        And I got some tools and gear
        That I can camp with in the woods
        The kid's got a brand new ten speed
        He's really ridin' good.

        Yeah S&H Green Stamps
        Make this truckin' fun
        I can bring home a little extra
        With S&H, on my run
        I keep my family happy
        They sure like it fine
        When I bring home S&H Green Stamps,
        The lick'em, stick'em on kind.

WOMAN: Hey kids, Daddy's coming home
        I'll bet he's got enough S&H Green Stamps for that
        new barbecue we've been wanting.

FIGURE 17-12

Musical commercial.   The "trucker" commercial reflects the fact that the company does a substantial business with truck stops across the country.

plus a series of spot announcements make the best combination of local advertising media available for your purposes, and you buy a schedule of spot time on the local radio station. You purchase minute spots, to be extended over a period of six weeks.

- You can simply have those commercials typed, along with instructions as to how they should be read, and send them to the radio station, instructing the station representative on which days to read which announcements. Then a local announcer will be assigned to your account and will deliver the spots as you have written them.
- You can hire an announcer in your own town (whose voice you like and whose delivery you can control through rehearsals), have a tape made of all the announcements, one after the other, and send that tape to the radio station in your new market. They will then play the designated tape at the time you request it, instead of having one of their own announcers read the material.

Both techniques have their advantages. If your messages are simple and straightforward, and do not require a highly dramatic or specialized type of voice, the first way is generally preferred, since it is less expensive.

If you wish to control the manner of delivery, in regard to emphasis and pace, the tape is your answer.

Of course, the first technique, that of sending the station the script for your announcements, is workable only when you have a straight commercial, handled by an announcer only. When you wish your spots to be dramatic, or to contain music or gimmicks, they necessarily must be taped. The local radio station could hardly afford to charge you the little they do for a spot announcement of a few seconds, and also stage a musical production for you.

Another situation that will become familiar to you is the writing of a commercial that will be taped for a 50-second segment. The last 10-seconds will be delivered live by a station announcer. You will write the 10-second "tag" as well as the 50-second portion.

Sometimes, too, you will have a musical introduction, called "intro," that runs for a few seconds before the announcer begins talking and you may end with music, too. In other cases, the music will continue under the announcer's voice throughout the commercial and then come up strongly at the end.

Advertiser:	The National Observer
Teaser:	"Social Security"
Station:	WOR
Agency:	Ellentuck & Springer

Do you realize that you don't have to pay Social Security? That you could get a much better deal from private retirement plans? This important information comes from a recent story in the National Observer, the national weekly newspaper that helps you cope with life. Each week it's packed with stimulating articles and news--the kind that zeroes in on people, issues and events that affect your life. News you'll want to share with family and friends. But find out for yourself. Right now you can save 40 percent off the newsstand price by ordering a full year of the National Observer for only 15 dollars. That's less than twenty-nine cents a week. To order, call 212-582-2000 for guaranteed satisfaction. If, after reading the first three issues you're not happy, just write "Cancel" across the invoice and you'll not owe one penny. Call now--212-582-2000 to order 52 fascinating weeks of the National Observer for only 15 dollars.

FIGURE 17-13

Persuasive radio commercial.   Several principles of effective radio commercial writing are demonstrated in this commercial:
- Easy conversational style that uses contractions, conversational bridges, and sentence fragments.
- A fast, interesting beginning.
- A call for action at the end.
- Repetition of the telephone number.

Extra creative helps

If you're working with local advertisers, there are a number of helps available to you. For one, there are the area radio stations. Many have extensive

SSC&B Inc. *Advertising*
575 LEXINGTON AVENUE, NEW YORK, N.Y. 10022
212-688-1600

	BROADCAST
SSC&B JOB NO.	
CLIENT	S&H
PRODUCT	Green Stamps
BROADCAST MEDIUM	Radio
LENGTH OF COMM.	
DATE TYPED	

. . . .

SON: So what do you think of the apartment, folks?

MOM: So far so good, Sonny. I love your vestibule.

SON: Mom, this isn't the vestibule. It's the whole apartment.

MOM: Sonny. Come back home!

DAD: Now Mother! He's got everything he needs, right on one
          wall. Stove. Refrigerator. Bathtub.

SON: Look. This piece of plywood comes down on top of the tub
          and presto! It's the dining room.

DAD: Get a load of the refrigerator. Mother.

MOM: Hmmm. Canadian bacon. Mushrooms. Sirloin steak!. . .
          How can you eat steak on your income?

SON: Easy. I shop at a place that gives good value and S&H
          Green Stamps. That way I save something on everything I
          buy.

DAD: Take a leaf out of the kid's book, Mother! He's eating
          better than we are.

MOM: That'll be quite enough, Dad. And what are you saving
          your Green Stamps for, Sonny?

SON: A charcoal grill. For the patio.

MOM: The patio?

SON: Yeah . . . Right here on the fire escape.

ANNCR: Saving money's hard. Saving S&H Green Stamps is easy.
          It happens automatically, every time you shop an S&H
          place. Shop National Tea. It's an S&H place.

FIGURE 17-14

Humorous commercial.   As this commercial demonstrates, the two-voice commercial can be effective when it is used with skillful humor. This commercial is entertaining, but it also presents a good selling message for the advertiser.

libraries of music and sound effects upon which you can draw. It's up to you to find out what's available. Keep a list in your desk and use every opportunity to draw upon the station resources to make your commercials lively and different. One trouble is that too many copywriters aren't energetic enough in finding out the availability of these helps. Another is that most stations don't volunteer to give you the information. You must dig it out yourself. Once you get your music or sound effects list, however, it can be an immense help to you in creating commercials that are out of the ordinary.

Another help is the "jingle house." This is the industry term for organizations that whip up with amazing speed music and lyrics that can be used by local advertisers. The companies have on call gifted writers and musicians who provide music and lyrics for any type of product often at a surprisingly low cost. Perhaps you ask for a 10-second musical intro and ending, complete with lyrics. As the copywriter you then write 40 seconds of straight copy in between the 10-second introduction and the 10-second ending.

To draw upon the service of the jingle house you simply tell them what you want to accomplish in the commercial, give them facts about the product or

service to be sold, and possibly some past copy in order that they can see your general advertising strategy. Utilize every such help you can find. Although the straight commercial is still a powerful sales agent, try for the variety that music and sound effects can give you whether you obtain them from your local stations, or from an out-of-town jingle house.

FIGURE 17-15

Humorous radio commercial.

SSC&B Inc. *Advertising*
575 LEXINGTON AVENUE, NEW YORK, N.Y. 10022
212-688-1600

	BROADCAST
SSC&B JOB NO.	
CLIENT	S&H
PRODUCT	Green Stamps
BROADCAST MEDIUM	Radio
LENGTH OF COMM.	
DATE TYPED	

. . . .

SYLVIA: (WITH HEAVY COLD) Doctor, you came on a house call.
          You're so dedicated!

DR: What dedicated. I'm your Uncle and we live in the same
          building.

SYLVIA: (COUGHS).

DR: You're a sick girl. What have you been doing to
          yourself?

SYLVIA: Food shopping.

DR: So?

SYLVIA: 17 stores a day. It's inside, outside, air conditioning,
          meat freezers, hot chicken rotisseries . . . hot, cold,
          cold, hot . . .

DR: Yes, yes, Sylvia. You're a comparison shopper now?

SYLVIA: I'm a homemaker. I save a penny here, a penny there.

DR: Right now, you'll stay in bed and drink lots of hot
          lemonade . . .

SYLVIA: With lemons six for a dollar?

DR: I'm coming to that. When you're up again, shop a market
          that gives S&H Green Stamps. That way you save something
          every time you buy anything . . . specials and everything
          else! And you don't run yourself into the ground.

SYLVIA: I feel better already.

DR: Good. I'll just leave the bill here on the night table.

ANNCR: Saving money's hard. Saving S&H Green Stamps is easy.
          It happens automatically . . . every time you shop an
          S&H place. Shop National Tea. It's an S&H place!

CALL FOR ACTION AT THE END

Books, plays, and motion pictures come to a climax at the end. So should radio commercials. Your climax is when you ask your listener to do something, or when you make a suggestion. There is hardly a radio commercial that should not ask for action. Examples:

See this bargain today.

Drop in. Learn for yourself.

Find out why National Bank is called the "Friendly" bank.

Let our experienced investment counselors help you.

Why delay? Enjoy your home now. Get a quickly arranged home improvement loan.

Warm up these chilly days with a steaming bowl of chowder.

Beat the heat with a cool lemonade.

Learn to play the organ in two easy lessons.

Think it over, and then see us about terms.

Calling for action doesn't mean that you actually expect instantaneous obedience from the listener. A request for action does, however, give vitality to the ending. Without the unmistakable call for action, your commercial ending lacks punch. Furthermore people, being what they are, need prodding. Who knows how many tires have been bought because an announcer said: "Don't drive another mile on those worn-out tires. It's illegal and it's unsafe. See your tire dealer today!"

(SFX Moog synthesizer)

SHOE: Hello. I'm a worn-out tennis shoe. (SFX synthesizer) And I want to tell you right now it ain't easy being walked on your whole life. Believe me, I know. You rip and tear and squirm and jerk and screech and bleach and stand around all day. Try to imagine what it's like to be tumble-dried, for crying out loud. I've had it. Let those new guys down at Adam's Department Store have a chance. I'm talking about those Nikes, Adidas, Converse and those AAU's. They're rough and they're tough, and they can take it. You'll find them all at Adam's Department Store in sporting goods. Me? I gotta go now. My top's all worn out. (SFX synthesizer up and out).

FIGURE 17-16

Humorous radio using personification.   As a variation, the technique of having a product talk is useful. Instead of an object, it could be a dog, or a cat, or a fish. This approach allows a chance for a good sales message.

NOW TO SUM UP

Although this book does not give you any pat formulas for writing copy in its different forms, it is time in this chapter to put down as guides for radio writing some of the points we have made and to add a couple of additional points. All of these are fundamentals which you should review periodically to be sure you're not straying too far from what we know to be successful elements of radio commercial writing.

1. Keep copy points to a minimum in deference to:
   a. The human mind's incapacity to absorb very much solely through the ear.
   b. The fact that your average radio listener is usually only a half-listener and will have difficulty enough catching one idea, let alone two or three.

2. Make pictures with words. You are not writing for television. If that package you're pushing has blue stripes, suggest to your listener that he look for the blue-striped package. If it's a round container, call it a "round container."
3. Repeat important words, elements, and names. Remember the inattentive listener. The first time he barely hears you, but the second time he may have that pencil ready to take down what you're saying. Repetition is especially important if you're giving a telephone number. As a general principle, don't bother giving a telephone number unless you plan to repeat it. Ninety-nine out of 100 persons will never catch the number the first time the announcer gives it, but there's an outside chance that the number will be remembered, or jotted down, if it is repeated. The same advice applies to the giving of addresses. As for the repetition of product names or the advertiser's name, there is no fixed rule but many writers automatically try to get a name in near the beginning, the middle, and the end.
4. Get attention at the very start. You don't have to scream to get attention at the start, but you should come over "big" in some way to distract the listener from what he is doing at the moment, whether washing dishes, polishing the family car, or putting furniture in order. How can you be "big"? Achieve bigness through music, unusual voices, the kind of words you use, the sound effects you achieve.
5. Persuade, don't scream. While a number of success stories—especially in local advertising—have been built by the "screamers," you'll do better in the long run to lead listeners to your way of thinking than to lash them with shrieking messages.

FIGURE 17-17

Humorous commercial.   Imitation of soap operas is a favorite device of writers of humorous radio commercials—a device that seems to be effective despite its frequent use.

(SFX soap opera music up and under)

ANNCR: Lassiter's Garden Supply presents another chapter in the continuing saga of "As The Leaf Turns."

GWENDOLYN: (distraught) I don't understand you, Rex. I took you into my home, showered you with attention. Why, I told you my innermost secrets and introduced you to great music. Yet, you've never responded. There's no life in you. I'm so afraid I've lost you.

(SFX music up)

ANNCR: Poor Gwendolyn. If only she'd bought her Rex begonia from Lassiter's Garden Supply where only the strongest, healthiest plants are sold. At Lassiter's the friendly pros will tell you all you need to know about plant placement, care and feeding. Then the music and small talk is up to you. And now, back to our story.

GWENDOLYN: Oh, Rex. I know we can make a fresh start at Lassiter's Garden Supply.

(SFX soap opera up and out)

---

6. Avoid the overworked superlatives and the trite, insincere, glib radio patter. Any comedian working for a laugh can always get it by imitating radio commercials because there are so many that sound ridiculous even without parodying. Does yours?

7. Make dialogue believable and unforced. Again, as in point 6, even comedians who are not usually very funny can slay audiences with take-offs on TV or radio copy. Finest target is the two-voice commercial with two supposed housewives, or with a husband-wife combination. It's almost impossible to deliver a believable, serious commercial with the entire message handled by two actors. Set your stage if you will, with the characters from "life" but leave them quickly and let the announcer do the selling. Exceptions to this rule are frankly humorous commercials in which obvious spoofing occurs.

8. Never forget you're writing for the ear. This point, of course, sums up everything previously said about short words, alliteration, unpleasant sounds. Radio writing is not print copy, and it is not television copy. It borrows from both, but it has its own unique areas. Above all, radio copy is conversational because the ear is attuned to the sound, flow, and nuances of conversation.

9. Watch your word count. Pace your commercial for understandability and sincerity. To be certain that you're not too far above or below your time limitations, count your words and use a stopwatch. You look like an amateur each time your commercial runs over the time. Be right!

10. In almost all commercials make your endings strong, positive, and action-suggesting. Naturally, in institutional approaches and certain humorous commercials, the big push at the end is inappropriate, but in the "let's-move-merchandise-from-the-shelves" type of commercial, ask for the order.

18

Garnering Sales with Television, Part A

So we come to television; "Mr. Big" to the average neophyte. If you're typical, you'd like to be a good writer of print copy, but you yearn to write television copy because the mere idea fascinates you. Its scope, influence, and sales power makes television the exciting medium. "Here, at last," you may say, "is what advertising creativity is all about."

Because of television's demands, a new breed of writers has evolved since television's first commercial was telecast. Today's television commercial writers not only have the selling instinct needed by any copywriter but also have a whole range of talents not required by other advertising writers.

To practice their craft intelligently they must understand the problems and techniques of the producers and cameramen. This is a whole complicated world in itself. Ideally, they should know staging, acting, and the theater. If they are involved in animated television commercials, they should possess knowledge of the complicated art of putting such commercials together. But also it is imperative that they have an above-average imagination often tinged with a touch of zaniness because humdrum writers have no part in the humorous and sometimes mad world of animated creation. As copywriters they may be dealing with producers of animation, an enormously creative group. Without knowing enough about their craft, they cannot command their respect.

One of the problems of television writing is that writers cannot sit back satisfied when they have turned out his script. On one side they have put down the video ideas, and on the otherside the words to be said by the characters on the video side. Next, a storyboard will be made. Copywriters begin to feel a little more certain of what the completed production might be like but they are still a long way from home. The type of voices, of acting, musical background will determine the final success of the commercial but

only when the first prints come back from the producers (called "answer" prints) will writer, client and others have any solid inkling of the finished product. It is apparent that the more writers know about all that goes on after they evolve original commercial script, the less guesswork there will be about the commerical that finally goes on the air.

IT'S SIMPLER IN RADIO AND PRINT

Contrast all this uncertainty and complication with the delightful simplicity of the average radio commercial, or print advertisement. A print writer does his headline, body copy, gets a rough layout from his artist and the finished advertisement is simply a refinement of what he has already done. At a similar stage in the television commercial script, he has merely begun and by the end of the production process the commercial could be a resounding flop.

Of course, not all television commercials depend upon way-out imagination. Many commercials of the demonstration type are clear-cut from the beginning and may be likened to the straight-line copy described in the listing of body copy types. Probably there are more routine television commercials than highly creative commercials and writers can make a good living turning out adequate, if undistinguished, television commercials. If they have that creative spark, however, that enables them to come up with the creative point of difference, the rewards for such writing can be enormous. One such idea can make a fantastic difference in the marketplace as shown by the "Don't squeeze the Charmin" campaign of Procter & Gamble.

Make no mistake about it, the world of television commercial writing is a different world. There are new rules, new techniques, and new demands but it's a fascinating world for the truly creative person.

FIGURE 18-1

Award winning dramatized commercials.   Originality in presentation has obtained much attention for this product. The two commercials (Figures 18-1 and 18-2) in photoboard form demonstrate radically different approaches within the same campaign. Each registers the product name strongly.

With various creative and technical production factors combining to make the television commercial more complex than any other form of advertising today, there is indeed a critical need for trained, competent television personnel.

FIRST AND LAST, A VISUAL MEDIUM

Television is a visual medium. Ideally, your television copy theme should be one that simply puts into words a piece of action seen on the screen. The best television copy is the least obtrusive copy; it does not call attention to itself. In writing it, you are less concerned with copy as such than either the radio or print copywriter. You are after significant action and ways of bringing it about. You are on your way to achieving these ends if, after writing a final script, you can evaluate it in this manner: block off the audio portion and read through the video to see if it makes an interesting, logical, fluid series of pictures. If you can grasp a basic, solid message from the video alone, you may indeed make a comfortable living from writing television commercials.

In this medium, however, you will not enjoy the freedom allowed the print writer. For example, his typical advertisement employs a headline, major illustration and subhead to convey the essential sales story. Nor does television afford the set finality of the printed picture to establish and sustain a mood while your copy carries on at length. It is dangerous in television to rely heavily on a single visual impression. Further, you cannot spread your commercial like a print advertisement, whose full page can accommodate a multitude of sales points, many more than even a two-minute commercial. Too many points are bad enough in print, impossible in television.

Even more difficult are the problems of the radio writer moving into television, for he is accustomed to writing for the ear exclusively, and the ear is much slower than the eye. For radio, each thought transition must be gradual; word pictures must be drawn carefully with clear definition, and verbal overemphasis is often required to drive home a point.

But television neither needs nor wants these standard radio techniques. In radio, words have always done the job. To relinquish this to the camera is one of the hardest and most essential things for the radio writer to learn about television. As a television copywriter, you will do well to heed the admonition, "Don't tell me—show me."

NEED FOR TRAINED CREATIVE WRITING

Most helpful to you in creating effective television commercials will be an imaginative visual sense, in order to develop and exploit to its fullest, the potential of television for imagery and product demonstration. Your creative writing talents will determine the extent to which you can communicate ideas with imagination, using words and pictures your audience will readily understand. This translation of ideas demands precise knowledge of the audience to be reached, for unless you understand the viewer they will never understand your message. People buy ideas, not things. Behind each product must lie the idea of what it will do for the buyer: an honest promise. Your idea developed with freshness, originality, and imagination will result in a more effective commercial—an idea which will be retained and acted upon by the viewer at the point of sale.

"Originality," however, can be dangerous according to Rosser Reeves, once board chairman of Ted Bates & Co., a New York agency with a huge percentage of its billings in television. In his book, *Reality in Advertising,* Reeves raised warning signals about the preoccupation with originality that can lead writers to absurd extremes. In searching after the different, the clever, and the unusual, or in attempting to imitate some truly original approach, writers can forget that an advertising campaign is not designed to express their individual ego or talent for entertaining. Rather, it is a functional tool whose purpose is to fully inform the public via maximum projection of the message. Forget the aesthetics and deal with the realities. Bring the basic claim to life with ideas, information, and specific visual interpretations that speak convincingly about why your product is better.

This is trained creative writing. The more of it you can develop and use, the better quarterback you will be on the creative team. Also, it is necessary to understand the value of simple, honest, persuasive copy with powerful graphic interpretations. This calls for a knowledge of your product, your product's market, consumer research, company policies, and whatever taboos the client has stipulated. A familiarity with competing products is helpful. In addition, you may also be required to coordinate television with the client's print campaign.

If you are a quarterback for your creative team, you will be able to prevent most of the failures and eliminate much of the waste and extravagance in the production techniques and their application to the television commercial, the greater service you will render—and the larger salary you'll be able to command. In making a one-minute commercial on film, you may well be the hub of a task force of one hundred, which means working with account executives, television directors, actors, producers, cameramen, technicians, and union personnel.

BIC BUTANE LIGHTER

CLIENT: Bic Pen Corp.

TITLE: "True Stories"

CODE NO.: WBBL6357

LENGTH: :30

(SFX: MUSIC UNDER THROUGHOUT) PAINTER: I dropped this Bic lighter in a can of paint this morning.

Now it's working fine.

WIFE: Oscar has always had the problem of keeping his grip when he flicks his Bic.

MAN: That truck ran over my Bic Lighter.

But even under tremendous pressure, I can still flick my Bic.

(VO): Flicking your Bic has become America's favorite pastime.

So we hear lots of stories about people whose Bic's flick through thin and thick.

FARMER: Last year I lost this, planting potatoes. Now I just found it,

Can you imagine what it's like not to flick your Bic for a whole year?

Wells, Rich, Greene, Inc.

FIGURE 18-2

Award winning dramatized commercial.

Naturally, you will have plenty of expert assistance from specialists in each of the many fields, but to handle your part of the production, the commercial, you should learn the important features of these other fields.

Budget bugaboos

While your agency's television director will usually control production and costs, this does not give you license to turn out ideas without regard to limitations imposed by a budget. You will learn by experience that it is wiser in building your commercial to avoid costly scenes that will invite price-cutting surgery later and thereby endanger the continuity of the whole script.

Another factor that now complicates cost control is the mechanics of union negotiations on payment of actors, announcers, and vocalists in television commercials. Codes of the SAG (Screen Actors Guild) and the AFTRA (American Federation of Television and Radio Artists) call for original "session" fees plus repayments to talent, depending on where and how many times a particular commercial is used. Unless this detail is carefully calculated at the start and budgeted accordingly, it can cost the sponsor many times his actual production investment.

Only with experience, of course, can you learn such calculation, and you may never be required to do any such figuring. But, the fact remains that the accomplished television copywriter is a many-faceted being—salesperson, psychologist, dramatist, film craftsman, and bookkeeper. And as such, you may take part in planning sessions, production briefings, and many of the various stages of actual production. You can make all of these efforts more productive and efficient from the beginning with good writing—the best insurance against faulty interpretation and costly production.

EXPLOIT TELEVISION'S STRONG POINTS

Never forget, as you fashion a commercial, that television is: a)a visual medium; b) an action medium. You put your stress on the video portion, and you make that portion active and dynamic, not a series of still-life shots. By so doing, you'll be exploiting the medium's strong points.

Similarly (and this is shared to some degree with radio commercials), television commercials draw upon drama. This dramatic quality is especially suited to demonstration commercials that utilize sight and sound and thus generate a more powerful sales story than any other mass medium.

WHAT CAN YOU DO ABOUT THE NEGATIVE ASPECTS?

With all its positive attributes, television has its sore spots. One of these is cost, a factor you can't control very much except to write commercials that

ANNCR: Today we're talking to the original "Share the Ride with a Friend" man.

Uh, you sir, are Noah of Noah's Ark Fame.

NOAH: That's right. I had two lizards, two monkeys, two snails,

two snakes and two rhinos get together and share the ride.

ANNCR: Uh, huh.
NOAH: Two falcons...boy, were they hard to get aboard.

ANNCR: Well, one of the great things about Carpooling is all the money you can save.
NOAH: Absolutely!

ANNCR: Then actually when you did do the whole number with the...
NOAH: whole number...is that a thing you say nowadays...?

ANNCR: That's   a   current terminology.
NOAH: Yea, O.K. fine.

ANNCR: So today the best thing you could advise people to do would...
NOAH: Share the Ride.

It worked out for us and so when you share a ride with somebody, make an animal noise--it's kinda fun.

ANNCR: Uh, by the way, did you call it carpooling way back then?

NOAH: No, we did not have that word. We called it Kalaka.

ANNCR: Kalaka. Is that the same...
NOAH: Kalaka, yes. In Babylonian, that meant carpool.
ANNCR: Oh, yes.
NOAH: Yea.

SINGERS: DOUBLE UP EVERY MORNIN' DOUBLE UP GOIN' HOME AT NIGHT. DOUBLE UP

EVERY DAY, IT'S A BETTER WAY. YOU'RE GONNA' HAVE MORE FUN TOGETHER.

BEATS DRIVIN' ALONE.

FIGURE 18-3

Animated commercial.   Animation is often used to put over serious messages. Because of the entertainment approach, a subject can be discussed without "preaching." The light touch is disarming.

The Advertising Council, Inc.

are effective, yet relatively inexpensive to produce.

Like radio, television is a transitory medium. Unless your commercial is outstanding, it may get only a brief glance or no glance. Perhaps it's boring in its concept, or perhaps it offers nothing of benefit or entertainment to hold the viewer. Such poor writing on your part can contribute to the commercial's lack of registration on the mind of the viewers so that later they can't even recall the name of the advertiser, or the advertised product.

Your commercial may be viewed as an intrusion, an unwelcome interruption (as in a tense moment in the Super Bowl) which means that you'd better make the message interesting and worthwhile to at least partially overcome the resentment its appearance has caused.

Television advertising can be embarrassingly intimate in its probing invasion into our methods of dress and hygiene. Such poking about into our habits in the bathroom, bedroom, and closets causes emotions ranging from annoyance to downright revulsion and outrage. You'd better develop a considerate, sensitive touch in writing commercials in a period when the viewers are assailed by messages for bras, pantyhose, feminine hygiene, deodorants, toilet-bowl cleaners, toilet papers, breath-sweeteners, foot-smell remedies, dandruff-removers, pimple-cures, and nasal-drip relief.

Nothing seems too intimate for exploitation by television commercials and great is the outcry among a sizable portion of the viewers. Are you going to contribute to the assault upon good taste, or will your commercials establish a proper tone yet sell your product? Here's a challenge you must meet.

In today's better educated, more cynical, and quick-to-resent society, the television commercial is too often viewed as insulting and demeaning. Unfortunately, the charge is true of many commercials that portray men and women as mindless idiots who react to advertised products (or talk about them) like subnormal children, or who are portrayed in silly little dramas that totally lack any semblance to real life.

What is your goal—to perpetuate this attack on the good sense of the viewer, or to lift the quality of television commercial writing to the point where it will be acceptable among people of intelligence, sensitivity, and good taste? It had better be the latter because the voices are loud in the land against today's television commercials.

WHAT DOES THE VIEWER HAVE A RIGHT TO EXPECT?

Above all else, there is believability.

This should be present in claims for and demonstrations of products. There should be the honest promise of a believable benefit expressed in understandable language. Useful information should replace the extravagant, unsubstantiated claim. Change your captive audience to a captivated audience by giving them commercials they can believe, unlike so many of the paid, or so-called unrehearsed testimonials that stretch credibility. Cynically, the audience has come to believe that anyone—stars or people-on-the-street—will say what the advertiser wishes him to say if the money is sufficient. Move away from "bombast, brag, and boast" to "simple, useful, and believable."

Then, too, there is respect.

Women, the target of so many television commercials, are loud in their resentment of the women portrayed in commercials. You've seen them a thousand times exclaiming over products, discussing trivia as if their entire days were filled with vacuous pursuits and still more vacuous language. Slice-of-life commercials have been special offenders depicting women whose chief concern in life seems to be ring-around-the-collar, or ring-around-the-bathtub. In this day of an awakening awareness of women to their role in society, too many commercials fail to give women respect for their significant contributions out of, as well as in, the home.

Lastly, there is naturalness.

Natural conversation. Natural situations. Television, more than any other medium, seems to eschew these two. It is not natural for two persons to talk for full 30 seconds, or 60 seconds, about a product—especially in the high-pitched, overly enthusiastic way of the supposedly real-life people shown on the screen. As a viewer, you know that this is so and you reject what is said as unnatural and, hence, as largely unbelievable.

And then there are the wild gyrations of the youthful set as they seem to get high on soft drinks. A succession of quick shots showing youth in high gear driving beach buggies, skydiving, hang-gliding, dashing into the surf, racing down the beach, riding motorcycles, and turning somersaults on the ski slopes picture an exhilaration no soft drink has ever been known to contribute. All this is mood stuff, of course, but it is unnatural like so much of television that substitutes mood for more solid material. In the case of soft drinks there is some excuse because there is really very little to write about such products, but still, the frantic pace of such commercials is part of the approach to selling in commercials that causes people to separate advertising talk from real talk and television life from real life.

New Musical Commercial Sells LAND O LAKES MARGARINE, From America's No. 1 Butter Maker

FIGURE 18-4

Humorous animated and live action commercial.   Combining live television and animation, this commercial with the cows taking a speaking and singing role has been a favorite with television audiences. Notice that live television is used to build up sensory appeal and package identification.

FIGURE 18-5

Personality salesperson commercial.   Many manufacturers have found it useful to associate their products with well-known persons who act as company spokespeople over a long period of time. A presentation of the product by such a person lends credibility to a sales talk and enhances product identification.

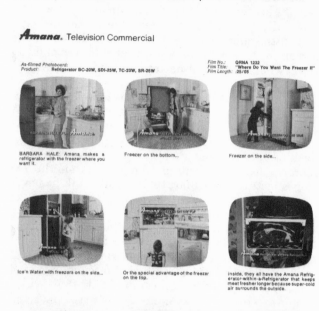

IDEAS, THE START OF THE COMMERCIAL

Where do you begin in writing a television commercial? The first step is the evolution of the idea. Your idea must strike at such basic motivations of the viewer as: love, ambition, self-preservation, economy. It should be developed with imagination and tempered with a knowledge of the medium and the advertiser's needs, as well as the consumer's desires. By applying simple reasoning, you will find that the product to be advertised contains within itself such sources of ideas as: what is new about the product; what benefits it offers to the user; the experience of these consumers with the product; its advantages over competitive products; and its basic value.

In an effective presentation, you must touch the right motivational button and stimulate desire for the product and its benefits. In short, you must enunciate a basic formula stated by Horace S. Schwerin of the Schwerin Research Corp:

Sales Idea x Strength of Presentation = Commercial Efficiency. The motivating force of the sales idea, multiplied by the strength with which it is put over, equals the effectiveness of your commercial effort.

Keep in mind that the greatest opportunity this medium offers is that of demonstration—demonstration to sell. Demonstrate the new feature, the benefit, the advantage, and where applicable, the price. Show the product; how it works; how it saves; how easy it is to use; how it makes one more attractive or more popular. When price is an important factor, superimpose it on the screen to make it seem even more of a bargain and to make it that much more memorable.

Another point is simplicity. While advantages of the product are important don't try to make your television commercial a catalog of all these advantages. If it has a dozen or more advantages, that's great for the advertiser but not for the commercial. Time is needed to put across a point, which means the selling story must be boiled down to one principal point, or possibly two or three. Just be sure the selling story has enough time to register on the viewer's mind, and that there is time at the conclusion to sum it up with a convincing repetition.

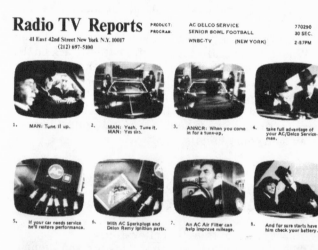

FIGURE 18-6

Dramatized humorous commercial.   Much of the effect of this commercial is achieved through the casting of gangster types—appearance and voices are important to the commercial's success. These are qualities hard to visualize when the commercial is in script or storyboard form.

DEFINING THE PROBLEM

Television commercials vary in length, cost and production techniques, depending on the specific jobs they are intended to perform. Such variations call for definition of the problem, a matter that may or may not lie within your province as copywriter. The problem deals with such factors as overall sales objectives, location and identification of primary customers, and the limitations of budget. Are you going to hit targets singly or in number? Your commercials should be designed with a basic sales objective in mind: winning new customers; holding regular ones; increasing use per capita; forcing distribution; improving dealer relations; building prestige and good will; and even impressing stockholders.

PROGRAM OR SPOT?

Your commercials must also take into account whether they are to be used for program or spot presentation. To present the commercial in what he feels is the proper environment, an advertiser will often buy (through his advertising agency) a specific type of entertainment or information program, network or local. Often, the advertiser and the product become identified, for better or worse, with the program and/or its star. Commercials used within these programs are usually a minute or longer and can be "live" or on film or tape. Some advertisers follow the practice of using live commercials with a live program and film picture quality as seen by the viewer. However, with the advent of television tape and its live quality, this problem is easily overcome.

BBDO
Batten, Barton, Durstine & Osborn, Inc.

Client:	PEPSICO, INC.		Time:	60 SECONDS
Product	PEPSI COLA	Title	Comml No.	

VIDEO	AUDIO
STATION WAGON WITH FAMILY IN IT PULLS UP IN FRONT OF HOUSE	(MUSIC UNDER)
GRANDMOTHER DESCENDING FROM STAIRS OF HOUSE TO MEET FAMILY	You're the Pepsi
GRANDMOTHER EMBRACING CHILD	Generation
FAMILY & GRANDMOTHER EMBRACING	Come and Have a Pepsi Day.
CUT TO LITTLE BOY ON HORSE	(MUSIC UNDER)
GROUP OF PEOPLE RIDING HORSES	C'mon, c'mon, c'mon and taste the Pepsi way.
LITTLE BOY ON HORSE	C'mon, c'mon, c'mon and
CLOSE UP OF GRAB SHOT OF PEPSI IN ICE	have a Pepsi day.
CLOSE UP OF GIRL ON HORSE HOLDING BOTTLE OF PEPSI	Wrap a thirsty smile around it
MAN DRINKING BOTTLE OF PEPSI	raise a Pepsi up and down it.
CLOSE UP OF LITTLE BOY MAKING ICE CREAM	C'mon, c'mon
GRANDMOTHER SERVING STEAKS OFF BARBECUE	C'mon, c'mon
MAN TAKING CORN ON THE COB OFF PLATE	C'mon
MOTHER AND CHILD ON HORSE	Have a Pepsi day.
SUPER: HAVE A PEPSI DAY.	

FIGURE 18-7

Script for 30-second commercial.   Fourteen scenes and one superimposition are used in this 30-second commercial. Full use of video is made in the commercials for this campaign. Only forty-eight words are needed on the audio side because the video properly carries the selling burden.

Spot television advertising is placed by advertisers on a market-by-market basis orginating in the individual market where it is telecast. The advertisement may consist of an 8-second—10-second commercial announcement known as an "ID" (for station identification). It may also be a twenty-second, thirty-second, sixty-second announcement between programs; or within a local program or a network participating program in which a number of advertisers have bought spot time. Spot commercials are almost always on film or tape. They come at the viewer from all angles and in all forms, and because many of them are irritating, they are the kind of advertising people usually complain about when they point an accusing finger at television commercials.

Program or spot: advantages and disadvantages

There are advantages to the advertiser in both program and spot presentation of commercials. A network program offers an advertiser prestige and a huge framework within which he can sell his individual products. He is also provided with a kind of mirror that reflects the total philosophy and public relations effort of the company itself. Network program commercials assure the advertiser of the same quality of presentation and emphasis in each market. These programs lend themselves readily to merchandising to dealers and distributors in order to impress them with the extent of national advertising support behind the products they handle. Network television, well positioned as to time and type of program, is a franchise that can obtain large audiences and a loyalty that may carry over into consumer loyalty to the products advertised on the program.

Such advertising calls, however, for a large investment and, moreover, the important elements of time and program may not be readily available. There is also the further disadvantage of a long-term commitment that is required, the minimum being thirteen weeks, with some time—and—talent combinations asking for twenty-six- and thirty-nine-week commitments.

Spot commercials have the advantage of extreme flexibility with regard to market, station and time selection. Once the spot schedule is established, it may be used to rotate various products of the sponsor and thus permit multiple brands to support the overall budget. Local, regional, and seasonal sales drives may be supported as required by the product marketing problems. Spot announcements can be merchandised to a sales organization, as well as by that organization at the local retail level. Spots deliver maximum efficiency per advertising dollar, especially for advertisers with an established, frequently purchased, brand name product. Their dollar is spent almost entirely for circulation, with no major program expenditure to achieve that circulation. Spot announcements develop a high degree of sales penetration through their greater frequency daily and weekly. They are also effective selling tools for advertisers who wish to change their campaigns with the season or weather.

Spots are the choice when budget or the availability of broadcast time on networks prevents use of programs. In this respect, the cost factor in SAG talent fees for programs often discourages an advertiser, and turns him to using spot commercials. The advertiser who does this must expect lower recall of both his brand name and sales points.

COMMERCIAL LENGTH VERSUS EFFECTIVENESS

Sixty in seconds is not a magic number in terms of commercial effectiveness. Optimum effectiveness has been measured at from 71 to 100 seconds, with a sharp falling off beyond that point. Very good performance is attained, however, by shorter-length commercials especially the now dominant 30-second commercials. In terms of audience appeal, the pattern has changed, with viewers apparently preferring the shorter commercial.

FIGURE 18-8

Low-cost, taped commercial.   Taped at a television station, this commercial avoided complications and use of inept local actors. The "cameo" lighting spotlights the action so that no background shows. Other commercials in the series showed a man's hands framing a picture, a woman's hands planting a terrarium, etc. In each instance, after showing such action, a dissolve took the viewer to the finished product in the next scene. Not all television commercials are Hollywood productions. The beginner, especially away from the big cities, may have to do commercials such as this for low-budget advertisers. Done with care, they may be very good commercials.

A commercial's length depends upon the theme, approach, and specific product advantages. Different sales stories may vary in their complexity. For example, a good demonstration commercial may require sixty seconds, every second of which will be useful and interesting to the viewer. A product, in contrast, that has nothing to demonstrate and no high degree of product-interest might be a bore as the subject matter of a sixty-second commercial. Give it thirty seconds or even ten seconds if the idea of the product can be grasped easily by viewers. As the copywriter you're usually going to be told how long a commercial you're supposed to write. Thus, this is a subject that doesn't concern you much unless you are permitted to participate in precampaign planning sessions.

HOW MUCH REPETITION?

Having decided on program as opposed to the spot presentation of your commercial, it is well to keep in mind certain principles about another factor: repetition. Viewer knowledge increases with repetition up to a certain point, when indifference or psychological deafness and blindness set in. It is difficult, if not impossible to measure at what point this mental tuning-out takes place, but there are four factors that seem to relate specifically to any commercial's life expectancy:

- Its frequency of broadcast,
- Its content as it affects the viewer,
- Variety of presentation in a given series,
- Techniques used in commercial construction.

Many advertisers have been successful with a minimum of well-constructed and oft-repeated messages. Skillfully built and judiciously scheduled, a spot can be used for many months, even years. Another can run its course in a few weeks in a heavy saturation campaign, yet still have been effective and economical. Kellogg's Rice Krispies ran a $3,700 cartoon jingle fifty times in a row on a children's program and burned it out like a meteor. Yet it served its purpose well, at a cost-per-showing of less than $75.

How acceptable a commercial is refers not to how much a viewer likes it but to its "what's-in-it-for-me" content and how well it entertains, informs, and holds forth a promised benefit. A film series should focus on a central theme for greatest impact throughout the series, but varied repetition is the key here, particularly in the manner in which the commercial begins. Beer commercials are much the same in any given series, but the variety of ways in which they capture attention at the outset makes for interest. Singing jingles combined with animated cartoons are a combination with long life-expectancy, especially if the commercial spot is used intermittently. You cannot, however, expect to repeat too often live action films in which memorable characters or settings are featured, since viewers tend to pick apart your commercial with each repetition.

STATION BREAK SPOTS

Let's examine more closely at this point the shorter of the spot commercials, the ten- and twenty-second station break television spots, which can best be viewed as the rifle bullets of this medium. Here you encounter the challenge of brevity, plus the need for simple, clear-cut selling ideas expressed with visual impact. It may be simpler to write a five or ten minute film script than a ten-second television spot.

You will be tempted in building spot commercials to crowd too much material into both audio and video presentations, which will only result in a confused and meaningless jumble of words and scenes from which your viewer will derive little. Again, concentrate on the video or visual in your commmercial, since this is what must remain with the viewer after your brief message. Remember, however, the sound or audio plays an important role, too, enabling the viewer to hear you even if he has left the room.

Advantages

Both the twenty-second commercial and the ten-second station identification (ID) spot have the advantage over a one-minute commercial in their ability to sustain a much stronger sales pitch and the fact that they can be repeated more often than their longer cousin. They are also easier to schedule for more intensive coverage on a number of stations, and thus are effective in coping with local sales problems.

The ID spot, chiefly a "reminder" type of advertising, can be built in two ways. The shared ID is one which is on the television screen for a full ten seconds, but shares its picture with the station's call letters in the upper right corner. It gives you eight seconds of sound. The full-screen ID is one which advertisers generally prefer. It does not share its video with the station; however, the picture is only seven and one-fourth seconds long, with 6 seconds of sound. (The twenty-second station break commercial permits full-time use of video, with eighteen seconds of sound.)

Disadvantages

The ID is a commercial form that must fight hard for identity and leaves small margin for error. Its brief moments of sound-and-picture glory are almost always preceded by the closing commercial of the preceding program and a chain break. It is immediately followed by the first commercial of the next program. In spite of its physical limitations, the ID can do a fine selling job as both a reminder for impulse-type items and as a supporting element for concurrent campaigns for big-ticket advertisers in television and other media.

To detract attention from surrounding commercials, station break commercials often employ cartoons, which are particularly effective because they read well. Since this is primarily reminder advertising, the sponsor's name must be indelibly identified, probably along with a slogan or an important selling point. It is better not to resort to camera tricks, such as dissolves or wipes, where action on the screen is involved. Stay with a basic setting and be content to move component parts in and out for the sake of fluidity. Hold to the premise, if possible, that the sponsor's signature or logotype should be on-camera for at least half, if not more, of the allotted ten seconds.

BBDO
Batten, Barton, Durstine & Osborn, Inc.

| Client: | PEPSICO, INC. | | Time: | 60 SECONDS |
| Product | PEPSI COLA | Title | Comml No: | |

VIDEO	AUDIO
PEOPLE GETTING OUT OF CAR	(Music under)
GRANDMOTHER COMES DOWN STEPS	A smile can wake the sun up
EVERYONE HUGS GRANDMOTHER	to what your world can be, and with every brand new moment you're alive, you're feelin' free
SHOT OF EVERYONE SITTING AROUND DRINKING PEPSI BIG GIRL AND LITTLE GIRL ON HORSE	Make this day a celebration
CU OF MAN DRINKING PEPSI AND GRINNING	Come and taste the Pepsi Way.
CU OF LITTLE GIRL RIDING SHEEP	Life is what is should be
SHOT OF HORSE AND RIDER CROSSING RIVER	when you have a Pepsi day.
SHOT OF HORSES RUNNING THROUGH WATER	C'mon, c'mon, c'mon and taste the Pepsi way.
SHOT OF TRUCK APPROACHING	C'mon, c'mon, c'mon
CU OF HANDS GRABBING PEPSI FROM COOLER	and have a Pepsi day.
CU OF GIRL DRINKING	Wrap a thirsty smile around it
CU OF MAN DRINKING	Raise a Pepsi up and down it
CU OF MAN GRINNING	C'mon, c'mon
SHOT OF GIRL ON HORSEBACK	and have a Pepsi day.
SHOT OF GIRL ON HORSE	C'mon, c'mon and
SHOT OF MEN RUNNING HORSES INTO CORRAL	make this day a celebration. C'mon, c'mon and
SHOT OF FOOD ON GRILL SHOT OF PEOPLE AT THE TABLE PASSING FOOD AROUND	join the Pepsi generation.
CU OF LITTLE BOY WINDING MUSIC BOX	C'mon, c'mon
CU OF MAN AT THE TABLE	C'mon, c'mon
SHOT OF TWO GIRLS ON HORSE ZOOM IN ON LITTLE GIRL SUPER OVER	Have a Pepsi Day!

FIGURE 18-9

Script for 60-second television commercial.   Notice that in this lively commercial, typical of the series, there are twenty-five camera shots. This makes for an action-filled commercial very suitable for a product that is associated with good times and that does not need pondering or demonstrations.

BUILDING A GOOD STATION BREAK SPOT

While the ID can be a single spot repeated often, or part of a family series, there seems to be a fairly basic structure involved in writing a successful version.

This usually calls for a headline or principal "reason why"; and once this is set, it is a matter of using it in the audio and dramatizing it in the video. Such commercials are in contrast to those contrived and complicated by local advertisers who seek to make major productions out of the precious seven to eight seconds allotted by the ID. It is enough to succeed in registering one point strongly in even a one-minute or longer commercial, let alone trying to do more in an ID.

In constructing the twenty-second commercial, select the dominant sales point and simply polish that point to its finest. This commercial has the ideal length for the cartoon singing jingle, which thus makes it a good opening or closing for a one-minute spot. While the point is often made that the one-minute should be constructed so that twenty-second commercials can be edited from it, you will be safer in writing the shorter version first, in its own right. Having done this well, the minute version will readily permit amplification of sales points made in the shorter length commercial, with possible addition of secondary points. The use of the established twenty-second jingle, either at the opening or closing of a series of one-minute spots, can serve as an institutional or identification bridge that maintains continuity and recognition for the series.

The success stories of advertisers who have used the station break spot to advantage are numerous, and many of them have achieved this success with little or no other advertising. One of these, a watch company, used this formula:

> Buy five or six spots a week on a station and hold them for all year use. Try to reach the entire family by buying spots in prime time (8:30 p.m. to 10:00 p.m.) with adjacencies to good shows, if possible. Buy a volume in spots commensurate with the company's sales in the particular market.

Another advertiser who had done a strong selling job with spots summed up the situation:

> Spots give us more coverage with the flexibility to handle sales problems peculiar to different areas. We can adjust our product commercials according to regional preferences in flavor, for instance.

While minutes give an advertiser more elbow room and more prestige, selling can be done effectively in many instances with the thirty-second spot and the ten-second ID. Just as many advertisers have succeeded using the full page, so can television advertising succeed using full, traditional one-minute commercial, in spot or program framework.

DEVELOPING THE STORYBOARD

Where do you, as the writer, start to develop a television commercial script? There is no better method of script presentation and description than that of a storyboard, the technique used by virtually all advertising agencies and successful film producers. The "storyboard" is a series of small sketches

Needham, Harper & Steers, Inc.
900 Third Avenue, New York, New York 10022
(212) 758-7600

CLIENT: XEROX CORPORATION
PRODUCT: XEROX 9200 DUPLICATING SYSTEM
AS FILMED TV COMM'L NO: OXNC7090
TITLE: "MONKS"
[PAGE 1]
DATE: 11/22/
LENGTH: 90 SEC.

1. (MUSIC UNDER BAROQUE) (MONKS CHORUS UNDER)   2. ANNCR: (VO) Ever since people started recording information,   3. there's been a need to duplicate it.   4. (MUSIC)

5. (MUSIC)   6. (MUSIC)   7. (MUSIC)   8. (MUSIC)

9. FATHER: Very nice work, Brother Dominick.   10. BROTHER DOMINICK: Thank you, FATHER; Very nice.   11. FATHER: Now, I would like 500 more sets!   12. (MUTTERING PAINFULLY TO HIMSELF AS HE WALKS AWAY.)

13. (SFX: CLOSES DOOR)   14. (SFX: BUS)   15.(SFX: STREET NOISE)   16. (SFX: OFFICE NOISE) STEPHENS: Brother Dominick. How are you?

1. BROTHER DOMINICK: Could you do a big job for me?   2. ANNCR: (VO) Xerox has developed an amazing machine that's unlike anything we've ever made.   3. The Xerox 9200 Duplicating System.   4. It automatically feeds and cycles originals ...

5. Has a computerized programmer that coordinates the entire system.   6. Can duplicate, reduce and assemble a virtually limitless number of complete sets ...   7. And does it all at the incredible rate of 2 pages per second.   8. The Xerox 9200 Duplicating System.

9. BROTHER DOMINICK: Here are your sets, Father.   10. FATHER: What? BROTHER DOMINICK: The 500 sets you asked for.   11. FATHER: (GLANCES UPWARD) It's a miracle!   12. (MONKS CHORUS)

FIGURE 18-10

Script for 90-second dramatized humorous commercial.   Although this was a highly entertaining commercial, it is also very informative providing that good combination of entertainment and vigorous selling. Because of the genuine entertainment value, the 90-second length posed no problem. However, avoid such length unless your commercial is truly interesting.

with accompanying description of action plus audio copy that gives an advertiser an approximate conception of what the commercial will be upon completion. It is a sort of halfway point between the birth of the original idea and the finished film.

Storyboards are preferable to written scripts for a number of reasons. Since the commercial will be presented through a medium in which the visual image is paramount in importance, it facilitates production to think in terms of pictures from the beginning. Furthermore, since a number of people may read and be called upon to approve a script, it is probable that each will have a personal visualization of how the story will appear on the screen. If a storyboard is prepared, all concerned will think in terms of the pictures shown. Each can check the staging and action as the commercial is actually shot. Also any errors in visualization from the standpoint of company policy or product value will be apparent, and can be corrected before actual production begins.

A properly designed story can also be utilized as a shooting script that suggests camera angles and staging as a preliminary layout for set designs or backgrounds, and as a guide for the film editor when the film is cut. Close-ups, camera moves, and optional effects can all be indicated. The director is also aided by the storyboard when planning the action and staging of the film to obtain the desired dramatic effect.

STORYBOARDS ARE STARTING POINTS

A print writer switching to television finds immediately that there's a big difference between a print layout and a television storyboard. In general, the copywriter, account executives, client and production people can tell from a print layout just about what the published advertisement will look like. In contrast, the filmed commercial that is finally produced from a storyboard is usually going to be vastly different from the storyboard. Thus, it takes a professional with plenty of experience and imagination to judge what is going to result from the incorporating of unusual voices, beguiling characters, superb music, dazzling color, energetic motion, and striking sound effects—none of which is truly conveyed by the storyboard.

Actually, the process works both ways. The storyboard idea may look good and the finished product poor. Or, the storyboard may convey little that gives a clue as to the outstanding commercial that will be developed finally from the idea. One of the problems in doing a storyboard is that it is necessarily brief compared to the finished film which is divided into frames that speed through the projector 24 to the second, or 1,440 to the minute.

Sometimes the problem isn't overwhelming as in the case of a simple demonstration commercial that has only two to five scene changes involving two, or possibly, one performer. On the other hand, a commercial such as the typical Pepsi-Cola or Coca-Cola commercial is difficult to storyboard for full understanding. How can you convey in detail all those quick shots, optical gimmicks, sound effects, numerous people, music, frantic action and background scenes? You can't. You simply call for enough storyboard frames to serve as a rough guide. You're at the mercy of the production house to bring those few cold pictures to life.

It's especially difficult to plot in advance the exact time each of those frames will require in the finished film. Furthermore, some scenes need more accompanying copy to explain them and thus more frames. The exact time they need is hard to tell in advance. Other scenes convey ideas in a fraction of a second, requiring only a glance of the viewer. They may need no accompanying copy.

Because of the limitations of the storyboard, it can be viewed only as a starting point. It can never be a rigid blueprint for the finished commercial. In fact, some producers don't even want to see a storyboard. Loftily, they may say: "Forget the storyboard. Just

FIGURE 18-11

Celebrity presenter commercial.   Use of a well-known person and humor make this a memorable commercial. Notice how strongly the name Hefty is stressed in the dialogue, in package display, and in the use of superimposition. Such emphasis should insure good identification for the product.

FIGURE 18-12

Dramatized television commercial in storyboard form.   From such rough storyboards the filmed commercial evolves, often changed significantly in the final version that appears on viewers' television sets.

tell us about the product, your objectives, and we'll do the rest." This kind of attitude may be even more pronounced when you ask for animated commercials, the infinite subtleties of which cannot be conveyed by a few storyboard frames.

VIDEO:

AUDIO:

ESTABLISH RIVER, BOAT AND PEOPLE.

SFX: RIVER, WIND, ETC.

ANNCR: (VO) Pabst Blue Ribbon wouldn't dare challenge anyone

CUT TO CU OF BOATMAN AND OTHERS.

to take on the raging Colorado

DISSOLVES AND CUTS THROUGH SCENES OF WILD RAPIDS.

in a wooden boat...

SFX: RAPIDS

unless you know what you're doing.

CUT TO MS OF BOAT BEING PULLED UP ON SHORE.

It's the kind of challenge that's just not for everyone.

CUT TO OPENING HATCH TO REVEAL BEER.

But we do challenge everyone to discover

SERIES OF CUTS/ DISSOLVES THROUGH PRODUCT ENJOYMENT ...INCLUDING POUR.

a better tasting premium beer.

Taste and compare Pabst Blue Ribbon

with the beer you're now drinking.

We set the standard for quality as America's first premium beer.

DISSOLVE TO MORTICE OF GROUP ON BEACH, INSIDE PABST LOGO ON GLASS.

And we bet you'll taste the difference our quality makes.

PULL BACK TO REVEAL BEER GLASS ON DARK BACKGROUND...LOGO MORTICE BECOMES LOGO.

Pabst. Since 1844,

Pabst. Since 1844. The quality has always come through.

SUPER: PABST. SINCE 1844. THE QUALITY HAS ALWAYS COME THROUGH.

the quality has always come through.

Pabst. Since 1844. The quality has always come through.

Storyboards can be too detailed

A word of caution is needed here to point out that too detailed and rigid a storyboard is not always the best one. Much depends on the type of producer who will take over from your storyboard to put the commercial on film. If he is a truly creative producer, you will be shortcutting your commercial by imposing too exacting directions upon him. He may have ideas about enacting some of your scenes in a manner to make them much more forceful. Or he might have suggestions on how to cut costs by repeating the use of a certain setting or dropping a bit of action that lends only minor support to the story. Such a producer can be a tremendous asset, so it is best to give this talented team member a green light with a storyboard that leaves him room for his own creative contributions.

Only through experience with such a producer or by his long standing reputation can you know when to construct a loose storyboard that takes advantage of this "bonus" talent. Other producers will follow you too unquestioningly, investing no creativity of their own in the commercial. Storyboards for these producers must spell everything out in minute detail. If you know, therefore, with what producer you will be working, build your storyboard to get maximum utilization of his talent. You may even want to consider, if you are working with an unimaginative producer, using a "third column" in your script in which to analyze and explain objectives and to elaborate on the handling desired in the video and audio columns.

BALANCE OF VIDEO AND AUDIO

A basic problem in writing your television commercial, regardless of its length, is the proper balance of video and audio. Be cautious about pacing the visual side of the commercial too fast and using too many scene changes. The main trouble, however, lies not with scenes being too long or too short but with uneven pacing. Long scenes too often are followed by jet-speed, short ones. This uneven pace stems from approaching the commercials sales points with words rather than pictures. You may find one point easy to express in a few words and then accord this point a correspondingly short visual. The more involved points get prolonged visuals. This is working the wrong way. The brief copy point should either not be visualized at all or its audio should be extended sufficiently to cover a visual of comfortable length.

It must be remembered that it is a mistake to pace your audio for television as fast as you would for the typical hard-sell radio commercial. Your audience in television has to follow video as well as audio, which makes it difficult to grasp a television sound track that is paced too fast. This pacing problem is particularly acute in film commercials where the announcer succeeds in getting in the full message only by racing through the script at breakneck speed.

These cautions do not apply to the mood commercials mentioned earlier in the chapter. In a soft drink commercial, to illustrate, you are not trying to register product points. Your aim may simply be to associate the drink with youth, good times, and activity. To acomplish this you run scenes in rapid succession with no need to let any of them linger on the screen. Together, with equally fast-paced music and off-screen announcing, you create whirlwind action and the mood you're seeking.

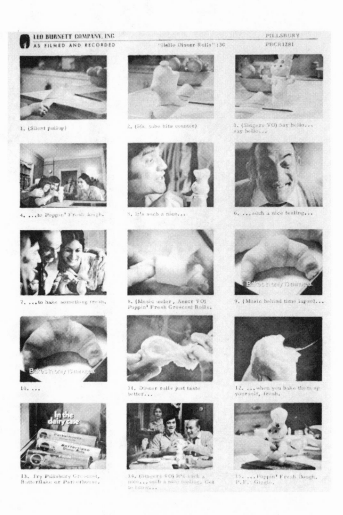

FIGURE 18-13

Stop-action and live-action film television commercial in photoboard form.   The hero of this 30-second commercial is discussed in the following observation by one of the agency writers working on the Pillsbury account:

"It's his near human quality, I'm sure that's responsible for his overwhelming success. People get involved with him. They sing with him. Dance with him. Belly-poke him. And in return, he gives them both encouragement and ideas.

"That's where the challenge comes when you sit down and try to write for him—to try to rehumanize instead of dehumanize him. It's easy to use Poppin' Fresh simply as an awareness device but you've got to remember that his durability lies in human involvement. That's why you have to give him a meaningful role within the context of each commercial as if he were the lead player in a 30-second drama. And it all has to be cute and human.''

PILLSBURY COMPANY
30-Second Film
"WHO BAKED CRESCENTS"
CRESCENT DINNER ROLLS

1. OPEN ON TRAY OF HOT
   CRESCENTS.

   SONG: WELL WHO BAKED
         THOSE MARVELOUS
         CRESCENTS?

2. PULL BACK, OLDER GIRL
   HOLDING TRAY. LITTLE
   GIRLS HELPING, MOM IN
   BACKGROUND.
   SONG: WE REALLY LIKE TO
         KNOW
   GIRLS: We did!

3. GIRL PUTTING ROLLS INTO
   BASKET.

   SONG: WITH PILLSBURY
         POPPIN' FRESH DOUGH.

4. GIRL WITH PACKAGE TO
   CAMERA. GIRLS IN
   BACKGROUND.

   OLDER GIRL: The next best
   thing to eating hot rolls.

5. CU, LITTLE GIRL FOLDING
   CRESCENT ROLL DOUGHBOY
   STANDING BY.

   (VO) is the fun we have
   making them.

6. LITTLE GIRL IS PLEASED.

   LITTLE GIRL: I did it!

7. ROLL ON BAKING SHEET

   SONG: YES THEY BAKED

8. BAKE-UP

   those crescent rolls

9. BREAK SHOT

   With Poppin' Fresh Dough.

10. DAD BREAKS ROLL FOR STEAM
    SHOT. FAMILY IN
    BACKGROUND.

    DAD: They did it!

11. DOUGHBOY WITH PACKAGE.

    SONG: WITH PILLSBURY
          POPPIN' FRESH
          DOUGH.

IN THE
REFRIGERATED CASE

12. BELLYPOKE.

    DOUGHBOY: (GIGGLE).

FIGURE 18-14

Combination television commercial—stop motion and live action, in storyboard form.   Doughboy, the Pillsbury doll, gets as many as 200 "love" letters a week. Because of his popularity, he has become a sort of corporate spokesperson in the United States and abroad. To give him movement, he is shot one frame at a time, moved slightly, and then shot again. Thus he is photographed twenty-four times for each second he appears on camera. He is almost always shown in package shots because he reinforces Pillsbury's brand identity and adds attention value.

An airline might use this technique if its aim is to emphasize all the interesting places to which it can take you rather than to stress any particular feature such as on-time arrivals, safety, the type of aircraft, or the service. Similarly, a hotel could run through a rapid series of shots highlighting its attractions—the pool, the sauna, the dining rooms, the roof garden, the nearby ocean beach.

For most commercials, however, don't race—<u>pace</u>. Be active but not frantic.

HOW MANY? THE WORD COUNT

Most radio announcers read comfortably at 160 to 170 words a minute, and others considerably faster. A governor of Nebraska was once clocked at 487 words a minute in an election campaign speech. Obviously, such verbal fluidity is well beyond the speed of the television viewer's understanding. You will find that 135 words a minute (w.p.m.) will fit nicely into many live-action commercials, although for the most part you will need fewer than that. Recommendations often range from 80 to more than 130 w.p.m., but experience has shown that a rule of thumb of 2 words per second usually works out consistently well.

Delivery rate is rather hard to define because of pauses and the fact that many commercials use more than one speaker. One study of 350 one-minute commercials by word-count analysis compared this data with effectiveness results for the same commercials. The most effective comercials ranged in word count from 101 to 140, demonstrating that a moderate speaking pace was desired over extremes of too many or too few words a minute.

Having a certain delivery rate, however, is no assurance of successful commercial writing. Some outstanding commercials have used no words; others more than the usual word count. A sensible speaking pace can be a contributing factor, of course, but the important thing is the quality of your words, not their quantity. Quantity, as it applies to the shorter commercials, would be: 20 words for the ten-second spot; 40 words for the twenty-second spot and 60 to 65 words for the thirty-second spot. The one-minute commercial will usually take well with 120-135 words; but if the announcer is on camera, give him less to say and, if he must demonstrate, still less than that. The ground rules say that a twenty-second

sound track cannot run over eighteen seconds, nor a one-minute track over fifty-eight seconds. You will be safer aiming for a shorter count, such as sixteen or seventeen seconds on the short spot, 25 to 26 on the thirty, and fifty-five or fifty-six seconds in the one-minute version. This will permit an easier pace and more flexibility in your commercials. Remember, too, in production it's much simpler to stretch than to tighten.

AND NOT TOO MANY SCENES, EITHER!

What has been said here about pacing the audio holds true for the video portion of your television commercial. Don't confuse your viewers with too many scenes or those that are too busy and distract from your sales story. You can avoid cutting scenes too short by allowing a minimum of three seconds for viewers to orient themselves to any new scene. Scenes can also run too long, so keep in mind that after six seconds something had better move, or perhaps the viewer will. Either a different camera angle or some action within the scene can provide movement to prevent a scene from becoming static.

FIGURE 18-15

Humorous commercial.   For this type of product, good-natured humor is desirable for putting across the basic point. Television is especially good for a campaign of this type because voices and expressions can deliver the message without offense. Also, the commercial gives ample chance to register the product name in spoken words and visually.

A single scene that is properly plotted out for action and camera angles can sustain interest for twenty or thirty seconds in a commercial. Ordinarily, however, you will want to think in terms of five or six seconds or more per scene. For more important visuals such as establishing a person, demonstrating, or major copy point, you may want to use ten to twenty seconds or more.

One television researcher found that the average "poor" commercial had one scene per seven seconds, while the average "good" commercial (one that increased brand preference) had one scene per thirteen seconds. Also, too many voices, as well as too many scenes, cut down remembrance.

There is no firm rule about the number of scenes in a commercial, but here are a few general measures that will serve to guide you: No more than two scenes in a ten-second spot; four in a twenty-second spot; and ten in a 30-second spot. Keep in mind that to the viewer a closeup from a previous shot is not considered a new scene.

To show the futility of trying to set up firm guidelines, a study conducted during the writing of this book found that thirty-second commercials were averaging eight to ten scenes; these were definite scene changes, not merely changes of camera angles or distance.

HOLD DOWN THE COST

When writing a commercial, think of cost. If your storyboard calls for five on-camera principal performers, do some rethinking. Could you rewrite and accomplish your goals with four or three, or even two performers? Remember, an on-camera session fee will run into hundreds of dollars for each person playing a major role whether he is called a "player" by SAG (Screen Actors Guild), or a "principal" by AFTRA (American Federation of Television and Radio Artists), for videotape commercials. This session fee pays for one use of the commercial on the network.

If the commercial is to be used in a major way over the networks, each player or principal must be given a re-use, or residual, payment for every time the commercial is shown. Even off-camera announcers and singers are given such payments, although in lesser amounts.

When you call for a person in the commercial to speak, handle, or react to the product, that person becomes a player. Others, such as stunt people and specialty dancers, are classified as players, too.

Because you've called for an unusual number of players, or principals, it may well be that the subsequent re-use payments can cost the client more than the charge for the commercial air-time. Assess the value to be gained by the lavish use of players against the added cost. Sometimes you may judge that the use of the extra players will result in a more powerful commercial that will better achieve advertising objectives. If not—then cut down.

Sitting at your typewriter it's easy to call for location shooting, but it's not so simple to lug all the people, props, cameras and other equipment to the location—and it can be frightfully expensive. Once again, the question: Is it worth it? Sometimes the answer must be yes. If you can't honestly say yes, there are ways around the problem. You could use a stock shot of the location as background, a special crew (without actors) could go to the spot to get such a shot, you could use stills to establish the location. Actually, one shot may be all you need to fix the location in the viewer's mind and to provide the atmosphere you want.

Lastly, you can run up costs by asking for effects and shots that are more complicated than they need to be to put over your message. Do you need that view from the helicopter, that fisheye shot, the telephoto shot, the extreme close-ups? Some of the most effective television is simple television, and simple television can be less expensive. Think about it.

For a thorough, practical discussion on this matter of controlling costs, read: *Controlling Your TV Commercial Costs* by Arthur Bellaire. This volume is published by Crain Books, 740 Rush Street, Chicago, Illinois 60611.

19

Garnering Sales with Television, Part B

It would be pleasant to tell you that as a copywriter you are going to decide just how your television commercials will be reproduced. Not so. Typically, you'll be told to write the commercials, and you'll be told also whether they'll be "live," "film," or "tape." You don't argue. Drawing upon your knowledge of each, you write your commercial to fit the requirements of the technique you've been told will be used.

LIVE, FILM, OR TAPE?

Live refers to action seen on the television screen as it takes place right in the studio before the television camera. Film commercials are those shot in a studio, on location outdoors, or wherever there is a suitable site for the desired action. Tape (video tape) is a system that records sound and pictures simultaneously on magnetic tape.

Live television production offers lower cost for the one-time commercial. It can also be produced in less time than film, from the written script to the actual production on camera. Live commercials can, of course, be changed in wording or action at the very last minute, a not insignificant advantage to an advertiser, especially in a keenly competitive situation.

On the other side, many of the most deadly commercials are done live in station studios, very often for low-budget local advertisers. To supply some kind of interest, the writer very often calls for props to be supplied by the client, the station, or sometimes the advertising agency. These may be mixed in with slides. Also, the announcer may appear at the opening and close. Occasionally, if the station has a good film library, a writer may use stock shots effectively in a live commercial.

Since the development of videotape, live studio, or live location shots, have been used less and less. If you must write live commercials, use every bit of imagi-nation you can in drawing upon the resources of the client and the station. Sometimes, however, if you have a personable announcer with a forceful delivery, it may be advisable to let him make a straight, sincere presentation and use few, if any, props.

Film television production is logical when plans call for repeated telecasting of the commercial. Likewise, film offers realism through on-location shooting, especially with outdoor scenes. A very wide latitude in production is possible through a variety of sets, optical tricks, and careful editing. Today, almost any approach is possible for the writer of film commercials because the production people are used to coming up with ingenious ways to supply film answers for those crazy ideas of those crazy copywriters. If you're working with film, therefore, let your creativity run. If your ideas can be put on film, they will be; if they can't, you'll soon find out but you've lost nothing by trying for a different approach.

Tape production offers such amazing fidelity and instant playback capabilities that it's been called "instant film," in its blending of the best of live and film techniques. Immediate playback, of course, is important. If, for example, your commercial calls for the use of amateur talent, such as executives of your client's company, you can almost count on them to fluff lines, or to commit some other speaking or acting error. The playback reveals this. If it does, the scene is done again, and again, and again until an acceptable take is achieved. Tape has been a great boon to local advertising because it makes possible the utilization of local talent and resources in a way not possible with live-studio production.

At first, tape was limited in special effects. Now, as a writer, you can call for such effects and optical tricks—all at low cost. In fact, compared to film (not live studio) tape costs are lower for shooting and processing. Also, tape can record and store a month's worth of commercials in one day.

Some other tape pluses

- <u>Easier client approval.</u> Before a commercial is finally approved by a major advertiser, it usually goes through numerous hands. Tape makes it possible for many, if not all, of those concerned with passing upon a commercial to be present and to make necessary revisions immediately, thanks to quick playback.
- <u>Alternate versions and testing.</u> Two or more versions of a commercial are easily permitted with tape. Changes in settings or new approaches suggested on the spot are less costly. Also, with alternate versions, a commercial can be pretested quickly via research before actual telecast to determine the most effective approach. Some larger videotape production houses employ closed-circuit testing facilities for such purposes.
- <u>Man-hour savings.</u> Time schedules in pretape days of live and film television tied down creative and technical people. Now this talent can be utilized more efficiently within the compact time schedules of tape. Furthermore, tape offers such flexibility that new scenes can be inserted in existing spots in an hour. Sound tracks can be erased and recorded anew in less time than that. Tape thus puts television ahead of newspaper in the all-important factor of advertising flexibility.

Viewers don't care

Whether a commercial is live, film, or tape matters not to the viewer. At their best, the final results obtained by the three methods are virtually indistinguishable. Viewers simply want to see a commercial that holds their interest and will reward them for the time invested in watching it. The real importance here is that you as a television writer know how to work with each, especially with videotape which, with its many production advantages, has given rise to a new breed of writer who knows well the potentials of both live and film techniques.

TYPES OF COMMERCIALS

What are the types of commercials you may be required to write? Some are classified as "soft" or "hard sell"—labels which refer more to the tone of copy rather than to the commercial's effectiveness. One might also set up classifications such as reason why and emotional commercials. In order to be more to the point break them down according to their source of authority:

Straight sales pitch
Personality salesperson
Dramatization
Demonstration
Testimonial
Production (song-and-dance)

Straight sales pitch. The first of the basic, live-action types is the so-called stand-up commercial, in which the announcer, seated or standing, delivers a straight sales pitch, usually stressing price advantage or reason-why claims. The speaker is unknown to the majority of the audience and uses no mood or other atmosphere setting to slide into the story. The speaker needs a well-constructed story and probably some props, charts, graphs, or other attention-getting visual devices to help put across the story effectively. The straight salesperson will deliver the commercial in one of three ways: a) punchy, fast-paced and repetitive in the manner of the pitchman role; b) informally and conversationally, like a friendly sales clerk talking over the counter; c) casually, even ad-libbing, like a neighbor discussing the weather over the backyard fence. Which technique will work best? Very often this will be determined at rehearsals where you, the copywriter, must be ready to adapt and revise your script on the spot to whatever changes in copy or delivery seem called for at the time.

Personality salesperson. Personality salespeople are quite another type, for here are stars with certain names, fame, and following, and it is expected that their audience will lend a very receptive ear to whatever they say or sell. These personalities seldom work directly from the commercial scripts provided by the sponsor's agency. Instead, the agency simply supplies a fact sheet about the product to be advertised, and the personalities (or their staff) will expand on this material in their own style.

One super-star who sold practically every product category available to radio and television had this to say about commercials:

> It takes me a half a minute to say hello, so rehearsed, well-written commercials are not for me. I believe in my product and I give my audience credit for having brains of their own. I imagine how I would feel in the listener's or viewer's place. I established part of my reputation by poking fun at the carefully prepared scripts of ad agencies and at some of the silly ideas used to trick people into trying the product. But I never razzed the product—it was the guy who wrote the commercial that I was after.

Also classified with this personality group are the "star" salespeople who, although not performers on the program, have built names and followings of their own, often in other entertainment fields.

It is the naturalness and believability of such sales personalities that make their commercial endorsements effective. They must have established themselves as known and likable characters, with appealing appearance, voice, and mannerisms in order to

FIGURE 19-1

Personality salesperson commercial.   The use of an outstanding personality can spell success for a product or service. Celebrity endorsements have been used increasingly in recent years and with good results.

The Superstar in Rent-A-Car

"Check-out"

O.J.: When you're in a rush, take it from O.J. Simpson. There's only one superstar in rent-a-car. Hertz.

Others claim to be fast, but nobody has more . . .

to do it faster.

More pros to execute the toughest performance standards.

More cars. More locations.

First with every good idea to speed up service.

Like the # 1 Club.

Before you get there your form is filled out,

car's preassigned.

WOMAN: Go, O.J.! Go!

O.J.: Rent a Ford fast from Hertz.

The Superstar in rent-a-car.

build a loyal audience. In using such personalities in a television commercial, it is important to avoid being so glib, expert and perfect in presentation of the message that the individual sacrifices his qualities of warmth and naturalness.

Dramatizations. Akin to personality commercials and most often used on comedy, musical and dramatic programs are dramatizations. These commercials are usually done by lesser known members of the show's cast and may be done straight or dramatized in the roles these people play on the program.

Demonstrations. There are several kinds of demonstration that can be used as part or all of a given commercial:

- Product versatility, to acquaint viewers with new and interesting uses.
- Product in use, to show its works, what it does.
- Before-and-after, to prove results in use.
- Extreme example, dramatic proof of quality, as in Timex watch commercials that subjected a watch to rugged treatment to prove it "takes a licking and keeps on ticking." Torture tests on proving grounds likewise aim to prove superiority of one make of automobile over another.
- Competitive tests, to show superiority over competitor, as in various washing or sudsing tests that seek to show that one brand of soap or detergent produces whiter washes.

Demonstration commercials rely heavily on film-tape production in order to cover periods of time necessary to illustrate points of superiority in use. The full application of a home permanent can be filmed or taped and then simply edited to required length, showing key sales points. Film and tape also permit use of split screens and other optical devices to lend additional impact and drama to before-and-after and competitive-test commercials of the demonstration type.

In recent years, the Federal Trade Commission has insisted that product demonstrations be literally true. In the past, in contrast, glycerine was substituted for ice cream because the latter melted before scenes could be shot. Under the new rules, if the product being advertised is ice cream, then ice cream must be used in the scene, not a nonmelting substitute. This means that the ice cream must be kept cold until the last seconds before shooting, and then rushed on to the set for a quick shot.

Such literalness has greatly increased the cost of shooting many commercials. Copywriters writing for television must keep in mind this requirement of literal honesty in every product demonstration they call for. This is in contrast to television's earlier days when a maker of glass for auto windows demonstrated the clarity of the product by removing the windows. This supposedly gave the viewer a true idea of just what it was like to be looking through an auto window using the advertiser's glass. The courts ruled against the advertiser in a court case and said that future commercials must use the window glass.

At one time, because of the difficulty of showing many products on television, production shortcuts were taken and given legal approval. Those days are gone. Write accordingly.

Testimonials. Commercials in which screen stars, sports heroes, and prominent figures from all walks of life are used as salespeople are a proved type of commercial. The main problem in this type of commercial is to avoid staginess and artificiality. The viewer is all too ready to disbelieve the words of your prominent personality unless you phrase the message in comfortable, conversational language that fits your star salesperson. Keep the testimonial brief, natural and believable, for even professional actors are not always capable of adjusting to selling roles. The same precautions must be observed in testimonials featuring satisfied users or so-called passers-by in the interview type of testimonial commercial. Don't ask these obviously ordinary people to speak, complicated and unreal sounding advertising phrases in praise of your product. It simply will not be swallowed by your viewers.

Exercise care in the casting of these commercials, too, if you have a voice in the matter. Try to use people who are not too beautiful or handsome, but who have faces with character that can quickly win over viewers. In television, there is not always time for viewers to take their eyes off the attractive face and to get in step with your message. Use familiar, comfortable settings well within the experience of the viewers so

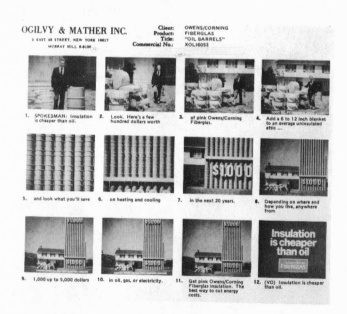

FIGURE 19-2

Dramatic demonstration commercial.   It would take a very blasé television viewer to overlook the demonstraton shown here. As the drums pile up higher than the house in the background, the effect is spectacular. The point about insulation's value is made with great strength.

they do not have to reorient their minds to an unusual setting before grasping your message. If your commercial is filmed or taped, get enough footage of a particular interview to catch facets of personality and unexpected conversational phrases that no prepared script could ever conjure up for the nonprofessional performer. Subsequent editing can then cull the highlights of the interview for commercial use.

Song-and-dance productions. Often with extensive choreography and original music, song-and-dance productions are a type of commercial that only the large, blue-chip advertisers can afford. Most often they are used by advertisers of soft drinks, beauty preparations, and automobiles, and they are definitely an art form that skillfully combines entertainment values with emotional selling. With its sweeping movement, intricate dance routines and the need for synchronization with lip movements, this type of commercial is usually produced on film or tape, preferably the latter, to insure a professional job.

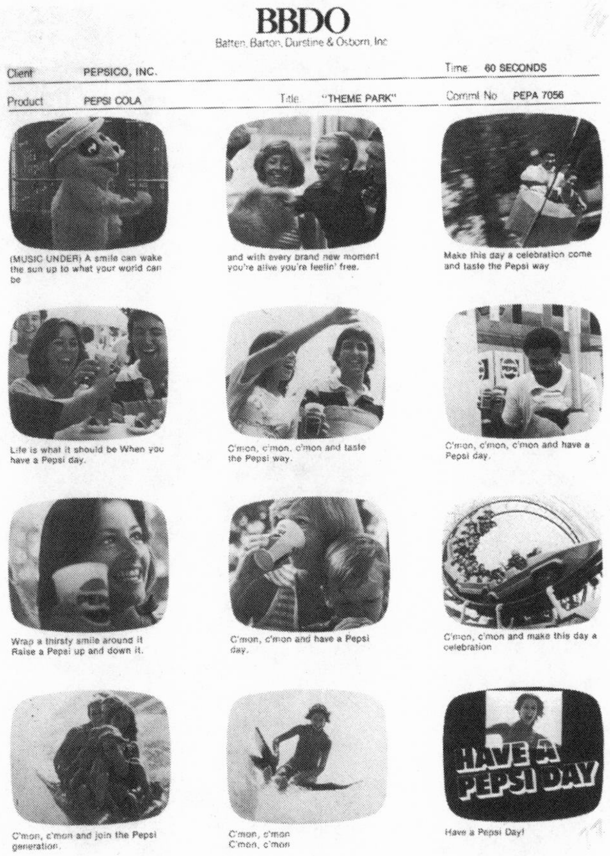

FIGURE 19-3

Production commercial.   While this is not a "production" in the sense that it uses song-and-dance teams, it _does_ use much action, music, many characters. It is a production in the full sense of the word and is ideally suited for a fun-type of product.

TO ANIMATE OR NOT TO ANIMATE

In originating the story idea for a television commercial you must decide which approach is best suited to the product or service being advertised. Your aim, of course, is to choose the approach that will initiate the greatest number of sales and develop good will for the sponsor-client. You must also decide, probably with the help of others, what production technique will show your chosen idea to best advantage. Each assignment calls for individual treatment; a story or technique that proves successful in one case may be a failure in another. It is hoped that you and your producer will have had enough experience in the field to know what can or cannot be animated, and whether the idea or product can be shown to advantage by the use of such a technique. You'd be surprised how many times you'll have to answer no to animation as the best possible method for advertising your product. If you're undecided about using animation as opposed to demonstration, use demonstration if your product has to be demonstrated for full sales effectiveness. Don't substitute cuteness for sales impact. If you decide that animation is the right method for the job, keep the following creative elements of that technique in mind:

Product character or trademark. Animation should fit the trademark or trade character naturally, without being forced. If your character is a Disney-type cartoon—full-animation drawing with rounded lines, full shading, and natural features—it won't fit well with a highly stylized, modern art treatment. Work with your producer to develop animation characters that will save you time, money and are well suited to the story you want to tell.

Setting and staging. Keep it simple and inexpensive, yet effective, for setting and staging for animation are as important as for live-action films. Your message is on the screen only briefly, so give your cartoon characters and product full attention by eliminating distracting backgrounds. Use simple lines, for instance, to denote cabinets for a kitchen scene. Staging is equally as important as background, so if your action can take place in one location, don't have characters chasing through many different scenes. If you want special effects, such as opticals that make products glow, sparkle or change, write them into your original storyboards. Extra production charges are made if you want to work them in later.

Movement of characters. Try to keep the movements of animated characters similar to those of a human being in the same situation. Remember that movement in animation should be exaggerated to be appreciated by viewers. Be sure they see that your character's wink is a wink, that a look of surprise is very surprised, lest these pieces of action be missed. Allow sufficient time for the movement to be grasped by viewers. Try to plan your animated spots rather loosely so that there is time for little bits of side action

228

KELLY , NASON
INCORPORATED
Advertising

Client: CHURCH & DWIGHT CO. INC.

Product: ARM & HAMMER BAKING SODA

Type: TV

Title: **WHAT TOOK YOU SO LONG**

Comm'l. No.:   **ZCTB-3145**

Length: **30 SECONDS**

MUFFLED SOUNDS OF ARGUING:
Help, Help! Keep your smelly hands
off me, etc.

OLD BOX: Remember me? I'm the
box of Baking Soda you left in the
refrigerator...Back then I could really
absorb those food odors...

ONION: Onion Power!!!

OLD BOX: Ah, if a new box doesn't
show up soon, a lot of food's gonna
get spoiled. ...Aah!

BAD FOODS: Oh oh!

GOODS FOODS: We're saved!!!

NEW BOX: You foods are gonna keep
your smells to yourselves!!!

BAD FOODS: Party Pooper!!!

ANNCR: If you can't remember the
last time you changed the
Baking Soda...

ANNCR: It's probably time to change
it again.

NEW BOX: Any last words?

OLD BOX: What took you so long?

that can give your commercial added interest and longer life.

Copy and narration. Consider the soundtrack of your commercial as consisting of two parts: the voice or narrative, and the music and sound effects. The best animated spots are written with a maximum of 85 to 100 words, rather than the 120 to 135 live-action count. This leaves room for the previously-mentioned bits of action that can enhance your effort. Give your character time to speak effectively, and write copy to fit the character's intended voice, rather than try to bend a character to fit copy.

Music and sound effects. These lend mood, action, tone, and emphasis that can "make" your animated commercial. If you are using offbeat or stylized art treatment, make the music suitable. Be sure the tempo of the music blends with your type of animation. Sound effects give impact and originality to your spot. If you want them, be sure to leave enough time for them in your script. They seldom fit when you try to squeeze them in later.

Timing the entire spot. Don't drag or zoom through your commercial. Good timing usually means writing a minute spot for 55 seconds, leaving some precious seconds available for consumption along the way. It is difficult to time an animated commercial because of the need to consider copy, music, and action. There's no surefire solution, but one of the safest approaches is to act out the commercial in its entirety.

Product package and logotype. With simple handling, animation (and stop-action photography) can do great things for your package or product. If your package has illustrations that are not in character with your style of animation, use artwork representation rather than the real package. You can use a matching dissolve from the artwork to the real package or logotype at the end of the spot. Emphasize important features of your package by bringing the elements off the box to full screen, as with a logotype that bounces off the package and then back on.

RECOMMENDED: ANIMATION PLUS LIVE ACTION

It is the consensus of almost all those who have worked with animation over a long period that the all-cartoon commercial should be approached with caution, for its promise generally outruns its performance. The main danger of pure animation is its

FIGURE 19-4

Pure animation.   Despite the light-hearted approach used in this commercial, it makes a strong point for the product—a good comination of entertainment and sell.

FIGURE 19-5

Pure animation.   "Pure" refers to fact that this commercial is entirely in animation. It does, however, combine the action with music. As in most animated commercials, the video dominates. Only sixty-nine words are used by the singers and the characters. Although the audio helps put over the message, the commercial would still make a point if no words were used. Notice the last frame in which the superimposed line is also sung by the voice-over singers.

over-commitment to entertainment at the cost of sacrificing copy ideas. The viewer is beguiled into enjoyment without being sold. The judicious use, however, of animation in conjunction with live action has much to recommend it. There are two basic types of this hybrid commercial: a) an opening animated segment (often comic or clever but containing the germ of the product story) is followed with a live straight sell; and b) a straightforward sales presentation that moves into animation after a live opening, usually to illustrate a product's "reason-why" story. The first type is best exemplified by commercials that often use an animated character with a catchy jingle, as an opening and then move into live-action scenes of the product in use. The second hybrid type is most often seen in commercials for patent remedies, which often employ diagrammatic views of visceral plumbing to illustrate the nature of their internal action. In

STAR-KIST TUNA TV COMMERCIAL
"FOOTBALL" HZST6040
Charlie's got the ball, but he can't score on Star-Kist.

This is one of the four new Charlie the Tuna Star-Kist TV commercials.
It will appear on all three networks and in important spot TV markets.

WALLY: Charlie - -
CHARLIE: Yeah?
WALLY: How d'ya play football?

CHARLIE: Easy - - you hand this
to a friend - -

WALLY: Yeah.
CHARLIE: - - and everybody else
jumps on him.

(SFX: CHARGING FEET)

(SFX: CHARGING FEET)

CHARLIE: It's a good taste
activity - -

college guys do it all the time.

Right Star-Kist.

WALLY: But Charlie, Star-Kist
doesn't want tunas with good taste - -
Star-Kist wants tunas that taste good.

ANNCR: Sorry Charlie - -

Only good tasting tuna get to be
Star-Kist.

Good tasting one hundred per
cent tuna fillet.

GIRL: This is good tasting tuna.

CHARLIE: Get good taste - -
get Star-Kist.

(SFX: FOOTSTEPS RUNNING)

FIGURE 19-6

Combination of animation and live action.   For years these entertaining commercials have amused viewers and sold the product.

either case, the flexibility of the live-plus-animated commercial allows the advertiser to blend exaggerated hyperbole or humor with naturalistic demonstration, to charm the viewer while selling him.

Combining live action and animation is effective, but can be expensive. An economical method is to use animated characters over still-photo shots of your product, giving you the depth of live action with the adaptability of animation. Another way of reducing expense is to use the same segment of animation to open or close an entire series of film spots. This lets you use your budget for animation of better quality or for more spots.

In trying to determine whether to use "live-on-film" or animated commercials for your particular product, there are some general considerations you'll recognize as helpful. Food products normally lend themselves better to television presentation with live action. The realism which can be gained by showing real people preparing and enjoying meals will almost always sell better than the cartoon characters with whom people cannot identify. The sales points of a new car, likewise, can best be demonstrated by actually showing a real person driving it, rather than showing drawings of the car.

Cosmetic selling usually needs the realism of beautiful people whose hair, lips, complexion and overall charm cannot possibly be captured in animation. On the other hand, many times you will be selling a service instead of a branded product. Sometimes when doing so, you can expect more memorability and attention if you invent an animated character to tell your story. Insurance selling, gasoline advertising, and bank and loan association commercials all lend themselves to the use of animation.

PRODUCTION TECHNIQUES

Assuming you are committed to the use of film (or tape) television commercials, there are five basic production techniques available to you:

- Live action
- Cartoon
- Stop motion
- Photo animation
- Puppets.

Live action

Similar to human, personal experience is the most believable technique in television commercials, live action. Viewers can identify with the action on the

screen and relate your commercial message to their own experience. While cartoons and puppets are figments of a fantasy world and stop-motion and photo animation are products of camera trickery, live action has the quality of genuine reality. There are two main types of live-action commercials: a) narrative style with the voices off-screen; and b) dialogue style with one or more persons speaking on screen, to each other or the audience.

Narrative style is less expensive, yet it has longer life expectancy because the speaker or speakers are not seen repeating the same story over and over, and thereby suffering loss of credulity. Narrative live action lends itself best to: demonstration, where the product is shown in use, with a voice presenting the sales story from off-screen; exposition, to set a scene quickly; human interest, to show family or other emotional settings; and appetite appeal, to show tempting dishes with the announcer's voice off-screen.

Dialogue has particular advantages for: personality commercials in which a name star or well-known announcer does the selling, job; testimonials by actual users; key copylines spoken by an actor as one part of a longer commercial.

The cost of live-action films, narrative or dialogue, varies a great deal because of the many factors involved: cast, settings, props, location trips, etc. Here again the matter of the SAG code and residual fees to talent used in live-action commercials has tended to switch some advertisers to other techniques. The move away from live action is not always wise, for its basic reality and faculty for reaching out to meet the viewer on common ground makes live action the most useful technique in television commercials.

Cartoon

As a television technique the cartoon is fun. It is high in viewer interest and it is probably lowest in cost per showing. While it wins interest quickly, it nonetheless lacks depth of penetration because it sacrifices credibility. Because viewers enjoy cartoons but don't believe them, most experienced advertisers will follow the cartoon segment of their commercials with real people using the product and repeating its benefits.

Cartoons are most effective for: gaining interest, at the opening of a spot by presenting some whimsical or fantastic situation, or an unusual character; trademark character, either the actual company or product trademark or one devised for purposes of a given campaign; personalizing the product, whereby a can of wax takes on life and personality with a cartoon face; fantasy, which enables just about any character or thing to do just about any type of action—an exercise in exaggeration to stimulate the imagination; singing jingles, because bouncy rhythms and cartoons are naturals that comprise one of television's longest-lived types of commercials.

FIGURE 19-7

Live action commercial with a twist.   The "twist" here is the thundering off-screen voice that delivers most of the product information in an important way that captures viewer attention. Notice the strong use of superimposition of words, usually a repetition of words that have been spoken.

GREY ADVERTISING, INC.

Client:	Drackett Co.	Date:	9/7
Product:	Drano	Code No.:	BMDR6023
Title:	"Talking Drano"		

Length: 30 seconds

1. CU woman (Susan) working at sink.

(SFX: Thunder)

MAN: (voice like that of giant or genie) Susan Warren,

2. CU Susan. Looks up startled as she holds Drano in hand.

MAN: where are you going with that Crystal Drano?

3. CU Susan looking toward voice, still holding can of Drano.

SUSAN: I'm unclogging my sink.

4. MCU of Susan and sink. Super words at top of screen: YOU MAY NEVER GET ANOTHER CLOG!

MAN: Suppose I tell you, you may never get another clog.

5. MCU Susan.

SUSAN: Come on. How?

6. ECU of sink drain. Super words at bottom of screen: USE WITH CAUTION. READ LABEL CAREFULLY.

MAN: You're using a tablespoon of Drano, right?

7. CU Susan looking sober. Super words at bottom of screen.

SUSAN: Sure. It works.

8. CU Susan looking sober.

MAN: Just do that every week. Only costs 6¢.

9. CU Susan looking alarmed.

SUSAN: Every week? Won't it hurt my pipes?

10. MCU Susan. Super words at top of screen: WOULD DRANO LET YOU HURT YOUR PIPES?

MAN: (in great, thundering voice) Would Drano let you hurt your pipes?

11. CU Susan looking up gratefully at voice.

SUSAN: Okay. Okay. Drano once a week, and...

12. CU can of Drano. Super words at top of screen: YOU MAY NEVER GET ANOTHER CLOG!

MAN: You may never get another clog.

There are three grades among cartoons: full animation, limited animation, and "grow" or "scratch-off" cartoon, in order of decreasing cost and effectiveness. Cost depends largely on what moves in your cartoon, since as many as seven artists may work on each frame of a full-animation cartoon. At 24 frames per second, this means as many as 1,440 drawings may be needed for a one-minute spot. It thus behooves you to use no more characters than absolutely necessary in your commercial, and to work closely with your animation director to make maximum use of cycles of the same sequence of pictures wherever possible, especially for backgrounds. A limited animation, which costs about half as much as full, makes full use of cycles, often shows only extremes of facial expression and relies heavily on camera movement and lens tricks. The grow cartoon cuts costs in two again. It works with a single drawing, photographed from the rear as lines are scratched off on successive frames. When projected in the opposite direction, the cartoon seems to grow or be drawn on the screen.

Cartoons are honest fun and, as such, can do a selling job for impulse-purchase types of products. Where there is substantial reason-why for the purchaser to buy, cartoons need support from live action, as previously discussed.

Making the hundreds of drawings necessary to depict movement in animated commercials has always required a huge amount of expensive art time. Just having a character lift her arm above her head can, for instance, entail many drawings because each drawing depicts only the slightest movement upward. Now, computers have stepped into the art and can be used to supply the detailed drawings for certain types of animation. They don't replace artists, but they relieve them of the tedious line-by-line renderings of animated movement.

Stop motion

The ingenious technique that makes inanimate objects come to life is stop motion. This type of animation is accomplished by using a camera adjusted to move one or two frames at a time. Between exposures the objects are moved slightly or changed with the thought of continuous action when projected at normal speed. Stop action should be confined to inanimate objects, since actors cannot remain in one position long enough for this type of shooting. This technique provides an impressive way to introduce packaged products. For example, a number of packages shown unevenly spaced on a table suddenly assemble themselves into a neat display. The scene cuts to a close-up, then one package unwraps itself, and out hops the product. Automobile doors open and close by themselves, or packages march across the screen.

The advantages offered by stop motion relate to: personalizing the product, as in the marching cigarettes or other products that are made to fly, dance, walk, zoom or take themselves apart; mechanical action, as in fitting parts of a motor or showing how attachments are used on appliances; and demonstration, without human hands, as in a commercial showing a wall oven that opens itself and a roast slides out. In the first of these advantages, stop motion shares with cartoons the ability to personalize a product, while in the last it vies with live action in its faculty for demonstration. It seems advisable here, too, to combine stop motion with a followup live action, pairing up the interest-rouser with the realistic demonstration.

FIGURE 19-8

Live action dramatized commercial.   Identification for the company name is the aim of this commercial used in a well-known campaign.

BFGoodrich

"POPS" :30

1st MAN: What kind o' tires are those, son?

2nd MAN: Goodrich Radials, Gramps.

1st MAN: I don't remember having those.

What's he done with those...

2nd MAN: Radials, Gramps, He rotated them so they'll last longer.

And the Goodrich dealer said it'll save me money.

1st MAN: I don't remember rotating tires either. Who makes those?

2nd MAN: Goodrich, Gramps.

1st MAN: Oh, I remember them.

The fellows with the blimp.

The most beautiful sight I ever saw. Floatin' up there...

ANNCR: (VO) Tires you can trust. B.F. Goodrich. The Other Guys.

Photo animation

The technique that sends bottles spinning and boxes zooming across the televiewer's screen is photo animation. It is the method that the low-budget advertiser can use to excellent advantage to achieve impressive effects, largely through the camera's movement and optical tricks. It has been called "Fotan" by many producers and the technique lends itself best to: special announcements, in which titles and tricks are the main elements, as in coming attractions for movies; signatures at the end of most commercials in which the package, logotype or slogan pop on to the screen, often in synchronization with voice copy; retouching products, as in appliances of chrome and glass, using still photographs which are then reproduced on motion picture film with dissolves or other optical tricks to achieve a dramatic effect; catalog of products, where an inclusive line of related items can be presented quickly, clearly and, again, with startling pop-on effect.

Photo animation is not advisable to use with live action, for it works only with separate still photographs or drawings. To move an inanimate object in a live-action scene involves costly optical treatment. An example of Fotan at work was shown on behalf of a liquidizer that made tomato juice out of tomatoes, cole slaw out of cabbage, and crushed ice out of ice cubes. Still photos of the original items were shown at top left of the screen. They moved in procession to the center and were whirled downward in the appliance and finally emerged at bottom right as completed dishes. Truly graphic!

Puppets

As a television production technique, puppets have enjoyed only a fair success. The creation and manipulation of them, usually as trademark characters, have been too limited to achieve best results. There are three types of puppets used for television commercials: string, hand, and stop-motion puppets. The first two types require the continuity of a regular program to establish viewer interest. "Kukla, Fran, and Ollie" were notably successful among hand puppets, principally because of their creator's skill in investing them with all the characteristics of human beings. The frame-by-frame or stop-motion puppets have achieved most renown in this area for they show expression, animation, and characterization without the need for manipulation by hand or string and without the limitation of one-expression faces. These puppets operate within miniature scale settings and are photographed one frame at a time, with the doll's body being moved and its head changed to match the next move called for in the commercial.

Summary of best uses of techniques

Live action (narrative) is best used for demonstration, human interest, and exposition.

Live action (dialogue) is best used for testimonials, personality commercials, dramatic spots, and key copylines.

Cartoon (full animation) is best used for developing trademark characters, personalizing products, exaggeration and fantasy, and singing jingles.

Stop motion is best used for demonstration, mechanical action, and personalizing product.

Photo animation is best used for titles and signatures, retouching products, and catalog of products.

Puppets (stop-motion type) are best used for trademark characters and singing jingles.

WHO'S THE SPONSOR? WHAT'S THE PRODUCT?

A dismaying fact of life for the television advertiser is that a huge portion of the viewing audience cannot remember whose commercials they saw on a show they have watched night after night—this, despite the millions poured into television advertising by the advertiser.

Only one viewer in four may be able to identify the sponsor of a show, or the product advertised on it. Sometimes the figure goes even lower. Furthermore, in addition to lack of identification, there is misidentification wherein the viewer credits a competitor and names his product as the one advertised on a show. Thus, Post cereal may be identified as Kellogg's, or Goodrich as Goodyear.

What with television clutter, offering a profusion of thirty-second commercials, billboards, promos, local program break spots, and public service commercials, it's no surprise that the viewer is hazy about who is advertising what product.

As the writer, what can you do to improve the showing for your client? First, of course, you use a strong, selling idea in the commercial. In addition, here are some devices and approaches that may help memorability and sponsor or product identification:

Avoid themes too much like your competitor's. This is especially true if your product is not the leader in the field. Any confusion about the identity of the advertiser tends strongly to result in the leader being remembered, not the runnerup.

Establish a strong campaign theme. When you know the theme is good, fight to keep it going. When advertisers change a campaign theme, they risk confusion and throw away the recognition they have built up. With confusion comes lack of identification or misidentification.

Use a strong presenter for the product. A likable, believable presenter can do wonders for product identification if used consistently over a long period of time, especially if the presenter puts on an interesting demonstration of the product. A good example is shown in various television commercials for coffeemakers. After a while, the name of the presenter and your product are automatically linked—a link that becomes even stronger if you use the presenter in print copy, too. A possible danger in the use of a strong presenter is that the audience will remember the presenter, not the product, because of interest in the presenter. Careful creative work, however, can avoid the problem.

Use powerful demonstrations. There's good memorability in a realistic demonstration, much more so than a mere relating of product facts. Watch out for comparative demonstrations, however, because if your product is being demonstrated against the leader's product, his product may be credited with your product's better performance. Comparative advertising is, in fact, a dangerous technique that can turn on you. If your demonstration has great strength in itself, you may not wish to take the risk of a comparative demonstration.

Make the product-name registration strong. Use techniques that enable you to bring in the name emphatically and frequently, not just in the opening and close. Likewise, the more you can keep your product on camera, the better for identification. Weaving the product and product name (and package) into commercials is a particular talent of Stan Freberg's whose humorous commercials have sold great quantities of his clients' products. Without diminishing interest or humor, he works in the name of the advertiser's product frequently as in one commercial that showed a theater of people shouting the name of the product as it was flashed on the screen. No television viewer could fail to know what product was advertised in <u>that</u> commercial.

Other techniques for emphasis

- Call for close-ups to be more vivid and personal—and do it quickly. If you start with an establishing shot, use it for only a few seconds.
- Develop your video first. If you write the audio before the video, you're simply writing a radio commercial with pictures and thus chancing a loss of the inherent drama in a commercial that emphasises the visual.
- Use superimposition when you want reinforcement. The "super" should be used sparingly, but when it is, you'll increase the impact by saying in the audio the words flashed on the screen. Limit the number of words on the screen.
- Occasionally use the split screen to hold attention. A two-way split is easier for the viewer to follow, but the four-way split can be an attention-getter.

SOME FINAL POINTS OF EVALUATION

Before concluding this chapter, it may be profitable to imagine that you have a finished television commercial script in front of you. How can you size up its potential? Its creative worth? Its practicability from a production standpoint? Here are a few telegraphic queries on areas of your commercial that have been discussed in this chapter and which you'll do well to keep in mind in reading and evaluating the scripts which you may be writing:

- Does the video tell the story without audio, and how well?
- Is the video fully graphic (specifying technique, describing staging and camera action)?

FIGURE 19-9

Rough storyboard for a demonstration commercial.   This first rough storyboard was prepared for presentation to the client and for production purposes. Inevitably, changes will be made in the final version—changes suggested by the client, the production people, the creative department, and others involved with the commercial.

- Does the audio "listen" well (language, pacing)?
- Do the audio and video complement each other and are they correctly timed for each other (act it out)?
- Are there too many scenes (can some be omitted)? Do you need more scenes?
- How well have you identified the product?
- Does your script win attention quickly and promise an honest benefit?
- How well have you "demonstrated"?
- Have you provided a strong visualization of the one major claim that will linger in the viewer's memory?
- Could a competitive brand be substituted easily and fit well? (Better not.)
- Is it believable? (Always ask this.)
- Are you proud to say you wrote it?

FIGURE 19-10

Final version of demonstration commercial shown in Figure 19-9.   Inspection of the rough storyboard and this photoboard version will reveal a number of changes. The photoboard was distributed to retailers to let them know about the upcoming spot. This is a common practice. Incidentally, the commercial was judged among the "100 best" for the year it was used.

SUMMARY

Nobody can tell you exactly how to write a television commercial. Nobody can tell you exactly what to say or what to show. These are things that can come to you only with time and experience. In this chapter you have been given an idea of what you will be expected to know about television commercial writing and, to a lesser extent, production.

Remember however, that as television improves technically and creatively, the scope of your activities in the field will broaden and the challenge to your resources will be greater. Only by increasing its effectiveness can the television commercial pay the everincreasing bill. This will increase your responsibility considerably.

A BRIEF GLOSSARY OF TELEVISION TERMS

The following glossary has some of the more frequently used terms in preparing and producing a commercial. As you study them, keep in mind that this is a book about copywriting and not television production. For those interested, there are detailed texts on television production.

ACROSS THE BOARD.   A program scheduled three, five, or six days a week at the same time.

AD LIB.   Impromptu action or speech not written into script; or, in music, to play parts not in the music.

ADJACENCIES.   Shows (on same station) immediately preceding and following the program referred to.

AFM.   American Federation of Musicians.

AFTRA.   American Federation of Television and Radio Artists.

ANGLE SHOT.   Camera shot of the subject taken from any position except straight.

ANIMATE.   To arrange and film static drawings or objects so that when the photographs are shown cinematographically, they produce the illusion of movement.

ASCAP.   American Society of Composers, Authors, and Publishers, which licenses public performances of music of its members and collects royalties.

BACKGROUND   OR   REAR-VIEW   PROJECTION.   Special technique whereby a wanted scene drawn from special photo or stock library is projected on a translucent screen which acts as a background for a studio set.

BACK-TIME.   To time a script backwards from end to beginning, with running time indicated every 15 seconds or less in the margin of the script, to keep the show "on the nose."

BALOP.   Short for balopticon, which is a projection mechanism used in television to project objects, photographs, and still pictures on to the mosaic element of television tube.

BILLBOARD.   Announcement at the beginning of show which lists people starred or featured.

BIT.   Small appearance or few lines in show. One who plays it is called a "bit player."

BMI.   Broadcast Music, Inc., competitors of ASCAP.

BOOM.   Crane-like device for suspending microphone or camera in mid-air and moving it from one position to another.

BRIDGE.   Slide, picture, sound effects, or music used to cover a jump in time or other break in continuity.

CAMERA OR CUE LIGHT. Red light on front of camera which is lit only when camera is on the air.

CAMERA RIGHT-LEFT. Indication of direction in a setting as viewed from the point of view of the camera or televiewer.

CAMERA SHOTS. (Referring to people) Head shot, only the head; Shoulder shot, shoulders and head; Full shot, entire person. (Referring to objects) CU, close-up or narrow angle picture limited to object or part of it; no background; MCU, medium close-up; TCU, tight close-up; LS, long shot in which figures are smaller than frame and sensation of distance is achieved; FoS, follow shot in which camera follows talent; RevS, reverse shot in which same object already on one camera is picked up from an exactly opposite angle by another camera; DI-DU, dolly in and up. DO-DB, dolly out and back.

CLEAR A NUMBER. To get legal permission to use specific musical selection.

COVER SHOT. Wide angle television picture to alternate (for contrast) with close-up.

COW-CATCHER. Isolated commercial at start of show which advertises a product of the sponsor not mentioned in program itself.

CUT. Switch directly from one camera picture to another and speed up action for dramatic effect.

D.B. Delayed broadcast of a live show.

DISSOLVE. Fading out of one picture as another fades in; to denote passage of time and present smooth sequence of shots.

DOLLY. Movable fixture or carriage for carrying camera (and cameraman) about during taking of shots.

DOUBLE SPOTTING. Also triple spotting. Station practice of placing a second or third commercial right after the first.

DOWN-AND-UNDER. Direction given to a musician or sound effects person to bring down playing level and sneak under dialogue lines that follow.

DUBBING. Mixing several soundtracks and recording them on a single film.

ET. Electrical transcription, usually 33-1/3 rpm's.

FANFARE. Few bars of music (usually trumpets) to herald start of show or commercial.

FILM CUE. Perforation in film to indicate time remaining.

FLUFF. Any mistake, action, word or phrase accidentally included, resulting in an imperfect sound or picture.

HIATUS. Summer period, usually weeks, during which sponsor may discontinue his program, but thereafter resume his time period until the next hiatus.

HIGHLIGHT. Emphasizing a subject or scene by special lighting or painting to make it stand out from the rest of the picture.

HOOK. Program device used to attract tangible response from the audience; for example, an offer, a contest, etc.

ID. TV station identification or call letters (or 10-second commercial).

IDIOT CARDS. Cue sheets attached to the front of camera, or blackboard and printed reminder sheets out of camera range to prompt talent in delivering lines.

INHERITED AUDIENCE. Portion of a program's audience which listened to preceding show on same station.

KILL. To strike out or remove part or all of a scene, set, action or show.

LEAD-IN. Words spoken by announcer or narrator at beginning of show or commercial to set a scene or recapitulate some previous action.

LIP SYNC. Direct recording of sound from scene that is being filmed; usually refers to film commercials in which actors can be seen with lips moving.

LIVE. "On-the-spot" television of events or people in contrast to transmission of film, videotape or kinescope material.

LOCAL. Show or commercial originating in local station as contrasted to network.

MAKE GOOD. Offer to sponsor of comparable facilities as substitute for TV show or announcement cancelled because of emergency; or offer to repeat a commercial, without charge for time, because of some mistake or faulty transmission.

MONITORING. To check show or spot content and transmission with on-the-air picture.

NARTB. National Association of Radio and Television Broadcasters.

OPTICAL. Trick effect done mechanically, permitting the combining of two or more pictures in one, creating wipes, montages, dissolves, fades and other effects.

PACKAGE. Special show or series of shows bought by an advertiser, which includes all components ready to telecast.

PAD. To add action, sound, or any other material to fill the required on-the-air time.

PAN. Gradual swinging of camera to left or right across a scene to see segments of it as camera moves.

PARTICIPATING PROGRAM. A single TV show sponsored by more than one advertiser.

PLAY-BACK. Reproduction of a soundtrack in studio during film shooting to enable action or additional sound or both to be synchronized with action; also, playing or recording for audition or reference purposes immediately after spot is made.

PLUG. Mention of a name, show or advertised product; or, loosely speaking, the commercial announcement.

PROCESS SHOT. Film combining real photography with projected backgrounds or model sets or drawings.

PROJECTORS. Used in TV for still material. They include: Balop, which takes cards or opaques (no transparencies); balop card size is usually 3″ x 4″ or 6″ x 8″. Also, Projectall, which takes both opaque cards and transparencies or slides; card size is 3″ x 4″; slides, 2″ x 2″.

PUNCH IT. To accent or emphasize an action, sound effect, music, or line of dialogue.

RATING. Percentage of a statistical sample of TV viewers interviewed personally, checked by telephone, or noted in viewing diary, who reported viewing a specific TV show.

RESIDUALS. Payments (required by the Screen Actors Guild) to talent for each broadcast of each film commercial on each network program per thirteen weeks' usage. If same commercial is used in spot markets, payment is additional per quarter.

SAG. Screen Actors Guild.

SEGUE (pronounced seg-way). Usually the transition from one musical number to another without any break or talk.

SETS-IN-USE. Percentage of all TV homes in a given locality whose sets are tuned in at a specific time, regardless of the station being viewed.

SFX. Abbreviation for sound effects.

SHARE-OF-AUDIENCE. Percentage of viewers watching a given show or station based on the total sets-in-use.

SLIDE. Usually refers to still art work, titles, photographs or film which are picked up or projected upon camera tube. Slides are of two types: transparent or opaque, their size varying according to station projection method used.

SPONSOR IDENTIFICATION. Percentage of viewers of a show or personality who can identify the name of the sponsor or are familiar with specific data about the product advertised on TV.

SPOT TV. Market-by-market buying of TV time (programs, announcements, participations, station breaks). It affords flexibility in adapting a TV ad campaign to time zone, seasonal variations, special merchandising plans, etc.

STATION TIME. Portion of a station's schedule not normally available for network programs; totals three out of every six clock hours.

STOP MOTION. Film taken by exposing one frame instead of a number of frames at a time. Objects are usually moved by hand a fraction of an inch for each exposure according to a set pattern.

TAKE. Single shot picture or scene held by TV camera; also, command to switch directly from one picture or camera to another, as "ready one—take one."

TALENT COST. Expense or cost (for music, talent, etc.) of a show or commercial aside from the time charge.

TELEFEX. Rear-view projection system for special effects, backgrounds, etc.

TELEPROMPTER. Rolling script device for talent who have difficulty in learning lines. Lines are printed large enough to be read at distance on sheet which revolves, keeping pace with show's action.

TRANSCRIPTION. Recording of highest quality, usually at 33-1/3 rpm, especially made for telecast or broadcast.

UNDER. Show that does not use all its allotted time; also, to sustain and subordinate one facet of the drama or situation under another.

VIDEOTAPE. A system that records both sound and pictures simultaneously on magnetic tape; offers great advantage of immediate playback plus exceptionally fine picture fidelity. In one day, commercials can be completed on tape that previously took three weeks in running through film processing.

VO OR VOICE-OVER. Narration-type recording as opposed to lip sync or live sound; also, voice-over narration where voice talent is not seen.

WIPE. Transition from one scene or image to another in which new scene replaces old one in some gradually increasing geometric pattern, that is, circle (circle in, circle out), square (expanding square), fan, roll, etc.

WORD COUNT. Number of words that will fit comfortably into a commercial of a specific length. Rule of thumb for television commercials is 2 words per second, although count will vary depending on type of commercial. Word count for radio is higher, approximating 170 words per minute spot.

ZIP-PAN. Effect obtained by swinging camera so quickly around from one point of rest to another that between the two the picture is blurred.

CAMERA SHOTS

Sooner, or later, if you work in television you must learn to distinguish between the various distances represented by the terms "long shot," "close-up," and others. There's no precision in these terms in the sense of their being defined in a definite number of feet. The following guide makes particular reference to the package so often the central object in television commercials:

Tight close-up (TCU). Camera brings viewer so close he gets startling detail—perhaps a portion of a package or can, such as the product name, or trademark. Often used for this purpose. Depending upon where you work, might also be called ECU (Extreme close-up) or VCU (Very close-up).

Close-up (CU). Here you zero in on an object, or part of an object. Instead of just the product name, as in the TCU, you get the entire package in the camera's eye. Instead of just the lips of a person, you get the whole face, or possibly head and shoulders. Extraneous details are omitted in the close-up.

Medium close-up. You draw back from the close-up. You still see the package, but you also see that it's on a table with a mixing bowl and other items. As the viewer, you sense that the package is important, but you see it in relation to other objects.

Medium shot. (MS). The package loses some of its importance in this shot in which some details are lost as if the viewer had backed up a few feet from the MCU position. He sees the MCU objects, but now he may see them in relation to people in the spot.

Medium long shot (MLS). You're close enough to recognize characters but far enough back to include items in the setting (such as the package) and to convey some of the background setting.

Long shot (LS). Often this is called an "establishing" shot. It might include barely recognizable people, along with an entire room setting, but the package is now just one of many objects and may not even be noticed. The long shot, used outdoors, may be panoramic in its showing of trees, a portion of a lake, and people who may be discerned as individuals.

Extreme long shot (ELS). As a panoramic shot this can take in a vast expanse of desert, mountains, or a whole lake. People can be detected but not as individuals. Again, like the long shot, this may be an establishing device to introduce dramatically what is to follow. Needless to say, we've lost our package entirely.

The Copywriter's Helper: Research

A copywriter in a small advertising agency is talking: "No. We don't use research. Our clients can't afford it, and with our small profit margin, we can't afford to pay for it ourselves. So we get along on experience and common sense."

We hear from a mail order copywriter: "Research? Of course. There's no guesswork around here. We test by results and that includes every element: headlines, body copy, illustrations, effect of color, coupons, timing, position, nature of the offer, etc., etc."

The big advertising agency copywriter says: "Yes. Our clients are sophisticated advertisers. They budget a healthy sum for research. Much of it is initiated and paid for by their market research division which also gets into copytesting. A lesser amount is paid for out of our funds. As for techniques, we draw upon everything from the simplest types to motivational research and G&R's impact testing. It's a great help, but we still do many ads that simply reflect judgment."

Perhaps you will set up your own homemade research method. Many copywriters do. Retail copypeople, for example, have devised so many individual copy-checking systems that it is impossible to list them all. Some are very good; others are very bad.

YOU CAN'T BE SURE

Since the first piece of copy was written, there has never been any real certainty regarding the effect of copy upon the consumer prior to its actual publication. There have been many uncertainties. From the start it was known that consumer reaction to advertisements was variable. An appeal that worked during one year might fail the next year. Even on a day-to-day or week-to-week basis the success of advertisements is uncertain. There have been attempts to take the uncertainty out of advertising. "Foolproof" systems have been devised to eliminate guesswork in copy. Consumers and their reactions to copy appeals, headlines, and illustrations have been studied as scientists study the beetle and his activities. It would be pleasant to relate that the research has been completely successful—but it hasn't. There are still uncertainties. As long as people themselves are so uncertain, there will always be a quantity of "by guess and by gosh" in copywriting. The weather, the political picture, the news, epidemics, and a thousand other variables can affect the success of a piece of copy. If any one of the variables is hard at work, the most scientifically conceived job of copywriting can fail.

Most copy-researchers admit the variables. They admit that it is difficult to predict the exact degree of success or failure for any single piece of copy. They can merely predict that the copy should be successful or unsuccessful. Copy research is greatly concerned with development of techniques for measuring copy's effectiveness before its appearance in print or in radio commercials—and then with analyzing why it failed or succeeded after its appearance. Some smart advertisers are high-readership advocates. They reason, "If they don't read it, they won't buy it because they don't know about it." Opponents say, "If a thousand persons read but only one buys, high readership means nothing. Advertisements pay off on conviction, not mere readership." Many advertising people believe in checklists. Others ridicule their use. Some say that only in returns from mail-order advertising can copy effectiveness be measured. Many will refute the assertion by pointing out the innumerable variables that will affect results even in this situation. There are, therefore, many measuring techinques for copy but certainly no complete agreement on them.

As a copywriter you should know what's going on. You should know the merits and faults of the different testing techniques, but you must be careful to avoid two dangerous traps:

- Don't let yourself become so sold on any one method of copy research that you are blinded to the merits of other types of research. Remember, there is no perfect research method.
- Don't get so bogged down in the mazes of copy research that you forget to write copy that is vigorous, spontaneous, and alive. There is no substitute for the warm, human writing that digs down deep into the consumers' desires and makes them want to buy your product—just because you've produced persuasive copy born out of humanness, intuition, and plain, good writing. You can be too scientific in your copy approach and tangle yourself in formula.

It is useful, however, to make some pre and post analysis. Such research often stops the advertiser from plunging into an expensive but foolish campaign. It also indicates need for a change in a current campaign. You can save much money and effort if you understand proper research techniques.

PRETEST AND POSTTEST TECHNIQUES

Think of the copy-research techniques as falling into two general groups: before (pretest) and after (posttest).

On the before side you can apply such techniques as:

- Focused group interviews
- Checklist
- Inquiry or direct-response tests
- Split-run tests
- Readability tests (Flesch formula)
- Eye camera tests
- Motivational research

On the after side:

- Readership study (recognition, identification, recall, and impact method)
- Tachistoscope
- Sales test

The remainder of this chapter will consider the methods of researching copy before publication or broadcast and then will consider the techniques used after publication.

FOCUSED GROUP INTERVIEWS (CONSUMER PANEL)

Sometime, if you haven't already done so, you will probably try out some copy on other students, your wife, your secretary, your mother, or strangers. "Just trying to get consumer reaction," you'll explain. The focused group interview is a more elaborate way to do the same thing.

Instead of arbitrarily selecting one person as your guinea pig, you will select a number of persons. Each will be a typical potential buyer of the product for which you are testing the copy. In addition to being typical, group members must also be interested—that is, "interested in the product." Copy for MODEL chewing tobacco should not be submitted to group members who have not, and never will, use this type of product. The group's rating of your advertising helps you determine possible reader-reaction in advance of publication. If the group members can never be interested in your product, they are not competent to rate your advertisements, since what would appeal to them would not, in many cases, appeal to the regular or potential user.

Order-of-merit ranking. A focused group ranks different advertisements for the same product. Two or more advertisements are presented to the individual members who are asked to indicate, "Which of these advertisements do you like best?" or "Which of these advertisements would be most likely to make you want to buy the product?" All advertisements are thus rated until they are ranked in order of preference. This is sometimes called order-of-merit ranking.

Paired-comparison technique. Another method is the paired-comparison technique, wherein advertisements are judged in pairs. The respondent picks what he thinks is the better advertisement in each pair. Then, through elimination, the best of all the advertisements is selected. Usually this system is used for choosing an approach, format, or theme rather than individual advertisements in one pattern.

Many times different elements of the advertisements are rated. For instance, your advertisements might be identical except for the headlines, which will be rated in comparison with each other. The next rating will compare illustrations, the next copy appeal, and so on.

Focused group interviews do in a group what depth interviews do on an individual basis. A group leader by introducing stimuli (advertisements, parts of advertisements, products, packages) thus stirs an informal discussion among the six to twelve persons in the group. An interesting result of group interviews is the sometimes startling frankness with which group members will discuss subjects that could hardly be approached in the individual depth interview. Likewise, because group members usually try hard to contribute, it will often be found that the group will contribute more points and more talk than will be obtained from the individual interview.

Why the focused group method is used

Although the focused group method has been useful for indicating how an advertisement might fare in the final published form, it has faults mixed with its virtues. On the plus side of the focused group method:

Good results. In many instances there has been a satisfactory correlation between group ratings and selling power of the advertisements rated. This correlation has been good enough, despite the faults of the method, to justify its continued use in pretesting copy.

Speed. Once the group has been selected, the job of rating the advertisements can ordinarily be done speedily and easily.

Moderate cost. A few interviewers equipped with copies of comprehensive layouts can do the whole job. A good many advertisements or separate advertising elements can be rated in one session, thus reducing the cost per unit tested.

Consumer viewpoint. You tend to overlook the consumer in some forms of copy research. You think of appeals, copy approach, or the market. The focused group makes you think of the market in terms of persons who view advertisements with like, dislike, or indifference. If you follow the ratings of a focused group, you are being guided by the preferences of a representative segment of your consumer target rather than by your personal, and possibly isolated, judgment. Too, your respondents are classified as to age, work, income, and other aspects.

Focused group testing has its difficulties

As in the case of most copy-research methods, it is easier to pick flaws in the group interview than to find virtues. The following list doesn't condemn the method as useless but provides you with some reservations. It should also indicate to you some weaknesses to avoid should you attempt to set up a group.

Respondents. Finding the right person to serve on a consumer group is vital to the success of the method. Determining just what is "typical" and then finding persons who fit that description is likely to be a slow, tedious task. The requirement that such persons be "interested" in a particular product provides a double complication.

Difficult to make conclusions. The questions usually asked of a consumer group fail to obtain a final answer. Examine the two questions again: Which of these advertisements do you like better? Which of these two advertisements would be more likely to make you want to buy the product?

The first question has nothing to do with sales potential. The respondents may like the advertisement because the illustration features a beautiful person. The rest of the layout may please them; they might even read and like the copy. All this, however, might not have the slightest influence in making them buy the spark plugs being advertised. Their favorable answer for a particular advertisement was based upon subjective factors having nothing to do with influencing them to buy.

The second question, although it is aimed more at determining buying behavior, asks respondents to indicate how they might act. There is a great difference between a person's intentions and subsequent

actions. Some copy evaluators have combined the answers to the two questions. The combining is not practical. One question measures liking for an advertisement on a basis entirely removed from buying behavior. The other attempts to measure buying potential. Combining these two unlikes is tricky and conclusions thus derived would be questionable.

Separating elements is dangerous. Although there is some value in dissecting advertising elements and letting the group judge headlines, illustration, and other items individually, the process is somewhat unrealistic. A person thumbing through a magazine is looking at advertisements, not headlines or illustrations. The general rating seems to be more accurate, according to the findings of the Advertising Research Foundation. Probably the best procedure is to use both methods—individual element rating and general rating. Both should then be analyzed carefully before the findings are accepted. It seems dubious in any event that final judgment of an advertisement should be based on a rating of the separate parts. Remember, some women taken feature by feature are not attractive. Assemble the features and you may have a charming result. An advertisement taken by sections may not be noteworthy. Combine elements and the result is often a persuasive, compelling advertisement.

Group members become copy "experts." Almost everyone feels competent to criticize advertisements. Group members thus frequently forget their consumer function and begin to act like copy chiefs. The tendency causes real trouble, since the group members thus are no longer "typical" consumer prospects. Instead, they have become professional critics. When they no longer view the advertisements with a consumer's eyes, their usefulness as group members has ended.

Hard to compare more than two advertisements. Although many consumer groups are asked to compare more than two advertisements at a time, it is often questionable that more than two should be compared—at the most three. The fewer the elements to be considered, the more reliable the judgment is likely to be. Thus the paired-comparison method may be preferable to that which gives the respondent the task of giving rank order to six different advertisements. If he does his job conscientiously, the respondent will probably be confused as he considers all the elements found in six advertisements. It is difficult enough to obtain reliable opinions from consumer groups without complicating the task further by confusing them. The paired-comparison method at least eliminates some of the confusion.

Size of the sample. Although the trend has been toward small samples, the sample size may often have to be varied for different types of products, or if the voting is so close on certain advertisements that the advertiser must ask for additional votes.

Impractical for certain items. Some products of

infrequent purchase such as figure skates or short-wave transmitters are not suitable for group interviews. Such products call for unusual promotions; ordinary testing procedures are not so suited to them as to ordinary items of everyday purchase like cereals, milk, or coffee.

Prestige factor is operative. Group interviewing, like any procedure requiring decision on the part of respondents is often inaccurate because of the respondents' pride or vanity. Respondents not wanting to admit that a sexy illustration is appealing, will vote against it although under actual reading conditions the same illustration would win delighted attention. Intellectuals might be unwilling to admit that motion picture star endorsements attract and convince them. As long as people are subject to vanity, the prestige factor will be at work in situations like those set up by the group copy-testing procedure.

Test measures standings—not quality of advertisement. Respondents are asked to rate advertisements in 1-2-3 order. This system is followed whether advertisements are good or bad. In some tests all the advertisements might be poor. The rating would simply indicate which was the least objectionable. The No. 1 advertisement might be used because the group voted for it, not because it had merit.

Campaigns are overlooked. Most national advertising is campaign advertising. One advertisement, by itself, might not have the push and appeal that it has as one of a series of advertisements. Yet the consumer group may be asked to judge an individual advertisement, ignoring the cumulative effect of the campaign. For instance, a *Ladies' Home Journal* advertisement featuring the campaign idea "Never underestimate the power of a woman" becomes powerful through repetition, as does the *Philadelphia Bulletin* advertisement which tells you that "In Philadelphia nearly everyone reads the Bulletin." Although it is unlikely that such advertisements would ever be used in group testing (since they are not for consumer products), they provide a good illustration of the point being made here.

In both campaigns, the usual reader, when glancing over a particular advertisement, is not reading one advertisement but is receiving the smashing impact of all the advertisements of a given series. Perhaps such a person was half-sold before reading this last advertisement, which acted as a sales clincher. Our reader has been sold by the campaign. Any one advertisement in the campaign might not have sold this person. Yet the consumer group judges one advertisement in an attempt to answer the question "Which advertisement would be most likely to make you buy the product?" That one advertisement might fit in very poorly with the campaign, and with most national advertisers the campaign is the important consideration. That is why, in many cases, national advertisers will continue to emphasize a campaign even though it is tempting to put all the

emphasis on a current prize contest. Long-run considerations, however, are not necessarily a part of a consumer group's thinking.

Conditions are not natural. No matter how skilled the interviewer, or how well the questions are phrased, the conditions under which the consumer group operates are not normal home-reading conditions. The group member cannot help being less casual than in reading in the home. In this test this person is on the alert for faults; the very act of comparing is unrealistic. Certainly, the usual reader will not match advertisements against each other. Also reading under group conditions allows undivided attention to the individual advertisements. Under more usual conditions, there would be the competition from surrounding advertisements. There would be unfavorable position. In finished printed form, one advertisement might gain over another through better type, use of color, and other mechanical factors.

Summary of focused group interviewing

To sum up, the focused group method is used so widely that you should know how it works. You should know that it has some virtues and many faults. Let it guide you, but have the proper reservations. Get in the habit of questioning the results of this or any other copy-testing method. They are all fallible. All these faults will not be present in each use of the focused group method. Clever researchers can eliminate nearly all the difficulties. The test will never be free from all the faults, however—a fact to keep in mind.

For television and radio commercial testing, the group method offers the same virtues and shortcomings as in print testing.

CHECKLISTS

Before you engage in the use of checklists, you had better clarify the meaning of the term. (See Appendix for examples of checklists.)

Practically everyone who has written copy has used a checklist at one time or another. Usually, the list will be a simple little affair—a casual reminder to put in certain important elements such as the slogan, price mention, and selling conditions. Other checklists bring in more elements to watch for. They keep the copywriter on the track without attempting to provide any scientific preevaluation as to the effectiveness of the advertisements.

The checklist, in its ultimate form, goes beyond reminding. It attempts, as in the case of the elaborate systems worked out a number of years ago, to serve as a yardstick for preevaluating the effectiveness of advertising. So confident were the proponents of checklist evaluations that they made assertions such as one man's that through use of his system, you could tell a good advertisement from a bad advertisement before publication in nine minutes flat.

Some of the opponents, however, assert that:

1. Originators of checklist evaluation techniques are engaged in a meaningless battle of points with each such originator simply trying to outdo the other in dreaming up new point lists
2. Checklist preevaluation methods hamstring, originality
3. Copywriters use points by instinct
4. Personal judgment is overemphasized in the checklist system.

Checklists—criticisms

Since sooner or later you will probably be engaged in a discussion of checklists, the four arguments just given are examined here.

Checklists degenerate in a battle of points. True enough. If you use a formal checklist, devised by someone else, you can become a victim of the point battle as you compare the list with someone else's. The best procedure is to avoid long lists because the longer and more complicated the checklist, the less usable it is on a day-to-day basis.

Checklists hamstring originality. "Creative work cannot be written according to a cut-and-dried formula. The checklist provides a mechanical crutch for the copywriter which, if followed, generally would tend to make all advertisements look the same." So go the comments of many copywriters. An illustration of how intensely some advertising people feel about this is provided by the example of one very large agency which threw one of its biggest accounts out of the "shop" when the account insisted on adoption of a checklist system by the agency copywriters working on the account's copy.

Checklist originators deny that their systems choke newness and sparkle in copy. Rather, they say, using a good checklist as a guide, the original writer can produce freely, confident that writing is channeled more effectively for sales-getting. The checklist merely systematizes a job that often has no system.

Copywriters use points by instinct, so checklists are useless. Most copywriters argue that they incorporate the necessary points in their writing without using any "system." They suspect the checklist as an attempt by research people to invade the copywriter's field. "Possibly all right for beginners but not for the experienced person" is a frequent comment about checklists. The comment is valid in the case of many copywriters who, through long practice, automatically use attention-getting, selling points in everything they turn out. Other writers—beginners and some old hands—might well adopt some system to keep them on the track in their thinking. The best copywriters in the field might occasionally use a checklist to remind themselves of the fundamentals that sometimes slip away from them as they become more advanced in their jobs.

Since checklists contain nothing new, but simply present everconstant, faithful sales points, they can be a great comfort to the beginner and an occasional aid to skilled copywriters.

Personal judgment is overemphasized. Any checklist, say the critics, is basically a personal judgment on what elements are needed to make an advertisement successful. Any copywriter can, they continue, evolve his own list. Even in using a checklist to evaluate an advertisement, the interpretation is a matter for individual judgment. That this criticism has some truth is borne out by situations wherein persons using the same checklist evaluating system arrive at radically different results in their ratings of the same advertisement. In short, one person may have more skill in applying the checklist than another, or both may be equally skilled but differ entirely in their use of the system. The method then becomes no better than the ability of the persons who use it.

About the most conclusive thing to say of the checklist is that it's up to you. It's a quick, inexpensive way to evaluate an advertisement—one of the quickest and most inexpensive. If you use a checklist be sure that you don't let it make you write like an automaton, and that you retain your good judgment.

INQUIRY TESTS (DIRECT RESPONSE)

The idea behind inquiry testing is simple. You run advertisements and you judge their relative effectiveness by the number of inquiries they bring. These inquiries may result from a hidden offer buried in the copy, or from a coupon offer, openly made, inviting purchases or inquiries.

The hidden offer rids the advertiser of professional coupon-clippers and inquiries from the curious. It also indicates extent of reading, but results in fewer inquiries or sales than does the coupon offer.

In the usual inquiry test, different advertisements are run at different times in the same publication, or at the same time in different publications. Results are then compared.

SPLIT-RUN TESTS

Another version of the inquiry test is the split-run test. This test has some of the advantages or disadvantages of the usual inquiry test plus some advantages and disadvantages of its own.

"Split-run" refers to the practice of testing advertisements by running two or more versions of the same advertisement on the same press run but on different presses of a newspaper or magazine. Thus, Advertisement A may be exactly like Advertisement B except for the headline. Each advertisement in the case of a newspaper will go out on the same day, in the same position in the paper. From the response to the advertisement, the advertiser can tell which of the two headlines was more effective. In the case of a magazine, as many as four versions of the same advertisement will go out and each may be distributed in a different area. Response will be judged relative readership by the coupon return, or by the replies to a hidden offer—one or the other may be employed in such tests. Any element of the advertisement may be checked—copy, illustration, headline. In some instance, the advertiser will test four entirely different advertisements.

You may wonder why this form of testing is not classified with the after (post) copy-testing techniques instead of the before-list. Like inquiry, or direct-response testing, it could be. It is placed in the before group simply because such testing usually precedes general use of the winning advertisement or advertisement elements. Normally, the advertisements would not have been run before the split-run test. In this sense, therefore, the test is a before-publication test. A fact you should realize, too, is that although several hundred newspapers offer split-run service only a few magazines offer split-run, so such testing is quite limited in its scope for magazines.

What split-run offers the researcher

Parallels running conditions. The trouble with so many copy-testing methods is that they are unrealistic. The researchers set up situations which are artificial despite all efforts to make them otherwise. The split-run test, on the other hand, gives the advertiser an almost perfect simulation of conditions under which the advertisements will be run. There will be no tampering with actual reading conditions; there will be no dependence upon the skill of interviewers. Instead, the advertisement readers will read as they always do—right in their homes and unaware that they are taking part in a test. Their response to the advertisements will give an excellent, although not completely reliable, comparison of the effectiveness of the test advertisements.

Test itself produces business. An obvious advantage of split-run testing is that the test pulls in business, unlike other tests which produce nothing but information. A split-run test may promote the product just as well and bring in just as much business as any other advertising used for the product.

Checks geographical differences. That sections of the country, or even sections of a city, vary in their response to different products, copy appeals, and so forth, is well known. Magazine-reading habits, for example, differ greatly in different cities. One tomato-sauce manufacturer found that sales were very good in one city while very poor in another. A TV star who gets a good rating on the West Coast may fare poorly in the South and Midwest but will get a good rating on the East Coast. This is the sort of thing that will vex you or any other advertising person. The split-run test can help you out since it provides a means of checking the power of your appeals in four different sections covered by a magazine. The split-run provides you with a method of making such a

check. As one magazine executive, whose publication offers split-run testing facilities, has explained it, split-runs make possible:

> Pretesting before general release, eliminating ineffective advertisements; comparison of campaign theme and ideas; development of the presentation; evaluation of different headlines; measuring various illustrative treatments; comparing four color to black and white or to black and one color; exploring different layout techniques; comparison of the relative values of various hidden offers.

Weaknesses in split-run tests

The coupon or inquiry return from split-run advertisements is not necessarily a true measure of the relative effectiveness of the advertisements. Here are some considerations:

- It is difficult to use split-run for measuring effectiveness of general advertisements. The method is suited to mail order advertisements. To make a mail order advertisement out of a general advertisement for purposes of the test can distort the true picture of reader reaction to a general advertisement run under normal conditions.
- Since most of your readers won't reply to your test advertisements, respondents may not give a fair indication of your readership. Also, you learn nothing in the split-run about people who don't send in the coupon.
- Mail returns may not give a true evaluation of potential store sales. The kind of people who reply to your coupon or hidden offer often are not typical of the kind of people who come into a store to buy the product. Children, professional "coupon clippers," and many women make a business of replying to advertisements carrying offers despite the fact that they have no real interest in the product. Split-run using hidden offers can avoid this difficulty somewhat.
- Unlike some other copy-testing methods, the split-run reveals nothing about the readers. You know nothing about the way they read the advertisement, their economic or social status, or whether anything in the advertisement actually appealed to them or whether they were just "curious."

Split-run advantages mentioned in the preceding discussion apply to conventional inquiry tests, too, except for the checking of geographical differences. The split-run, however, wins over the conventional inquiry testing in its control over position and time elements. With all test advertisements running at the same time in the same position, you can get a better idea of the comparative drawing power of the copy and other advertisement elements, since extraneous variables are thus reduced. As for the disadvantages, they are essentially the same for conventional inquiry and split-run testing.

Split-run television tests

Split-run television testing is available through the split-cable offered on cable television (CATV). Described simply, the cable station makes it possible to show different commercials in different households simultaneously. Any television commercial can be blanked out and another commercial substituted at any time. Later, surveys may be made by phone, mail, or personal interviews to get viewers' opinions. The technique is especially good for evaluating a campaign that involves a number of different commercials. Furthermore, by checking viewers after the commercial exposures, the television researcher can learn the personal and demographic characteristics of the respondents—not always possible in testing through print split-run.

ADDITIONAL PRETESTS FOR TELEVISION

In addition to testing procedures that can be used for both print and broadcast, such as group discussion and split-run, there are some that are used solely by television researchers. All of these cannot be described here because researchers continue to find many new ways to ascertain viewers' reactions to commercials. Included here, however, are three techniques—in-home camera testing, theater projections, and on-the-air tests. They will be described only briefly because of space limitations.

In-home camera testing

The in-home camera test takes pictures of viewers watching television in the home. To do this, an in-home camera (Dynascope) is coupled with the television set and a timer. Discovered by the test is whether the person tested is watching during the commercial. Just as important, the device reveals the attention given to the commercial while it is being shown.

Theater projections

Many different techniques are used for a theater projection type of testing in which 300 to 400 persons may be invited to a theater for the private screening of some "new television material." Usually, the audience will see entertainment programs and television commercials. Later, the audience is asked for their reactions to the commercials, such information as comprehension, brand-name recall, likes-dislikes, interest, and believability. There might even be group discussions to obtain full information. Much television copy has been, and is tested, in these "laboratory" theaters.

On-the-air tests

Under the on-the-air testing method, the respondents do not know they are taking part in a test. The test commercial is aired in one, or a few cities. The advertiser's test commercial may be used on a regular program in one city while the present commercial runs in other cities as usual. Sometimes, the advertiser may buy a new time period in selected cities for a local participation, or a spot. Following the airing, viewers who saw the new commercial are interviewed (usually by telephone) to find out their brand attitudes, their ability to playback the commercial message, and their brand knowledge. These are compared with those of people who did not see the new commercial but saw the existing commercial.

READABILITY TESTS

There can be some question that this discussion of readability properly fits into a chapter on testing. A person might ask, Isn't readability (and the Flesch formula) concerned with writing style and thus more appropriate in another chapter? Furthermore, isn't the Flesch formula, in particular, concerned more with postpublication analysis than pretesting?

To the first question, it may be said that if a writer examines copy in terms of readability principles—or has a researcher do it—before it is set in print in final form, it is possible to greatly increase its effectiveness. Thus, it seems proper to discuss readability in this research chapter even though there is no denying that readability principles are writing principles and can be used as such by the copywriter.

To the second question, it may be said that readability research can be used for pretesting or posttesting but it seems more sensible to apply it in pretesting and thus avoid the use of writing that is less efficient than it should be.

Some years ago, United Press, worried that they were writing "over" their readers, made a thorough study of their wire stories. They found among other things that out of 100 United Press stories going out in a single day, the average sentence length was 29 words—the average length of lead sentences was 33 words. Yet comfortable reading for the mass of the population is a sentence length of around 20 words. UP found that although they were averaging around 30 words for their sentences, current magazines ran about as follows:

Magazine	Average Sentence Length
Time	16 words
Reader's Digest	18 words
Atlantic Monthly	24 words

United Press editors found that in addition to writing long sentences, their writers were also using too many long, complex words. Alarmed by the trend, the wire service began a writing reform within the organization. Sentences were shortened, language was simplified, and readability, according to tests, increased noticeably and quickly.

What was true of United Press has been true of almost every organization writing to the public—magazines, newspapers, advertisers. Sentences have been too long, words too long, and the writing impersonal. The three factors make a marvelous recipe for low readership. During labor-management difficulties, publications are usually crowded with good-sized advertisements from both sides explaining their viewpoints. In such issues, involving the general public welfare, it can be assumed that both sides are anxious that the greatest possible number of people read their messages. Controversial advertisements of this type, you would think, would be designed for easy digestion. Not so. Most of them are ponderously written. The language level is beyond the ordinary reader. They are often written like treatises on economics. Neither labor nor management seems able to speak the language of the people—nor to write that language so that the majority of people are convinced and will respond.

Thanks to readership studies you know that Advertisement A gets 55 percent readership and Advertisement B gets 20 percent. But why? It might have been the headline, illustration, or position in the publication. There are many ways to account for the difference. One of the most important is this matter of readability. Was the copy a chore to read or did it run off smoothly under your glance? What made the difference in readability between A and B? How do you actually measure readability? At least some of the answers to these questions have been supplied by a former Vienna lawyer, Dr. Rudolph Flesch, whose readability formula you can learn and apply quickly to your copy or anyone else's copy.

Flesch formula

Basis for the Flesch formula are four elements as they appear in 100-word samples of writing:

- Average sentence length.
- Average number of syllables.
- Percentage of personal words.
- Percentage of personal sentences.

These are no magic ingredients. Flesch has simply expressed mathematically what writers have always known; short words and short sentences make for easier reading. In sentences, for example, the Flesch table points out that about 88 percent of the population can understand without difficulty sentences that fall in the "Fairly Easy" category. Such sentences average 14 words; their syllable count is 139 per 100 words. "Very Difficult" writing, in contrast, is suitable to only about 4.5 percent of the population. Here the average sentence runs 29 or more words and the syllable count soars to 192.

Personal words. An interesting facet of the Flesch formula is the stress on the use of personal words and personal sentences in order to achieve what is termed a high "interest" factor. Words such as "people, folks" (plus personal names and personal pronouns) are classified as "personal" words. Personal sentences include: spoken sentences set off by quotation marks; questions, commands, and other

sentences addressed directly to the reader; exclamations; and incomplete sentences whose meaning must be inferred from the context. A classification of "dull" writing has no personal sentences and contains only 2 percent or less personal words per 100 words. Typical users of such writing are scientific magazines which, however absorbing to their limited audience, would be found dull by the mass audience. "Highly Interesting" in contrast, has 10 personal words; and 43 percent of personal sentences.

For years, young writers have been told—"write simply; write on the level of your readers." It is not easy to decide what kind of writing is suited to the different levels. Because a folksy advertisement gets a good Flesch rating, and thus can be read by most of the adult readers, does not mean that all advertisements must be written in folksy style. Certainly if you are selling a mass-appeal item, write in the way that will appeal to the biggest possible portion of that market. However, if you are writing *New Yorker* copy for a very expensive product, you will not be addressing a mass readership. The readers you want to reach probably will be affluent and appreciate precision instruments. They probably will have an educational background which enables them to surmount easily a "Difficult" Flesch rating of the advertisement.

By no means should a copywriter write consciously to the Flesch or any other formula. The system is simply a device to tell you whether your writing is geared in readability to the various segments of your readership. That the method has some practicality is evident in its adoption by a number of advertising agencies and publications. The formula is applicable to any kind of writing and, as a matter of fact, has been used widely to determine readability of the editorial content of magazines and newspapers.

A significant point coming out of the Flesch formula is the degree of correlation between Flesch rating results and readership studies such as the magazine reports of Daniel Starch and of the Continuing Study of Newspaper Reading.

The principal danger in the use of the Flesch system is that writers might adopt it too literally. It would be oversimplification to believe that all you must do to write good copy is to write short words, short sentences, and throw in a personal reference now and then. Thought and writing skill must still be used by the copywriter. The Flesch formula does nothing but wave a warning when the copy begins to clank. Because copywriters can read their copy easily often makes them forget that others won't have a similarly easy time reading it. The Flesch system acts as a warning that:

These sentences are too long.

Only half your readers will understand this.

Don't forget your readers are human; they like personal references to themselves or other human beings.

Secondly, be cautioned that the Flesch formula cannot be applied literally to radio or television writing since a good radio announcer can make material that looks difficult to the eye seem hearable when it is read out loud. Through skillful phrasing and intonation the announcer breaks long sentences into easily assimilated phrases. Even long, unusual words that would daunt the reader of a printed page will "sound easy" when delivered by a good announcer or actor.

In conclusion, don't use the Flesch system as a mold for your writing. Flesch doesn't measure literary excellence or selling effectiveness, but how well you reach your audience. A formula should not be used constantly if you are to maintain elasticity in your writing. Use it occasionally as a sort of checkup on your writing. Employed in this manner, it can help your writing to be more consistently readable—especially if you are writing to a mass market.

EYE-CAMERA TESTS

A film record of the path of the eye over an advertisement is made by the eye-camera. Not only does the eye-camera indicate eye direction, but it also indicates how long a reader's glance remains on any one section of the advertisement. Although the eye-camera is probably more suited to long-range advertisement research than to copy testing individual advertisements, it can be useful in the latter activity. It can, for example, indicate the relative pulling power of the various advertisement elements. It can answer the question as to whether the subject is merely a headline reader or whether he reads body copy, too. Also, the eye-camera may reveal the extent of reading, although under the test conditions necessary for an eye-camera test the subject is rather far away from home-reading conditions.

Undoubtedly the eye-camera can reveal the mechanics of eye-flow. The greatest use for the eye-camera is in determining the correct mechanical structure of the advertisement. It tells nothing of what the subject thinks about the advertisement, or how he might react to it. It simply indicates how to arrange the advertising elements for the most logical, thorough, and easiest readership. In this sense it may be considered even more useful as a layout-testing device than as a means for testing copy. It can be argued, however, that interest in copy can be indicated by the length of time the eye rests upon it. As a counter-argument, it may be that the subject had to spend much time on a particular section because it was so difficult to understand.

Daniel Starch, in his *Factors in Readership Measurements*, has said:

> Photographic records of eye movements measure precisely where the eyes look and how long they look while they read. Such records are probably affected to some extent by the artificial conditions that attend laboratory reading. However, it seems reasonable that eye-camera tests broadly measure the relative amounts of text that would be read under normal conditions.

Continuing to talk about eye-cameras, Starch pointed to strong correlation between eye-camera results and magazine readership test results. Thus, if an advertisement checked in a Starch readership study was classified high in "Read-Most" results ("Read-Most" refers to those readers who have read 50 percent or more of the reading matter of an advertisement), it tended to be scanned a longer time during eye-camera tests. You can see how this works when you examine the following table:

	Read-Most Readership Percentage	Rank	Eye-Camera Reading Time Seconds	Rank
Swans Down Cake Flour	15.2%	1	4.9	1
National Dairy Products	7.0	2	3.2	3
Grape Nuts Flakes	6.3	3	3.2	3
Ivory Soap	4.2	4	2.3	5.5
Palmolive Soap	2.5	5	2.3	5.5
Tavern Home Products	2.4	6	4.0	2
Trushay Lotion	2.0	7	2.2	7
Elizabeth Arden	1.0	8	1.7	8
Jolly Pop Corn	0.8	9	1.0	10
Chevrolet	0.4	10	1.1	9
Everglaze Chintz	0.3	11	0.6	11

Another approach using photography is to measure eye-pupil dilation. When the respondent is looking at an advertisement, his pupil dilations or contractions are photographed. Contraction of the pupil is interpreted as indicating a negative response to the material observed; dilation is considered to show a positive, or favorable, response.

MOTIVATIONAL RESEARCH

Researchers know that very often the answer they can obtain from a respondent is not the true answer to the question that was asked. The true answer is hidden in the subconscious. Even the respondent is not aware of it. An advertising researcher, therefore, in probing for reactions about a product or a campaign may, if using ordinary research techniques, obtain a set of answers that will not reveal the real feelings of the respondents. To dig under the surface advertising has, in the last few years, used motivational research. This form of investigation draws heavily upon psychology, laws underlying thinking, learning, and actions, and sociology, the study of mass behavior. MR, as it is familiarly called by advertising people has been used before or after campaigns have been run; thus it fits into postpublication copy research as well as prepublication. Also, it must not merely be thought of as a copy research tool since its findings are used to establish a rationale for the whole marketing process.

Motivational research practitioners usually proceed on the assumption that they do not know what their investigation may uncover since irrational behavior, drives, impulses, fears and desires may cause people to act as they do toward the product or situation being studied. Out of a study may come reasons respondents could tell the ordinary researcher but probably will not.

Most motivational research is concerned with the subconscious level in which there are strong motivating forces that the individual respondent does not recognize. Other thinking levels, of course, are the outer level that those about us can see, and the conscious inner level of personality, a sort of private dream world. This, too, is an area for motivational probing.

Although there are many ways to obtain information, a good portion of motivational research depends upon depth interviewing and projective approaches.

FIGURE 20-1

The Photo-Graphic Brandt Eye-Camera.   The light on the subject's head hits the area observed by the reader, but, since it is infra-red, cannot be seen by the subject. The 16mm spectoscopic film in the camera, however, records both content observed and the infra-red spot. Thus the exact location, duration, and sequence of every fixation are recorded.

Courtesy Dr. Edmund W. J. Faison, President, Visual Research International.

Depth interviews. Of course, depth interviews are not the exclusive province of motivational researchers; all types of researchers have conducted depth interviews for years. Such interviews may last one or two hours during which questions are asked that seem, and often are, quite indirect but which, nevertheless, center around the problems investigated. Unsuspected motivations are often unearthed through these interviews.

Projective approaches. Most strongly identified with motivational research are projective approaches. These frequently use the following techniques:

- Free-word association. Typically, respondents are given lists of words, one at a time, and asked to respond with the first word that comes to mind. Judgment is made on the basis of the frequency with which a word may come up, or how long it takes for the word to appear.

- Sentence completion. Respondents finish a series of incomplete sentences. A respondent will be guided along a certain direction but, if correctly handled will not know what data is to be obtained.
- Picture responses. An illustration is shown to the respondent who then interprets the illustration or tells its story.

A sort of madness overcame portions of the advertising industry when motivational research first appeared as a tool of advertising researchers. Swiftly people began using motivational research who had no knowledge of its meaning or techniques. Many times ordinary consumer surveys might have obtained more information for them and at considerably lower cost. Of late, however, the fever has subsided as advertising people have become aware of the limitations of MR, as well as its virtues. While much hitherto buried information has been obtained through motivational research, its use brings up questions among the companies, advertising agencies, and the media that employ it. For example, who is going to validate the results among the average businesspeople who pay for the research? How can these businesspeople judge the validity of the work conducted by psychologists? Too, the businesspeople ask how they are to judge the accuracy of the techniques used when arguments persist among the motivational researchers themselves, not only about the techniques for getting the information but about the interpretation of the results obtained.

Regardless of the doubts and queries and the uneasiness of businesspeople suddenly wading in the esoteric terminology of the psychologist, motivational research, properly conducted, is here to stay. It will remain in some form or other because it helps reduce guesswork in advertising creation by giving copywriters answers to those eternal questions: "What do they really like or dislike?" "What do they really want?" "What do they really think?"

The absorption of creative advertising people with these questions is illustrated by the use during the past few years of such techniques as psychogalvanometer testing and hypnosis. The former, utilizing an instrument greatly akin to the "lie detector" police work, has been used to measure involuntary reactions to various advertising stimuli. A number of media and large companies have tried this form of testing. Both galvanometer testing and the use of hypnosis, like the use of motivational research, evidence the advertising person's discontent with the surface answers obtained through conventional survey methods.

ADDITIONAL PUBLICATION PRETEST TECHNIQUES

The following methods are classed as pretests in the sense that they give advertisers reactions of respondents to advertisements that have been prepared for viewing but which have not been run yet in the whole publication run of newspapers or magazines.

This "pre-view" reaction saves the advertiser the cost of running ineffective advertisements by trying out new approaches in a limited way. As you will see, however, such testing can, in itself, be expensive. The three methods to be discussed briefly here are folio testing, dummy publications, and tip-ins.

Folio testing

"Folio" here is an abbreviation for portfolio, or a folder of advertisements shown to a cross-section of respondents, usually in their homes. A number of methods may be followed in this kind of testing. Advertisements, for example, may be shown to respondents one by one and questions asked about each before the next advertisement is shown, or the respondent may look over all the advertisements before questions are asked. Advertisements are scored one against another, or each against averages. From this, the advertisements are positioned as higher or lower in performance according to each standard of measurement covered by the questionnaire. Usually no more than eight advertisements are shown in one folio interview.

Dummy publications

The "dummy" publication is a magazine or newspaper that has been prepared especially for test purposes. It contains editorial material and possibly fifteen to twenty advertisements. Copies of the publication are given to a cross-section of people who are directed to read the publication in a normal fashion. An interviewer, they are informed, will visit them to question them about what they have read. The questions reveal advertising recall, advertising impact, and a possible increased interest in buying the products advertised. Although this is an expensive testing method, it has been useful in reproducing posttest scores using the same questions asked of those respondents who have read the dummy publications.

Tip-ins

A "tip-in" is a page that is glued to the gutter of a real magazine in such a way that a reader cannot tell it from the regular pages. In newspapers, an insert page may be used. On the page will be a pretest advertisement, plus another advertisement. The tip-in will be inserted in a specified number of copies of a publication—magazine or newspaper—before the publication's release date. These copies are then distributed to enough people to furnish the desired sample size. Later, the persons who have read the publication with the tip-in page are questioned in a manner similar to that used for the dummy publications previously described. One possible advantage of the tip-in method over dummy publication testing is that the reading situation is more natural because a real publication is used. This may be offset somewhat by the fact that the tip-in copies are planted with readers, not being bought as usual at newsstands or by subscription.

READERSHIP STUDIES

The advertisement has been published. No advertiser alive can help wanting to know certain things about that advertisement. How many persons read it? How thoroughly did they read? How much advertiser and product identification was created? How well do the readers remember the advertisement? What features of the advertisement obtained the best readership? All these questions and more are answered to a degree by readership studies undertaken after publication of the advertisement.

RESEARCHING COPY AFTER PUBLICATION

Arguments have been heard about readership techniques from the time they were first used. You may be sure of one thing, however. You will always have some form of readership study. Like them or not, you will need to know the various methods, and you should determine which one you believe in most firmly. You should learn readership terminology and the mechanical procedures for detecting misleading readership research.

The readership report, like radio and TV ratings, has become an obsession in some circles. The magic percentage figures of readership studies are hypnotic. They lull the advertiser into satisfaction with his advertising or they goad him into anger. With many advertisers a high percentage of readership is the final test of an advertisement's success. "The readership reports say we're on the right track," says the person who produced the advertisement. The advertiser leans back satisfied. Yet, there are so many variables to consider in readership reports that you will be a very wise copywriter never to accept a readership report at face value. Look behind the figures. Don't let the mesmerizing effect of good readership keep you from setting off on new copy trails. An evil of the reports is that they encourage status quo advertising. "We're going along fine," cries a cautious executive. "The readership reports are good. Why endanger our success with that new technique?" The hesitancy is understandable. Yet, new ideas are the life of advertising. New ideas are responsible for increased sales and higher manufacturing output. If you rely too slavishly on readership reports, you will find a good formula, and you will never leave it. Some advertisers have done well under that system. Most advertising, however, has been flexible. Most advertisers have been willing to try for the greater reward—have been willing to experiment.

Many good advertising ideas would have been lost had satisfied executives refused to experiment. Yet such refusals are frequent when readership figures for present campaigns are good. A bit of the gambler is needed to desert the high readership campaign for the bold, new idea.

Advertising Achievement Awards. Readex calls special attention to and has prepared special award certificates for the following advertisements which have achieved outstanding reader interest in comparison with all other ads in this issue.

Interest	Size	Page	Advertiser
53%	2c4	14-5	American Hoist & Derrick Company
39	2c4	12-3	Terex Division of General Motors
38	2c4	10-11	Clark Equipment Company
38	1c4	5	Warner & Swasey

Advertisements by Product Classification in Order of Interest

Tractors, Loaders, Scrapers, Wagons & Attachments

Interest	Size	Page	Advertisement
39%	2c4	12-3	Terex 82-40T Crawler
35	2c4	36-7	Allis-Chalmers HD-41
30	2c4	46-7	MF Equipment
27	2c4	50-1	Trojan Loaders
25	1	125	Ateco Attachments
24	2c4	88-9	Long 5-N-1 Super 16
23	2c4	28-9	Int'l. Harvester 25C Crawler
23	1r	75	New Holland L-35 Loader
18	1c4	2	Caterpillar Wheel Loaders

69%	Total reader interest in one or more ads.
77%	Highest total reader interest recorded in 12 reports.
49%	Most interesting single ad in 12 reports.

Shovels, Draglines, Backhoes, Backhoe/Loaders & Attachments

Interest	Size	Page	Advertisement
38%	2c4	10-11	Clark Lima 945
38	1c4	5	Warner & Swasey Gradall

47%	Total reader interest in one or more ads.
69%	Highest total reader interest recorded in 12 reports.
55%	Most interesting single ad in 12 reports.

Cranes, Hoists & Attachments

Interest	Size	Page	Advertisement
53%	2c4	14-5	American Hoist Cranes
36	1c4	30	Northwest Truck Crane
31	1c4	2C	Link-Belt Speeder Crane
28	1c4	16	Grove RT Cranes
18	1c4	113	Koehring 1510 Skytrak
5	1/4	139	Equipment Systems Products

63%	Total reader interest in one or more ads.
84%	Highest total reader interest recorded in 12 reports.
59%	Most interesting single ad in 12 reports.

Key to symbols: Under the heading of "size" numerals indicate ad size. Letters following numeral show color. No letter following indicates black & white. Example:

1b - 1 page blue; 1/2 g - 1/2 page green; 2c4 - 2 page 4 color.

b - blue	c4 - 4 color	φ - orange	y-yellow
br - brown	g - green	r - red	

Under the heading of "page," the letters "a, b, etc." indicate an insert following the page mentioned.

FIGURE 20-2

Typical page from Readex Reader Interest report.   Readex, a posttesting method, measures interest, not observation. Readers report only what they found of interest.

READEX, INC., Reader Interest Research,
140 Quail Street
St. Paul, Minnesota 55115.

Assume, as you read now about readership study techniques, that there is misinformation in the best of them—and some good in most of them. What you find—good or bad—will depend upon your capacity for objective analysis.

Testing by recognition

"What do you usually read?" "What advertisements did you see in yesterday's paper?" This type of recall questioning was used for years to determine advertisement reading. Opinions were obtained, but not actual behavior. As mentioned before, you will find a big area between what people say they do and what they actually do.

Recognition testing (which is based on presenting published material to find out what has actually been read) ignores opinion. Actual reading behavior is measured. A widely known newspaper-readership study using the recognition principle was the Continuing Study of Newspaper Readership.[1] In magazine readership studies, Daniel Starch & Staff are probably best known among research organizations using recognition testing.

A quick glance at the technique used in the Continuing Study and the Starch study will show you how newspaper and magazine studies are conducted. Some of the essential differences in analyzing readership of the two media will be uncovered. Other prominent studies that employed the recognition methods were the Continuing Study of Farm Publications, and

[1]The Studies ended in 1952 because by then it was felt that further studies would simply duplicate information already obtained, but individual newspapers using the same methodology have continued to obtain readership information.

the Continuing Study of Magazine Audiences conducted by Crossley Incorporated. Both introduced new twists in the procedure, but the recognition principle guided their technique.

Continuing Study of Newspaper Readership. An interviewer went over a newspaper with a person who said that he had read the issue of the newspaper being tested. The reader pointed out every news item, picture, and advertisement he had read in the test issue. Reading of local advertisements was recorded in terms of how many men and women read the advertisement. National advertisements were checked also for reading of headlines, illustrations, and copy blocks. Reading totals for the approximately 450 men and women interviewed for each study were totaled and added to the accumulative totals for the more than 100 Continuing Studies that were made for newspapers before the studies were discontinued.

Advertisement Readership Service, Daniel Starch & Staff, Inc. Interviewers check respondents on reading of advertisements one-half page or larger in a number of national publications. Respondents are divided equally among men and women. The advertisement as a whole is checked on a three-way basis:

1. Noted. Reader has seen the advertisement.
2. Advertiser-associated. Reader has seen or read the advertisement enough to know the product or advertiser.
3. Read-most. Reader has read 50 percent or more of the advertisement's reading matter.

Parts of the advertisement—headline, subheads, text units, illustrations, and logotypes—are also checked for observation and reading.

In addition to determining the percentage of reading for advertisements and their component parts, the Starch service also provides cost ratios of the advertisements and ranks them in terms of dollars spent to obtain readers. These figures are refined to the point where the studies tell the advertiser just how much it costs merely to get the advertisement seen, or seen and associated, or read most. Thus you might get a high cost for the "seen" classification, but your copy may be read so well that a high percentage of those who read the advertisement read most of the copy. Your cost ratio for Read-Most would then be low.

The real value of recognition studies is in cumulative studies. It would be foolish to let one study entirely influence an important decision. You can compare that one study, however, with other studies. The cumulative figures can show you whether your copy was "on" or "off." The principal strength of readership studies is in the long-trend aspect. As study piles on study, you see certain appeals pulling consistently. Certain ideas pull every time—others fail consistently. The studies attempt to give the "why." At this point two other techniques used for recognition testing should be mentioned.

Weak spots in recognition testing

Poor memory, dishonesty, false pride, either in combination or singly, reduce the believability. Sometimes magazine researchers attempt to measure the effect of the three factors by setting up a "confusion control." Thus they ask people to point out advertisements they have read in a certain magazine. The advertisements have not yet appeared in any publication but have been so cleverly inserted in the test issue that the respondents think they are already-run advertisements. The researcher finds out how much the reading of such advertisements totals and makes a statistical allowance for this confusion factor in the final figures. So many people become honestly confused in readership tests that an allowance must be made for this "honest" confusion. Marlboro advertisements, for example, have a strong family resemblance. It is easy to think that you have seen a specific Marlboro advertisement when actually you are remembering not that advertisement but the impression created by the series. Other persons, ashamed to admit they read certain items, skip by them when being interviewed. Thus the accuracy of the readership percentage is reduced.

STARCH READERSHIP AVERAGES BY PRODUCT CLASS, SIZE & COLOR

READER'S DIGEST W

These are the average readership scores for all advertisements studied in 1973-1974 issues of this magazine. All figures are percentages.

By comparing scores for your advertisement with these averages, you have an answer to the question "Did my advertisement achieve average, above average, or below average readership?"

	1P4				1P2				1P				2/3P4			
	NO.	N	A	R	NO.	N	A	R	NO.	N	A	R	NO.	N	A	R
INSURANCE					17	20	15	5	28	20	14	5				
LIFE, GROUP & MEDICAL					5	24	20	7	7	24	19	6				
FIRE, CASUALTY & OTHER					12	19	14	5	21	19	11	4				
OFFICE EQUIP., STAT., & SUPP.	5	37	30	8					5	32	25	4				
OFFICE MACHINES & EQUIPMENT									5	32	25	4				
INDUSTRIAL MATERIALS	5	40	32	9												
TOILETRIES & TOILET GOODS	79	37	31	6	19	36	33	11	40	34	28	9				
COSMETICS & BEAUTY AIDS									17	34	26	14				
PERSONAL HYGIENE PRODUCTS	67	34	28	5	9	29	26	8	19	31	27	5				
BATH TOILETRIES/MISC GOODS					8	44	41	14								
HAIR PRODUCTS	6	49	43	9												
DRUGS & REMEDIES	40	37	33	7	21	15	12	5	37	26	21	7				
MEDICINES/PROPRIETARY REMS	40	37	33	7	21	15	12	5	35	26	20	7				
FOOD & FOOD PRODUCTS	93	51	45	12												
COOKING PROD. & SEASONINGS	23	54	49	14												
PREPARED FOODS	33	50	46	10												
FRUITS & VEGETABLES	9	48	39	11												
FOOD BEVERAGES	15	50	42	12												
COMBINATION COPY & GEN'L PR	7	49	45	10												
SMOKING MATERIALS	5	34	27	7												
MISC SMOKING MATERIALS	5	34	27	7												
JEWELRY,OPT'L GOODS & CAMERAS	34	47	37	15					5	39	32	11				
JEWELRY & WATCHES	20	47	34	15					5	39	32	11				
CAMERAS & PHOTO SUPPLIES	14	49	42	16												
SPORTING GOODS & TOYS	17	32	23	5												
BOATS & MOTORS	8	21	13	2												
BICYCLES, MOTORCYCLES	7	40	30	6												
MISCELLANEOUS	41	40	33	7					8	29	22	8				
LUGGAGE & LEATHER GOODS	14	47	40	11												
PETS & PET SUPPLIES	23	34	28	4												
MISCELLANEOUS									6	33	25	10				
RETAIL &/OR DIRECT BY MAIL	9	33	27	5												
HOUSEHOLD FURNISHINGS	10	53	42	12												
HOUSEHOLD EQUIPMENT & SUPPLIES	54	42	35	8												
MAJOR APPLIANCES	40	41	34	8												
OTHER APPLIANCES & EQUIP	9	44	36	9												
HOUSEHOLD ACCESS./MISC. SUP	5	47	40	9												
RADIOS/TV SETS/PHONO/MUSC.INST	17	44	34	9												
R&D/TV/PHONO/TAPE RECORDERS	16	44	34	9												
SOAPS, CLEANSERS, & POLISHES	11	47	43	11												
BUILDING MAT.,EQUIP., & FIXT.	11	27	19	5												
BUILDING MATERIALS	5	23	13	4												
PROTECTIVE COATINGS & FIN.	5	27	21	3												
AUTOMOTIVE/AUTO. ACCESS./EQUIP	106	27	19	5	10	15	10	2	13	23	18	5				
PASSENGER CARS & VEHICLES	59	33	24	5					7	31	24	7				
COMM. TRUCKS/VEH. & LEASING	23	23	15	2												
TIRES & TUBES	5	19	14	1					5	16	11	2				
AUTO ACCESS., EQUIP., MISC.	17	15	9	1	9	15	11	2								
GASOLINE, LUBRICANTS & FUELS	10	18	13	2												
GAS/OIL(TRANS)/DEALER SERV.	8	16	11	2												
TRAVEL, HOTELS, & RESORTS	6	44	35	9												

Three percentages are shown for each size of space: Noted, Associated, Read Most. Where fewer than five ads were studied, averages are now shown. All sizes include bleed & non-bleed advertisements.

FIGURE 20-3

Average readership scores.   Advertisers who want to see how close their advertisements come to the averages obtained by competitors in their category can study pages such as this one.

Courtesy Daniel Starch & Staff, Inc.

All reading is not reported. Often respondents will say firmly, "No, I didn't read that advertisement." Quite often the interviewer will accept the negative answer instead of making certain that the respondent has not actually read the advertisement. Much reading is not declared by the respondent. If respondents fail to tell you what they have read, you are helpless. There is no way to correct for this factor, nor to validate your findings. The man conducting the test has nothing to work from. As one researcher has ruefully said, "If certain product advertising get no more readers than the surveys sometimes report, the products would have to be pulled off the market."

Recognition study measures memory or observation; it does not indicate sales or conviction power. This is probably the strongest objection to readership studies as a whole. Proponents of recognition studies, such as Daniel Starch, have attempted to show that there is a relationship between high readership and high sales. Starch has said, (*Factors in Readership Measurements*) "In general, the more readers an advertisement attracts and the more completely it is read, the more sales are produced by that advertisement—except that some types of copy treatment actually repel buyers. The more reading there is of such advertisements, the less buying there is." Opponents point to many advertisements which obtained low readership but which pulled big coupon returns—and vice versa. "You can't sell 'em if they don't see your advertisement" is the usual report. The answer to that is, of course, that a thousand persons may see your advertisement yet no one will buy the product.

Many times, too, short copy will rate higher in Starch's Read-Most figures than will long copy. Yet the lower-rated long-copy advertisement will often far outsell the other because the readers it sells it "hooks."

In a sense, high readership and sales might be in opposite corners of the ring. You may have devised your advertisement for high readership. Tricky, unusual features may get you your high figures, but you may have worked so hard for attention that you crowded out a powerful selling message. You may be full of pride when you see the Starch reports, but your sales manager may feel a different emotion when looking over falling sales.

The real readership is the readership of your sales story by people who may subsequently buy—not general, casual readership. You should ask, "How many prospects read our message?" A diamond advertisement might get high readership among older readers sighing for romance. The diamond salesperson will trade a dozen older readers, however, for one, young bride-to-be; she represents prospect readership.

STARCH
READERSHIP REPORT

For the private use of purchasers only. Reproduction of this report in whole or in part is prohibited. Any reference to this report or any figures in this report in publishers' or advertising agencies' paid advertising or in their printed promotion pieces, must be submitted to the Starch Organization before release. Reference by name to competitive publications or advertisements is expressly prohibited. Use of this report or any figures from this report by non-subscribers is expressly prohibited.

Conclusions drawn from figures shown in this report may not be represented as the opinion of the Starch Organization

PAGE 1

46 ADS 1/2 PAGE AND OVER
READER'S DIGEST JULY

WOMEN READERS

PRODUCT CATEGORIES			COST	RANK IN ISSUE		PERCENTAGES			READERS PER DOLLAR			COST RATIOS		
PAGE	SIZE & COLOR	ADVERTISER	PENNIES PER READER	BY NUMBER OF READERS	BY COST PER READER	NOTED	ASSOCIATED	READ MOST	NOTED	ASSOCIATED	READ MOST	NOTED	ASSOCIATED	READ MOST
		COMMUNICATION/PUBLIC UTILITY												
41	H1/2P	BELL TELEPHONE SYSTEM G P	.7	32	6	30	27	10	163	147	54	131	135	360
153	H1/2P	BELL TELEPHONE SYSTEM G P	.7	32	6	29	27	11-	158	147	60	127	135	400
215	H1/2P	BELL TELEPHONE SYSTEM G P	.6	29	2	32	29	9	174	158	49	140	145	327
		OFFICE MACHINES/EQUIPMENT												
134	1S4	IBM CORPORATION G P	1.9	23	41	41	39	9	55	52	12	44	48	80
		MFRS. MATERIALS/SUPPLIES												
160	1S4B	UNITED STATES STEEL CORP G P	2.9	35	45	33	26	4	44	35	5	35	32	33
		PASSENGER CARS/VEHICLES												
1	1P4B	CHEVROLET CARS	1.1	27	31	52	34	4	139	91	11	112	[illegible]	[illegible]
2	1S4B	CHEVROLET CARS	1.6	11	40	62	47	5	83	63	7	67	[illegible]	47
139	1P4B	FORD GRANADA CARS	.9	11	15	58	[illegible]	6	145	117	[illegible]	[illegible]	[illegible]	100
		TIRES/TUBES												
140	H1/2S B	FIRESTONE RADIAL TIRES	1.4	37	39	28	23	3	84	69	9	68	63	60
		AUTO ACCESSORIES/EQUIPMENT												
159	1P	AC-DELCO AUTOMOTIVE PARTS	2.8	45	43	21	12	4	63	36	12	51	33	[illegible]
		GASOLINE/OIL/DEALER SERVICES												
136	1P5B	QUAKER STATE MOTOR OIL	2.8	44	43	17	16	3	39	36	7	31	33	47
		COSMETICS/BEAUTY AIDS												
162	1P4B	COPPERTONE SUPER SHADE	.8	7	9	55	57	5	[illegible]	[illegible]	12	116	121	80
		PERSONAL HYGIENE PRODUCTS												
8	1P4B	BAN ROLL-ON ANTI-PERSPIRANT	.9	15	19	49	45	3	122	112	7	98	103	47
30	1P4B	SCOPE MOUTHWASH	.7	5	8	54	54	4	135	135	10	109	124	67
133	1P4B	CREST TOOTH PASTE	.7	2	3	63	61	3	157	152	7	127	139	47
155	1P4B	TAMPAX TAMPONS	1.0	22	28	45	40	5	112	100	12	90	92	80
179	1P4B	CLOSE-UP TOOTHPASTE OFFER	.8	10	13	52	50	9-	130	125	22	105	115	147
183	H1/2P2	CUSHION GRIP DENTAL ADHESIVE	.9	30	24	31	31	3	108	108	15	87	99	100
195	1P B	EZO DENTAL CUSHIONS	1.1	29	22	32	29	3	96	87	9	77	80	60
214	H1/2P4	ORAFIX DENTURE ADHESIVE	1.2	42	35	24	19	3	109	82	14	88	75	93
		MEDICINES/PROPRIETARY REMEDY												
9	1P4B	EXCEDRIN TABLETS	.9	15	19	50	45	3	125	112	7	101	103	47
21	1P4B	SOLARCAINE SUN CARE PRODS	.9	18	22	52	44	6	130	110	15	105	101	100
22	H1/2P4B	CRUEX MEDICATED POWDER	.8	31	10	35	29	9-	159	127	41	126	117	273
23	H1/2P4	AFTATE FOOT CARE PRODUCTS	1.2	41	34	20	19	4	91	86	18	73	79	120
152	V1/2P	PRIMATENE TABLETS	1.0	42	29	22	13	1	120	98	5	97	90	33
182	H1/2P2B	CORRECTOL LAXATIVE	.8	37	14	25	23	3	128	118	15	103	108	100
207	1P2	ANACIN TABLETS	1.4	35	38	37	26	7	104	73	20	84	67	133
211	1P	STRESSTABS 600 VITAMINS	1.2	32	36	28	27	9	84	81	27	68	74	180
219	1P2	PREPARATION H SUPP/OINTMENT	3.2	46	46	22	11	4	62	31	11	50	28	73
		PREPARED FOODS												
151	1P4B	KRAFT DINNERS	.8	8	13	56	51	11	140	127	27	113	117	180
173	1P4B	CHEF BOY-AR-DEE RAVIOLI	.9	11	15	59	47	5	147	117	12	119	107	80

- FEWER THAN 50 WORDS IN AD.

FIGURE 20-4

Magazine readership scores. The figures shown here are from a Starch Report on an issue of the *Reader's Digest.* In addition to giving readership scores, cost ratios are provided in the right-hand column that tell relative costs for achieving readership costs for achieving readership scores in the categories of "Noted," "Associated," and "Read Most."

Recognition testing has its good points, too

Regardless of the lack of conviction-measuring, recognition studies do give an adequate (if not entirely reliable) idea of the observation and reading obtained by a particular advertisement. Even hard-boiled mail-order people, the kind always screaming for "direct results," use a form of advertising which they didn't try generally until readership studies proved it effective—the editorial technique. Yet mail-order people scoff almost in unison at readership studies. "Sales, not readership" is their motto.

As already mentioned, the recognition study measures actual reading behavior—a more reliable measurement than that obtained through opinion or what the respondents say they have read.

The method is useful for comparing readership of different campaign advertisements, or competitors' advertisements, too. Unlike mail-order advertising, newspaper or magazine advertising may run a long time before sales results show that advertisements are not being read. A readership survey gives the advertiser a reasonably quick and accurate method of checking advertising effectiveness. Poor format, for example, might discourage readership. One advertiser provides backing for this point. Readership was poor on an advertisement he felt certain contained effective copy. When he examined the advertisement critically he discovered the trouble—the format was dull, conventional, lifeless. Using the same copy but giving it a new dress, he tried again. This time he inserted several lively illustrations instead of one drab one. Copy was broken into small doses. Captions were plentiful. The advertisement was a success!

A warning should be made here. When comparing readership results, say in a Starch report, you should compare products in the same group. Your most valid comparison in readership is made with your competitor's advertising. Comparing your readership with that of a noncompetitor is a meaningless sort of activity.

Recognition testing—good or bad?

Results from recognition studies have pointed the way to many techniques now used by copywriters. Recipes in food copy, for example, were shown from the first readership study to assure almost good attention from readers. Editorial techniques, shown by readership studies to get high readership, have been used more and more. Questions on layout and position have been settled through recognition studies. Such fundamental questions as "Will people read long copy?" "Does small type stop reading?" have been answered by recognition studies.

Not one, but many, studies have provided the answers. Questions are still being settled. A mass of evidence is becoming available as recognition studies pile up. Admitted that the conclusions are averages; they cannot be projected to every individual case. Still they point the way. The long-range value of the studies is obvious. Consider vitamins, for instance. For years advertisement copy that could squeeze vitamins in somewhere had almost automatically good readership. Then it was noticed through recognition studies that vitamins were not catching so many readers—the vitamin honeymoon was over and food advertisers began to think of other appeals.

Recognition studies are usually praised by those advertisers whose advertisements get high readership. They are often called unrealistic and silly by advertisers who happen to produce low readership advertising. Despite the latter group, you will profit from the findings of recognition studies. They have been useful to advertising men for some years now. They can help you.

Measurement of separate advertisements. Respondents are shown a number of advertisements cut out from a newspaper or magazine. They select advertisements they think they have seen published. They are then asked detailed questions about each of the advertisements. An advantage of this method is that the interviewer can thus lessen the influence of nearby editorial matter on the reading of advertisements. Often in recognition tests, respondents will answer that they have seen an advertisement simply because thay have read the editorial matter near it. Also, since the advertisement is taken out of the usual reading sequence of the magazine, there is no

chance for this factor to inflate the claimed reading. The method, of course, still has the usual disadvantages found in recognition testing.

FIGURE 20-5

Page from a "Starched" issue of a magazine.   Starch reports, a form of recognition testing of the posttest type, show readership for the advertisement as a whole and for different elements in an advertisement. In this page from the *Reader's Digest,* the readership figures are very high for men and women, especially the women.

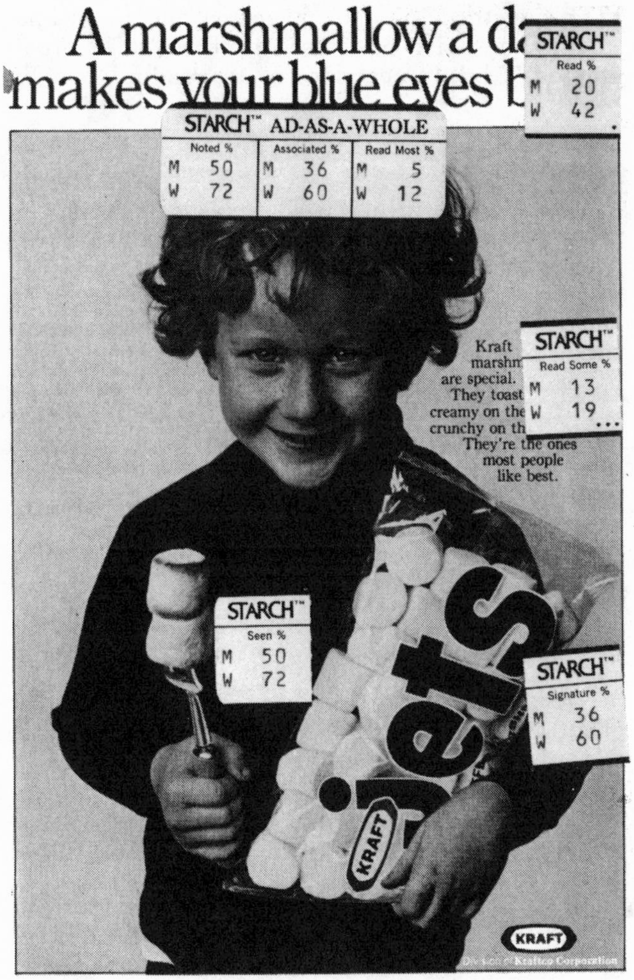

Controlled recognition testing. A number of techniques have been worked out to correct the interview error occasioned by respondents' dishonesty or faulty memory. Some of these techniques require control groups. In a typical situation one group has seen the advertisements, the other has not. Reading differences are then balanced.

Another technique, the system of "confusion control" already described, uses the standard procedure of showing advertisements that have been run and others that have not. By using a simple formula the researchers can weed out the unreliable interviews and come out with a close estimate of actual readership. The formula for this type of testing runs like this:

1. One-hundred persons are interviewed.
2. Three persons claimed readership of an advertisement not yet published.
3. Thirty-three persons indicate readership of an advertisement that has run.
4. Subtract 3 from 100 (97).
5. Subtract 3 from 33 (30).
6. Readership is 30 persons out of 97 or 30.9 percent.

This method, used in magazine and newspaper studies, has also been used by the Traffic Audit Bureau (TAB) in analyzing poster reading.

Identification test

A typical identification test proceeds like this: You are shown an advertisement in which all identifying features have been inked or pasted out. You are then asked to identify the advertisement by indicating what company, product, or service is being advertised. The rest of the advertisements in the newspaper or magazine have been "masked." Whether the results from identification testing are meaningful is debatable. Some advertisers feel, however, that high identification of their advertisements gives an important clue to the success of the advertising—especially in campaign advertising, since the advertiser wants assurance that the campaign idea and format are going over.

Recall tests

A recall test tries to determine what you remember about an advertisement. Unlike in the recognition test, usually no advertisement is shown. The recall test aims at determining the positive, lasting impressions made by an advertisement some time after it has run. Brand-consciousness is probably measured better through recall testing than through any other method. Since no advertisement is shown, respondents must yank up facts about the advertising out of their minds without help from their visual sense. This form of testing is best administered by research experts, since the posing of th questions and interpretation of results are jobs for a specialist. Three forms of recall testing dominate:

■ Unaided recall.
■ Aided recall.
■ Triple associates.

Unaided recall. This form of recall testing is used very little. It consists of asking questions that provide no starting clue on which the respondent may base his answer. Information obtained from the vague questions that must be asked yield vague results. For instance, you might be asked, "What radio commercials do you remember hearing lately?" The same question might be asked about advertisements you have seen. Without any assistance from the interviewer, you are thus forced to pull out into the light some of the hundreds of advertisement impressions jostling themselves in your mind. Trying to attach some meaning to the answers is a nightmare for the researcher.

On an individual basis it is almost impossible to isolate the factors that would cause you, as the respondent, to name some particular advertisement and not some other advertisement. On a mass basis, it would take a terrifying number of interviews to bring out any usable facts. Supposing, for example, you were asked, "What recent advertising copy has impressed you most?" Picture the possible answers to this question. Think of the interviews needed to develop any worthwhile facts. Then think of the countless variables that might have brought the answers. For practical copy testing you may forget the unaided recall.

Aided recall. Advertisers spend millions to create brand-consciousness. This "burning" of the brand on the consumer is one of advertising's most important jobs. "How well is our advertising putting our brand across?" is a question of quivering interest if you want consumers to walk into a store to ask for Wheaties, or Ivory Soap, or Zenith. One of aided recall's particular jobs is to indicate what brand a consumer thinks of when a certain type of product is mentioned, such as: tooth paste—Pepsodent; tires—Goodyear; canned soup—Campbell's. Perhaps you feel that testing brand-consciousness is quite apart from copy testing. In a sense your feeling is justified, since such testing doesn't delve deeply into the copy as do readership tests, and checklists. Lack of brand-recognition may, however, indicate that little association is being created between a type of product and a certain brand. Poor copy may be one of the reasons for lack of identification. Other reasons might be faults in the position of advertisements, illustrations, media, timing, and campaign continuity.

What is the principal importance of the aided recall test? Simply this: It indicates at least the beginning of an association between the brand and a product. Scientific illustrating, expert copy, and page advertisements are useless if such association isn't made. If, when you want a blanket or chewing gum, you don't think of brands to fill your requirements such as North Star or Wrigley's Spearmint, then the copywriter, artists, and other advertisement creators have wasted their time. If they have succeeded, the recall test will indicate not only the success of your advertising but also the relative failure of your competitors in obtaining brand-consciousness.

The aided recall using a question, "Can you name a brand of shaving cream you have seen or heard advertised recently?" is virtually useless for single advertisements but can be useful for measuring campaign impact. From the answers, you learn whether the campaign is moving forward or is failing to impress consumers.

Aided recall—impact testing. One of the more interesting forms of recall testing is provided in Impact testing in which respondents "play back" for interviewers what they remember of advertising they have seen in magazines read in a recent period. Gallup & Robinson, a well-known advertising research organization, has led the field in impact testing. The company has some of the biggest names in American advertising as clients. These clients, who pay substantial fees for impact testing of each product they advertise, are informed by Gallup & Robinson what has been good and what has been bad about their advertising as revealed in each impact testing procedure that has been carried out. This information is given to clients on a regular basis in "clinics" that are usually conducted by Gallup & Robinson in the client's offices.

The test itself consists of a long interview that lasts one or two hours. Persons are approved as respondents after first proving that they have actually read the magazine being used for test purposes. They are then shown names of all products which have been advertised in full page or double page advertisements. The next job is to tell what they remember of the advertisements that they think they remember seeing in the magazine issue. When they tell what they remember they are, in research parlance, "playing back" the advertiser's message. What the advertiser hopes will appear in the playback are:

- Sales points or arguments.
- The advertiser's principal message.
- Reasons for buying.
- What ideas were obtained.
- What went through respondents' minds as they read.

It is obvious from a glance at these points that impact testing goes considerably beyond recognition testing in that its objective is to measure the effect of exposure to advertising rather than to determine mere reading of the copy message. Idea registration and buying urge may often be determined from impact testing. While the aims of impact testing, like those of motivational research, are to dig deeper than the surface to determine what to put into advertising or to determine what makes advertising work, the method has its difficulties. Expense of such research is one factor since costs of the method limit its use rather generally to the larger advertisers with big-budget campaigns. This limitation is unfortunate since many smaller advertisers are thus frozen out and, as is very often the case, they are the ones who could profit most from using impact testing.

Another criticism, often expressed by researchers, is that the method is too difficult. The procedure is "understimulating" which means that the clues given for recall are so weak that an advertising impression has to be massive before it can be recalled. Those who criticize impact testing in this manner, on the other hand, often call the recognition method, as used by Starch, "overstimulating." This means that exposure to advertisements during interviews is often more intense and longer than during normal reading of the magazine. Although there is some validity in the charge that the impact method is difficult, the fact remains that a great amount of copy guidance is obtained from impact interviews. Advertisers who employ impact research use it for long periods and seem satisfied.

Speaking of aided recall testing in general, it must be conceded that a single advertisement has so little chance to catch attention and sink the brand harpoon into the reader that you might well think of aided recall as used mostly for campaign testing. Yet the very success of a campaign destroys, to some extent, the chance of using aided recall testing to measure the effect of the campaign copy. Take Lucky Strikes, for instance. If you were asked what brand of cigarettes you had seen advertised recently, the answer might pop out, "Lucky Strikes." Actually you may have seen more advertising by Marlboros, Winstons, or Chesterfield. Over the years, however, Lucky Strike had possibly built more impact than any other single brand. Your answer, then, was not impelled by recent observation but from the piled-up impressions of years. To use aided recall testing for current advertising of a leading product such as Luckies, you would need to refer to some unusual feature that had not been used in past years such as a slogan, illustration, or headline. This kind of testing, although a form of aided recall, has been given a more impressive title, the "triple associates test."

Triple associates test. Suppose someone came up to you and asked, "What automobile advertises 'Big car quality at lowest cost.'" If at the time Chevrolet was so advertising, and you answered, "Chevrolet," you would have made the three-way connection sought in the triple associates test. Here are the three factors:

- Product—low-price automobile.
- Brand—Chevrolet.
- Copy theme—Big car quality at lowest cost.

As you can see, you are given two elements—the type of product and the theme. Then you supply the brand, thus making the third association. You might not be given the theme exactly as it is used. The question might read, "What automobile advertises that it gives the value of a big car at a lower cost?"

Finding the extent of the association of brand with copy theme is the principal goal of the triple associates test. The information is used for determining campaign effectiveness only. Although the advertiser wants to develop high identification of his copy theme, he is even more hopeful that the triple associates test will connect brand and theme.

Consumer recognition of the theme for itself is of little value. In some campaigns, actual harm has been revealed when it was discovered that consumers associated the copy themes with the wrong products. The uncovering of such misinformation is another value of the triple associates test. If the advertiser discovers that a high percentage of the consumers are identifying the company's copy theme with a competitor's product, then the advertisers should scan the advertising carefully—especially if the campaign has been running for some time.

Sales increases may be due to many factors other than the effectiveness of current advertising. A rising sales curve may be the final result of good advertising that appeared a number of months ago. It may, also, be due to improved selling methods, a change in the price levels, a more favorable business climate.

Should your triple associates test show bad results, you might, in view of the preceding, do some worrying about your advertising even though sales curves are going up. The upward trend might exist despite the advertising.

As in aided-recall testing, you must be careful if you are the dominant advertiser. To illustrate, imagine that you are the first peanut advertiser to promote vacuum-packed peanuts. Imagine further that you are the only really big peanut advertiser. Suppose for your triple associates test you ask, "What peanuts are vacuum-packed?" How much reliability could you place in the findings when many persons could guess your brand—if they didn't know. To get around this difficulty, you can ask the consumers to indicate by brand which of several products are vacuum-packed. In this list you might name such products as coffee, soup, pickles, peanuts, and shoe-string potatoes. If the respondents included peanuts among the several products vacuum-packed, you would know that your advertising of the feature was making an impression. Similar testing conducted at regular intervals should tell you whether your campaign theme and brand recognition were becoming stronger or weaker.

To sum up—think of the following in connection with the triple associates test: a) It is an excellent way to determine brand and theme association in campaign advertising. b) Through this test you can often obtain a more reliable indication of the success of your advertising than you will get from rising sales. Many times, moreover, you will find a strong correlation between sales and high brand- and theme-awareness and vice versa. c) On the negative side, don't forget—as in so many tests of copy, the results don't necessarily measure conviction or selling power. You can establish superb recognition of theme and brand but the consumers may buy your competitor's product. Often it's easier to capture attention than conviction—especially if you depend on "irritating" consumers into becoming aware of you. In such cases the triple associates test results may look good despite what consumers may actually think of your product and your advertising.

COMMUNISCOPE (TACHISTOSCOPE) TESTS

The section on impact testing mentioned that critics have called the Starch technique "overstimulating" and the impact method "understimulating." An answer to these asserted weaknesses was, according to its sponsors, Communiscope testing. This form of testing was begun because its originators believed neither recognition nor impact testing provided measurements sensitive enough to produce statistically significant differences among most printed advertisements.

A long-used testing device, the tachistoscope, provides the principal means for Communiscope research. This device is a slide projector hooked to an electric timer. In the test situation, advertisements on slides are flashed rapidly before respondents who then play back what they have seen. Backers of the Communiscope method assert that respondents will be stimulated enough to remember whether they have seen the advertisements and what they remember about them, but they will not be overstimulated by having been given so much time to look that they "learned" the advertisement while the test was administered.

Test reports will give three types of information to clients: percentage of adults in the United States who recognize and recall the advertisement checked; what impression and meaning was derived from the advertisement; respondent's emotional reaction to the advertisement.

A criticism of Communiscope testing by those who favor recognition testing is that it is impossible to measure exposure to advertising and the influence of the advertising on those exposed to it at the same time. These critics add that the importance of memorability has been overstressed since it cannot be assumed that the reader who can play back the contents of an advertisement has necessarily been favorably influenced by the advertisement—nor does failure to play the advertisement back prove that the advertisement has had no influence.

From the viewpoint of supporters of the impact method, Communiscope testing fails to supply the interpretive data and analysis supplied by the former.

COPY TESTING THROUGH SALES TESTS

You will find sales tests mentioned in many books as a form of copy testing. It is true that the efficiency of different copy approaches is discovered in sales tests. Also, it is true that packaging, pricing, choice of media, labor conditions, income trends, salespeople, inventory controls, and other elements affect results of sales tests. The form of advertising—position, advertising size, frequency—are tested as much as the copy itself. Since copy is just one of the forces being examined in sales tests, it does not seem necessary for this book to dip very far into the subject. Copy has been the principal object of analysis in other copy-testing procedures—since you are close to such tests. The sales tests, on the contrary, are closer to the market-research people, or the sales department. You will probably not have actual contact with such tests except to supply the original copy for the campaign. After that, you lose sight of the test as the sales and marketing people move in. A sales test, briefly explained, goes something like this:

You decide to test the effect of your advertising in two markets. One of the market areas is considered a "control" area. The other is the "test" area. Three or more cities are usually found in each area. The new campaign will be used in the test section. In the control area you will either a) run no advertising or b) continue to run your old campaign. Sales results in the two areas will then be compared by checking store inventories in selected stores before, during, and after the advertising is run.

Possibly you will run a different campaign in each of the test cities. The results will enable you to compare the campaigns against one another as well as against the control cities.

Some advertising people believe only in a sales test, because they look upon the test as operating under "actual" conditions as opposed to "artificial" conditions of other forms of copy research. Yet many factors make the sales tests extremely difficult to control. Results must be examined with great care to avoid erroneous conclusions. Some of the difficulties:

- Selection of appropriate control and test cities.
- Sales ability of salespeople in the different areas. Poor salespeople in the test cities and good salespeople in the control cities might throw the whole test off, since the new campaign might thus show poor sales despite effective advertising.
- Dealer reaction. Unless dealers cooperate equally in all the test areas, sales variations will occur quite apart from the advertising.
- Competitive advertising and sales efforts may vary from city to city during the test period.
- Media differences are hard to control. Some newspapers and radio stations are much more aggressive than others in their merchandising promotions. They do a vigorous job of backing up the advertisers. Also, they may vary greatly in the amount of reader or listening interest they command.
- Unusual weather conditions during the test may affect sales results. A paralyzing snow storm affecting one of the cities might affect its sales record negatively.

Think of the factors named. When you realize that there are many other variables and that, in addition, a sales test is expensive and time-consuming, you can see why it is not of great concern to you.

GENERAL CONCLUSIONS ABOUT TESTING

An effort should be made to keep up with research methods and organizations. Some of these have been discussed in this chapter. Any alert copywriter should know about the many studies performed for business publication advertisers, as well as the complicated world of television research.

There are, in addition, others that may or may not be important to you depending on the nature of your work and where you work. Do not let the virtues of any one system blind you to its faults. Be everlastingly critical. Do not let testing replace good sense. Good sense must be used in analyzing and applying copy testing. Consider the Flesch formula, for example. Your copy will, according to the readability formula receive an equally high rating if the copy is printed backwards or if the sentences are jumbled. Since the word count, and personal references are the same in either case, the readability score will be the same. Good sense is the final determinant of copy effectiveness in this case—as it is in every copy-testing method.

Your judgment of sales points, human nature, and effective writing style are the important factors in copywriting. The copy tests are your assistants; they'll never be your boss. The best businesspeople and the best copywriter get off the track occasionally. Copy research is valuable if it does nothing but reduce the margin of error in the guesses of advertising men. It can unkink the thumb in the famous "rule of thumb" measurement you have heard so much about. When you lose touch with the market and the consumer, copy testing may bring you back. If you were to be asked the principal values of copy testing, you might answer:

- To determine before publication what copy style, copy approach, or copy appeals are likely to obtain the greatest readership and/or sales conviction.
- To determine after publication the quantitative and qualitative aspects of readership and thus to indicate what copy techniques should be continued, discontinued, or modified for future use.
- To obtain through cumulative findings a body of information about copy that advertisers may use to produce advertising of the greatest efficiency—advertising that will cost the advertiser less in time, effort, and money because it avoids the mistakes of the past.

21

Protect the Consumer and Yourself: Know the Legal Rules

You may, if you're writing copy for certain types of products (such as headache remedies, cold cures, soaps, certain food products and cigarettes) be working harder to please the lawyers than the clients. As you type, you have a haunted feeling. Just over your shoulder you can sense stern-visaged representatives of the Federal Trade Commission, the Food and Drug Administration, the Better Business Bureau, and others whose job it is to protect the consumer.

Are they frowning as they read your copy? You fervently hope not because your client will be less than enchanted if your copy drags him into the courts.

Before you worry unduly about legal trouble, however, remember that of the millions of words of copy produced each year, only a small percentage will get the writer into any kind of legal trouble. Most products and services have nothing about them that would cause a writer to turn out copy that could lead to legal action. Furthermore, if you find yourself assigned to products or services that are troublesome legally, you'll be given the first day on the job a set of legal "do's and don'ts" that apply. By observing these cautions, using common sense, and being guided by your innate sense of honesty, you'll keep yourself, your client, and your agency out of trouble.

The single most important principle is to get the facts and make certain they are correct. Any attempt to write copy about a product or service without knowing in complete detail exactly what it is and does will invite legal difficulties. It must be emphasized, though, that even telling the absolute truth is not always enough. Each sentence in an advertisement, considered separately, may be literally true and yet the entire advertisement as a whole may be misleading. This can come about because statements that ought to be made are omitted, or because the advertisement is composed or set up in such a way as to create a misleading impression. If the copy can be understood in two different ways, the advertiser is not excused just because one of its meanings can be sustained as accurate.

It is essential to bear in mind also that most consumers are trusting and unsophisticated people. It is not a defense to a charge of false advertising to show that a particularly intelligent and acute reader should have been able to figure out the true meaning of the copy. The standard to be applied is not the level of intelligence of the average purchaser, but of someone even less knowledgeable than that.

Television creates its own special problems for the copywriter. The visual portion of a TV commercial may be misleading even though the off-camera voice is telling the exact truth; or the audio may be the means of misrepresenting the picture that appears on the screen. Product demonstrations, in particular, must be genuine, and the accompanying dialogue must be honest and accurate.

TRICKINESS AND PUFFERY

There is no point in trying to be tricky when writing advertising copy. Short term gains in sales possibly might result, but in the long run such a policy can do only harm to the advertiser. This can come about through loss of good will from disillusioned customers even though no government agency ever may get around to commencing a legal proceeding designed to force the discontinuance of the misleading copy.

Thus far in this introductory section, we have been dealing with the category of what generally are called "product claims." To show that the law is not completely arbitrary, there is another recognized category known as "puffery" or "puffing." Under this heading come the harmless exaggerations that are expressions of opinion rather than claims of some objective quality or characteristic for the product. For example, even the most gullible consumer is considered capable of grappling with the fact that such statements as "the best of its kind," "the most beautiful," or "the finest" might not be literally true. This does not mean that a false objective claim can be legalized by disguising it in the form of a statement of opinion. If an automobile will not get fifty miles to a gallon of gas, the advertisement still will be misleading even if the statement is put in the form of the manufacturer's opinion that, "I believe this car will get fifty miles to the gallon."

The difference is between a representation that induces the purchase and one that does not. Consumers who buy "the funniest book you ever read" can expect to be amused, but they don't really expect the advertiser to be able to prove the superlative.

Product claims and statements of opinion, of course, are not the only areas in which legal problems arise in advertising. Permission to use copyrighted material, defamatory statements, the right to use a person's name or picture, proper trademark usage, and idea piracy are just some of the other areas where an awareness in advance of the possible legal pitfalls may save a great deal of trouble and expense that otherwise might be encountered. An attempt will be made here to discuss those topics that are most likely to affect the work of the copywriter.

FEDERAL TRADE COMMISSION

The one government agency most concerned with problems of advertising is the Federal Trade Commission (FTC). This agency, under the Federal Trade Commission Act, has broad authority to proceed against "deceptive acts or practices" in almost all kinds of commercial activity. The theory of the law is that false or misleading advertising, like other deceptive acts and practices, is an unfair method of competition. If a false advertisement succeeds in its purpose, it will give the advertiser an unfair advantage over his truthful competitors. But false advertising is an offense even though no competitors are hurt, because the Federal Trade Commission Act is also designed to protect consumers. The Federal Trade Commission constantly brings numerous cease-and-desist proceedings under this law.

The Federal Trade Commission also functions in several other and different ways. It issues advertising guides, trade practice rules and standard rules. In addition to the Federal Trade Commission Act itself, which is phrased in broad general terms as indicated, the Federal Trade Commission administers several special statutes dealing with particular fields of commerce, including margarine, wool, fur and textile products.

FALSE AND MISLEADING ADVERTISING IN GENERAL

The Federal Trade Commission is concerned with so many different varieties of false and misleading advertising that it is almost impossible to categorize all of them. There are, however, certain specific areas of difficulty that constantly recur in advertising cases brought by the Federal Trade Commission. Some of those with particular interest to advertising copywriters are discussed in the succeeding sections.

Guarantees

There seems to be a common temptation to use the word "guaranteed" rather loosely. It is a very rare occurrence when advertisers actually guarantee a product unconditionally, but that is the way the word "guaranteed" will be construed legally unless any conditions that may be attached to the offer are clearly in the advertisement.

If, for example, advertisers mean that they merely will replace a defective article rather than refund the purchase price, then the advertisement must say so. If the guarantee is limited in terms of time, then this must be stated clearly. If the guarantee applies only to defective parts rather than to the entire article, then the advertisement should make this clear. Frequently there are extra charges, such as shipping expenses for the defective merchandise or the return of the repaired article; these conditions must be set forth clearly in the advertisement.

A "money-back" guarantee means that the customer is entitled to a cash refund, not just a credit slip or an exchange of merchandise. The expression "satisfaction or your money back" should not be used unless the advertiser is willing to let the customers be the sole judge of whether they are satisfied.

Similar words such as "warranty" or "warranted" also require the same treatment as "guarantee." The word "bonded" signifies something more. This should not be used in advertising unless an actual bond has been posted by the advertiser to insure that the customer will get what he is promised under the terms of the guarantee or warranty.

An example of a suitably stated guarantee with certain limitations might be, "Guaranteed against defective materials and workmanship for ninety days." But this guarantee would not be fulfilled merely by shipping a replacement part under circumstances where the customer had to pay an installation charge, shipping expenses, or the like. In all cases the true nature of the guarantee must be disclosed clearly; there should be no doubt about what the advertiser is willing to do and what, if anything, the customer will have to do in order to obtain the benefit of the guarantee.

Premiums

When an article of merchandise is offered as a premium, it is essential for the copywriter to learn as much as possible about the premium, just as he must learn about the product of the advertiser itself. A misdescribed premium is the responsibility of the advertiser, not of the manufacturer of the premium merchandise.

The most common problem arising out of the use of premiums is a misrepresentation of their value. Sometimes advertisers who are extremely careful when making claims about their own products are somewhat less careful in describing the premiums that they offer. If an advertisement states that a premium is worth a certain amount or has a value of a stated sum, that amount should be the price at which the premium merchandise actually is sold customarily when offered for sale on its own.

Premium offers also raise a multitude of problems under separate state laws. In order to make it practical to use premiums in national distribution, it is common to take two precautions. In the first place, premium coupons have a cash value assigned to them. This ordinarily is a nominal sum like 1/10 of a cent, but the manufacturer must be prepared to redeem the coupons in cash at that rate on demand. Secondly, the coupon traditionally carries what is called a "nullification clause" reading somewhat along the following lines: "This offer void in any state where prohibited, taxed, or otherwise restricted."

Any premium offer on a large scale also may raise serious questions under federal and local tax laws, but these are not the responsibility of the copywriter and obviously are outside the scope of this discussion.

Contests, lotteries, and sweepstakes

A true contest is a perfectly lawful advertising method. Legal difficulties arise in two principal ways. The first is when the advertiser fails to give the full details of the contest. In that case it frequently turns out to be some sort of a "come-on" device that will cost the reader much more than he ever anticipated in extra fees for tie-breaking puzzles or some other hidden requirement. The second is when it is not a true contest at all, but is a lottery because the element of chance is present. This not only violates the Federal Trade Commission Act as an unfair method of competition, but also is an offense under numerous other laws, state and federal.

Just as in the case of a guarantee, the key to proper contest advertising is to make certain that all of the details are given clearly and unequivocally in the advertisements. This means more than a complicated list of rules in small type that a highly intelligent person might be able to figure out with close attention to detail.

One famous contest case went all the way to the United States Supreme Court. The advertisement gave the impression that it was a "rebus," or picture puzzle, contest with an entry fee of $3. Actually, when you examined the fine print, you could find out with very careful analysis that there was a required $9 entrance fee and, in addition, that it might be necessary to pay as much as a total of $42 in order to continue with the tie-breakers. On the basis of the advertiser's own past experience, it was clear that this really was an essay contest to break the ties that were bound to develop. The statistics showed that 90,000 people had

submitted answers to the first eighty puzzles. Of these, 35,000 solved all eighty. The first set of tie-breakers was completed by 27,000 people. Eventually it was necessary, under the obscure language of one of the rules, to write a competitive letter on the subject. "The Puzzle I Found Most Interesting and Educational in This Contest."

This particular contest was involved in a Post Office Department fraud order case rather than a Federal Trade Commission cease-and-desist proceeding. The general principles, of course, are the same. The key finding of the Postmaster General which the United States Supreme Court upheld was that the advertisements for this puzzle contest had been "deliberately contrived to divert readers' attention from material but adroitly obscured facts."

A lottery is not a contest at all; it involves a payment (or other legal consideration) in exchange for the chance to win a prize. All three elements—chance, consideration, and prize—must be present or the promotion is not a lottery.

There ordinarily is no difficulty in determining whether a prize is involved. If no prize were offered, there would be no contest.

Chance means that the participant has no way of controlling the result. It may be understood as the opposite of skill. An essay contest in which awards are given for merit by impartial judges is perfectly satisfactory because there is no element of chance present; but a baseball contest that requires listing the standings of the teams in both the American and National leagues at the end of a particular month is something completely outside the possibility of control by the participant. It is guesswork, or chance, and not skill.

Consideration generally is found in the entrance requirements. For example, buying some breakfast cereal in order to get the coupon from the back of the box is enough to constitute consideration. It does not matter that the price of the cereal was not increased when the coupon was added to the back of the box. The consumer bought that particular box of cereal when otherwise he might not have purchased any, or have purchased a different brand, and that is sufficient to satisfy the requirement of consideration. The familiar provision for using a "reasonable facsimile" of the entry blank is included in order to avoid a violation of the lottery laws by eliminating the element of consideration.

A prize lawfully may be awarded by chance if there is absolutely no charge or obligation of any kind. So-called sweepstakes, with coupons distributed free to all comers, fall in this category. Conversely, if a prize is given for true skill as distinguished from chance, then it is not unlawful to charge a consideration for permission to enter the contest.

"Good purpose," incidentally, does not excuse a lottery. Although enforcement officials rarely crack down on fund-raising drawings for charities, enterprises of this sort technically are lotteries just as if they were operated for advertising purposes or for private gain.

Testimonials and endorsements

An advertiser cannot escape responsibility for a false or misleading product claim by putting it in the mouth of an endorser. Testimonials and endorsements must be true and free from misleading statements. Merely because someone is willing to write a letter saying that a particular drug cured a disease does not mean that this necessarily is so, even though the author of the letter believes it to be true.

The Federal Trade Commission will take action against advertisements containing testimonials given by people who are not competent to pass judgment upon the accuracy of the statements of opinion that they are making. There is a great deal of difference between a baseball player saying that he eats a particular brand of bread and likes it, and the same baseball player saying that eating a particular brand of bread has a beneficial effect upon his health.

There is nothing wrong about paying for a testimonial. The fact that the endorser receives some compensation for giving the testimonial need not be disclosed in the advertisement.

It is improper to take words or sentences out of context. A testimonial should be given in its entirety; or at least the portion that is used should not create a different impression from what the complete text would have implied if given in full.

When testimonials are used in advertising, they must be genuine. The natural tendency of any reader of an advertisement containing a testimonial or endorsement is to believe that a real person gave it. A fictitious endorsement, therefore, is an unfair trade practice.

The use of a testimonial also implies automatically that it is reasonably current. If the endorser no longer uses the product or if the product has been so changed since the date of the testimonial that the endorsement no longer fairly applies to the product which is advertised, then the testimonial should be discontinued.

A public opinion poll or market survey is the equivalent of a testimonial on a mass scale and its results must be used with corresponding care. In addition, reference to a poll or survey in advertising copy will be construed as a representation that proper sampling techniques were used and that the sample was of meaningful size.

"ADVERTISING GUIDES"

On several occasions, the Federal Trade Commission has issued what it calls "Advertising Guides." These are detailed statements that constitute basic policy developed by the Federal Trade Commission in specific business areas and compiled essentially for the use of its own staff. They are released also to the public, particularly for the guidance of advertisers, in the interest of obtaining voluntary cooperation and avoiding legal proceedings.

Deceptive pricing

Claims of special savings, extra discounts, less than the usual price and reductions from ticketed prices, have been among the most troublesome problems faced by Federal Trade Commission enforcement officials. The Deceptive Pricing Advertising Guides go into these problems in explicit detail. Examples of both approved and disapproved types of statements are given, along with the basic principles that will satisfy Federal Trade Commission requirements. A statement, for instance, that there is a reduction or saving from a specified retail price, or from the advertiser's usual or customary retail price, is improper if an artificial markup has been used to provide the basis for the claim of a saving. The claim is equally improper if it is based on infrequent or isolated sales, or on a price that was charged some substantial time in the past, unless, of course, these facts are stated clearly and adequately. The saving or reduction must be from the usual and customary retail price of the article in the particular trading area where the statement is made, and the saving or reduction must be from the advertiser's usual and customary retail price charged for the article in the regular course of business.

Certain words and phrases are recognized as representations when an article is being offered for sale to the consuming public at a saving from the usual or customary retail price. Obviously, these should not be used unless the claim is true. Examples of words or phrases of this type are: "special purchase," "clearance," "marked down from stock," "exceptional purchase," "manufacturer's close-out," "advance sale."

Preticketing with fictitiously high prices comes in for special attention in these advertising guides. No article should be preticketed with any figure that exceeds the price at which it is sold usually and customarily in the trading area where it is offered for sale. In this connection, the Federal Trade Commission points out that those who distribute preticketed price figures are chargeable with knowledge of the ordinary business facts of life concerning what happens to articles for which they furnish the preticketed prices. The same basic principle applies to the use of the preticketed price in advertising copy. The manufacturer may be held responsible for exaggerated prices in national advertising even though it is the retailer who misuses the figures; and the retailer will not be excused merely because it was the manufacturer who first advertised the fictitious price.

"Two for the Price of One" sales are prohibited unless the sales price for the two articles is the advertiser's usual and customary retail price for the single article in the recent regular course of his business. Similarly, half-price sales or one-cent sales are improper unless the represented saving in price is true with relation to the advertiser's usual and customary retail price for the article in the recent regular course of his business. If the special offer is conditioned on the purchase of additional merchandise, then all terms or conditions imposed must be disclosed conspicuously in connection with the offer.

The key point to remember is that the word "price" itself constitutes an implication that the figure given is the usual and customary price charged by the advertiser in the recent regular course of his business in the trading area reached by the advertisement. This rule must be the starting point for all price advertising.

Tires and tubes

The Federal Trade Commission advertising guides for tires and tubes grew out of a long series of proceedings involving misleading terminology and various types of exaggerated product claims in this industry. One of the guides, for example, states that manufacturers should not use deceptive designations for the different grades of their products. If the first line tire of a particular manufacturer is designated "standard," then the same manufacturer's tires of a lower quality should not be designated as "super standard." If discontinued models or obsolete designs are offered, those facts must be stated clearly. Used products must be described adequately, so that it is clear they are not new. Terms such as "nutread" and "snow tread" do not constitute sufficient disclosure of this fact.

The unqualified use of absolute terms such as "skid proof," "blow-out proof" and "puncture proof" is improper unless the product really affords complete and absolute protection under any and all driving conditions.

The term "ply" is defined in technical detail. Tire advertising should contain an adequate statement of the identity of the fabric or other material used in the construction of the ply. Statements implying that tires possess a specified number of plies are not to be used unless this is the fact. The term "ply rating" is an index of tire strength and does not necessarily represent the number of cord plies in a particular tire. If a term such as "eight-ply rating" is used to describe a tire containing fewer than eight plies, then the statement must be accompanied by a conspicuous disclosure of the actual number of plies in the tire.

These technical provisions are included here as an illustration of the degree of detail into which the Federal Trade Commission goes on appropriate occasions. Obviously, it would be foolhardy to write copy for automobile tires without studying the Federal Trade Commission's Tire Advertising Guides carefully.

TRADE PRACTICE RULES

Still another function of the Federal Trade Commission is the promulgation of trade practice rules. Typically, these are quite complex and detailed sets of regulations worked out by members of the Federal Trade Commission staff in conference with representatives of a broad segment of the industry affected. They put the requirements of the Federal Trade Commission Act into concrete form as applied to that particular industry.

Over the years, trade practice rules have been issued by the Federal Trade Commission for dozens of different industries. A few will be referred to here, largely for the purpose of indicating by example the fact that it is highly important for copywriters to determine whether trade practice rules exist in the industry with which they are concerned and to make certain they are familiar with them in detail if that turns out to be so.

Watches

A watch either is waterproof or it is not. In order to describe it as waterproof, the case must be of such composition and construction as to be impervious to moisture through immersion for the life of the watch. The Federal Trade Commission trade practice rules include details of a specific test that requires complete immersion for at least five minutes in water under atmospheric pressure of 15 pounds per square inch and for at least an additional five minutes in water under atmospheric pressure of at least 35 pounds per square inch without admitting any water. If a watch does not pass this test, it may not be described as waterproof, although, possibly, it may be described correctly as "water-resistant" or "water-repellent." Here, too, a specific test has been promulgated by the Federal Trade Commission.

Similarly, the terms "shock-proof," "jar-proof," "magnetic" and "regulated" are defined carefully. Improper use of any of these terms will be considered a violation of the principles of the Federal Trade Commission Act.

Radio and television sets

One of the problems peculiar to this industry is the number of tubes in a radio or television set. Rectifier tubes, so-called ballast tubes, lamps used only for illumination, resistors of the plugin type and other devices must not be counted in stating the number of tubes.

When describing the size of the picture tube in a television set, the horizontal measurement is required. The trade practice rules permit the use of the diagonal measurement only if it is also stated, in immediate conjunction with that figure, that it is a diagonal measurement and if the horizontal figure is given in addition. Only a tolerance of plus or minus 1/8 inch is permitted in quoting the figures for the dimensions of the picture tube.

It is an unfair trade practice to sell any radio or television set as a discontinued model unless the manufacturer has discontinued it entirely and replaced it on the market with a new set or model. This means a new model embodying specific, material changes in appearance, mechanical design or function, with the addition of new features to perform new functions.

The terms "rebuilt" and "factory rebuilt" also are discussed in detail. It is improper to use such words unless the product has been dismantled and reconstructed, with badly worn and defective or missing parts either repaired or replaced with new parts. If the term "factory rebuilt" is used, then the rebuilding must have been done at a factory or under the supervision or control of the factory of the original manufacturer.

Products made of "gold"

The use of the word "gold" creates a number of problems in the industry. The unqalified word "gold," or its abbreviation, cannot be used alone unless the part of the product so described is composed throughout of gold of 24 karat fineness. The word "gold" cannot be used at all to describe an alloy of less than 10 karat fineness. When the gold is more than 10 karat but less than 24 karat, the karat fineness must be shown in immediate conjunction with the word "gold."

Terms such as "duragold" or "goldene" may not be used unless the article is made of pure gold or of an alloy of at least 10 karat fineness. No phrase or representation indicating the substance, charm, quality or beauty of gold may be used properly unless the article is of at least 10 karat fineness.

"Gold filled," "rolled-gold plate," "gold flashed" and similar terms also are described in terms of their technical definitions. It is an unfair trade practice to use any of these terms under circumstances where they do not meet the requirements laid down in the trade practice rules.

Correspondence schools

A school may not adopt a name which gives a misleading or deceptive impression. Under specific Federal Trade Commission rulings, for example, the word "college" cannot be used by a school unless it is an institution of high learning empowered to confer degrees and possessing a faculty of instructors in various branches of learning. The faculty and equipment of the school must not be misrepresented by illustration or otherwise. Words such as "federal" and "national" may not be used in such a way as to represent by implication that the school has any connection with the federal government. The word "foundation" is improper as part of the name for a private commercial school.

It is an unfair trade practice to make deceptive statements concerning probable earnings or opportunities in any vocation for which the school offers a course of instruction. It is improper to claim that taking a particular course necessarily will bring about a certain result, such as learning to play a musical instrument, or learning to perform a particular trade skillfully. It is also unfair to indicate in advertising that only qualified applicants are accepted when the fact of the matter is that anyone paying the purchase price will be received as a student.

Luggage

The correct name of the material from which the luggage is manufactured must be stated. Luggage not made of leather, of course, must not be misdescribed. It is also an unfair trade practice to use tradenames that are misleading because they suggest the presence of genuine leather in a product made from imitation leather, or the presence of one variety of leather in a product made from a different variety.

Even genuine leather frequently is processed in such a way as to indicate that it is leather of a different type. The words "genuine," "real," "natural," and the like may not be used to describe leather that has been embossed or processed to simulate a different kind, grade, type, or quality. The facts must be disclosed in detail when the product is advertised. For example, "top-grain cowhide," "imitation pig grain" or "split cowhide, embossed design" are appropriate terms that explain what the leather is and what finish has been applied to it.

Top grain leather is the best grade. The trade practice rules provide specifically that leather from which either a layer of the top surface or grain, or a so-called buffing, has been removed shall not be considered top grain leather. In addition, terms such as "waterproof," "water repellent," "dust-proof," "warp-proof" or the like should not be used unless they are literally true of the product.

STANDARD RULES

In connection with its trade practice conference work, the Federal Trade Commission has published two standard rules with the announcement that they are prescribed for inclusion in every set of trade practice rules issued thereafter. It is clear that these can be taken as expressions of the Federal Trade Commission's policy and the standard rules therefore are treated as having general application.

One of these rules deals with push money, that is, payments by manufacturers to retail sales clerks. But copywriters have very little concern with it. The other rule deals with the tricky question of the proper use of the word "free," and this is of considerable interest to copywriters.

The Standard "Free" Rule prohibits the use of the word "free" under circumstances where there has been a reduction in the ordinary and usual price of the product, or its quality, or its quantity or size. This applies to the merchandise that is required to be purchased in order to obtain whatever it is that the advertiser is offering "free." In other words, neither the price, the quality, nor the quantity of the regular merchandise can be juggled in order to absorb some or all of the cost of the supposedly free merchandise.

In addition, if the free merchandise is not truly an unconditional gift, then all of the conditions or obligations affecting its acquisition must be set forth clearly and conspicuously "so as to leave no reasonable probability that the terms of the offer will be misunderstood." A disclosure in the form of a footnote is not considered sufficient compliance by the Federal Trade Commission. The rule specifically requires that this disclosure must appear in close conjunction with the word "free" wherever that word first appears in each advertisement.

SPECIAL STATUTES

As indicated, the Federal Trade Commission is charged with the duty of enforcing a group of special statutes dealing with specific products or industries in addition to its general powers under the Federal Trade Commission Act. During the past few years, it has become increasingly common to find specific statutes of this sort introduced into Congress, and there may be more of them from time to time. Each of the principal ones now in effect will be discussed briefly.

Oleomargarine

A special law provides that no advertisement for oleomargarine (or margarine) may contain a representation by statement, word, device, symbol, or any other method that the oleomargarine offered for sale is a dairy product. This means that dairy terms may not be used in writing copy for margarine. Specific examples of prohibited advertising statements are "churned to delicate sweet creamy goodness," "always country fresh," and "the same day to day freshness which characterizes our other dairy products."

The law specifically permits a truthful, accurate and full statement of all the ingredients contained in the oleomargarine. On this basis, some manufacturers have added actual butter, apparently for the principal purpose of being able to advertise that fact. The Federal Trade Commission prohibits any emphasis in margarine advertising on an unstated percentage of butter content. If butter is added, the percentage must be set forth clearly and conspicuously or the advertisement will be considered misleading in a material respect.

Wool products

The Wool Products Labeling Act defines "wool," "reprocessed wool" and "reused wool." It requires a clear and explicit statement of the true composition of any wool product, and also a statement of other fibers in addition to wool if there are any such contained in the product. Although this law deals specifically with labeling, the same principles are applied as a matter of policy to the advertising of wool products and the rules and regulations under the Wool Products Labeling Act should be consulted in preparing advertising copy for any product containing wool.

"Wool" means the fiber from the fleece of the sheep or lamb, or the hair of the angora or cashmere goat. It also may include the so-called specialty fibers, which derive from the hair of the camel, alpaca, llama or vicuna. Accordingly, it is proper to use just the word "wool" or terms such as "alpaca," "camel hair," "llama," "vicuna," "cashmere," or "mohair" if in fact the fiber is that type of wool. If, however, the fiber is reprocessed or reused, those words also must be included in order to avoid misleading the public.

The key facts that must be shown are the kind of wool involved and its percentage by weight. In addition, if 5 percent or more of any other fiber is included in the total fabric, the presence of this fiber also must be disclosed. And the weight of any nonfiber that is used as loading or filling must be disclosed with its proper percentage stated prominently.

Fur products

The Wool Products Labeling Act was followed by a Fur Products Labeling Act. Unlike its predecessor this statute does apply to advertising by its terms.

Since there are so many different types of fur and they come from so many different parts of the world, the principal objective of the Fur Products Labeling Act is to make certain that the true type of fur is named and that the country of origin is given in all instances. A Fur Products Name Guide has been issued by the Federal Trade Commission in which the name of the animal can be looked up and checked according to its scientific designation. The country of origin, of course, must be determined and disclosed.

The Fur Act also contains detailed regulations about disclosures of the method of construction. Terms such as "pointing," "bleaching," "dyeing" and "blending" are defined and the circumstances under which they may be used are set forth.

Trade names or trademarks may not be used if they might create a misleading impression concerning the character of the product, the name of the animal producing the fur, or its geographical or zoological origin.

Textile fiber products

The most recent special statute in this series assigned to the Federal Trade Commission for administration is the Textile Fiber Products Identification Act. Like the Fur Act, this statute specifically applies to advertising as well as labeling.

If any fibers are mentioned at all, the correct generic name of each fiber present in the amount of more than 5 percent of the total fiber weight of the product must appear. Detailed regulations have been issued by the Federal Trade Commission including a list of definitions of generic names for manufactured fibers.

In advertising any textile fiber product, all parts of the required information must be stated in immediate conjunction with each other, in legible and conspicuous type or lettering of equal size and prominence. The generic names of the fibers that are present in amounts of more than 5 percent must be listed in the order of their predominance by weight. If any fiber is present in an amount of 5 percent or less, then the list of ingredients must be followed by the designation "other fiber" or "other fibers" to make this fact plain.

Specific examples of various types of approved expressions are given in the regulations. The following statements, for instance, would be appropriate for use in advertising: 60 percent cotton, 40 percent rayon, exclusive of ornamentation; all nylon, exclusive of elastic and all cotton except 1 percent nylon added to neck band.

An imported textile fiber product must be marked with the name of the country where it was processed or manufactured. This requirement applies where the form of an imported textile fiber product is not basically changed even though it is processed in the United States, such as by finishing and dyeing. However, a textile fiber product manufactured in the United States from imported materials need not disclose the name of the country where the textile originally was made or processed.

RED FLAG WORDS

The watchful eyes of the Federal Trade Commission's alert staff are particularly sensitive to certain "red flag" words. The copywriter, too, must learn to recognize the danger signals. This does not mean that these words may never be used, but only that particular care is required because they are so easy to misuse. The presence of a red flag word frequently is an indication that the entire basic thought of an advertisement is wrong from the legal viewpoint. Of course, it is entirely possible to violate the Federal Trade Commission Act without using a single word on this list, but experience has shown that these are the ones most likely to create legal difficulties.

It would be futile to attempt a complete list of red flag words; there is no such thing and, even if there were, the passage of time would eliminate some old ones and add others. A few important examples will be discussed to illustrate the general principles involved in avoiding trouble. The fundamental idea is to make sure that you know just what the words mean and that your product can fulfill the promises contained in them.

Two such words have been discussed already—"free" and "guarantee." They are such troublemakers that they have been treated separately. The following are some additional sources of difficulty. Notice that a good many of these red flag words apply particularly to drug and cosmetic copy. Advertising for such products is watched with special zeal because these products affect physical and mental welfare. At one time, the Federal Trade Commission analyzed 915 of its cases and found that from all the different classifications of commodities, 65 percent of the questioned advertising copy related to drug products and 14.4 percent to cosmetics. In other words, almost 80 percent of all questioned copy fell into these two classes.

Banish, rid, stop, correct, end. Each of these five words says to the consumer, "This is the last of your trouble—it's all over now—permanently and forever." There may be times when you can use these words in their literal meaning. Too often, however, the Federal Trade Commission finds them used inaccurately—if not dishonestly.

Words in this group probably have been more used and abused in drug copy than in any other type of advertising. See if the following examples don't look familiar: Banish sleepless nights. Rid yourself of constipation. Stop psoriasis. Correct sluggish liver conditions. End headaches. Each of these statements promises relief to sufferers—permanent relief. It is the permanency feature that makes the Federal Trade Commission balk. Permanent relief means cure, and drugs seldom cure.

Cosmetic copy often uses these words carelessly, also. It is too easy to write: Acne sufferers—rid yourself of unsightly pimples. Ashamed of your hands? Banish roughness.

To generalize—think before you use these words. Consider whether your claims are truthful. Ask yourself, "Can my product cure, fix or remedy permanently the condition under discussion?" If you can't answer that it does, you'd better use a different word, or qualify your statement with "can help rid you of . . ."

Cure, remedy, therapeutic, curative. Millions of people suffer chronically from myriad ailments—ulcers, varicose veins, eye trouble, headaches, arthritis. Each of these afflicted persons is anxious for relief. Some of them swallow gallons of patent medicines led on by unthinking or untruthful copywriters who promise "cure" or "remedy."

Unfortunately, real cures are rare. The proper procedure for the copywriter is to find out what the product actually has accomplished and claim only that it will relieve specific symptoms—not cure the disease (unless the manufacturer is certain that it really will).

"Remedy" is put in the same class as "cure" by the Federal Trade Commission. "Therapeutic" and "curative" are eyed suspiciously also.

Drug copy isn't the only type using these red flag words. Cosmetics, soaps, tooth pastes and foods are only a few of the other products that slip one of these words into their copy on occasion. All four of them are alarm signals.

Blemish-free, clear, smooth. There are few forms of mental suffering so acute as that felt by people who have bad complexions. Since they are so extremely susceptible to advertising promising them skin that is blemish-free, clear or smooth, the Federal Trade Commission has been especially critical of such copy. Here are some points to remember in writing copy for a product used for skin care. If the product is applied externally and you promise that it will make the skin blemish-free, you must:

1. Establish the fact that the skin is blemished because of external factors and not because of a systemic condition.

2. Indicate that the product can be effective only if the cause of the blemishes is external.
3. Be sure your statements are based on proved facts. If the product is taken internally, then reverse the procedure of steps 1 and 2.

"Clear," as applied to skin, is interpreted as blemish-free. Think of this definition when you use the word. Then set up conditions as you do when you use the expression "blemish-free" itself.

A "smooth" skin normally is difficult to promise unless you establish the fact that a) the skin is already rough because of some specified treatment or condition; and b) the regular use of your product will bring a change. Be sure that the manufacturer has support for your claim. It is better, incidentally, to stick to the comparative in this case. An outright promise of smooth skin through use of a product is easy to make but very difficult to fulfill. Many complexions will never become smooth through use of any product, but they may get smoother than they were. Be satisfied with that.

Safe, harmless. When you say unqualifiedly that a product is "safe" or "harmless," you are asking for trouble. Humans have a fiendish capacity for proving you're wrong whether you're writing about drugs, electrical apparatus, machinery, or even baby products. To say that a product is safe or harmless under all conditions is like saying a gun is unloaded. Too often you're mistaken.

Suppose a drug product is advertised as "safe" or "harmless." The Federal Trade Commission immediately wants to know a) Isn't it possible that certain persons may be allergic to one or more of its ingredients? b) Can all persons reading the statement rely on the fact that the preparation will not harm them?

Improper use of these red flag words in copy is more than just false advertising. Suppose a person does suffer from using the product because it turned out not to be safe or harmless. There is the basis for a possible damage claim.

So far as the law is concerned, when you say your product is safe you don't mean safe to a certain degree. You mean completely safe. The same thing goes for "harmless." If you're not sure, don't use either of the words.

Science, scientific, test, evidence, proof, research. Use these words, singly or in combination, and the credulous public conjures up visions of test tubes, microscopes and long hours spent in the laboratory by white-coated men with Vandyke beards. If what you are writing is a television commercial, the picture may be right there on the tube to reinforce the impression created by the words. Yet this group of red flag words probably has been the most abused of all.

Scientists themselves use these words with great restraint. They imply a careful, systematic investigation conducted under unbiased conditions by experts who are trying to find out the truth, not to prove that their employer's brand has a slight edge over its competitors in some particular respect. Perhaps your company's laboratory discovers something about a product that you can translate into a copy claim. Do the findings of a couple of chemists become "science"? Because an informal poll of ordinary practicing physicians shows a slight favoring of your product, does this constitute "overwhelming scientific proof" that your product is superior? When you stop to think about the fact that even eminent scientists often honestly disagree, you can realize how extremely inaccurate and misleading an impression can be created by the careless use of these red flag words.

Approach "science" with humility and use "proof" and "evidence" sparingly. If you have substantial evidence to back you and if your use of the terms is literally true, then, of course, you would be foolish not to employ this very strong copy approach. Otherwise be careful.

Doctor, laboratory. These red flag words have much the same kind of built-in trouble potential as the group last discussed. A doctor's recommendation is considered a precious asset for any kind of product that can either help you or hurt you. "Laboratory" goes right along with it because that is where doctors frequently get their inspiration. But beware of the temptation to be anything but scrupulously accurate in your use of these terms. The Federal Trade Commission, knowing how gullible the public is about doctors' recommendations, is hypersensitive to copy of that type.

If you want to keep your "doctor" copy out of legal turmoil, here are a few points to bear in mind:

- Make sure the "doctors" to whom you refer are genuine physicians, licensed to practice medicine by a recognized governmental authority.
- If they are not such doctors, then make it very clear just what kind of "doctors" they are for instance, doctors of naturopathy or chiropractors.
- Avoid the unqualified, representation that a preparation is "a doctor's prescription." If true, the statement "formulated in accordance with" a doctor's prescription is acceptable. But be sure of your facts.
- Don't make a blanket statement of medical approval for your product based upon an informal survey which asked doctors for their personal preference or for a "less harmful than Product X" type of statement; these and similar limited expressions of opinion actually don't amount to recommendations.
- If an analysis by doctors reveals an insignificant advantage for your product over your competitor's product, don't blast forth with a claim of superiority. In the past, cigarette advertising sometimes was characterized by this kind of magnification of infinitesimal differences, without revealing to the public the fact that all brands contain substantial quantities of the substance involved in the analysis. Such things make cynics of the doctors and the public.

Often the word "laboratory" is used simultaneously with "doctor." The principal caution to observe with this word is that you must not refer to "our laboratory" when the client does not operate a control or research laboratory in connection with its organization. At the same time, don't mention laboratory and doctors together unless the doctors actually did their research in the laboratory from which you assert they obtained their facts. Otherwise, you may have them approving research which they would not have endorsed according to their own ideas of research methods.

The word "laboratory" is viewed suspiciously whether or not doctors are mentioned in the same advertising copy. The strict attitude of the Federal Trade Commission is shown by a series of cases in which manufacturers were forbidden to use "laboratories" as part of a trade or corporate name because they did not actually operate any laboratory.

New. The Federal Trade Commission usually won't believe that, if a product has been used for a time, it can be restored entirely to its original state through the use or application of your product. Whenever your copy asserts that the product stays "just like new" despite age, use and abuse, get ready to defend your statements. "New" to the Federal Trade Commission means fresh—no different from the day you bought it. Remember that picture when you write "looks like new." Also keep in mind that the phrases "works like new" or "lasts like new" are subject to cynical legal scrutiny.

The scrutiny becomes especially watchful when the advertiser says that a process will make something old work like new. A "better performance" claim may very well be accurate and do a good selling job without ever getting attention from the Federal Trade Commission, while the little word "new" in the copy is waving the red flag and asking for trouble, which frequently comes.

Another facet to the use of the word "new" affects those advertisers who use "new" interminably in their advertising and on packages thus giving the impression that the product is actually a new product, or a newly-improved product. Generally, the Federal Trade Commission has taken the position that "new" should not be used to describe a product that has been in use for more than six months. Furthermore, it may be used properly only when the product is truly new, or has been changed in a substantial respect. The word, moreover, does not apply to mere changes in packaging.

Although no more red flag words will be discussed, there are, of course, many more than have been presented here. The purpose in providing this partial list is twofold: to make you cautious in the use of these specific words; and to alert you to the necessity for honesty and accuracy that is the basic legal guide to all copywriting.

FOOD AND DRUG ADMINISTRATION

The Food and Drug Administration exercises control over a tremendously wide area of the entire American economy. Food is our country's largest single industry. Drugs are among the most widely advertised of all items. In addition, the Food and Drug Administration has jurisdiction over "devices," which are defined as instruments or apparatus for use in the diagnosis, cure or treatment of disease or to affect the structure or function of the body of humans or animals. This includes everything from a fever thermometer to a massage machine. And last but by no means least come cosmetics, which the law defines to include articles intended to be "rubbed, poured, sprinkled or sprayed on, introduced into or otherwise applied to the human body or any part thereof for cleansing, beautifying, promoting attractiveness or altering the appearance," with the single exception of soap.

The Food and Drug Administration is concerned primarily with the false or misleading labeling of products under its control. From the standpoint of the advertising copywriter, the principal problem, therefore, is package copy. Any literature, however, that accompanies a product has been ruled to be part of its "labeling" and leaflets, brochures or the like also come under the jurisdiction of the Food and Drug Administration when they are designed to accompany the product at the time and place of sale. Other types of advertising for products controlled by the Food and Drug Administration are supervised by the Federal Trade Commission under its general powers over false and misleading advertising, but obviously it would be inviting trouble to make a statement in advertising copy that would go against the prohibitions of the Food and Drug Administration if it happened to appear on a label.

The statute under which the Food and Drug Administration operates deals specifically with the question of labeling that becomes misleading by failure to state what should have been included. The law provides that, in determining whether labeling is misleading, there shall be taken into account not only representations made or suggested, but also the extent to which there is a failure to reveal facts which are material in the light of any representations that are made. There also is a specific provision that any information required to be on a label must be placed prominently, with such conspicuousness and in such terms as to make it likely to be read and understood by the ordinary individual, under customary conditions of purchase and use, for the particular product involved.

Numerous detailed provisions are made for a great variety of specific products, some in the law itself and others in the voluminous regulations that have been issued from time to time by the Food and Drug Administration. Particularly worthy of mention is the fact that the statute provides for the Food and Drug Administration to issue definitions and standards of identity for foods, and many such have been published for a great variety of edible products. These definitions and standards of identity typically prescribe minimum quality standards that a product must meet in order to be entitled to bear that name. If the particular product for which you are writing copy fails to satisfy these standards, then it is not proper to use what you might think is its ordinary name. For example, if cocoa contains less than 10 percent of cacao fat, it must be sold as "low-fat cocoa"; and only if it contains more than 22 percent cacao fat can it be called "breakfast cocoa." Obviously, this is the kind of factual detail that must be checked before copy is prepared.

If no standard of identity has been established for any particular food, then it must be labeled to disclose each ingredient by name—except for spices, colorings and flavorings, which may be declared simply as such. There are provisions also for exemptions from these requirements, and the Food and Drug Administration has exempted various foods for various reasons. In a number of instances the indications are that these exemptions are only temporary and definitions and standards of identity may be issued at a later date.

Drugs and devices must be labeled with adequate directions for use. Special mention must be made where a drug is liable to deteriorate. New drugs may not be offered for sale at all unless they have been tested adequately and approved. Drugs listed in standard formularies such as the United States Pharmacopoeia must be labeled with their official names, and any differences of strength, quality, or purity from the official standards must be stated conspicuously on the label.

Cosmetics are subject to misbranding and false labeling restrictions similar to those affecting foods, except that there is no provision for definitions and standards of identity with respect to cosmetics. It should be noted that a product may be both a drug and cosmetic. The claim on the label made by the manufacturer concerning its function will determine which set of legal requirements the product must fulfill. It is possible that the identical product can be sold under two different labels for two different purposes, in one case as a drug and in the other as a cosmetic.

POSTAL SERVICE

The United States Postal Service exercises control over advertising in two main areas. The first of these affects advertising that depends on the use of the mails. This includes both direct mail advertising and mail order advertising. For example, a lottery or any fraudulent scheme, that is, a plan for obtaining money or property through the mails by means of false pretenses, is a violation of the postal laws. The Postal Service need not even take the offender to court. It can conduct an administrative proceeding, and if it finds a violation has been committed, the Postmaser at the local office is directed to stamp the word "Fraudulent" on all mail addressed to the offending party and return it to the sender. Postmasters also are instructed not to pay any money orders drawn in favor of such a party.

Secondly, in addition to this direct method of control, the Postal Service exercises indirect control over advertising carried in any publication that goes through the mails. This comes about because of the very valuable second-class mailing privilege which amounts to a government subsidy in favor of periodicals that have what is called a "public character," that is, that contain news, literature, scientific information or the like, and have a legitimate list of subscribers. The Postal Service has the power to revoke second-class mailing privileges if the periodical fails to maintain its so-called public character. It is theoretically possible that advertising misrepresentations might be sufficient to warrant this type of extreme action, although there seems to be no record of its ever having been done.

The particular concern of the copywriter with the second-class mailing privilege is that, while any periodical which has this privilege may contain advertising, the advertising must be clearly indicated as such. If an advertisement is written and set up so that it gives the appearance of being editorial matter, then the word "advertisement" itself must appear as an identifying symbol in sufficiently conspicuous type and placement so that it will be readily noticeable to the reader. Failure to comply may lead to revocation of the periodical's second-class mailing privilege.

FEDERAL COMMUNICATIONS COMMISSION

The Federal Communications Commission also exercises an indirect type of control over advertising. Radio and television advertising is subject to the general supervision of the Federal Trade Commission just as advertising in print media is. The Federal Communications Commission, however, licenses every radio and television station and it is one of the overall conditions of such a license that the station must operate in what the law calls the "public interest, convenience and necessity."

If the Federal Communications Commission should find that, because of advertising misrepresentations or any other reason, a station has not been operating within this quoted statutory purpose, then it has the power to revoke or refuse to renew the station's license. This power obviously can be a potent one.

While the Federal Communications Commission has criticized false and misleading advertising, it is the Federal Communication Commission's general policy not to take any specific action with respect to this type of offense, but rather to bring the matter to the attention of the Federal Trade Commission. But the Federal Communications Commission has indicated its disapproval of advertising by physicians, clergymen and persons offering advice on marriage or family matters. It also has disapproved advertising of lotteries, contraceptive devices, and hard liquor. All such advertising practices jeopardize the licensee's chances of securing a renewal of his license, which ordinarily runs for a period of only one year at a time.

The Commission has been known to bring to the attention of a station (informally) what it considers objectionable advertising. This method of procedure can be extremely effective since few stations would care to risk the loss of their broadcasting franchises and some would be unwilling even to risk the publicity of a public hearing in connection with a renewal application.

BUREAU OF ALCOHOL, TOBACCO, AND FIREARMS

The Bureau of Alcohol, Tobacco and Firearms is charged with the responsibility, among other things, of administering the Federal Alcohol Administration Act. On this basis, the Bureau of Alcohol, Tobacco, and Firearms imposes on the liquor industry what is almost without doubt the most detailed and severe set of controls that any industry in the country must face in its advertising practices.

The Bureau of Alcohol, Tobacco and Firearms exercises supervision over distilled spirits, wine and malt beverages. Its control starts basically with the labels to be used on the products. There are detailed regulations setting forth what must appear on the labels and no label can be used on an alcoholic product unless it has been approved by the Bureau of Alcohol, Tobacco and Firearms in advance.

The next step is direct control over the advertising of the products. The class and type of the beverage must appear in every advertisement. These must be stated conspicuously, and the designation in the advertising copy must be the same as that on the approved label for the product. Detailed information about alcoholic content is required for distilled spirits, but statements of alcoholic content are prohibited in advertisements of malt beverages and wine. The name and address of the company responsible for the advertisement always must be included. It may be the distiller, the distributor or the importer in proper cases. The name and address of the advertiser, the class and type of the product and the alcoholic content (in the case of distilled spirits) are the so-called mandatories in liquor advertising.

The Bureau of Alcohol, Tobacco and Firearms regulations also prohibit certain types of advertising statements specifically. These include false or misleading statements; disparagement of competing products; obscene or indecent statements; misleading representations relating to analysis, standards or tests; and guarantees which, irrespective of their truth or falsity, are likely to mislead the consumer;

other prohibited types of advertising include statements indicating authorization by any municipal, state or federal government; the use of certain words such as "bonded" (unless the product in fact is bottled in bond), "pure," and "double distilled"; claims of curative or therapeutic value; misleading statements as to place of origin; and many others. In particular, no statement concerning an alcoholic beverage may be used in advertising if it is inconsistent with any statement on the labeling of the product itself.

OTHER FEDERAL LAWS

There are certain specialized industries in which still other Federal agencies exercise specific control over advertising. For example, the Securities and Exchange Commission has the power to stop the sale of a security if its advertising contains an untrue statement of a material fact, or if it fails to state a material fact necessary to make the advertising not misleading in the light of all the circumstances. The Federal Aviation Agency has control over advertising by airlines of their passenger and freight services.

There are other federal statutes that apply to particular products and some of them contain labeling and advertising controls. Among these are the Economic Poisons Act, which governs insecticides, fungicides and similar products; and the Federal Seed Act.

Another group of statutes deals specifically with the use in advertising of particular symbols or representations, including the laws which prohibit the use of the American flag, the Red Cross symbol, the 4-H Club emblem, Smokey Bear as originated by the U.S. Forestry Service and a number of others. A leading advertising agency once had to scrap a filmed television commercial because the magic letters "FBI" were mentioned in a flippant manner; the Federal Bureau of Investigation called the agency's attention to a law making the use of those initials in advertising a misdemeanor.

These statutes are so specialized in nature that it would be impractical to discuss all of them in detail. They are mentioned primarily to indicate the necessity for checking in each instance to find out before preparing copy whether or not some special law deals with the subject.

OBSCENITY

It is hardly necessary to point out that obscene advertising is improper. However, there are legal as well as moral objections to obscenity. The problem here is one of definition. Standards of taste vary from community to community and even more noticeably from time to time. Nevertheless, a writer should have no great difficulty in drawing the line between obscenity and acceptable copy. Although poor taste is not in itself unlawful, it cetainly is disapproved by most advertisers. A copywriter who avoids poor taste almost automatically will avoid any question of violation of the obscenity laws.

COPYRIGHT

We are not concerned here with the technique of protecting an advertisement under copyright laws, but rather with the problem of using somebody else's copyrighted material as part of your advertising copy. There are many misconceptions about the right to use such material, whether in quoted or paraphrased form.

A copyright does not protect the basic idea of the author. An advertising copywriter, therefore, is privileged to use the basic ideas contained in anything that he may read. But copying the exact language, or closely paraphrasing the way in which the original author expressed his idea, is an infringement if the original work is protected by copyright. The same rule applies to art as well as to copy.

It is sometimes thought that copyright infringement occurs only when the fact of copying is concealed, that is, when the copier attempts to pass off the work as his own. This is not so. The mere fact that the source is acknowledged does not prevent the use from being an infringement of copyright. Actual consent of the copyright owner must be secured. A fee freqently is charged for this privilege, but that is something that must be arranged in advance, because the copyright owner may decide to withhold permission altogether.

Fair use

The one basic exception to this rule is the doctrine of what the law calls "fair use." It is this exception that makes it possible, for example, for reviewers to quote passages from books that they are reviewing and for a scientist to copy from the works of others in the same field in order to be able to comment on scientific developments. It is important, however, to bear in mind that the purpose for which the copyrighted material is to be used is a definite limitation of the scope of the doctrine of fair use. Specifically, to take even a small extract from a copyrighted work and use it in a commercial advertisement is not fair use. This point was made unmistakably in a case involving the Liggett & Myers Tobacco Company which copied, although not in exactly the same words, just three sentences from a doctor's book about the human voice which made some favorable comments about the use of tobacco. Specific credit was given for the source of the quotation, but no permission had been obtained to use it.

The case went to court and the decision was in favor of the copyright proprietor. There must be "substantial" copying to constitute infringement, but this does not necessarily mean a large quantity. The court decided in this case that even three sentences amounted to a substantial copying under the circumstances because of the relative importance of the material that was taken. It was decided also that the use was not a "fair use" because it was for a purely commercial purpose.

Copyrighted music

Another common misconception has to do with music, which is also subject to copyright if the proper formalities are observed. There is a widespread impression that so long as no more than eight bars of a popular song are borrowed, there can be no infringement of copyright. This is clearly wrong. The same basic standards apply to the infringement of a musical copyright as to a literary copyright. In other words, was the part taken from the copyrighted work substantial and was the use a fair one? The distinctive characteristics of the melody or the lyrics of a popular song can be expressed in fewer than eight bars. It is, therefore, not safe to use the words of a song unless permission has been granted or it has been checked and found to be in the public domain.

Copyright does not protect the title of a work. On the other hand, this does not mean that everyone necessarily is free to use a title. The practice of commercial tie-ins of all types is so common today that titles of books, plays, motion pictures, songs, and even comic strips have become highly important commercial properties. Although it does not constitute a technical copyright infringement to use someone else's title, this may be prohibited by general principles of unfair competition in order to protect its exploitation values. The legal test is whether the public is likely to infer that there is some connection between the title as used in advertising and the work on which the title originally appeared. If so, the title may not be used without permission.

LIBEL

To libel somebody means to injure his reputation by making a false statement that will subject him to ridicule or contempt in the community, particularly if it would tend to cause damage to the victim in his business or profession. The penalties for libel can be severe. It is a complete defense to a charge of libel if the defamatory statement can be proved true in fact, but the possibility of such a situation developing out of advertising copy is remote. Most of the litigated cases in which individuals have been libeled by means of advertising involved false testimonials.

Libel can be committed by a radio or television broadcast as well as by a printed advertisement. Libel also can be committed by pictures. The use of a professional model is no assurance against a suit for libel. The usual form of model release, which will be discussed in the succeeding section, does not waive any rights under libel laws. One particularly well-known case involved an advertising photograph. The angle at which the picture was taken and the way in which the light fell created an obscene impression that was not noticed by the people who prepared the advertisement. The model sued on the theory that this was damaging to his reputation and the court agreed that the photograph was libelous. Protection against this unfortunate kind of result can be secured by having the model approve the finished layout.

It is possible to libel a business or a product as well as a person. While this is difficult to establish as a legal proposition under the laws pertaining to libel, disparagement of competitors and their products also constitutes an unfair method of competition within the meaning of the Federal Trade Commission Act and, therefore, may bring on a Federal Trade Commission proceeding.

RIGHTS OF PRIVACY AND PUBLICITY

The use in advertising of the name or picture of a person without his consent constitutes a violation of his right of privacy. In New York State, this right is created by specific legislation which requires that the consent be in writing. In most other states, the same rule of law prevails through decisions of the courts, although oral consent may be enough. Utah and Virginia have specific statutes similar to that of New York. The New York statute, however, is limited to living persons. Utah and Virginia go further and give the heirs of a deceased person the right to complain about the unauthorized use of his name or picture. When preparing copy for national advertising, obviously the most restrictive of all these laws must be taken into account.

It is this right of privacy that makes it necessary to obtain a release from every model who poses for artwork or photography. Similarly, an endorsement or testimonial cannot be used without a release from the person whose name is to appear in connection with it. Anyone who is legally an infant must have his or her parent or legal guardian sign the release in order for it to be valid.

Releases frequently are limited in their scope. A model release, for example, may permit only the use of the picture of the person and not his or her true name. Furthermore, the right to use a picture does not always carry with it the right to use words in connection with the picture indicating that the model endorses a product or service. Even a release from a person permitting his name to be used as an endorser does not necessarily include the right to create a statement praising the product and attribute it to the person as though it were his own words. In addition, as indicated in the preceding section, the possession of a model release in the customary form does not excuse libel, so that a photograph covered by a release might be used in conjunction with libelous words in such a way as to violate the legal rights of the model.

Decisions of the courts have recognized that the right of privacy is somewhat out of step with the facts of modern commercial life. For example, figures in the entertainment and sports world frequently have no desire for privacy in the same way that an ordinary citizen does; they seek publicity actively. As a result of court decisions, therefore, the right of privacy of such persons has been limited on the theory that the person has given up his right of privacy by making himself into a public figure. This does not apply, however, to strict commercial uses such as advertising. A magazine or newspaper can use a publicity still of a motion picture star for editorial purposes, but it cannot be used as part of an advertisement without a release.

In recent years, the courts have considered the right of publicity as something distinct from the right of privacy. Only a public figure possesses this right of publicity. It is the law's recognition of the fact that the name and picture of a personality in the entertainment or sports world has a definite commercial value for endorsements, testimonials, and the like. Accordingly, the use of the name or picture of such a person for advertising purposes without written consent may give rise to a claim for substantial damages.

It will be desirable, occasionally, to use a personal name in advertising and the copywriter may devise a fictitious name for that purpose. This always creates the risk that unknowingly the fictitious name will turn out to be borne by some real person who will make his complaint known. It then becomes a difficult if not impossible task to prove that the name in the advertisement did not refer to the actual living person. In order to avoid such problems, some agencies maintain files of cleared names, generally persons on their own staffs or working for their clients who have consented to the use of their names in advertising. Even if a duplicate of such a name should turn up in the form of another person, the advertiser or agency always can go to the release file to establish that the cleared name is the one that was used in the copy. This will not, of course, excuse the use of a celebrity's name even if by coincidence the agency has an employee bearing the same name who is willing to sign a release.

Consideration of the rights of privacy may take you into strange bypaths. For example, an agency copywriter prepared an advertisement for a bank. In the advertisement was a list of bank customers who had won prizes as a result of a drawing in the bank during an opening day celebration.

Looking over the list, the copywriter was worried because the names were being published without the consent of those concerned. Checking with a lawyer, the copywriter read the New York Privacy Statute (50-51) of the Civil Rights Act which says:

Section 50:
A person, firm or corporation that uses for advertising purposes or for the purpose of trade, the name, portrait or picture of any living person without having first obtained the written consent of such person, or if a minor of his or her guardian, shall be guilty of a misdemeanor.
Section 51:
Any person (whose name is so used) may also sue and recover damages.

Suppose, the copywriter asked, one of the women winners received a number of nuisance telephone calls as the result of her name appearing in the newspaper advertisement. Among these might be obscene calls, and calls from salespeople. Could she, under the statute, sue the bank on the basis that she had not authorized the publishing of her name? Not being sure of the answer, the agency advised the client to omit the list of winners even though it added local interest to the advertisement, and the advertisement had already been set in print.

Although it is likely that no ill would have come from publishing the list of winners, in such cases it is better to err on the side of caution because we are in a period presently when consumers sue quickly for real or fancied violations of their rights.

PROPER TRADEMARK USAGE

Basic trademark principles have been discussed earlier. The purpose of this section is to describe the proper ways of using trademarks and brand names in advertising in order to avoid the possible loss of the valuable legal rights that a trademark represents. Some trademarks have become associated so completely with the products to which they are attached that they are treated by the public as merely a name for the product rather than an identification of one particular brand of that product. When a trademark literally becomes a household word in this way, it has ceased to be a trademark and no single manufacturer any longer has the exclusive right to use it on his product. The tremendous investment that may have gone into establishing the trademark and creating a brand image through extensive advertising has been lost to the advertiser. The question is an important one for advertising copywriters because the improper use of a trademark in advertising can give the public the impression that it is a generic term instead of a brand name, and that is what it will become very quickly under such circumstances.

Another indication of the seriousness of the problem is to list a few well-known products whose commonly accepted names today once were the valued trademarks of particular manufacturers. These include aspirin, lanolin, milk of magnesia, celluloid, kerosene, shredded wheat, linoleum, cellophane and escalator. In order to preserve a trademark, it must be kept in mind that it indicates only one particular variety of the product and is not the name of the product itself.

Grammatically, a trademark is a proper adjective. A trademark must be identified as such in all advertising, which means that at a bare minimum it requires an initial capital letter. There are many other typographical methods by which to give distinctive treatment to a trademark so that there will be no doubt of what it is. It may be run, for example, in all-caps or placed in quotation marks; it may be set in a distinctive typeface, or the manufacturer's logo may be included in the body copy.

A trademark should be so designated by actual notice to that effect at least on its first or most conspicuous appearance in any given advertisement. If the trademark has been registered in the United States Patent and Trademark Office (and this requires a legal check) use the official circle-R notice ® or the abbreviation Reg. U.S. Pat. and TM Off. If it has not been registered, then use the abbreviation TM or the word "trademark." The notice may be in the form of a footnote referred to by an asterisk.

Another way to indicate clearly that a trademark is not merely the name of the product is to use the word "brand" in connection with it. When the copy talks about the "XYZ brand" of a certain product, there can be no doubt that XYZ is the brand name or trademark and not the generic name of the product itself.

Furthermore, if you use the generic name of the product every time you refer to the trademark, you will avoid the possibility of creating a situation where the public will start the loose usage of the term

Xerox vs. xerox.

Our Xerox trademark is among our most valuable assets.

So it's important to us that you know how it should be used. And how it should not.

If you spell Xerox with a small x, you're making a big mistake.

Since a trademark is by definition a proper adjective, it should always be capitalized.

At the same time, using a capital X doesn't give you the right to use it in a way that's wrong.

Even with a big X, you can't make

a Xerox, you can't go to the Xerox and you can't Xerox anything. Ever.

As long as you use a big X, however, you can make copies on the Xerox copier, you can go to the Xerox computer and you can read a Xerox publication.

So remember, whenever you're writing our name, use a capital letter.

After all, isn't that the way you write your name?

XEROX

FIGURE 21-1

Advertisement stressing proper use of a trademark name. Xerox has been vigilant in calling attention to the use of its trademark in order to prevent the name from becoming generic. Other advertisements have emphasized the importance of capitalizing the name and using it as an adjective—not as a noun or verb.

that eventually leads to its loss of trademark significance. If aspirin had been sold as aspirin pain-relieving tablets instead of just as aspirin, the trademark might have been preserved.

A simple way to test your copy for this purpose is to omit the trademark from the sentence in which it is used. A complete thought still should be expressed. For example, "See the latest XYZ toaster at your local appliance store," not "See the latest XYZ at your local appliance store."

A good trademark exists only in one form and the copywriter should stick to it. Don't make up fanciful words containing the trademark and don't use it in the wrong grammatical form. As stated above, a trademark is a proper adjective. It should not be used as a noun, in the plural, as a verb, in the possessive, or as an adjective that describes some quality of the goods.

It is not uncommon for trademarks to be used under license agreements from their owners. Under such circumstances, the licensee's package and advertising copy should contain an appropriate legend stating the facts in order to preserve the legal rights of the trademark owner. A typical notice for this purpose would be in the form: "Manufactured by XYZ Corporation under authority of ABC Company."

Many companies publish manuals giving specific directions on how their trademarks are to be used. These manuals are prepared very largely for the use of advertising copywriters, and it goes without saying that you should follow such a manual if one has been issued by the advertiser on whose product you are working.

COMPARATIVE ADVERTISING

Direct reference to competitive products or services in advertising once was a rarity that people considered in bad taste or even morally reprehensible. In recent years, following a period when veiled references to "Brand X" were in vogue, a substantial amount of advertising has appeared in which competitors are mentioned specifically. No longer is a product or service simply "the best on the market"; instead, many advertisers do not hesitate to identify the competition and make direct comparisons. Philosophical questions of morals or ethics are outside the scope of this chapter, but does comparative advertising raise any legal questions?

In order to identify a competitor in advertising, it almost invariably is necessary to use his trademark so that the public will understand the comparison. For that reason, the legality of comparative advertising has been tested most often in the framework of lawsuits claiming trademark infringement. In one extreme case, a manufacturer of low-priced domestic perfume advertised that his product duplicated the exact scent of "Chanel No. 5," a famous and expensive brand of French perfume. When this use of the Chanel trademark was attacked, the court responded by ruling that there was nothing wrong about referring to a competitive product by its trademark, provided that the comparative advertising was strictly accurate.

In accordance with this ruling, the prevailing view is that comparative advertising is legally permissible so long as there is no misrepresentation. But if inaccurate or untrue statements are made, the advertisement can be attacked as false disparagement of the competitive product or service as well as trademark infringement and substantial damages might be awarded. It has been pointed out repeatedly that strict accuracy is the basic legal requirement a copywriter must bear in mind; this brief discussion shows why that requirement must be observed with special care when the advertisement makes a direct reference to competitive products or services.

IDEA PIRACY

It has been explained that a copyright does not protect the basic idea of any literary or artistic work. Nevertheless, some ideas are treated as property by the law and, like other forms of property, they can be stolen.

One of the constant problems that plagues advertising agencies and advertisers alike is the unsolicited idea. An astonishing number of people constantly are engaged in attempting to present what they consider novel merchandising ideas, catchy advertising slogans, and similar helpful thoughts which they confidently expect will bring them substantial remuneration. The fact of the matter is that professionals are much better at thinking up advertising ideas and slogans than amateurs. Even if the unsolicited idea has merit, it frequently turns out to be simply a duplication of an idea that is already in the company's files as the result of studies by its own staff or the staff of its advertising agency. Yet it is sometimes an impossible task to persuade the member of the public who submitted the unsolicited idea that it was not his particular brainchild that was stolen.

Idea piracy suits are a nuisance and can be extremely expensive. As a result, many large advertisers and advertising agencies have set up standard procedures by which they attempt to protect themselves from receiving unsolicited ideas in the first place; or, if they do, to receive them only when the submitter of the idea has signed a written release in advance that will protect the agency and the advertiser from the risk of any litigation. It is important for copywriters to learn just what system their own employer follows for dealing with situations of this kind.

The copywriter may very well be exposed to friends or acquaintances from outside the profession who are sure they have a "wonderful idea" to submit. When faced with such a situation, the copywriter would be well advised to refuse to listen to the idea, but explain as politely as possible that the employer has a standard policy either not to consider ideas from the outside at all, or to consider them only when submitted in writing and accompanied by an appropriate standard form of signed release, whatever the case may be. Considerable difficulty, expense, and eventual hard feelings can be avoided through this precautionary technique.

STATE LAWS

The greater part of our discussion thus far has dealt with federal laws. These, of course, apply to all national advertising. They also apply to a great deal of local advertising because either the advertising itself or the product crosses state lines, and thus involves interstate commerce which is under the control of the federal government.

It is necessary to know in addition that practically all of the states have their own individual laws dealing with advertising in one way or another. Writing copy for strictly local advertising, such as that for a retail store to run in a local newspaper, obviously involves the law of the particular state. Unfortunately, the situation is even more complicated than this, for states have the right to pass judgment on advertising that affects their local interests even though the same advertising simultaneously may be subject to federal controls. To take one specific example, a number of states have their own advertising requirements for liquor. Advertising copy to appear in such a state must comply with the regulations of the Federal Bureau of Alcohol, Tobacco and Firearms and also with the requirements of the local authorities.

Most of the states have enacted laws, based on the model statute recommended by *Printers' Ink*, prohibiting untrue, deceptive or misleading advertising. These are criminal statutes which provide for a fine and imprisonment, as distinguished from laws such as the Federal Trade Commission Act under which the typical penalty is an order to cease and desist. Because of the severe punishment, these state laws are not enforced very frequently. Local authorities seem to be reluctant to proceed criminally in such cases.

Some states are even stricter than the federal government in their legal approach to the lottery problem. There are parts of the country where the offering of a prize by chance is prohibited even if no payment or other consideration is required from the entrant. The theory of these state laws is that awarding prizes by chance is a form of gambling, which they consider both immoral and illegal whether the chance must be paid for or not. As these laws are interpreted, the required legal element of consideration is found in the benefit derived by the sponsor.

The typical state also has a miscellaneous collection of other statutes covering specific areas of commerce, that generally deal with advertising along with other phases of the business involved. Among the industries regulated in this manner in many states are small loan companies, employment agencies, optometrists and opticians, barbers and hairdressers, and real estate brokers. In addition, many states have their own Pure Food and Drug laws and practically all states prohibit obscene or indecent advertising. Intoxicating beverages are a special case, as already indicated, and the specific law of each state must be checked if liquor advertising is involved.

CONSUMERISM AND THE COPYWRITER

Sometimes laments are heard from creative people about the maze of legal regulations that have grown out of the consumerism movement. Fear is expressed that creativity will suffer as copywriters attempt to work within the limitations of the ever-increasing rules, guidelines and prohibitions.

An agency executive, Allen Rosenshine, vice president of Batten, Barton, Durstine & Osborn, had these words of comfort for creative people:

Maybe the legal restrictions have become so stringent that we just can't do product demonstrations anymore.

Well, I don't believe that.

What I DO believe is that we are tending to shy away from the legal problems rather than trying to meet them head on. If we look long enough and hard enough we will find something meaningful about the product that is worth saying, and can be said legally.

If we can't, then we have a basis for a client recommendation to the effect that a product improvement is necessary. And even if it isn't the big breakthrough product improvement that will bring competition to its knees, as long as it makes sense conceptually, there is no reason why the creative department can't advertise it dramatically, but within the bounds of legal propriety.

That's exactly the kind of creative imagination that clients have been paying for in the first place.

And even if we can't make open ended comparisons anymore; even if we CAN'T say a product is "better" without saying "better than what," that is not the end of advertising.

Even if we CAN'T say "our product is the best you can buy," that's not the end of advertising either . . .

I suggest we spend our time more productively if we work out our own set of guidelines that would enable us to work within the current—or even projected—legal restrictions.[1]

Influence of the consumerism movement

During the past several years, pressures exerted by consumer interest groups and the addition of some activists to the Federal Trade Commission staff have

---

[1]Speech delivered to the Eastern Regional Conference of the American Association of Advertising Agencies, June 5, 1972, New York City.

influenced the adoption by the Commission of new techniques for dealing with false and misleading advertising, particularly requirements for corrective advertising and for the substantiation of product claims.

Orders requiring corrective advertising are based on the theory that false and deceptive claims have a residual effect on the consumer so that conventional orders to discontinue the misrepresentations are insufficient to protect the public. Instead, the Federal Trade Commission now requests in many cases (and some advertisers have agreed to supply as part of the settlement of Federal Trade Commission complaints against them) positive statements that will dissipate the misleading claims. A typical order requires that 25 percent of advertising expenditures for the product in question for a period of one year must be devoted to advertisements, approved in advance by the Federal Trade Commission, stating that previous claims were subject to misinterpretation and giving the true facts; for example, that "Profile" bread is not effective for weight reduction.

The Federal Trade Commission's advertising substantiation program was launched by a resolution adopted in 1971 that is based on the Federal Trade Commission's statutory authority to require the filing of special reports to aid its investigations. Orders calling for the submission of documents, including test reports and testimonials, to support advertising claims concerning safety, performance, quality and competitive prices, have gone out to various manufacturers of such products as television sets, air conditioners, pet food, electric razors, toothpaste and detergents. These orders refer to specific product claims for which substantiation must be furnished, for instance: Sani Flush kills common household germs in 15 seconds, Tabby Canned meets 100 percent of a cat's daily nutritional needs, Ajax Liquid contains more ammonia than any competing product. The Federal Trade Commission reserves the right to make public any of the materials submitted in response to these special orders and also to release reports of its own to inform the public about the response or lack of response to its requests for substantiation.

An example of a substantiation case, widely reported in the media, occurred in 1977 when General Electric agreed to a Federal Trade Commission consent settlement. The agreement, published by the Commission for public comment, enjoined General Electric from claiming superiority over a competing product unless the nature of the superiority was specified, or was discernible to the consumer. The case stemmed from the company's statement that its television sets required less servicing than competing sets. Under the Federal Trade Commission settlement, the company could not claim greater dependability or reliability without giving particulars. Furthermore, it could not claim superiority if it knew of inconsistent or contrary evidence.

CONCLUSION

It may very well seem that the task of keeping up with this enormous array of legal requirements is beyond the capacity of any single individual. Fortunately, the basic responsibility ordinarily is not the copywriter's alone. This is true particularly in a large advertising agency, which either will have its own staff of lawyers or use the services of an outside law firm to check copy for compliance with legal requirements.

It is, nevertheless, of great importance for the copywriter to have at least a minimal familiarity with the kinds of legal problems that do exist. A conscientious copywriter not only will acquire as much information as possible about the product or service on which he is working, but also about the kinds of legal restrictions that may apply to the particular industry involved.

The fundamental source of information about the product or service, of course, is the advertiser itself. The details may come directly, or more likely indirectly—through the account executive or supervisor in his place of employment. In the case of an advertising agency, information about legal requirements can come from the agency's own staff or from the client. In addition, many industries have trade associations that provide tremendous quantities of helpful information. Better Business Bureaus also are sources of extremely valuable assistance. The National Better Business Bureau, Inc. publishes *Do's and Don'ts in Advertising Copy,* an excellent loose-leaf volume that is kept up to date with monthly revisions.

A number of industries have their own self-imposed codes of regulations. As a practical matter, although these do not have the force of law, it is essential that they be followed. Some well-known examples are the codes of The National Association of Broadcasters, The Distilled Spirits Institute and The Motion Picture Association of America.

The copywriter should strive to be informed in order that legal difficulties may be avoided. Two basic rules that the Federal Trade Commission likes to emphasize are enough in themselves to constitute a condensed code of principles for advertising copywriting: a) Laws are made to protect the trusting as well as the suspicious; b) Advertisements are not intended to be dissected carefully with a dictionary at hand, but rather to produce an impression upon prospective purchasers. Keeping these simple rules in mind will solve many of the legal problems in advertising copywriting.

CORRECTIVE ADVERTISING— EXAMPLES AND EFFECT

Some examples of legal orders for corrective advertising demonstrate the process at work:

Example 1:   A swimming pool company was required to devote 25 percent of the space in all its advertisements for one year to a statement that the Federal Trade Commission had questioned its advertising practices. The company had been accused of bait and switch advertising, false guarantees and misrepresentation of credit terms.

Example 2:   An appliance retailer was fined and jailed for falsely advertising stereo equipment. In addition, he was required to run a series of newspaper advertisements that said prominently: FALSE ADVERTISING IS STEALING.

Example 3:   A bread company agreed to run corrective advertising for a year that corrected the unsubstantiated claim that the bread was particularly effective for reducing weight. Twenty-five percent of its advertising was to be devoted to the correction.

As a copywriter, you may do your client real harm if you're the one directly responsible for such offending claims. Evidence of this is research which shows that the reputation of the affected company is hurt when corrective advertising is run. According to Harold J. Kassarjian, reseacher, attitude scores tend to drop significantly on the variables of honesty and sincerity when corrective advertising appears.[2] Deceptive advertisements seemingly are perceived as a result of dishonesty and insincerity, and not as a mistake due to lack of experience.

One interesting sidelight, however, is that corrective advertising does not seem to reduce the credibility of all advertising in general.

[2] Harold J. Kassarjian, "Applications of Consumer Behavior to the Field of Advertising," reprinted from *Journal of Advertising,* Vol. 3, Summer, 1974, pp. 10-15, in Ronald D. Michman and Donald W. Jugenheimer, *Strategic Advertising Decisions: Selected Readings* (Columbus, Ohio, Grid Inc., 1976), p. 73.

22

One Last Look at Being a Copywriter

You're sitting in your office at 5:30 on Friday afternoon, staring at the sheet in front of you. Across the top, the account executive has scrawled: "Sorry, but the client doesn't buy this approach and I think he's right. Let's talk Monday a.m. earliest. Meanwhile, better come up with some more ideas—good ones."

"Some weekend," you think. "Mad at the client. Even madder at the account executive because he didn't sell my idea. And that little dig about good ideas. Where am I going to come up with a better idea? This was my better idea—a real barn-burner even though those clunks couldn't appreciate it."

At such moments, you wonder why you refused that insurance job, or the chance to take management training in the department store. Yet, despite the discouragement, you know in your heart that you're glad you're in copy. You do have moments of depressing failure, but if you had wanted a job that didn't have ups and downs, you'd have elected to be a bank teller, or a retail sales clerk.

YOU'RE IN BUSINESS WHEN YOU'RE IN COPY

Purple drapes, a cathedral-like hush, and sweet violin music playing softly in the background—these were provided (the story goes) to create the right mood for one temperamental advertising-agency copywriter in the fabulous 1920s.

During this period, when advertising billings were beginning to zoom, copywriters could do no wrong. If they wanted mood background, the indulgent advertisers let them have it. The copywriter was a favorite actor in a dizzy drama of lush profits.

Today's copywriters are likely to be less coddled than the copywriters who worked during the period from the end of World War I until the 1929 crash. They were credited then with the sensitivity of any

other "artiste." They were littérateures who condescended to work at the prosaic job of selling soap, automobiles, and washing machines.

When the crash came, advertising emerged from the golden haze. The era of advertising research began. Advertising became a serious, painstaking business instead of a madcap adventure. Copywriters pulled down the purple drapes and looked out soberly upon the smoky city below. They were no longer artists with taken-for-granted temperamental rights. They were businesspeople.

Not all copywriters, admittedly, have given up the idea that they are apart from the ordinary businesspeople. Generally, however, most of today's copywriters think of themselves as businesspeople—not artists.

IF ALL YOU WANT IS SLOGAN WRITING, FORGET IT

Most people in the general public have only the vaguest idea of a copywriter's work and some of these ideas have been colored by exaggerations of motion pictures and trashy novels that "tell the truth" about the advertising business.

Very deep-rooted is the idea that the usual copywriter is a glib "sloganeer." A sizable portion of the public, including many businesspeople who should know better, think of copywriting in terms of writing clever slogans. Countless persons, desiring entrance into advertising and the copywriting field, have been armed with nothing more potent than a firm belief that they could "turn out slogans." The fact that "99 and - $^{44}/_{100}$% pure," "Say it with flowers," and others have become a part of the American vernacular, has helped create the illusion that copywriting is basically slogan writing.

279

The duties of a copywriter, although practically unknown to most persons, do not discourage advertising aspirants. Persons who might, for example, question their ability to do satisfactory work in the research department or the media department of a company will apply very confidently for a copywriter's position. Without advertising knowledge or experience, applicants will try unhesitatingly to enter this tough, competitive field. When their applications are received indifferently or without too much serious consideration, the applicants are hurt and amazed.

BEING A GOOD WRITER ISN'T ENOUGH

Just what is there about copywriting which makes it seem easy and desirable? The answer is that there is almost 100 percent ignorance among nonadvertising folk of just what copywriters are supposed to do—and what they get paid for doing it. They have no comprehension of the hard work and supplementary knowledge that must accompany a copywriter's expected ability in writing.

Advertising managers, like newspaper editors, are continually squashing the hopes of applicants who have little else in their personal sales kit than an alleged flair for writing. Because of letter-writing ability, or a succession of A's on high-school or college themes, the youthful men and women of self-asserted literary merit feel that writing advertising or newspaper copy is merely an extension of the writing they have already done. Everyone thinks he can write because everyone has to write at one time or another. How many times have you looked at an advertisement and said to yourself, "And they call that copywriting! Why didn't they do it this way?" The world is filled with people who feel they could do a better job of writing advertisements than the persons who make their living as copywriters. Under the delusion that they "could do it better," the uninitiated approach the copywriting field eagerly and confidently.

WHICH IS HARDER— COPYWRITING OR REPORTING?

Reporting and copywriting demand ability, knowledge, and experience far beyond a surface facility in writing. Requirements for the two occupations are similar in some points. In both, for instance, it is vital to understand people and to use that understanding in the fashioning of lucid material.

A copywriter, like a reporter, must be analytical, observant, and thorough. Each has specialized knowledge fitting him for his work. Where, for example, the aspiring reporter might find it advantageous to obtain a background in political science and labor economics, the future copywriter might acquire a knowledge of sociology and mass psychology.

Despite certain points of similarity between the two occupations, it is perhaps more difficult to prepare for a copywriter's job than for that of a reporter. A journalism school, granted normal intelligence and aptitude on the part of the student, can teach the student the celebrated 5 W's formula. Having mastered the rather stylized forms of newswriting, the intelligent journalism school graduate can do a creditable beginning job for most newspapers.

The fact that copywriting is less precise than newswriting and less amenable to "formula" writing makes the task of teaching copywriting in school somewhat more arduous than the teaching of newswriting. Take the writing of crime stories. Any reporter who has worked a police beat has developed a format for crime stories. Depending on his ability, he can vary the writing within his format, but essentially he follows a rather definite writing pattern. His work is made easier and faster if he follows the pattern. You have no such formula to help you in copywriting. You cannot use as a crutch any mechanical style of writing to make your job easier. Each advertisement is custom-built to time or space requirements and to the product.

What makes your preparation for copywriting work even more difficult is the fact that the copywriter as a businessman must know business matters. Before you sit down at the typewriter, you should have a background of business experience that enables you to write copy intelligently and competently. The knowledge of selling, of merchandise, or of general business procedure gained from this experience gives you confidence.

The copywriter adds another element to writing that is not present in the news story. This is the element of persuasion. Whereas the reporter gives the facts without embellishment, the copywriter while also giving facts must add words and sentences that will cause readers to take action. His words must create a mood, an excitement, and a desire for the goods or services he is selling. Not for him is mere recital of facts. He must sell, as well as tell. As anyone knows who has done face to face selling, persuading a reluctant prospect to a course of action can be difficult. Yet this is what the copywriter must do in every advertisement he prepares.

To sum up, copywriting like reporting demands much more than facility with words. Whether it is more difficult to become a good copywriter than a good reporter is debatable, but there is no debating the assertion that copywriting calls for hard and extensive preparatory work.

Copywriters are anonymous

Although copywriters may write top-flight copy, may develop slogans, trade names, and descriptive phrases that become a part of the nation's idiom, they may never be identified with their work. Copywriters are anonymous. They are among the thousands of businessmen who do their jobs day after day— efficiently and unknown. Here again the copywriter is removed from the class of the artiste.

Not for the copywriter is the acclaim of the by-line newspaper reporter or of the motion picture scenario writer. If the only satisfaction you get out of writing is the glow you feel when people talk about your work, then copywriting will give you only limited satisfaction, since the only people who will know what you have written are those who are associated with you in business. As a copywriter you are just another salesperson peddling merchandise and ideas.

WHAT YOU CAN EARN

Salaries for copywriters are generally thought to be much higher than they are. Although top agency copywriters draw very high pay, many beginning copywriters start with salaries little better than that of office boys.

Skill in copywriting, however, is rewarded as well as in any other business activity. Some advertising agency copy chiefs, to illustrate, are paid huge salaries, but for every high-salaried person there are hundreds of copywriters who earn modest salaries. The high salaries paid to relatively few copywriters have, unfortunately, been so widely publicized that the beginner is led into thinking that all copywriters are paid bountifully.

If you are able to check the salaries paid to copywriters in the different kinds of advertising activity—retail, agency, newspaper, business concerns, or radio—you will soon discover that such copywriters are paid no better and no worse than are persons of comparable skill in most other fields of business activity. A few make the top-bracket figures—most make average salaries.

HURRY! HURRY! HURRY!

Like the newspaper reporter, copywriters are hounded by deadlines. If they are nervous types, they will find the work taxing. Day after day, month after month, they will be hurried, always conscious of publishing or broadcasting dates. What field of advertising is most trying on the nerves of the copywriter? It is difficult to say.

The retail field, in which the artists, copywriters, and production people are just a step ahead of the publishing date, is full of worry for persons who like to do thoughtful, careful work. As one retail copywriter said, "There's an empty feeling in turning out copy this way. I'm always haunted by the consciousness that this hurried, rush-rush work is not my best work. I'd like to work in an agency where the deadlines are farther apart."

The retail copywriter typically sighs for the green fields of agency copywriting. All the way down the line, agency copywriters are envied. But what is the situation with the agency copywriter? Is the job relatively easy? Actually, they voice almost exactly the same complaint heard from the retail copywriters.

True, the deadlines are not usually daily deadlines, but they are seemingly always behind the schedule. Then, there is always the unexpected presentation, the new account, or the quick revision. All these call for hurry-up writing dashed off to the accompaniment of the impatient jigging of the copy chiefs or clients waiting for the copywriter to get through.

Copywriting provides little quiet, leisurely writing. The copywriter is a businessperson who writes under hard-driving business conditions for other businesspeople who have no time for creative temperament. Copywriters produce work quickly—and good work, too, or out they go.

Still, many successful copywriters feel that they do their very best work when under extreme pressure. Like athletes you may often find inspiration when circumstances force you to do the "impossible." If you're the type who can rise to the urgency of the moment, you will find the pressure stimulating.

NEEDED—MENTAL AND PHYSICAL STAMINA

The drain on the copywriter's creative talent is considerable. Where a successful magazine writer might make a good living turning out a few articles or stories a year and have a chance to rest up between efforts, copywriters must turn out a quantity of good writing daily. Each day they search for new ways to write headlines, slogans, body copy, commercials, and direct-mail pieces.

If you, as a copywriter, are assigned miscellaneous accounts, you must adjust yourself rapidly to each new product that you write about. You are expected to give a fresh twist to your copy in order that you may satisfy the probing and skeptical examination by executives of the client company. Such quantity writing puts a great strain on your freshness and originality.

The working hours of copywriters are likely to be irregular. When an emergency arises (and emergencies are always arising), you are expected to stay on the job day and night until your part of the work is done. Overtime is a part of creative work. Then, too, as a conscientious copywriter, you are likely to take your work with you wherever you go. As you walk down the street, you may see new uses for the products that you write copy about. You jot down the ideas before they escape you. At night you squirm in your bed, musing over a new approach for a current campaign. Finally, unable to get back to sleep, you snap on the light, sketch the idea, and wait impatiently for morning in order that you may give your sizzler the test of daylight examination.

The combination of irregular hours and work which creates nervous tension makes good health an important requisite for copywriters. Obviously, you don't need the muscles of a Samson, but if you can bounce out each day fresh and vigorous—all the better. Health and an ability to take each new assignment as it comes are important in the profession.

Unless you reach top levels, you cannot expect pampering in your working conditions. You are more likely, as an average copywriter, to work in a crowded little cubicle piled high with proofs, unfinished work, and samples of products about which you are writing. Some copywriters, in fact, seem to work best in an office that many persons might consider hopelessly littered. If you're the usual copywriter, you cannot expect specialized work to bring specialized working conditions. Although your work may be important, you are just part of the business of creating advertising that will sell, and you carry on your function in a business office.

REWARDS OF COPYWRITING

Up to this point, the "cold water" approach has been employed in discussing the career of a beginning advertising copywriter. Any copywriting book must describe the negative aspects. Such frankness is necessary because of the general misconceptions regarding copywriting. When you start your first copywriting job, you should do so eagerly but not with a feeling that you are about to enter a never-never land divorced from the usual business world.

Before discouraging you further, however, it is only sensible to point out that there are agreeable sides to the life of a copywriter. To those who can stand the pace, the work is deeply satisfying. Copywriters may grumble, threaten to quit, fight with the boss, but they know deep down that it would be difficult to find any other work that they would like so well.

The lure of the copywriter's job is compounded of varied factors. Some of these factors mean more to one person than to another. You, for example, might experience a never-ending thrill in the creative side of the work. Seeing your copy in *Reader's Digest* or *The New Yorker* or hearing your commercial over a national network—these moments are your bonus for the hours of word-hammering. Reading your writing in print is a satisfaction whether the words appear in a country weekly, a huge metropolitan daily, or a national magazine. Although much of the copywriter's work is mere common sense put into selling words, some efforts fall into the classification of sheer creativeness. Such work is a joy to perform, never routine, always satisfying.

Good copy serves a vital function

Copywriters might derive satisfaction from the important part they have in the movement of goods. They realize that all the manufacturing skill and marketing genius behind a product are wasted unless their words convince the customers they should buy the product. To these copywriters comes a sense of usefulness in the business picture, the feeling that they are "movers of goods."

This feeling of being useful is vital to the copywriter. Your work is better if you can feel that it is of service in the social and economic sense. Admittedly, the utility of many products is so questionable that you feel no glow in having written the copy that makes goods move from the producer to the consumer. On the other hand, if the product is beneficial to the user, you are gratified that you can inform users about the product and that you can cause them to buy it. One of your real pleasures is to see the sales curve rise as a result of a successful advertisement or series of advertisements. You soon discover that if your copy doesn't sell, it represents so much wasted effort. The successful copywriter and the sales department are never far apart.

If you feel that you are part of business, if you see your work as contributing to the marketing pattern, you are likely to be a better copywriter. You then see the marketing pattern as it is concerned with the product research and sales plans behind the goods advertised. You include in your working knapsack some knowledge of the manufacturing difficulties and even the legal aspects such as the patent rights, trademark details, and regulations affecting the distribution of the products you write about.

You're part of the total effort

You are aware, too, of the many things that happen after you have punched out copy on your typewriter. You know that untruths or careless wording may cause trouble with such groups as the Radio and Periodical Division of the Federal Trade Commission, or the Better Business Bureau, or the Federal Security Agency administering the Federal Food and Drug Act. Possibly your words might cause consumer "kickback" which will make the sales department storm and ask angrily, "Who wrote this?" Copy, you realize, is a sharp-edged business tool, part of the marketing process involving you, salespeople, wholesalers, retailers, consumers, manufacturers, research people, and all others engaged in business. You have an obligation to all of these and especially to the consumers who, like you, are entitled to honest, competently written copy in order that they may make the best possible use of their money when they purchase goods.

It is very necessary for you to obtain a feeling which has been described aptly as "togetherness." Without the feeling, you write copy in a void. With the consciousness of the whole job, you attain unity in your copy.

In a sense, you must also look upon yourself as a merchant who has goods to sell. Your words either take the place of salespeople or make the salesperson's job more productive by acting as the door opener. They tell the truth about the goods, but they tell the truth persuasively—so much so that the reader is given a reason to buy. Again, you must, above all, become a part of the vital business of moving goods.

RETAIL COPYWRITERS ARE MERCHANTS

The feeling of being a "merchant" must be especially strong in the department store copywriter. True, some of these writers merely sit in their tiny offices in the advertising department. By preference, these "sitters" deal with goods—not with people, and not with the big, dynamic selling process of modern retailing. They become wrapped up in their task of writing words—countless words—about merchandise. Such copywriters are not businesspeople-writers. They have the writer's viewpoint only. It is not enough.

The retail copywriter—the good one—must be a part of the retail business. If you write newspaper advertisements for an aggressive department store, you have the privilege of learning merchandising in its most vigorous form. Some of the best copy in any business activity is turned out daily at such stores as Marshall Field & Company, Macy's, Pogues', and Bullock's. Do the men or women copywriters turning out these words learn to do so by spinning them out in their offices, far removed from the bargain-hunters in the basement? No! These writers become a part of the business scene. They get out of their offices and into the store.

They talk to buyers. From them they can learn merchandising, fashions, trade-talk, prices, and customer likes and dislikes. The topnotch retail copywriters learn the jobs of other people in the store, too. The salespeople, in direct contact with the customers, can provide much grist for copy. A personal service shopper can be pumped for comments made by customers. In the retail trade, the learning of all the functions and services of a department store is known as acquiring the "whole-store" viewpoint. The acquisition of such a viewpoint by you, the retail copywriter, is a part of your training as a businessperson and hence—a better copywriter.

IF YOU'RE GOOD, YOU HAVE PRESTIGE

If you have become a good copywriter, you will derive satisfaction from your standing in the business community and in the firm for which you work. Although it has been pointed out that good copywriters are not coddled as artists, they are definitely treated with respect as an important type of worker.

If you are in an agency, you are one of a relatively small group of specialists. To picture this, assume that XYZ agency has lined up a new account through the work of its new-business person. The account executive who is to service the account has been approved. The agency's financial stability and business integrity have been found satisfactory by the client. Despite the foregoing—the fast-talking and persuasive new-businessperson, the charming and efficient account executive, the firm's unquestioned integrity—all these will mean nothing if the agency cannot, through you, furnish good selling copy. Copy

is a last and very important link in the manufacturer-agency-consumer chain. As the welder of the link, you are an important person. Yours is the final responsibility.

A retail copywriter has the same sort of prestige. The men and women who write the copy for Ohrbach's, Wanamaker's, Hudson's, and Famous-Barr are solidly established in the business community. In addition to having developed the ability to write selling copy, they have stored in their brains an accumulation of valuable knowledge about products, merchandising, and other general business facts. So long as advertising is used in the mass distribution of goods, there will be need for skilled copywriters, especially in retail advertising—the biggest field of all.

Mediocrity in copywriting brings the usual reward of mediocrity. Skill in the profession enables you, the possessor, to name your ticket in the advertising world.

ONE LAST WORD

Now that you have been pummeled by rules, warned against this, and told to do that, you might think back over what has been said. If you do, you'll find that the following are some of the principal conclusions:

There is no easy road to copywriting ability. Throughout the book we have made a sincere effort to deglamorize copywriting. You were told that copywriting is not Hollywoodish; that as a copywriter you will not be a petted, pampered artist. You will be a businessperson in a business office. You'll be important—yes. You will not, however, have special prerogatives and working conditions. If you think of yourself always as a businessperson you'll be better off. You're expected to know how to write, but you must remember that your writing is a tool of business, not a stepladder to literary prominence. If copywriting ability were easy to acquire, there'd be no need for this book, for advertising copy courses, for the slow apprentice system so often found in agencies and retail stores—nor would copywriters be paid so well. But copywriting is not easy to learn. It's an exacting craft which a very few learn easily and the great majority learn through trial and error, perseverance and instruction. Some never learn it.

Skill in one kind of copywriting does not automatically transfer to other types of copywriting. Competent copywriters can usually write all kinds of copy. An agency copywriter, for example, because he handles diversified accounts, often attains proficiency in almost every type and style of copy. The fact remains, however, that a person who has done nothing but radio or television copy has learned techniques different from those of the copy person who has spent all his time on magazine or newspaper copy. The retail writer who began in department store copywriting and has remained in it is in a little world of her own which has its own problems.

Even within the same field, there are pronounced differences. In Chicago, for example, Carson, Pirie, Scott & Company, the widely known State Street department store, develops the "Carson" copy approach. Copy and art treatment are distinctive enough to identify advertisements as "Carson's" advertisements, establishing the store's character and individuality unmistakably. The store's copy people, ever mindful of their great rival, Marshall Field & Company, strive constantly to be different from Field's. The same thing is true of nearly all big cities—big stores through their copy and art treatment build up individuality. Thus a successful writer for one store may be so thoroughly indoctrinated into certain copy techniques that she must consciously adapt herself to the general approach used by another store if she changes jobs.

Then, look at mail-order and fashion copy. The first is stripped of nonsense. It's direct, detailed, and slugs the message home. The customer gets up from the floor groggy with facts. He knows just how to order. He probably even knows how many seams were put in that pair of overalls he's asked about. Fashion copy, on the other hand, is normally light, fluffy, and inclined to substitute atmosphere for facts. Perhaps each writer could take over the other's job. In a good many cases, however, it is doubtful that such a switchover could be made without considerable flexibility on the part of the copywriter.

As a last warning on the point that a certain adjustment is needed in order to switch from one kind of copy to another—think about the industrial magazine advertising writer. Consider the technical knowledge needed to write industrial advertisements. Think again, then, of your fashion writer, or your average writer of consumer copy. The airy, nonsensical touch of the fashion copywriter would be out of place in a hard-selling advertisement for steam boilers. Some writers can do both types of copy. Others never can.

To sum up: Each copywriting job makes use of the basic human appeals, but differences in writing style, media, and subject matter make it difficult to say that because you have mastered one copywriting job you can necessarily master them all—no more than a master steamfitter can become a grade A carpenter even though both of them are in the building trade and are handy with tools.

Copy research, like copywriting, has no final answer. You have probably noticed that this book handled copy testing as if it were capable of blowing up at any time. Copy testing and other forms of research *are* explosive. Some of the most violent advertising arguments are concerned with research methods. If you picked up the idea that we don't espouse any one kind of copy testing, that we find some good and bad points in all the methods, that we think copy testing is very important and that you should learn some of the methods—then the research section did its job. Most of all, we hoped that you would decide, after finishing the chapter, that you would always keep an open mind about copy testing, always looking for the good and bad points of each system.

Education, work experience, and personality are important elements in copywriting success. Although there are and have been successful copywriters with no more education than one might pick up from McGuffey's Fourth Grade Reader, education—especially college education—is an advantage to copywriters. You must gather that there are certain courses of study that are more suited to a copywriting career than others, but this doesn't mean a copywriter can't profit from almost any course of study. Although advertising, newswriting, and such courses are directly applicable to a copy career, a course in history, economic geography, or sociology might provide a background that could be very useful some day.

As for work experience, we depart from American tradition by suggesting that you try several jobs. Work experience is ideally composed of writing and selling, with an accent on diversity of experience. A sort of composite reporter-salesperson may have floated before your eyes as the ideal precopywriter. That's our ideal, too.

Quite a stress must be placed on the copywriter's personality. Of course, you can find some good copy people who shy from human contact. They're the exceptions. Unless you like people and share the usual enthusiasms, annoyances, and disappointments of most people, you are handicapped as a copywriter. And, too, if you are overly sensitive to criticism of your work, you'll suffer as your fellow-workers or bosses roughly and caustically criticize what you consider your choicest copy. Also, your personality must be adaptable to the creative demands of copywriting. You work hard, long, and fast in most copy jobs. Unless you are willing, and capable of doing so, we advise you to think carefully before you enter copywriting.

Your conscience and good taste should make you an "honest" copywriter. There have been so many high-sounding and painfully moral treatises turned out under the title of "Honesty in Advertising" that we've decided to be different. We assume that you have been well indoctrinated into the ethics of truth and honesty in advertising. Our approach is to point out that it's just plain silly to write untruthful copy. We believe this firmly. On one side, you have the law ready to pounce if you transgress. We hope very earnestly that the sections involving points about which the Federal Trade Commission is very sensitive will help you avoid trouble with that body. On the other side are the consumers of your products. Their buying power is an effective inducement to honesty. Sooner or later the cheat and fraud is discovered and, when he is, he loses sales.

We have discussed the practical inducements to honest advertising. When you are dealing with the public—the very young and the very old, the shrewd and the feeble-minded, the very poor and the very rich— your own conscience, also, should dictate honesty. In your person-to-person contacts you wouldn't cheat a subnormal or a charity case out of one cent, yet, through their copy, a lot of your fellow copywriters can bilk thousands of people. It's a matter of extending your conscience beyond what you're writing and visualizing the undiscerning people who will buy your product because you tell them to. The saying "Let your conscience be your guide" can be most apropos in this instance—only be sure to put your conscience in order before you write copy.

As a closing note, remember that nowhere have we said, "this is the way and the only way to write copy." If you put any of the book's principles to work, remember that each copy job is just a little different from the one before. Learn what we have said and then make allowances and adjustments when you apply our ideas to your individual situation. Among the copywriter's greatest assets are flexibility and skill in adjusting to the needs of the individual copy assignment.

Appendix

The appendix contains such helps and suggestions as:

- Copyfitting guides
- Type specimen sheet
- Proofreading marks
- Ad rating systems (several)
- Evaluation checklist
- Copywriting marking code

What you find in this section should be useful on many occasions. It is material for the working copywriter, or for the student who is working at learning copywriting. Too often material in a book appendix is never looked at. In this case, such neglect would be a pity since every item in *this* appendix should be useful to you at one time or another.

COPYFITTING GUIDES

Even experienced copywriters can write too much copy for the space. Beginning writers consistently do so. Seldom does anyone write too little copy for the space, but this can happen, too.

There are complicated copyfitting systems that require mathematics, or call it arithmetic, that will help you. Then, there are crude word-count systems that are based on an average number of words per line, multiplied by the number of lines to achieve the total.

The first system is too time-taking for the impatient copywriter, and the second too inaccurate. On the latter point, for example, "honorificabilituditadibus" is counted as one word. So is the letter "a." Radio writers can be thrown off by multisyllable words, too.

Figure A-1 is a page from a type specimen book. You are given in this page type sizes from tiny 5-point type all the way to 36 point. Body type usually ends at 12 points. For newspaper copy 10- to 11-point type is desirable with 11-point type being especially good for easy reading.

You must remember if you use this type specimen page as a guide that a 10- or 11-point type in one face may take more or less room than 10- or 11-point type in another face. Still, if you're careful enough to be guided by the pages reproduced here, your chances of being markedly wrong in your copyfitting for the usual advertisement are remote.

For a quick idea of how much copy you should write, find out the length of lines in your body text. Let's say that the line is 4 inches long. Assume, too, that you've decided upon 11-point size. Since you discover that 11-point type fits 15 characters to the inch, 4 inches will take 60 characters. Set your typewriter for 60 characters and then type away.

Naturally, you'll have to determine how many lines deep your copy is to go. Decide that and multiply 60 by the number of lines to get the total number of characters. Usually, however, all you need to know is the character count per line and then you simply type the number of lines needed. You normally don't worry about the total number of characters although sometimes you may be told to write a piece of copy with a limit of 780 characters, or 900, or some other figure.

Remember these type specimen pages if you're in doubt about how much copy to write. They can save you much reworking of copy, not to mention the embarrassment of having your copy returned for pruning.

PROOFREADING

You'll be asked to proof your own work, and sometimes that of others. Likewise, someone may be proofing yours. When you use the standard proofreading symbols and methods, you're using a common language of the writer, editor, and printer.

In Figure A-2 is a simple listing of proofreading marks. For most copywriters this listing is sufficient. If, however, you find that you need a proofreading guide more elaborate than this, write to Mergenthaler Linotype Company, Mergenthaler Drive, P.O. Box 82 Plainfield, New York 11803.

An incidental piece of information that might be useful to you is that there is no proofreading symbol for the underline. When you underline a word, a printer automatically will set it in italics. To make sure that he understands that you want an underline, put a line under the word or phrase and then on the side of the sheet use these words: "Printer. Underscore, not *italics.*"

8½ pt.

Printing has performed a role of achievement unparalleled in the re
PRINTING HAS PERFORMED A ROLE OF ACHIEVEMENT UNPA
PRINTING HAS PERFORMED A ROLE OF ACHIEVEMENT UNPA 1234567890
Printing has performed a role of achievement unparalleled in the rev
PRINTING HAS PERFORMED A ROLE OF ACHIEVEMENT U 456

9 pt.

Printing has performed a role of achievement unparalleled in th
PRINTING HAS PERFORMED A ROLE OF ACHIEVEMENT U
PRINTING HAS PERFORMED A ROLE OF ACHIEVEMENT U 1234567890
Printing has performed a role of achievement unparalleled in the
PRINTING HAS PERFORMED A ROLE OF ACHIEVEME 789

10 pt.

Printing has performed a role of achievement unparalleled
PRINTING HAS PERFORMED A ROLE OF ACHIEVEME
PRINTING HAS PERFORMED A ROLE OF ACHIEVEM 1234567890
Printing has performed a role of achievement unparalleled
PRINTING HAS PERFORMED A ROLE OF ACHIE 123

11 pt.

Printing has performed a role of achievement unpara
PRINTING HAS PERFORMED A ROLE OF ACHIEV
PRINTING HAS PERFORMED A ROLE OF AC 1234567890
Printing has performed a role of achievement unparal
PRINTING HAS PERFORMED A ROLE OF AC 456

12 pt.

Printing has performed a role of achievement un
PRINTING HAS PERFORMED A ROLE OF AC
PRINTING HAS PERFORMED A ROLE OF 1234567890
Printing has performed a role of achievement unp
PRINTING HAS PERFORMED A ROLE OF 789

14 pt.

Printing has performed a role of achieve
PRINTING HAS PERFORMED A ROLE
PRINTING HAS PERFORMED A RO 1234567890
Printing has performed a role of achievem
PRINTING HAS PERFORMED A RO 123

5 pt.

Printing has performed a role of achievement unparalleled in the revelation of new horizons, and in emphasizing t
he potentials of social and cultural development. The invention of printing stands at the peak of man's broad civiliz
PRINTING HAS PERFORMED A ROLE OF ACHIEVEMENT UNPARALLELED IN THE REVELATION OF NEW
PRINTING HAS PERFORMED A ROLE OF ACHIEVEMENT UNPARALLELED IN THE REVELATION OF NEW HORIZONS 1234567890
Printing has performed a role of achievement unparalleled in the revelation of new horizons, and in emphasizing in th
PRINTING HAS PERFORMED A ROLE OF ACHIEVEMENT UNPARALLELED IN THE REVELATION OF 123

5½ pt.

Printing has performed a role of achievement unparalleled in the revelation of new horizons, and in emph
asizing the potentials of social and cultural development. The invention of printing stands at the peak of m
PRINTING HAS PERFORMED A ROLE OF ACHIEVEMENT UNPARALLELED IN THE REVELATION
PRINTING HAS PERFORMED A ROLE OF ACHIEVEMENT UNPARALLELED IN THE REVELATION OF NEW 1234567890
Printing has performed a role of achievement unparalleled in the revelation of new horizons, and in emphas
PRINTING HAS PERFORMED A ROLE OF ACHIEVEMENT UNPARALLELED IN THE REVEL 456

6 pt.

Printing has performed a role of achievement unparalleled in the revelation of new horizons, and
in emphasizing the potentials of social and cultural development. The invention of printing stand
PRINTING HAS PERFORMED A ROLE OF ACHIEVEMENT UNPARALLELED IN THE REVEL
PRINTING HAS PERFORMED A ROLE OF ACHIEVEMENT UNPARALLELED IN THE REVELATION o 1234567890
Printing has performed a role of achievement unparalleled in the revelation of new horizons, and
PRINTING HAS PERFORMED A ROLE OF ACHIEVEMENT UNPARALLELED IN THE R 789

6½ pt.

Printing has performed a role of achievement unparalleled in the revelation of new horizo
ns, and in emphasizing the potentials of social and cultural development. The invention of
PRINTING HAS PERFORMED A ROLE OF ACHIEVEMENT UNPARALLELED IN THE
PRINTING HAS PERFORMED A ROLE OF ACHIEVEMENT UNPARALLELED IN THE REV 1234567890
Printing has performed a role of achievement unparalleled in the revelation of new horizon
PRINTING HAS PERFORMED A ROLE OF ACHIEVEMENT UNPARALLELED IN 123

7 pt.

Printing has performed a role of achievement unparalleled in the revelation of new
horizons, and in emphasizing the potentials of social and cultural development. Th
PRINTING HAS PERFORMED A ROLE OF ACHIEVEMENT UNPARALLELED IN
PRINTING HAS PERFORMED A ROLE OF ACHIEVEMENT UNPARALLELED IN T 1234567890
Printing has performed a role of achievement unparalleled in the revelation of new
PRINTING HAS PERFORMED A ROLE OF ACHIEVEMENT UNPARALLE 456

7½ pt.

Printing has performed a role of achievement unparalleled in the revelation o
f new horizons, and in emphasizing the potentials of social and cultural develo
PRINTING HAS PERFORMED A ROLE OF ACHIEVEMENT UNPARALLE
PRINTING HAS PERFORMED A ROLE OF ACHIEVEMENT UNPARALLE 1234567890
Printing has performed a role of achievement unparalleled in the revelation of
PRINTING HAS PERFORMED A ROLE OF ACHIEVEMENT UNPARA 789

8 pt.

Printing has performed a role of achievement unparalleled in the revelat
PRINTING HAS PERFORMED A ROLE OF ACHIEVEMENT UNPARAL
PRINTING HAS PERFORMED A ROLE OF ACHIEVEMENT UNPARALLE 1234567890
Printing has performed a role of achievement unparalleled in the revelatio
PRINTING HAS PERFORMED A ROLE OF ACHIEVEMENT UNP 123

Characters per pica: 5 pt—4.5; 5½ pt—4.1; 6 pt—3.8; 6½ pt—3.5; 7 pt—3.2; 7½ pt—3.0; 8 pt—2.8; 8½ pt—2.7; 9 pt—2.5; 10 pt—2.3; 11 pt—2.1; 12 pt—1.9; 14 pt—1.6; 16 pt—1.4

FIGURE A-1 Type specimen sheet.

Courtesy Rochester Monotype Composition Co.

CHECKLISTS, RATING SYSTEMS, AND EVALUATION METHODS

In the chapter on advertising research you read about checklists. For usual copywriters a checklist is merely a simple list of product points. For instance, if they were writing about a flashlight they might list:

- Floats.
- Casts beam half mile.
- Waterproof.
- Shatterproof plastic.
- Three long-life batteries.
- Lightweight.
- Can be focused.
- One-year guarantee.

PROOFREADERS' MARKS

OPERATIONAL SIGNS		TYPOGRAPHICAL SIGNS	
ℐ	Delete	lc	Lowercase capital letter
⌒	Close up; delete space	cap	Capitalize lowercase letter
ℐ	Delete and close up	sc	Set in small capitals
#	Insert space	ital	Set in italic type
eq #	Make space between words equal; make leading between lines equal	rom	Set in roman type
hr #	Insert hair space	bf	Set in boldface type
ls	Letterspace	wf	Wrong font; set in correct type
¶	Begin new paragraph	✗	Reset broken letter
no ¶	Run paragraphs together	⊙	Reverse (type upside down)
☐	Move type one em from left or right		PUNCTUATION MARKS
⅃	Move right	⋀	Insert comma
⊏	Move left	⋁	Insert apostrophe (or single quotation mark)
⅃⊏	Center		
⊓	Move up	⋁⋁	Insert quotation marks
⊔	Move down	⊙	Insert period
⹀	Straighten type; align horizontally	?	Insert question mark
‖	Align vertically	;/	Insert semicolon
tr	Transpose	:/	Insert colon
sp	Spell out	=/	Insert hyphen
stet	Let it stand	M	Insert em dash
⌄	Push down type	N	Insert en dash

FIGURE A-2 Proofreader's marks.

Courtesy University of Chicago Press, *A Manual of Style*, 12th edition.

For the conscientious copywriter ever anxious to improve performance, there are many systems and methods that have been written by men in agencies and companies. Most copywriters pay little attention to these. This is unfortunate since much is to be gained by using these suggestions either before, or after, writing copy.

Following are a number of systems. Perhaps one or more might be of great help to you.

Copywriting system 1

Some years ago, David Ogilvy, noted advertising man and author, offered the following scoring system for rating the mechanical or physical aspects of an advertisement. His suggestions are as valid today.

To use this, assume that the advertisement begins with a score of 100. Then deduct points according to whatever transgression has been committed. It is dubious that any advertisement will obtain 100 points when you rate it in this manner. The scoring system has much merit, however, in making the copywriter and artist painfully aware of some very important principles.

On the content side, Mr. Ogilvy decries a) any advertisement which is obviously dishonest; b) an advertisement which would obviously be considered indecent or blasphemous by more than 5 percent of the readers of the publication in which it appears; and c) any advertisement which is an obvious imitation of another advertiser's advertisement.

Layout and Printing Factors	Points Deducted
1. Graphic technique obtrudes itself between the copywriter and the reader.	17
2. Illustration is lazy—it does not work hard at selling the product.	11
3. It requires more than a split second for the reader to identify the kind of product being advertised.	10
4. Brand name is not visible at a glance.	9
5. Layout looks more like an advertisement than an editorial page.	7
6. Illustration lacks "story appeal," something interesting happening.	6
7. A drawing is used instead of a photograph.	6
8. Layout is cluttered or complicated.	5
9. There is more than one place to begin reading.	4
10. Type is used self-consciously for purpose of design.	4
11. Body copy is set in reverse or in a tint.	4
12. Any illustration appears without a caption.	3
13. Illustration is defaced in any way, for example, by having the headline run into it.	2
14. Illustration is any shape other than rectangular.	2
15. Headline is set in more than one typeface.	2
16. Body copy is set in a sans serif face.	2
17. Measure is wider than 40 characters.	2
18. Long copy is not broken with crossheads.	2
19. First paragraph is more than 12 words.	1
20. Paragraphs are squared up.	1

Copywriting system 2

You will find the following suggestions in two parts. In the first part you'll find major considerations to think about in your advertisement. By the way, this material applies to newspaper or magazine advertisements but the suggestion about including telephone numbers and hours in item 5 would apply specifically to newspaper advertisements.

In the second part, the scoring sheet enables you to determine how well the six major considerations have been applied.

WARNING. Don't apply this too literally to all advertisements. In fact, you can't apply it to all advertisements. For example, there are splendid corporate, or institutional advertisements that would rate poorly if judged by this system. There are image-building advertisements that would fare badly, too. In short, before you use this copywriting system, be sure that your subject matter, technique, or objective is suitable. If so, use. If not, don't use.

1. **A theme.** Can the sales message in the ad be stated in a simple declarative sentence?

2. **Headline.** A good headline includes the company name and a reader benefit. It should also be selective so the reader knows whether or not the ad is directed at him. And, of course, the headline should be simple enough to be clearly understood.

3. **Illustration.** The illustration should attract readers and help tell the story or reinforce the main sales point of the ad. If possible, it should show the product in use.

4. **Text or body copy.** The text should follow the headline, amplifying user benefits, explaining and offering proof that the product or service being advertised is a good one. And the text should end with an action close. It should tell the reader what to do next and it should make it easy for him to do it.

5. **Signature.** The ad should end with the company name clear and visible. Address (complete with zip code), phone number and hours open for business should be included.

6. **Ad layout.** The ad layout is nothing more than the arrangement of items two, three, four, and five. It should be planned to draw readers into the ad, guide them through it, and visually present the image the advertiser wants to present.

Scoring sheet for evaluating an ad

Item	Score
Can the main sales point be stated in a simple declarative sentence?	1
Does the headline mention company or brand name?	1
Does the headline promise a benefit?	2
Does the headline select the people the ad wants to talk to?	1
Is the headline simple and easy to understand?	1
Does the headline promise something new?	1
Does the illustration show the product in use?	1
Is the illustration attention-getting?	1
Does the illustration show user benefits?	1
Are there supplemental photos, drawings, or charts to add interest and help sell the product?	1
Does the text repeat the benefit in the headline and amplify on it?	1
Does the copy back up claims with proof?	1
Does the copy present the whole story?	1
Does the ad have an action close that tells the reader what to do next?	1
Is the company name, address, phone number and hours included in the ad?	1
Does the ad attract the reader's attention?	1
Is there a logical visual path through the ad?	1
Does the ad convey the company's image?	1

16 or more	excellent
13 to 15	good
10 to 12	fair
9 or less	poor

"Best Way to Judge Your Company's Ads: Score Them" *Sales Management*, September 18, 1972.

Reprinted by permission from *Sales Management, The Marketing Magazine*, copyright Sales Management, Inc.

Copywriting system 3

One major corporation established the following "communications checkpoints" as criteria for its review-rating program. The objective was to determine whether an advertisement was above average, below average, or average in qualitative terms. Many company advertising departments establish such guidelines to judge their own output and that of their advertising agencies.

1. Does the advertisement offer a reward for the reader's time and attention? A benefit to the user? News? Service? Does it entertain or amuse?
2. Does the advertisement avoid the necessity for metal work by the reader? Is the headline specific, clear and direct? Does the illustration work hard to support the sales message? Is the layout simple and orderly, avoiding clutter?
3. Does it provide validation and support for the sales claim? By demonstrations? By tests? By case history or testimonial? By guarantee?
4. Does it exploit the principle of repetition? Is the story told in the headline? Again in the illustration? Again in the copy?
5. Does the treatment avoid the stereotype? Is it arresting? Fresh?
6. Is the total effect modern and advanced?

Copywriting system 4

In Figure A-3 you will find material aimed especially at the copywriter who is creating newspaper advertising, especially advertising for retail stores. The basic ideas and the copy came from the Bureau of Advertising of the American Newspaper Publishers Association. The material had been published in the Bureau's *Annual Retail Advertising Plan Book*. It was also used as a mailer sent out by one newspaper to help local merchants and others prepare better advertisements. It is reproduced as it appeared in the February, 1973, International Newspaper Promotion Association Copy Service Newsletter, edited by James B. McGrew, of the Lancaster Newspapers, Inc., Lancaster, Pennsylvania.

Copywriting system 5

In the following pages you will find an elaborate advertising evaluation checklist that can be used: a) to check your own work; b) to check the work of someone else and thus give him a valuable critique. Used in this way, it would eliminate the infuriatingly vague type of comment expressed in the words: "I don't like it, but I can't tell you exactly why."

This checklist, thus, can be used by the copywriter or by the copy chief. It is not, as you can see, a casual, once-over-lightly evaluation since it embraces headlines, body copy, layout, illustration, and typography.

The person using this evaluation system on a regular basis might wish to work out a point scoring system and evolve a total for the "perfect" advertisement. Thus advertisements could be judged in terms of how far or how close they are to a perfect rating.

FIGURE A-3 The ten essentials of a good advertisement.

Dear Advertiser,

The increasing complexity of retailing — such as the rapid growth and diversity of competition, changing customer shopping habits and the continuing squeeze on profits — has made it vitally important that merchants get full value from their advertising dollars.

The newspaper ad is the retailer's best store window and salesman. Nearly everyone reads a daily newspaper, and readers shop the newspaper for good values. Yet, the effectiveness of advertising varies widely. In terms of readership and sales results, some ads are far more successful than others.

The most important single factor determining how many people will read any newspaper ad is the skill and technique used in preparing the ad.

The following suggestions for copy and layout are drawn from several studies. When effectively used, these techniques and rules generally increase readership

LANCASTER NEWSPAPERS, INC.
8 W. King St., Lancaster, Penna. 17604

essentials of a good ad

1 make your ads easily recognizable

Advertisements which are distinctive in their use of art, layout techniques and type faces usually enjoy higher readership than run - of - the - mill advertising. Make your ads distinctively different in appearance from the advertising of your competitors. Then keep your ads' appearance consistent. This way, readers will recognize your ads even before they read them.

2 use a simple layout

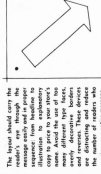

The layout should carry the reader's eye through the message easily and in proper sequence: from headline to illustration to explanatory copy to price to your store's name. Avoid the use of too many different type faces, overly decorative borders and reverses. These devices are distracting and reduce the number of readers who receive your entire message.

3 use a dominant element

— a large picture or headline — to insure quick visibility. Photographs and realistic drawings have about equal attention-getting value, but photographs of real people win more readership. So do action pictures. Photographs of local people or places also have high attention value. Use good art work. It will pay off in extra readership.

4 use a prominent benefit headline

The first question a reader asks of an ad is: "What's in it for me?" Select the main benefit which your merchandise offers and feature it in a compelling headline. "How to" headlines encourage full copy readership, as do headlines which include specific information or helpful suggestions. Your headline will be easier to read if it is black-on-white and not printed over part of an illustration.

5 let your white space work for you

NAME

Don't overcrowd your ad. White space is an important layout element in newspaper advertising. White space focuses the reader's attention on your ad and will make your headline and illustration stand out. When a "crowded" ad is necessary, such as for a sale, departmentalize your items so that the reader can find his way through them easily.

6 make your copy complete

COPY

Sizes and colors available are important, pertinent information. Your copy should be enthusiastic, sincere. A block of copy written in complete sentences is easier to read than one composed of phrases and random words. In designing the layout of a copy block, use a boldface lead-in. Small pictures in sequence will often help readership. Don't be too clever, or use unusual or difficult words.

7 state price or range of prices

Don't be afraid to quote your price. Readers often overestimate omitted prices. If the advertised price is high, explain why the item represents a good value — perhaps because of superior materials or workmanship, or extra features. If the price is low, support it with factual statements which create belief, such as information on your close-out sale, special purchase or clearance.

8 specify branded merchandise

BRAND

If the item is a known brand, say so in your advertising. Manufacturers spend large sums to sell their goods, and you can capitalize on their advertising while enhancing the reputation of your store by featuring branded items. Using the brand name may also qualify the ad for co-operative advertising allowances from the manufacturer.

9 include related items

Make two sales instead of one by offering related items along with a featured one. For instance, when a dishwasher is advertised, also show a disposal, or if you're advertising a dress or suit you can increase potential sales by also including shoes, hats or handbag in the same ad.

10 urge your readers to buy now

NOW

Ask for the sale. You can stimulate prompt action by using such phrases as "limited supply" or "this week only." If mail-order coupons are included in your ads, provide spaces large enough for customers to fill them in easily. Don't generalize, be specific at all times.

Formal and controversial evaluation systems from the past. The Townsend system was originally based upon twenty-seven points of evaluation for national advertising. They were:

1. Identification
2. Attention
3. Interest
4. Proof
5. Timing
6. Good quality
7. The proposition
8. Consumer acceptance
9. Personality—you
10. Sincerity
11. Focus
12. Poor quality
13. Loss (if prospect doesn't buy)
14. Who (testimonial of prominent user)
15. The request for action
16. Association
17. The command to act
18. Aim
19. The main appeals
20. The instinct for life
21. The instinct to reproduce life
22. The instinct for bodily comfort
23. The instinct for personal importance
24. The instinct to enjoy the five senses
25. Layout and illustration
26. Sequence
27. Type

The twenty-seven points were subsequently reduced to nine points for retail advertising. Here is the shortened list:

The Townsend Nine Standard Method for Rating Retail Advertising

A. Headlines and subheads
   No. 1 Identification—memory
   No. 2 Main appeals—featured
   No. 3 Reasons why—subheads
B. Copy
   No. 4 Main appeals—copy interest
   No. 5 Quality—proof—belief
   No. 6 The proposition—action
C. Layout and illustration
   No. 7 Sequence
   No. 8 Main appeals—illustrated
   No. 9 Identification—style

The Townsend backers said that the twenty-seven points were not "created," but were simply identified as basic to all copy and each was given an approximate value. Thus, a copywriting novice could tell quickly whether his, or someone else's copy, had the elements to make an effective advertisement.

Dr. Charles M. Edwards, expert in retail advertising research, in turn worked out a complicated formula using 671 points for checking retail advertising. This formula was not for the novice but for the skilled researcher. Yet it is often mentioned among the checklist system. It was used extensively for evaluating copy of the R.H. Macy department store in New York City, but Dr. Edwards felt that in most stores no more than 14 to 22 points were of vital significance.

Another checklist system that received wide attention was the Thompson-Luce method, which used thirty-five factors assertedly controlling reader interest.

The factors were assembled on the basis of exhaustive analysis of readership studies. Each one of the thirty-five was consistently present in high readership copy, according to the method's originators. For instance, news interest might appear five times as frequently in high-ranking advertisements. A picture of a famous man might appear three times as frequently. A forecast of the probability of success was made on the basis of proper incorporation of the points.

From these examples you may see some aptness in the term "battle of the points." Although there was merit in each of the systems, it was difficult for copy people to know just which system was the best or whether *any* such system was sound.

Copywriting system 6

The copywriting marking code in Figure A-5 has been used for some years to grade advertising campaigns turned in as term projects. On the other paper of the student will be placed the code letter and number to tell him the nature of his transgression.

It is included here as a guide to warn of the many faults to be found in advertising copy and layouts. The "Analysis" referred to on the bottom is the market and creative analysis each student provides. This analysis is done before the copy is written.

FIGURE A-4 Advertising evaulation checklist.

Headline

Over-all, is the headline:	10-8 Strong	7-5 Average	4-0 Weak	POINTS
	_____	_____	_____	_____
1. Does the headline relate to the product?	Closely	Fairly	Poorly	
	_____	_____	_____	_____

_____

_____

_____

2. Does the headline contain a benefit?	Strong	Fair	Weak	
	_____	_____	_____	_____

_____

_____

_____

3. Is head lively and full of action?	Lively	Fairly lively	Static	
	_____	_____	_____	_____

_____

_____

_____

4. Is headline tied in well with opening copy?	Very	Slightly	Not at all	
	_____	_____	_____	_____

_____

_____

_____

5. Is headline tied in well with illustration? Very Slightly Not at all

_____ _____ _____   _____

_____

_____

_____

6. Is headline aimed directly at prospect-reader of publication? Very directly Fairly well Not at all

_____ _____ _____   _____

_____

_____

_____

Miscellaneous Comments

_____

_____

_____

Body Copy

Over-all, is the body copy strong, average, weak? 10-8 Strong 7-5 Average 4-0 Weak

_____ _____ _____   _____

_____

_____

_____

1. Is copy well-organized in progressing logically from beginning to end? Very well organized Fairly well organized Poorly organized

_____ _____ _____   _____

_____

_____

_____

2. Does copy start out fast and
    interestingly?

    Very   Fairly   Starts slow,
    well   well   uninterest-
    ing

    _____   _____   _____   _____

    _____

    _____

    _____

3. Copy identifies company and/or
    product?

    Strongly   Fairly   Not at
               well   all

    _____   _____   _____   _____

    _____

    _____

    _____

4. Copy stresses main benefit?

    Strongly   Moderately   Poorly

    _____   _____   _____   _____

    _____

    _____

    _____

5. Copy stresses subsidiary benefits?

    Strongly   Fairly   Poorly
               well

    _____   _____   _____   _____

    _____

    _____

    _____

6. Copy written in language of prospect-
    reader?

    Very much   Fairly   Not at
    so   well   all

    _____   _____   _____   _____

    _____

    _____

    _____

7. Can copy be called helpful?

Very helpful	Fairly helpful	Not helpful	
———	———	———	———

————————————————————————

————————————————————————

————————————————————————

8. Are copy claims believable?

Quite believable	Fairly believable	Not believable	
———	———	———	———

————————————————————————

————————————————————————

————————————————————————

9. Copy ending urge to action or some other positive manner?

Strong	Average	Weak	
———	———	———	———

————————————————————————

————————————————————————

————————————————————————

Miscellaneous Comments

————————————————————————

————————————————————————

————————————————————————

————————————————————————

Layout, Illustration, Typography

Over-all, is the total physical effect of the ad effective in achieving sales objectives, campaign objectives, or other objectives?

10-8 Very	7-5 Fairly so	4-0 Not at all	
———	———	———	———

————————————————————————

————————————————————————

————————————————————————

1. Is headline strong enough physically
    to achieve impact?

Strong impact	Fair impact	Little impact	
———	———	———	———

_____

_____

_____

2. Is main illustration strong enough
    physically to achieve impact?

Strong impact	Fair impact	Little impact	
———	———	———	———

_____

_____

_____

3. Is main illustration interesting to
    prospect-reader?

Very interesting	Fairly interesting	Not interesting	
———	———	———	———

_____

_____

_____

4. Is copy typographically easy to read?

Very easy	Fairly easy	Hard to read	
———	———	———	———

_____

_____

_____

5. Is size of ad space suitable to accomplish
    ad objectives?

Very suitable	Fairly suitable	Not suitable	
———	———	———	———

_____

_____

_____

6. Is layout technique (drawing or photo) suitable for purposes of ad?

Very suitable   Fairly suitable   Not suitable

_____   _____   _____   _____

_____

_____

_____

7. Does logo stand out?

Very well   Fairly well   Poorly

_____   _____   _____   _____

_____

_____

_____

8. Does layout "track" well in leading the reader logically through the ad?

Very well   Fairly well   Poorly

_____   _____   _____   _____

_____

_____

_____

Miscellaneous Comments

_____

_____

_____

FIGURE A-5 Copywriting marking code.

Layout and Typography

L-1 sloppy lettering
L-2 poor balance
L-3 coupon badly-designed (crowded, too little room to write, no sell)
L-4 headline and/or logo too small to get attention
L-5 headline is jammed against top
L-6 illustration idea dull, or not appropriate
L-7 too empty looking
L-8 just generally amateurish
L-9 use some small illustrations to liven up your ad, or to better explain the product
L-10 your layout has no focal point
L-11 your illustration is too small
L-12 your layout is sloppy
L-13 copy lines are set in too wide a measure
L-14 copy blocks are too small
L-15 layout (or certain sections of it) looks crowded
L-16 too much solid, unbroken type
L-17 too much material run together. Don't obscure points by running them together. List for easy reading.
L-18 layout cut up into too many elements

Copy

C-1 poor writing
C-2 skimpy copy treatment
C-3 illogical writing; doesn't fit in well, or doesn't make sense
C-4 writing is confusing
C-5 take too long to get started
C-6 writing is awkward
C-7 trite, worn-out, or cliche-ridden language
C-8 too fancy or literary for audience
C-9 needlessly negative
C-10 language is artificial, unnatural, or stilted—or all three
C-11 you don't make clear just what you're selling
C-12 your writing is too impersonal
C-13 you don't get excited enough
C-14 don't jam too many ideas in one sentence or paragraph
C-15 dull, lifeless slogan
C-16 poor product name
C-17 you don't stress the U.S.P. or point of difference

C-18 copy isn't geared well to the medium you're using
C-19 you fail to stress the most important point
C-20 too sweeping a claim
C-21 statement is misleading
C-22 unbelievable
C-23 exaggerated

Technical and Grammatical Faults

C-24 unsupported comparative
C-25 grammar is incorrect
C-26 antecedent is not clear
C-27 bad punctuation
C-28 use paragraphs
C-29 your writing lacks transition
C-30 use active tense
C-31 avoid this backward "newspaperese"
C-32 write complete sentences
C-33 I'd prefer more cohesive writing rather than a mere listing of points a la catalog copy
C-34 wrong spelling

Headlines

C-35 weak headline—doesn't interest or doesn't sell
C-36 head (or copy) lacks benefit or direct personal appeal to reader
C-37 not a good tie-in of headline and opening body copy
C-38 you should use some subheads
C-39 headline isn't specific enough
C-40 headline doesn't involve the reader

General Faults

C-41 you fail to use principles taught you this semester (in writing, merchandising techniques, in physical form, copy style, etc.)
C-42 wrong form
C-43 too much copy for space (or paragraph, or point being made)
C-44 too much "we" or company viewpoint
C-45 company's promotional backing out sold hard enough, or specifically enough.
C-46 you're emphasizing the weaker appeal
C-47 not enough difference between your various ads
C-48 need more product details
C-49 need fewer product details
C-50 should use product name here
C-51 weak ending
C-52 doesn't end with urge to act

Analysis

A-1   superficial ideas or execution
A-2   you've aimed at wrong market(s)
A-3   analysis is badly-written
A-4   you haven't done a thorough job

A-5   no discussion (or not enough) of differences for different media
A-6   you fail to pinpoint your market(s) definitively
A-7   reasoning seems faulty here
A-8   too dogmatic here
A-9   you don't dig deeply enough

Index